welc

"EXTRA" WORK f ... y for those interested in working as background actors in the entertainment industry. Our intention is to provide you with the tools necessary to MARKET YOURSELF most effectively for work in films, TV, commercials, music videos and more. You can rest assured you have the most comprehensive information available because we provide the nuts and bolts for finding work!

We work directly with Casting Directors so you have the most current information and are following the CORRECT PROCEDURES for finding work.

You see, we want you to find work – and lots of it – so then you can tell others how cool this book is. And the person referring you to us will prove to be an honest soul. Now some words from our lame, overpriced lawyers:

dumb disclaimer:

This is simply a Guide/Directory containing information about extras casting agencies, independent Casting Directors, and other casting resources. These listings are only intended to inform you, the Background Actor, about work possibilities. Please note that the places or people mentioned are not rated or recommended – just listed, that's all. Furthermore, purchasing this darn book does not guarantee employment.

Produced By:

HOLLYWOOD OS®
400 South Beverly Drive, Suite 307
Beverly Hills, CA 90212

PHONE: 310-289-9400
FAX: 310-277-3088
E-MAIL: Info@HollywoodOS.com
WEBSITE: www.HollywoodOS.com

Twenty-four – 2006

ISBN: 1-893899-24-1

ISSN: 1522-306X

• thank you!

- To the reputable Casting Companies who use & support HOLLYWOOD OS®. Thanks for making my little company grow! You are simply a delight to work with.
- Mom(s) & Dad(s) & Sexy Grandparents!
- Jimmy, Jerry, The Dot (and her hot hair), Mike, Assaf, Andrew, Howard. Thanks for believing. Dreams do come true.
- Samro - the happiest intern ever!
- Sean Tohidi - webdude extraordinaire.
- You - the Reader/Dreamer are appreciated.

credits •

EDITORIAL AND OPERATIONS

Angela Bertolino • CEO
Angela@HollywoodOS.com

Jared Tweedie • EDITOR
Jared@HollywoodOS.com

Behnoosh Khalili • CBS
HollywoodOS@aol.com

John Berner • CORPORATE STRATEGIST
John@HollywoodOS.com

Stuart Smith • ADVERTISING
Stuart@HollywoodOS.com

EDITORIAL AND CORPORATE HEADQUARTERS

400 S. Beverly Drive, Suite 307
Beverly Hills, CA 90212
(310) 289-9400
Website: www.HollywoodOS.com
Advertising Fax: (310) 277-3088
Editorial Fax: (310) 277-3088

"EXTRA" WORK for Brain Surgeons®
• Volume xxxiv, 2006 •

Hollywood Operating System® originally founded in 1997 by Angela Bertolino and Carla Lewis, owned by Angela Bertolino. ISBN: 1-893899-24-1, ISSN: 1522-306X

Printed in Canada

book application

into ...this directory... 

...so you want to be listed...

getting...

- **APPLICATION for an**
  "EXTRA" WORK for Brain Surgeons®
  LISTING – it's FREE!

- Complete this application and return by mail, fax or email:

HOLLYWOOD OS®
400 South Beverly Drive, Suite 307
Beverly Hills, CA 90212
FAX: 310-277-3088
EMAIL: Info@HollywoodOS.com

YOUR NAME: ______________________________

COMPANY NAME: ______________________________

COMPANY CATEGORY:
____
(i.e. extras casting company, calling service, independent CD)

ADDRESS: ______________________________
____
____

PHONE (for publication): ______________________________

PHONE (private): ______________________________

FAX: ______________________________

EMAIL: ______________________________

WEBSITE: ______________________________

Please include one or more of the following:

- A Resumé
- Letters of Reference
- Company Profile/History

This will expedite the processing of your application. A member of our staff will be in touch with you regarding your application and will forward you the necessary follow-up paperwork.

Thank you for your interest.

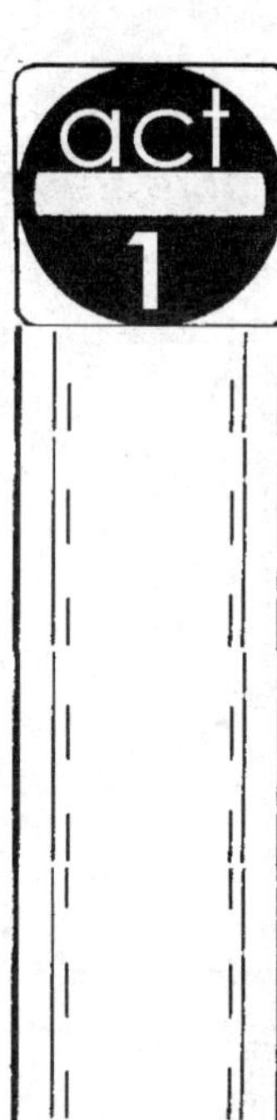

getting started

sag & aftra

act 3

non-union

extras casting: tv, film, music videos & more

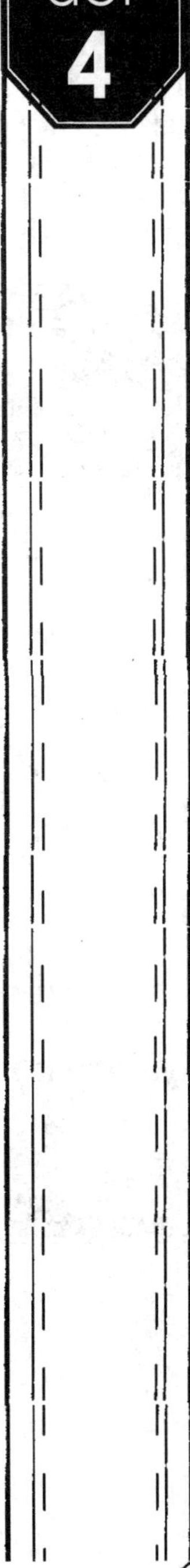

act 4

extras casting: tv, film, music videos & more (cont'd)

act 5

extras casting: soap operas

act 6

extras casting: commercials

act 7

services & such

services & such (cont'd)

act 7 cont'd

principals & kids

fabulous other

fabulous other (cont'd)

act 9 →

intro

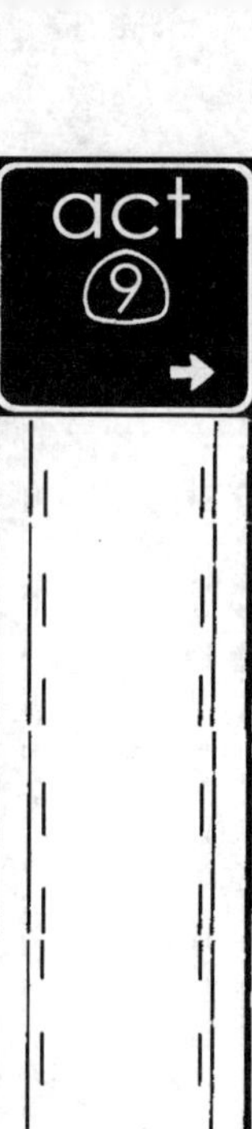

fabulous other (cont'd)

fabulous other (cont'd)

act 9 →

act 10

reference

Welcome to

"EXTRA" WORK for Brain Surgeons®

by 

From An Author

Where to begin? I moved here from uneventful Sacramento (contain your laughter, I know) in 1995, where I had written, produced and hosted two television programs: *Everyone's a Critic* and *Get Real*. These shows were geared toward the teenage market and aired throughout Northern California. Out of sheer curiosity, I fell into extra work, where I met Carla on the set of some cheesy cable movie. As it turned out, she had been "scammed" out of thousands of dollars on the modeling circuit. I had had a similar experience in the acting arena, also having shelled out thousands of well-earned dollars to so-called casting agencies that charged me up the wazoo, supposedly "guaranteeing" me work and convincing me I needed to spend millions of dollars on bad headshots. WHATEVER. Little did I know that this was all totally unnecessary. I was pressured into spending money because these places apparently were "swamped" with only three alleged spots left to cast. Upon hearing this blessed information, I of course felt the intense need to speed around in L.A. rush-hour traffic to find these scammy places and spend hundreds of dollars so I could land that next big gig. Only months later did I learn that the AVERAGE registration fee was less than $20 at that time. In fact, some places were even FREE. Oops!

This happened to me on many occasions. I was never once booked through any of these pricey places and have since learned a great deal about this business. The problem that exists (even today) is the simple fact that no one — not one single person or institution — ever guided me in the right direction. Here I was spending hundreds of dollars a week, registering at all of these bogus companies because each of these places sounded like a dream come true. I was told everything I wanted to hear and I believed it all. God, I was blonde!

Extra work is an oddity in itself — and there is so much of it out here in Los Angeles! It's like this: People do not share information with you because, let's be honest, they don't want you to land the next job before they do. Everyone keeps casting information to themselves so that the other person inquiring cannot move ahead. This was so frustrating. How is anyone supposed to learn and not get scammed, for cryin' out loud?!

When I moved to Los Angeles, I thought doing extra work would be a fun and enjoyable experience. The more I learned about various casting companies and the way the industry operated, the more disen-

chanted I became. Very political. I did extra work for the sheer chance of meeting great people and observing the industry at work — I considered it a paid education. In trying to get work, it certainly would have behooved me to know who was casting what projects and what types of people Casting Directors were looking for. This information simply wasn't available — period. It would have been nice to know how I could have marketed myself more effectively instead of just sitting around waiting for the damn phone to ring!

Upon discussing our experiences, I tried to convince Carla there was a need for an objective, unbiased launching point for those interested in finding work in the entertainment industry. It's amazing: Not one company existed to help Actors and Extras alike. After a few weeks of blowing off my brilliant brainstorm, Carla finally gave in to the idea of publishing our first cockamamie directory, thus founding our company, **HOLLYWOOD OS**®. It was in the Costco parking lot that the title **"EXTRA" WORK for Brain Surgeons**® was conceived.

Even today, our readers usually fall into one of three categories:

- New to the industry and do not know where to start
- Familiar with the industry but too busy to research new opportunities
- CDs who keep the book on their coffee tables (or in their bathrooms)

Since our 1997 inception, we have taken our company, **HOLLYWOOD OS**®, a step further by offering an online casting information subscription service that is updated 24 hours a day, seven days a week. It is used by both Casting Directors seeking talent and Actors seeking work. We also publish a children's directory, **KIDS' ACTING for Brain Surgeons**™ , for parents and their actor children, and a quarterly magazine, **HOLLYWOOD OS**® The Casting Magazine, an extension of updated information for the casting community at large.

Throughout the **HOLLYWOOD OS**® evolution, our primary objective has remained the same: to give talent an honest perspective of the entertainment industry. We list the facts as they are directly reported out of Casting Directors' mouths or from their illegible faxes. In writing our first volume of **"EXTRA" WORK for Brain Surgeons**®, we did what we wished someone had done for us — help to educate ACTORS, EXTRAS and PARENTS with the facts in finding and/or offering them legitimate work. We are a service at your disposal whether you purchase our book or not — it doesn't matter. Your input allows us to grow and learn and provide a better service. Feel free to drop us an email at HollywoodOS@aol.com or give us a call! What we care about is the background community gaining more respect and supplying you with accurate, current information. And let me tell you, if we have done that, we have succeeded. WE ARE HERE TO HELP YOU! **HOLLYWOOD OS**® looks forward to improving this industry and setting new standards, but most of all, we want you working, dammit! Thanks for reading!

Best of luck,

Angela Bertolino,
CEO, Owner
HOLLYWOOD OPERATING SYSTEM®

Welcome to "EXTRA" WORK for Brain Surgeons®

by HOLLYWOOD OS®

From A Founder

I began in this industry at the age of fifteen, when I moved to California from Atlanta, with the glorious dream of modeling. I soon found myself naively paying thousands of dollars at a supposed "modeling school": John Casablancas. I was eventually armed with a portfolio of headshots, but that was about it. Now what? Like a lot of newcomers, I did not know what my next step should be. A few years later, my "counselor" at the "modeling school" recommended I go to this company called Star Casting. She told me it was for a part in a movie called *Major League*. I had no concept of the "acting world," much less "extra work." I went to Star Casting, completed the paperwork and a few days later, I was called with a job. Cool. It was a featured bit where I wore a black T-shirt with "Wild Thing I Think I Love You" and Charlie Sheen's picture on it. All I had to do was walk down the street, turn around, make a number one signal, and continue walking. It took more than twenty takes — ooops. Nevertheless, I was hooked.

Then I worked for Star Casting periodically for the next few years and in college I registered with Tina Real Casting and Background San Diego. Extra work was a fun part-time job for me. Then the Screen Extras Guild merged with the Screen Actors Guild (SAG) and I quickly became a SAG member. With my trusty SAG card in hand, I decided to register with some Los Angeles casting agencies. I remember looking in the phone book trying to find legitimate casting agencies with whom I could register. After college, I gave myself one year to do nothing but extra work.

Armed with my pager, cell phone and a silly piece of folded and refolded paper containing a crude list of casting phone numbers, I found work on my own, averaging three days a week by being a versatile and professional background actor. I had a ton of looks, several wigs, access to upscale cars, and I fell into the ever-so-popular 18-to-look-younger booking category. I visited casting offices very little and instead was obsessed with calling the hotlines. That's how I did it: I was a casting hotline junkie.

After that year of working 100 percent as a background actor, I quit. I moved to San Francisco for graduate study in Multimedia. Okay, I did not entirely quit. I did register with a few extras casting companies in San Francisco. After a year of study, I finally ended up back in Los Angeles where Angela devised this cockamamie plan to write books

act one

and create a company that would help the casting community. We could write about what we knew and I could still tinker with my nifty computer. (**HOLLYWOOD OPERATING SYSTEM**® is named after MAC Operating System. Cool, huh?)

Once we began research for our first issue (it was on purple paper!), we were surprised that there were so many casting agencies. I remember reviewing our notes and asking, "Who the #$%* is this Tammy Smith casting person?" and "Who the #$%* is Debe Waisman and how does she have so many shows?" I thought I knew everyone. Boy, did I still have a lot to learn!

HOLLYWOOD OS® has achieved a lot since we began this entertaining and challenging journey in 1997. We have solidified our position as the leading resource for Extras Casting information and then some. Former *Back Stage West*® journalist Thomas Mills (Tombudsman) named us the "Unofficial Overseers of the Background Community" a few years back. Basically, we set out to do what we wish someone would have done for us. From day one, this was the model we worked from in providing our readers with our casting information and services.

With every endeavor and publication, we are constantly brainstorming new ideas to benefit the casting community and to ensure our reputation remains as honest and trusted as ever. The **HOLLYWOOD OS**® mission has always been to help talent find work. Angela and I write from a combined personal perspective with a dash of sarcasm. We shoot from the hip and write from the heart.

CARLA UPDATE:
I recently relinquished my daily duties at **HOLLYWOOD OS**® and have since branched out on my own to launch an independent casting company. As a full-time Casting Director, I personally cast Actors and Extras on music videos, commercials, print jobs, feature films, infomercials and television shows on a daily basis. This hands-on natural progression further complements my primary desire to help talent find work. And casting is fun! Nowadays, how many people can say they love their job?!

Carla Lewis,
Original Co-Founder
HOLLYWOOD OPERATING SYSTEM®

About & Why HOLLYWOOD OPERATING SYSTEM® was founded!

Since its 1997 inception, **HOLLYWOOD OPERATING SYSTEM®** (or **HOLLYWOOD OS®** as it is better known) was born out of a need in the multi-faceted entertainment industry for a legitimate resource for newcomers and seasoned professionals seeking reliable casting information and guidance.

Scam-busting is a top priority at the **HOLLYWOOD OS®** office – a battle that is fought daily. Many dubious companies lure in innocent, unsuspecting souls by advertising in non-industry publications, soliciting on telephone polls, and posting bogus casting calls on websites in hopes of taking these people for obscene amounts of money with nothing in return. **HOLLYWOOD OS®** is an advocate for those taken advantage of in such unscrupulous ways.

Angela Bertolino, Founder/Owner/CEO, and Carla Lewis, Co-Founder of **HOLLYWOOD OS®**, have both served for the city attorney's office as expert witnesses on casting scams in Southern California, beginning with the successful conviction of Premiere Casting in 1999. Their directory **"EXTRA" WORK for Brain Surgeons®** was distributed throughout the courtroom as the material of reference. **HOLLYWOOD OS®** launched that very publication over eight years ago when the founders were duped out of scads of money by fraudulent companies claiming they could book them as extras and make them stars. At that time there was no tool available for talent to guide them through the maze of misinformation about the acting trade, so Angela Bertolino and Carla Lewis set out to create that tool for others. Out of this, the book **"EXTRA" WORK for Brain Surgeons®** was created.

The well-respected industry publication Back Stage West® touted **"EXTRA" WORK for Brain Surgeons®** as "one of the Top 10 books" for new actors in LA to buy. Casting Directors throughout Southern California have also praised the publication for its insightful, humorous, no-holds-barred approach to helping talent find legitimate, paying work in the industry.

Currently **HOLLYWOOD OS®** produces three publications sold at newstands and bookstores: **"EXTRA" WORK for Brain Surgeons®**, **KIDS' ACTING for Brain Surgeons™**, and **HOLLYWOOD OS®** – The Casting Magazine. Through the publication of their directory **"EXTRA" WORK for Brain Surgeons®**, **HOLLYWOOD OS®** has become known as the authority in extras casting information. This **HOLLYWOOD OS®** publication provides Southern California talent with the tools necessary to start out as a background actor. **"EXTRA" WORK for Brain Surgeons®** is the most comprehensive and complete extras casting directory that exists. The 400+ page book breaks down the basics for background actors as well as addressing the tricky stuff, like the language of labor laws, how to join the Screen Actors Guild, what companies to avoid and much, much more. For the last four years, **"EXTRA" WORK for Brain Surgeons®** has served as the textbook/manual for the prestigious Directors Guild of America's DGA Training Program for new Assistant Directors.

In addition to the annual directory, **HOLLYWOOD OS®** also publishes a guide for parents who want to get their children involved in the industry. **KIDS' ACTING for Brain Surgeons™** takes a no-holds-barred approach to informing parents and young performers about working in the uncertain world of show business. With so many scams across America, this book is a must-read for any parent or guardian who wants to learn about the potential pitfalls and "scammy" sales tactics parents can face when trying to get their children started in the fields of acting or modeling.

HOLLYWOOD OS® also publishes **HOLLYWOOD OS®** - The Casting Magazine. This publication is released quarterly, serving as the perfect complement to the directories. Featured articles focus on a wide array of topics, but ultimately every magazine is targeted to the actor – background actors and principal talent alike – as well as child actors and their parents. With its abundance of updated casting information, casting news, production listings, columns about getting work in the industry, and interviews with some of the top Extra and Principal Casting Directors in the industry, **HOLLYWOOD OS®** - The Casting Magazine is the only magazine exclusively dedicated to this realm of the acting trade.

In 1998 **HOLLYWOOD OS®** launched a subscription-based website where actors, casting directors, entertainment and production team members can participate in an active online community for the entire industry. Once one subscribes, they receive a bundle subscription package consisting of the hard copy print materials in addition to the online access and advance casting notices. The **HOLLYWOOD OS®** website has become an industry lifesaver for the casting community. You see, Extra and Principal Casting Directors are able to post their daily casting details, what types of talent they are seeking and which projects they are casting. Subscribing Actors are able to log in, 24 hours a day, seven days a week, read through the casting information and submit themselves to the various commercials, print jobs, feature films, music videos, infomercials and television shows posted on the website.

Best of all, the company philosophy of no fees has expanded in scope, geared toward benefiting the Actor's best interests. To ensure that everyone, of all walks of life, are given a casting opportunity, the **HOLLYWOOD OS®** Talent Search Engine is free of charge to anyone who wishes to be included and searchable by Casting Directors. Actors of all ages, shapes and sizes are able to come into the office, complete the paperwork, take a free digital photo and fill out an online profile for free. No registration fee, no commission.

The Casting Directors are now able to cast with ease, utilizing the Talent Search Engine to locate Actors and Minors of a specific skill set or characteristic. The efficiency of the **HOLLYWOOD OS®** website has helped change the way casting is done. No more headshots, no more sole reliance on hard copy files, no more messengering over files.

The **HOLLYWOOD OPERATING SYSTEM**® is electronic and instant. This interactive website is yet another means for productions, casting directors and talent to connect, communicate and book projects.

For years Angela Bertolino and her company **HOLLYWOOD OPERATING SYSTEM**® have worked hard to revolutionize the entertainment and casting industry. With its continual growth and rock-solid reputation, **HOLLYWOOD OS**® looks forward to surprising its fan base with many more exciting developments in the near future.

Thank you,
HOLLYWOOD OPERATING SYSTEM®

Extra! Extra!
Read all about ya!

act one

So You Want To Be An Extra, Do Ya?!

Well, first things first, kids!
The term "extra" has been enhanced in
the following ways . . .

• EXTRA •

A.) Atmosphere
B.) Background Actor
C.) Background Artist
D.) Background Talent
E.) The Artist Formally Known as Extra
F.) Background Support Team
G.) Moving Prop (laugh!)
H.) Prop With an Appetite (laugh again!)

Nevertheless, we are going to use the term "extra" – just to annoy the good ole kids on the EVER-PRODUCTIVE SAG Background Actors Committee – kidding, folks! Actually, we have less of a chance of misspelling the word EXTRA as opposed to BACKGROUND ARTIST, and to answer your next question, no, we are NOT changing the title of our book **"EXTRA" WORK for Brain Surgeons**® to *"BACKGROUND ACTING" for Brain Surgeons*™ – hopefully you will understand why – say it out loud for goodness sakes! We will be using the term "extra" only to simplify things throughout the course of this politically incorrect publication – so please, DO NOT view our use of the term "extra" as condescending or derogatory. It's not. And it's not intended to be. Swell.

An "Extra" is an actor usually placed in the background who does NOT SPEAK. There are just a few exceptions and these EXTRAS WHO MAY SPEAK (but don't get paid any more) are:

- Extras who mumble non-distinct words commonly known as "walla wallas" or "omnies."
- Groups of 5 or more who say in unison traditional things like, "Go team!" or "Hooray!"
- Groups of 15 or more who are photographed as a group and who say the same lines in unison (though the rules for this are a bit different in Commercials).

SAG, AFTRA, Non-Union . . .
Cliff Note version – what's it all mean?!

act one

SAG EXTRA or UNION EXTRA:

Usually refers to members of the Screen Actors Guild (SAG). On most SAG projects (film, television, commercials, CD-ROMs, etc.) there is a required minimum number of "contract covered positions" which must be filled by extra performers. If, for some reason, the required minimum number of contract covered positions is not filled by talent who are already members of the Screen Actors Guild, a Non-Union (Non-SAG) person will be hired and paid under a SAG background contract covered position. When a Non-SAG (Non-Union) person is hired under a union contract, they receive union pay and are given a "Taft Hartley."

The base rate is $122 for 8 hours, meaning you are paid AT LEAST $122 whether you are at work for one minute or for the entire 8 hours. After that, SAG members receive time and a half for the next four hours and double time from the twelfth to sixteenth hour. The sixteenth hour is the Golden hour and you receive "Golden Time," which is your base rate for each additional hour or fraction thereof.

SAG extras cast in commercials (the MOST LUCRATIVE extra work around town) receive a somewhat different base rate which is almost three times the regular $122/8 rate (currently $291.80/8) – unless, of course, you are asked to work on a weekend or holiday – for this travesty you receive an ADDITIONAL DAY'S PAY.

The initiation fee to join SAG is "reconfigured" every July 1st. In English, the reconfiguration means THE PRICE WILL MOST LIKELY GO UP. So, come July 1, 2006, you can expect the initiation fee to go up $40 or $50 bucks or so. For recorded info about new membership, call: 323-549-6772.

NON-UNION EXTRA:

This refers to anyone who is not a member of SAG – most often including AFTRA members. The base rate is usually $54 for 8 hours ($6.75/hour, the state-mandated minimum wage as of Jan. 1, 2002) when working for film and television. Then from the eighth to the tenth hour the overtime rate is time and a half. After the tenth hour the overtime rate increases to double time. Sometimes there is a FLAT rate. This means you are paid a flat amount for the entire day – whether you work ten minutes or ten hours you are still paid the same amount. For those of you who are given the opportunity to do Non-Union commercial work, the base rate is usually between $100 - $150 for 12 hours (it still can't legally be less than $6.75/hour + OT). Additionally, music videos often pay much higher as well. Usually anywhere from $75 to $200.

If You Are Non-Union, Vouchers Are Your Friends, People!*
(*at least as we go to press . . .)

If you work as an extra – SAG or Non-Union – the way you will normally be paid is through a "VOUCHER." Once you "CHECK IN" on a set, you will be given this form (a voucher) to complete, so bring a pen that works. Complete both sides of the voucher (there is often I-9 tax info on the back – see our nifty samples on the pages that follow). At the end of the day, you turn in the voucher. This voucher is processed by a payroll company and you are then mailed a check. The info filled out on the voucher includes your name, address, social security number and fun stuff like that. The voucher also includes your pay rate. That's how the term "SAG VOUCHER" came about. A SAG voucher is essentially a voucher paid at the SAG pay rate. It used to be the case that once you had worked under the union contract three times (been paid the SAG extra rate), you were eligible to join SAG (if you're reading this early in 2006 – it may still be in effect). Recently, this policy has been under scrutiny. Stay tuned because change is most likely afoot (but slow in coming).

**** NOTEWORTHY DISCLAIMER:***
The three-voucher mode of entry into the Screen Actors Guild may be changing as we go to press. Keep up with our **HOLLYWOOD OS®** *magazines for the latest news or contact the SAG hotline for this change: 1-800-807-4188.*

AFTRA EXTRA:

The American Federation of Television and Radio Artists, simply known as AFTRA, is ALSO a UNION. However, just to keep things confusing, when the terms UNION and NON-UNION are used, AFTRA Members who are NOT SAG members usually fall into the NON-UNION CATEGORY. Did you catch that? (Need an adult alcoholic beverage yet?) AFTRA, unlike SAG, allows anyone to join. All you have to do is pay the initiation fee of $1,300 and the first installment of biannual dues ($63.90 as of November 2004). AFTRA handles many TV shows and all Soap Operas. The minimum pay for working on most AFTRA programs is $92.25 for 8 hours ($92.25/8). Plus, if you are asked to provide your own clothing for a scene and it is approved by the wardrobe department, you will then be paid an additional $10 for your clothing (under most AFTRA contracts).

Because AFTRA handles so many types of shows, running different lengths in time, it is very complicated to break down the various rates of pay in this tiny paragraph. We suggest you do go get that adult alcoholic beverage and check Act 2 for detailed pay information on AFTRA.

EXTRA VOUCHER

UPS
UNIVERSAL PAYROLL SERVICE INC.
11340 W. OLYMPIC BLVD
SUITE 110
LOS ANGELES, CA 90064
(310) 478-6360 INQUIRIES 3-5 pm PST

FORM ULA101

☐ UNION   SAG NO. ________
☐ WAIVER/TAFT HARTLEY
☐ NON-UNION

021386

PLEASE PRINT
MAKING MULTIPLE COPIES

NAME (LAST) ***PRINT CLEARLY!*** (FIRST) | PRODUCTION CO. | TYPE OF CALL

SOCIAL SECURITY # (MUST be provided in order to be paid) ☐☐☐ — ☐☐ — ☐☐☐☐ | PRODUCTION TITLE | APPROVED FOR PAYMENT

MARITAL STATUS M☐ S☐ | NO. DEPENDENTS ______ | EXEMPT ☐ IF EXEMPT, YEAR ______ | BASIC WAGE RATE | 1ST MEAL OUT IN | 2ND MEAL OUT IN | TRAVEL TIME LEAVE : AM PM ARRIVE : AM PM

DATE WORKED | WORK STATE | NON DEDUCTIBLE BKFST OUT IN | STARTING TIME AM PM | DISMISSAL TIME AM PM | TOTAL HOURS

	AMOUNT		AMOUNT		AMOUNT		AMOUNT		AMOUNT
WARDROBE		MILEAGE		AUTO		WET ☐ SMOKE ☐		WALKAWAY	
PROPS		MEAL PENALTY		FITTING		NIGHT PREMIUM		BUMP/ALLOWANCES	
								ADJUSTMENTS	

COMMENTS: UNION CODE ☐   ▼ **DO NOT WRITE IN THIS SPACE** ▼

"I agree to accept the sum properly computed based upon the times and the basic wage rate shown as payment in full for all services heretofore rendered by me for the company named. I further agree that the said sum, less all deductions required by law, may be paid to me by negotiable check issued by said company, said check to be addressed to me at my last reported address. I hereby give the said company all rights of every kind and character whatsoever in and to all work heretofore done and all poses, acts, plays and appearances heretofore made by me for it, as well as in and to the right to use my name and photographs, either still or moving, for commercial and advertising purposes. I further give the said company the right to reproduce in any manner whatsoever any recordation heretofore made by said company of my voice and all instrumental, musical, or other sound effects produced by me. I further agree that in the event of a retake of all or of any of the scenes in which I participate, or if additional scenes are required (whether originally contemplated or not) I will return to work and render my services in such scenes at the same basic rate of compensation as that paid me for the original taking."

TYPE OF WORK	HOURS	AMOUNT	ACCOUNT CODE
DAY			
1.5			
2.0			
WET/ SMOKE			
TOTAL PAYMENT ▶			

SIGN HERE (If minor, Parent or Guardian Must Sign) X   ☐ **"X" BOX IF NEW ADDRESS**

ADDRESS   TELEPHONE ( )

CITY   STATE   ZIP CODE _ _ _ _ _ — _ _ _ _

EMPLOYER IDENTIFICATION NUMBER **36-3919852**

UPS COPY

I-9 on back MUST be completed to be paid.

Sample Voucher

EMPLOYMENT ELIGIBILITY VERIFICATION (Form I-9)

LAST NAME	FIRST	MIDDLE	BIRTH NAME	BIRTH DATE
Write your last name here	Write your first name here	Write your middle name here	Write your birth name here	Write your birth date here

STREET ADDRESS	CITY	STATE	ZIP	SOCIAL SECURITY NUMBER
Write your complete address on this line (print clearly)				Write your Social Security Number here

I attest, under penalty of perjury, that I am (check a box):

☑ 1. A citizen or national of the United States. ☐ 2. An alien lawfully admitted for permanent residence (Alien Number A ______). ☐ 3. An alien authorized by the Immigration and Naturalization Service to work in the United States (Alien Number A ______, or Admission Number ______ expiration of employment authorization, if any ______).

I attest, under penalty of perjury, the documents that I have presented as evidence of identity and employment eligibility are genuine and relate to me.

I am aware that federal law provides for imprisonment and/or fine for any false statements or use of false documents in connection with this certificate.

SIGNATURE	PREPARER TRANSLATOR CERTIFICATION	SIGNATURE	PRINT NAME
X Sign your name here	((To be completed if prepared by person other than employee). I attest, under penalty of perjury, that the above was prepared by me at the request of the named individual and is based on all information of which I have any knowledge.		
DATE Write today's date		ADDRESS	

EMPLOYER REVIEW AND VERIFICATION: Examine one document from List A and check the appropriate box. *OR* examine one document from List B *and* one from List C and check the appropriate boxes. Provide the *Document Identification Number* and *Expiration Date* for the document checked.

List A Documents that Establish Identity and Employment Eligibility	List B Documents that Establish Identity	List C Documents that Establish Employment Eligibility
☐ 1. United States Passport ☐ 2. Certificate of United States Citizenship ☐ 3. Certificate of Naturalization ☐ 4. Unexpired foreign passport with attached Employment Authorization ☐ 5. Alien Registration Card with photograph *Document Identification* # ______ *Expiration Date (if any)* ______	☑ 1. A State-Issued driver's license or a State-issued I.D. card with a photograph, or information, including name, sex, date of birth, height, weight, and color of eyes. (Specify State) CA ☐ 2. U.S. Military Card ☐ 3. Other (Specify document and issuing authority) *Document Identification* # Write Drivers License Number Here *Expiration Date (if any)* Write Expiration Date Here	☑ 1. Original Social Security Number Card (other than a card stating it is not valid for employment) ☐ 2. A birth certificate issued by State, county or municipal authority bearing a seal or other certification ☐ 3. Unexpired INS Employment Authorization Specify form. *Document Identification* # Write Social Security Number Here *Expiration Date (if any)* ______

CERTIFICATION I attest, under penalty of perjury, that I have examined the documents presented by the above individual, that they appear to be genuine and to relate to the individual named, and that the individual, to the best of my knowlege, is eligible to work in the United States.

SIGNATURE	TITLE	EMPLOYER
X		PAYROLL SERVICE

Sample I-9 Form
(Answer the questions as they apply to you.)

• Understanding

The Extras Casting Industry

1 **LEVEL ONE:** starting point = production

Needs Background Talent

PRODUCTION opts to cast the Background themselves =
In-House Casting
(the end)

PRODUCTION opts to hire ONE of the following types of
Extras Casting Companies

2 **LEVEL TWO:** extras casting companies

a. Team FREE
Extras Casting Company with FREE Registration & No Talent Commissions.

b. Team Pay Me ONCE & Be Done With It
Extras Casting Company that charges Talent a Fee but does not take Talent Commissions.

c. Team Pay Me Once & Pay Me Per Job
Extras Casting Company that charges Talent a Fee and also takes Talent Commissions.

3 **LEVEL THREE:** third party talent services

any number of these companies may be called to assist

Team Calling Monthly
•
Calling Services

The Minor Team
•
Children's Casting Co's

Team Show Me ALL The Money
•
Yearly Fee Co's

Special Teams
•
Specialty Casting

Team Dot Com
•
Internet Listing Co's

LEVEL ONE: starting point – production

This is the actual feature film, television show, commercial, etc. Each production either hires a specific Extras Casting company or opts to do the casting themselves (in-house). When the Casting is done "IN-HOUSE" there are no registration fees and no commissions taken from extra performers. When production hires an Extras Casting company there can be fees involved for extra performers.

LEVEL TWO: *extras casting companies*

When an Extras Casting company is hired by PRODUCTION to cast a project they are usually paid a percentage of what the extra performers earn on the show. So you better believe Extras Casting wants you to go into overtime because the more you make – the more production pays them for casting. Because production hires only ONE Extras Casting company to cast their show/project, it is a good idea to register with multiple extras casting companies. The more you register with, the more projects/jobs you will have access to.

a.) TEAM "FREE"

These Extras Casting companies offer free registration and do not take a percentage from Non-Union extras (union commissions are forbidden by SAG and AFTRA). TEAM FREE Extras Casting companies register talent by mail only and usually meet with talent in person via open calls and/or periodic visiting and registration sessions. All extra performers should register with TEAM FREE Extras Casting companies as it is a FREE process. Also on TEAM FREE are Independent Casting Directors who cast on a project-by- project basis. See ACT 4 for individual contact info and procedures.

b.) TEAM "PAY ME ONCE AND BE DONE WITH IT"

These Extras Casting companies charge a one-time fee of some sort (photo fee, registration fee, etc.). These Casting companies typically have an office where you are able to register and visit. These companies DO NOT take a percentage from the Non-Union performer.

c.) TEAM "PAY ME ONCE AND PAY ME PER JOB"

These Extras Casting companies typically operate similar to Type B extras Casting companies except for the fact that they also take a percentage from the Non-Union performer's paycheck. These companies take a commission from both production and the Non-Union extras. They must not take commissions that would bring your earnings below the state-mandated minimum wage or they could find themselves with a lawsuit on their hands – like the class action suit against Central Casting that resulted in background actors receiving a settlement in 2002.

LEVEL THREE: *third party talent services*

These companies are typically NOT hired by production companies. Instead they are called upon by the Level 2 extras casting companies. The Extras Casting companies do not pay the Level 3 companies for their services. The Level 3 companies make their money by charging the extra performer a fee, a commission or both.

a.) TEAM "CALLING MONTHLY"

Calling Services usually charge a monthly fee (often between $45 - $90) to mediate between the extra performer and the extras casting company. These services will arrange your schedule and book you for work. They vouch for your availabilty, so having more than one service can lead to some major schedule meltdowns. Calling Services provide extras casting companies with pictures of their members. Some charge a commission per job (whether you're Union or not) as opposed to a flat monthly fee and some charge it on top of the monthly fee.

b.) TEAM DOT COM

With the innovation of computers and such this team was inevitable. Internet listing companies provide a searchable database of talent via the Internet. But do your research – it does you no good to spend money for a webpage on a site that Casting Directors don't use!

c.) THE "MINOR" TEAM

Children's casting companies charge a fee and a commission from the child's paycheck (SAG, AFTRA and Non-Union). The majority of the extras casting companies rely on these children's casting companies when booking minors since this is their specific function.

d.) "SPECIAL" TEAMS

Specialty Casting companies/organizations are for talent with a specific look/talent (i.e., military, bikers, etc.). These companies/organizations often negotiate for a higher rate of pay for their members and offer the extras casting company a one-stop shop when seeking their specialized type. There are various fees associated with these kinds of groups.

e.) TEAM "SHOW ME ALL OF THE MONEY"

Yearly Fee companies typically advertise a great deal – usually in non-industry publications (and here's the kicker – they claim to cast other companies' projects). They charge a large up-front lump sum averaging $100 or more per year. Many claim to operate similar to Calling Services in that extras casting companies supposedly call them when seeking talent and the "Yearly Fee Company" will then book their members on the project. . . supposedly.

act one

• *Fun Introduction*

(NO SKIPPING THIS SECTION, PEOPLE - WE SAW THAT!!)

You were going to SKIP THIS SECTION, you were going to SKIP this page – We DO NOT THINK SO, buddy! Even if you have read this before, last month or last winter, you may consider reading it again. WHY, you ask? Ideas, marketing strategies, thought-provoking run-on sentences, the use of many – unnecessary – d-a-s-h-e-s – incorrect grammer (see, we even spell grammar wrong), and useful tips run amuck on the following pages (we do this on purpose, it keeps your attention span in check).

Whether you are an "extra god" or if you are just plain new to the entertainment industry, this section applies to EVERYONE – Got it?! It is muy importanté! (Spanish for VERY Important, or so we think, it has been a while and now that we think about it, didn't we take Cantonese in high school?!)

On the following pages we are going to outline a step-by-step guideline /process for you to obtain extra work. Be on the lookout for capitalized terminology. Some of it you may know, while unfamiliar industry terms may be new. We've tried to Brain Surgeon(ify) what they mean.

• *Finding Work*

Ultimately, the key factors to working in this industry are RESEARCHING job possibilities, MARKETING yourself, and maintaining a level of PROFESSIONALISM that Casting Directors will remember. Extra Work is a job like any other job and should be taken seriously! Heck, you ARE getting paid.

Casting Directors are just looking for good people, with good attitudes (aside from bribes and gifts...) who will do an exceptional job on the set! In all seriousness, and in the overall realm of things, treat the Casting Directors as YOU would want to be treated if you were in THEIR shoes – suck up to them, harass them . . . (no, we're kidding, kids – pay attention to sarcasm!) If you follow the guidelines set forth in this book – you should be pretty darn OK without all the butt-kissing. They have a job to do, you have a job to do. Everyone does what's expected of them and everybody wins!

• *Read Act 4, Act 5, Act 6 & Act 7*

Before we get started, we first want to stress the importance of reading Act 4, Act 5, Act 6 and Act 7. Thoroughly read about EACH and every extras casting agency listed and how they operate. You should make notes and COMPARE the following information:

• Credits
• Commissions
• Registration Fees

Please use ALL of the information contained within these pages to decide which agencies are right for you. Do not forget to pay close attention to those that are FREE or that offer IN-HOUSE CASTING – like the soaps! They have FREE REGISTRATION or SUBMISSION, so take advantage of this – and why the heck not?! It is FREE!

• Registration Fees

Registration type fees in extra work often exist. However, not all agency fees are the same. They have all kinds of names and fancy reasons to charge people – regardless of whether or not talent is affiliated with any sort of union. There is a Computer Imaging Fee, or a Registration Fee, a Photo Fee, and how about a Parking Fee? There's the good'ole Processing Fee, the ever-hip Digital Photo Fee, the Orientation Fee and our personal fave, the"Safety and Security Course" fee. (Sometimes we are surprised there isn't a VISITING FEE!!) Are all of these enhanced terms legit, you ask? Well, unfortunately, the answer is YES – however, just remember, these fees are typically a ONE-TIME deal! Be sure to pay attention to the following:

• There are No Guarantees of Work
• Average Fee is no more than $25
• Registration Fees are One Time only

Any agency that asks for or requires a yearly fee sounds subject to making outlandish promises, not to mention charging way too much money. The average registration fee IS TYPICALLY LESS than the newly inflated $25 and again, that should be a one-time fee. (See, it is not that bad, but we know that a fee here and a fee there can add up quickly – hence our ADORATION of FREE REGISTRATION AGENCIES!) This is also why we try to list many recent credits each agency or CD has. Carefully go through each page and decipher if the agency has had A LOT of work recently or a MINIMAL amount (we try to list their recent credits for a reason, duh). See if you feel it's worth your time or trouble to register with them. This will help you determine the volume and quality of their work before you plop down any dough.

• Agencies Charging Over the Average Fee

There are indeed a number of agencies in this publication that charge OVER $25. Again we cover this topic in-depth in Act 4, but to make a long story short – we include these agencies in **"EXTRA" WORK for Brain Surgeons®** because these agencies DO have work. You just need to determine for yourself whether paying the annual fee is worth your well-earned moo-lah.

Many so-called agencies that advertise in non-industry publications charge well OVER $100 – promising guaranteed work (some may even advertise in the *Los Angeles Times* and generally claim to cast other people's projects). Be careful of "guarantees" and understand, spending that amount of money is

just NOT NECESSARY (unless you are bored & really wealthy) because there are lots of FREE (or nominal-fee) agencies who really DO have work! For more on these supposed companies, check out their dubious practices in Act 9, aptly titled *Fabulous Other*.

- Check out the Better Business Bureau
- Casting Companies typically do not charge 100s of dollars
- Again, read Act 9 at the end of this book

Checklist of Information

Next (especially if you are new), COMPLETE THE CHECKLIST OF GENERAL INFORMATION later in this Act. It can serve as a mini resumé of sorts. This way, when you register with agencies you will be prepared – if you DO NOT fill it out, chances are, you will find yourself asking for a measuring tape at the casting office (unprofessional). Please, for the love of God, know your measurements and bring a photo! (more about that later) If you are prepared, you are viewed as more professional – this is a good thing. Also, when you are registering via mail, be sure to include ALL of that SAME information along with a photo.

Get Registered With The Free Places

As we mentioned, there are places with FREE Registration!! Get registered with these cool cats! You do not need to go and visit these places as most of them accept submissions by mail only. Some of these FREE registration folks, however, have given **HOLLYWOOD OS**® their registration cards to pass along to you. Simply stop by our office Monday - Friday, from 1PM-4PM.

You do not have to complete the registration cards to get registered with most of them, although, it is a good idea - it's more of an official document! Instead, you may also mail a basic 3"x5" photo (as discussed in "The 3"x5" Lecture" later in this chapter) along with your "General Information" and anything else listed in their individual sections. This will cost you less than a buck and is well worth the investment – especially if you get booked!

The same basic procedure applies to those in-house/soap opera casting folks – it's also FREE. Hurry up, you have NO EXCUSES! If you are already registered with some of the agencies listed, you are definitely a step ahead of most people at this stage.

Do Your Research

Now you need to take things a step further. Develop a strategy – this, my friends, is your homework! Analyze who has the most work. (look in the latest **HOLLYWOOD OS**® magazine or www.HollywoodOS.com for these extras casting listings/information!) Scope out other trade magazines like *Back Stage West*®, *Variety*® and *The Hollywood Reporter*®. Another good idea is to check CD's hotlines regularly and mail them CURRENT snapshots or postcards with a note saying you are still interested in working. If you can visit (be aware days and times vary), be sure to plan your visiting route based on who has the MOST work – this way you will save gas and not spend so much darn time in traffic!

Market Yourself

Next, visualize yourself as the Casting Director – what would you respond best to? (BEHAVE, FOLKS – no first-class tickets to Aruba!!) How about unique photos? Sending snapshots of yourself in diverse looks shows enthusiasm and allows Casting Directors to visualize you in more than one category for work.

(NOTE: Different LOOKS are NOT different poses, shoes, shirts, or ties. Different looks ARE really different CHARACTERS in drastically different attire!)

You DO NOT NEED to go out and spend hundreds of dollars to do this. Borrow a friend with a camera and take some color 3"x5" photos of yourself WAIST-UP, against a WHITE BACKGROUND – this is the basic format and is perfectly acceptable. Again, see "The 3"x5" Lecture" for more exciting information.

Getting Booked

The ART of being a background artist – essentially you are a non-speaking actor! First and foremost, in order to work as an extra, you've got to get booked. Essentially, this means you were contacted by an agency or Casting Director and they asked you if you were available to work on a set. If the answer is "yes" you were available to work, the Casting Director will typically "book" you on the call. CONGRATULATIONS, this is half the battle! Now comes the responsibility – you will be asked to confirm, show up, and act professionally while working on set. It is your responsibility to make it to the set. If you know you have a dental appointment for the next day, do not show up on set expecting to be excused early to get your teeth fixed. This is not school, people – your parents cannot write you a frickin'note! It is exceedingly important that you are available the entire day. Given that the average workday is around 12 hours, expect to be on set a heck of a long time.

Flake Factor Disclaimer

Not showing up is a huge, huge mistake. Not showing up and not having the courtesy to call and inform the Casting Director is even worse. We have had numerous complaints from busy Casting Directors who are getting flaked on. This, my friends, is not good. If a Casting Director takes the time to submit you for a project, please make the effort to show up. If you have a Calling Service, chances are you have been hand-selected by either the Casting Director, the service, or both. If you do not show up, they will hear about it. This is where much of the lack of professionalism comes into play. What makes you think that Casting Director will ever hire you again? When you do not show up, you undermine the work efforts of the casting company. The lack of responsible people reflects poorly on the Casting Director. And what happens if not only you don't show up, but ten other people choose not to show up as well? What if the Casting Director gets fired because of this? Do you think the producers of that show will ever hire that company again knowing they have provided unprofessional, unreliable people? Extras have the ability to play with Casting Directors' livelihoods and reputations.

act one

Be Prepared, People

With that vent session said, understand that the Casting Director is SWAMPED! When you receive a call for work, please do not ask unnecessary questions (i.e., what the movie/TV show/commercial is about or who is in it). If everyone asked such questions, the Casting Director would never be able to cast!

Instead, have a PEN and PAPER READY & MAKE SURE YOU OBTAIN the following INFORMATION from the Casting Director:

- Call Time
- Location (Thomas Guide Coordinates or *Yahoo! Maps*)
- Who to check in with
- What to bring (Clothing colors, seasonal, etc.)
- Emergency Number (Always call if you are late)

If you were booked through your Calling Service they should provide you with all of this essential information (including which extras casting agency booked you).

Calling Services

For those of you who are new, a Calling Service is kinda like the agent of the extra world – except you have to pay them a monthly fee to book you. In a nutshell, Calling Services are not Casting Directors – they are companies that you pay a monthly fee (usually from $45 to $90) or a percentage to manage your schedule and keep your availability and picture accessible to Casting Directors on a daily basis. Your service is authorized to accept work calls on your behalf and vouch for your availability. Some people enjoy the challenge of booking themselves, others do not and would rather pay someone to manage their affairs. It's all up to the individual to do his or her research to determine if this is the way to go. Our best advice to the newcomer is try it on your own first! If you find yourself frustrated and/or not getting booked, then perhaps a service is for you. There are some really good Calling Services and some really lousy services, do your homework. There is a section in this Act about Calling Services, we suggest you peruse it.

Double No-No

"DOUBLE BOOKING" yourself is definitely not a wise decision, so don't do it! For those who are not familiar with this term, it simply means do not book yourself or commit yourself to two different shows for the same day. This always leads to some sort of God-forsaken trouble. Unfortunately with extra work, when it rains, it pours and when it's dead, it's DEAD. Double booking yourself is a no-win situation for you. It's not like you can show up to two different sets. Even if you have two completely opposite call times for the same day, this can still lead to a load of trouble. And do not have your friends try to show up and be you – replacing yourself with your buddies is a VERY bad idea! What if your redheaded self was picture-picked by the Director and your blonde buddy shows up claiming to be you – busted! Not only are you dead meat with the Casting Director, the Casting Director is dead meat with the darn production company and then the agency that hired you thinks you're a flake, then you end up looking like a moron. See what we mean? This could have a snowballing "BLACKBALL" effect! (meaning – NO ONE will want to book you again). Also random – NO boozing on set – seriously, we've heard stories!!

Here's a little lesson: Three thought-they-were-clever background performers accept a *Rainbow* (now *Jeff Olan Casting*) job which was filming on a studio lot. Once they checked in, they proceeded to walk over to the next sound stage and "SPEC" a *Central* show. A SPEC is someone who shows up to a set who is not OFFICIALLY booked. They show up in hopes of being added to the call. Well anyway, as luck would have it, these three clowns got on the *Central/Cenex* job next door. Unfortunately for them, the *Rainbow* and *Central* coordinators compared notes at lunch and voilá – BUSTED!! This is an excellent example of how one could alienate two agencies in a matter of minutes (and jeopardize future work with either casting company).

Call Time

Now, when you are given a "CALL TIME," it is very important that you understand that this is the time you are to report to work. The general rule of thumb is – when you arrive on time, you are late. Huh? What we mean is, it is always a good idea to be EARLY (15 minutes is industry standard). Also, when you show up, please do not ask, "How long do you think we'll be here?" This gets tiresome and probably puts some Assistant Directors in a bad mood – especially if you have 50-plus extras asking the same darn question. How annoying! No offense. If you are lucky, you will get an awesome Assistant Director – who is not overworked – and he or she will explain the scene you are in and give you a rough estimate of how long you may be there. Keep in mind, "how long you will be there" is most often not known – it varies from day to day, show to show. So don't think the "A.D." (ASSISTANT DIRECTOR) or Coordinator is holding out on you by not telling you – they just don't know!! All we can say is that you will "be there" until they get the shots they need that have been scheduled for the day. The rule of thumb is that the typical day is around 12 hours, FYI.

Check In

Now that you have been briefed and have confirmed your information, it is very important that you know where your "LOCATION" to the set is. Oftentimes Casting Directors will give you your location on a Thomas Guide coordinate and page number or supply you with an address and zip code so you can *Yahoo! Maps* the locale. It would be an excellent idea to look up the directions the night before so that you can determine how long it will take you to get to where you are going. This way you can map out how bad traffic will be. Nothing could be worse than showing up late on your first day – not a good impression to make!

Great – so you beat traffic, you got there on time – now what? Do I just sit around? Hell no! Find an A.D. and immediately "CHECK IN" upon arrival – this will save everyone a headache, because they know that you arrived safely on set. Sometimes a "PRODUCTION ASSISTANT," "SET COORDINATOR" or even the Casting Director will check you in – it all depends on how large the call is. In any event, the person you will check in with is the person who will mark your name down on some "SKINS" (the working extra roll call, like in school).

Once you have been checked off, you will then be given your "VOUCHER." A voucher is basically your time card and contains all of your vital information (address, phone numbers, social security, dependents, etc.) so that your paycheck may be issued and mailed to you.

In addition to clocking in with your "IN TIME," you will also jot down your meal breaks, sign your John Hancock and fill in your "OUT TIME" (departure time, but we will explain this later!). Basically it's like this, if you haven't been given a voucher, chances are the A.D. doesn't know that you're there. This is not good! Also, for those of you who are New Kids on The Block (did we just say that? Anyway...) do not show up on the set asking where your trailer is – not a good idea. You are an extra, (i.e., background actor) not Leonardo DiCaprio. Therefore, unfortunately, you will NOT be given a trailer. Sorry – we know, it sucks!

Wardrobe & Selections

Let's talk about "WARDROBE" for a minute. The reason you were booked on this call was because you were available, you were either the right type/age group/ethnicity, and you fit the proper sizes or you had the right type of wardrobe.

Now, when Casting Directors call you to confirm your booking, they will tell you what type of wardrobe to bring. This is very important – do not blow off bringing wardrobe, people! DO NOT lie and say you have a particular color suit if you really don't! Do what is asked of you and bring the specific type that was instructed or requested. Be honest about your wardrobe when the Casting Director is booking you. If you do lie, you better do so before the stores close.

After you have checked in, an A.D. will often tell you to eat (especially if you arrive early on a morning call) and shove you off to the happy Wardrobe department. Make sure you have your voucher and have your name written on it before you get in line at the wardrobe trailer. You should come to work dressed and ready to work – otherwise known as "CAMERA READY." Wardrobe will look at what you are wearing and the clothes you brought and tell you what they want you to wear. Word to the wise – never, never, under any circumstances, bring clothes that you feel ridiculously uncomfortable in. The wardrobe department is weird like this – let's say you bring some skintight spandex dress from 1987. Let's say you hate this dress. Let's say you brought it but you didn't mean to. When Wardrobe begins rummaging through your bag to find a hip outfit, they will inevitably pick out that blasted outfit! WHY, you ask? Well, Wardrobe Department has a sixth sense and can smell what you passionately loathe. They will undoubtedly stick you in that Spandex Schpeel all day long! The moral of this story is do not bring stuff you hate – but you didn't hear this from us, so shhh. . . FYI: It is against the California State Law for wardrobe to clothe you in previously worn and not laundered clothing.

The only way really around this is to make sure you have brought several "SELECTIONS." This will only benefit you. We know lugging around your big one-ton luggage bags sucks, but if the Wardrobe Department likes what you have brought to the set, and if you are asked to change into the outfits, you will often be paid a "WARDROBE BUMP" (or "CHANGE") for every change you are requested to wear on camera. It simply has to be your clothing – cool! The wardrobe bump is not designed to cover your chiropractic bills from lugging your clothing – it is designed to pay your cleaning expenses for the clothing worn on camera. Think of this bump as a cleaning fee. The first outfit (on SAG film/TV jobs) you are photographed in is "FREE," it's part of your "BASE RATE."

Your current base rate is listed on your voucher. For Non-Union talent your rate is $54 dollars for 8 hours and for SAG members, your base rate is $122 for 8 hours (at least until July 2006). The next outfit of your own clothes that you are asked to change into is a wardrobe change. You are paid only for changing into outfits you have provided.

For SAG members, the wardrobe issue is a little different. According to the SAG contract, SAG members are to receive payment for ALL changes or selections of clothing requested by production and relayed to you via the Casting Director. For more information, see your boring SAG contract.

If wardrobe does not select any of your clothing, do not take their disapproval of your clothing personally. They might be going for a specific look or you might be in the same color as the star. Please do not bring red, white or black clothes unless asked. Usually the Director of Photography (D.P.) hates these colors. Also, do not bring clothing with obvious logos on them (like the *Nike*® swoosh). Production would first need permission to photograph the logo and that is a whole other can of worms! Always bring or wear soft-soled shoes appropriate to your wardrobe. Girls: it's an excellent idea to have your high-heeled shoes soled with soft rubber and to get small crutch tips for the heels.

If everyone is in soft-soled shoes the "SOUND DEPARTMENT" has a much better chance of getting all of the dialogue recorded. If the wardrobe department gives you some of their stylish clothes to wear, they will ask for your voucher and keep it until the end of the day when you return their clothing. (Your voucher is kinda like collateral for their stuff – this is why your name should be on your voucher!) Additionally, if you change into something provided by wardrobe, it doesn't count as a wardrobe change. Sorry, folks!

• Hair & Make-Up Ready

After wardrobe, you will often be excused to go to hair and make-up – yes, we said hair and make-up (even background actors, oftentimes, have touch-ups and style changes)! You will either be approved or fixed. If the film is a period piece, you can bet that the hair and make-up department will have a field day primping and prepping you for the scene. Girls should ALWAYS arrive made-up (appropriately – do not go and get valley-girled up!) with their hair done. And boys, well, boys should take a shower and smell good! Shaving is also a fabulous idea (unless asked specifically not to) No party hangover looks, people!

• Prop This

After this whole check-in nonsense, the wardrobe fiasco and the hair/make-up adventure, you may then be asked to go to the "PROP TRUCK" where the "PROPERTY DEPARTMENT" (the people in charge of giving out props) will give you whatever the appropriate props are depending on what you were booked as. Students will get notebooks and backpacks and cops will get guns and badges. FYI: if you are working as a cop, just know that all cops should give their guns to a propman before leaving for lunch. Sometimes you are asked to bring props of your own to the set, (i.e., sporting goods, luggage – you get the idea). If this is the case, and casting specifically booked you for this and/or asked you to supply your own props, you will be given a "BUMP" on your voucher. All this means is that you will be given additional money for supplying your own props. (But this isn't guaranteed for Non-Union gigs - so ask!)

• Holding Schmolding

Next – after blasted breakfast, after visiting blasted wardrobe, after changing into your blasted wardrobe, after blasted hair, after blasted make-up, and after blasted props, you will then be instructed to hang out in "HOLDING." Holding is just what is sounds like. Oftentimes it's like this small, cramped, tank-like area where the extras are expected to hang out and schmooze with each other. That's schmoozing, not snoozing!

Although Holding is not the most exciting place in the darn world, you will hear good gossip and listen to fellow extras brag about what they have been "FEATURED" in. When someone is featured, they are clearly seen on screen in the scene. When extras are featured, however, this does not necessarily result in more pay.

Chairs should always be provided for both the SAG and Non-Union talent as this is mandatory and specifically stated in the California State Laws. However, it's a good idea to bring your own folding chair because it's probably a lot more comfortable than the lame chairs the production will likely provide. Remember you are at work, so don't bring pillows and take a snooze.

• Brain Surgeon Pop Quiz

Okay, you are in Holding . . . the Assistant Director (A.D.) comes in & wants volunteers for the next scene. You . . .

a.) *Hide under the table (like Angela).*

b.) *Excuse yourself to use the restroom (like sexy Samro).*

c.) *Volunteer to go to set and work.*

d.) *Pretend to tie your shoe (like Carla). Has the same effect as answer "A."*

• Score Card

- If you picked **a.)** Give yourself 5 points for picking the right instinctive response.
- If you picked **b.)** Give yourself 1 point – you're a wimp! Sit down!
- If you picked **c.)** Give yourself 10 points and keep quiet (no one needs to see you jumping up and down, it's only a multiple-choice quiz).
- If you picked - **d.)** Give yourself 7 points for being more clever than Angie.

• Craft(y) Service

In Holding there should also be a meager "CRAFT SERVICE" table set up (weak food table) comprised of stale coffee, hard doughnuts and bruised fruits (only if the production is cheap, that is!). Big budget projects generally have kick ass (for those over 19, this means rad or outstanding) crafty (slang for "Craft Service") tables. If you are lucky you may be able to sit down and munch some breakfast without the A.D. yapping at you to hurry up and be on your way to work. "HURRY UP AND WAIT" will soon be an over-used term/concept you will quickly become familiar with. It is imperative you stay in the designated holding area. The A.D.'s must be able to find you quickly if and when you are needed.

If, for any reason, you need to leave the Holding area please tell an A.D. where you are going (i.e., the bathroom, the phone, or the smoking area). When you go to Craft Service (if it is outside the Holding area) don't treat it like a hang-out spot – get your grub and return to the official Holding area.

While On Set

Always be prepared to get off your rear end and work already. That's what you are getting paid to do anyway, right? Remember, this is a job – not a party! You are getting paid. The A.D. will appreciate the fact that you volunteered and she/he may remember this cooperative behavior later on. Besides, this only increases your chances of being given "SPECIAL BUSINESS" (sounds kinda kinky, we know...) and everyone wants to be given that special instruction of interacting with the principal actors (who knows? It could result in an added bump on your paycheck). Remember this, people – you will never get "UPGRADED" if you just sit around and sleep in holding. Make yourself useful and be enthusiastic – A.D.'s will appreciate this (and it could result in more days of work, or other cool things).

TIP: If an Assistant Director is asking how tall people are – pay attention!! The A.D. is most likely looking to "upgrade" someone to a "STAND-IN" or "PHOTO DOUBLE." This means more money and possibly more days on the show!

When the Assistant Director brings you to the set, please try not to talk or flirt. Usually when you go into the set the crew is still lighting and it's very important that they are able to hear the Director of Photography and the "GAFFER." The crew makes enough noise on their own and the background shouldn't add to it – it just makes the day longer. The crew and the cast can be evil – they'll get you in trouble. For example, the 1st A.D. won't care that you haven't seen Joe Grip since his son's wedding; the 1st A.D. will only care that you are talking. BUSTED! Don't let them get you in trouble. Don't talk to them on the set. This is one of the most important rules!

Background Action

Remember, the crew is supposed to be working SILENTLY and the A.D. is trying to determine what "BACKGROUND ACTION" or movement to give you in the scene. Once you have been instructed to do something in the scene, please continue to remain silent and allow the other crew members to work. Pay attention to the A.D.'s – they are your bosses in the extra world – they are the big cheeses you need to give your undivided attention to.

Next, the cast and crew will "BLOCK OUT" or rehearse the scene with "SECOND TEAM" – otherwise known as "Stand-Ins." Essentially, Stand-Ins do just that – they are hired to "stand in" for the principal actors for lighting purposes and camera angles while the actor reviews his or her lines with the director. More often than not, the Stand-In will resemble the person he or she is standing in for. This job is very important because as a Stand-In, you must memorize the exact actions as the principal actor. A good Stand-In must be responsible, attentive and alert while working. For more information, see "Stand-In 101" later in Act 1.

Anyway – by this time you have rehearsed your background action several times and are now confident that you are ready for the real thing – however, let us suggest just one more tip! For example, if the scene is in a hallway

act one

and you have been asked to stand in the hallway having "conversation" with a fellow background player, this does not mean to really speak – this means you should "PANTOMIME" or pretend to talk and mouth the words as if you are having that real conversation. Please, for the love of God, remember that you are a background actor which in the truest of definitions means you are being paid NOT to speak. Talking in the middle of a scene will get you canned!

When the Director yells out, "Background Action," this is your chance to show the A.D. what you are made of – this is your "CUE" to begin your movement in the scene. The A.D. will tell you when and where to make a cross and who to stop and deal with. Unfortunately, because there is so much going on, the A.D. doesn't usually have time to give you a motivational pep talk or a character. At this point, you should know what the scene is, where it takes place, and what kind of people you are playing – heck, you have rehearsed it hundreds of times!

We know it may sound cheesy, but create a character for yourself and a reason for every cross. Stop and "talk" to Jill - not just because the A.D. told you to, but because you want to congratulate her on a promotion or find out how last night's softball game went (REMEMBER: always miming!). The possibilities for making the background "live" are endless. The more meaning and motivation you put into each cross or encounter with another extra, the better the scene and the show will look when it airs. We've all seen a show where the background is making crosses across an office only because the A.D. told them to make a cross. We call it the "ZOMBIE CROSS." Try to avoid it and you'll end up looking much more real on TV and on film.

• *Cut The Cheese*

After the the director yells, "CUT," this does not mean you are excused to go off to Holding for Happy Hour. Usually there is an area set up for "CAST CHAIRS". Newcomers are not always aware of this, but cast chairs are not set up for the background talent. It would NOT be a wise decision to sit in these chairs. Cast members are provided chairs for two reasons. The first reason is that it's in their contract. The second reason (most important for the 2nd A.D.): if the production has an area for the cast, they will usually sit there and it makes it easier for the A.D.'s to find them when they are needed. If background talent is sitting in their chairs, the cast won't be – they will be off at craft service ruining their make-up!

• *Okay. . . Random. . .*

Although it doesn't happen often, in the event of an earthquake (yeah, that's what we said – "Hey, it happened to me once!" claims Angela. *Angie, are you sure that's coffee you're drinking?*)... yes, an earthquake on the set/sound stage. Well, the first thing you should do is be glad you're not on its epicenter, then look up and see where you are. They tell us that the only bad thing that happens in a quake on stage is that sometimes things shake off the scaffolding. If you are standing under one, just move into a clear area. If the stage needs to be evacuated, please exit through the stage doors – don't head for the big loading doors unless you see that they are already open. Just remember you should probably meet up with the A.D. outside, that way they can get a head count and make sure everyone got off the stage safely. See, random!

act one

Wrapping it Up

Okay, now let's say you've worked (yeah!!) and you are sent back to Holding – don't go back to your table/bed and risk the chance of drool dripping from your mouth. Stay alive for God-sakes! And when it is time for you to "WRAP" (end of your day) please no pushing or shoving to sign out. Be nice.

You must return any props the Prop Department had supplied you with and then return any clothing the Wardrobe Department may have supplied you with. The A.D. will usually meet you in the holding area to sign you out. At that time they should briefly review lunch time and tell you the "OUT TIME" (when you... that's right, kids – sign out and go home).

Please remember, if the Holding area is a disaster, you can bet your bottom dollar that the A.D. will not release you until all of the coffee cups and candy wrappers are carefully placed in that ever-so-handy trash can. It's safe to assume they would appreciate your cooperation in cleaning up the Holding area voluntarily. It is amazing how many people actually resist doing this. The lack of cooperation on the part of extras to clean up after themselves only causes a lack of respect among those who do background work. It is also safe to bet that those A.D.'s will notice those few willing individuals who assist in cleaning up the overall mess. Remember, in order to gain respect, you must earn respect and this is definitely an excellent way to prove yourself. Cheesy, but true.

At this point, after all is said and done, you will probably be released. You will either walk to where your car is parked or catch a "SHUTTLE VAN" (a way cool *Scooby-Doo*-like party van that transports the extras and crew members to and from the location to holding or where your car is parked). If this is the case, please do not run all over each other to catch the shuttle van. Be respectful of those individuals who need help getting into these cramped vans. It is respectful to fill the back seats first – especially if you are a young tyke! Luggage bags are heavy, so make a point to think of others first. On that note, be polite to those who are not "SPRING CHICKENS" (people over 65). Let THEM into the van and assist them first. Chivalry is not dead, people, let's have some darn respect. (Being nice, by the way, is so very "IN" right now.)

Background Attitude

There are a lot of really good professional extras around who are usually willing to answer questions and explain stuff. Don't be afraid to ask questions – talk to them, they won't bite! The only way you will learn more about how this industry works is by asking.

Background actors can be nice, mean and every variation in between. There will be those fellow background actors who THINK they know everything. We're here to say, "be very careful who you listen to and for how long." You can listen to everybody, of course, but be careful what you believe. Many a know-it-all will try to get background actors in an uproar over any little thing, claim to know dismissal times, etc., and this will make for a most unpleasant on-set experience.

• Professionalism Disclaimer/Final Note:

There are some folks out there who are professional background actors. This is all they do. It is their profession. There are others who do this once in a while or as a stepping stone to other work.

No matter what your goal or objective is, you want someone to hire you. If you want to increase your chances, take heed to the previous few pages. Be professional. You have to be. We try to make the whole "learning" experience of extra work FUN, but remember, the bottom line is – it's a JOB!

We realize that, too often, background actors are treated with flat-out contempt from both production and casting. They are treated like "extras." Unfortunately, those treating you that way are not practicing what they preach. They obviously either hate their job or have fixated on a few background actors who may have acted unprofessionally in the past. So now these people are taking their frustration out on everyone. Essentially, they have contempt for the entire group of background actors (or the industry itself) because of a lack of professionalism they experienced with a few "bad eggs." What they do not realize is that this very contempt is a flagrant expression of their own unprofessionalism.

What we're trying to say is that you should attempt to be the better one, the bigger person, and not let these types of people get to you. If you do, and you react, you are perpetuating preconceived notions about background actors and continuing the destructive cycle.

We would like nothing more than to see the entire industry of "Background Acting" granted a little more respect. We believe that the merging of SAG and SEG (Screen Extras Guild) has helped. It blurred the line between "Background" and "Actor." By promoting professionalism, we at **HOLLYWOOD OS**® are trying to blur – even blend – that line even more.

Good luck and have oodles of FUN!!

NOTEWORTHY DISCLAIMER:
At press time, again,the three-voucher mode of entry is changing to a "points system." Keep up with your slammin' **HOLLYWOOD OS**® *- Casting Magazine for the latest news or contact SAG directly!*

The Right Place At The Slammin' Right Time Route:

Get yourself hired on a SAG project as a Day Player or Principal. In other words, convince someone to pay you to talk – this is quite a feat and not often accomplished by Non-Union talent... but it can happen!

36DD Blonde Bombshell / Fabio Route:

Find your sexy self on a SAG project working in some capacity, and out of nowhere the Director, Producer, A.D. – someone with clout decides you should be upgraded!

The Good Old "Extra" Route:

Getting hired as a SAG extra three times used to be the most common way talent became eligible to join SAG. However, this means is no longer valid. Beginning some time in 2006 (maybe!), SAG will institute a "points" system which will give value to all vouchers an extra receives. BG actors can also earn points by participating in SAG-sponsored activities that support professionalism within the Guild.

For the latest, check SAG's hotline set up specifically for this change: **1-800-807-4188** or call SAG's Membership Info Line: **323-549-6772**

Will Vouchers Still Help Me?:

As far as we can tell right now, YES! It looks as though you can still collect SAG vouchers as in the past, but it will take more then three of them to be eligible to join SAG. On most SAG projects there are a MINIMUM number of SAG vouchers which must be used each day (i.e., 19 for TV shows, 50 for feature films, etc.) In theory, SAG vouchers are to be given to SAG talent. In the event the Casting Director is unable to find a SAG member who fits the requirements of the job, a Non-SAG member may be hired (essentially, by default). This happy Non-SAG person has now obtained a SAG voucher.

Let's Break This Down:

Let's say a given SAG TV Show needs 19 men who are over 6' with their ow L.A.P.D. uniform and that is all the background talent they will be using that day. If Extras Casting can find only 10 SAG members who meet these requirements, they most likely will turn to their NON-SAG files to finish casting the call.

Those Non-SAG members who are then cast will be given SAG vouchers. This is because the first 19 people booked must be hired as SAG Talent (per the SAG contract). This example illustrates the importance for all talent to be as diverse as possible in their look, wardrobe, special skills and abilities.

Let's say a given feature film is using 100 background actors in a restaurant scene. At the end of the day, production realizes they have not completed filming a certain section of the room and they need to re-call the talent seated in that section. If they will be using only 30 background artists the next day and re-call that section of the room, everyone will be given a SAG voucher, whether they are SAG or not. This occurs because of the minimum number of SAG talent who must be hired on most SAG feature films each day. This example illustrates the point that it is good to get out there and work as much as possible, because anything can happen!

Less Official Ways To Go About Getting Your Vouchers!

Call the hotlines early in the morning. If there is a rush call, and you fit the bill and are ready to go AND it is a SAG job (lots of variables – but it happens) then you might just get the job, thus the voucher. We believe a SAG voucher will be worth more "points" than a Non-Union voucher in SAG's new "points system."

Register With Agencies Outside Of Los Angeles

These include Oxnard and San Diego. Remember the rule about using a minimum number of SAG vouchers each day? Well, realize the SAG talent is CONCENTRATED in the L.A. area. There are fewer SAG members in Oxnard and San Diego for Casting Directors to choose from – so again by default, more SAG vouchers are given to Non-SAG talent by agencies residing in those areas.

1-800-BUY-SAG-V. . . (Angela, Behave!!)

Yes, there are corrupt means of obtaining these little jewels – we feel they are pathetic. Agencies and/or organizations supporting them degrade the integrity of the Screen Actors Guild and its membership.

We have been told horror stories of talent buying vouchers – yuck! This is one main reason why the new "points system" is reportedly being adopted.

Voucher Tip #1:

Call the *Central Casting* Union line for rush calls as well. If you find SAG vouchers still hold more value than Non-Union vouchers once the point system is in place, and you hear a "car call" on the *Central* hotline – you might consider renting a car (could be cheap)– if it is indeed a SAG job – realize you are paid $35 extra for a car call in addition to the SAG base rate – it might just be worth it! Yeah, we know we told you that earlier in the chapter – but you folks are always skipping around!!

Voucher Tip #2:

Market yourself. Casting Directors will use a variety of resources to fill their calls. Online, for example, when they put up a casting notice they are often looking for something highly specific or seeking a background actor with a certain skill or trait.

Talent submit to the casting notice and write a personal note in their submission to the Casting Director. This would generally contain the level of your expertise, or you listing your qualifications, etc.

Of course, if after exhausting their search they cannot locate the appropriate SAG talent, they will then look to those appropriate in the pool of Non-Union talent. It is then that the Casting Directors will give out vouchers to those fitting the casting needs. Make sense?

So, you want to be a Stand-In or a Photo Double, ...do ya?

Great – join the crowd! But first things first – there is a hell of a lot more to STANDING IN than many of you may think. Oftentimes, a great majority of the Standing-In is done when the background is not present and entails more than just STANDING AROUND as commonly perceived. Obtaining that first Stand-In position is a lot like getting that first SAG voucher. However, any regular Stand-In will tell you, word of mouth is your best friend. You better know what to do when given a chance so you can be requested again and again which is exactly how most Stand-In's are hired!

Before we officially get started, let's define "Standing-In" and "Photo-Doubling" with a couple examples from the back of our swell (and massive) glossary.

STAND-IN: Also known as part of the "Second Team," these background actors are used as substitutes for featured players or principal actors so the D.P. (Director of Photography) can set lights and rehearse camera moves.

PHOTO DOUBLE: When talent is hired to take the place of the Principal actor. This could also be a Hand Double, Foot Double, Leg Double, or a Butt Double (this is needed more than you know and for actors you would not think – no joke!).

....SAG, AFTRA & Non-Union

Stand-In's and Photo Doubles can be SAG, AFTRA or Non-Union, it simply depends on what union affiliation the production falls under. Non-Union talent work on, yep, you guessed it, Non-Union projects!

If it is an AFTRA project, AFTRA Members or Non-Union talent who are willing to work AFTRA will be hired.

If it is a SAG project, then SAG members who best fit the specific criteria will be hired. If the appropriate SAG members cannot be found in the pool of SAG talent, Non-Union background *actors, who fit the criteria, are usually given a "SAG VOUCHER." As we have mentioned before, entry into the Screen Actors Guild via three vouchers is changing. At this time, however, it does look as though Non-Union talent can still earn SAG vouchers because these SAG vouchers will be worth more POINTS than Non-Union vouchers in SAG's new "points system."*

Part of the Crew

Just for the record, you do NOT work for the actor you are Standing In or Photo Doubling for. Realize that you work for the D.P. (Director of Photography) NOT the A.D.'s (Assistant Directors) as in background work. Stand-Ins are technically part of the Camera Department (and no, people, this does not mean you get to ride shotgun in the camera truck!).

Stand-In's Working as Extras

Interestingly enough, however, Stand-In's can also be used as background actors in the shot if needed, whether you are SAG or Non-Union. For the most part, they really need you to be paying attention to your job, so this doesn't really happen very often. Even though you are doing double duty, you are not entitled to an increase in pay on feature films or television. However, when working as a SAG extra and a stand-in on Commercials, you are entitled to two checks.

Stand-In's Working as Photo Doubles

Now, if you are Standing In as a SAG member and asked to photo double, there is a specific photo double/special ability rate of $132 for 8 hours (until July 2006) that will be adjusted on your voucher. That specific rate is for SAG members only. Non-Union stand-ins may negotiate a bump, but nothing is really set in stone.

Television

Well, we'll tell ya one thing, Standing In on an episodic television show is one hell of an intense, attention-demanding job. Unlike other Stand-In gigs, the television Stand-In may even require a bit of actor in ya! For the most part, you must not only Stand-In, but you are (often) required to know and memorize your actor's character's lines. Yeah, you read that right! You see, on the days of rehearsal, the principal actors are not present. The "CAMERAMEN" (people operating the cameras) and the "DIRECTOR" (the director, duh, come on, people...) heavily rely on you to "BLOCK" (the way in which the camera moves in the scene) the scene line by line, page by page, shot by shot, must be on, the appropriate "MARKS" (the position you were placed at by the A.D., director or D.P.) at the appropriate time and recite the dialogue sentence by sentence. Good Lord! If it's a "MULTI-CAMERA SHOW" (usually using four cameras), this demanding type of Standing In is most common on sitcoms. Obviously it requires a lot of professionalism, coordination, memorization, and a concise note-taking ability. Super-skilled folks needed for this type of work only – no time for any screwing up or screwing around on these shows!

Let's Talk Dollars, Baby

It's true what you've heard. Many people do make a living Standing In professionally. And if you are SAG, why the hell not – it doesn't pay half bad?! As you'll read, the base rate for Standing In is $137 for 8 hours (until July 2006 - of course). Considering the average day on a feature film is around 12 hours a day, throw in mileage, a couple of meal penalties and tack on the overtime, you are looking at a pretty decent daily paycheck! You may be looking at anywhere from $150 to $350+ bucks per day!

AFTRA members can also make bank. At $24 an hour with a 2-hour minimum for an 8 hour day, you are looking at $192 bucks. Considering the average day is, again, often 12 hours, we are talking about grossing around $288 bucks. Throw in that mileage and some random meal penalties and now you're really making some big smack-a-roos!

Non-Union background actors generally receive a considerable amount less when hired to work on Non-Union projects. That base rate for 8 hours can be anywhere from $75 to $100, depending on what the Casting Director tried to negotiate/finagle with production.

Although you are making good money, the only foreseeable drawback is the long-term commitment (for some gigs) and the exhausting hours. Working 12 to 14 hours a day can grow tiresome after a while. . . unless, of course, you are just laughing all the way to the ATM machine – in which case, thank your lucky stars!!

Now that we've covered most of the commonly asked questions, let's go through the art of Standing-In.

Step One

After arriving to set early, the very first thing your professional self should do is report to the wardrobe department. (As you will often encounter, these folks are a barrel of hip fun.) You should be prepared with the same color shirt as your actor – this is known as "COLOR COVER." If it is an ongoing Stand-In gig, go to wardrobe the night before so you can bring the correct color(s) for the next day. This is a sign of a seasoned Stand-In.

Step Two

Secondly, you will need to obtain your "SIDES" (sides are a mini-version of the script containing the scenes filmed for that day). You usually obtain these little bad boys from the 2nd A.D. or a Production Assistant. You will utilize these, refer to these, make notes on these and keep them with you at all times so that you are prepared.

Your Role

At this point your role is to, yup, watch and study rehearsal. In taking notes, you should observe EVERY detail of your actor's character's movement (Speed of Walk, Direction of Turns, On Which Line of Dialogue Movement Is Initiated/Ended, All Points In Which Your Character Stops, etc.). Your focus should be glued on what is going on around you.

Your Job

Once the crew (that means you too) has seen the rehearsal, the "FIRST TEAM" (The Principals/Actors) are usually excused to relax or finish getting ready and the "SECOND TEAM" (that would be you, the Stand-In) takes over. As the term "Second Team" implies – you are a "team" and should work together – no egos please!!

act one

At this point you work through the camera "blocking" (again, the way in which the camera moves in the scene) and stand in the "STOP MARKS" (your marks with fluorescent tape) as the "GAFFERS" (Lighting Technicians) set the lights.

Once the set is ready, "First Team" is invited back. There is usually a FINAL rehearsal and then the scene is shot. Once you hear, "PICTURE'S UP" (the Director is ready to shoot the scene) you are able to relax a little – this is your down time (this does not mean take a drooly snooze or grocery shop at craft service). The next term you should listen for is, "NEW DEAL." Upon hearing "New Deal," you should march your happy self back to the set and watch the next rehearsal, as we get ready for yet another scene.

The following is a list of pointers that may help you further your quest to become a "Stand-In" GOD or GODDESS:

• EMULATING YOUR ACTOR
Do not look into the camera when "Standing In." Look in the direction that the actor looks and try as best as you can to emulate the mood/attitude of your actor's character in every scene.

• TALKING
Talking on your cell phone, flirting with the crew, gossiping about the actor, painting your nails, eating olives, picking your nose, doing your hair, applying your lipstick, listening to a football game, and playing with your vibrating... pager while "Standing-In" generally does not go over very well. Although you work for the D.P., you better bet the A.D. (Assistant Director) is keeping an eye on you and the A.D. is the person who reports back to extras casting – so stay quiet and attentive – and you will be considered super-professional and maybe you'll get kudos (accolades, not the candy).

• SIDES
Always ask for "sides" from a P.A. or the 2nd A.D. or 2nd, 2nd A.D. – not the First A.D., the D.P. or the actor. Try to have your "sides" available and a working pen ready before rehearsal. NOTE: always make sure your pen has ink.

• CALL TIME
Your call time is when you are expected on set – be prepared to arrive early so you can eat, talk about last night's episode of *Desperate Housewives* and see wardrobe before your call time. Remember, everyone wants your job and you want to keep it. Yes, technically you could skip wardrobe and have a P.A. (Production Assistant) get you the correct color to wear, but that is not the professional way of doing things.

• KEY TERMINOLOGY
Understand the terms we have presented to you in this article. It is important terminology that you will hear over and over when Standing In – it's imperative that you know what they mean (this is why we have repeated them and their definitions, so repetitively throughout this damn well-written article)!

• MARKS
If you are "Standing-In" and your mark is changed, (you are told to adjust your position) make sure the tape on the floor/chair/whatever is also changed.

• COLOR COVER
The very first thing you do when you get to set - yup, you guessed it! Check in with wardrobe before arriving on set to get your proper "color cover."

• SHOES WITH HEELS
Different healed shoes, making you an inch or two or three taller will enable you to qualify for more jobs and make your height more flexible.

• WIGS
Obtain wigs as backup. It will diversify and increase your booking odds.

• STAND-IN/PHOTO DOUBLE RESUMÉ
Start keeping track of your credits and create a specific resumé for this type of work. The most important information you should list would be the year, the project and the actor. Listing any wigs or props you may have is also a good idea. There is an example of a resumé at the end of this Act.

STAND-IN WORK: 2005 - "Cinderella Man," Russell Crowe
1998 - "Southie," Jimmy Cummings

PHOTO DOUBLE: 2005 - "The Eye," Renee Zellweger
2004 - "Ray," Jamie Foxx

• BE PROFESSIONAL
Essentially, perform as PROFESSIONALLY as possible and never forget this is a job, not Jazzercise. Obtaining Stand-In work is an interesting phenomenon. There are professional Stand-Ins who follow particular actors from project to project or those who work for a particular D.P.

Take your time as a Stand-In to be an excellent learning opportunity. You are literally in the center of everything and your main function is TO STAND THERE, LISTEN and OBSERVE. The more you KNOW about what is happening around you, the more of an asset you are to the entire crew.

Politics Suck

Unfortunately, like everything in life, there is a flip side to Standing-In. Oftentimes, individuals who are "Politicals" are HIRED DUE TO PERSONAL FAVORITISM or better yet – FAMILY RELATION – and NO, not usually to the actor. As you may or may not know, Hollywood is a "political environment" so you better bet this occurs quite often. This is why it is ever so important to know how to perform your job well once given a chance. The "Politicals" may outnumber the "Professionals" but those who are "Professional" stand out and are genuinely appreciated. This, oftentimes, will lead to you being requested back.

Final Bit of Babble

There you have it – "How To Be A Stand-In/Photo Double 101" – We hope we covered the bases. If we left out some specific stuff or left things unclear – PLEASE drop us an email at info@HollywoodOS.com. With that in mind, treat this article as an overview only – NOT an absolute and we'll ALL be happy.

act one

Calling Service, Schmalling Service...

Do I need one and how do I know who's good?!

What the heck is a Calling Service?

Good question. In theory, a Calling Service is a pretty nifty idea – they are like the extras casting agent you pay a monthly fee to. The officially dry and boring **HOLLYWOOD OS**® definition: a 3rd party organization to which you pay a monthly fee to obtain work for you. They receive bookings from the agencies actually hired by production.

1.) A company that is paid a monthly fee to manage your schedule, to keep your availability and picture accessible to casting on a daily basis and is authorized to accept work on your behalf.

2.) A liaison between Casting Directors and Extras. (They are NOT Casting Directors and should NEVER guarantee jobs to Extras.)

Calling Services work for YOU

It's supposed to be that simple. YOU pay THEM to find YOU work. You pay them, thus employ them – an interesting concept – to find YOU work and manage YOUR "extra work" schedule. In return, they respect you and provide you with a quality service. You're not laughing right now, are ya? In a perfect world, this is HOW a Calling Service would treat you and SHOULD treat you. Enough said.

How do I know if I need to hire one?

If you are not a go-getter, but want to work as an extra, this may be an option you consider. (This obviously applies to those who are flat-out lazy by the way... in case you missed that polite implication of NOT being a "go-getter.") In any event, if you want to work as an extra (periodically or rather sporadically depending on the quality of your service) and you lack the confidence or do not have the patience to try to book yourself, by all means, this may be just the answer you are seeking.

Now, do not for a moment think we are recommending getting a Calling Service without RESEARCHING and INVESTIGATING. There are many people out there who date everyone in town and work plenty... did we say that out loud?! But seriously, there are many people who hustle their little J. Lo booties on their own – many are even SAG – and manage to get themselves booked quite a bit. Some people work it and market themselves while others simply don't have the drive nor the patience to do it on their own – that's where a Calling Service can come in handy.

Secondly, if you live super-duper far away and calling the hotlines gets to be more expensive than the actual $45 to $90 bucks a month it would cost to have a Calling Service, then it might be a wise idea for you to get one if it'll decrease your phone bill. With so many cellular plans available today and endless amounts of minutes this may no longer be a factor!

If you live within the local calling area and will NOT be billed for local frickin' toll calls – which are more expensive than calling our families in Frankfurt (why the heck is that?!) – and you feel like a Calling Service could decrease your expenses, (and increase your chances of getting booked) by all means, maybe you should get one! You're a clever brain surgeon - heck, you bought this darn book - do more detective work!

act one

Interviewing a Calling Service

There are a couple of really good Calling Services out there which provide a great service and there are some extremely disorganized fellas and chicitas who have created this stigma that all Calling Services stink! (It's the whole bad apple concept.) So how the heck are you gonna find the good ones?! Excellent question, people! Read below.

ASK QUESTIONS - remember, YOU are the one doing the hiring here!

1.) Do you know anyone with this Calling Service, in your age category/type?

2.) Does the Calling Service have a good reputation amongst your peers? This means good or even great. Not "so-so." Not "not so bad." Those are not good answers.

3.) How many people are on their roster and do they have a limited number of clients? If they don't, they should. How else can you expect to work?

4.) How many people on their roster are in your type/age group?

5.) Are they even seeking or looking for your type?

6.) How often do they claim they can work you? And is there a guarantee of work? If so, what is that guarantee – a money-back guarantee for instance or a box of rocks?

7.) Can you afford the monthly fee and is the service worth it when figuring in all the above factors?

8.) What if the service doesn't book you for that month – do you still have to pay the monthly fee or is it waived? Say, "waived," please.

9.) Does the service claim to be all SAG, then take on new Non-Union talent and offer a new service called the "Voucher Package Deal"? (This is very bad, by the way. Very.)

10.) Does the service constantly book you only to have you replace someone else? Does that sound, ah, sketchy? Yep.

The bottom line for interviewing

Question the Calling Service you are about to employ. Pretend it's a job interview and YOU are interviewing THEM for a job – a job to represent you, your livelihood and your financial stability. Question them, it's okay, that's your right. Ask them the questions that pertain to finding you work because THEY ARE WORKING FOR YOU! Don't let them intimidate you or tell you otherwise. Definitely do not let them bully you around like you are chopped liver! If they give you attitude, move on!

A Good Calling Service

A good Calling Service has a limited number of clients on their roster, a limited number of people in your age/type category and can honestly tell you what your odds are of working. A good Calling Service is respectful and appreciative that you are a client. They may not charge you for the month if they haven't booked you, AND they NEVER sell SAG vouchers. Be aware, stay awake – don't let 'em scam you!

A Crappy Calling Service

A lame Calling Service registers everyone and their mother and their mother's mother and their mother's mother's brother's uncle's next-door neighbor's husband. A sucky calling service treats you as if they own you, speaks down to you and blatantly disregards the fact that YOU pay them. Do not deal with power-tripping Calling Services – there are a few. Enough said.

Damaging Effects

Constantly switching from one service to another could prove to be detrimental to your career. When a Casting Director wants to book you, they do not have the luxury of time to horse around and hunt down every Calling Service and number change you had. Moving from one service to another only confuses the poor frustrated Casting Director. If your file hasn't been updated with new information, it becomes too hard to catch up with you and your soap opera lifestyle. This will undoubtedly have a negative effect. Because your file is not current, they may view you as flaky and may not even consider booking you any longer. If you are too high maintence to keep up with, they may even toss you from their files and memory bank all together. Sucks to be you at this point, we know. The moral of this story is to stay current, kids.

Advantages

In this fast-paced industry, if you are not easily located in thirty seconds, the job offer that was open a second ago, is now filled by someone who was easily found. Therefore, it makes sense that a GOOD service who provides a good service would be beneficial to your career. It makes sense to have someone speak on your behalf and vouch for your availability/schedule. The bottom line is that if they are booking you on a regular basis, you are a step ahead of many other people.

Disadvantages

It's a job in itself to make the rounds visiting and marketing yourself, but ultimately more beneficial. By promoting yourself and trying to get the work on your own, you develop relationships with the casting community. They become familiar with your work ethic, look, professionalism and reliability. When you are with a service, the service does the work for you, so you don't really build those strong relationships with the Casting Directors. They only really get to know you through your service, which could serve in the long run as a disadvantage - especially if you move around and change services and contact numbers as we mentioned.

Tips for letting them know you want work

Believe it or not, Calling Services are regular schmoes, just like you and me. They have a fast-paced, time-restricted, attention-demanding, detail-oriented job. This is why it's important to not bug them too much. They want to complete their job just as smoothly and expediently as possible. They have many Casting Directors breathing down their necks. There are several non-intrusive, polite ways to let them know you are alive and kicking for more work. Visiting them on a monthly basis (NOT daily, that can get a bit old) to say hello, sending a nice postcard, and dropping them a line on the phone (again, not daily, but once – in a while if you haven't been booked).

"EXTRA" WORK for Animals

PET XING

Rules & Regulations for Working With Your Pets

• What is the American Humane Association?
The Film and Television Unit of the *American Humane Association* is an organization partially funded by the Screen Actors Guild with the purpose of protecting all animals on set and any people who may be involved with any claim that a particular production was not nice to the cute critters on set.

• When are They Used?
We recently learned that all owners of animals that work on a set MUST have a license to have that animal on set with them – this includes background actors! Originally, we were led to believe that the production was supposed to notify the *American Humane Association* whenever animals were to be used and an *AHA* rep was supposed to always be on set. Period. Well, now the news gets more complicated.

• When are They NOT Used?
If a production is using an animal not supplied by a USDA-certified animal trainer/supplier, the animal's owner must obtain a USDA Exhibitor's License waiver BEFORE the animal can work on set.

It's easy enough to apply for this waiver and the license if you feel you will work often enough with your pets to warrant a license. The cost is a $40 annual fee for this license (one-time waiver is free).

When you apply for the exhibitor's license, it is $10 up front, the USDA sends a representative out to inspect your animal holding area (i.e., kennel, condo, or other doggie abode) and make sure living conditions for the little buggers are all shipshape, then you pay the $30 balance to get the license. The $40 per year covers 1 to 5 animals.

The dilemma arises since most background actors aren't aware that they need a license and (to further the chaos) AHA literature reads: "AH discourages a production's use of an extra's dog in lieu of a professionally trained animal." The key word being "discourages." Yet other AH literature insists the animal owner MUST obtain a Exhibitor's License or its equivalent waiver. English, people!

• Animals are Rock Stars too!
Ex-Creative-Dictator-turned-Casting-Director Carla Lewis has previously worked many times with her poodles. She had never encountered the *American Humane Association* on set and never knew she needed a license. Luckily, the last time she worked (with three dogs) there was an *AHA* rep there to show her the way. She had her very own dog assistant all day – how cool is that? The representative is there to hang with the animals and make sure they are comfortable. This meant the dogs didn't have to join Carla in the honeywagon and she did not have to look lame when the pups needed to stay in the shade or when, between takes, they needed water. Truly, her animals were treated like First Team – with their own personal assistant!!

• Pets' Best Interests

Okay, so what's all this mean for background actors who want to work on set with their pets? Our calls to both the AHA and USDA provided some insight, but did not particularly bode well for extras – in terms of their financial obligation to comply with licenses. Both organizations insist that a license is required for pets that background actors want to use on sets. Contacts at both agencies wanted us to remind you that all of this is for "the best interests and care" of your animals.

• Come on, Parents, get it together already!

While productions could get in trouble with the USDA for using pets without licenses, it is ultimately up to the animals' owners to be sure their pets have current exhibitor's licenses. (Duh, what the hell is your pet supposed to do, make an appointment and drive its happy self down to the local office?)

It will make your day on set all the more fun, luxurious and relaxing (maybe bring a lovely crossword puzzle or something for your pet to work on during it's downtime) and it protects production from any whacked-out claims that animals were hurt or mistreated. So be sure to call the AHA and learn the lowdown on licenses and waivers to ensure your pet's safety!

Here's a tip: if you're going to plunk down the cash for your pooch's license, you might also makeup a doggy postcard to let casters know about your buddy's certification.

• Who to Contact

For information on obtaining a waiver or an exhibitor's license for your pet contact the USDA Western Regional office: 970-494-7478

• When You are Booked with Your Pets

Call/Notify the AMERICAN HUMANE ASSOCIATION if you and your (non-rent paying) pet are booked.

PHONE: 888-301-3541

OFFICE: 818-501-0123

WEBSITE: www.AHAfilm.org

LOCAL LOS ANGELES OFFICE:
AHA
15366 Dickens Street
Sherman Oaks, CA 91403

AMERICAN HUMANE ASSOCIATION

• *Some Basic Facts (from the "AHA GUIDELINES")*

"American Humane Association is the only organization authorized by the entertainment industry to monitor the use of animals in film and television productions (per SAG/Producer's Codified Agreement)."

"During filming, AHA monitors the animal action, steps in as needed to protect the animals, and documents how each scene is accomplished as well as the level of care the animals receive during the production. After a production has wrapped, AHA rates and reviews the project as to its treatment of the animal actors. AHA responds to public and media inquiries about productions throughout their release life."

• *Basic Principles*

1.) No animal will be killed or injured for the sake of a film production.

2.) If an animal must be treated inhumanely to perform, then that animal should not be used.

3.) Animals are NOT props. (Even if they are supplied by the props department. Huh? Moving on.)

4.) AHA Guidelines apply to all animals used in the production, even if the animal is used as background.

5.) "ANIMAL" means all sentient* creatures - including birds, fish, reptiles and insects.

* *How's that for a million $$ word? Cool, huh? Yeah, we thought so.*

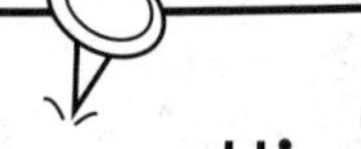

cool tips for getting work!

1.) You MUST HAVE a Pager or a Cell Phone

Not only MUST you have a pager or cell phone (or both), but you must carry the darn thing around at all times! At this stage in the industry, you can never be too accessible. You should also make a practice of keeping the silly thing on VIBRATE. Given the nature of Murphy's Law, you will usually be paged/called when your car stereo is too loud to hear it or you are on set and the Director has just called, "ACTION!" Do it as a courtesy too – other people's pagers and cell phones are known to sound off when you are stuck in holding, so you have to listen to the ever-famous technological mating calls that are sounding off all around you.

Given the nature of this industry and the number of people available and perfectly capable of fulfilling a given job you are being considered for, you must be accessible. Casting Directors are busy people with a job to do. They are on a mission to book a call and you need to be ready to respond. So when you get a page or a call, don't dilly-dally about calling back. The best way to handle a page is to call back as soon as possible and the easiest way to do this (especially on set) is to have a nifty cellular phone and a pen and paper.

Yes indeed, cell phones are your friends. Take a look at the payphone line at lunch on any given set and I am sure you will agree (if you can even find a payphone these days!). If used in moderation and out of necessity, a cellular phone will undoubtedly pay for itself each month – especially considering the tax write-off potential!!

If you don't already have an answering machine. . . you are in the wrong business (and quite possibly the wrong decade). Speaking of answering machines, or any form of voice mail, being "cute" on your outgoing message is truly not so "cute" to the busy casting world. Musical intros have got to go!! Bad comedy routines – even worse. Simply state your name and let the darn thing beep already!! Imagine making 100+ calls each day – then imagine listening to 100+ messages. Who would you want to book? Short and simple always wins.

2.) Versatility = More Bookings = MORE Work!

How many times have you heard really random requests on the Casting Hotlines (i.e., a guy missing his left thumb and half of his forefinger)? Casting is faced with booking a wide variety of "types" each day. The more diverse you are in your look or the more props and wardrobe you have access to – the better for you (but please do not chop off your thumb just because it might get you booked with your favorite celebrity)!

cool tips for getting work!

Wardrobe Tips for Dudes

- Get yourself an L.A.P.D. or police uniform – think how often you see police officers on TV or in movies (plus, chicks dig a guy in a uniform).
- Black combat boots
- White T-shirts
- Hair products
- Tuxedo
- Nice suits (not mean ones)

Wardrobe Tips for Chicks

- Get a nurse's uniform!
- A pair of low black pumps (use insoles to make them as comfortable as possible – rubber soles are ideal, this way they do not make ANY noise on set!)
- A pair of white tennis shoes
- Soft rollers (you know, the kind that you can sleep in – period films usually ask women to show up with their hair in rollers!)

We've been told by many backgrounders that a great place for uniforms is *Uniforms Depot* in Reseda: 818-343-7554 (but call first – they're closed on Sundays & Mondays!)

These are simply things we have heard repeatedly! Your WARDROBE IS MORE IMPORTANT THAN YOU THINK!! When it comes to upgrades, it is often dependent on HOW YOU LOOK! (i.e., If the Wardrobe Department puts you in a uniform, you are usually given special business.) The best way for you to keep your clothes neat is to carry them in a lightweight hanging bag. You should NOT cram your clothing into a duffel bag. No one wants to look at your wrinkled clothing! It would be well worth your money to invest in a hanging bag with lots of pockets or get something with wheels like a flight attendant!

3.) Car Call = Mo' Money!!

If you hear a UNION CAR CALL – RENT A DARN CAR! You are walking into a $122 base rate plus $35 for the car – that's $157 just for showing up! Or better yet, steal one, get caught speeding on the six o'clock news, and become an instant celebrity – even BAD publicity is good publicity. Right? Okay, maybe not.

4.) Wigs Rock!!

If you are a female and serious about Standing-In – don't be afraid to get yourself an army of wigs. Furthermore, wigs are your best buddy when coping with rush calls! In a simple nutshell, showing casting your versatility (via photos) shows your enthusiasm. It shows your dedication and your drive to accommodate.

cool tips for getting work!

5.) Photos, Photos & More Photos!!

As for photos, here is THE NUMBER ONE THING you MUST remember. Always, always write your name, union status and phone number on the back of each and every photo you submit to casting (unless instructed otherwise). This goes for headshots, too! Feel free to attach that resumé to the back. But paper clips don't cut it and staples can literally cut! Your best bet is to glue your resumé to the back or flat-out handwrite your darn info!! Just be sure your name AND contact information is PERMANENTLY ATTACHED to your photos – ALL of them!! If you remember anything, remember this:

The Easier It Is For Casting To Book You,
The Quicker And More Readily
You Will Be Booked!

Back to the PHOTO DISCUSSION – your best tool for finding work as a background performer is a 3"x5" photo against a white background (it's the headshot of the extra world)! Casting wants to see what you REALLY look like, not some airbrushed version of what you COULD look like or a dated version of what you DID look like. What matters is what you will look like when you get to the set. Being cast from your "Glamour Shots" proofs will do you more harm than good – in the event you cannot recreate the look casting believed they were casting. Our best advice is to take 3"x5"'s of yourself often. Take them of yourself in different "looks" (from homeless to formal) – be diverse and STAY CURRENT!

Some Neato Ideas:

- Upscale Business
- Punk or "Freak"
- Homeless
- Hip & Trendy
- Period Looks (1950's, 1960's, etc.)
- Formal Wear
- Bathing Suit

Quite often, production companies request to choose extras from photos. The MORE versatile you are, the greater your chances to get the jobs that are "hand-picked." It is a wise decision to have extra copies printed and ready for submission. If you organize these various looks and photos in advance, you can save money by shopping around at thrift stores and garage sales!!

cool tips for getting work!

6.) Things You Should Bring To Set:

- Pen & your I.D.
- A darn comfy folding chair
- This nifty book
- Spare change for anti-cellular folks (always have a roll of quarters or some change in your car – some lots charge for parking & it's better to be safe than sorry!)
- A deck of cards (I am going blind, nil...)
- A warm jacket

7.) Things Better Left at Home...

- Friends NOT booked on the show
- In-Laws NOT booked on the show
- Anything that makes noise
- Valuables
- Cameras
- A negative attitude

8.) Things to Help You Get There!

- A reliable mode of transpo (um, a car...)
- An alarm clock!!
- A *Thomas Guide Map Book* – many times your directions to the set will include a Thomas Guide coordinate.

9.) Quick Do's & Don'ts

PLEASE, PLEASE, PLEASE......

DO BE camera ready.
DO BE on stage with your voucher in hand at your call time.
DO BE professional at all times.
DO HAVE your clothing hung up – not crumpled up.
DO BE prepared to work at least 12 hours.
DO BE happy – you are working, after all!!

PLEASE, PLEASE, PLEASE......

DO NOT show up without the proper wardrobe.
DO NOT arrive late to set.
DO NOT fail to show up to set – no flaking!
DO NOT constantly complain about food.
DO NOT sleep while you are supposed to be working.
DO NOT hide out while you're supposed to be working.
DO NOT fail to clean up after yourself.
DO NOT talk during the scene.
DO NOT have a bad attitude.
DO NOT cross in front of a light as you will make an ugly shadow on whatever it's lighting (& maybe get beat up by the D.P. & his crew!)

"pro"fessionalism tips

No Long Messages on Your Answering Machine . . .
Casting Directors are busy and often do not have the time and/or patience to listen to your favorite song or your lame rendition of *Budweiser*'s "Whassup!?!? Commercial" before leaving you a work-related message. If you want to be professional – have a short, concise outgoing message and save the song and dance for Saturday night soirees!

When You Arrive on a Set . . .
The first rule of thumb is to be ON TIME. Nothing irritates an Assistant Director more than people showing up late! Always get your voucher the minute you get to set, and hang on to it for the entire day, (unless wardrobe takes it) until wrap. If you were sent to replace someone, know that person's full name when you check in. If you were sent on a rush call, tell the A.D. that you were sent on a rush call, and which Casting Director booked you. Always bring at least two choices of wardrobe unless you were told specifically not to bring choices, then hang out.

We Have Heard Complaints . . .
The most common complaints include showing up late, asking for a SAG voucher, not bringing the correct wardrobe (or not enough choices), wandering off from the Holding area, trying to call in for work when needed on set, disappearing (hiding) for long periods of time without telling someone, and refusing to do as told by an A.D. in the scene. We cannot tell you how many times we have heard about phone calls from irate A.D.'s saying that a Non-Union extra refused to do a cross because they thought it was not appropriate for their "character." Hello – ARE YOU KIDDING?!? Unless maniacal Michael Bay is forcing you to follow SEXY Ben Affleck through waist-high flames in *Pearl Harbor*, just do it!

Getting Paid . . .
When it comes to getting paid, those who are new always assume it is the Casting Director's responsibility. This is absolutely NOT the case. When you work, you are handed a voucher. The voucher you receive is the paperwork the background artist needs to fill out accurately in order to get paid. On the voucher is the name of the payroll company (i.e., *Entertainment Partners*, *Universal Payroll Service*, *Sessions*, etc.). It is the payroll company who is the official employer of record. If you do not receive your check in the mail after waiting for two weeks or so, please do not call the Casting Director and ask where your check is. The Casting Director does not deal with the monetary aspect. Should there be any problems or concerns about payment, please contact the payroll company to iron out any wrinkles.

"pro"fessionalism tips

Who Originally Booked You . . .
When you arrive to set, please remember the name of the Casting Director that booked you. If you have been booked through a Calling Service, do not forget to ask who the project was booked through and what you were booked as because if an A.D. asks you on set, and you name your Calling Service, chances are he or she will not know who that is and this could create confusion.

Hurry Up & Wait . . .
Hour-long series and feature films are similar in that each scene will be done over and over, until the director feels it is right. This can be very boring, especially if you're not in the scene. To bide your time, the best advice we can give is to read, write, or talk to other extras, but do not wander off anywhere without telling a Production Assistant or Assistant Director.

Pay Attention People!
It is imperative that you listen carefully, not only to the dialogue in the scene, but also to the Assistant Director. You'll need to know where to go and how to go there, or what to do and how to do it when working on set – WITHOUT disrupting the scene. Working on a sitcom is a true test of a good extra. You'll probably get a copy of the script as well so that you're aware of what's happening in each scene.

Talking On the Set When the Crew is Trying to Work Typically Does Not Go Over Too Well . . .
Try to keep quiet while you are on the set – understand you are all individuals but you are often perceived by the crew as a group, "the background," and if ONE person sets a bad example – you ALL end up getting reprimanded. It is unfortunate to see a group of people who, on the whole, are genuinely trying to do the best job they can – but then a handful of people goof off and the entire group is chastised for it. This initiates an unnecessary cycle of apathy. There are too many professionals being brought down by those who do not understand what it means to be professional. If more people saw the larger picture, perhaps everyone's job would be easier and more respected. Essentially, take pride in your work because you asked for this job as did your peers.

If You are Recalled To Set. . .
Don't tell the A.D., "I can't come back, I have another job tomorrow." A recall takes precedence over any new booking regardless of which company booked you – every casting company in town knows this rule and will communicate with each other if necessary when a recall takes place. Don't worry, you're not going to make anybody mad, unless you don't show up for the recall and/or don't call the company that booked you for the next day. Communication is key.

"pro"fessionalism tips

Maintain a Positive Attitude . . .
Negative attitudes bring everyone down. We do not wish to preach (that's annoying). We just want to point out the fact that for every job you get – think of all of the people who wish they were working. So be happy to be working. Stand out, stay true, and in time you will undoubtedly find your efforts do pay off.

As Far as Casting Directors are Concerned . . .
They hear everything from A.D.'s and production companies. If you were uncooperative on set, or showed up late, odds are the CD knows about it, and they don't like being yelled at by their clients because you didn't do YOUR job. Please don't make them look bad by being unprofessional – that includes saying, "I wasn't told to bring an overcoat." They know you were told to do so and saying anything other than the truth just makes you look stupid. Extra work should be considered a real job – if an A.D. decided not to show up and not call anybody, he or she would be fired immediately. As an extra, you should treat each assignment the same as you would a regular job. Okay? Okay. Lecture over. This one, anyway. We'll lecture again – that you can be sure of! We just love to go on and on and... okay, you get it. Woo-hoo!

FINALLY . . .
Whatever you do,
respect the company who gave you
the job by performing in a
professional manner
(Corny maybe, but practical!).

marketing tips

How can I best market myself
in the world of extra work?...

act one

postcards! •

Many Casting Directors we list in this publication suggest that you not only update your information on a REGULAR basis, they suggest you KEEP IN TOUCH with them via a POSTCARD. Check out Act 4 and see for yourself which CD's like them and what they say about um!

You see, postcards (as opposed to headshots) are a CHEAPER, more RELIABLE way of getting through to a Casting Director to let them know you are available to work.

First of all, if you get a photo postcard in the mail, you don't need to take the time to open it, take it out and throw away the envelope (all of which can be time-consuming with stacks upon stacks of BORING MANILA ENVELOPES).

With all the stuff that arrives daily to casting offices, it must be refreshing to get a photo postcard that's not intrusive and is easy to handle. Postcards practically come with a guarantee that someone will look at it (at least the mailman... kidding)! No opening anything and making clutter. The postcard arrives – READY TO BE SEEN. Ta-dah! Yeah, baby! Yeah!

Also, let's factor in costs. Photo postcards are currently ONLY 23¢ to mail, which IS NEARLY A THIRD of what it costs to mail a darn headshot and God knows that can get expensive. There are photo reproduction houses that have special deals for photo postcards – some rates as low as $65 - $75 for 500 postcards (TALK ABOUT SAVING TIME AND MONEY)!

And guess what? You can take your own photos with a disposable camera and gets prints that can be used as postcards! Just write directly on the back of the picture like you would a postcard and send them in the mail!

Just another TIP TO CONSIDER when trying to market yourself in an effective and inexpensive way.

Okay, that's all (for now, of course). Good luck!

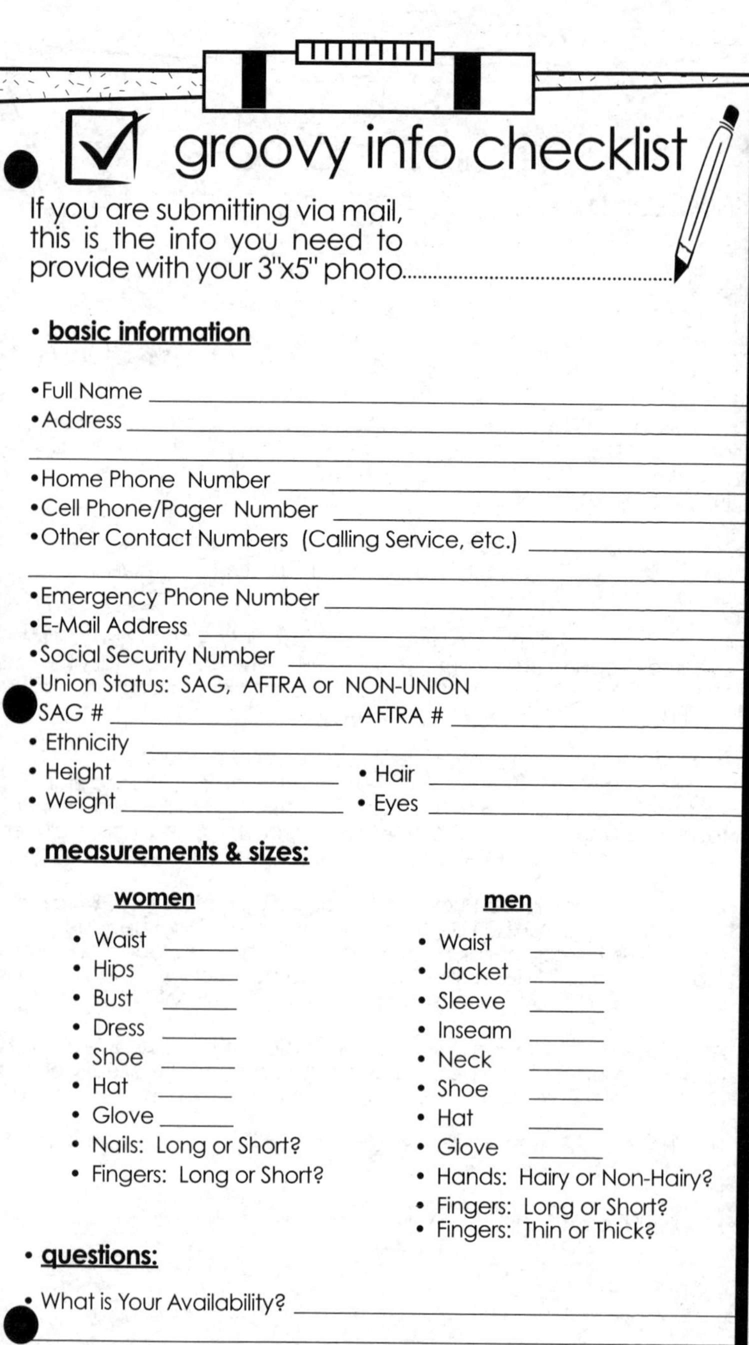

groovy info checklist

If you are submitting via mail, this is the info you need to provide with your 3"x5" photo..

- **basic information**

- Full Name ______________________
- Address ______________________

____
- Home Phone Number ______________________
- Cell Phone/Pager Number ______________________
- Other Contact Numbers (Calling Service, etc.) ______________________

____
- Emergency Phone Number ______________________
- E-Mail Address ______________________
- Social Security Number ______________________
- Union Status: SAG, AFTRA or NON-UNION

SAG # ______________ AFTRA # ______________
- Ethnicity ______________________
- Height ______________ • Hair ______________
- Weight ______________ • Eyes ______________

- **measurements & sizes:**

women

- Waist ______
- Hips ______
- Bust ______
- Dress ______
- Shoe ______
- Hat ______
- Glove ______
- Nails: Long or Short?
- Fingers: Long or Short?

men

- Waist ______
- Jacket ______
- Sleeve ______
- Inseam ______
- Neck ______
- Shoe ______
- Hat ______
- Glove ______
- Hands: Hairy or Non-Hairy?
- Fingers: Long or Short?
- Fingers: Thin or Thick?

- **questions:**

- What is Your Availability? ______________________

____

____

act one

groovy info checklist

If you are submitting via mail, this is the info you need to provide with your 3"x5" photo

- Do you own a tux/evening gown? (please describe) ______
- How many suits do you own? (please describe) ______
- Do you have tattoos or piercings? (please describe ______
- Will you work in smoke or water? ______
  Will you work all night? ______
- Do you have driving restrictions? (please describe) ______
- Do you mind working in a gay scene? ______
- Will you do nudity or semi-nudity? ______
- Do you have Stand-In/Photo Double experience? ______
  (if so, on what, and for whom?) ______

- **auto information**

Type of Car(s) ______
Year(s) ______
Model(s) ______
Condition ______

- **pets**

Kind ______
Size ______
Color ______
Temperament ______
(Consider all the people your animal will be around)

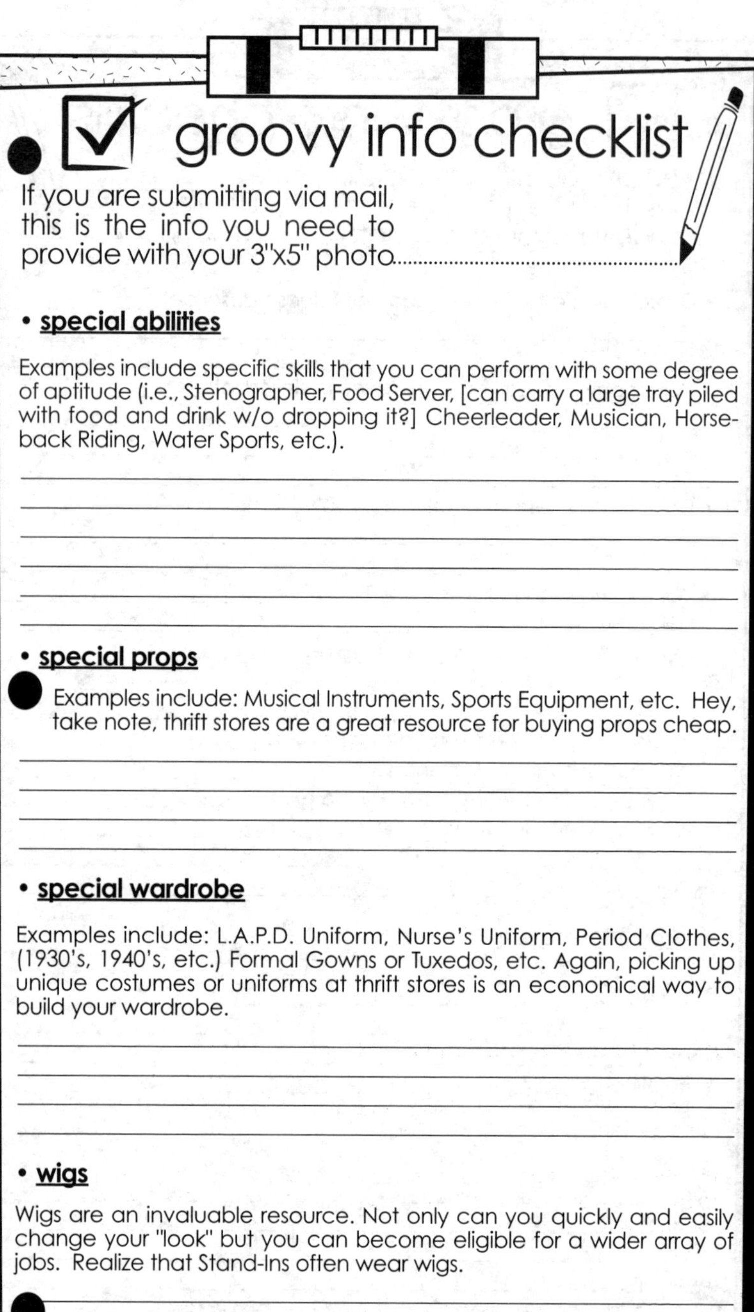

groovy info checklist

If you are submitting via mail, this is the info you need to provide with your 3"x5" photo.........

- **special abilities**

Examples include specific skills that you can perform with some degree of aptitude (i.e., Stenographer, Food Server, [can carry a large tray piled with food and drink w/o dropping it?] Cheerleader, Musician, Horse-back Riding, Water Sports, etc.).

- **special props**

Examples include: Musical Instruments, Sports Equipment, etc. Hey, take note, thrift stores are a great resource for buying props cheap.

- **special wardrobe**

Examples include: L.A.P.D. Uniform, Nurse's Uniform, Period Clothes, (1930's, 1940's, etc.) Formal Gowns or Tuxedos, etc. Again, picking up unique costumes or uniforms at thrift stores is an economical way to build your wardrobe.

- **wigs**

Wigs are an invaluable resource. Not only can you quickly and easily change your "look" but you can become eligible for a wider array of jobs. Realize that Stand-Ins often wear wigs.

the 3" x 5" photo lecture

When registering, the MOST IMPORTANT tool you should have are photographs..........

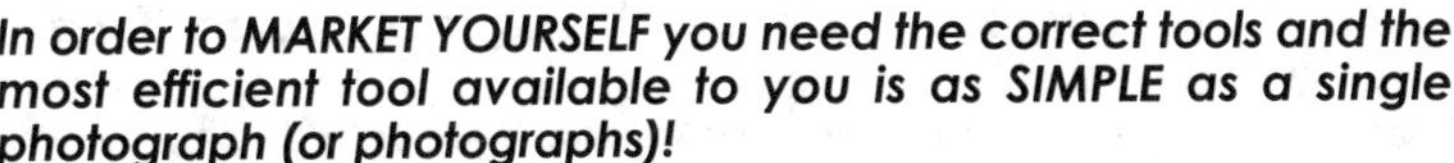

In order to MARKET YOURSELF you need the correct tools and the most efficient tool available to you is as SIMPLE as a single photograph (or photographs)!

We're not talking about a headshot here, people, but simply small photos. The standard format is a 3"x5" color snapshot against a white background. The idea surrounding this resides in the fundamental nature of extras casting. Most often, extras are cast to portray real people, and the Casting Director needs to see what you REALLY look like – not an airbrushed, digitally retouched version that would require hours in the makeup trailer or extensive lighting to recreate. Therefore, snapshots of what you will look like when you arrive on the set just make sense.

Secondly, headshots are difficult to store and file. Small photos are easily attached to your information file or scanned into the computer. The chances of the Casting Director coming across your 3"x5" when casting is higher than casting you from your headshot.

Thirdly, most agencies will take a photo of you when you register. If you do not have your own photos to submit, the one taken at the Casting Office is what will be referenced when considering you for employment – WHAT IF IT IS JUST NOT A GOOD PHOTO? The only way to be sure is to submit YOUR OWN. Submitting photos in the industry standard format will relay a message of professionalism – a quality every Casting Director seeks in their talent. It is a modest investment, much more economical than headshots, and truly the most effective tool when seeking extra work. It is also a practical and efficient way to "try out" a photographer.

It is up to you to market yo'self.

Many people working as background talent ultimately want to work as principal actors and are starting with extra work to make connections, gain experience, get their SAG card or possibly maintain their insurance (if already SAG). In any event, headshots are a necessity for the next stage – and wouldn't it be nice to have a working relationship and familiarity with a photographer when you are ready for headshots?

the 3" x 5" photo lecture

When registering, the MOST IMPORTANT tool you should have are photographs

One of the biggest challenges background talent faces is being typecast!

Because there are so many people who want to work, it is easy for Casting Directors to mentally place talent in a category and ONLY consider them for the jobs which require that "type." 3"x5"s can help you overcome this obstacle if you submit not just one photo, BUT SEVERAL – each showing you as a completely different "type" (always be sure to indicate the date the photo was taken).

Examples of 3"X5" photos . . .

Upscale, cocktail gowns, casual clothes, homeless, punk, formal (gown, tux), uniform (police, tennis, nurse, military, clergy), bathing suit, wet suit, western, your car, your pet, your bike, etc.

The more diversely you present yourself, the more jobs you will be considered for. Having a supply of different "looks" will also prove invaluable when you hear that "type" requested on the hotline. If you are prepared, you can submit right away. The sooner you respond, the higher your chances of getting the job. There is absolutely no way you can be prepared for everything – you hear some rather odd requests on the hotlines these days!! Nevertheless, if you take your days of not working as time to visit thrift stores and garage sales – I am sure you will find "types" or "looks" you never imagined yourself portraying.

Our beloved Carla purchased a $5 Postal Worker shirt while in a thrift store searching for old Levis. She found out *The Game* was filming locally in San Francisco and was looking for people with uniforms. She ended up getting a 4-day job simply because she had this silly shirt and she earned over a thousand dollars! Now this story has absolutely nothing to do with 3"x5"s but it does relate to the importance of being unique – having things less common – because you never know. If you have such items and have photos ready to submit, we have no doubt your efforts WILL pay off.

FINAL NOTE:

Remember, YOU are your OWN PRODUCT & YOU are your OWN AGENT at this stage of "The Game" (there, we tied it in).

"extra" resumé tips

How do I shlop one together if I don't have any darn credits?

act one

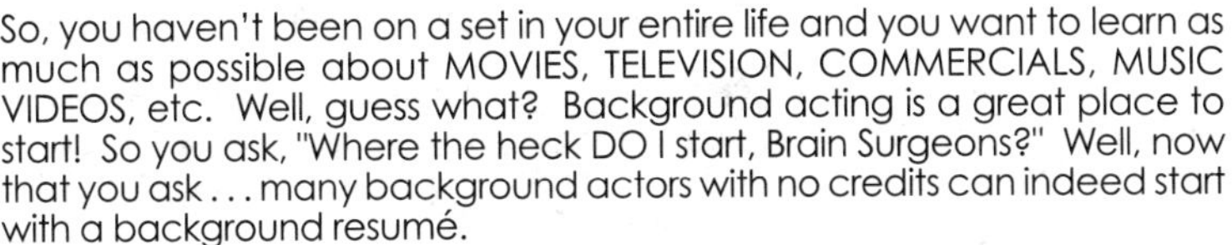

So, you haven't been on a set in your entire life and you want to learn as much as possible about MOVIES, TELEVISION, COMMERCIALS, MUSIC VIDEOS, etc. Well, guess what? Background acting is a great place to start! So you ask, "Where the heck DO I start, Brain Surgeons?" Well, now that you ask . . . many background actors with no credits can indeed start with a background resumé.

Run to that frighteningly cramped closet full of odds and ends. Brace yourself for an avalanche of memories, including Aunt Edna's Muumuu and Uncle Ed's yellow polyester jumpsuit. These articles of clothing are really hidden treasures, plus you might find twenty bucks long-forgotten in a pocket or two. Then put together some of the most diverse outfits you own and jot them down. Come on, have fun with this!

DUCK! Grandpa Joe's false teeth are dive-bombing you from the top shelf (a groovy prop, by the way). Next, fish out that stethoscope, guitar, tap shoes, and all the sports equipment, and wigs, etc., and make a list of props. Try to think of as many objects as possible… the more the merrier!

Now think about all your special skills – many of which you use with the above props, right?! Also include past job experience, because you never know when a waitress, secretary or Kung Fu expert will be needed for a scene. That strong sense of balance, those clerical skills or "The Death Grip" could be extremely handy in a given scene!

Know your REAL sizes – no cheating!!!
Grab a measuring tape and find out your exact sizes:

BOYS	GIRLS
Neck	Bust
Jacket	Waist
Waist	Hips
Inseam	Dress
Sleeve	
Hat	

Hat Tip: By the way, for hat size, measure your head and divide it by π (pi, 3.14)… YES, we're completely serious! You take the number of inches of that noggin' of yours and divide that by 3.14!

Example: Your head measures 22"
22 divided by 3.14 = 7 (almost equals ≠) So your hat size is 7!

Okay, enough Mathematics, people!

"extra" resumé tips

How do I shlop one together if I don't have any darn credits?

Now you need full-color, 3"x5" photos of your sexy body in those outfits, waist-up against a white background. Unfortunately, a photograph of you hanging off the side of a mountain is not exactly what we're looking for. I know it shows off the buff bod, the outfit, the props and your super skill . . . but you need to be a little bit bigger than a thumbnail on a scenic backdrop!

Now Comes The Background Actor's Resumé!

- ☑ Your resumé should begin with your name, centered.
- ☑ List gender and union status.
- ☑ Next list all of your contact information.
- ☑ Next come those sexy physical descriptions/measurements. Remember MEN, you don't need to measure "Bust" . . . I'm sure the WOMEN can measure that without your assistance.
- ☑ Okay, pull out those pictures and list that incredible wardrobe! The more versatile you are, the more you'll work. (WIGS, UNDER THAT PROP CATEGORY, ARE ALSO A BIG PLUS!)
- ☑ Now, we're sure you found more "things" in that closet than you bargained for! No, that slice of stale/moldy pizza isn't a prop. Props should be functional, not edible!
- ☑ Now comes that car, you stallion! Include make, model, color and condition. Don't include the story of your best friend vomiting in the back seat! Also, FYI, your car won't be very popular with Casting Directors if it's red, white or black – these colors don't work for filming!
- ☑ Those incredible special skills come next! Please list what you can do fairly well. Just because you have balls doesn't mean you can juggle them!
- ☑ Last comes your "Stand-In" experience. This is your most recent work of "Standing-In" for another actor who is your shape, size and height, so cameras and lighting have a person to focus on.

See the next page for a SAMPLE Background Actor's Resumé:

Joey Schmoey
SAG/AFTRA
Male

HOME: 310-555-1212
PAGER: 310-555-1212
CELL: 310-555-1212

AGE RANGE: 25-35
HAIR: Black
EYES: Brown
HEIGHT: 6'
WEIGHT: 190
ETHNICITY: African American

WAIST: 34
(if female, also use Waist)
JACKET: 46
(if female, replace using Bust)
NECK: 16
(if female, replace using Hips)
INSEAM: 33
(if female, replace using Dress)
SLEEVE: 35
SHOE: 12
HAT: 7

WARDROBE:
(2) Single-Breasted Suit - Black, Gray
(3) Double-Breasted Suits - Black, Blue, Green
(1) Single-Breasted Tux - Black

Athletic Wear, Bathing Suit, Formal Evening, Fatigues, Grunge, Hip-Hop, Homeless, Karate Uniform, Police Uniform, Scrubs, Skater, Surfer, Waiter, Western/Country Attire

PROPS: Luggage, Bike, Roller Blades, Camera, Boxing Equipment, Soccer Ball, Tennis Racquet, Laptop, (1) Short Brown Wig, (1) Long Blonde Wig

CAR: 2003 Honda Civic EX, 4 Door, Hunter Green, Excellent Condition

SPECIAL SKILLS: Disco Dancing, Baseball, Basketball, Volleyball, Karate, Track & Field, Rollerblading, Figure Skating, Water-Skiing, Wrestling, Juggling, Bartending, Billiards, Firearms, Improv, Magician, Waiter, Stenographer

STAND-IN WORK:
2005 - "Miami Vice," Jamie Foxx
2004 - "Hitch," Will Smith

PHOTO DOUBLE:
2005 - "Batman Begins," Morgan Freeman
2004 - "Man on Fire," Denzel Washington

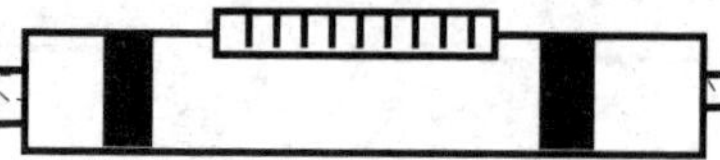

Are you a Brain Surgeon?!

Okay, so you bought the book, but are you really a Brain Surgeon? To get ahead in this business, you have to know what is expected of you. Take this test and rock the world with your knowledge! (See our answer key at the end. . . we'll scold you then if you screw up!)

Okay, here goes. . . two-part quiz, two minutes to do it and, of course, that Number 2 pencil. . . Alright you can have more than two minutes. Three . . . ten. .? Oh, whatever. . . get going!

PART ONE: Multiple Choice Quiz

1.) When a Casting Director wants to reach you regarding work do you:

a.) Have a pager or a cell phone?
b.) Have only a home answering machine?
c.) Have an old number on file from your refuge in Wisconsin?
d.) Have a home phone with no machine?

2.) If you have an answering device of some sort, is your outgoing message:

a.) Short and to the point?
b.) A melodic anthem to your ex sung by an *American Idol* finalist?
c.) A five minute stand-up routine that you stole from Johnny Knoxville?
d.) A never-ending series of beeps, blurps, hisses and hums?

3.) When you receive a page do you:

a.) Call back ASAP?
b.) Call back when you feel like it cuz you're busy watching *Buffy*?
c.) Call back when you feel like it and still expect the job to be available?
d.) Call back days later and ask if there is anything else going on?

4.) When you are told to bring wardrobe to the set do you:

a.) Carefully select your wardrobe that most fits the call and bring it in a hanging bag?
b.) Carefully select your wardrobe that most fits the call and stuff it in your purse or a tiny little duffel bag?
c.) Disregard what you were told to bring and bring what looks best on you? (Blue is your color after all – it goes with your eyes.)
d.) Wear your favorite outfit and bring nothing – toting the attitude, "Take it or leave it baby"!?

act one

5.) When you are requested for work and asked about your availability you should:

a.) Answer the question with either of two simple responses, "Yes, I am available for the entire day no matter how long" or "No, I am not available, but thanks for considering me."
b.) Ask when the call time is in hopes that your previously scheduled event will not conflict. (Keep in mind that call times are not set in stone and may change at the last minute. This could cause a problem for both you and the Casting Director if you are not available when production decides at the last minute that the call time is now three hours earlier than previously determined.)
c.) Realize that you are already booked but opt to ask what the project is and the rate of pay. This gives the Casting Director the feeling that you would flake on them if "something better" came up.
d.) Accept the job no matter what and find someone to cover for you in the event you couldn't, wouldn't or simply didn't feel like showing up.

6.) The first thing you should do when arriving to set is:

a.) Check in and follow the instructions of the person you checked in with.
b.) Ask for a SAG voucher and ask how long you will be there.
c.) Go directly to catering for some yummy grub before checking in.
d.) Take a nap.

7.) Are you:

a.) A genuinely nice person trying to make your way in this business?
b.) A money-hungry pain in the rump?
c.) A grievance monger?
d.) An "I-hate-extra-work-just-give-me-my-darn-SAG-voucher-joy-to-be-around" dude or dudette?

Now for the fun TRUE or FALSE portion of our exam...
(is that No.2 pencil still sharp and ready, boys and girls?)

PART TWO: True or False

1.) True or False:
Always ask to leave at lunch for an audition. Don't worry if you were established in the shot before lunch and the very act of you leaving puts the entire production on hold. Don't worry about the bad position that you are putting the coordinator or A.D. in when you ask to leave. If you are late coming back the entire production should always be happy to just sit on the clock and wait for you. The person authorizing you to leave will not get in trouble. Not at all. No problem. No sweat. Good luck on the audition, darn it!

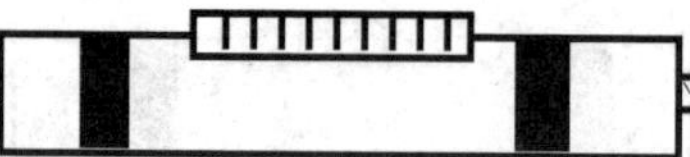

2.) True or False:
When receiving a call, make sure to call the number back that shows up in that cool little screen on your cell or home caller ID. Don't worry if it is a private number to the casting office – just call the number back and explain to whomever answers that you need to be dealt with because someone called you. Be sure to do this before checking the message (if any) that was left for you as this is certainly the best number to call back on (especially if it's the CD's home residence)!

3.) True or False:
When returning a page, simply use your first name and be sure to sound like a stoner: "Hey, dude, it's Chris, you like paged me?" This will not create any confusion at all, as you are probably the only "Chris" in their files and you sound very intelligent and "book-able."

4.) True or False:
Submit photos of yourself in costumes that you don't actually own but that the wardrobe department on various shows have dressed you in. This way casting can see how you would look if you were to play this character or that character. Completely disregard the fact that casting might assume that you actually do own the perfect pair of purple and pink polka-dotted painter's pants. Too bad you'll have to tell them that you don't (um, thank God) and that the CD was wasting his or her time.

OKAY, how'd you do, folks?

If you answered:

"**A**" to ALL the Multiple-Choice Questions AND False to ALL the **True or False** questions... Congratulations! You are a Brain Surgeon (you rock!) and you can go on you merry way to Act 2.

If you answered **B, C or D** to the Multiple-Choice questions AND **True** to ANY of the **True or False** questions, chances are, you simply don't rock and you have hurt your chances of gaining future employment as a background actor. Ouch. Not rocking? No jobs? Double-ouch!

Now since you failed, IF YOU FAILED, (all BRAIN SURGEONS can skip ahead with our blessings), you MUST read or *re-read* this entire Act 1 again and MEMORIZE it – possible pop quiz on Tuesday!

SCREEN ACTORS GUILD

Just a Li'l Introduction To SAG, What It Is, What It Does...

(or what it's supposed to do)

The Purpose Of SAG

Basically, SAG has two main goals:

1.) To provide and negotiate competitive wages for its members.

2.) To ensure safe, secure, and the best working conditions possible for its members.

SAG does not provide, procure or otherwise guarantee employment for its members like most other labor unions do. Members must find their own work and take the required steps to develop and hone their skills in order to land that coveted role. SAG does, however, offer a variety of programs and activities to help its members in search of work. They often have industry outreach programs and seminars to help their members find and then land acting gigs. SAG's main priority, however, is looking after your well-being on set once you have been hired by a production – in terms of wages and working conditions.

This means that members are responsible for finding their own agency representation if they need, want or require it. This is particularly important for those SAG members seeking principal roles in TV and film since most auditions or avenues to such parts require agency representation (see Act 8 for a list of SAG-franchised talent agencies in the LA area). If you are mainly a background actor or wish only to pursue extra work in TV and films, professional agency representation is not necessary.

How Much Does It Cost?

"Show me the money!" Okay, you don't have to show me (or us for that matter). But you do have to show them fancy folks at SAG. Actually, you gotta do more than show it to them. You have to hand over the cold hard cash (or plastic)! What's it gonna cost ya? The initiation fee (which now includes your first semiannual basic dues of $50) is currently $1,440. (And if you read Act 1 like a good Brain Surgeon, you would already know this; if you did already read it, congrats, you're reinforcing your brain cells and that be – we mean – that is A VERY GOOD THING!)

Okay, now that we've broken down some of the basics for you, you can get all the delirium-inducing details on the pages that follow. As fully updated for the 2006 edition of **"EXTRA" WORK for Brain Surgeons**® as SAG and our printer allow (things change so quickly around here!) you'll find the latest changes and additions to pay rates, requirements, standards and crazy contractual language! Oh, it's so much fun, we can hardly stand it. Happy reading!

How Do I Become A SAG Member?

If you're considering joining SAG, you should understand that you must meet one of the following criteria:

1.) You must be cast and hired to work in a principal or speaking role for a SAG signatory producer.

2.) You must have a minimum of one year's membership and principal work in an affiliated performers' union (i.e., AFTRA).

3.) You must be cast and hired to work in an extra role for a SAG signatory producer at full SAG rates and conditions for a minimum of three workdays. *(This route of entry is set to change in 2006/2007, but the specifics of that change remain unconfirmed at press time.)*

Additionally, at the time of joining SAG, a performer must pay an initiation fee plus the first half of his/her annual dues for that year (currently: $1,440).

Basically, once you become eligible to join SAG, you are allowed to work for thirty days without having to join SAG. After that time, if you wish to continue working as a SAG actor you must officially join the Union (SAG) if you want to accept or partake in any Union work after that thirty-day window. This is known as the federal Taft-Hartley law and applies to California, New York, and most other states.

It is at this point that many potential "professional actors" find themselves facing a hard decision. Why? Well, when a new member joins the Screen Actors Guild, he or she is agreeing, from that point forward, to abide by all the rules and regulations of the Screen Actors Guild, as spelled out in their Union Constitution and bylaws. These establish the member's rights as a professional, union actor, and also specify the member's responsibilities and obligations. What does that last part mean? Well, any member who is found in violation of any of their rules (know your rules) is subject to serious fines and disciplinary action by a panel of your Union peers. And the first and foremost of all the SAG rules is called (quite appropriately) Rule One: "You may not agree to work for any producer who is not signatory to the applicable SAG contract."

IMPORTANT NOTE:

As mentioned in Act 1, the "three voucher" eligibility requirement is changing. Back in October 2003, SAG's National Board unanimously voted to adopt the recommendation of the National Background Actors Committee which would replace the three-voucher eligibility rule with a new points-earning system. How will this work? Change seems slooow in coming.

There will be two routes for entry into SAG via background work and one route via participation in other "activities" that promote professionalism among SAG members. All routes will use the points system for entry. You will acquire "points" for each SAG voucher and each Non-Union voucher you receive. These vouchers must be received through work on a SAG-signatory project. You will also acquire "points" for the activities designated by SAG as "points-earning" projects. The big questions are:

- ***HOW MANY POINTS IS EACH SAG VOUCHER WORTH?***
- ***HOW MANY POINTS IS EACH NON-UNION VOUCHER WORTH?***
- ***HOW MANY POINTS IS EACH SAG ACTIVITY WORTH?***
- ***HOW MANY POINTS DO I NEED TO JOIN SAG?***

Answers to these queries have yet to be determined, but should be forthcoming sometime in 2006 (or so we're told). They were orignally to be forthcoming in 2004 and 2005, but budgetary problems forced a delay in the implementation of the new system. So, while rumors abound at press time, the "official" ins-and-outs of the "point system" have yet to be announced. A Transition Committee has been set up at SAG to answer all questions in the interim. But for the most up-to-date information regarding this situation, check out the SAG website at www.sag.org or call the hotline specifically set up for this change: 1-800-807-4188.

act two

Problems on the set?!
Who the heck do you call at SAG?!

If you call after hours or on the weekend, you will be connected to a series of options. Fun. Choose the appropriate option and you will be connected to the answering service and their ever-so-helpful personnel.

During NORMAL BUSINESS hours: 323-549-6879

At that time, you must STATE the following information:

1.) The problem
2.) Your location
3.) The name of the show
4.) A pager/phone/contact number (if possible)
5.) Changed call times
6.) Craft service problems
7.) Meal period violations
8.) Improper voucher notes

NOTE: *You do NOT have to give your name.*

If AFTER HOURS or weekends: 323-954-1600

Please limit your after-hours and weekend calls to SERIOUS SAFETY ISSUES.

AFTER HOURS: After hours are weekends or Monday - Friday after 5PM.

F.Y.I.: *Changed call times are examples of situations that can and should be handled during normal business hours.*

Indie Film SAG Contracts

In addition to its world famous Theatrical and TV contract, SAG also has a number of other contracts to cover low (or no) budget film productions looking to employ professional-type SAG talent. SAG views these projects as coming in five different flavors, and has created separate Agreements for each of them:

1.) Student Films
2.) Short Films
3.) Ultra-Low Budget
4.) Modified Low Budget
5.) Low Budget

• Student Films. . .

Are, y'know, those weird, interesting, exacerbating, boring, terrifying little flicks shot by the next generation of Spielbergs-In-Training who haunt the campuses of UCLA, and USC, and other such dens of cinematic learnification. They're great ways for actors to build up a reel, they also usually pay in pizza - and SAG is cool with this, more or less. Basically you're going to be working for "Deferred" pay, which means you don't get jack unless the film is picked up for some sort of distribution. Which is very unlikey to happen. These are projects you do for fun and experience. Especially for Background Actors, since they are not covered at all under the Student Film Agreement - so, according to the folks in the SAG Theatrical office, even the theoretical deferred pay won't be coming your way.

SAG defines a student film as (and we're paraphrasing here) a project made by a film student at an accredited school, whose primary purpose is for exhibition in the classroom or student film festivals or as part of the student's "visual resumé." It is permitted a maximum run time of 35 minutes, a total budget of $35,000, and cannot exceed 20 total shooting days or 6 weeks (whichever comes first).

• Short Films. . .

Are, well, um...short. Basically a student film made by non-students primarily as a learning experience and exhibition for award consideration (so film festivals are fair game). SAG defines a short film as a flick with a total budget of less than $50,000 and a run time of under 35 minutes. More deferred pay for the actors. And again, no special considerations for Background in the contract.

• Ultra-Low Budget. . .

Projects are indie films with budgets not to exceed $200,000 ($500,000 including all the deferred pay). They are films made primarily for non-commercial reasons. They can be distributed theatrically, but not made with the intention of going straight to cable or DVD. The nice part about these films - some of the performers actually get paid! Woo! Unfortunately not the Background, who, again, are not covered! Boo! Principal performers pull in a day rate of $100 smack-a-roos!

Modified Low Budget. . .

Projects are films budgeted under $625,000 (or $937,500 if the Producer meets certain diversity in casting criteria). The film can be produced for an initial theatrical release. While the friendly lady at the Background Department at SAG denies that Background Actors are covered under this agreement, the contract itself says otherwise. The pay for background on these projects is the standard $122/$132/$137 as broken down in the main contract summary (see p. 73).

• Modified Low Principal Rates:

Day Performer	$268.00
Weekly Performer	$933.00
Solo/Duo Singer on Daily Contract	$289.00
Solo/Duo Singer on Weekly Contract	$933.00

act two

Low Budget. . .

Projects are pretty much the same as the Modified Low Budget films (since the Modifications in the *Modified* Low Budget Agreement were made relative to this Agreement). The big differences are in the budget of the film ($2.5 million max) and in the pay rates for principals. Also, the production only has to employ 30 SAG Background actors before they can hire Non-Union (as opposed to the 50 required in the standard contract). Background pay rates, however, are the same as above.

• Low Budget Principal Rates:

Day Performer	$504.00
Weekly Performer	$1,752.00
Solo/Duo Singer on Daily Contract	$544.00
Solo/Duo Singer on Daily Contract	$1,752.00

There are of course a zillion little rules and regulations peppered throughout these Agreements. Keep in mind, this is just a Brain Surgeon(-ifyed) sysnopsis/summary of these independant contracts.

If you're looking for super-specific specifics, take a look at the contract summaries at:

www.sag.org or www.sagindie.com/contracts.

SAG in LA vs. SAG in NY (Bummer):

While the job description is the same, SAG Background actors in LA seem to get the short end of the stick compared to their counterparts on the east coast. The new SAG Background contract looks (at press time anyway) like it won't be doing much to correct for these discrepencies, but hope springs eternal.

The facts:

- N.Y. Background get "night premium" pay on movies and TV, but LA Background do not.
- N.Y. Background get "double time" pay after only 10 hours on set; LA Background don't get it until after 12 hours.
- In N.Y. the first 85 Background hired on a movie are on SAG vouchers, but in LA it's only the first 50.
- In N.Y. the first 25 Background hired on a TV show, in addition to all the stand-ins, are on SAG vouchers; in LA it's only the first 19 (plus 1 stand-in).
- The N.Y. Background zone has a 300 mile radius, but the LA background zone is only 75 miles.

SAG Rate Increase Schedule:
Theatrical Motion Picture & TV

Current thru 7-1-07

The salary rates for background actors working under Screen Actors Guild Basic and Television Agreements and AFTRA Exhibit A will increase by 3% on 7/1/06, and 3% on 7/1/07.

• Current

General	$ 122
Background Actor Special Ability	$ 132
Background Actor Stand-in	$ 137

• As of 7/1/06

General	$ 126
Background Actor Special Ability	$ 136
Background Actor Stand-in	$ 141

• As of 7/1/07

General	$ 130
Background Actor Special Ability	$ 140
Background Actor Stand-in	$ 145

INCREASES IN JOBS!

Background Actors Schedule X-I covered background actor numbers in television will increase from 16 to 19 plus one stand-in, a total of 20. In theatrical motion pictures, the Schedule X-I numbers for covered background actors increase from 45 to 50.

The unions estimate that over the term of the agreement this will result in more than 50,000 additional union jobs in television and more than 25,000 additional union jobs in feature films.

SAG Minimum Rates Contract:
Theatrical Motion Picture & TV

10-01-05 thru 7-01-06

DAY PERFORMERS:	
Performer	$678
Stunt Performer/Coordinator*	$678
WEEKLY PERFORMERS:	
Performer	$2,352
Stunt Performer/Coordinator*	$2,525
DANCERS:	
Solo/Duo (Day/Week)	$678 / $2,179
3 – 8 (Day/Week)	$594 / $1,997
9 + (Day/Week)	$519 / $1,816
Rehearsal Rate (Day)	$398
SINGERS (Theatrical: on and off screen and Television: on camera)	
Solo & Duo (Day/Week)	$732 / $2,352
Groups 3 - 8 (Day/Week)	$643 / $2,157
Groups 9+ (Day/Week)	$561 / $1,962
Mouthing 1-16 (Day)	$537
Mouthing 17+ (Day)	$419
SINGERS (Television, daily, off camera)	
Solo & Duo	$732
Groups 3-8	$388
Groups 9+	$334
3-DAY PERFORMERS (Television)	
Performer & Singer (1/2 or 1hr. show)	$1,714
Stunt Performer (1/2 or 1hr. show)	$1,853
Performer, Singer or Stunt Performer (11/2 or 2hr. show)	$2,018
"MAJOR ROLE" PERFORMERS (Television)	
1/2 hour programs	$3,644
1 hour programs	$5,831
MULTIPLE PICTURES (Television, Weekly)	
1/2 hour and 1 hour show performers	$1,741
1 1/2 hour show performers	$2,046
2 hour show performers	$2,414
TELEVISION SERIES (1/2 hour)	
13 out of 13 episodes	$2,352
7-12 episodes	$2,691
6 or less episodes	$3,139
TELEVISION SERIES (1 hour)	
13 out of 13 episodes	$2,828
7-12 episodes	$3,156
6 or less episodes	$3,691
TELEVISION SERIES (1 1/2 hours)	
13 out of 13 episodes	$3,767
1-12 episodes	$4,268

*Stunt Coordinator employed at less than "flat deal" minimum

Background Actors 2001 Theatrical Films & Television Digest

Applicable in the Los Angeles, San Diego, Las Vegas, San Francisco, Hawaii, and Sacramento Zones.

Reproduced for HOLLYWOOD OS® with permission from the Screen Actors Guild. Questions? Call the fabulous ever-so-helpful Production Services at 323-549-6811

act two

This is a digest of rates and working conditions applicable to Background Actors in the West Coast background zones in theatrical motion pictures and television. The rates are effective as of July 1, 2001, and extended through June 30, 2005.

It is intended to provide a readily available source to answer the most frequently asked questions. If further information is needed concerning specific contract terms, contact your local Guild office. Remember, this is only a summary of the Basic Agreement and not intended as a substitute.

SCREEN ACTORS GUILD
National Headquarters
5757 Wilshire Boulevard
Los Angeles, CA 90036-3600
Main Switchboard: 323-954-1600
Production Services: 323-549-6811

SAG Branch Offices

LAS VEGAS
3900 Paradise Road, Suite 162
Las Vegas, Nevada 89109
702-737-8818

SAN FRANCISCO
350 Sansome Street, Suite 900
San Francisco, California 94104
415-391-7510

HAWAII
949 Kapiolani Boulevard, #105
Honolulu, Hawaii 96814
808-596-0388

SAN DIEGO
7676 Hazard Center Drive, #500
San Diego, California 92108
619-497-2510

• NON-SIGNATORY PROJECTS •
SAG members may not work as Background Actors on non-signatory projects filming within the background zones.

• SAG JURISDICTION •
SAG members who are working as Background Actors within SAG's jurisdiction cannot work for less than the contract-covered wage.

• NON-COVERED JOBS •
Members may not work the non-covered jobs that are available after the required SAG covered Background Actors are hired.

Background Actors
2001 Contract Summary Theatrical & TV Digest
Table of Contents

SECTION NUMBER

RATES

Minimum Daily Rate Scale

	7/1/05 - 6/30/06
Background Actor	$122
Special Ability / Photo Double	$132
Stand-In	$137
Choreographed Swimmers and Skaters	$284 (West Coast)

Under the terms of the 1998 Agreement, the rates and numbers for Background Actors have been fixed for a term of six years (ending June 30, 2004).

The 1998 agreement (with additional rate hikes) has been extended until June 30, 2005. **A spankin' new 2006 agreement should be taking effect as we publish, so check www.SAG.org regularly (but all our groovy rate info is the latest).**

Weekly rates are five times the daily rates and shall include a guarantee of five consecutive days of employment.

Definitions

act two

• GENERAL BACKGROUND: Performer of atmospheric business which includes the normal actions, gestures and facial expressions of the Background Actor's assignment.

• SPECIAL ABILITY BACKGROUND ACTOR: Background Actor specifically called and assigned to perform work requiring special skill such as tennis, golf, choreographed social dancing (including square dancing), swimming, skating, riding animals, driving livestock, non-professional singing (in groups of 16 or less), mouthing to playback in groups of 16 or less, professional or organized athletic sports (including officiating and running), amputees, driving which requires a special skill and a special license (such as truck driving but not cab driving), motorcycle driving, insert work and practical card dealing.

• STAND-IN: Background Actor used as a substitute for another actor for purposes of focusing shots, setting lights, etc., but is not actually photographed. Stand-Ins may also be used as General Background.

•PHOTOGRAPHIC DOUBLE: Background Actor who is actually photographed as a substitute for another actor. A General Background Actor who is required to do photographic doubling shall receive the Special Ability rate.

• DAY PERFORMER: A Performer who delivers a speech or line of dialogue. A Background Actor must be upgraded to Day Performer if directed to speak, except in the case of "omnies".

• OMNIES: Any speech sounds used as general background noise rather than for its meaning. Atmospheric words such as indistinguishable background chatter in a party or restaurant scene.

Payments In Addition To Basic Daily Rate

(adjustments added to the basic daily wage)

Hazardous Work

Producer shall notify Background Actor at time of booking if any rough or dangerous work is involved. If no notice is received, Background Actor may refuse such work and receive a one-half check or payment for actual hours worked, whichever is greater. However, if other General Background Actor work is available, Producer may keep the Background Actor to do such work at full rate. No discrimination shall be permitted against such Background Actor for such refusal. Background Actors who accept hazardous work shall be entitled to additional compensation in an amount to be agreed upon between the Background Actor and the Producer *before the performance of such work.*

The amount of this adjustment shall be listed on the Background Actor's daily voucher.

Producer will provide immediate access to "qualified medical personnel" whenever hazardous work is to be performed.

2 Wet Work/Smoke Work

A Background Actor required to get wet (including rain work) shall receive an additional $14 added to the basic daily rate unless wearing swimming or surfing gear required for the scene. Any Background Actor not notified of wet work at the time of the call may refuse to perform such work and will receive one-half pay.

Background Actors working in smoke shall receive an additional $14 added to the basic daily rate.

Any Background Actor not notified of smoke work at the time of the call may refuse to perform such work and will receive one-half pay.

If a Background Actor refuses wet or smoke work, the Producer may keep the Background Actor to perform other General Background work, if it is available.

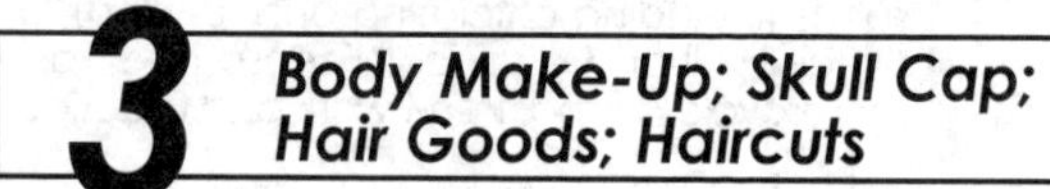

3 Body Make-Up; Skull Cap; Hair Goods; Haircuts

A Background Actor who is directed to and does have body make-up or oil applied to more than fifty percent (50%) of his/her body, and/or is required to and does wear a rubber skull cap, and/or is required to and does wear hair goods affixed with spirit gum (specified as wigs, beards, sideburns, mustaches or goatees), and/or who at the time of his employment is required to and does wear his own natural full-grown beard as a condition of employment, shall be entitled to additional compensation of $18.00 per day added to the basic daily rate. When a Background Actor is required to and does furnish his/her own hairpiece, he/she shall be paid additional compensation of $18.00 per day, added to the basic daily rate.

Any Background Actor required to get a haircut must be notified at the time of booking. If notice is not given, the Background Actor may refuse the job on arrival without prejudice, but will not be entitled to compensation. A haircut may not be required more than two (2) working days prior to the date of work.

4 Rehearsals

Rehearsal time is work time, whether on a day prior to filming or on the same day.

5 Costume Fittings

If on a day prior to work call, payment is one-quarter of daily rate for work call for up to 2 hours; additional time is payable at 1/16 of daily rate for each additional 30 minutes or fraction thereof. If fitted, he/she is guaranteed at least one day's pay from that company.

Wardrobe Allowance

Producer may require a Background Actor to report in formal attire (tuxedo, tailcoat or full length formal gown) for which the Background Actor shall receive $18.00 for maintenance. Producer may require a Background Actor to report in non-formal attire without extra payment. If Producer requires or requests a Background Actor to bring additional complete changes of wardrobe, the Background Actor shall receive $9.00 per day for the first such complete change and $6.25 per day for each additional change. Payment is for all changes requested, whether used or not. Performer may not be required to leave wardrobe overnight; if the Background Actor agrees to do so, daily wardrobe allowance is paid for each day so held.

Damage to Wardrobe or Property

A Background Actor must file a lost or damaged property report with Producer prior to leaving the set the day of work. Producer must provide a form for the purpose of filing such claim.

Please do not bring valuables to the set. If you must, make sure you notify the company and make special arrangements for safekeeping.

act two

INTERVIEW FEES

Background Actors reporting for interviews shall receive an allowance for the first two (2) hours of the interview in the amount of one-quarter (1/4) check. For additional time of the interview, Background Actors shall be paid in units of two (2) hours at the specified regular hourly rate for the call being filled.

In addition, Background Actors required to bring the following shall receive the indicated additional payment:

Requested Wardrobe	•	1/2 the applicable allowance rate
Requested Pet, Auto, Prop	•	1/2 the applicable allowance rate

PERSONAL PROPS

Background actors required to furnish the following shall receive the indicated additional payments:

Pets, Personal Accessories – Allowances Per Day:

Pets:	$23.00
Golf Clubs - Set With Bag:	$12.00
Tennis racket: *(no additional pay if paid for tennis outfit)*	$5.50
Luggage (per piece):	$5.50
Camera:	$5.50
Skis and Poles:	$12.00

For Props not listed above. . .
(the Background Actor must negotiate a fee at time of booking.

3 *Autos, Etc. Allowances Per Day*

Auto	$35.00
Trailer	$19.00
Bicycle	$12.00
Moped	$15.00
Motorcycle	$35.00
Police Motorcycle	$50.00
Skates/Skateboard	$5.50

Automobile Allowance of $.30 per mile roundtrip, computed from Producer' base to location within studio zone. (In Los Angeles, if no Producer's base mileage is computed from the corner of Beverly Boulevard and La Cienega. The Producer agrees to pay thirty cents (30¢) a mile for all miles traveled by th Background Actor upon the Producer's instructions.

SIXTEEN HOUR VIOLATION

One day's pay for each hour (or fraction thereof) beyond 16 hours. Meal break wardrobe and prop return, and travel time are included in calculating 16 hour A Background Actor employed in excess of 16 hours in any one day of 24 hour shall receive this additional amount except in circumstances beyond th control of the Producer. Production considerations or conditions are not consic ered to be beyond Producer's control.

MEAL PERIODS

Meal period must be at least 1/2 hour but not more than one hour in duratio (and is not counted as part of paid work time). Producer shall be allowed twelve minute grace period before the assessment of damages for mea period violation if camera is in the actual course of photography.

N.D. Meals (non-deductible meals) may only be called within the first two hours of the call time, are 15 minutes in length during which the Background Actor must be free of all activity including wardrobe, makeup, and hair, must be a meal appropriate to the time of day, and must be given only for the purpose of aligning the Background Actors' meal times with the crew meal times.

When crew members' meal period is shorter than that of Background Actors', crew members may be served before Background Actors are served. When this situation occurs, no time shall be deducted from work time until the Background Actors are given the opportunity to get in line for the actual feeding of the Background Actors.

• Meal Period Violations •

First 1/2 hour of delay or fraction thereof	$7.50
Second 1/2 hour of delay or fraction thereof	$10.00
Each additional 1/2 hour of delay or fraction thereof	$12.50

A Background Actor who does not receive a meal break within the first 6 hours after time of call shall receive the above meal penalties. Other meal breaks are due within 6 hours after the end of the previous meal break. Only one meal break may be deducted from work time within the first 8 hours of work.

• MEAL ALLOWANCE

Whenever the Producer supplies meals or other food or hot drinks or pays any money for meals to the cast and crew, Producer shall supply the same to all Background Actors. "Meal" means an adequate, well-balanced serving of a variety of wholesome, nutritious foods. Snacks such as hot dogs or hamburgers shall not constitute a meal.

6 OVERTIME

The regular work day is eight (8) consecutive hours (excluding meal periods). The 9th, 10th, 11th and 12th hours are payable at time-and-a-half in tenths of an hour (6 minute units). Work beyond the 12th hour is payable at double-time in tenths of an hour (6 minute units).

7 WARDROBE

a Allowance

Producer may request performer to report in normal attire without additional payment.

First complete change	$9.00 per day
Each additional change	$6.25 per day
Formal attire	$18.00 per day
Police Uniform	$36.00 per day

Payment is for all changes requested, whether used or not. Performer may not be required to leave wardrobe overnight; if the Background Actor agrees to do so, daily wardrobe allowance is paid for each day so held.

b Removal

Wardrobe removal time shall be counted as work time for all purposes includin computation of overtime, unless wardrobe is supplied by the background acto The background actor shall be dismissed as soon as his/her wardrobe c property is turned in.

C Non-Normal Wardrobe

Background Actors may not be required to report in out-of-season, period dres or in other non-normal wardrobe if the Background Actor utilizes publi transportation.

8 *SIXTH & SEVENTH DAY & HOLIDAYS WORKED*

The regular studio workweek shall consist of any five (5) consecutive days ou of any seven (7) consecutive days commencing with the first of such five (5 days. However, the five (5) consecutive day requirement shall be assignec to a schedule that calls for him/her to work, for example, on Monday anc Tuesday, with Wednesday and Thursday as the regular days off, and i followed by work on Friday through the following Tuesday.

• HOLIDAYS

- New Year's Day
- Memorial Day
- Thanksgiving Day
- Christmas Day
- President's Day
- Independence Day
- The Day *After* Thanksgiving Day (this is a Friday)
- Good Friday
- Labor Day

Above shall ALL be recognized holidays.

If any of the above holidays falls on Saturday, the preceding Friday shall be considered the holiday and if a holiday falls on Sunday, the following Monda shall be considered the holiday, except that on overnight locations, Saturda holidays will be recognized on Saturday. Got that?!

• PROVISIONS FOR HOLIDAYS NOT WORKED

Studio employment: Allowance of one (1) day's pay at straight time if the Background Actor is employed by Producer the day before and the day afte any of the above named nine (9) holidays.

• OVERNIGHT LOCATION EMPLOYMENT

Allowance of one (1) day's pay at straight time.

• PROVISIONS FOR HOLIDAYS WORKED

Double daily wage.

Overtime premium payments shall not be compounded or pyramided and sha be paid at the highest applicable premium rate only.

CROWD WORK

Minimum number of Registered Background Actors before Non-Registered persons may be employed on same day:

Features	(45 - Background)
Television	(16 - Background)

• STAND-INS

(1.) Stand-Ins are included in the count of covered Background Actors in theatrical motion pictures.
(2.) Stand-Ins are included in the count of covered Background Actors in long form television motion pictures.
(3.) One stand-in per day shall be excluded from the count of covered Background Actors in short form television.

NUDITY

Background Actors must be notified in advance of required nudity. Set must be closed and no still photography permitted without Background Actor's prior written consent. If not notified, the Background Actor may refuse to work and shall receive full day's pay. Employment as a nude body double is paid at the principal day rate.

11 WORKING IN A HIGHER CLASSIFICATION

If any part of the work day is worked at a higher rate than the rate under which the Background Actor is called for work, the higher rate shall prevail for that entire work day. If the Background Actor is called back for the next day and the Producer intends that he/she shall revert to the rate at which he/she was originally hired, the Background Actor must be notified of such intention at the time of the callback.

12 CALLBACKS

If the Background Actor is established in the film so that he/she cannot be replaced and if the Producer requires his/her services on the following work day and notifies the Background Actor of this by giving him/her a definite callback, the Background Actor shall report for the following work day.

If the Background Actor is given a definite callback, and such callback is canceled before 4:30 p.m. of the day preceding the work date, there is no payment due.

act two

13 AVAILABILITIES & BOOKINGS

Asking for availability does not obligate either the actor or the Producer. Availabilities are not bookings. Example: A casting director calls you and says "There is a two-day shoot next Monday and Tuesday; are you available?" and you reply " yes" and are told to call back on Sunday for details. When you call you are given all the necessary information (time, place, wardrobe) for Monday, but Tuesday is not mentioned. At this point you should ask "Am I booked for Tuesday?" Many casting directors would like to give the impression that the Background Actor is obligated to hold the second day, but this is not true. If you specifically ask whether or not you are "booked" you can avoid losing any other potential work.

14 CANCELLATIONS

The Background Actor is entitled to a full day's pay for cancellation of an initial work call except if due to illness in principal cast, fire, flood, or other similar catastrophe or national emergency. In the event of such cancellation, the Background Actor will be entitled to a half-check. If the Background Actor is notified of such cancellation before 6:00 p.m. of the work day previous to the work date, the Background Actor will not be entitled to the half-check.

15 WEATHER PERMIT CALLS

The Background Actor must be advised at the time of booking that a call is "weather permitting" and the type of weather required to shoot the scene. If such a call is canceled or postponed due to unsuitable weather, a half day's pay shall be due. Producer may require up to 4 hours of work for rehearsal, etc., but performer may not be recorded or photographed. Producer cannot request the Background Actor to call in the early morning hours of the following day for a possible "weather permitting" call. If Background Actor is held for more than 4 hours, an additional one half check is due.

16 PAYMENT REQUIREMENTS

The Background Actor will be paid by check to be mailed by the Thursday following the week of employment.

Late payment damages will be assessed at $3.00 per day (excluding Saturday, Sunday & Holidays) not to exceed twenty-five (25) days or $75.00.

17 TRAVEL / TRANSPORTATION

When a Background Actor is required to report at any studio zone location, Producer shall either furnish transportation to the Background Actor or, at Producer's option, may require the Background Actor to report at such location, in which latter case Producer will allow mileage of $.30 per mile computed between the studio and the zone location. The Producer shall have the right to require the Background Actor to report (subject to the same mileage allowance between the studio and the pick-up point) to a pick-up point from where the Background Actor will be transported to the location.

Background Actors shall be dismissed at the place of reporting. If Producer transports the Background Actor, this shall be counted as work time, payable in tenths of an hour and shall be considered in computing overtime, if any.

18 SANITARY PROVISIONS

The following shall be provided:

(a) Pure drinking water.

(b) A seat for each Background Actor.

(c) A stretcher or cot to be used as a stretcher.

(d) Separate dressing rooms for actors of each sex.

(e) Separate dressing rooms for children of each sex.

(f) Adequate provisions for proper and safe keeping of Background Actor's clothing during work.

(g) Adequate, clean and sanitary, individually screened toilet facilities, toilet paper, soap and paper towels or individual towels. Sanitary napkins must be obtainable.

Background Actors may refuse to change wardrobe if not provided with a place of privacy and comfort. Dressing rooms with adequate lighting to be provided. Buses and rest rooms are not considered acceptable places to change. Buses used as holding areas must have lights and proper seasonal climate control. Violations subject to grievance or Cooperative Committee, at the Guild's option.

19 AGENT'S FEE

Background Actors employed at scale shall not be required to pay commission to an agent. Any agent's fee shall be borne by the Producer.

20 HIRING

(a) No Background Actor shall be hired due to personal favoritism.

(b) Rotation of work shall be established to such reasonable degree as may be possible and practical.

(c) Producer will not hire a Background Actor who is currently on the payroll of the Producer or any of its hiring, casting or payroll agencies, except upon written waiver by the Guild.

(d) No fee, gift or other remuneration shall be demanded or accepted by any person having authority to hire, employ or direct services of Background Actors.

(e) Non-discrimination: producer will make every effort to cast Background Actors belonging to all groups in all types of roles, having regard for requirements of suitability for the role so the American scene may be realistically portrayed.

Producers agree not to discriminate on basis of geographic residence.

UNION SECURITY

If the Background Actor owes dues to the Guild at the time of employment, or if the performer is considered a "must-pay", the Producer may be liable to pay liquidated damages to the Guild in the amount of $436.00. "Must-pays" are performers who are not SAG members but have worked under SAG jurisdiction more than 30 days prior to this new work call.

***ADDITIONAL INFORMATION TIP:* See the complete 2001 SAG Codified Basic Agreement or contact the Screen Actors Guild.**

22 *EXTERIOR WORK OR WORK IN SEVERE CLIMATIC CONDITIONS*

Background Actors are to be notified in advance of any exterior work or work in severe climatic conditions, if known. In addition, Producer will provide reasonable protection from severe climatic conditions and when wearing out of season wardrobe.

23 *WORKING WITH EXPLOSIVES*

If a Background Actor is rigged with any type of explosive device (including squibs), the Background Actor must be upgraded to a Principal Performer and must be permitted to consult with the stunt coordinator and special effects person. The upgraded Background Actor may be brought back on subsequent days in the same role as a Background Actor.

24 *MINORS*

Minors working as Background Actors are now entitled to the same working conditions with regard to working hours as those working as Principal Performers.

***WEBSITE TIP:* For more specific information on any of the above, contact SAG or check out their most recent contracts online at www.sag.org**

Screen Actors Guild
PRODUCERS PENSION & HEALTH PLANS

Health Plan Eligibility Rules

Office: 818-954-9400
Hours: M-F, 8:30am - 4:30pm

act two

Eligibility for the Screen Actors Guild Producers Health Plan is established through employment with the producers who have signed Collective Bargaining Agreements with the Screen Actors Guild. If you meet:

(1) The minimum **dollar amount** of reported earnings (or)

(2) A minimum of **number of days** of covered employment within four consecutive calendar quarters, you will be eligible for one year of coverage for yourself and your qualified dependents. See the charts below for eligibility requirements.

PLAN II

Base Earnings Period	Minimum Earnings	Benefit Period
Jan.1, 02 to Dec. 31, 02	• $7,500 or 60	• April 1, 03 to Mar. 31, 04
Jan.1, 03 to Dec. 31, 03	• $9,000 or 61	• April 1, 04 to Mar. 31, 05
Jan.1, 04 to Dec. 31, 04	• $9,500 or 62	• April 1, 05 to Mar. 31, 06
Jan.1, 05 to Dec. 31, 05	• $10,000 or 63	• April 1, 06 to Mar. 31, 07
Jan.1, 06 to Dec. 31, 06	• $10,500 or 64	• April 1, 07 to Mar. 31, 08
Jan.1, 07 to Dec. 31, 07	• $11,000 or 65	• April 1, 08 to Mar. 31, 09

PLAN I

Base Earnings Period	Minimum Earnings or # of Days	Benefit Period
Jan.1, 02 to Dec. 31, 02	• $15,000	• April 1, 03 to Mar. 31, 04
Jan.1, 03 to Dec. 31, 03	• $20,000	• April 1, 04 to Mar. 31, 05
Jan.1, 04 to Dec. 31, 04	• $21,500	• April 1, 05 to Mar. 31, 06
Jan.1, 05 to Dec. 31, 05	• $23,000	• April 1, 06 to Mar. 31, 07
Jan.1, 06 to Dec. 31, 06	• $24,500	• April 1, 07 to Mar. 31, 08
Jan.1, 07 to Dec. 31, 07	• $26,000	• April 1, 08 to Mar. 31, 09

Once you have attained the minimum earning requirement for either of the Plans outlined, your eligibility will run for one full year before reevaluation occurs. In addition to meeting the eligibility requirements, you will also be responsible for a quarterly premium of $150 for Plan I participants and $195 for Plan II participants. Quarterly premiums are due quarterly (there's a surprise!) and in advance of the due date or your coverage will be terminated.

Participants cannot qualify for Plan I and Plan II simultaneously. You will be enrolled in the first Plan for which you meet the earnings test and your eligibility will run for one full year. Subsequent earnings are not used until the next base earnings period which will then be measured to determine your continuing eligibility status. Please review the section entitled Maintaining Eligibility.

Plan I and Plan II provide different benefit schedules. The benefit schedule for each plan is described in your Summary Plan Description booklet. Senior Performer's eligibility rules and benefits are also described in this booklet. If you would like a copy of the Summary Plan Description, contact the Plan Office.

Spouses & Dependents

The legal spouse and dependent children (under 19 years old) of the participant are covered as well. Same-sex domestic partners are also covered. Contact the plan office for rules and verification procedures.

Maintaining Eligibility

In order for eligibility to continue without interruption you must continue to generate the minimum earnings requirement in the necessary period as outlined below:

Base Earnings Period If you meet the minimum earnings requirement in this period.	**Benefits Period** You will be eligible for this period.
• ***January 1 through December 31***	• ***April 1 through March 31***
• ***April 1 through March 31***	• ***July 1 through June 30***
• ***July 1 through June 30***	• ***October 1 through September 30***
• ***October 1 through September 30***	• ***January 1 through December 31***

Once you have established eligibility, your base earnings period and benefits period do not change unless you have a break in coverage.

Covered Earnings

Covered earnings (sessions and residuals) are those which require contributions to be made to the Pension and Health Plans by producers who are signatory to the Screen Actors Guild contracts in connection with employment in theatrical motion pictures, television motion pictures, television commercials, industrial and educational motion pictures, and interactive media projects.

Non-Covered Earnings

Non-Covered earnings are those which do not require contributions to be made to the Pension and Health Plans. For example:

1.) Payments for various penalties and allowances such as meal penalties, late call, payments for rest period violation, traveling expenses, lodging or living expenses, interest on delinquent payments, reimbursement for special hairdress, for wardrobe damage, for the use of personal automobile, or other equipment, are not included.

2.) Some residual payments are not applicable for Pension and Health Plan eligibility purposes.

3.) Earnings in excess of the theatrical and television contribution limits are also not covered. For a schedule of the applicable contribution "ceiling," please contact the Plan Office: 818-954-9400 - or - Website: www.sagph.org

Alternative Health Coverage for SAG Members

Finally, some good news for SAG members who need health insurance, but who are finding it difficult to meet the new, higher minimum requirements of SAG's Producers Pension & Health Plans (discussed on the previous pages).

If you are a current, paid-up SAG member for at least 30 days prior to effective start dates of coverage, you may be eligible for low-cost health insurance through The Entertainment Industry Group Insurance Trust (TEIGIT). They offer insurance options for those employed in qualifying entertainment unions – and SAG is definitely one of them.

You must live in certain states to qualify, but the good news for all you Hollywood background actors is that all California SAG members are eligible to fill out an enrollment form! The plan doesn't cover anyone over the age of 64, but it can cover spouses, domestic partners and dependents.

Enrollment could be automatic for members who meet the eligibility requirements, from the get-go (i.e., SAG members who have been in the Union more than thirty days and are under the age of 64).

WEBSITE TIP:
For more information on specific plans and rates - check them out on the web: www.teigit.com

act two

The Purpose of AFTRA

AFTRA represents its members in four major areas:

1.) News and broadcasting

2.) Entertainment programming

3.) The recording business

4.) Commercials, non-broadcast, industrial and educational media

This union represents professional performers and broadcasters in television, radio, sound recordings, non-broadcast/industrial programming and new technologies such as interactive programming and CD-ROMs.

Much like SAG, AFTRA negotiates and enforces agreements that guarantee minimum (but never maximum) salaries, safe working conditions and health and retirement benefits for its members. In fact (a little bit of trivia here), AFTRA was the first industry union to establish employer-paid health and retirement plans for members and their dependents who qualify. How cool is that? For more detailed information about the AFTRA Health & Retirement Funds visit its website (www.aftrahr.com).

AFTRA even has a separate tax-exempt organization, The AFTRA Foundation, funded entirely by voluntary contributions, that works in other significant ways to benefit its members. How about an AFTRA scholarship available to AFTRA members and their dependents through the AFTRA Heller Memorial Foundation? Not bad, huh? Local AFTRA chapters also offer all sorts of different programs designed to assist members who live and work in or around each particular area. They publish guides with talent contact information and distribute them to local producers, agents and casting directors.

They also conduct workshops to help members with resumé writing and audition techniques as well as other types of seminars where members can meet agents, managers, and casting directors who hire talent. Call Member Services (323-634-8213 for schedules and more information). They've got other perks too, so check out their website www.aftra.org and see if joining AFTRA is something for you!

How Do I Become an AFTRA Member?

If you were paying attention, we told you in Act 1, but we like ya, so we'll tell ya again! Now be good and pay attention this time you bad boy/girl/actor/background-Brain-Surgeon!) Any person who has performed or INTENDS to perform in AFTRA's jurisdiction is eligible for membership. What does that mean? Well, ANYONE who wants to join AFTRA can join! But...

How Much Does It Cost To Join AFTRA?

You gotta pay your dues, dude! New members must pay a one-time initiation fee plus union dues covering the first dues period. How much is that? One thousand, three hundred cool, cold $1 bills for the initiation fee ($1,300 bucks, kids) effective November 1, 2004, plus $63.90 minimum dues for the first dues period (for a grand total of $1,363.90). After joining, a member's dues are based on his or her earnings in AFTRA's jurisdiction during the prior year. You are billed twice a year for AFTRA dues – each May 1st and November 1st.

act two

Alright, now those are just some tasty tid-bits to get you started. The pages that follow break down pay rates for various types of programming, include some snazzy contract-type stuff that even we Brain Surgeons have a hard time demystifying (boy, we like that $100 word!), and other fun stuff – so, get reading already and learn all there is to learn about AFTRA! But, wait...

The Current & Tricky Dilemma of AFTRA Pay Rates. . .

As we've stated above, on the next few pages we have broken down some basic pay rates for you, our wonderful readers. The tricky dilemma to which we refer in our aptly subtitled section is that some parts of the AFTRA contract expire on November 15th of each year. Some contractual stuff is valid for a three-year period, while other rates are revised and adjusted every year. Make sure to double check that the particular rates that apply to your situation are still current.

What Does That Mean For You If You Are An AFTRA Member?

It means, we've tried to be as current and accurate as possible, but different AFTRA contracts are in flux at different times so this is no easy task. Also take into consideration that AFTRA must jointly negotiate with SAG on some specific contracts too (all the more important with new digital filming technology). Why are we sharing all this? Because these contract negotiations can happen every year and with a SAG/AFTRA merger forever looming... well, it's because we just love to talk (well, write) and because we always want you to have the latest, greatest, and most up-to-date information possible when picking up this directory. So, use the rates that follow as a guide, but if you are an AFTRA member or are concerned about fluctuations in pay rates, or want the end-all in answers about things other than soaps and TV shows, contact AFTRA (323-634-8100) or consult their website: www.aftra.org

AFTRA
Demystifying AFTRA Television
HOLLYWOOD OS® Condensed Cheat Sheet

act two

1 AFTRA DAYTIME SERIAL (SOAP) RATES FOR BACKGROUND ACTORS*

Program	Extras	Rate	Amount
Half-hour Program	(Less than 20 Extras)	• 8.5 Hr. Rate	: $108 /8.5hrs.
Half-hour Program	(More than 20 Extras)	• 8.5 Hr. Rate	: $86.40 /8.5hrs.
One Hour Program	(Less than 20 Extras)	• 9 Hr. Rate	: $140 /9hrs.
One Hour Program	(More than 20 Extras)	• 9 Hr. Rate	: $112 /9hrs.

*If you are informed at the time of the booking that 20 or more extra performers will be used, your rate is 20% less.

• STAND-IN FOR ALL DAYTIME SERIALS
$24/Hour – 2 Hour Minimum

There is an "Under-5" or "5 lines or less" category for daytime serials.

• "UNDER 5" DEFINED FOR ALL DAYTIME SERIALS
You are given a speaking part consisting of 5 lines or less or you perform without speaking but your character/action is integral to the scene.

• OVERTIME FOR ALL DAYTIME SERIALS
Time and 1/2, pro rata, after 8 hours

2 AFTRA DRAMATIC PROGRAM RATES FOR BACKGROUND ACTORS
(Primetime, Non-Primetime & Syndication)

General Background

Currently $92.25/ 8hrs.

Special Ability

Currently $102.25/ 8hrs.

• STAND-IN FOR DRAMATIC PROGRAMS
$24/Hour – 2 Hour Minimum

There is NOT an "Under-5" category for Primetime dramatic programs. If you are given a speaking part, you are upgraded to Principal status.

• OVERTIME FOR DRAMATIC PROGRAMS
Time and 1/2, pro rata, after 8 hours.

AFTRA MEAL PENALTIES FOR TELEVISION

After the first 6 hours, you are to be given a 1-hour lunch break. There is a grace period of 12 minutes (like SAG) before the Meal Penalty begins. If you are not broken after 6 hours (plus the Grace Period, if applicable) you will receive a flat $25 for the violation. If, during the same job, you go into Meal Penalty for a Second Meal (i.e. dinner) you will be paid a flat $35 for the violation ($60 Total: $25 for the first (i.e. lunch) and $35 for the second (i.e. dinner.) You may be broken for a half-hour for the second meal, while the first meal break must be for an hour. If you are broken for a second meal but the second meal is not catered, the meal penalty is $27.50.

AFTRA VARIETY SHOW RATES FOR EXTRA PERFORMERS*

Half-hour Program	(Less than 30 Extras)	• 8 Hr. Rate	: $115 /8hrs.
Half-hour Program	(More than 30 Extras)	• 8 Hr. Rate	: $92 /8hrs.
One Hour Program	(Less than 30 Extras)	• 9 Hr. Rate	: $146 /9hrs.
One Hour Program	(More than 30 Extras)	• 9 Hr. Rate	: $116.80 /9hrs.
One & 1/2 Hour Prog.	(Less than 30 Extras)	• 11.5 Hr. Rate	: $178/11.5hrs.
One & 1/2 Hour Prog.	(More than 30 Extras)	• 11.5 Hr. Rate	: $142.40/11.5hrs.
Two Hour Program	(Less than 30 Extras)	• 11.5 Hr. Rate	: $210 /11.5hrs.
Two Hour Program	(More than 30 Extras)	• 11.5 Hr. Rate	: $168/11.5hrs.

*If you are informed at the time of the booking that 30 or more Extra Performers will be used, your rate is 20% less.

• OVERTIME FOR EXTRA PERFORMERS
Overtime Penalties will begin after 9 hours – the base rate may be spread over two consecutive work days totaling 11.5 hours.

RATES FOR PROGRAMS
(Other Than Variety or Serials)

General Extra
Currently $92.25/ 8hrs.

Special Ability
Currently $102.25/ 8hrs.

• STAND-IN OTHER THAN VARIETY OR SERIALS
$24/Hour – 2 Hour Minimum

• "UNDER 5" OTHER THAN VARIETY OR SERIALS
You are given a speaking part consisting of 5 lines or less or you perform without speaking but your character/action is integral to the scene.

AFTRA WARDROBE FOR TELEVISION

• COMPLETE OUTFIT
$10 for each COMPLETE OUTFIT you wear on camera *(including your first)*
(ed. note: The Contract states $10 per Garment, not "complete outfit" – hmm. . ?)

- FORMAL ATTIRE

$25 for Formal Attire

AFTRA NON-BROADCAST/INDUSTRIAL CODE RATES

These rates apply to the first 10 Extra Performers employed per day for each Industrial program produced.

	11/06-4/08
General Extra	$119
Special Ability Extra (Stand-In, Photo Double, Hand Model)	$131
Silent Bit Extra	$ 222.50

8 AFTRA INTERACTIVE MEDIA AGREEMENT FOR EXTRA PERFORMERS

All Fees are PER PROGRAM.	7/05-1/06	1/06 - 1/07
General Extra	$118	$122
Special Ability/Stand-In	$142	$146

AFTRA NATIONAL PUBLIC TELEVISION AGREEMENT

(Informational / Educational Programs, Cultural / Entertainment Programs.)

All Fees are PER PROGRAM.	11/06-4/08
Extra/Walk-On	$119
Stand-In	$131
Silent Bit Background	$222.50
Specialty Wardrobe (Uniforms/Costumes)	$12
Regular Wardrobe	$10
Formal Attire	$25

10 AFTRA TV RECORDED COMMERCIALS CONTRACT FOR EXTRA PERFORMERS

• SESSIONS •	10/30/03 -10/29/06
Unlimited	$291.80
13-Week	$169.40
Extension	$218.50

• ADDITIONAL PAY •	
Wet, Smoke, Snow, Dust (Natural or Artificial)	$40.00
Body Makeup	$31.40
Wardrobe (Regular)	$16.90
Evening/Pre-1950 Wardrobe	$28.20
Uniform/Costume	$28.20

• ADDITIONAL PAY (continued) •	10/30/0-10/29/06
Mileage	$0.345/mi
Skates/ Skate Board	$9.05
Bicycle	$12.05
Moped	$18.05
Night Premium (8pm-1am)	+10%
Night Premium (1am-6am)	+20%
MPV (First 1/2 Hour)	$25.00
MPV (Second 1/2 Hour)	$25.00
MPV (Third 1/2 Hour, etc.)	$50.00
Late Pay	$2.50/day
Fitting (2 Hours Max)	1/4 check
Auto/ Motorcycle	$36.05
Cable 1st Commercial, w/ 1 yr use	$275
Add Cable Commercials in day, each	$68.75

• COMMERCIAL INTEGRATION FEES •	
Standard	$291.80
Cable (1 yr)	$216.80

11 AFTRA NATIONAL CODE OF FAIR PRACTICE FOR NETWORK TELEVISION BROADCASTING

• AFTRA'S DEFINITION OF WALK-ONS AND EXTRAS •

Walk-ons and extras are those performers who do not speak any lines whatsoever as individuals but who may be heard, singly or in concert, as part of a group or crowd.

The extra rate shall be applicable for the performance, singly or in concert, of ordinary business including actions, gestures, and facial expressions portraying the extra performer's assignment.

Walk-on or extra shall be upgraded to the five-line-or-less category if he or she meets any one of the following three conditions in a scene:

(i) is addressed individually by a principal performer

(ii) is alone in the scene;

(iii) speaks individually as part of a group or crowd; and provided that such walk-on or extra receives more than minimal direction and portrays a point essential to the story.

A performer engaged as a walk-on or extra who is subsequently directed to speak at least one line not as part of a group or crowd shall be paid the applicable principal or five-line-or-less rate.

Performers who speak no lines but who nevertheless portray a major part in the program shall be paid the applicable principal performer rate.

12 SIXTH & SEVENTH DAY & HOLIDAYS WORKED

• AFTRA RECOGNIZES THE SAME HOLIDAYS AS SAG•

- New Year's Day
- President's Day
- Good Friday
- Memorial Day
- Independence Day
- Labor Day
- Thanksgiving Day
- The Day *After* Thanksgiving Day (this is a Friday)
- Christmas Day

Above shall ALL be recognized holidays. Saying that you should still always double check that the specific AFTRA contract you're working under recognizes any specific holiday.

If any of the above holidays falls on Saturday, the preceding Friday shall be considered the holiday and if a holiday falls on Sunday, the following Monday shall be considered the holiday, except that on overnight locations, Saturday holidays will be recognized on Saturday. Got that?!

***NOTE:**

The AFTRA contract can vary from show to show. For the definitive answer to rate or rule query, please contact the AFTRA representative assigned to the show in question.

American Federation of Television & Radio Artists

AFTRA HEALTH PLANS

Health Plan Eligibility Rules

Phone: 800-562-4690

act two

AFTRA Health Plans are administered by the AFTRA Health Fund, an independent organization directed, in part, by Union representatives. The AFTRA Health Fund was founded in 1955, and was the first fund of its kind to provide health benefits for performers and their families.

AFTRA Branch Offices

LOS ANGELES
5757 Wilshire Boulevard
Los Angeles, CA 90028
323-937-3631
800-562-4690

NEW YORK
261 Madison Avenue
New York, NY 10016
212-499-4800
800-562-4690

The Plans

There are two different health plans available to eligible AFTRA members: the Individual Health Plan and the Family Health Plan. Both plans offer: hospital, major medical, prescription drug, mental health and chemical dependency, wellness, and dental programs.

Becoming and Staying Eligible

Eligibility for the plans is determined by the covered earnings (we'll explain this phrase in a sec) you make over four consecutive calendar quarters (most folks call it a "year").

If you've brought home more than $10,000 in covered earnings, but less than $30,000 in covered earnings, during the previous year, you are eligible for the Individual Health Plan. The Individual Health Plan covers the performer, but not his or her dependents (though you can usually purchase additional coverage for them through the Family Health Plan).

If you've made MORE then $30,000 in covered earnings during the previous year, you are eligible for the Family Health Plan. The Family Health Plan covers both the performer and his or her dependents (in case you've got spouses and kids and domestic partners and those types of folks you want to look out for).

Schedule of Effective Dates for Coverage

Generally you will become eligible to join the health plan on the first day of the second calendar quarter following the quarter in which you meet the minimum covered earning requirements. It's not as confusing as it sounds.

Check Out The Dates Below:

Qualify By:	**Coverage Begins:**
• ***September 30***	• ***January 1***
• ***December 31***	• ***April 1***
• ***March 31***	• ***July 1***
• ***June 30***	• ***October 1***

Covered Earnings

Covered earnings are those payments made to you by a contributing employer for work under a collective bargaining agreement that provides for contributions to the AFTRA Health Fund.

act two

Spouses & Dependents

Dependents eligible for coverage under the AFTRA Health Plans include: legal spouses, domestic partners, unmarried children until they reach the ripe old age of 21 (or 23 if they are full-time students), and unmarried children of any age with certain physical or mental handicaps.

Fun Factoids

Here's a grab bag of interesting and odd little facts we came across while poring through the not-so-fine print of the AFTRA Health Plans:

The Accidental Death & Dismemberment Insurance included in the coverage pays out exactly $9,000 for the accidental loss of a foot.

If you are eligible for the SAG Producers Health Plan, but have failed to pay the premiums (and thus aren't getting health coverage from the gang at SAG), the AFTRA Health Plan will still process your claims as if the SAG Plan were your primary health insurance (basically the AFTRA plan pays a lot less of the medical bill than they would otherwise).

The AFTRA Plan will toss you 10 grand if you permanently lose your voice. Unless, of course, that loss of voice occurred as a result of a war (so all you background actors out there moonlighting as mercenaries had better be careful).

AFTRA offers a Senior Citizen Health Program that compliments the coverage provided by Medicare.

Learn More

To find out more specifics about the AFTRA Health Plans, call them at one of the numbers listed above, or go to www.aftrahr.com and check out the mountains of info they've got waiting for you.

SAG & AFTRA Pay Cheat Sheet

The following is for quick reference - read contracts for specific information that may be different for the show you're working. When you're working on a basic cable program, (*Comedy Central* or *E!* shows, for instance), the AFTRA rates/terms and conditions are determined on a show-by-show basis. Therefore, the pay rate, if they pay meal penalties, etc., is dependent upon the contract that particular show worked out with AFTRA. It is in your own best interest to contact the union rep. for the show in question so you know exactly what you are paid for and under what conditions.

Item	SAG Theatrical/ SAG Television	SAG or AFTRA Commercial	AFTRA TV	AFTRA Interactive	AFTRA Industrial
Background Talent	$122/8	$291.80			
Stand-In	$137/8	$291.80			
Pets	$23	$24.40			
Camera	$5.50	$5.84			
Luggage	$5.50/piece	$5.84			
Skis/Golf Clubs & Bag	$12	$12.73			
Tennis Racquet	$5.50	$5.84			
Binoculars/Opera Glasses	$5.50	$5.84			
Large Portable Radios	$5.50	$5.84			
Skates/Skateboard	$5.50	$9.05			
Auto	$35	$36.05	$0	$0	$0
Trailer	$19	$36.05			
Bicycle	$12	$12.05			
Moped	$15	$12.05			
Motorcycle	$35	$36.05			
Smoke/Wet Work	$14	$40*	$0	$0	$0
Dust/Snow Work	$14	$40*	$0	$0	$0
Body Make-up	$18	$31.40		$16	
Skull-Cap	$18	$31.40		$16	
Hair Goods	$18	$31.40	$12	$16	
Beard	$18	$31.40 (see contract)			
Wardrobe 1st outfit	$0	$17.20	$10		
Wardrobe Change	$9	$17.20	$10	$15	$16
Each Addl. Change	$6.25	$17.20	$10		$5.50
Wardrobe (Formal)	$18	$28.65	$25	$25	$27
Police Uniform	$36				
First MPV	$7.50	$25.00		$25	$25
Second MPV	$10	$25.00 (see contract)		$35	$35
Third MPV, etc.	$12.50	$50.00 (see contract)		$50	$50
Night Work (8PM-1AM)	none	+10%	$0	$0	$0
Night Work (1AM- 6AM)	none	+20%	$0	$0	$0

* You are paid a single $40 adjustment if you work in any or all of the following: smoke, wet, dust or snow.

frequently asked...

Background actors' frequently asked questions

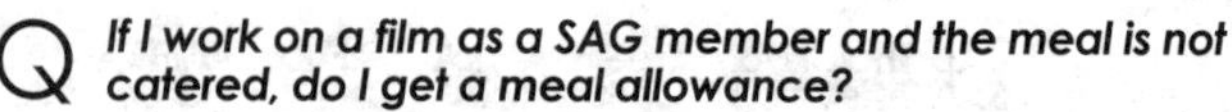

Q ***If I work on a film as a SAG member and the meal is not catered, do I get a meal allowance?***

A You are entitled to whatever the crew gets. If the crew gets a meal allowance, you are entitled to the same.

Q ***If I volunteer a line as a background actor, doesn't that entitle me to an upgrade to Day Performer?***

A If you think a scene would be further enhanced by dialogue, you can ask if that's what the director wants. Let him or her make that determination. Otherwise, a volunteered line cannot be considered as a basis for an upgrade. If you simply add the dialogue yourself without approval, the Guild will not pursue a claim on your behalf, even if your line remains in the final version of the film.

Q ***Can anything be done if a Casting Director has not hired me for a long time to perform work as a background actor?***

A The collective bargaining agreement reads: "Rotation work shall be established to such reasonable degree as may be possible and practical." Also, please keep in mind that SAG is not a hiring hall and cannot guarantee employment for its members.

Q ***What obligation do I have to a Casting Director who asks for my availability for certain days?***

A An availability inquiry is not a booking. You should advise the Casting Director if you are available on the dates specified. However, if you are not definitely booked, you have no obligation to keep those days available if you get another offer of employment. A "hold" is not a booking. In order to be clear about whether you are booked and the company is obligated to pay you in the event of a cancellation, you should ask the question, "Is this a booking?"

frequently asked...

Background actors' frequently asked questions...

Q ***If I am upgraded to a principal role, how is my salary calculated for that day?***

A You will receive a pro rata share of your background actor's salary based on the number of hours you worked under that contract plus the full daily wage for your principal work. For example, suppose you report to the set at 7AM, work as a background actor until 12PM (noon), at which time you are upgraded to a principal performer, and work until 8PM as a principal. In this scenario, you will be paid 5/8ths of your background actor's rate (5 hours of work as a background actor)and the full principal's rate. If you have negotiated a rate higher than the minimum wage, your salary will be based on that negotiated amount. At the time you are upgraded, your clock, for purposes of overtime, starts over: no overtime is due until you have worked more than 8 hours as a principal.

Q ***Are there any time limits within which a claim must be filed?***

A Yes. A claim other than an upgrade must be filed with the producer within 30 days of the date of knowledge of the violation, which is, in general, the date you received or should have received your paycheck. This provision means that SAG has 30 days from the date of knowledge of the violation in which to process your claim, investigate the facts and send it to the producer. NOTE: You DO NOT have 30 days in which to send your claim to SAG. Please notify the Guild as soon as you realize there has been a violation so that SAG will have sufficient time to file your claim within the 30 day filing limit.

For upgrades, SAG has 90 days from the date of knowledge in which to send your claim to the producer. If you have been directed to speak, please notify the Guild as soon as possible. Your upgrade does not depend on whether the line was used in the final cut: the issue is whether you were directed to and did speak on camera, not whether the line stays in the movie. If you wait until the film comes out in theatres or television, the filing deadline will have passed and the Guild will be unable to act on your behalf.

frequently asked...

Background actors' frequently asked questions

Q ***Does SAG's affirmative action policy apply to background actors?***

A Yes. Schedule X-1, Section 45, sets forth the policy of Non-Discrimination with respect to background actors. This policy affirms the Producer's and SAG's commitment to non-discrimination and fair employment in hiring background actors for all types of roles with respect to sex, race, age, color, creed, national origin, marital status, disability, or sexual orientation. The Producers shall also make every effort to include minorities, women, performers with disabilities, and performers over 40 in the casting of motion pictures and television productions.

Q ***What are my contractual rights when offered work of a hazardous nature?***

A Schedule X-1, Section 7, together with other applicable sections, such as Section 9 ("Wet, Snow and Smoke Work"), define these rights. The Producer must advise the background actor regarding any hazardous or dangerous work to be performed, and the extra performer has the right to refuse the work and receive a one-half check or compensation for actual time worked, whichever is greater, if he/she is not so notified. However, if you refuse the hazardous work, the Producer may keep you on the set to do other general background acting.

If you are asked to perform hazardous work and have been hired on a minimum check, you have the right to negotiate with the Producer for additional compensation before you perform the action.

Q ***If I'm not a member of AFTRA, can I accept a booking on an AFTRA show?***

A Short answer: yes, with certain provisions. Oops, guess that last part unshortened the answer. If you've never worked an AFTRA job before, you can feel free to accept the role. Once you've taken that first job you have 30 more days to work as many more AFTRA jobs as you can book. After that, you must join AFTRA to continue working shows which fall under their jurisdiction.

frequently asked...

Background actors' frequently asked questions

Q ***Once I've started working AFTRA jobs, will AFTRA take my paychecks?***

A Once you're past the 30 day grace period (see the preceding question) during which you can work AFTRA jobs without joining the union, AFTRA expects you to either join and pay the initiation fee of (as of this printing) $1,300 or stop accepting AFTRA jobs. If you choose to join and don't want to pay the fee, AFTRA will allow you to work it off. Basically, they'll take your paychecks from AFTRA gigs until you're all paid up on your fees. After that, the checks are all yours.

Q ***If I'm in the middle of a high stakes poker game in holding and I'm called to set just as I've been dealt a royal flush, should I fold and get to work or blow off the 2nd AD so I can rake in $5.75 in nickels?***

A Whoa...rough decision. Hmmmm. That is a deep and ponder-worthy question if ever there was one. A question for the ages. On one hand, no extra role in the world is going to give you the satisfaction of being known as the legendary card shark of holding. On the other hand, if you don't do your job, you'll never be back in holding because you won't be working again. Catch-22 much? Hmmm. Hmmm. Hmmm. Oh yeah...GO DO YOUR JOB! Jeesh. You wacky kids.

professional conduct

Reminder of professional conduct for professional performers..

- <u>NOTES</u> • The professional performer is always prepared to take down the reporting location, date and time of a call, as well as the required wardrobe.
- <u>LEAVING SET</u> • Once you are hired, you have been hired until released by the production company. In short, do not leave early and do not ask to leave early.
- <u>BOOKING CONFLICTS</u> • Immediately notify Casting Director of potential conflicts caused by other bookings.
- <u>PREPAREDNESS</u> • Make sure that you arrive on the set on time, with the required outfits and/or props. Production companies have the right to dismiss without payment any performer who is not on time. It is better to arrive early than to report late (imagine that?).
- <u>SAG CARD</u> • Always carry your current, paid-up SAG card or receipt of payment from the Membership Department if you are SAG.
- <u>BEHAVIOR</u> • Be courteous and attentive.
- <u>VOUCHER</u> • Remember: Fill out your contract or voucher with care, making sure all information appears on all copies. Keep your own records of hours worked, meal breaks, etc. Make sure you note all personal wardrobe and props supplied at the request of Producer.
- "<u>HURRY UP & WAIT!</u>" • Bring along some busy work. Part of working sometimes requires hours of idleness on the set. Remember: Down time on the set is still considered work time.
- <u>LEAVING SET</u> • Never leave the set without getting approval from the Assistant Director.
- <u>SMOKING</u> • Smoke only in designated areas. This is a matter of courtesy to your fellow performers.

RATED:* PBS - *Professional Behavior Suggested

In order to be recognized by others as a professional performer & to protect the dignity of the entire acting profession, members are advised of the aforementioned guidelines.

SAG MEMBERSHIP ORIENTATION •

This orientation offers SAG members (new and old) a brief overview of the Guild's history and the procedures necessary to maximize your SAG membership. Whether you are a new member or an old member, all are encouraged to attend this orientation to be informed on all Guild practices. Call 323-549-6418.

SAG ASSISTANCE FUND •

This Fund provides emergency relief and financial aid to those who qualify. They allocated over $1 million to qualified SAG members during the 2000 commercial strike. Call 323-549-6773.

act two

SAG CONSERVATORY •

These workshops and seminars generally run from mid-October through May of the following year. The conservatory is designed to help SAG actors develop their skills as actors. You must apply for an application once a year in order to participate. Call 323-856-7736.

SAG COLD-READING SEMINARS & SHOWCASES •

The cold-reading seminars are held on the second and third Wednesday of every month. The showcases are held on the fourth Tuesday of each month. You must call 323-549-6435 to sign up in advance as there is a limited number of actors who can participate in each session. The Info Hotline is 323-937-3441 and it lists the recent seminar dates and call-in dates for reservations. For more info, call the SAG Casting Committee at 323-549-6540 (the office is manned by an all-volunteer staff, so expect to get voicemail).

SAG VOLUNTEER INCOME TAX ASSISTANCE •

Taxes suck – we need all the help we can get, right?! This service provides detailed training and extensive review in tax forms so actors may properly complete what is needed. April 15th is the dreaded day (as we're sure you know all too well). Call 323-954-1600 for more information as tax season approaches!

SAVVY EMPLOYEE •

SAG members can get some pretty good deals on tickets to movies (*AMC, Mann's* & more) and theme parks (*Universal, Knott's, Sea World*) and things that aren't available to the general public! Woo-hoo for SAG! Tickets can be ordered at www.savvyemployee.com or you can order over the phone: 310-828-8107. There are other perks for dining out, etc. Check the web, man! Be sure to specify SAG as your affiliation.

SAG CONVERSATIONS •

This monthly speaker series features established Guild members sharing their experiences with current members. Call SAG to ask for more info or reserve a spot, 323-549-6488. You must include your name (as listed by SAG), SAG ID number, phone number and the date of the event when you are requesting a specific date/speaker – and there is no admittance without reservations. Reservations are accepted until seats are filled.

FINANCIAL LIFE RAFT WORKSHOPS •

These seminars are meant to help SAG members get their finances in order, and stay afloat financially today and for the future. The workshops are held in the James Cagney Room at SAG's main headquarters. Call 323-549-6668 for more information, scheduling and reservations.

JOHN L. DALES SCHOLARSHIP FUND •

This program provides a certain number of scholarships each year to SAG members and the children of members. There are "regular" scholarships intended for college educations. There are also "transitional" scholarships for those wishing to make a career change and in need of further education. Of course the catch is that you need to have earned $30,000 in the Guild's jurisdiction. Yowzers! If you're the offspring of a Guild member, your parent must have aggregate earnings of $60,000 earned in the Guild's jurisdiction in order for you to qualify. If you're doing that much extra work, who has time for school??! The applicant must submit Financial Aid Forms, income tax returns, transcripts and all sorts of embarrassing stuff you might rather not reveal. For more information about this scholarship or more specific requirements, call 323-549-6708.

BOOKPALS (PERFORMING ARTISTS FOR LITERACY IN SCHOOLS) •

Here's your chance to give something back! BookPALS is a SAG program to promote literacy among the young ones of California. Actors like you visit elementary schools in local neighborhoods and read aloud to children week after week. It can be a fun way to help out the kids, plus you can hone those acting skills by reading to a live, captive audience!

CATASTROPHIC HEALTH FUND •

This fund provides grants to eligible SAG members or dependents who suffer from catastrophic illness or injury (hence the name) and can't afford the SAG Health Plan. Call 323-549-6773.

HEALTHY FAMILIES •

For members who do not qualify for the SAG Health Plan, the Healthy Families Program is a state and federally funded health coverage program for children with family incomes above the level eligible for no cost Medi-Cal and below 250% of the federal income guidelines ($36,576 for a family of three). Log on to www.sag.org for more information.

THE INTERNET MOVIE DATABASE - IMDB.COM •

You know that site where you go to learn who's who in which and what hot or not-so-hot movie? Yeah, well now you can upgrade to their "professional version" which offers enhanced production listings, box office tallies, an entertainment industry calendar and more. Subscribe online (www.imdb.com) with promotional code 'SAGWEB' for a 30% discount.

THE HOLLYWOOD REPORTER •

SAG members get half off the published newsstand price. You can order the insider's mag by calling 323-525-2150. Members outside Los Angeles can call toll free at 1-866-525-2150.

VARIETY.COM •

SAG-sters can save 70% on a yearly subscription to the online version of the popular industry magazine. Variety.com contains everything that appears in the daily and weekly magazine plus archived articles and more. Just go to www.variety.com/sag2005 to receive the special SAG rate.

AFTRA-SAG FEDERAL CREDIT UNION •

SAG and AFTRA members are eligible to join this credit union, as are their family members and domestic partners. They offer everything you might expect from your average bank, as well as services designed specifically for actors (such as residual deposit). For more information go to www.aftrasagfcu.com or call the LA branch at 323-461-3041.

THE SHOWCASE PROJECT •

Performances are held at the AFTRA offices approximately every other month. Members of AFTRA can perform a scene for casting directors and/or agents. For more information, or to register, call 323-634-8262.

AFTRA CASTING FILE •

AFTRA has a file of pictures and resumés comprised of paid-up members of the LA chapter. This file is for members who are available to do extra and Stand-In work on AFTRA programs. Supposedly, producers and casting representatives often call and request names and home numbers of AFTRA members from this file. TO SUBMIT, send your picture and resumé to: Extra File c/o AFTRA, 5757 Wilshire Boulevard, Suite 900, Los Angeles, CA 90036.

SENIOR PERFORMERS CASTING SHOWCASE •

Offers cold readings once every month to seniors who want to keep their skills sharp. To qualify you must be a senior (50+) and a current, paid-up member of AFTRA (or SAG). Appointments are required. Call 323-634-8240 for the next date.

ACTORS' WORK PROGRAM •

This organization offers alternative career planning for current AFTRA members who seek employment outside the realm of in-front-of-the-camera work. Training, resumé writing, and other career planning services are offered to qualified members. Call 323-933-9244 for more information.

SIGHT SINGING CLASSES •

Sight Singing Classes are scheduled every month or so at the local LA chapter. Space is limited so AFTRA members who want to participate should call 323-634-8144 for placement in the program.

Some of these services/offers are independent of SAG and the discounts or deals are up to the discretion of the specific company offering its service(s) to members. Check with each individual company to validate the offers or see if the services are still being offered or are available. Check out the SAG website (member perks): www.sag.org and the AFTRA website: www.aftra.org

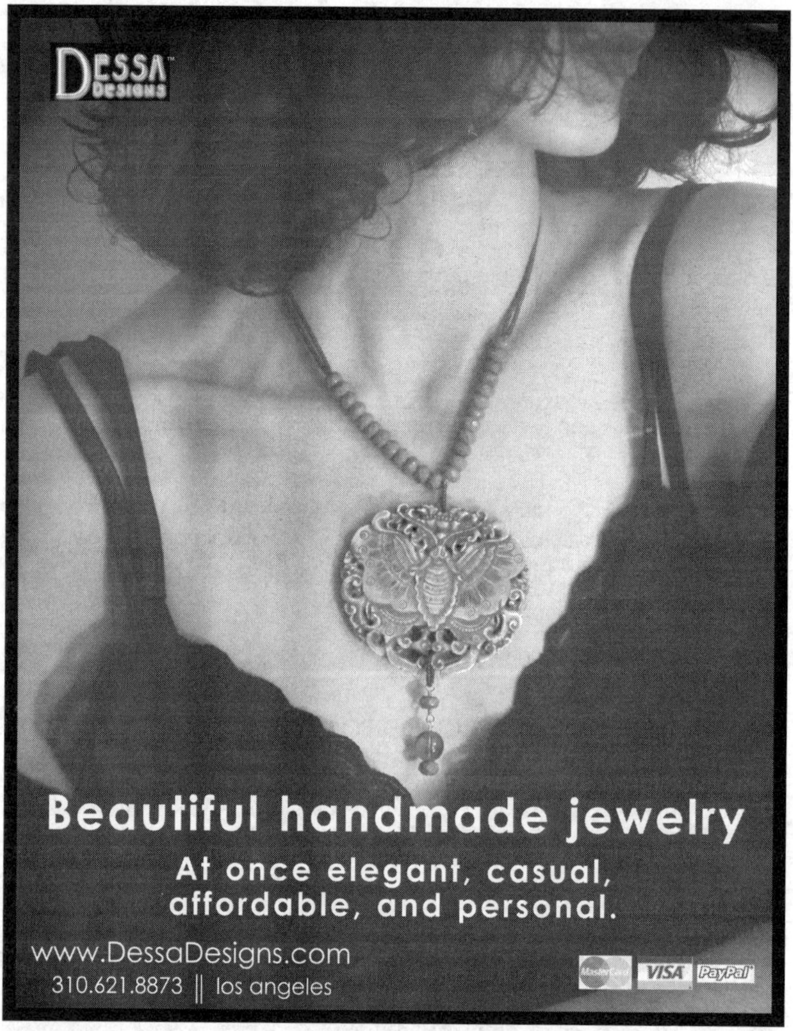
DESSA DESIGNS
Beautiful handmade jewelry
At once elegant, casual,
affordable, and personal.
www.DessaDesigns.com
310.621.8873 || los angeles
VISA PayPal

California State
Labor Laws Summary

The following is an interpretation of the California Labor Laws as deemed by HOLLYWOOD OS®. The basis for these statements are referenced in the parentheses which point to the actual LAW.

We have provided this reference section to help you better understand the LAWS that are written to protect background performers. The final interpretation of the Labor Laws are up to the Labor Commissioner.

Labor Laws "Brain Surgeon (-ified)"

Following our streamlined interpretation, you will find:

1.) The actual California State Labor Laws.

2.) Procedures for filing a claim.

3.) The testimony of one background actor who filed an actual claim. It serves as an example, so you'll have references in the event you feel your labor rights were violated while on set and you want to file a claim yourself.

act three

The following California State Labor Laws primarily pertain to Non-Union Extra performers. Extra Performers working under the SAG or AFTRA contract are already covered by a collective bargaining agreement (3.J). All NON-UNION Extra Performers (2.G) employed (2.K) in the Motion Picture Industry (2.D) in the state of California are protected by the California State Labor Law.

• Minimum Wage

As of January 1, 2002, minimum wage is \$6.75/hour (4.A) or \$54/8 for extra performers.

• Overtime

If you are employed for more than 8 hours, you are to receive time and 1/2 for the 9th and 10th hours worked and double time for all hours worked after the 10th hour until the 16th hour (3.D.1) It is ILLEGAL for Extra Performers to be employed for more than 16 hours – from call time to wrap (3.1.a).

• Hours Worked

Hours worked includes all of the time that you are "subject to the control of the employer." (2.H) From the moment you receive your voucher (call time), until you have signed out and returned to your car (if you were shuttled) you are "subject to the control of the employer."

• Turnaround

There is a 10 hour turnaround when working consecutive days on the same show. This means, your call time must be at least 10 hours later than the previous day's wrap. (3.F)

• Lunchtime

Extra Performers must be relieved of ALL DUTY and a suitable place for eating must be designated for the meal to count as time off the clock. (11.B) & (11.D)

• Meals

When working after 12 midnight, production MUST provide you with Hot Meals and Hot Drinks. (3.G)

" 'Meal' means an adequate, well-balanced serving of a variety of wholesome, nutritious foods." (10.A)

• Meal Penalties

It is ILLEGAL for production to not break Extra Performers for a meal after 6 hours. Meal breaks may be between 30 minutes & 1 hour. After every 6 hours of employment, meal breaks must be given. (11.A) If production fails to do so, they owe the Extra Performers an additional hour's wage. (11.C)

• Rest Breaks

Extra Performers must be given a rest period of 10 minutes for every consecutive four hours (or major fraction) of working on set. (12.A) If production fails to do so, they owe the Extra Performers an additional hour's wage. (12.B)

• Transportation

If you rely on public transportation, are working at night, and wrap after the last scheduled public transportation time – it is production's responsibility to get you home. (3.H)

• Wardrobe

Production is responsible for the safekeeping of Extra Performer's clothing. (13.A)

• Changing Area

Production must provide "reasonable privacy and comfort" for wardrobe changes. Changing areas must be clean and separate from bathroom stalls. (13.A)

• Holding

Extras holding must be in an area separate from the bathrooms. (13.B)

Extra Performers must be provided with chairs in holding. (14.A & B)

Extras holding must not be less than 68˚. (15.C)

• Uniform Rentals

When Extra performers are hired to wear a uniform, the uniform is to be provided and maintained by the employer. (9.A) California Labor law does not distinguish a dollar amount for such rental and cleaning for the Extra Performer who provides his or her own uniform. Our best advice is to follow the allowances set forth by the Screen Actors Guild.

• Equipment Rentals

When Extra performers are hired to use specific tools or equipment, the tools or equipment are to be provided and maintained by the employer. (9.B) California Labor law does not distinguish a dollar amount for such rental and maintenance for the Extra Performer who provides his or her own tools or equipment. Our best advice is to follow the allowances set forth by the Screen Actors Guild.

• Discrimination

It is ILLEGAL to "blackball" or discharge or discriminate against any talent who files a claim due to a Labor law violation. (98.6.a)

• Claim Fines

If production does not adhere to California State Labor Laws, they are subject to a fine of $50-$100 per claim filed. (20.A.1 & 20.A.2 & 1199)

It is an unfortunate reality that many productions are not aware of these Labor Laws. Again, these are laws. They are written to protect Non-Union extra performers. If you discover that production is violating your labor rights, you should assume they are unaware of these labor laws and politely inform them of your rights. The situation should then immediately be corrected and/or you are compensated to your satisfaction.

• Golden Time

If you had worked over 16 hours, we previously suggested that you should request "Golden Time" (like your SAG counterparts receive) which is your base rate for the day (currently $54/8) for each additional hour required on set in excess of 16 hours from your call time. We, at **HOLLYWOOD OS**®, learned by a closer examination of Labor Laws, however, that it appears to be ILLEGAL for Non-Union to work more than 16 hours – check out our little ditty at the end of this Act.

It is also illegal for production to discharge you for standing up for your labor rights and it is illegal for anyone to attempt to "blackball" you for trying to enforce your labor rights. If production does not adhere to your labor rights, you are strongly encouraged to file a claim with the Labor Commissioner (instructions are listed at the end of this chapter as well as a sample claim form).

We, at **HOLLYWOOD OS**®, believe that the entire industry would be better served if these laws were to be enforced.

The only way they will be enforced is if:

a.) You POLITELY let production know they exist.

AND

b.) You FILE CLAIMS when your rights are disregarded.

When productions who blatantly disregard your labor rights are fined $50-$100 per person, per infraction (or more)they will think twice the next time. Let's face it, these Labor Laws really do not call for anything extraordinary. The sooner production realizes this, the sooner they will find less apathy among the Non-Union ranks. What comes around goes around.

Extra Performer
Motion Picture Labor Laws

HOLLYWOOD OS® has been granted permission by the California Labor Board to publish the Labor Laws pertaining to the Motion Picture Industry and specifically, the laws pertaining to extra performers.

INDUSTRIAL WELFARE COMMISSION ORDER NO. 12-2001 REGULATING WAGES, HOURS AND WORKING CONDITIONS IN THE MOTION PICTURE INDUSTRY (Effective January 1, 2001 as amended & updated as of January 1, 2006)

1 APPLICABILITY OF ORDER

This order shall apply to all persons employed in the motion picture industry, including extra players, teachers, and welfare workers, whether paid on a time, piece rate, commission, or other basis, except that:

(A) Provisions of Sections 3 through 12 of this Order shall not apply to persons employed in administrative, executive, or professional capacities. The following requirements shall apply in determining whether an employee's duties meet the test to qualify for an exemption from those sections:

(1) Executive Exemption. A person employed in an executive capacity means any employee:

(a) Whose duties and responsibilities involve the management of the enterprise in which he is employed or of a customarily recognized department or subdivision thereof; and

(b) Who customarily and regularly directs the work of two or more other employees therein; and

(c) Who has the authority to hire or fire other employees or whose suggestions and recommendations as to the hiring or firing and as to the advancement and promotion or any other change of status of other employees will be given particular weight; and

(d) Who customarily and regularly exercises discretion and independent judgment; and

(e) Who is primarily engaged in duties which meet the test of the exemption. The activities constituting exempt work and non-exempt work shall be construed in the same manner as such items are construed in the following regulations under the Fair Labor Standards Act effective as of the date of this order: (29 C.F.R. §§ 541.102, 541.104-111, 541.115-116).

Exempt work shall include, for example, all work that is directly and closely related to exempt work and work which is properly viewed as a means for carrying out exempt functions. The work actually performed by the employee during the course of the workweek must, first and foremost, be examined and the amount of time the employee spends on such work, together with the employer's realistic expectations and the realistic requirements of the job, shall be considered in determining whether the employee satisfies this requirement.

(f) Such an employee must also earn a monthly salary equivalent to no less than two times the state minimum wage for full-time employment. Full-time employment is defined in Labor Code § 515(c) as 40 hours per week.

(2) Administrative Exemption. A person employed in an administrative capacity means any employee:

(a) Whose duties and responsibilities involve either:

(1) The performance of office or non-manual work directly related to management policies or general business operations of his employer or his employer's customers, or

(2) The performance of functions in the administration of a school system, or educational establishment or institution, or of a department of subdivision thereof, in work directly related to the academic instruction or training carried on therein; and

(b) Who customarily and regularly exercises discretion and independent judgment; and

(c) Who regularly and directly assists a proprietor, or an employee employed in a bona fide executive or administrative capacity (as such terms are defined for purposes of this section), or

(d) Who performs under only general supervision work along specialized or technical lines requiring special training, experience, or knowledge, or

(e) Who executes under only general supervision special assignments and tasks, and

(f) Who is primarily engaged in duties which meet the test of the exemption. The activities constituting exempt work and non-exempt work shall be construed in the same manner as such terms are construed in the following regulations under the Fair Labor Standards Act effective as of the date of this order: (29 C.F.R. §§ 541.201-205, 541.207-208, 541.210, 541.215). Exempt work shall include, for example, all work that is directly and closely related to exempt work and work which is properly viewed as a means for carrying out exempt functions. The work actually performed by the employee during the course of the workweek must, first and foremost, be examined and the amount of time the employee spends on such work, together with the employer's realistic expectations and the realistic requirements of the job, shall be considered in determining whether the employee satisfies this requirement.

(g) Such employee must also earn a monthly salary equivalent to no less than two times the state minimum wage for full-time employment. Full-time employment is defined in Labor Code § 515(c) as 40 hours per week.

(3) Professional Exemption. A person employed in a professional capacity means any employee who meets all of the following requirements:

(a) Who is licensed or certified by the State of California and is primarily engaged in the practice of one of the following recognized professions: law, medicine, dentistry, optometry, architecture, engineering, teaching, or accounting; or

(b) Who is primarily engaged in an occupation commonly recognized as a learned or artistic profession. For the purposes of this subsection, "learned or artistic profession" means an employee who is primarily engaged in the performance of:

(i) Work requiring knowledge of an advanced type in a field or science or learning customarily acquired by a prolonged course of specialized intellectual instruction and study, as distinguished from a general academic education and from an apprenticeship, and from training in the performance of routine mental, manual, or physical processes, or work that is an essential part of or necessarily incident to any of the above work; or

(ii) Work that is original and creative in character in a recognized field of artistic endeavor (as opposed to work which can be produced by a person endowed with general manual or intellectual ability and training), and the result of which depends primarily on the invention, imagination, or talent of the employee or work that is an essential part of or necessarily incident to any of the above work; and

(iii) Whose work is predominantly intellectual and varied in character (as opposed to routine mental, manual, mechanical, or physical work) and is of such character that the output produced or the result accomplished cannot be standardized in relation to a given period of time.

(c) Who customarily and regularly exercises discretion and independent judgment in the performance of duties set forth in subparagraphs (a) and (b).

(d) Who earns a monthly salary equivalent to no less than two times the state minimum wage for full-time employment. Full-time employment is defined in Labor Code §515 (c) as 40 hours per week.

(e) Subparagraph (b) above is intended to be construed in accordance with the following provisions of federal law as they existed as of the date of this Wage Order: 29 C.F.R. §§ 541.207, 541.301 (a)-(d), 541.302, 541.306, 541.307, 541.308, and 541.310.

(f) Notwithstanding the provisions of this subparagraph, pharmacists employed to engage in the practice of pharmacy, and registered nurses employed to engage in the practice of nursing, shall not be considered exempt professional employees, nor shall they be considered exempt from coverage for the purposes of this subparagraph unless they individually meet the criteria established for exemption as executive or administrative employees.

(g) Notwithstanding subparagraph (f), the following advanced practice nurses shall be exempt from provisions of this subsection:

(i) Certified nurse midwives who are primarily engaged in performing duties for which certification is required pursuant to Article 2.5 (commencing with Section 2746) of Chapter 6 of Division 2 of the Business and Professions Code.

(ii) Certified nurse anesthetists who are primarily engaged in performing duties for which certification is required pursuant to Article 7 (commencing with Section 2825) of Chapter 6 of Division 2 of the Business and Professions Code.

(iii) Certified nurse practitioners who are primarily engaged in performing duties for which certification is required pursuant to Article 8 (commencing with Section 2834) of Chapter 6 of Division 2 of the Business and Professions Code.

(iv) Nothing in this subparagraph shall exempt the occupations set forth in clauses (i),(ii), and (iii) from meeting the requirements of subsection 1(A)(3)(a)–(d), above

(h) Except as provided in subparagraph (i), an employee in the computer software field who is paid on an hourly basis shall be exempt, if all of the following apply:

(i) The employee is primarily engaged in work that is intellectual or creative and that requires the exercise of discretion and independent judgment. The employee is primarily engaged in duties that consist of one or more of the following:

(ii) The application of systems analysis techniques and procedures, including consulting with users to determine hardware, software, or system functional specifications.

- The design, development, documentation, analysis, creation, testing, or modification of computer systems or programs, including prototypes, based on and related to, user or system design specifications.

- The documentation, testing, creation, or modification of computer programs related to the design of software or hardware for computer operating systems.

(iii) The employee is highly skilled and is proficient in the theoretical and practical application of highly specialized information to computer systems analysis, programming, and software engineering. A job title shall not be determinative of the applicability of this exemption.

(iv) The employee's hourly rate of pay is not less than forty-five dollars and eighty-four cents($45.84). The Division of Labor Statistics and Research shall adjust this pay rate on October 1 of each year to be effective on January 1 of the following year by an amount equal to the percentage increase in the California Consumer Price Index for Urban Wage Earners and Clerical Workers.

(i) The exemption provided in subparagraph (h) does not apply to an employee if any of the following apply:

(i) The employee is a trainee or employee in an entry-level position who is learning to become proficient in the theoretical and practical application of highly specialized information to computer systems analysis, programming, and software engineering.

(ii) The employee is in a computer-related occupation but has not attained the level of skill and expertise necessary to work independently and without close supervision.

(iii) The employee is engaged in the operation of computers or in the manufacture, repair, or maintenance of computer hardware and related equipment.

(iv) The employee is an engineer, drafter, machinist, or other professional whose work is highly dependent upon or facilitated by the use of computers and computer software programs and who is skilled in computer-aided design software, including CAD/CAM, but who is not in a computer systems analysis or programming occupation.

(v) The employee is a writer engaged in writing material, including box labels, product descriptions, documentation, promotional material, setup and installa-

tion instructions, and other similar written information, either for print or for on-screen media or who writes or provides content material intended to be read by customers, subscribers, or visitors to computer-related media such as the World Wide Web or CD-ROMs.

(vi) The employee is engaged in any of the activities set forth in subparagraph (h) for the purpose of creating imagery for effects used in the motion picture, television, or theatrical industry.

(B) Except as provided in sections 1, 2, 4, 10, and 20, the provisions of this Order shall not apply to any employees directly employed by the State or any political subdivision thereof, including any city, county, or special district.

(C) Except as provided in sections 1, 2, 4, 10, and 20, the provisions of this Order shall not apply to professional actors.

(D) The provisions of this Order shall not apply to outside salespersons.

(E) Provisions of this Order shall not apply to any individual who is the parent, spouse, child, or legally adopted child of the employer.

(F) The provisions of this Order shall not apply to any individual participating in a national service program, such as AmeriCorps, carried out using assistance provided under Section 12571 of Title 42 of the United States Code. (See Stat. 2000, ch. 365, amending Labor Code § 1171.)

2 DEFINITIONS

(A) An "alternative workweek schedule" means any regularly scheduled workweek requiring an employee to work more than eight (8) hours in a 24-hour period.

(B) "Commission" means the Industrial Welfare Commission of the State of California.

(C) "Division" means the Division of Labor Standards Enforcement of the State of California.

(D) "Employ" means to engage, suffer, or permit to work.

(E) "Employee" means any person employed by an employer.

(F) "Employer" means any person as defined in Section 18 of the Labor Code, who directly or indirectly, or through an agent or any other person, employs or exercises control over the wages, hours, or working conditions of any person.

(G) "Extra Player" means any person employed by an employer in the production of motion pictures to perform any work, including but not limited to that of a general extra, stand-in, photographic double, sports player, silent bit, or dress extra; or as extras employed in dancing, skating, swimming, diving, riding, driving, or singing; or as extras employed to perform any other actions, gestures, facial expressions, or pantomime.

(H) "Hours worked" means the time during which an employee is subject to the control of an employer, and includes all the time the employee is suffered or permitted to work, whether or not required to do so.

(I) "Location" means any place other than the studio premises of the employer, at which the employer shoots all or a portion of a motion picture.

(J) "Minor" means, for the purpose of this Order, any person under the age of eighteen (18) years.

(K) "Motion Picture Industry" means any industry, business or establishment operated for the purpose of motion picture or television film production, or primarily allied with theatrical or television motion picture productions, including but not limited to motion pictures for entertainment, commercial, religious, or educational purposes, whether made by film, tape, or otherwise.

(L) "Outside Salesperson" means any person, 18 years of age or over, who customarily and regularly works more than half the working time away from the employer's place of business selling tangible or intangible items or obtaining orders or contracts for products, services or use of facilities.

(M) "Primarily" as used in Section 1, Applicability, means more than one-half the employee's work time.

(N) "Shift" means designated hours of work by an employee, with a designated beginning time and ending time.

(O) "Split shift" means a work schedule which is interrupted by non-paid non-working periods established by the employer, other than bona fide rest or meal periods.

(P) "Wages" includes all amounts for labor performed by employees of every description, whether the amount is fixed or ascertained by the standard of time, task, piece, commission basis, or other method of calculation.

(Q) "Workday" and "day" mean any consecutive 24-hour period beginning at the same time each calendar day.

(R) "Workweek" and "week" mean any seven (7) consecutive days, starting with the same calendar day each week. "Workweek" is a fixed and regularly recurring period of 168 hours, seven (7) consecutive 24-hour periods.

3 HOURS AND DAYS OF WORK

(A) Daily Overtime - General Provisions

(1) The following overtime provisions are applicable to employees eighteen (18) years of age or over and to employees sixteen (16) or seventeen (17) years of age who are not required by law to attend school and are not otherwise prohibited by law from engaging in the subject work. Such employees shall not be employed more than eight (8) hours in any workday or more than forty (40) hours in any workweek unless the employee receives one and one-half (1 1/2) times such employee's regular rate of pay for all hours worked over forty (40) hours in the workweek. Eight (8) hours of labor constitutes a day's work. Employment beyond eight (8) hours in any workday or more than six (6) days in any workweek is permissible provided the employee is compensated for such overtime as follows:

(a) Employees may be employed up to a maximum of sixteen (16) hours including meal periods in any one day from the time they are required and do

report until dismissed, provided the employee is compensated for such overtime at not less than:

(1) For daily employees and weekly employees, excluding weekly employees guaranteed more than forty (40) hours a workweek and "on call" employees, one and one-half ($1^1/_2$) times the employee's regular rate of pay for all hours worked in excess of eight (8) hours up to and including twelve (12) hours in any one workday, and for the first eight (8) hours worked on the seventh (7th) consecutive day of work in a workweek; and

(2) Double the employee's regular rate of pay for all hours worked in excess of twelve (12) hours in any workday, and for all hours worked in excess of eight (8) hours on the seventh (7th) consecutive day of work in a workweek.

(3) Overtime payments shall not be compounded and all payments made by the employer for daily overtime on the basis herein above specified shall be applied toward any sum for weekly overtime.

(4) The overtime rate of compensation required to be paid to a non-exempt full-time salaried employee shall be computed by using the employee's regular hourly salary as one fortieth (1/40) of the employee's weekly salary.

(B) Alternative Workweek Schedules

act three

(1) No employer shall be deemed to have violated the daily overtime provisions by instituting, pursuant to the election procedures set forth in this wage order, a regularly scheduled alternative workweek schedule of not more than ten (10) hours per day within a forty (40) hour workweek without the payment of an overtime rate of compensation. All work performed in any workday beyond the schedule established by the agreement up to twelve (12) hours a day or beyond forty (40) hours per week shall be paid at one and one-half ($1^1/_2$) times the employee's regular rate of pay. All work performed in excess of twelve (12) hours per day and any work in excess of eight (8) hours on those days worked beyond the regularly scheduled number of workdays established by the alternative workweek agreement shall be paid at double the employee's regular rate of pay. Any alternative workweek agreement adopted pursuant to this section shall provide for not less than four (4) hours of work in any shift. Nothing in this section shall prohibit an employer, at the request of the employee, to substitute one day of work for another day of the same length in the shift provided by the alternative workweek agreement on an occasional basis to meet the personal needs of the employee without the payment of overtime. No hours paid at either one and one-half ($1^1/_2$) or double the regular rate of pay shall be included in determining when forty (40) hours have been worked for the purpose of computing overtime compensation.

(2) Any agreement adopted pursuant to this section shall provide not less than two consecutive days off within a workweek.

(3) If an employer, whose employees have adopted an alternative workweek agreement permitted by this order requires an employee to work fewer hours than those that are regularly scheduled by the agreement, the employer shall pay the employee overtime compensation at a rate of one and one-half ($1^1/_2$) times the employee's regular rate of pay for all hours worked in excess of eight (8) hours, and double the employee's regular rate of pay for all hours worked in excess of twelve (12) hours for the day the employee is required to work the reduced hours.

(4) An employer shall not reduce an employee's regular rate of hourly pay as a

result of the adoption, repeal or nullification of an alternative workweek schedule.

(5) An employer shall explore any available reasonable alternative means of accommodating the religious belief or observance of an affected employee that conflicts with an adopted alternative workweek schedule, in the manner provided by subdivision (j) of Section 12940 of the Government Code.

(6) An employer shall make a reasonable effort to find a work schedule not to exceed eight (8) hours in a workday, in order to accommodate any affected employee who was eligible to vote in an election authorized by this Section and who is unable to work the alternative workweek schedule established as the result of that election.

(7) An employer shall be permitted, but not required, to provide a work schedule not to exceed eight (8) hours in a workday to accommodate any employee who is hired after the date of the election and who is unable to work the alternative workweek schedule established by the election.

(8) Arrangements adopted in a secret ballot election held pursuant to this order prior to 1998, or under the rules in effect prior to 1998, and before the performance of the work, shall remain valid after July 1, 2000, provided that the results of the election are reported by the employer to the Division of Labor Statistics and Research by January 1, 2001, in accordance with the requirements of Section C below (Election Procedures). If an employee was voluntarily working an alternative workweek schedule of not more than ten (10) hours a day as of July 1, 1999, that alternative workweek schedule was based on an individual agreement made after January 1, 1998, between the employee and employer, and the employee submitted, and the employer approved, a written request on or before May 30, 2000, to continue the agreement, the employee may continue to work that alternative workweek schedule without payment of an overtime rate of compensation for the hours provided in the agreement. An employee may revoke his or her voluntary authorization to continue such a schedule with thirty (30) days written notice to the employer. New arrangements can only be entered into pursuant to the provisions of this section.

(C) Election Procedures.
Election procedures for the adoption and repeal of alternative workweek schedules require the following:

(1) Each proposal for an alternative workweek schedule shall be in the form of a written agreement proposed by the employer. The proposed agreement must designate a regularly scheduled alternative workweek in which the specified number of work days and work hours are regularly recurring. The actual days worked within that alternative workweek schedule need not be specified. The employer may propose a single work schedule that would become the standard schedule for workers in the work unit, or a menu of work schedule options, from which each employee in the unit would be entitled to choose. If the employer proposes a menu of work schedule options, the employee may, with the approval of the employer, move from one menu option to another.

(2) In order to be valid, the proposed alternative workweek schedule must be adopted in a secret ballot election, before the performance of work, by at least a two-thirds (2/3) vote of the affected employees in the work unit. The election shall be held during regular working hours at the employees' work site. For purposes of this subsection, "affected employees in the work unit" may include all employees in a readily identifiable work unit, such as a division, a department, a job classification, a shift, a separate physical location, or a recognized

subdivision of any such work unit. A work unit may consist of an individual employee as long as the criteria for an identifiable work unit in this subsection is met.

(3) Prior to the secret ballot vote, any employer who proposed to institute an alternative workweek schedule shall have made a disclosure in writing to the affected employees, including the effects of the proposed arrangement on the employees' wages, hours, and benefits. Such a disclosure shall include meeting(s), duly noticed, held at least fourteen (14) days prior to voting, for the specific purpose of discussing the effects of the alternative workweek schedule. An employer shall provide that disclosure in a non-English language, as well as in English, if at least five (5) percent of the affected employees primarily speak that non-English language. The employer shall mail the written disclosure to employees who do not attend the meeting. Failure to comply with this paragraph shall make the election null and void.

(4) Any election to establish or repeal an alternative workweek schedule shall be held at the work site of the affected employees. The employer shall bear the costs of conducting any election held pursuant to this section. Upon a complaint by an affected employee, and after an investigation by the Labor Commissioner, the Labor Commissioner may require the employer to select a neutral third party to conduct the election.

(5) Any type of alternative workweek schedule that is authorized by the Labor Code may be repealed by the affected employees. Upon a petition of one-third (1/3) of the affected employees, a new secret ballot election shall be held and a two-thirds (2/3) vote of the affected employees shall be required to reverse the alternative workweek schedule. The election to repeal the alternative workweek schedule shall be held not more than 30 days after the petition is submitted to the employer, except that the election shall be held not less than twelve (12) months after the date that the same group of employees voted in an election held to adopt or repeal an alternative workweek schedule. The election shall take place during regular working hours at the employees' work site. If the alternative workweek schedule is revoked, the employer shall comply within sixty (60) days. Upon proper showing of undue hardship, the Division of Labor Standards Enforcement may grant an extension of time for compliance.

(6) Only secret ballots may be cast by affected employees in the work unit at any election held pursuant to this Section. The results of any election conducted pursuant to this Section shall be reported by the employer to the Division of Labor Statistics and Research within thirty (30) days after the results are final, and the report of election results shall be a public document. The report shall include the final tally of the vote, the size of the unit, and the nature of the business of the employer.

(7) Employees affected by a change in the work hours resulting from the adoption of an alternative workweek schedule may not be required to work those new work hours for at least thirty (30) days after the announcement of the final results of the election.

(8) Employers shall not intimidate or coerce employees to vote either in support of or in opposition to a proposed alternative workweek. No employees shall be discharged or discriminated against for expressing opinions concerning the alternative workweek election or for opposing or supporting its adoption or repeal. However, nothing in this section shall prohibit an employer from expressing his/her position concerning that alternative workweek to the affected employees. A violation of this paragraph shall be subject to Labor Code section 98 et seq.

(D) Extra players employed in excess of eight (8) hours in any workday from the time the extra player is required and does report until dismissed, shall be paid daily overtime compensation as follows:

(1) One and one-half (1 1/2) times the extra player's rate of pay for the ninth (9th) and tenth (10th) work hours of employment and not less than double the extra player's rate of pay for all hours worked thereafter, computed in units of one-tenth (1/10) hours.

(2) Weekly overtime. The total sum paid to an extra player who works more than forty (40) hours in such workweek for a particular employer shall be the extra player's regular hourly rate of pay times forty (40), plus one and one-half (1 1/2) times such regular hourly rate of pay for all hours worked in excess of forty (40) during such workweek. The regular hourly rate shall be determined by dividing the amount of the weekly salary by the number of regular hours in a workweek.

(3) An extra player employed by the week shall receive payment of daily overtime for all hours or fractions thereof worked beyond eight (8) hours in any workday on which such daily overtime occurs as provided above, provided that overtime payments shall not be compounded and all payments made by the employer for daily overtime on the basis herein above specified shall be applied toward any sum due for weekly overtime.

(E) One and one-half (1 1/2) times a minor's regular rate of pay shall be paid for all hours worked on the sixth (6th) consecutive workday except that minors sixteen (16) and seventeen (17) years old who are not required by law to attend school and may therefore be employed for the same hours as an adult are subject to subsections (A), (B), (C) or (D) above.

(VIOLATIONS OF CHILD LABOR LAWS are subject to civil penalties of from $500 to $10,000 as well as to criminal penalties. Refer to California Labor Code Sections 1285 to 1312 and 1390 to 1399 for additional restrictions on the employment of minors and for descriptions of criminal and civil penalties for violation of the child labor laws. Employers should ask school districts about any required work permits.)

(F) No employee shall be required to report to work unless ten (10) hours have elapsed since the termination of the previous day's employment.

(G) Hot meals and hot drinks shall be provided for employees who are required to work after 12 o'clock midnight, except off-production employees regularly scheduled to work after midnight.

(H) When employees are required to work at night and are not dismissed in time to permit their return to their homes by public service transportation, transportation shall be provided by the employer.

(I) The provisions of Labor Code §§ 551 and 552 regarding one (1) day's rest in seven (7) shall not be construed to prevent an accumulation of days of rest when the nature of the employment reasonably requires the employee to work seven (7) or more consecutive days; provided, however, that in each calendar month, the employee shall receive the equivalent of one (1) day's rest in seven (7).

(J) Except as provided in subsections (E) and (I), this section shall not apply to any employee covered by a valid collective bargaining agreement if the agreement expressly provides for the wages, hours of work, and working conditions of the employees, and if the agreement provides premium wage rates for all overtime hours worked and a regular hourly rate of pay for those employees of not less than thirty (30) percent more than the state minimum wage.

(K) Notwithstanding subsection (J) above, where the employer and a labor organization representing employees of the employer have entered into a valid collective bargaining agreement pertaining to the hours of work of the employees, the requirement regarding the equivalent of one (1) day's rest in seven (7) (see subsection (I) above) shall apply, unless the agreement expressly provides otherwise.

(L) If an employer approves a written request of an employee to make-up work time that is or would be lost as a result of a personal obligation of the employee, the hours of that make-up work time, if performed in the same workweek in which the work time was lost, may not be counted toward computing the total number of hours worked in a day for purposes of the overtime requirements, except for hours in excess of eleven (11) hours of work in one (1) day or forty (40) hours of work in one (1) workweek. If an employee knows in advance that he or she will be requesting make-up time for a personal obligation that will recur at a fixed time over a succession of weeks, the employee may request to make-up work time for up to four (4) weeks in advance; provided, however, that the make-up work must be performed in the same week that the work time was lost. An employee shall provide a signed written request for each occasion that the employee makes a request to make-up work time pursuant to this subsection. While an employer may inform an employee of this make-up time option, the employer is prohibited from encouraging or otherwise soliciting an employee to request the employer's approval to take personal time off and make-up the work hours within the same workweek pursuant to this subsection.

MINIMUM WAGES

(A) Every employer shall pay to each employee wages not less than six dollars and seventy five cents ($6.75) per hour for all hours worked, effective January 1, 2002, except:

(1) LEARNERS. Employees during their first one hundred and sixty (160) hours of employment in occupations in which they have no previous similar or related experience, may be paid not less than eighty-five percent (85%) of the minimum wage rounded to the nearest nickel.

(B) Every employer shall pay to each employee, on the established payday for the period involved, not less than the applicable minimum wage for all hours worked in the payroll period, whether the remuneration is measured by time, piece, commission, or otherwise.

(C) When an employee works a split shift, one hour's pay at the minimum wage shall be paid in addition to the minimum wage for that workday, except when the employee resides at the place of employment.

(D) The provisions of this section shall not apply to apprentices regularly indentured under the State Division of Apprenticeship Standards.

REPORTING TIME PAY

(A) Each workday an employee is required to report for work and does report, but is not put to work or is furnished less than half said employee's usual or scheduled day's work, the employee shall be paid for half the usual or scheduled day's work, but in no event for less than two (2) hours nor more than four (4) hours, at the employee's regular rate of pay, which shall not be less than the minimum wage.

(B) If an employee is required to report for work a second time in any one workday and is furnished less than two hours of work on the second reporting, said employee shall be paid for two hours at the employee's regular rate of pay, which shall not be less than the minimum wage.

(C) The foregoing reporting time pay provisions are not applicable when:

(1) Operations cannot commence or continue due to threats to employees or property; or when recommended by civil authorities; or

(2) Public utilities fail to supply electricity, water, or gas, or there is a failure in the public utilities, or sewer system; or

(3) The interruption of work is caused by an Act of God or other cause not within the employer's control.

(D) This section shall not apply to an employee on paid standby status who is called to perform assigned work at a time other than the employee's scheduled reporting time.

6 LICENSES FOR DISABLED WORKERS

act three

(A) A license may be issued by the Division authorizing employment of a person whose earning capacity is impaired by physical disability or mental deficiency at less than the minimum wage. Such licenses shall be granted only upon joint application of employer and employee and employee's representative if any.

(B) A special license may be issued to a nonprofit organization such as a sheltered workshop or rehabilitation facility fixing special minimum rates to enable the employment of such persons without requiring individual licenses of such employees.

(C) All such licenses and special licenses shall be renewed on a yearly basis or more frequently at the discretion of the Division. See California Labor Code, Sections 1191 and 1191.5.

7 RECORDS

(A) Every employer shall keep accurate information with respect to each employee including the following:

(1) Full name, home address, occupation and social security number.

(2) Birth date, if under 18 years, and designation as a minor.

(3) Time records showing when the employee begins and ends each work period. Meal periods, split shift intervals and total daily hours worked shall also be recorded. Meal periods during which operations cease and authorized rest periods need not be recorded.

(4) Total wages paid each payroll period, including value of board, lodging, or other compensation actually furnished to the employee.

(5) Total hours worked in the payroll period and applicable rates of pay. This information shall be made readily available to the employee upon reasonable request.

(6) When a piece rate or incentive plan is in operation, piece rates or an explanation of the incentive plan formula shall be provided to employees. An accurate production record shall be maintained by the employer.

(B) Every employer shall semimonthly or at the time of each payment of wages furnish each employee, either as a detachable part of the check, draft, or voucher paying the employee's wages, or separately, an itemized statement in writing showing: (1) all deductions; (2) the inclusive dates of the period for which the employee is paid; (3) the name of the employee or the employee's social security number; and (4) the name of the employer, provided all deductions made on written orders of the employee may be aggregated and shown as one item.

(C) All required records shall be in the English language and in ink or other indelible form, properly dated, showing month, day and year, and shall be kept on file by the employer for at least three years at the place of employment or at a central location within the State of California. An employee's records shall be available for inspection by the employee upon reasonable request.

(D) Clocks shall be provided in all major work areas or within reasonable distance thereto insofar as practicable.

CASH SHORTAGE AND BREAKAGE

No employer shall make any deduction from the wage or require any reimbursement from an employee for any cash shortage, breakage, or loss of equipment, unless it can be shown that the shortage, breakage, or loss is caused by a dishonest or willful act, or by the gross negligence of the employee.

UNIFORMS AND EQUIPMENT

(A) When uniforms are required by the employer to be worn by the employee as a condition of employment, such uniforms shall be provided and maintained by the employer. The term "uniform" includes wearing apparel and accessories of distinctive design or color.

NOTE: This section shall not apply to protective apparel regulated by the Occupational Safety and Health Standards Board.

(B) When tools or equipment are required by the employer or are necessary to the performance of a job, such tools and equipment shall be provided and maintained by the employer, except that an employee whose wages are at least two (2) times the minimum wage provided herein may be required to provide and maintain hand tools and equipment customarily required by the trade or craft. This subsection (B) shall not apply to apprentices regularly indentured under the State Division of Apprenticeship Standards.

NOTE: This section shall not apply to protective equipment and safety devices on tools regulated by the Occupational Safety and Health Standards Board.

A reasonable deposit may be required as security for the return of the items furnished by the employer under provisions of subsections (A) and (B) of this section upon issuance of a receipt to the employee for such deposit. Such deposits shall be made pursuant to Section 400 and following of the Labor Code or an employer with the prior written authorization of the employee may deduct from the employee's last check the cost of an item furnished pursuant to (A) and (B) above in the event said item is not returned. No deduction shall be made at any time for normal wear and tear. All items furnished by the employer shall be returned by the employee upon completion of the job.

10 MEALS AND LODGING

(A) "Meal" means an adequate, well-balanced serving of a variety of wholesome, nutritious foods.

(B) "Lodging" means living accommodations available to the employee for full-time occupancy which are adequate, decent, and sanitary according to usual and customary standards. Employees shall not be required to share a bed.

(C) Meals or lodging may not be credited against the minimum wage without a voluntary written agreement between the employer and the employee. When credit for meals or lodging is used to meet part of the employer's minimum wage obligation, the amounts so credited may not be more than the following:

EFFECTIVE DATE: **January 1, 2002**

Lodging:

Rooms occupied alone....................................$31.75 per week

Room shared...$26.20 per week

Apartment two-thirds (2/3) of the ordinary rental value, and in no event more than..............................$381.20 per month

Where a couple are both employed by the employer, two-thirds (2/3) of the ordinary rental value, and in no event more than...$563.90 per month

Meals:

Breakfast.. $2.45

Lunch.. $3.35

Dinner.. $4.50

(D) Meals evaluated as part of the minimum wage must be bona fide meals consistent with the employee's work shift. Deductions shall not be made for meals not received nor lodging not used.

(E) If, as a condition of employment, the employee must live at the place of employment or occupy quarters owned or under the control of the employer, then the employer may not charge rent in excess of the values listed herein.

11 MEAL PERIODS

(A) No employer shall employ any person for a work period of more than six (6) hours without a meal period of not less than thirty (30) minutes, nor more than one (1) hour. Subsequent meal period for all employees shall be called not later than six (6) hours after the termination of the preceding meal period.

(B) Unless the employee is relieved of all duty during a thirty (30) minute meal period, the meal period shall be considered an "on duty" meal period and counted as time worked. An "on duty" meal period shall be permitted only when the nature of the work prevents an employee from being relieved of all duty and when by written agreement between the parties an on-the-job paid meal period is agreed to. The written agreement shall state that the employee may, in writing, revoke the agreement at any time.

(C) If an employer fails to provide an employee a meal period in accordance with the applicable provisions of this Order, the employer shall pay the employee one (1) hour of pay at the employee's regular rate of compensation for each work day that the meal period is not provided.

(D) In all places of employment where employees are required to eat on the premises, a suitable place for that purpose shall be designated.

12 REST PERIODS

(A) Every employer shall authorize and permit all employees to take rest periods, which insofar as practicable shall be in the middle of each work period. The authorized rest period time shall be based on the total hours worked daily at the rate of ten (10) minutes net rest time per four (4) hours or major fraction thereof. However, a rest period need not be authorized for employees whose total daily work time is less than three and one-half (3 1/2) hours. Authorized rest period time shall be counted as hours worked for which there shall be no deduction from wages.

(B) If an employer fails to provide an employee a rest period in accordance with the applicable provisions of this Order, the employer shall pay the employee one (1) hour of pay at the employee's regular rate of compensation for each work day that the rest period is not provided.

(C) Swimmers, dancers, skaters, and other performers engaged in strenuous physical activities shall have additional interim rest periods during periods of actual rehearsal or shooting.

13 CHANGE ROOMS AND RESTING FACILITIES

(A) Employers shall provide suitable lockers, closets, or equivalent for the safekeeping of employees' outer clothing during working hours, and when required, for their work clothing during non-working hours. When the occupation requires a change of clothing, change rooms or equivalent space shall be provided in order that employees may change their clothing in reasonable

privacy and comfort. These rooms or spaces may be adjacent to but shall be separate from toilet rooms and shall be kept clean.

NOTE: This section shall not apply to change rooms and storage facilities regulated by the Occupational Safety and Health Standards Board.

(B) Suitable resting facilities shall be provided in an area separate from the toilet rooms and shall be available to employees during work hours.

14 SEATS

(A) All working employees shall be provided with suitable seats when the nature of the work reasonably permits the use of seats.

(B) When employees are not engaged in the active duties of their employment and the nature of the work requires standing, an adequate number of suitable seats shall be placed in reasonable proximity to the work area and employees shall be permitted to use such seats when it does not interfere with the performance of their duties

15 TEMPERATURE

(A) The temperature maintained in each work area shall provide reasonable comfort consistent with industry-wide standards for the nature of the process and the work performed.

(B) If excessive heat or humidity is created by the work process, the employer shall take all feasible means to reduce such excessive heat or humidity to a degree providing reasonable comfort. Where the nature of the employment requires a temperature of less than 60° F., a heated room shall be provided to which employees may retire for warmth, and such room shall be maintained at not less than 68°.

(C) A temperature of not less than 68° shall be maintained in the toilet rooms, resting rooms, and change rooms during hours of use.

(D) Federal and State energy guidelines shall prevail over any conflicting provision of this section.

16 ELEVATORS

Adequate elevator, escalator or similar service consistent with industry-wide standards for the nature of the process and the work performed shall be provided when employees are employed four floors or more above or below ground level.

17 EXEMPTIONS

If, in the opinion of the Division after due investigation, it is found that the enforcement of any provision contained in Section 7, Records; section 12, Rest

Periods; Section 13, Change Rooms and Resting Facilities; Section 14, Seats; Section 15, Temperature; or Section 16, Elevators, would not materially affect the welfare or comfort of employees and would work an undue hardship on the employer, exemption may be made at the discretion of the Division. Such exemptions shall be in writing to be effective and may be revoked after reasonable notice is given in writing. Application for exemption shall be made by the employer or by the employee and/or the employee's representative to the Division in writing. A copy of the application shall be posted at the place of employment at the time the application is filed with the Division.

18 FILING REPORTS
(See California Labor Code, Section 1174(a))

19 INSPECTION
(See California Labor Code, Section 1174)

20 PENALTIES
(See Labor Code, Section 1199)

act three

(A) In addition to any other civil penalties provided by law, any employer or any other person acting on behalf of the employer who violates, or causes to be violated, the provisions of this order, shall be subject to the civil penalty of:

(1) Initial Violation – $50.00 for each underpaid employee for each pay period during which the employee was underpaid in addition to the amount which is sufficient to recover unpaid wages.

(2) Subsequent Violations – $100.00 for each underpaid employee for each pay period during which the employee was underpaid in addition to an amount which is sufficient to recover unpaid wages.

(3) The affected employee shall receive payment of all wages recovered.

(B) The Labor Commissioner may also issue citations pursuant to Labor Code § 1197.1 for payment of wages for overtime work in violation of this order.

21 SEPARABILITY

If the application of any provision of this Order, or any section, subsection, subdivision, sentence, clause, phrase, word, or portion of this Order should be held invalid or unconstitutional or unauthorized or prohibited by statute, the remaining provisions thereof shall not be affected thereby, but shall continue to be given full force and effect as if the part so held invalid or unconstitutional had not been included herein.

22 POSTING OF ORDER

Every employer shall keep a copy of this Order posted in an area frequented by employees where it may be easily read during the work day. Where the location of work or other conditions make this impractical, every employer shall keep a copy of this Order and make it available to every employee upon request.

Excerpts From the Labor Code

SECTION 98.6.
(a) No person shall discharge or in any manner discriminate against any employee because such employee has filed any bona fide complaint or claim or instituted or caused to be instituted any proceeding under or relating to his rights, which are under the jurisdiction of the Labor Commissioner, or has testified or is about to testify in any such proceeding or because of the exercise by such employee on behalf of himself or others of any rights afforded him.

(b) Any employee who is discharged, threatened with discharge, demoted, suspended, or in any other manner discriminated against in the terms and conditions of such employment because such employee has made a bona fide complaint or claim to the division pursuant to this part shall be entitled to reinstatement and reimbursement for lost wages and work benefits caused by such acts of the employer. Any employer who willfully refuses to hire, promote, or otherwise restore an employee or former employee who has been determined to be eligible for such rehiring or promotion by a grievance procedure, arbitration or hearing authorized by law, is guilty of a misdemeanor. Note: Nothing in this act shall be construed to entitle an employee to reinstatement or reimbursement for lost wages or work benefits if such employee willfully misrepresents any facts to support a complaint or claim filed with the Labor Commissioner.

SECTION 201.
If an employer discharges an employee, the wages earned and unpaid at the time of discharge are due and payable immediately.

SECTION 201.5.
An employer who lays off a group of employees engaged in the production of motion pictures whose unusual or uncertain terms of employment require special computation in order to ascertain the amount due, shall be deemed to have made immediate payment within the meaning of Section 201 if the wages of such employees are paid within such reasonable time as may be necessary for computation or payment thereof; provided, however, that such reasonable time shall not exceed 24 hours after discharge excluding Saturdays, Sundays, and holidays; and provided further, such payment may be mailed and the date of mailing is the date of payment.

SECTION 202.
If an employee not having a written contract for a definite period quits his employment, his wages shall become due and payable not later than 72 hours thereafter, unless the employee has given 72 hours previous notice of his intention to quit, in which case the employee is entitled to his wages at the time of quitting.

SECTION 2800.
An employer shall in all cases indemnify his employee for losses caused by the employer's want of ordinary care.

SECTION 226.
(a) Every employer shall, semimonthly or at the time of each payment of wages, furnish each of his or her employees, either as a detachable part of the check, draft, or voucher paying the employee's wages, or separately when wages are paid by personal check or cash, an accurate itemized statement in writing showing (1) gross wages earned, (2) total hours worked by the employee, except for any employee whose compensation is solely based on a salary and who is exempt from payment of overtime under subdivision (a) of Section 515 or any applicable order of the Industrial Welfare Commission, (3) the number of piece-rate units earned and any applicable piece rate if the employee is paid on a piece-rate basis, (4) all deductions, provided that all deductions made on written orders of the employee may be aggregated and shown as one item, (5) net wages earned, (6) the inclusive dates of the period for which the employee is paid, (7) the name of the employee and his or her social security number, (8) the name and address of the legal entity that is the employer, and (9) all applicable hourly rates in effect during the pay period and the corresponding number of hours worked at each hourly rate by the employee. The deductions made from payments of wages shall be recorded in ink or other indelible form, properly dated, showing the month, day, and year, and a copy of the statement or a record of the deductions shall be kept on file by the employer for at least three years at the place of employment or at a central location within the State of California.

SECTION 1199.
Every employer or other person acting either individually or as an officer, agent, or employee of another person is guilty of a misdemeanor and is punishable by a fine of not less than one hundred dollars ($100) or by imprisonment for not less than 30 days, or by both, who does any of the following:

(a) Requires or causes any employee to work for longer hours than those fixed, or under conditions of labor prohibited by an order of the commission.

(b) Pays or causes to be paid to any employee a wage less than the minimum fixed by an order of the commission.

(c) Violates or refuses or neglects to comply with any provision of this chapter or any order or ruling of the commission.

SECTION 1391.2. (a)
Notwithstanding Sections 1391 and 1391.1, any minor under 18 years of age who has been graduated from a high school maintaining a four-year course above the eighth grade of the elementary schools, or who has had an equal amount of education in a private school or by private tuition, or who has been awarded a certificate of proficiency pursuant to Section 48412 of the Education Code, may be employed for the same hours as an adult may be employed in performing the same work.

(b) Notwithstanding the provisions of the orders of the Industrial Welfare Commission, no employer shall pay any minor described in this section in his employ at wage rates less than the rates paid to adult employees in the same establishment for the same quantity and quality of the same classification of work; provided, however, that nothing herein shall prohibit a variation of rates of pay for such minors and adult employees engaged in the same classification of work based upon a difference in seniority, length of service, ability, skill, difference in duties or services performed, whether regularly or occasionally, difference in the shift or time of day worked, hours of work, or other reasonable differentiation, when exercised in good faith.

California Codes
Labor Code Section for Advance-Fee Talent Services

HOLLYWOOD OS® has been granted permission by the California Labor Board to publish the Labor Laws pertaining to the Motion Picture Industry and specifically, the laws pertaining to extra performers and, thus, Advance-Fee talent services. Also included is the newly amended information for Labor Code 1701. For COMPLETE information, contact your your local DLSE office.

1701 For purposes of this chapter, the following terms have the following meanings:

(a) (1)"Advance fee" means any fee due from or paid by an artist prior to the artist obtaining actual employment as an artist or prior to the artist receiving actual earnings as an artist or that exceeds the actual earnings received by the artist as an artist.

(2) "Advance fee" does not include reimbursements for out-of-pocket costs actually incurred by the payee on behalf of the artist for services rendered or goods provided to the artist by an independent third party if all of the following conditions are met:

(A) The payee has no direct or indirect financial interest in the third party.

(B) The payee does not accept any referral fee or other consideration for referring the artist.

(C) The services rendered or goods provided for the out-of-pocket costs are not represented to be, and are not, a condition for the payee to register or list the artist with the payee.

(D) The payee maintains adequate records to establish that the amount to be reimbursed was actually advanced or owed to a third party and that the third party is not a person in which the payee has a direct or indirect financial interest or from which the payee receives any consideration for referring the artist.

(E) The burden of producing evidence to support a defense based upon an exemption or an exception provided in this paragraph is upon the person claiming it.

(b) "Advance-fee talent service" means a person who charges, attempts to charge, or receives an advance fee from an artist for one or more of the following:

(1) Procuring, offering, promising, or attempting to procure employment or engagements for the artist.

(2) Managing or directing the development or advancement of the artist's career as an artist.

(3) Career counseling, career consulting, vocational guidance, aptitude testing, evaluation, or planning, in each case relating to the preparation of the artist for employment as an artist.

(c) "Artist" or "artists" means persons who seek to become or are actors or actresses rendering services on the legitimate stage or in the production of motion pictures, radio artists, musical artists, musical organizations, directors of legitimate stage, motion picture and radio productions, musical directors, writers, cinematographers, composers, lyricists, arrangers, models, extras, and other artists or persons rendering professional services in motion picture, theatrical, radio, television, and other entertainment enterprises.

(d) "Fee" means any money or other valuable consideration paid or promised to be paid by or for an artist for services rendered or to be rendered by any person conducting the business of an advance-fee talent service.

(e) "Person" means any individual, company, society, firm, partnership, association, corporation, limited liability company, trust, or other organization.

1701.1. This chapter does not apply to any person exempt from regulation under the Employment Agency, Employment Counseling, and Job Listing Services Act (Title 2.91 (commencing with Section 1812.500) of Part 4 of Division 3 of the Civil Code) pursuant to paragraph (2) of subdivision (b) of Section 1812.501 or Section 1812.502 of the Civil Code.

1701.2. Compliance with this chapter does not satisfy or is not a substitute for the requirements mandated by any other applicable law, including the obligation to obtain a license under the Talent Agencies Act (Chapter 4 (commencing with Section 1700)), prior to procuring, offering, promising, or attempting to procure employment or engagements for artists.

1701.4. (a) Every contract or agreement between an artist and an advance-fee talent service for an advance fee shall be in writing. The contract shall contain all of the following provisions and the additional provisions, if any, as may be set forth in regulations adopted by the Labor Commissioner from time to time:

(1) The name, address, and telephone number of the advance-fee talent service, the artist to whom the services are to be provided, and the representative executing the contract on behalf of the advance-fee talent service.

(2) A description of the services to be performed, a statement when those services are to be provided, the duration of the contract, and refund provisions if the described services are not provided according to the contract.

(3) The amount of any fees to be charged to or collected from the artist receiving the services or any other person and the date or dates when those fees are required to be paid.

(4) The following statements, in type no smaller than 10-point boldface type and in close proximity to the artist's signature, shall be included in the contract:

Right To Refund

"If you pay all or any portion of a fee and you fail to receive the services promised or that you were led to believe would be performed, then (name of advance-fee talent service) shall, upon your request, return the amount paid by you within 48 hours of your request for a refund. If the refund is not made within 48 hours, then (name of advance-fee talent service) shall, in addition, pay you a sum equal to the amount of the refund."

Your Right To Cancel

(enter date of transaction)

You may cancel this contract for advance-fee talent services, without any penalty or obligation, if notice of cancellation is given, in writing, within 10 business days from the above date. To cancel this contract, mail or deliver a signed and dated copy of the following cancellation notice or any other written notice of cancellation, or send a telegram containing a notice of cancellation to (name of advance-fee talent service) at (address of its place of business), NOT LATER THAN MIDNIGHT OF (date). ONLY A TALENT AGENT LICENSED PURSUANT TO SECTION 1700.5 OF THE LABOR CODE MAY ENGAGE IN THE OCCUPATION OF PROCURING, OFFERING, PROMISING, OR ATTEMPTING TO PROCURE EMPLOYMENT OR ENGAGEMENTS FOR AN ARTIST.

Cancellation Notice

I hereby cancel this contract.

Dated: ______________________________

____

Artist's Signature.

(b) All contracts subject to this section shall be dated and shall be made and numbered consecutively in triplicate, the original and each copy to be signed by the artist and the person acting for the advance-fee talent service. The advance-fee talent service shall provide an original and one copy of the contract to the artist at the same time the artist signs the contract and before the artist or any person acting on his or her behalf becomes obligated to pay or pays any fee. The additional copy shall be kept on file at the advance-fee talent service's place of business.

(c) The full agreement between the parties shall be contained in a single document containing the elements set forth in this section.

(d) Any contract subject to this section that does not comply with subdivisions (a) to (c), inclusive, of this section shall be voidable at the election of the artist and, in that case, shall not be enforceable by the advance-fee talent service.

(e) Refunds shall be made as follows:

(1) In the event that an artist does not receive the services promised or that the artist was led to believe would be performed, the advance-fee talent service shall, upon demand therefor, repay the artist the fees collected for those services. If payment is not made within 48 hours after the artist's demand, the advance-fee talent service shall pay the artist an additional sum equal to the amount of the fee.

(2) In the event that an artist cancels the contract, the advance-fee talent service shall refund in full any advance fees demanded by the artist in writing within 10 business days after delivery of the demand to the advance-fee talent service, provided that the artist furnishes a notice of cancellation to the advance-fee talent service in the manner specified in paragraph (4) of subdivision (a). Unless repayment is made within 10 business days after the demand, the advance-fee talent service shall pay the artist an additional sum equal to the amount of the fee.

1701.5. (a) Every person engaging in the business of an advance-fee talent service shall keep and maintain records of the person's advance-fee talent service business. The records shall contain all of the following:

(1) The name and address of each artist employing that person as an advance-fee talent service.

(2) The amount of the advance fees paid by or for the artist during the term of the contract with the advance-fee talent service.

(3) A record of all advertisements by the advance-fee talent service, including the date and the publication in which the advertisement appeared, which shall be maintained for a period of three years following publication.

(4) Records described in subparagraph (D) of paragraph (2) of subdivision (a) of Section 1701.

(5) Any other information that the Labor Commissioner requires.

(b) All books, records, and other papers kept pursuant to this chapter by an advance-fee talent service shall be open at all reasonable hours to inspection by the Labor Commissioner and his or her representatives and to the representative of the Attorney General, any district attorney, or any city attorney. Every advance-fee talent service shall furnish to the Labor Commissioner and to the representative of the Attorney General, any district attorney, or any city attorney, upon request, a true copy of those books, records, and papers, or any portion thereof, and shall make reports as the Labor Commissioner requires.

(c) Every advance-fee talent service shall post in a conspicuous place in the office of the advance-fee talent service a printed copy of this chapter and of other statutes as may be specified by regulation of the Labor Commissioner. Those copies shall also contain the name and address of the officer charged with the enforcement of this chapter. The Labor Commissioner shall furnish to the advance-fee talent service printed copies of any statute required to be posted under this section.

1701.8. Prior to requesting any advance fee, an advance-fee talent service shall provide an artist with written disclosure of all of the following:

(a) The name, address, and telephone number of the advance-fee talent service, and evidence of compliance with any applicable bonding requirements, including the bond number, if any.

(b) A copy of the advance-fee talent service fee schedule and payment terms.

1701.10. (a) Prior to engaging in the business or acting in the capacity of an advance-fee talent service, a person shall file with the Labor Commissioner a bond in the amount of ten thousand dollars ($10,000) or a deposit in lieu of the bond pursuant to Section 995.710 of the Code of Civil Procedure. The bond shall be executed by a corporate surety qualified to do business in this state and conditioned upon compliance with this chapter. The total aggregate liability on the bond shall be limited to ten thousand dollars ($10,000). The bond may be terminated pursuant to Section 995.440 of, or Article 13 (commencing with Section 996.310) of Chapter 2 of Title 14 of Part 2 of, the Code of Civil Procedure.

(b) The bond required by this section shall be in favor of, and payable to, the people of the State of California and shall be for the benefit of any person damaged by any fraud, misstatement, misrepresentation, unlawful act or omission, or failure to provide the services of the advance-fee talent service while acting within the scope of that employment or agency.

(c) The Labor Commissioner shall charge and collect a filing fee to cover the cost of filing the bond or deposit.

(d) The Labor Commissioner shall enforce the provisions of this chapter that govern the filing and maintenance of bonds and deposits.

(e) (1) Whenever a deposit is made in lieu of the bond otherwise required by this section, the person asserting the claim against the deposit shall establish the claim by furnishing evidence to the Labor Commissioner of a money judgment entered by a court, together with evidence that the claimant is a person described in subdivision (b).

(2) When a claimant has established the claim with the Labor Commissioner, the Labor Commissioner shall review and approve the claim and enter the date of the approval thereon. The claim shall be designated an approved claim.

(3) When the first claim against a particular deposit has been approved, it shall not be paid until the expiration of a period of 240 days after the date of its approval by the Labor Commissioner. Subsequent claims that are approved by the Labor Commissioner within the same 240-day period shall similarly not be paid until the expiration of that 240-day period. Upon the expiration of the 240-day period, the Labor Commissioner shall pay all approved claims from that 240-day period in full unless the deposit is insufficient, in which case every approved claim shall be paid a pro rata share of the deposit.

(4) Whenever the Labor Commissioner approves the first claim against a particular deposit after the expiration of a 240-day period, the date of approval of that claim shall begin a new 240-day period to which paragraph (3) applies with respect to any amount remaining in the deposit.

(5) After a deposit is exhausted, no further claims shall be paid by the Labor Commissioner. Claimants who have had claims paid in full or in part pursuant to paragraph (3) or (4) shall not be required to return funds received from the deposit for the benefit of other claimants.

(6) Whenever a deposit has been made in lieu of a bond, the amount of the deposit shall not be subject to attachment, garnishment, or execution with respect to an action or judgment against the assignor of the deposit, other than as to an amount as no longer needed or required for the purposes of this chapter and that would otherwise be returned to the assignor of the deposit by the Labor Commissioner.

(7) The Labor Commissioner shall return a deposit two years from the date it receives written notification from the assignor of the deposit that the assignor has ceased to engage in the business or act in the capacity of an advance-fee talent service or has filed a bond pursuant to subdivision (a), provided that there are no outstanding claims against the deposit. The written notice shall include all of the following:

(A) The name, address, and telephone number of the assignor.

(B) The name, address, and telephone number of the bank at which the deposit is located.

(C) The account number of the deposit.

(D) A statement that the assignor is ceasing to engage in the business or act in the capacity of an advance-fee talent service or has filed a bond with the Labor Commissioner. The Labor Commissioner shall forward an acknowledgement of receipt of the written notice to the assignor at the address indicated therein, specifying the date of receipt of the written notice and the anticipated date of release of the deposit, provided there are then no outstanding claims against the deposit.

(8) A municipal or superior court may order the return of the deposit prior to the expiration of two years upon evidence satisfactory to the court that there are no outstanding claims against the deposit, or order the Labor Commissioner to retain the deposit for a specified period beyond the two years to resolve outstanding claims against the deposit.

(9) This subdivision applies to all deposits retained by the Labor Commissioner. The Labor Commissioner shall notify each assignor of a deposit it retains and of the applicability of this section.

(10) Compliance with Sections 1700.15 and 1700.16 of this code or Section 1812.503, 1812.510, or 1812.515 of the Civil Code shall satisfy the requirements of this section.

1701.12. An advance-fee talent service, or its agent or employee, may not do any of the following:

(a) Make, or cause to be made, any false, misleading, or deceptive advertisement or representation concerning the services the artist will receive or the costs the artist will incur.

(b) Publish or cause to be published any false, fraudulent, or misleading information, representation, notice, or advertisement.

(c) Give an artist any false information or make any false promise or misrepresentation concerning any engagement or employment, or make any false or misleading verbal or written promise or guarantee of any job or employment to an artist.

(d) Make any false promise or representation, by choice of name or otherwise, that the advance-fee talent service is a talent agency or will procure or attempt to procure employment or engagements for the artist as an artist.

(e) Charge or attempt to charge, directly or indirectly, an artist for registering or listing the artist for employment in the entertainment industry or as a customer of the advance-fee talent service.

(f) Charge or attempt to charge, directly or indirectly, an artist for creating or providing photographs, filmstrips, videotapes, audition tapes, demonstration reels, or other reproductions of the artist, casting or talent brochures, or other promotional materials for the artist.

(g) Charge or attempt to charge, directly or indirectly, an artist for creating or providing costumes for the artist.

(h) Charge or attempt to charge, directly or indirectly, an artist for providing lessons, coaching, or similar training for the artist.

(i) Charge or attempt to charge, directly or indirectly, an artist for providing auditions for the artist.

(j) Refer an artist to any person who charges the artist a fee for the services described in subdivisions (e) to (i), inclusive, in which the advance-fee talent service has a direct or indirect financial interest.

(k) Accept any compensation for referring an artist to any person charging the artist a fee for the services described in subdivisions (e) to (i), inclusive.

1701.13. A person who willfully violates any provision of this chapter is guilty of a misdemeanor. Each violation is punishable by imprisonment in the county jail for not more than one year, by a fine not exceeding ten thousand dollars ($10,000), or by both that fine and imprisonment. However, payment of restitution to an artist shall take precedence over the payment of a fine.

1701.15. The Attorney General, any district attorney, or any city attorney may institute an action for a violation of this chapter, including, but not limited to, an action to restrain and enjoin a violation.

1701.16. A person who is injured by any violation of this chapter or by the breach of a contract subject to this chapter may bring an action for recovery of damages or to restrain and enjoin a violation, or both. The amount awarded for damages for a violation of this chapter may be up to three times the damages actually incurred, but not less than the amount paid by the artist to the advance-fee talent service. When an advance-fee talent service refuses or is unwilling to pay damages awarded by a judgment that has become final, the judgment may be satisfied from the bond or deposit maintained by the Labor Commissioner. If the plaintiff prevails in an action under this chapter, the plaintiff shall be awarded reasonable attorney's fees and costs. If the court determines, by clear and convincing evidence, that the breach of contract or violation of this chapter was willful, the court, in its discretion, may award punitive damages in addition to any other amounts.

1701.17. The provisions of this chapter are not exclusive and do not relieve any person subject to this chapter from the duty to comply with all other laws.

1701.18. The remedies provided in this chapter are not exclusive and shall be in addition to any other remedies or procedures provided in any other law.

1701.19. Any waiver by the artist of the provisions of this chapter is deemed contrary to public policy and void and unenforceable. Any attempt by an advance-fee talent service to have an artist waive his or her rights under this chapter is a violation of this chapter.

1701.20. If any provision of this chapter or the application thereof to any person or circumstances is held unconstitutional, the remainder of the chapter and the application of that provision to other persons and circumstances shall not be affected thereby.

1701 ADVANCE FEE TALENT SERVICE ACT
(Newly Amended Labor Code, Section 1701)

On August 24th, 2004, Governor Schwarzenegger signed into law the following amendment to the Advance Fee Talent Service Act.

What it says, in a Brain Surgeon(ified) nutshell, is that talent representatives can no longer require actors to pay for services (such as photos or acting lessons) before accepting them as clients. So next time an "agent" tries to force you to pay an up-front fee before he'll represent you, tell him he's breaking the law. Hopefully make it harder for those scammy-type "agencies" and "managers" out there to trick unsuspecting actors out of their hard-earned moolah. It seems that charging talent "fees" in hopes that they will get cast may be big business. While this amendment seems crystal clear in the world of high pressure sales tactics and expensive scams and schemes, the real question is how this may affect the extras casting industry?

In reviewing each amended code, there seems to be an applicable implication directly to Casting Directors/Extras Casting Directors who charge kids, actors and background talent "Registration Fees," "Digital Fees," "Yearly Registration Fees," "Commercial Book Fees," "Photo Fees," "Computer Imaging Fees," all under a mandatory banner to get work via that company or service, with no guarentee of a darn gig.

In regard to calling services, we are unsure how this may affect them. Many calling services charge a "Registration Fee" in addition to a first month of service paid up front and your last month of service paid up front, which seem to qualify as advance fees. Only time will tell how this may be enforced and what the repercussions will be to those who violate the law. Hopefully this requested information will assist you further with whatever acting endeavors you persue.

SENATE BILL NO. 1687
CHAPTER 288
An act to amend Section 1701 of the Labor Code, relating to employment.

[Approved by Governor August 24, 2004. Filed with Secretary of State August 24, 2004.]

LEGISLATIVE COUNSEL'S DIGEST
SB 1687, Murray. Advance-fee talent services.

Existing law regulates agreements for advance-fee talent services, as defined, and includes the right to a refund of any advance fee paid and the right to cancel any contract for advance-fee talent services. Persons engaging in the business of advance-fee talent services are required to provide a written disclosure to the artist, file a bond with the Labor Commissioner, and maintain specified records. Advance-fee talent services are prohibited from, among other things, charging an artist for photographs or lessons.

Under existing law, any person who willfully violates any of these provisions is guilty of a misdemeanor. This bill would revise the definition of advance-fee talent service to include a person who charges, attempts to charge, or receives an advance fee from an artist for specified services, or for the purchase of any other product or service, including, but not limited to, creating or providing photographs or providing lessons, coaching, or similar training, in order to obtain from or through the advance-fee talent service one or more of the specified services. The bill would expand the list of services specified for purposes of this definition to include procuring, offering, promising, or attempting to procure auditions for the artist.

By expanding the scope of an existing crime by making the crime applicable to a new category of persons, the bill would impose a state-mandated local program. The California Constitution requires the state to reimburse local agencies and school districts for certain costs mandated by the state. Statutory provisions establish procedures for making that reimbursement. This bill would provide that no reimbursement is required by this act for a specified reason.

The people of the State of California do enact as follows:

SECTION 1. Section 1701 of the Labor Code is amended to read:

1701. For purposes of this chapter, the following terms have the following meanings:

(a) (1) ''Advance fee'' means any fee due from or paid by an artist prior to the artist obtaining actual employment as an artist or prior to the artist receiving actual earnings as an artist or that exceeds the actual earnings received by the artist as an artist.

(2) ''Advance fee'' does not include reimbursements for out-of-pocket costs actually incurred by the payee on behalf of the artist for services rendered or goods provided to the artist by an independent third party if all of the following conditions are met:

(A) The payee has no direct or indirect financial interest in the third party.

(B) The payee does not accept any referral fee or other consideration for referring the artist.

(C) The services rendered or goods provided for the out-of-pocket costs are not represented to be, and are not, a condition for the payee to register or list the artist with the payee.

(D) The payee maintains adequate records to establish that the amount to be reimbursed was actually advanced or owed to a third party and that the third party is not a person in which the payee has a direct or indirect financial interest or from which the payee receives any consideration for referring the artist.

(E) The burden of producing evidence to support a defense based upon an exemption or an exception provided in this paragraph is upon the person claiming it.

(b) ''Advance-fee talent service'' means a person who charges, attempts to charge, or receives an advance fee from an artist for one or more of the following, or for the purchase of any other product or service, including, but not limited to, those described in subdivisions (e) to (i), inclusive, of Section 1701.12, in order to obtain from or through the service one or more of the following:

(1) Procuring, offering, promising, or attempting to procure employment, engagements, or auditions for the artist.

(2) Managing or directing the development or advancement of the artist's career as an artist.

(3) Career counseling, career consulting, vocational guidance, aptitude testing, evaluation, or planning, in each case relating to the preparation of the artist for employment as an artist.

(c) ''Artist'' or ''artists'' means persons who seek to become or are actors or actresses rendering services on the legitimate stage or in the production of motion pictures, radio artists, musical artists, musical organizations, directors of legitimate stage, motion picture and radio productions, musical directors, writers, cinematographers, composers, lyricists, arrangers, models, extras, and other artists or persons rendering professional services in motion picture, theatrical, radio, television, and other entertainment enterprises.

(d) ''Fee'' means any money or other valuable consideration paid or promised to be paid by or for an artist for services rendered or to be rendered by any person conducting the business of an advance-fee talent service.

(e) ''Person'' means any individual, company, society, firm, partnership, association, corporation, limited liability company, trust, or other organization. SEC. 2. No reimbursement is required by this act pursuant to Section 6 of Article XIIIB of the California Constitution because the only costs that may be incurred by a local agency or school district will be incurred because this act creates a new crime or infraction, eliminates a crime or infraction, or changes the penalty for a crime or infraction, within the meaning of Section 17556 of the Government Code, or changes the definition of a crime within the meaning of Section 6 of Article XIIIB of the California Constitution.

• ADVANCE-FEE TALENT AGENCY LIST •

Please review the Advance-Fee Talent Agencies that are bonded, or were recently bonded, in the state of California on the next page.

Advance-Fee
Talent Services

As is now required by California law, all Advance-Fee Talent Services must register with the state to ensure that prospective clients know that they charge up-front fees for the services they provide.

The following companies are currently or were recently bonded in the state of California as Advance-Fee Talent Services as we go to press.

TSM Entertainment, Inc.
DBA John Robert Powers
20 Independence Circle
Chico, CA 95973
BOND CANCELLED

PRINCESSA, INC.
DBA John Robert Powers
416 B Street, Suite B
Santa Rosa, CA 95401
BOND CANCELLED

2ND DREAM ENTERTAINMENT, LLC
DBA John Robert Powers
27200 Turney Road, Suite 120
Valencia, CA 91355
BOND IN FILE

UNLIMITED CASTING, INC
DBA Unlimited Casting
511 N. La Cienega, Suite 210
West Hollywood, CA 90069
BOND IN FILE

INT'L ENT. & TALENT GROUP, INC.
DBA John Robert Powers
9220 Sunset Blvd., Suite 100
West Hollywood, CA 90069
BOND CANCELLED

SHANE, MCTISH & JULIAN
DBA John Robert Powers
505 Corona Mall
Corona, CA 92789
BOND CANCELLED

HOLLYWOOD TALENT ASSOCIATES, LLC
7825 Fay Avenue, Suite 200
La Jolla, CA 92037
BOND CANCELLED

STUART C. KINZEY
DBA Youth Entertainment Artists
230 Manhattan Avenue
Hermosa Beach, CA 90254
BOND IN FILE

TALENT ENTERTAINMENT NETWORK, INC.*
8833 Sunset Blvd., Suite 203
West Hollywood, CA 90069
BONDED AS LICENSED TALENT AGENT

WILLIAM RANDOLPH CLARK*
DBA W. Randolph Clark Company
13415 Ventura Blvd., Suite 3
Sherman Oaks, CA 91423
BONDED AS LICENSED TALENT AGENT

KIDS HOLLYWOOD CONNECTION, INC.
1151 Dove Street, Suite 225
Newport Beach, CA 92660
BOND IN FILE

JEANETTA DUMOUCHEL*
DBA SILVER SCREEN TALENT AGENCY
19925 Stevens Creek Blvd.
Cupertino, CA 95014
BONDED AS LICENSED TALENT AGENT

JO LEE ENTERPRISES, LLC.
DBA Associated American Artists
2221 West Olive Avenue, Suite L & M
Burbank, CA 91506-2619
BOND IN FILE

KENNA DEAN
Act Now Talent Group
14140 Ventura Blvd., Suite 203
Sherman Oaks, CA 91423
BOND IN FILE

act three

Read the detailed information about what Advance-Fee Talent Services are and what their obligation is to their clients on the previous pages.

* These are ALSO licensed talent agencies. They offer other advance-fee services that are separate from those services they offer their represented clients. They DO NOT ALWAYS require those they represent to pay advance fees. *William Randolph Clark* Company is SAG-franchised.

Department
of Industrial Relations

Division
of Labor Standards Enforcement

Policies & Procedures

For Wage Claim Processing Division of Labor Standards Enforcement (DLSE)

The purpose of the following section is to provide a basic overview of the Division of Labor Standards Enforcement's (DLSE) wage claim process and to outline the basic filing, conference, hearing and appeal procedures. Since this guide is not meant to be a definitive statement regarding the processing of wage claims, parties are strongly urged to read all forms received by them throughout the process. Failure to comply with each requirement of the process may result in the loss of important rights.

Summary Of The Procedures

Any employee who has a claim against his or her employer or former employer for unpaid wages or other compensation, which falls under the jurisdiction of the Labor Commissioner, may file a claim with DLSE which is under the direction of the State Labor Commissioner. The Labor Commissioner has no jurisdiction over those persons determined to be bona fide independent contractors or over employees of public agencies (for example, federal, state, county or municipal employees).

The Labor Commissioner, pursuant to the provisions of Labor Code Section 98 has established procedures for investigating wage complaints, which may include a conference and/or a hearing pursuant to Section 98 or both.

Sometimes claims are filed which are very complex and involve a large number of employees and records. Such claims will usually be investigated by DLSE's Bureau of Field Enforcement and not through the procedures described in this pamphlet. If this occurs, the parties will be so informed by the deputy handling the case. However, the majority of claims filed with DLSE are resolved through conferences and/or Section 98 hearings which are explained in this guide. If an interpreter will be needed, it is necessary that you advise the office immediately.

Filing A Complaint!

When You're Not Paid:

• An employee (claimant) alleging the non-payment of wages or other compensation by his or her employer (Defendant), must file a claim with a local office of DLSE to initiate investigation of the claim by the Labor Commissioner. So the time limit for filing a claim will be either two, three or four years from the date of the alleged non-payment, depending upon the underlying employment agreement or the type of claim. Claimants are advised to file a claim as soon as possible after the alleged non-payment.

• When filing the claim, the claimant should provide as much information and documentation as possible, including the legal name, location, and status (method of doing business, i.e., sole proprietorship, partnership, corporation) of the defendant employer or former employer.

• After the claim is assigned to a deputy labor commissioner (Deputy), he or she will determine, based on the circumstances of the claim, how best to proceed. Within thirty (30) days of the filing of the complaint, the Deputy shall notify the parties as to the specific action which will initially be taken regarding the claim:

1.) **Referral to a hearing**

2.) **Dismissal of the claim**

Not all cases will go to a conference before going to hearing. Moreover, many cases will be resolved informally before either a conference or a hearing is scheduled.

act three

The Conference

If it gets this far:

• If the decision has been made by the deputy to hold a conference, a Notice of Claim filed and Conference will be sent to both parties which will describe the claim, provide the date, time and place of the conference, and will direct the parties that they are expected to attend. The purpose of the conference is to determine if the claim can be resolved without a hearing.

• Both parties should bring any documentation to support their positions. However, the parties will not be under oath and the conference will be conducted informally.

• If the defendant fails to appear at the conference, in most cases, the claim will be scheduled for a hearing. If the claimant fails to appear, except for good cause shown, the claim will be dismissed.

• If the case is not resolved at the conference, the deputy will evaluate the parties' positions and documentation and will determine the appropriate action with regard to the claim – usually referral to a hearing or dismissal.

• If the defendant makes payment of the claim, or any part of the claim, directly to the claimant, the claimant must notify the Deputy. If the payment satisfies the claim in full, the case will be closed.

• The claimant may withdraw the claim, by written request to the Deputy, at any time before the conference or hearing.

The Hearing

They suck if it comes to this:

• If a hearing is scheduled (either after the claim is filed or after a conference), the parties will receive, either by certified mail and/or regular mail or by personal service, a Notice of Hearing (or Notice of Claim Filed and Hearing if no conference is deemed appropriate) which will set the date, time and place of the hearing.

• Although hearings are conducted in an informal setting, they are formal proceedings, as opposed to the conference. At the hearing the parties and witnesses testify under oath, and the proceedings are recorded.

• Each party has the following basic rights at the hearing:

1.) To be represented by an attorney or other party of his or her choosing.

2.) To present evidence.

3.) To testify in his or her own behalf.

4.) To have his or her own witnesses testify.

5.) To cross-examine the opposing party and witnesses.

6.) To explain evidence offered in support of his or her position and to rebut evidence offered in opposition.

7.) To have a translator present if necessary.

• The Hearing Officer has sole authority and discretion for the conduct of the hearing. He or she may:

1.) Explain the issues and the meaning of terms not understood by the parties.

2.) Set forth the order in which persons will testify, cross-examine and give rebuttal.

3.) Assist parties in the cross-examination of the opposing party and witnesses.

4.) Question parties and witnesses to obtain necessary facts.

5.) Accept and consider testimony and documents offered by the parties or witnesses.

6.) Take official notice of well-established matters of common knowledge and/or public records.

7.) Ascertain whether there are stipulations by the parties that may be entered into the record.

• The parties must bring all documents and/or records which will support their positions, such as pay vouchers, employment contracts, correspondence or other information. If available, the originals of all documents should be brought to the hearing, with copies for the other party and the Hearing Officer.

• If a document or record a party needs is in the possession of someone else, the party may apply to DLSE for a subpoena, at least 15 business days prior to the date of the hearing. The requesting party must submit, in writing, the reasons he or she feels the document is relevant and necessary. The requesting party has the responsibility for service on the opposing party, including any costs incurred by such service.

• Both parties are entitled to have witnesses at the hearing. Each party may arrange for witnesses to attend voluntarily or may apply to DLSE, at least 10 days prior to the date of the hearing, for issuance of a personal subpoena compelling the witness's attendance at the hearing. The same rules applicable to the issuance of a subpoena for documents, as described above, apply to the issuance of witness subpoenas.

• Changes in the date, time or place of the hearing will not be granted except upon the showing of extraordinary circumstances. The decision to grant such a request is within the sole discretion of the Hearing Officer and Senior Deputy and will be rare.

• If the claimant fails to attend the hearing, the case will be dismissed.

• If the defendant is served with a notice of hearing and fails to attend the hearing, the Hearing Officer will decide the matter on the evidence he or she receives from the claimant. (The hearing will not be rescheduled unless an application for relief under Labor Code Section 98(f) is granted.)

• The Hearing Officer is not bound by the rules of evidence and, therefore, has wide discretion in accepting evidence. He or she also has discretion in deciding whether the assessment of penalties is appropriate in a particular case.

• Within fifteen (15) days after the hearing, the Order, Decision or Award (ODA) of the Labor Commissioner will be filed in the DLSE office and served on the parties shortly thereafter. The ODA will set forth the decision and the amount awarded, if any, by the Hearing Officer.

Appeal To Civil Court

Either party, or both, pursuant to Labor Code Section 98.2, may appeal the Labor Commissioner's ODA to the Municipal or Superior Court, in accordance with the appropriate rules of jurisdiction. The party appealing may obtain a Notice of Appeal form from the Court or may request one from the DLSE office. The appeal must be filed in court within the time period set forth on the ODA, and a copy of the Notice of Appeal must be served on the Labor Commissioner and the opposing party. The court clerk will then set the matter for de novo hearing, which means the judge will hear the case again with each party having the opportunity to present evidence and witnesses.

In the case of an appeal by the defendant, DLSE may represent a claimant who is financially unable to afford counsel, in the appeal proceedings. The decision to represent the claimant is within the sound discretion of the assigned Deputy and the legal staff. The claimant must meet the financial criteria set forth by DLSE. The assigned Deputy will send to the claimant a Request for Attorney Representation along with a State of Financial Status which must be completed and returned to the DLSE office. If the claimant does not meet the requirements for representation, he or she will be notified in writing by the assigned Deputy of the reasons that DLSE will not be providing legal representation.

Department of Industrial Relations, Division of Labor Standards Enforcement OFFICES

Just in case any of the phone numbers or addresses have changed since or during our printing, you can also find local offices of the Division of Labor Standards Employment via the internet address listed below.

320 West 4th Street, Room 450
Los Angeles, CA 90013
(213) 620-6330

6150 Van Nuys Blvd., Room 206
Van Nuys, CA 91401
(818) 901-5315

300 Oceangate, Suite 302
Long Beach, CA 90802
(562) 590-5048

28 Civic Center Plaza, Room 625
Santa Ana, CA 92701
(714) 558-4910

411 E. Canon Perdido, Room 3
Santa Barbara, CA 93101
(805) 568-1222

464 West Fourth Street, Room 348
San Bernardino, CA 92401
(909) 383-4334

7575 Metropolitan Drive, Room 210
San Diego, CA 92108
(619) 220-5451

2031 Howe Avene, Suite 100
Sacramento, CA 95825
(916) 263-1811

50 "D" Street, Suite 360
Santa Rosa, CA 95404
(707) 576-2362

619 Second Street, Room 109
Eureka, CA 95501
(707) 445-6613

5555 California Ave., Suite 200
Bakersfield, CA 93309
(661) 395-2710

770 East Shaw Avenue, Room 315
Fresno, CA 93710
(559) 244-5340

31 East Channel Street, Room 317
Stockton, CA 95202
(209) 948-7770

455 Golden Gate Ave., 8th Floor
San Francisco, CA 94102
(415) 703-5300

1515 Clay Street, Suite 801
Oakland, CA 94612
(510) 622-3273

100 Paseo De San Antonio, Room 120
San Jose, CA 95113
(408) 277-1266

1870 N. Main Street, Suite 150
Salinas, CA 93906
(831) 443-3041

2115 Civic Center Drive, Room 17
Redding, CA 96001
(530) 225-2655

WEBSITE: www.dir.ca.gov/DLSE/districtoffices.htm

LABOR LAW INFO: 213-620-6330 (24 Hours a Day, 7 days a Week)

OFFICE HOURS: Generally open Monday-Friday, 9AM-5PM. (Call for Saturday hours or special, extended weekday hours.)

STATE OF CALIFORNIA - DEPARTMENT OF INDUSTRIAL RELATIONS
DIVISION OF LABOR STANDARDS ENFORCEMENT
STATE LABOR COMMISSIONER

FOR OFFICE USE ONLY - NO ESCRIBA EN ESTA SECCION		
Taken by	Wage Adjudication	
Date filed	Action	SIC Number

INITIAL REPORT OR CLAIM
REPORTE INICIAL O RECLAMO

PLEASE PRINT ALL INFORMATION / POR FAVOR ESCRIBA CON LETRA DE MOLDE TODA LA INFORMACIÓN

Your name / Su nombre | Interpreter needed / Interprete requerido ☐ Yes ☐ No | Social Security Number / No. de Seguro Social | Date of birth / Fecha de nacimiento

Your address – Number and street, apartment or space no. / Su domicilio - No. y calle, apartamento o no. de espacio | Home phone no. / Teléfono - casa ( ) | Work phone no. / current / No. de teléfono de su trabajo actual ( )

City, State, Zip Code / Ciudad, Zona Postal | California Driver's License No. / CA. I.D. Number / No. de Licencia de Conducir o Identificación de California

AGAINST / EN CONTRA

Name of business / Nombre del negocio

Address of business, City, State, Zip Code / Dirección del negocio, Ciudad, Zona Postal

☐ Corporation ☐ Sole owner ☐ Partnership ☐ LLC-LLP ☐ Bankruptcy ☐ Business sold ☐ Business closed

☐ Sociedad anonima ☐ Propietario ☐ Sociedad ☐ LLC-LLP ☐ Bancarrota ☐ Negocio vendido ☐ Negocio cerrado

Name of person in charge / Nombre de la persona a cargo | Telephone no. / No. de teléfono | Type of business / Tipo de negocio | No. of employees / No. de empleados

Type of work performed / Ocupación, tipo de trabajo hecho | Date of hire / Fecha de empleo | Public Works Project? / ¿Proyecto de Obras Públicas? ☐ Yes ☐ No | Was your job union? / ¿Pertenecía Ud. a un sindicato? ☐ Yes ☐ No

Location where work performed - Number. and Street, City, County, Zip Code / Lugar donde trabajó - No. de Calle, Ciudad, Condado, Zona Postal

WAGES - CONDITIONS OF EMPLOYMENT / SUELDO – CONDICIONES DE EMPLEO

Rate of pay - per hour, day, week or month, or piece rate (specify) / Tasa de pago –por hora, día, semana o mes (especifique) $ | Total hours worked / Total de horas Trabajadas: By day / Por día; By week / Por semana | Paid Overtime? / ¿Le pagaban el sobretiempo? ☐ Yes ☐ No

Are you still working for this employer? / ¿Aún sigue trabajando para este patrón? ☐ Yes ☐ No | ☐ Discharged / Despedido | ☐ Quit / Renuncié | On what date? / ¿En que fecha? | Were you paid at time of discharge? / ¿Le pagarón cuando lo despidierón? ☐ Yes ☐ No

If quit, did you give 72 hours notice? / ¿Si renunció, dió Ud. 72 horas de aviso? ☐ Yes ☐ No | Have you asked for your wages? / ¿Ha solicitado su sueldo? ☐ Yes ☐ No | If yes, on what date? / Si es que si, ¿en que fecha? | ☐ In person / En persona ☐ By mail / Por correo

How were you paid? / ¿Cómo le pagaban? ☐ By check / con cheque ☐ In cash / en efectivo | Given a deduction slip? ☐ Yes ☐ No / ¿Le dierón un talón de deducciones? | Did you keep a record of hours worked? ☐ Yes ☐ No / ¿Tiene récord de las horas trabajadas?

GROSS WAGES CLAIMED / GANANCIAS EN BRUTO RECLAMADAS

From (date) / De (Fecha) mo. / date / yr. | To (date) / A (Fecha) mo. / date / yr. | Number of hours, days, weeks or months (Specify: vacation, commission, expenses, overtime) / No. de horas, días semanas o meses reclamados (Especifique vacaciones, comisión, gastos, sobretiempo)

At the rate of - per hour, day, week or month (specify) / Al pago de - por hora, diá semana o mes (especifique) $ | Gross amount claimed / Cantidad en bruto reclamada | $

Brief explanation of issues (use additional sheet if necessary) / Breve explicación de los hechos (use papel adicional si es necesario) | Less amount paid: / Menos la candidad recibida | $

Amount claimed: / Cantidad o saldo reclamado: $

I hereby certify that this is a true statement to the best of my knowledge.
Por el presente, que esta es una declaración verídica conforme a mi conocimiento.

Signed: ______________________ Date: ______________________

DLSE FORM 1 / WAGE ADJUDICATION REV. 2/2000

When they break the law – you go get them!
A Sample Claim Form.

filing a claim

One woman's account of filing a claim – from one background actor to another..

A Special Letter:

- ***Experience on the "set from heck"***
- ***What she did about it***
- ***What she has to say to other background actors who find themselves in a similar situation***

"Not too long after I became an Extra, I was booked on a production as Non-Union Background Talent. The rate of pay was a bit over the usual minimum wage. I thought perhaps that was because SAG was on strike.

This production was astonishing in its complete disregard for most of the Extras. There was a complete lack of even the most elemental of things, like food and water. Most of us were treated as though we were less than cockroaches.

Because I had committed to work this shoot, I felt I had given my word to show up and stay for the duration. And like most of us, who are Non-Union, I was somewhat concerned that if I complained or spoke up, I would be blackballed and/or not booked again.

After waiting several weeks to be paid, the first check came and the amount was wrong. My phone calls to the payroll office were not returned. After making repeated phone calls, with no positive results, I began to get angry. I was still waiting to be paid! After all, I had done all that was asked of me and more. And all I wanted was to be paid for what I had been asked to do. I contacted **HOLLYWOOD OS®** for some advice and was encouraged to file a complaint with the California Labor Board. I got a copy of the CA Labor Laws as they apply to our industry and to my surprise, I found that the production company had not only violated several laws, they had done some things that were illegal to do to Non-Union Extras – such as insist we work past 16 hours.

Finally, I had had it & decided that if I didn't want to have to go through this kind of situation again, I had to do something about it. So I filed a complaint with the Labor Board. However, I didn't stop there. I was really angry now, as I still had not been paid the rest of what I was owed and I now had this

filing a claim

One woman's account of filing a claim – from one background actor to another..........

(CONT'D)

additional information. So I wrote to the company, in a very professional way, explaining my reasons for writing, as well as my position. This began a back and forth dialogue that lasted several weeks. Others were brought into it by the original company and I found myself explaining the situation over and over again. However, I was on a mission! I wanted to be properly compensated and if it made the road easier for other Non-Union performers, then all the better.

After a few months, I was beginning to think I was never going to see the money I was owed. Then, I received a phone call from the California Labor Commissioner assigned to my case. He asked me some questions and told me he was sending out the notices to all parties concerned and if I were to receive payment to let him know or be prepared to come to the scheduled hearing with my documents. I had, prior to filing with the Labor Board, sat down & figured out exactly what I had coming to me – not only in overtime, but when there was not an applicable law for Non-Union, I used the Union rates. It is amazing what a little piece of paper can do! All of a sudden there was a flurry of activity and a check for all that I was owed. All I had to do in return was sign a non-disclosure agreement and, of course, the company asserted they were not at fault.

The Labor Board does work for us! All it takes is a little perseverance, knowing you are in the right and being professional in your behavior and requests. It worked for me and it can and WILL work for you... and I am still working! Don't sit back and let yourself be taken advantage of because you are Non-Union!

This is something you (a person filing) HAVE to do on your own. Don't wait for others to back you up. You are mostly on your own, BUT if you have been mistreated or underpaid you MUST file as a matter of self-respect. It WILL take time to solve, BUT don't give up! Be persistent but professional. Do not stop writing to them – keep reminding them you are serious, you are right, and you are not going to go away. Believe me, companies DO NOT want to get into "it" with the Labor Board. The penalties they will have to pay to you for their "misbehavior" will be far in excess of what you are most likely asking for. If this helps anyone else I am glad... because as you folks at **HOLLYWOOD OS®** say, 'Non-Union does not mean non-human!' "

– One Totally (Fabulous) Anonymous Extra

break the law?

Pay the piper, baby! Two reports of labor law bewilderment

• Report #1

"Friends" made MILLIONS, extras FORCED to make LESS THAN minimum wage!

Just to be clear, we are not picking on *Friends* as the ONLY TV show extras got screwed on. And let's be honest, this has absolutely nothing to do with *Friends* or the production company. The predator here, folks, was a little company called *Central Casting*.

In fact, ten to one, unbeknownst even to production, it's actually ANY TV show *Central* cast where Non-Union extras got the big shaft. We say "unbeknownst" simply because, how mortifying to network television production if word leaked that they were stiffing the background actors – talk about an embarrassing and negative press bonanza. Good thing this practice has changed. Good work, *Central*!

Just what the heck are we talking about... if you're new to the extras casting community or have been living under a darn rock, perhaps you hadn't heard about the lawsuit which was settled in the summer of 2002. Your fellow background actors David Heim and Arlie Sego won a huge victory for *all* background actors.

How? Well, they challenged the biggest extras casting company in town for bringing their hourly wage below CA's minimum wage – a big-time, bottom-feeding, commission-taking boo-boo on the part of *Central Casting*.

Yup, you got it. *Central Casting* was taking commissions from Non-Union background actors' paychecks for years (how this happened in the first place is beyond us!) and this practice often resulted in Non-Union performers being paid less than the state-mandated minimum wage.

Ouch.

break the law?

Pay the piper, baby! Two reports of labor law bewilderment...

(CONT'D)

Thus, the 5% "agency fee" deductions which had been taken from backgrounders' paychecks were challenged and *Entertainment Partners/Central Casting/Cenex* stopped taking the illegal deductions in January 2001, to avoid any further complications to the already-sticky situation they found themselves in. If that's not an admission of guilt, we don't know what the heck is.

On July 19, 2002, the Superior Court of the State of California gave final approval to a settlement agreement on behalf of Non-Union extras who had this 5% agency fee deducted from their paychecks prior to January 1, 2001. So any background actor who worked Non-Union for *Central* between January 1997 and May 16, 2002, and had commissions taken from their paycheck, owe David and Arlie a big, fat hug or at least a very big "thank-you" since they challenged the "Big One" (*Central*) and won.

Background actors whose total deductions during this period were equal to or greater than $150 will receive a settlement award reflecting the full amount of their deductions. Class members whose agency fee deductions were less than $150 will unfortunately not be compensated. But the battle has been won. These heroes deserve much praise for their efforts and we are proud to know there are background actors out there who will fight for justice and never give up. *Central Casting* settled (duh, the obvious choice) and the good guys won.

Moral of the story – it's not a lost cause to speak up when your rights are being violated.

We thank these good men for continuing in the tradition of **HOLLYWOOD OS**® – always looking out for the background actors' best interests and putting themselves on the line for everyone.

break the law?

Pay the piper, baby! Two reports of labor law bewilderment.

• Report #2

22-Hour WORKDAY – Nothing "Golden" Here, Folks!

Okay, here's a doozy of a double-edged sword. Nobody's "paid the piper" on this one yet, but it's an interesting conundrum for sure (c'mon, Brain Surgeons, get out that dictionary if you need some help with our fancy-schmancy million dollar word)!

An influx of calls to the **HOLLYWOOD OS**® office regarding a 22-hour workday on the WB's *Gilmore Girls* prompted us to do a little investigating. The background actors who contacted us felt they had not been fairly compensated for the hours they worked on set. Unfortunately, their calls and our calls to the California Labor Board were uniformly dismissed since the talent were granted overtime pay and double time.

However, as we have interpreted the law, it states that it is illegal for Non-Union extra performers to work over 16 hours. Thus, it seems to us that paying double-time after the 16th hour doesn't disqualify the original law that states it is illegal to work over 16 hours regardless of compensation. A conundrum indeed (did you look it up yet?).

In earlier editions of **"EXTRA" WORK for Brain Surgeons**®, we stated that "Golden Time" on or beyond the 16th hour for Non-Union performers was "industry standard." What this meant was that most productions that held Non-Union performers to the 16th hour or beyond generally compensated Non-Union actors with "Golden Time" just like their SAG counterparts as a sign of courtesy and humane conditions. It is interesting to note, however, that even this uniformly accepted "Golden Time for Non-Union" practice appears to be illegal as the California law stands now. It seems the law of the land may need amending. SAG "Golden Time" is legal because California Labor Laws do not apply to those covered by a collective bargaining agreement (a.k.a. the SAG contract).

break the law?

Pay the piper, baby! Two reports of labor law bewilderment......................................

(CONT'D)

In addition, these background actors on *Gilmore* lost out on working the next day since their workday was twenty-two hours long – thus they each potentially lost a day's pay if they had been booked for work the next day. It appears they should also be compensated for that day's missed wage (a minimum of $54/8). We urged each and every one of the actors who contacted us to file a claim, pointing out the apparent loopholes in this law so that a resolution could be met – now and for the future. Sadly, we never heard any good news. Seems the CA Labor Board insisted that the BG were paid overtime in accordance with the law. Hhmm?

If nothing else, perhaps SOMEONE at the Labor Board will look at this law more carefully and reconfigure its language to see to it this riddle is solved once and for all. Apparently, this oversight is something that has been going on for years, but apparently the Labor Laws were never read carefully enough to catch the snafu. The law is the law and we're hoping a resolution comes of this sooner than later.

extras casting companies

The who, where and how-to of submitting for extra work

• *Dumb Disclaimer*

Before we get started, we just want to remind you that this is simply a guide with a listing of extras casting agencies and Casting Directors to inform you, the background actor, about work possibilities. Phone numbers, addresses, policies, fees, and staff members may change at any time without notice. Also note that the companies mentioned are not rated or recommended – just listed, that's all. Furthermore, purchasing this swell book does not guarantee employment. Duh!

Three Avenues Explored in this Act:

Now that we got that crap out of the way, let's get down to business! In the following chapter, you will find a variety of Casting Directors and/or casting companies where you can find work:

- Companies that charge a fee
- Companies that are FREE to register with
- Casting Directors that are FREE to submit to

• *Companies Not Listed*

In terms of the casting companies/agencies that are NOT listed in this directory, we are truly confused as to WHY any REPUTABLE agency would NOT respond to our phone calls, emails or faxes and PROVIDE US with complete and accurate information - in their OWN words. Essentially, we provide FREE ADVERTISING to the legitimate agencies listed in our kick-ass book. We do NOT charge or sell advertising space to casting agencies/directors, as that would do you, the job seeker, a disservice. Besides, charging them to be listed is even more preposterous – we would never want to limit ourselves in such a political way.

If YOU conducted a legitimate business, WHY WOULDN'T you want YOUR REPUTABLE AGENCY listed – with current, thorough information including your address and registration fees? The more information talent has about an agency – the less talent will call asking redundant questions. We can ONLY SPECULATE that these "supposed" agencies that do not take the time to fill out our casting questionnaire or return phone calls could possibly have something to hide or be ashamed of. We urge all of you to think twice before paying often high registration fees to agencies who are NOT interested in FREE ADVERTISING in a directory that's primary function is to inform and educate background actors.

extras casting companies

The who, where and how-to of submitting for extra work

• *Keep Us Posted!*

If by chance you hear of an agency or CD that is not listed in **"EXTRA" WORK for Brain Surgeons**® and they claim to have work for background actors, kids, principal actors, real people or whatever, feel free to e-mail us at info@HollywoodOS.com with your questions or concerns.

We'll do our best to find out what we can. Through our research, we may be able to shed some light on what is really going on. Some casting agencies or so-called casting agencies will claim to have projects and some will even name various projects that they are "supposedly" casting.

Please keep in mind that some agencies will do and say anything to get you to register – this is how they REALLY make their money because chances are, they were not hired by Production to cast the film or music video or what have you, they've claimed to have been hired for.

There are many extremely reputable agencies for you to choose from. Peruse this chapter carefully. Look at what each Casting Director or casting agency/company offers – and for how much! Hopefully, we have helped you in your "EXTRA" endeavor and warned you of a few hurdles along the way (read *Fabulous Other* in Act 9).

Okay, now read on and good luck, Brain Surgeons!

extras casting companies

The who, where and how-to of submitting for extra work

•Companies with Fees

First up, let's talk about the agencies that charge a fee. The average fee has increased (inflation, apparently). The new average is $20 - $25... not $200! And it should be a one-time deal people, NOT a yearly fee and NOT an endless parade of fees for this and fees for that.

Unlike other books that have been known to sell star ratings at $100 a pop, we DO NOT RATE the agencies in this book, nor do we have some lame, suck-up, kiss-ass, arbitrary "Top 10 List" to impress Casting Directors so we can try to get special treatment from them. Instead, we simply list casting companies along with the information you need, so YOU can make an informed decision as to which casting companies/Casting Directors are right for YOU INDIVIDUALLY.

A "Top 10 List" of agencies has no bearing on what companies are busy and reflective of what work is really out there for the type you may be cast as. Whether you are a fifty-something SAG member or hip and trendy Non-Union 18 to-look-younger, the amount of work would greatly vary. Some casting companies may only focus on certain types of projects that are generally specific to one age/look (i.e., music videos tend to use primarily hip and trendy twenty-somethings); other CD's may cast 100's of people daily in all categories. You just never know. It all depends on what type you are and what kinds of projects each casting company/Casting Director is currently casting.

WHO ARE WE to rate agencies? An agency which is right for one type of person MIGHT NOT be right for another – that is the fundamental reason that there are so many casting offices in the first place. If we were to accept money or kickbacks, we would be forced to censor ourselves and possibly be implored to tone down our sarcasm – HELL NO! THAT WOULD SIMPLY BE NO FUN (for Angie... "Hey, I heard that?!!"). Why on earth would we want to give a "Smiley Face," a "Thumbs-Up Sign," a "Frowning Face," or a "Five-Star Rating" to Casting Agencies who DO NOT have work? We would never want to mislead you and recommend agencies (because some come and go so quickly) that do not have work just so that those agencies can perhaps stay in business a little longer by charging outrageous registration fees to pay their rent. We don't think so, people!

So, remember the rule of thumb for singular, one-time Registration fees: $20 - $25 is now the going rate. $200 is absurd.

extras casting companies

The who, where and how-to of submitting for extra work..

•Companies with Free Registration

Next, to tell you about the super-cool folks who offer FREE registration, we present to our fine readers, Production Accountant turned Extras Casting Director, Mr. Pete Sutton:

"To charge and not guarantee work to people who are sometimes a paycheck away from homelessness not only goes against my religion and my upbringing, but also against the grain of the people who hire me, i.e., the production companies.

I make my money (as most casting companies do) at a negotiated percentage (usually 10%) of whatever my hired background makes. If I were to do the background payroll as well, I would make approximately 4% of the gross that the extra makes along with "The Float" (the time between the check deposited from the production company to me and the time the check is cashed by the extra).

If my expenses in running my operations (phone, fax, office supplies, office staff, insurance, rent, computers, etc.) were EVER to EXCEED my income, then it's either time to take down the shingle or start charging the people I cast a fee to register or to "photo image." But I DON'T THINK that's fair. Nobody's putting a gun to your head to do this work, but then again if I ever lose my mind and start charging you guys (many who are making minimum wage as it is), make sure you save a bullet for me."

You can register with Pete's *Mountain Ash Casting* and several other extras casting companies with FREE registration at **HOLLYWOOD OS**®.

Enough said.

extras casting companies

The who, where and how-to of submitting for extra work

•Companies with Free Submission

Now it's time to tell you about those people it is FREE to submit to (yes, FREE is good!). But, remember, these places DO NOT have registration like described on the previous page – you can SUBMIT only, NOT REGISTER. These companies/Casting Directors offer FREE SUBMISSION and they do not operate like regular extras casting companies. They do NOT maintain regular files. Until now, many of them have primarily dealt with AGENTS and MANAGERS when needing talent.

We at HOLLYWOOD OS® want to expose our readers to as many avenues to obtain work as possible but you must understand a few things. YOU MUST NOT CALL ASKING "HOW DO I REGISTER?" because these companies function a bit differently than you may be used to.

Companies like this do not have registration policies or call-in situations where you leave your availability, like you are used to with the majority of the Extras Casting Companies listed in this book. When they need talent they go through their submissions and contact you – period.

We have listed other companies like these in the past and they have quickly asked that they be removed because of the abundance of unnecessary and tiresome phone calls they received. Super rad Casting Director Tolley Casparis asked to be removed from from this main section because people kept calling her for work at all hours of the day and night - even though it specifically said NOT to call. We do not want to see this happen again. We want to provide you with cool contacts and paths for work, but you HAVE TO TRUST US when we advise you on how to (and how not to) contact CDs.

Thanks for reading this little preamble about certain CDs. The moral of the story is, DON'T CALL THEM – they will call you! Capeche (that's Italian for "got it" - not that we spelled it right - on purpose - duh)?!

Across The Board Casting

(a.k.a. People Finders)
5287 Sunset Blvd., 2nd Floor
Hollywood, CA 90027

Website:
n/a

Email:
castingboard@sbcglobal.net

Casting Directors/Staff
LaVonne & Carmen

Main Line:
818-974-9973

Registration Line:
818-760-0467

Info Line/Hotline:
818-754-2557

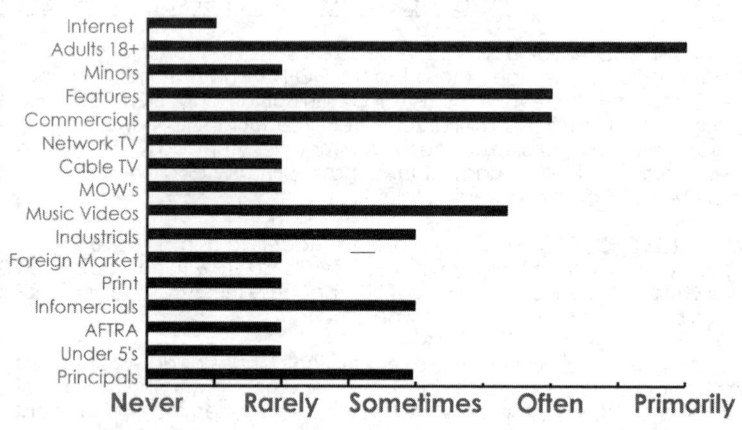

YEAR OPENED
2002

act four

CREDITS INCLUDE
Cook Off, Havana Rush, 50 Ways To Leave Your Lover, The Legend Of Pit Fighter, Disney's Brainiacs, Valentina's Tango, Great Escape Three, government training films, industrials and lots of audience work.

TYPE OF AGENCY
These independent Casting Directors usually work on independent features and student films casting both BG and principals. They also cast many industrials and book audience work for TV shows.

Company Fees	SAG Members	AFTRA & Non-Union Talent
Registration Fee:	$0	$0
Photo Fee:	$0	$0
Photo Update Fee:	$0	$0
TOTAL:	***$0***	***$0***

Across The Board Casting
(a.k.a. People Finders)

REGISTRATION
Registration is now FREE! All ages and ethnicities 18+ are welcome to submit hardcopy photographs along with your current sizes and contact information. You may also email over your super sexy photos directly to castingboard@sbcglobal.net.

VISITING
No regular visiting. Check in with the registration line periodically for any sporadic changes.

WHAT DO YOU APPRECIATE FROM YOUR BACKGROUND?
- Good or "great" attitude and professionalism.
- Be on time!

WHAT ARE SOME OF YOUR PET PEEVES?
- Being late or talent not showing up at all!
- Whining & ridiculous excuses.

DO YOU USE ON-LINE RESOURCES?
Across the Board makes use of **HOLLYWOOD OS**® when casting projects.

HAS BACKGROUND ACTING CHANGED IN RECENT YEARS?
LaVonne tells **HOS**®: "Yes, but our method has always been to select 'hand-picked' quality actors."

WHAT DO YOU SEE FOR THE FUTURE OF BACKGROUND CASTING?
LaVonne tells **HOS**®: "Continued quality work and representation."

COMPANY PHILOSOPHY
LaVonne tells **HOS**®: "To bring professional casting skills, experience, value and integrity to all projects while being of service."

IF YOU COULD TELL BACKGROUND ACTORS ANYTHING...
LaVonne tells **HOS**®: "Remember to pack your tool kit with some essentials: reliability, a good attitude, cooperation, respect, patience, integrity, professionalism, sense of humor, uniqueness... and a comfortable chair!"

Primary Contact Info

Main/Registration Line:
818-760-0467

E-Mail:
castingboard@sbcglobal.net

Sande Alessi Casting

(a.k.a. The Casting Couch, Inc.)
13731 Ventura Blvd.
Sherman Oaks, CA 91423

Website:
www.sandealessicasting.com

Email:
n/a

Casting Directors/Staff:
Sande Alessi, C.S.A., Kristan & Jennifer

Main Line:
n/a

Registration Line:
818-623-7040

Info Line/Hotine
818-771-5717

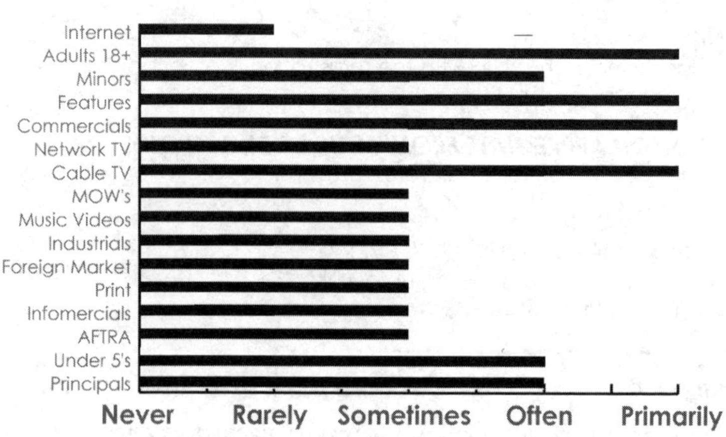

YEAR OPENED
1998

CREDITS INCLUDE
Fat Actress, War of The Worlds, The Terminal, Monster-In-Law, Pirates Of The Caribbean (1, 2, and 3), Raising Helen, American Wedding, I Heart Huckabees, Catch Me If You Can, Haunted Mansion, Minority Report, Six Feet Under, Goldmember, A.I., Curb Your Enthusiasm, Panic Room, Zoolander, The Wedding Planner, Austin Powers 2, Fight Club. Some commercial credits including: Hertz, Cingular, Ford, Best Buy, Pepsi and Adidas.

TYPE OF AGENCY
All ages and ethnicities.

Company Fees	SAG Members	AFTRA & Non-Union Talent
Registration Fee:	$20	$20
Photo Fee:	$0	$0
Commercial Book:	$5	$5
Photo Update Fee:	$10	$10
TOTAL:	***$20 or $25*** (cash only)	***$20 or $25*** (cash only)

Sande Alessi Casting
(a.k.a. The Casting Couch, Inc.)

REGISTRATION
Extras registration for *The Casting Couch* is held M-F, 11AM-3PM, at the address listed on the previous page. Arrive camera ready. Wear clothing that suits your look, but nothing white as they shoot your photo aginst a white background. Also, make sure you bring $20 cash to pay the cash only registration fee (and an extra $5 if you want to get into their commercial book).

PROCEDURE TO FOLLOW ONCE REGISTERED
You will be contacted if *The Casting Couch* has work for you. Keep in touch with the hotline on a regular basis. DO NOT call directly requesting work.

PHOTO & INFO UPDATES
If your look changes, there is a $10 fee for all photo updates, cash only. To update your information, you may email couchupdates@aol.com.

COMMERCIAL WORK
If you want to be considered for Commercial work, *The Couch* has a commercial book used to book talent for commercials. If you wish to be included in this, there is a $5 additional fee to be printed in this book.

VISITING
When visiting you should wear, "The nicest, most up-to-date business or casual outfit you own. Do NOT show up in jeans and a T-shirt – it tells us nothing about what you may have in your closet." Or use nifty postcards. Sande tells **HOS**®: "I love the postcards. It's like visiting by mail and stopping by to say 'hi' without the pesky phone call!"

ABOUT SPECING
Sande tells **HOS**®: "It is fine if they bring good clothes and look appropriate. We don't mind a well-prepared spec, but it's slim odds because our people always show up!"

GOOD THINGS TO DO
- Do carry yourself in a PROFESSIONAL manner on set and ARRIVE EARLY.
- Do have a pager and return pages promptly.
- Visit by mail on 3"x5" photos or postcards with your availability and phone numbers listed on the back.
- Do show up on time and in the correct wardrobe.
- Be honest if you have changed your look since registering.
- Be a short talker: say what needs to be said and avoid the unnecessary chat. While they like you (they called you for work) they have a job to finish and you will impress them most if you help them get that job done as efficiently as possible by being concise.

Sande Alessi Casting
(a.k.a. The Casting Couch, Inc.)

BAD THINGS TO DO

- Don't call to thank *The Casting Couch* for a job – if you want to say thanks, send a postcard. Understand "Thank-You" phone calls just slow the busy *Couch* down!! For those of you who STILL call to thank the casters for a job, we have been officially informed that they can "see right through that one!" Again, thank-you's are a good thing – just not via phone.
- Don't have a long outgoing message on your voice mail!
- "Don't hex our PA's and AD's" – We heard this happened on *Little Nicky* – not a good way to get recalled!
- Don't mail 8"x10"'s – they don't want them.
- Don't mention lack of work from *The Couch* when being called for work.
- Don't call for work, explaining you are registered (when you are not) and then explain to them that they can find your pictures at *Central Casting*.
- Don't be sticky-sweet-nice on the phone and then forget your Prozac and be an "ass" on set.
- Don't HOUND *The Couch* for SAG vouchers – ESPECIALLY if it is your first booking through them.
- Don't fail to explain that your look has changed from when you registered, when accepting a job.
- If you are not available for the day in question, don't ask for work on other days.
- Don't call *The Couch* with payroll problems – call payroll (see your voucher for the number)!
- Don't harass and/or take pictures of the principals on set.
- Don't fail to listen to the specifics on the Hotline. People will actually hear their type listed on the hotline and promptly hang up and call the office directly. This is bad and will not get you booked. The Hotline will usually give a Voicemail number to call if you fit the specifics on the Hotline – that is the number to call, kids!

IF YOU HAVE A PROBLEM ON SET

Sande tells **HOS**®: "Call us, then, if you are SAG, call SAG."

OBTAINING YOUR VOUCHERS

If you are still coveting SAG vouchers even with SAG's new rules, Sande says, "Go to set EARLY and offer to help the AD, get them a cup of coffee, etc. Later, after check-in, and now that he/she knows you, let them know you would like one. Keep in mind that the best time to ask for a voucher is on a call with less than fifty people. Work for a while Non-Union and then ask on a small day - not a call with over fifty people."

Sande Alessi Casting
(a.k.a. The Casting Couch, Inc.)

ADVICE TO SAG MEMBERS OVER 50
Sande tells **HOS**®: "Buy a really nice charcoal or navy suit (that fits)! Look like a MILLIONAIRE or SENATOR or DOCTOR" or something sophisticated!

ADVICE TO WANNABE SAG MEMBERS
The *Couchers* share with **HOS**®: "Don't join SAG to be a SAG extra. Join SAG to be a SAG ACTOR! Wait a while, get some Non-Union film credits on your resumé first, star in Non-Union films, shorts – then join SAG! Just because you're SAG doesn't mean you'll get an agent right away or speaking parts. SAG extras work much less than Non-Union. Don't send us a headshot with "extra" credits on your resumé – less is more! Tell us about your acting, training and skills – not your extra work! Use your own contact numbers (not your agent's) if you submit directly. We will always call in actors for auditions with or without agents or managers. If they submit you – we'll call them."

DO YOU USE CALLING SERVICES OR ON-LINE RESOURCES?
The Couchers prefer using their own database (which was created back in 1997 by **HOLLYWOOD OS**®), but when they cannot find the appropriate talent in their own files, they will look to Charlie Alessi's *Direct Line*.

HAS BACKGROUND ACTING CHANGED IN RECENT YEARS?
The Couchers tell **HOS**®: "The internet has really helped us to streamline. Now we're able to e-mail photos to the Director in minutes instead of pulling, printing and calling a messenger."

WHAT DO YOU SEE FOR THE FUTURE OF BACKGROUND CASTING?
Sande tells **HOS**®: "More Directors who want personalized service in extras casting versus the 'boiler room' type casting they have experienced in the past. Also, I see more use of the internet and virtual auditions."

IF YOU COULD TELL BACKGROUND ACTORS ANYTHING...
The Couchers tell **HOS**®: "When you go to set, go to learn and observe. Think of yourself as an actor – even if you are in a large crowd scene or a pedestrian walking down the street. This mentality will only help you. Act like a professional and you will be treated as such!"

Primary Contact Info

Registration Line:
818-623-7040

Hotline:
818-771-5717

All Locations Casting

(a.k.a. Makris Casting)
P.O. Box 518
Hermosa Beach, CA 90254

Website:
www.alllocationscasting.com

Email:
n/a

Casting Directors/Staff:
Shawn Makris & Marie Makris

Main Line:
310-372-6555

Registration Line:
n/a

Info Line/Hotine
n/a

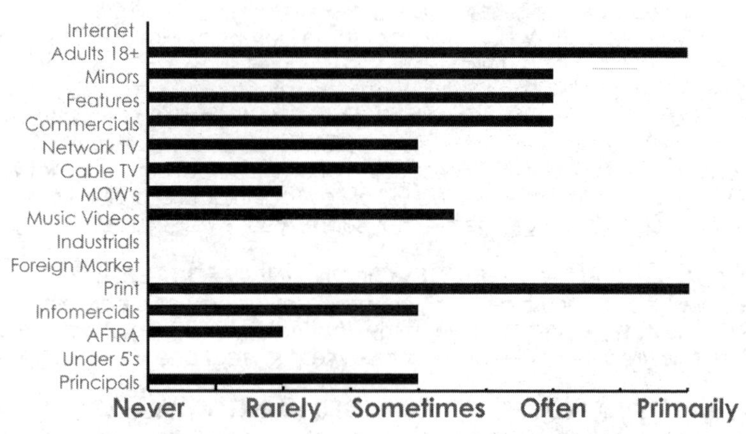

YEAR OPENED

2000

CREDITS INCLUDE

Blind Justice, First Daughter, Girls Will Be Girls, Mind Of The Married Man, Joy Ride (reshoots), *Don't Say A Word* (reshoots), commercials and print ads for American Airlines, Reader's Digest, Match.com, Powerbar, FOX Sports Network, Newsweek, Gateway, Best Buy, Isuzu, Northwest Mutual and more.

TYPE OF AGENCY

These folks primarily cast adults 18+ for a variety of projects.

Company Fees	SAG Members	AFTRA & Non-Union Talent
Registration Fee:	$0	$0
Photo Fee:	$0	$0
Photo Update Fee:	$0	$0
TOTAL:	***$0***	***$0***

act four

All Locations Casting
(a.k.a. Makris Casting)

REGISTRATION
You can grab a picture/headshot with a resumé stapled to the back and mail it directly to them. They ask that you not seal the envelope. Always keep your information current, and if your look should change, please mail them a new photo with all your new info!

You can also obtain a registration card for FREE:

- Stop by the **HOLLYWOOD OS**® office -or-
- Send a 6"x9" or larger SASE to **HOLLYWOOD OS**® specifying you wish to register with the extras casting companies that offer FREE REGISTRATION. You will then be sent official registration cards. Please include your name, phone number, Union status, and your gender (those named Chris, or Pat, or others with multi-purpose nomenclatures can confuse matters). Be sure six 39¢ stamps are attached to the SASE. Yippee!

ABOUT SPECING
Marie tells **HOS**®: "I don't encourage it!"

ALL LOCATIONS APPRECIATES
Marie tells **HOS**®: "Professionals. On time, camera-ready people."

ALL LOCATIONS PET PEEVES
- People who flake.
- People who show up on set with the incorrect wardrobe.
- People who show up somewhere "near" the set and wonder, "Where is everybody?"
- People who don't call when they're going to be late – always call!

DO YOU USE CALLING SERVICES OR ON-LINE RESOURCES?
All Locations primarily turns to **HOLLYWOOD OS**®, *Networks* or *Kids! Background Talent* when using such resources.

IF YOU COULD TELL BACKGROUND ACTORS ANYTHING...
Marie tells **HOS**®: "As a background actor you are representing yourself, your Casting Director, your Calling Service and your Union. Please live up to the expectations of all of them."

Primary Contact Info

Main Line:
310-372-6555

act four

Background Players

Crossroads of the World
6671 Sunset Blvd., Suite 1585-101
Hollywood, CA 90028

Website:
www.bgplayers.com

Email:
n/a

Casting Directors/Staff
David Anthony, Judy Cook, Robin, David, Shannon, Andrew, James & Sasha

Main Line:
323-790-0138

Registration Line:
323-790-0138, ext. 17

Info Line/Hotline:
(Boys) 323-692-5620
(Girls) 323-692-5622

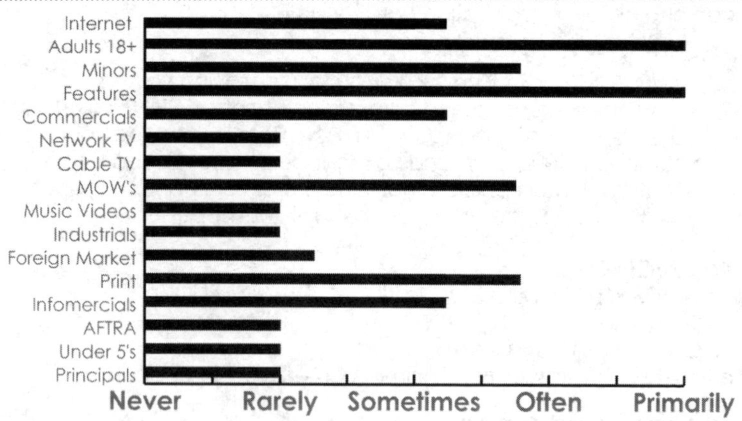

YEAR OPENED
1995

CREDITS INCLUDE
Inconceivable (Pilot), *September, Mr. Woodcock, Wannabe, Grilled, Dark Ride, In Good Company, After The Sunset, Intolerable Cruelty, Down In the Valley, Van Helsing, Serenity, Red Dragon, Rush Hour 2, The Man Who Wasn't There, The Hot Chick, The One, View From The Top, Big Momma's House, My First Mister, The Nutty Professor II, O' Brother, Where Art Thou?, Drowning Mona, Whatever it Takes, Panic, Splendor, Anywhere But Here, The Mod Squad, Pleasantville, Can't Hardly Wait, The Opposite of Sex, Wag the Dog, Phantoms, Trial and Error.*

Company Fees	SAG Members	AFTRA & Non-Union Talent
Registration Fee:	$0	$0
Photo Fee:	$20	$20
Photo Update Fee:	$5	$5
TOTAL:	***$20***	***$20***

act four

Background Players

TYPE OF AGENCY
Adults, 18 and older for mostly big feature films.

REGISTRATION
Any weekday by APPOINTMENT ONLY. Call Andrew at 323-790-0138, ext. 14 to make one. Bring your union cards (if you are union) and driver's license. Resumés are not important. Keep in touch with the hotline on a daily, hourly, minute-ly (not a word, we know) basis. New stuff can come up at any time.

ONLINE DATABASE
Background Players has decided to create an online database of all their groovy talent. Stay tuned for updates at their website: www.bgplayers.com.

ABOUT PHOTOS
Extras are allowed up to 4 different looks in their new system: cowboy, LAPD, business, casual, business-casual, whatever. The first look is included with the initial $20 fee, but the other 3 will cost you an extra $5 total.

VISITING
Visiting is also good – but this can be done only by registered talent on the 2nd Thursday of each month between 11AM -12:30PM.

PROCEDURE TO FOLLOW ONCE REGISTERED
Check the appropriate hotline for work and follow the instructions given, otherwise you will be called if they can use you. Casting notices are also placed online.

BACKGROUND COMMERCIAL DIVISION
In 2005, *BGP* teamed up with David Kang (formerly of *Networks Casting*) to form a separate Commercial Division simply named *Background Commercials.* They will have their own independent database. Headshots can be sent to the *BGP* address (Attn: Commercials Division); Registration is $20 plus a $5 photo fee. For more info, call the *Background Commercial* info line at 310-535-7749. Also check out *www.backgroundcommercials.com*

THE BACKGROUND PLAYERS DON'T LIST
- Don't call the office line BEFORE checking the hotline.
- Do not initiate casual conversations without first asking if they have time to sit and gab.
- Don't complain about not getting booked!
- "Don't stop by unannounced – especially when we're busy! As much as we love to see all of the friendly, talented people registered with us, unannounced visits to our office are still somewhat of a problem. Coming during visitation hours is the best bet."
- Don't call the office directly fishing for work.

Background Players

THE BACKGROUND PLAYERS DO LIST

- Do update your information regularly.
- Do give your FULL NAME when calling the office.
- Do send "Thank-You" notes for jobs you really enjoyed!
- Do check the hotline.
- Do keep your outgoing message on your pager/answering machine: "Short and Sweet!"
- Do have manners.
- Do volunteer selections when it comes to wardrobe.
- Do make *Background Players* look good by representing them well – what comes around goes around.

THOUGHTS ON SPECING

The *BGP* posse tell **HOLLYWOOD OS**®: "Specing is fine as long as they fit the look and wardrobe and are professional and responsible. They should be aware there is no guarantee of work."

ABOUT SAG VOUCHERS

BGP tells **HOS**®: "If one becomes available and the talent is appropriate then that person may receive a voucher. Ask but don't be pushy. There are no guarantees."

IF YOU COULD TELL BACKGROUND TALENT ANYTHING...

We just have to share this li'l ditty. Straight from the *BGP*'s mouths to you: "Please be cautious of body odor when visiting or working." Super random, but okay, then.

act four

Primary Contact Info

Registration Line:
323-790-0138, ext. 17

Guys' Hotline:
323-692-5620

Girls' Hotline:
323-692-5622

Background San Diego

4705 Ruffin Road
San Diego, CA 92123

Website:
www.backgroundsandiego.com

Email:
extras@backgroundsandiego.com

Casting Directors/Staff:
Vivienne Chang & Justin Foley

Main Line:
858-974-8970

Registration Line:
858-974-8970, ext. 477

Info Line/Hotline:
858-974-8974

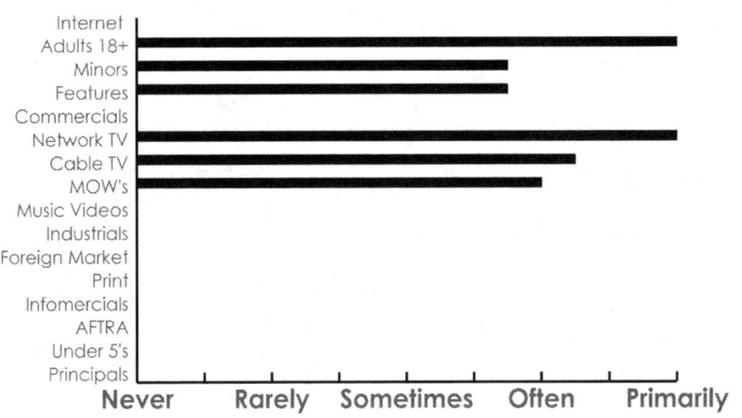

YEAR OPENED

1991

CREDITS INCLUDE

Veronica Mars, See Arnold Run, Perfect Husband, 18 Wheels of Justice, The Chronicle, Bring It On, How To Marry A Millionaire, Silk Stalkings, The Twelfth Lap, Renegade, The Tiger Woods Story, The Invisible Man (TV), Pensacola: Wings Of Gold, Vanishing Son, A Place For Annie, Home Invasion.

TYPE OF AGENCY

Primarily in-house casting for *Stu Segall Productions* which are filmed in the San Diego area. They seek all ages.

Company Fees	SAG Members	AFTRA & Non-Union Talent
Registration Fee:	$0	$0
Photo Fee:	$0	$0
Photo Update Fee:	$0	$0
TOTAL:	***$0***	***$0***

act four

Background San Diego

REGISTRATION

Check the hotline or website for exact dates of registration. *Background San Diego* is presently accepting registration applications through their website: *www.backgroundsandiego.com*. It's a quick and easy way to get the registration process started. You'll still have to go to their office in person during a formal registration, but at least the paperwork will be started before you get there!

Be sure you are a U.S. citizen and/or have a current working visa and bring:

- A current photo no larger than 8"x10" and a resumé (if you have one).
- Social Security card & Union card(s) – if you are SAG or AFTRA.
- If registering a minor, bring a photocopy of your child's work permit.

REGISTRATION FOR MINORS

Minors must have a current work permit. To get a work permit in San Diego, call the San Diego Labor Commission: 619-220-5451.

PROCEDURE TO FOLLOW ONCE REGISTERED

Once registered, check in NO MORE THAN ONCE every two weeks. If you have already registered with them and it has been OVER A YEAR since that date, you should call their main line to schedule an appointment to re-file because registration files expire after one year!

TIPS FOR GETTING WORK FROM BACKGROUND SAN DIEGO

- Don't accept a job and then not show up or show up late
- List ALL of your contact numbers and be PROFESSIONAL
- Send pictures with your new or different looks (L.A.P.D., etc.)
- Send "thank-you" notes for jobs you enjoyed

INSIDE SCOOP!

This is all for work in San Diego. You WILL NOT be reimbursed for mileage when driving down from L.A. – so please don't ask them! And, "no, we don't HAND OUT SAG vouchers!"

Primary Contact Info

Main Line:
858-974-8970

Registration Line:
858-974-8970, ext. 477

E-Mail:
extras@backgroundsandiego.com

Burbank Casting

224 E. Olive Ave., Suite 213
Burbank, CA 91502

Website:
www.burbankcasting.com

Email:
talent@burbankcasting.com

Casting Directors/Staff:
Michelle & Susan

Main Line:
818-559-2350

Registration Line:
818-559-2350

Info Line/Hotline:
818-559-2350

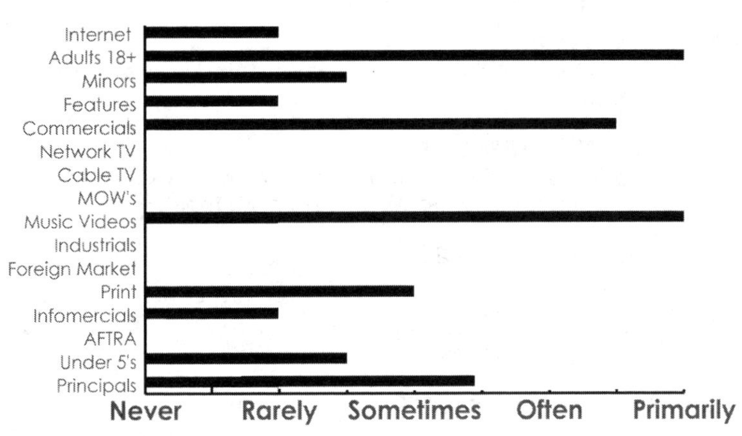

YEAR OPENED
2005

CREDITS INCLUDE
Commercials and print jobs for McDonald's, Cox Cable, Del Taco, Nissan, Comcast, Baskin & Robbins, Arby's, Toyota, ESPN, Fox Sports, Boost Mobile, along with several random music videos.

TYPE OF AGENCY
A new Extras Casting Company for commercials, features, music videos, print, television, etc.

Company Fees	SAG Members	AFTRA & Non-Union Talent
Registration Fee:	$40	$30
Photo Fee:	$0	$0
Photo Update Fee:	$0	$0
TOTAL:	***$40***	***$30***

act four

Burbank Casting

REGISTRATION
Dates and times are posted both on their Info Line and their website.

PROCEDURE TO FOLLOW ONCE REGISTERED
Check the hotline regularly for work. Feel free to leave your availabilty every week or two on their voicemail.

THOUGHTS ON SPECING
Michelle tells **HOLLYWOOD OS**®: "Non-Union is welcome to spec. I prefer no specs for SAG jobs."

BURBANK CASTING APPRECIATES
Michelle tells **HOS**®: "Taking pride in your work. Always being presentable in terms of hair, makeup and wardrobe. Staying close to set."

BURBANK CASTING PET PEEVES
- Tardiness.
- People who ask to leave set early.
- People who go missing on set.

DO YOU USE CALLING SERVICES?
Burbank Casting makes use of *Extras Management, Kids! Background Talent*.

DO YOU USE ONLINE RESOURCES?
Michelle and the gang use **HOLLYWOOD OS**® *and LA Casting.*

INSIDE SCOOP!
Michelle, formerly of *Idell James* fame, has busted out to start her very own spifftastic (it's a combination of "spiffy" and "fantastic" - uh, just go with it) Extras Casting agency. Rock on!

act four

Primary Contact Info

Main Line:
818-559-2350

E-Mail:
talent@burbankcasting.com

Casting Associates

3304 Sepulveda Blvd., Suite #1
Torrance, CA 90505

Website:
n/a

Email:
n/a

Casting Directors/Staff
Tracy Dixon, Joseph Hicks & David Kramer

Main Line:
310-364-0233

Registration Line:
310-364-0233

Info Line/Hotline:
310-366-5591

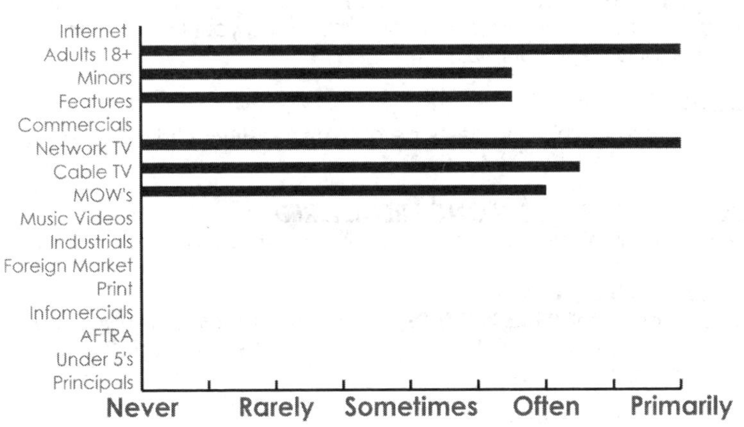

YEAR OPENED

2004

CREDITS INCLUDE

Rocky Balboa, The Breakup, Bottoms Up, The 40 Year-Old Virgin, Hollywood Vice, Skeleton Key (reshoots), *The Wedding Crashers, Alternative Medicine, Carnivale, The Island, Max Havoc: Curse of the Dragon*, various print jobs and lots of fabulous audience work. (Some individual credits from their *BGP* days are included).

Company Fees	SAG Members	AFTRA & Non-Union Talent
Registration Fee:	$0	$0
Photo Fee:	$20	$20
Photo Update Fee:	$0	$0
TOTAL:	***$20***	***$20***

act four

Casting Associates

TYPE OF AGENCY
They primarily cast adults 18+ for feature, print, and TV work, although they do accept minors with the proper entertainment paperwork.

REGISTRATION
Tuesdays and Thursdays from 11:30AM to 12:30PM. Info about Registration is available on the recorded Registration line. Bring your ID and Union cards, wardrobe, and know your sizes.

VISITING
Visiting is groovy – this can be done only by registered talent on Thursdays between 11:30AM -12:30PM.

PROCEDURE TO FOLLOW ONCE REGISTERED
Check the hotline often for work. You will be called if they can use you.

THOUGHTS ON SPECING
Tracy and crew tell **HOLLYWOOD OS**®: "We love specs, but they should be aware that if they do not fit the look and wardrobe of the call they may not be able to get on the call."

ABOUT SAG VOUCHERS
Tracy tells **HOS**®: "We do not give out SAG vouchers. If we are casting something specific and there are no available SAG members, we may cast a Non-Union talent."

CASTING ASSOCIATES APPRECIATES
Tracy tells **HOS**®: "People who make us look good with their professionalism, punctuality, great wardrobe, effort, ability to follow directions, and manners."

CASTING ASSOCIATES PET PEEVES
- People who complain about lack of work.
- People who call the office line without first checking the hotline.
- People who show up to visit on days other than the Visting Day.

DO YOU USE ON-LINE RESOURCES?
Casting Associates makes use of **HOLLYWOOD OS**®, *Now Casting, and LA Casting.*

THE FUTURE OF BACKGROUND CASTING...
Tracy tells **HOS**®: "It is going to get easier and easier as the use of online casting and emailing of pictures increases and becomes more common."

Casting Associates

INSIDE SCOOP!
Prior to starting their very own way-cool Casting Agency, Tracy Dixon and Joseph Hicks worked with *Background Players*. If you're in a snooping mood, check out each of these casting directors by typing in their names on www.imdb.com to peruse more of what they have worked on.

Primary Contact Info
Main/Registration Line: *310-364-0233*
Info/Hotline: *310-366-5591*

act four

Cattle Call Productions

P.O. Box 953
Victorville, CA 92393

Website:
www.cattlecallproductions.com

Email:
casting@cattlecallproductions.com

Casting Directors/Staff
Robert Middlebrooks

Main Line:
760-246-5376

Registration Line:
n/a

Info Line/Hotline:
n/a

YEAR OPENED

2003 (under new ownership)

CREDITS INCLUDE

Location casting for TV and film includes: *Wristcutters, X-Files, C.S.I., Sweet Valley High, The Animal, Circuit,* and commercials for Nintendo, Cadillac, Shakey's Pizza, and many more.

TYPE OF AGENCY

Primarily location casting in the Inland Empire and surrounding areas for talent of all ages. Those under 18 must have the proper entertainment work permit in order to join *Cattle Call*.

Company Fees	SAG Members	AFTRA & Non-Union Talent
Registration Fee:	$20	$20
Photo Fee:	$0	$0
Photo Update Fee:	$0	$0
TOTAL:	***$20***	***$20***

act four

Cattle Call Productions

REGISTRATION

You can get started online. Log on to their website and click on the link that leads you to the registration category (i.e., Adult Male Actor, Adult Female Actor, Under 18 Actor). Print out this page filling out all the appropriate information. BE SURE TO INCLUDE five headshots with your printed out registration form as well as a check or money order for $20. Mail it off to the address provided, then sit tight – you are registered with *Cattle Call Productions*.

PROCEDURE TO FOLLOW ONCE REGISTERED

As mentioned above, sit tight! They ask that background actors not call to check in for work. They will call you if and when a project is coming to the area. Casting notices are also placed on the **HOLLYWOOD OS**® website!

Primary Contact Info

Main Line:
760-246-5376

E-Mail:
cattlecallproduction@msn.com

act four

Central Casting
(a.k.a. Entertainment Partners)
220 South Flower Street
Burbank, CA 91502

Website:
www.centralcasting.org

Email:
n/a

Casting Directors/Staff
(see damn fine chart!)

Main Line:
818-562-2700

Registration Line:
818-562-2755

Recorded Information Lines:
(Non-Union Girls) 818-260-6130
(Non-Union Guys) 818-260-6120
(SAG/AFTRA Girls) 818-260-6110
(SAG/AFTRA Guys) 818-260-6100

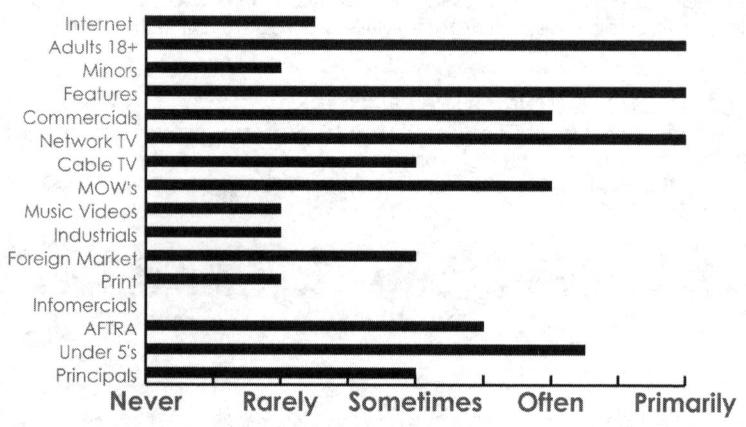

YEAR OPENED
The studios formed *Central* during the Depression in the 1920's.

CREDITS INCLUDE
Click, Night Stalker, Entourage, The Aviator, The O.C., Alias, Without A Trace, C.S.I., Threshold, Cold Case, Joey, ER, Judging Amy, Gilmore Girls, Invasion, Scrubs, Malcolm In The Middle, Will & Grace, My Name Is Earl, and the largest portion of network TV shows.

Company Fees	SAG Members	AFTRA & Non-Union Talent
Registration Fee:	$0	$0
Photo Fee:	$25	$25
Photo Update Fee:	$0	$0
Commissions:	0%	10%*
TOTAL:	***$25*** (cash only)	***$25+ COMMISSIONS*** (cash only)

*COMMISSIONS - Non-Union talent will have 10% deducted from their gross wages when they work on higher-based jobs that do not put the performer below the hourly minimum wage mandated by the California Labor Commission. No commissions taken from SAG & AFTRA talent per Union regulations.

act four

Central Casting
(a.k.a. Entertainment Partners)

TYPE OF AGENCY
For those who have been out of the loop for awhile. . . a few years ago *Central Casting* and *Cenex Casting* MERGED and are now operating under one name: *Central Casting*. Instead of having a Union division (*Central*) and a Non-Union division (*Cenex*) as before, they have 4 TEAMS. They are quite simply named: Teams 1, 2, 3 and 4. The TEAMS are comprised of Casting Directors who cast the Union Jobs and Casting Directors who cast the Non-Union jobs along with a few spiffy assistants to lend those ever-so-helpful hands when needed.

THE TEAMS
Because of the high turnover at *Central* in the last few years, we've been told that the Teams are perpetually in flux – and may change frequently. We've opted just to list the "who's" and you can place them WHERE yourself if and when positions become more permanent.

Central's current CD and Staff list is constantly changing. But as of this printing: Ajay, Adrrena, Ashley, Allen, Alex, Brad, Caitlin, Chris, Chad, Cindy, Doug, Farrah, Franklyn, Gary, Hans, Jeni, Jennifer, Jill, J.J., Julie, Lisa, Mandy, Marc, Mariann, Robert, Sabina, Summer, Tony and Travis.

• Team 1 CDs	• Team 2 CDs	• Team 3 CDs	• Team 4 CDs
SAG & AFTRA	SAG & AFTRA	SAG & AFTRA	SAG & AFTRA
NON-UNION	NON-UNION	NON-UNION	NON-UNION
Central Casting Assistants			

act four

Central Casting
(a.k.a. Entertainment Partners)

SAG REGISTRATION
SAG and AFTRA members may register on Tuesdays and Thursdays between 10:30AM and 11:30AM.

NON-UNION REGISTRATION
Non-Union talent may register on Mondays, Wednesdays and Fridays between 10:30AM and 11:30AM.

You can now download their registration form and complete it before you arrive. Technological advancements rock!

Be sure to know your sizes and be sure to bring:

- Current photo ID and original (non-laminated) Social Security card OR a receipt from the Social Security office OR
- Current photo ID and birth certificate OR current U.S. passport OR current green card.
- Current SAG card and /or your AFTRA Card (or a receipt from SAG or AFTRA) if you are union.
- AND CASH only (get a receipt - for Uncle Sam) for the photo fee – no checks or credit cards!

You Must Show Original Documents
– NO PHOTOCOPIES!

act four

CRAPPY NOTE
Apparently, you may need to re-register every two years - fun times! If you registered with *Central* before 2000 you are surely in trouble! March your happy-self back down to *Central* and re-register. Long lines – FUN TIMES, people! The good news - there is no fee or application charge for the new photo IF you're still in the computer.

PHOTO UPDATES
Photo updates because of change in appearance are at the discretion of the fine folks at *Central*. If they feel you need one, we're told there is no fee! If you want one because you simply don't like your photo, it'll cost you $10.

PROCEDURE TO FOLLOW ONCE REGISTERED
Call the Recorded Line for current casting needs. If you wish to respond to a casting request on the "Recorded Line," specific instructions will be given to you at that time about how to do so. If you are instructed to call a Casting Director directly, be sure to state your name and the first five digits of your Social Security number, and the particular project you are calling about. If you meet the preliminary needs for the job in question, the CD will most likely ask about your availability. Then take the conversation from there – always remembering to keep it short and sweet, people.

Central Casting
(a.k.a. Entertainment Partners)

VISITING
Visiting the Casting Directors at *Central* is allowed on a quarterly basis for registered members only. That's once every three ever-so-exciting months! Come prepared for a short visit – basically say "hi!" and "bye!" and get your keister out the door! They want to keep the line moving. This is when those photo updates we told you about earlier can be taken.

- SAG & AFTRA Talent: — Tuesdays 9AM-10AM
- Non-Union Talent: — Thursdays 9AM-10AM

Last names beginning with:	VISIT:
• A - D	1st Tues. or Thurs. of the month (depending on Union status)
• E - L	2nd Tues. or Thurs. of the month (depending on Union status)
• M - R	3rd Tues. or Thurs. of the month (depending on Union status)
• S - Z	4th Tues. or Thurs. of the month (depending on Union status)

If there is a 5th Tuesday – there is NO VISITING!
This visitation schedule is subject to change. . . lucky for you!

THE PURPOSE OF VISITING
Visiting allows talent to make file changes, drop off headshots, and in theory, it allows time for CASTING DIRECTORS to SCHMOOZE with BACKGROUND talent. This does not mean tea and crumpets, cookies and cola, or lounging around for hours. Do your best minute-or-less schmooze and move along. Additionally, bring your Union card (if applicable) and if you BRING photos (make sure your name, union status, phone number(s) and SS# information is listed on the back of all those you submit), otherwise you will not be allowed to enter "Club Central."

SPECIFICATIONS FOR THE COMMERCIAL BOOK
Central Casting supplies a handout detailing their requirements for their Commercial Book, so check with them for the latest info, but we'll try our best to break it down for you last we knew:

- 6 copies of a 3"x5" color photo, matte finish – NOT glossy!
- DO NOT write your name on back of these photos. INCLUDE your name and Social Security on a separate sheet of paper. Tricky!
- *Central* recommends and prefers that you use their spiffy photographer for their super-spiffy commercial book!

act four

Central Casting
(a.k.a. Entertainment Partners)

DAMN FINE PHONE CHART
Okay, moving on... check out the cool PHONE CHART below that breaks it all down for you! Did we mention... fun times...

Phone Numbers	Girls	Guys
SAG & AFTRA "Recorded Line"	818-260-6110	818-260-6100
SAG & AFTRA Registration Information	818-562-2755 (Press 1)	818-562-2755 (Press 1)
Emergency Number for SAG & AFTRA Talent	818-562-2700	818-562-2700
NON-UNION "Recorded Line"	818-260-6130	818-260-6120
NON-UNION Registration Information	818-562-2755 (Press 2)	818-562-2755 (Press 2)
Emergency Number for Non-Union Talent	818-562-2799	818-562-2799
TALENT Bulletin Board (Press 4 Digit Code & Number)	818-562-2966	
PAYROLL Monday - Friday, 3PM-5PM	818-729-6450	
FAX	818-260-9828	

act four

INSIDE SCOOP!
Yeah, we know, they have classy signs over there at "Club Central," basically saying they do not like **HOLLYWOOD OS**®. A while back we sent them several poster-sized versions of our logo, but apparently they did not want to put them up. Oh well, we should just sit back and be grateful. Hell, they've been so kind to give us free publicity all this time. I guess they really don't like us. Yeah, we understand. We wouldn't like us either if we published that we were taking money from Non-Union background actors, (see Act 3, page 131) forcing them to make less than minimum wage. We'd be perturbed too if we went to court and settled on paying talent back a few million dollars. Yuck. I wouldn't like us either.

Cline Entertainment

P.O. Box 3077
Apple Valley, CA 92307

Website:
www.clineentertainment.com

Email:
clineent@verizon.net

Casting Directors/Staff
Tammy & Robert

Main Line:
760-342-5398

Registration Line:
n/a

Info Line/Hotline:
n/a

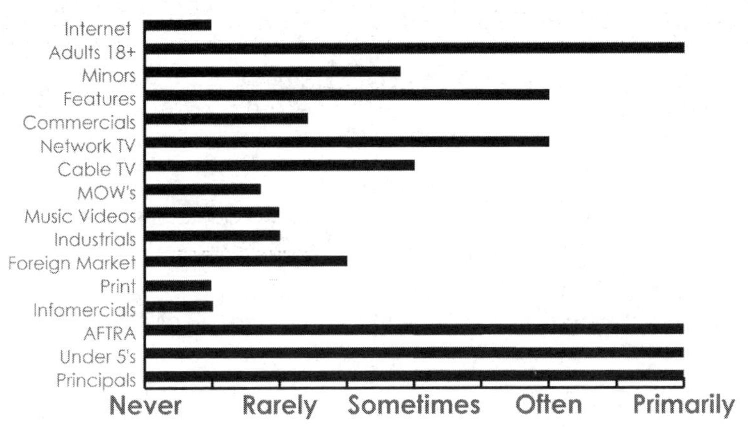

YEAR OPENED

2004

CREDITS INCLUDE

English as a Second Language, The Last Kennedy, Me & You & Everyone We Know, The Groom, National Geographic (Discovery documentary), *When You're Ready to Fall* (Music Video), and commercials for Casino Morongo, VW, and Ford.

TYPE OF AGENCY

Seeks all types of talent, adult and children alike. While Cline does cast the odd project in the LA area, the company's primary focus is work shooting in the "outer areas," such as Palmdale, Lancaster, Big Bear, etc.

Company Fees	SAG Members	AFTRA & Non-Union Talent
Registration Fee:	$0	$0
Photo Fee:	$0	$0
Photo Update Fee:	$0	$0
TOTAL:	***$0***	***$0***

act four

Cline Entertainment

REGISTRATION

Registration is done via their website, so it is of the utmost importance that your photos accurately represent you. Talent MUST supply the following in order to register: Current Snapshot, Sizes/Measurements, Special Abilities, Wardrobe, E-mail, Emergency Phone Number, and SAG info (obviously only if you're SAG).

PROCEDURE TO FOLLOW ONCE REGISTERED

New projects will be posted on www.clineentertainment.com under the "PROJECTS" heading, so check back regularly.

PET PEEVES

Cline tells us that they're none-to-fond of "complainers," folks who call in fishing for work and talent who ask for SAG vouchers.

TAMMY APPRECIATES

Honesty and reliablility, a good attitude, and a phone call if you're running late to set (which hopefully won't happen).

COMPANY PHILOSOPHY

Cline tells us: "We really are trying to make a good name for the background casting in the 'outer areas.' Our goal is to keep the filming in the U.S.A." Excellent!!

act four

Primary Contact Info

Main Line:
760-342-5398

Email:
clineent@verizon.net

Coleman Alexander Casting

12442 Laurel Terrace Drive
Studio City, CA 91604

Website:
www.colemanalexander.com

Email:
info@colemanalexander.com

Casting Directors/Staff
Reasheal, Rae & Carolyn

Main Line:
818-487-8520

Registration Line:
818-487-8520

Info Line/Hotline:
818-487-8520

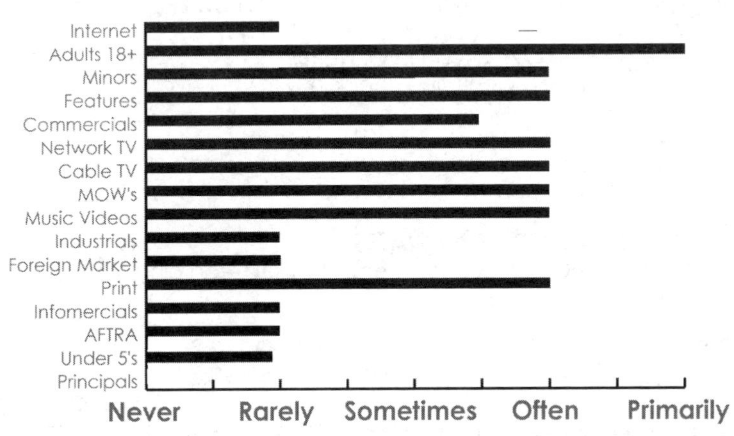

YEAR OPENED
2005

CREDITS INCLUDE
Casting Director Raesheal Monique is formerly of *Bill Dance Casting* and *Monica Cooper Casting*, where she worked on: *Kingdom Come, All About You, Moesha, The Parkers, The Steve Harvey Show* and various videos and commercials.

TYPE OF AGENCY
An extras casting company that deals primarily with Adults 18+ (though minors are welcome), and casts anything and everything from features to print work.

Company Fees	SAG Members	AFTRA & Non-Union Talent
Registration Fee:	$0	$0
Photo Fee:	$0	$0
Photo Update Fee:	$0	$0
TOTAL:	***$0***	***$0***

act four

Coleman Alexander Casting

REGISTRATION
No charge! Call or check their website for specific Registration days and times. Headshots, snapshots, and resumés are welcome, but not required. They are especially on the lookout for upscale men and women, children, unusual types and dancers. Note: Registration is now FREE! Cool.

PROCEDURE TO FOLLOW ONCE REGISTERED
Give them a call once a week and check in with your availability.

PET PEEVES
Raesheal says: "Tardiness, disconnected phone numbers, unnecessary phone calls, disruptive behavior on set, and no-shows!!"

COLEMAN ALEXANDER APPRECIATES
Reliability, professionalism, keeping [them] updated regarding any changes, and, last but not least, a great attitude!

WHAT SERVICES DOES COLEMAN ALEXANDER USE?
They use several different calling services, but would like to remain mum on which ones in particular. For online casting help they use HOLLYWOOD OS®, *Now Casting* and LA Casting.

WHAT IS THEIR POLICY ON SAG VOUCHERS?
Raesheal tells HOS®: "You must be in good standing with us. You must be reliable and responsible, and we only give them out when we have a real need to do so."

act four

HOW DO THEY FEEL ABOUT TALENT WHO SPEC THEIR SETS?
Four words: "Please don't do it."

COMPANY PHILOSOPHY
Coleman Alexander tells us: "Attitude is everything! With humility, patience and persistence, the sky is the limit." You go girl...

Primary Contact Info

Main Line:
818-487-8520

Email:
info@colemanalexander.com

Monica Cooper Casting & Associates

2850 Potomac Ave.
Los Angeles, CA 90016

Website:
www.makeithappenentertainment.com

Email:
monicacoopercasting@comcast.net

Casting Directors/Staff
Monica Cooper & Tai

Main Line:
213-613-1565

Registration Line:
n/a

Info Line/Hotline:
n/a

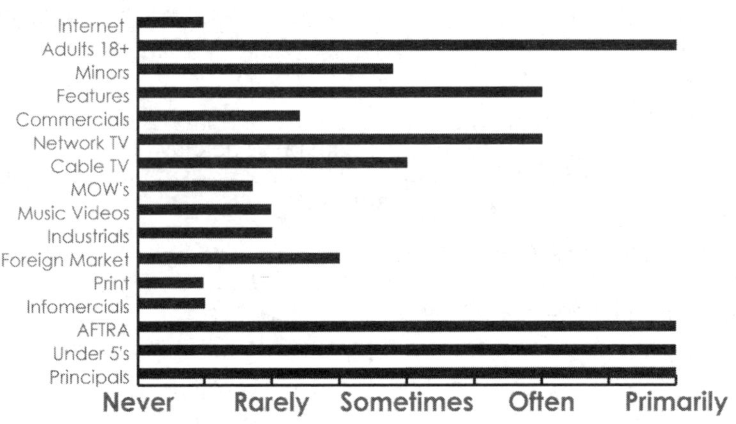

YEAR OPENED
1993

CREDITS INCLUDE
Waist Deep, Mind Games, Sucker Free City, Doggy Fizzle, The Parkers, The Steve Harvey Show, Moesha, A Fare to Remember, The Kirk Franklin Show, The Keenan Ivory Wayans Show, Caught Up, The Players Club, America's Most Wanted, How to be a Player, Gridlock, Sprung, Tales from the Hood, Friday, The Thin Line Between Love and Hate, B.A.P.S., Posse, Sunset Park, Panther, Ned & Stacey, Gregory Hines Project, Cupid, Claude's Crib, etc.

TYPE OF AGENCY
Monica seeks talent all ages and all ethnicities for her casting files.

Company Fees	SAG Members	AFTRA & Non-Union Talent
Registration Fee:	$0	$0
Photo Fee:	$0	$0
Photo Update Fee:	$0	$0
TOTAL:	***$0***	***$0***

act four

Monica Cooper Casting & Associates

REGISTRATION/VISITATION

None, zip, zero. Please NO visiting or drop-offs. Typically open calls are done as needed on a project by project basis.

PROCEDURE TO FOLLOW ONCE REGISTERED

Check in with the **HOLLYWOOD OS®** website. When *Monica Cooper* has a project, they post their casting notices there. Otherwise, sit tight and Monica and her Associates will call you when they have work for you.

PET PEEVES

Monica tells **HOS®**: "Talent who come to set with the wrong wardrobe or not enough wardrobe or those grumpy background actors who have chips on their shoulders!" Also: "Do not call us AFTER your call time to tell us you're running late. Call us BEFORE your call time."

MONICA COOPER APPRECIATES

Monica tells **HOS®**: "I love to see smiles on their faces. Enjoying themselves. A 'thank-you' is always appreciated."

INSIDE SCOOP!

From the mouth of Ms. Monica herself: "I'm not an employment agency or a call-in service. I provide a service to the Production Company and if you fit my current needs, you will be cast. No one is ever thrown by the wayside unless they call sounding ungrateful."

act four

Ms. Cooper founded the *One World Film and Television Society* as well as the annual *Carribean International Film Festival* (originally called the *Bahamas One World Film Festival*) which will take place every November.

"The *Caribbean International Film Festival* is for all independent filmmakers from all around the world," says Cooper, "and what a beautiful place to do it!" The festival looks to unite talented filmmakers from around the globe by showcasing their feature length films, shorts, and documentaries in a relaxing, inspiring environment. There's also a tribute to music videos that will add a Caribbean flair to the event, guest speakers and more. Check out the website: www.caribbeaninternationalfilmfestival.com

"*The One World Film and Television Society* began in January 2003 and is made up of writers, directors, producers, cinematographers, casting directors and newcomers alike, says Cooper".

Primary Contact Info

Email:
monicacoopercasting@comcast.net

Creative Extras Casting

(a.k.a. C.E.C.)
2461 Santa Monica Blvd., Suite 501
Santa Monica, CA 90404

Website:
n/a

Email:
cecasting@yahoo.com

Casting Directors/Staff
Vanessa Portillo

Main Line:
310-391-9041

Registration Line:
310-203-7860

Info Line/Hotline:
310-203-1459

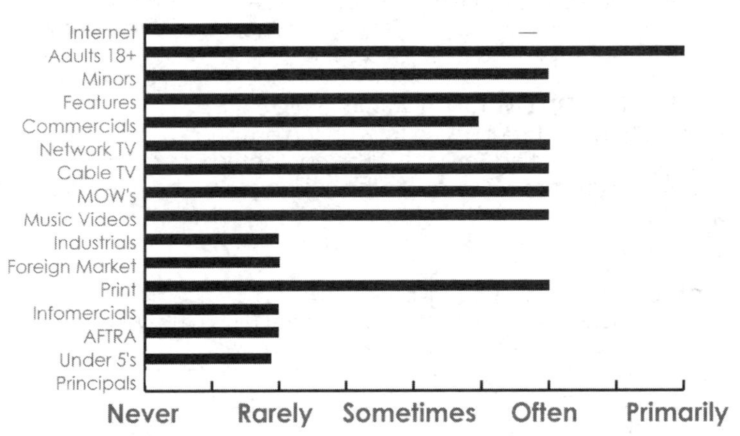

YEAR OPENED

1998

CREDITS INCLUDE

Boston Legal, Emily's Reasons Why Not, Boston Public, VIP, Live From Baghdad, Crocodile Dundee In L.A., The Country Bears, Snitch, The Home, The Homeroom, Mockingbird, Don't Sing, Risk, Sinful Temptation, Hawaiian Gardens, Private Call, The Girl Next Door, music videos and commercials.

TYPE OF AGENCY

Registers adults 18+, so you must be 18 or older and legal to work in the United States! When Vanessa needs minors, she primarily uses *Screen Children's Casting*.

Company Fees	SAG Members	AFTRA & Non-Union Talent
Registration Fee:	$0	$0
Photo Fee:	$0	$0
Photo Update Fee:	$0	$0
TOTAL:	***$0***	***$0***

act four

Creative Extras Casting
(a.k.a. C.E.C.)

REGISTRATION
By mail ONLY! Submit at least one 3"x5" color snapshot and/or a headshot along with all of your GENERAL INFORMATION. Be sure that your photo(s) best represent(s) what you really look like (no airbrushed versions). If you are interested in working in a bathing suit, be sure to submit a bathing suit photo. Include the following information on the back of EACH picture: name, phone #'s, service (if any), height, weight, sizes, Social Security #, Union status (SAG or AFTRA # if applicable), car type and color.

PROCEDURE TO FOLLOW ONCE REGISTERED
Non-Union folks should keep close tabs on the exciting *C.E.C.* hotline – otherwise, you (or your Calling Service) will be contacted when there is work for you. They very rarely put SAG work on the hotline. Do not call the office looking for work!

C.E.C. PET PEEVES
C.E.C. tells **HOS**®: "Cancelling jobs at the last minute, not showing up at all, keeping us on the phone too long. Bad attitudes don't fly with us. Don't argue with A.D.'s or production folks – it will get back to us & we won't use you!" Also "Non-Union people who think joining SAG will get them just as much work and then complaining about not working. I only hire SAG members who have been SAG for years whenever possible."

C.E.C. APPRECIATES
C.E.C. tells **HOS**®: "We always like it when our production companies call us and compliment our background, which happens frequently."

ADVICE FROM C.E.C.
C.E.C. tells **HOS**®: "Don't spend more than $25 to "register" with any company!! We don't charge you for a reason – you should keep the money you make and please, please, please we only want to hire those who have positive attitudes and are willing to give 110% to our production companies."

ABOUT SAG VOUCHERS
C.E.C. tells **HOS**®: "We don't give out SAG vouchers – they must be earned and the talent must be requested by the AD staff specifically... or recalled from set. Sorry, but we can't help you there. There are way too many SAG members and not enough SAG work."

ABOUT SPECING
C.E.C. tells **HOS**®: "As long as they are Non-Union and haven't worked the show recently, we're fine with it, but don't bother to spec if you're SAG."

Creative Extras Casting

(a.k.a. C.E.C.)

DO YOU USE CALLING SERVICES?

C.E.C. tells HOS® that when they rely on a Calling Service, they go the gamut from *Cameo* to *TCA*, from *Networks* to *Kalifornia Kasting* and *Atmosphere* - whomever can help them find the best background actor for the job.

DO YOU USE ON-LINE RESOURCES

The primary online resource *C.E.C.* uses is HOLLYWOOD OS®.

WHAT DO YOU SEE FOR THE FUTURE OF BACKGROUND CASTING?

Before Shannon left, she told HOS®: "I have been hiring background for 12 years now and things have changed so much. I am using Calling Services more often and we now use HOLLYWOOD OS® all the time." Also, "we hope that the required SAG count increases to at least 30 on television shows soon. This would help out tremendously and more TV shows booked through independent agencies would be nice."

INSIDE SCOOP!

C.E.C. says, "Sometimes things are hot and sometimes they're not. Be sure to check the hotline – you never know when a new project will pop up!" They also wanted us to tell you, "a good attitude will get you work in any agency in town. The independent extras casting agencies all talk to each other and if you're causing problems on set, we tell each other! So be on your best behavior at all times."

Primary Contact Info

Main Line:
310-391-9041

Registration Line:
310-203-7860

Info/Hotline:
310-203-1459

E-Mail:
cecasting@yahoo.com

Bill Dance Casting

4605 Lankershim Blvd., Suite 401
North Hollywood, CA 91602

Website:
www.billdancecasting.com

Email:
office_manager@billdancecasting.com

Casting Directors/Staff
Bill Dance, Terence Harris & Sheri Tucker

Main Line:
818-754-6634

Registration Line:
818-725-4209

Info Line/Hotline:
818-771-8450

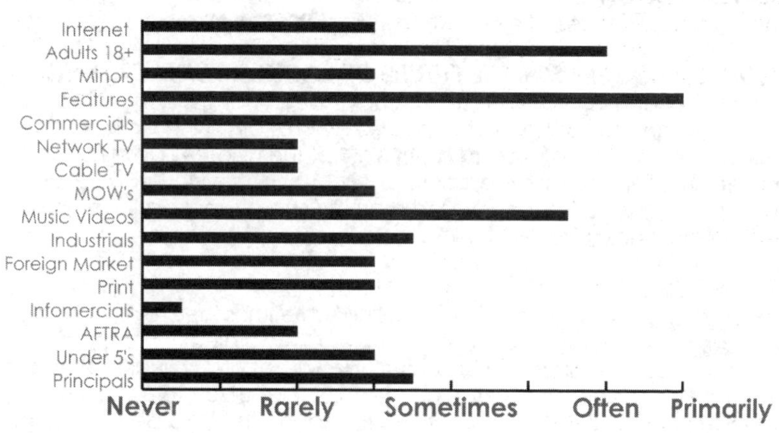

YEAR OPENED

1987

CREDITS INCLUDE

Hostage, Red Eye, Spanglish, Deadwood, Monster House, The Cat In The Hat, Seabiscuit, Legally Blonde 2, A Beautiful Mind, Down With Love, Phone Booth, Life As A House, American Pie 2, 61, Dr. Doolittle II, James Dean: An Invented Life, Tomcats, Confessions Of A Dangerous Mind, How the Grinch Stole Christmas, Snow Falling on Cedars, Boys & Girls, Things You Can Tell Just By Looking At Her, Deuce Bigelow, Fight Club, Stigmata, Ed TV, The Astronaut's Wife, Payback, 8 Millimeter, American History X, The Truman Show, Alien Resurrection, True Vinyl, She's So Lovely, Jerry Maguire, Ed Wood, 8MM, Steel Magnolias, Devil In A Blue Dress, Boys On The Side.*

Company Fees	SAG Members	AFTRA & Non-Union Talent
Registration Fee:	$25	$25
Photo Fee:	$0	$0
Photo Update Fee:	$5	$5
TOTAL:	***$25*** (cash only)	***$25*** (cash only)

act four

Bill Dance Casting

TYPE OF AGENCY
Adults ages 18+. When the clever folks at *Bill Dance Casting* need to cast minors they primarily utilize *Kids! Background, Studio Kids* and *Screen Children's.*

REGISTRATION
Call the Registration Line (818-725-4209) for upcoming days and times. There is a $25 cash Registration/Digital Processing Fee. Come knowing ALL of your sizes– you know the drill. Also, if you are Union – you MUST bring your Union card(s) – or a receipt of current payment from SAG or AFTRA. Orientation takes approximately one hour but you still need to arrive promptly at noon! Don't be tardy! Make a good first impression and it might land you a gig or two worth writing home about!

ABOUT PHOTOS
Your digital photo will be taken at Registration so dress appropriately. MEN should wear a suit and tie and WOMEN should wear a suit or dress upscale. You may also submit your own 3"x5"'s in different looks in addition to a photo of your car (if it is NOT red, white or black). Be sure the following info is on the back of all photos: name, address, phone number(s) and Union status.

COMMERCIAL BOOK
Submit the following: Professional 3/4 wallet-size photos against a white background wearing business attire. Be sure to list the following on the back of all photos taken: Union status, name, phone numbers, wardrobe sizes and SS#. If you have the above described photos, please submit to *Bill Dance Casting*, Attn: Commercial Book.

act four

PROCEDURE TO FOLLOW ONCE REGISTERED
Follow the instructions given to you when you registered. DO NOT call the Main Line to the office directly – you will do yourself more harm than good (we say that a lot, don't we?). If you are registered, you should check the Hotline/Information Line daily. Check the **HOLLYWOOD OS®** website, as many casting notices are often posted there regularly.

Oh, yes... also, it seems that folks like to stop by and visit – don't! There is a sign on the door that says, "Please don't stop in to 'Visit.'" As the folks at *Bill Dance* put it, that sign, "DOES MEAN YOU TOO!" So behave, background. Those who don't follow the rules or decide that the rules do not apply to them are doing themselves more harm than good (there we go again)!!

ABOUT SAG VOUCHERS
BDC tells **HOS®**: "We don't [give them out]. Do the Non-Union extra work. If they are missing a SAG extra, they can hand out vouchers on set in order to make the SAG count."

Bill Dance Casting

TIPS FOR GETTING BOOKED

- Call the Hotline/Information line and Non-Union talent should come to the "Open Calls" with big, wide smiles and lots of photos!
- Check the HOLLYWOOD OS® website – we post casting notices there often!
- When booked, arrive to set early and have the correct wardrobe.
- Send postcards with updated photos if your look changes!

THE BILL DANCE COMPANY PHILOSOPHY

BDC tells HOS®: "Be professional at all times. If you have this quality, casting directors will want to use you. Those who have a negative attitude or feel that Hollywood owes them are putting themselves in a losing battle."

WHAT A BACKGROUND ACTOR IS TO BILL DANCE CASTING

BDC tells HOS®: "Someone who enhances the scene. Background actors are not just bodies on the set. Many times they are featured and upgraded to day players. You just never know." Well, alrighty then!

IF YOU COULD TELL BACKGROUND ACTORS ANYTHING...

Bill Dance says: "Background work could be a launch pad to a career either as an actor or in production. Opportunities don't happen overnight. Keep at it. Eventually the breaks will happen. Also, perfect your craft if you want to act. We often [find new talent at] the theatre. Get in a [theatre] company where you are constantly working on your craft."

Primary Contact Info

Main Line:
818-754-6634

Registration Line:
818-725-4209

Info/Hotline:
818-771-8450

E-Mail:
office_manager@billdancecasting.com

Faceplant Casting

1335 N. La Brea Ave., Suite 2106
Hollywood, CA 90028

Website:
www.faceplantcasting.com

Email:
greg@faceplantcasting.com

Casting Directors/Staff
Greg Cotton

Main Line:
323-908-3607

Registration Line:
n/a

Info Line/Hotline:
n/a

YEAR OPENED
2005

CREDITS INCLUDE
Formerly of *Scottie's Bodies*, Greg has over 400 credits casting videos for everyone from Britney Spears to Snoop Dogg.

TYPE OF AGENCY
Greg is an Independent Casting Director who primarily casts adults for music videos, commercials, and print jobs. He's always looking for attractive 18-28 year old club types.

act four

Company Fees	SAG Members	AFTRA & Non-Union Talent
Registration Fee:	$0	$0
Photo Fee:	$0	$0
Photo Update Fee:	$0	$0
TOTAL:	***$0***	***$0***

Faceplant Casting

REGISTRATION
Registration is currently via email ONLY. Send a photo and your contact info to greg@faceplantcasting.com. All photos will be kept on file in his digital database.

PROCEDURE TO FOLLOW ONCE REGISTERED
If Greg has work for your type, he will contact you. He also looks for talent using *Extras Management*, **HOLLYWOOD OS**®, *Networks, LA Casting, and Actor's* Access.

FACEPLANT'S PET PEEVES
Greg tells **HOS**®: "Being late. Bringing only the shirt on your back. Asking how long the shoot will last."

FACEPLANT APPRECIATES
Greg says: "Being on time and having proper wardrobe."

ABOUT GIVING SAG VOUCHERS
Greg tells **HOS**®: "If I have the chance to... I do (to someone deserving)."

ABOUT SPECING
Greg tells **HOLLYWOOD OS**®: "Fine with me...ya never know!"

COMPANY PHILOSOPHY
Greg says: "Provide the best possible talent for every job! And be loyal to those loyal to me. Casting is 90% about relationships."

act four

IF YOU COULD TELL BACKGROUND ACTORS ANYTHING...
Greg says: "Be honest with yourself. Think before you submit. Be on time always. As CD's, we're the ones who get [EXPLETIVE DELETED] when you are late! It puts our future business with a production company in jeopardy. There are a lot of CD's to choose from."

INSIDE SCOOP!
Please DO NOT call or stop by the office asking for work. Greg is an Independent Casting Director, not an extras casting agency. Rest assured, you will be contacted if he can use you.

Primary Contact Info

Main Line:
323-908-3607

E-Mail:
greg@faceplantcasting.com

Debbie German Casting

2286 E. Carson Street, #141
Long Beach, CA 90807

Website:
n/a

Email:
dgcasting@earthlink.net

Casting Directors/Staff
Debbie & Greg German

Main Line:
n/a

Registration Line:
n/a

Info Line/Hotline:
562-981-3092

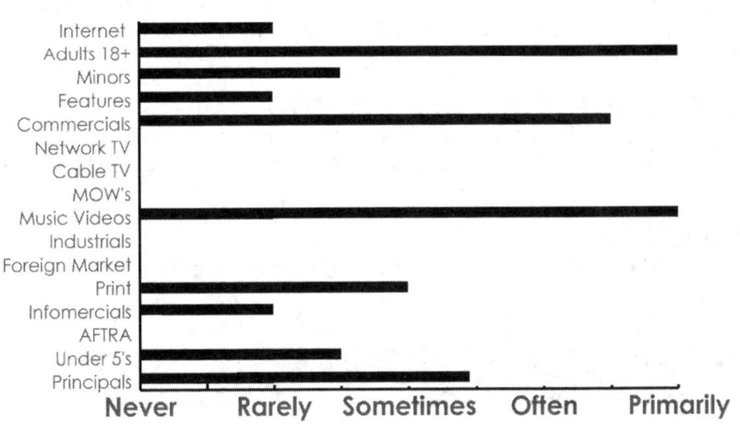

YEAR OPENED
2001

CREDITS INCLUDE
Feature film 42.4%, lots of music videos including Prince, 50 Cent, India.Arie, Snoop Dogg, Mariah Carey, Kelly Rowland, Dave Navarro, Sting, Fatboy Slim, Blink-182, Rachel Ferris, John Mayer, commercials for Honda, Orbit Gum, Slim Beauty Salon, Viceroy watches, and more.

TYPE OF AGENCY
Debbie primarily casts adults of all types for music videos, commercials, and print jobs in addition to principal casting and occasional feature film work.

Company Fees	SAG Members	AFTRA & Non-Union Talent
Registration Fee:	$0	$0
Photo Fee:	$0	$0
Photo Update Fee:	$0	$0
TOTAL:	***$0***	***$0***

act four

Debbie German Casting

REGISTRATION
No real Registration per se. Debbie mostly casts on a project-by-project basis. But you can mail current 3"x5" snapshots (or a headshot) with a resumé (if you have one) and all of your "General Information" – including contact numbers to the address listed. You can also send jpeg images when she has a current project – make sure each jpeg is labeled with your name and contact info. No stuffed or zipped files! She will contact you if there is work for you.

PROCEDURE TO FOLLOW ONCE REGISTERED
Feel free to check the hotline occasionally as projects often come up without much notice. She also places notices regularly on the **HOLLYWOOD OS**® website.

INSIDE SCOOP!
Debbie worked as a Casting Director at *Bill Dance Casting* before venturing out on her own in October of 2001.

Primary Contact Info

Hotline:
562-981-3092

E-Mail:
dgcasting@earthlink.net

Carol Grant Casting

5155 W. Rosecrans Ave., Box 1124
Hawthorne, CA 90250

Website:
www.carolgrantcasting.com

Email:
cgcasting@yahoo.com

Casting Directors/Staff
Carol Grant

Main Line:
n/a

Registration Line:
323-692-7779

Info Line/Hotline:
323-692-7779

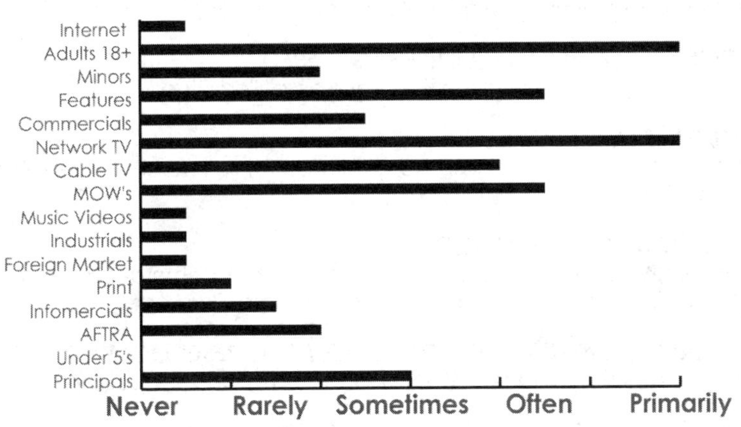

YEAR OPENED
2005

CREDITS INCLUDE
Garfield 2, Honor, What We Do Is Secret, The 3rd Rail, I'm Perfect. While working with both *Casting Associates* and *Background Players*, Carol cast many projects including: *40 Year-Old Virgin, Bottoms Up, The Wedding Crashers, Dodgeball, Havoc, Bad Santa, Hot Chick, Carnivale*, and *Lemony Snicket*.

TYPE OF AGENCY
Carol is an Independent CD who primarily casts Adults 18+ in features and television.

Company Fees	SAG Members	AFTRA & Non-Union Talent
Registration Fee:	$20	$20
Photo Fee:	$0	$0
Photo Update Fee:	$0	$0
TOTAL:	***$20***	***$20***

act four

Carol Grant Casting

REGISTRATION
Specific open calls and periodic registrations will be announced via her Hotline and Website.

PHOTO SUBMISSIONS
You may currently email over photos for consideration.

PROCEDURE TO FOLLOW ONCE REGISTERED
Check the hotline often for work. You will be called if they can use you.

THOUGHTS ON SPECING
Carol tells **HOS**®: "I love specs!" Guess it doesn't get much more straight-forward than that.

CAROL GRANT APPRECIATES
Carol tells **HOS**®: "...a winning attitude. Being on time, camera-ready with ID, a pen, SAG card if you're Union, and appropriate wardrobe."

DO YOU USE CALLING SERVICES OR ON-LINE RESOURCES?
Carol makes use of **HOLLYWOOD OS**®, *Now Casting, and LA Casting.*

IF YOU COULD TELL BACKGROUND ACTORS ANYTHING...
"When the AD's line you up before placing you on set...please perk up, stand tall, and be enthusiastic. I can't believe how many times I've seen talent hide behind a newspaper or a big coat, trying to sleep. Come on, folks! Time to be noticed!"

act four

INSIDE SCOOP!
Carol has worked as a casting director, first with *Background Players*, and, until recently, *Casting Associates*. While Carol has nothing but friendship and respect for her former casters she decided it was time to step out on her own. She wants folks to know that anyone who registered with *Casting Associates* during her tenure there is automatically registered with *Carol Grant Casting* as well.

Primary Contact Info

Hotline:
323-692-7779

E-Mail:
cgcasting@yahoo.com

Christopher Gray Casting

8271 Melrose Avenue, #100
Los Angeles, CA 90046

Website:
www.christophergraycasting.com

Email:
christophergraycas@yahoo.com

Casting Directors/Staff
Christopher Gray

Main Line:
323-658-1530

Registration Line:
n/a

Info Line/Hotline:
323-692-3139

YEAR OPENED

1987

CREDITS INCLUDE

Miami Vice, Barbershop, The Inside, Beauty Shop, Guess Who, Bride and Prejudice, Lackawanna Blues, Collateral, Cellular, Torque, The Path To War, City Of Angels, Heart Of A Champion, Frailty, Men Of Honor, Stuart Little, 15 Minutes, Rules Of Engagement, Why Do Fools Fall In Love?, How Stella Got Her Groove Back.

Company Fees	SAG Members	AFTRA & Non-Union Talent
Registration Fee:	$0	$0
Photo Fee:	$25*	$25*
Photo Update Fee:	$0	$0
Commissions:	0%	0%
TOTAL:	***$25**** (yearly, cash only)	***$25**** (yearly, cash only)

*Denotes mandatory yearly cash only "photo fee."

Christopher Gray Casting

TYPE OF AGENCY

All ages and ethnicities are welcome to register for extra work but children must have current Entertainment work permit and the appropriate Coogan paperwork in order.

REGISTRATION

You can register at *Christopher Gray Casting* daily from 9AM-4PM, but be sure to call first! You must have the proper ID's to prove that you are eligible to work in the United States (i.e., Driver's License, Social Security card, valid US passport, or other legally qualifying I-9 info). *CGC* has an annual fee, which means you must re-register each year if you wish to continue to be considered for work through these casters. Your registration expires one year from the day you sign up with them. The *CGC* casters will call you when your expiration approaches to remind you about the $25 for the upcoming year.

CHRISTOPHER GRAY CASTING APPRECIATES

Punctuality and people who come ready to work with the right wardrobe. Make a good first impression.

PET PEEVES

- People who are late or unprofessional.
- Background who want to or try to leave set before the call is done!

Primary Contact Info

Main Line:
323-658-1530

Info Line:
323-634-2969

Headquarters Casting

400 S. Beverly Drive, Suite 306
Beverly Hills, CA 90212

Website:
www.headquarterscasting.com

Email:
hqctalent@gmail.com

Casting Directors/Staff
Carla Lewis & Natasha

Main Line:
310-556-9006

Registration Line:
310-556-2626

Info Line/Hotline:
310-556-2626

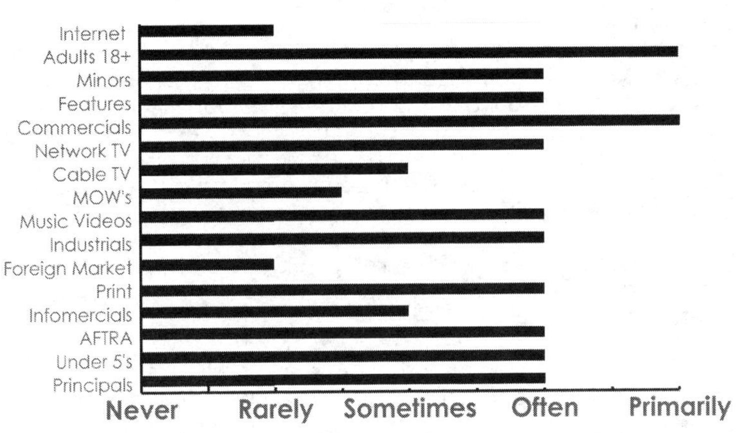

YEAR OPENED
2004

CREDITS INCLUDE
The Fast and the Furious 3, Jimmy Kimmel Live, Talk Show 45, Trust Me, Showbiz Show with David Spade, Jake in Progress, Girls Behaving Badly, All Souls Day, Guilty or Innocent, The Virgin of Juarez, Arc, Hallmark's Rescue, The Hunt for Bin Laden, Horns Of Hattin, Touched, Tournament of Dreams, Last Rites, Lords of Dogtown (reshoots), *Boys Behaving Badly, The Wizard of Gore,* industrials such as *OS6* and *OS7*, print jobs for BMW, Purina, ITW, Juicy Juice, Herbalife, Toyota, Nissan, commercials for Hummer, Verizon, XLA, Chrysler, LG Electronics, Jeep, Rolling Rock, Nike, Gap, Sony, *Bally*'s and music videos for Paula Rubio, No Motiv, Run DMC, Kid Rock, Avenged Sevenfold and Madonna.

Company Fees	SAG Members	AFTRA & Non-Union Talent
Registration Fee:	$0	$0
Photo Fee:	$0	$0
Photo Update Fee:	$0	$0
TOTAL:	***$0***	***$0***

act four

Headquarters Casting

TYPE OF AGENCY
All ages and all ethnicities, including minors who have a current work permit and Coogan bank account are encouraged to submit (kids are needed often). *Headquarters* also casts both principal actors and voice-over talent, in addition to outstanding background talent.

REGISTRATION
Hell yeah, it's FREE, baby! Registration for *Headquarters Casting* is held at the **HOLLYWOOD OS**® office. You should supply your own 3"x5" photo, waist-up, against a white background – obviously this is free, baby! If you are in a jam and do not have a photo of this type, you can have **HOS**® take your photo and have it duplicated and printed in the office for a nominal fee. You can use these photo printouts for ALL the companies that offer FREE REGISTRATION through the **HOS**® office. Make sure your photo represents you (i.e., if you are an upscale senatorial type, dress in a fabulous business suit. If you look like a tattooed rock star, with spiked purple hair, come in being that person. If you look like you could be in high school/college, come in looking as young as possible).

One mo' thing. Please, no headshots for extras casting registration. Sorry, folks, the majority of people simply don't look like their super glamorized, retouched headshot. However, your headshot WILL come in handy when *Headquarters* is casting principal work. Just make sure you have current contact numbers and an up-to-date resumé of sorts on the back.

When you come in, you will need to complete a *Headquarters Casting* hard copy registration card as well as some general paperwork that includes name, phone numbers, calling service (if any), height, weight, sizes, etc. You will also sit your booty down at a computer and type up your information into the **HOLLYWOOD OS**® *Talent Search Engine™*. This is free to do.

Be sure to know your sizes and bring the following information:

- Current photo ID and original (non-laminated) Social Security card OR a receipt from the Social Security office OR
- Current photo ID and birth certificate OR current U.S. passport OR current green card.
- Current SAG card and/or your AFTRA Card (or a receipt from SAG or AFTRA) if you are union.

It is also suggested that you have a car photo on file as well as a snapshot of your pet. Sometimes specific calls come up for both - it can't hurt! On the back of your photos, make sure all pertinent info/contact info is listed.

Headquarters Casting

REGISTRATION FOR MINORS
Bring a current snapshot and your own PHOTOCOPIES of the following:

- Child's current (non-expired) work permit
- Proof of your child's Coogan Account

PROCEDURE TO FOLLOW ONCE REGISTERED
If *Headquarters Casting* has work for your type, they will contact you. Absolutely NO phone calls fishing for work!

PHOTO UPDATES
If your look changes significantly, obtain and complete a new registration card – for free when you supply your own photo.

COMMERCIAL WORK
Headquarters casts commercials pretty often and recommends that you have a quality upscale photo on file for this purpose. There is no specific commercial book, limiting production - everyone can be considered.

VISITING/AUDITIONS
Check the *Headquarters Casting* Registration/Info line or the **HOLLYWOOD OS®** website for dates and times. Auditions are also held periodically for principal actors and voice-over talent to find the best actors for each job. If you have demo reels of either/or, please feel free to leave a copy for review.

GOOD THINGS TO DO
- Return phone calls as promptly as possible, but always LISTEN to the message left for you FIRST! Be professional, folks!
- Be brief and to the point when called requesting availability.
- Show up early to set with a sunny disposition, bring the proper wardrobe and represent *Headquarters* well – it will inevitably lead to more work!
- Always call the confirmation line and the office line if you need to cancel or are running significantly late to set.
- Understand that if a CD is in a casting pinch and is busy casting rush calls, they are under presure to book the gig and they likely won't have time to chit-chat on the phone. Don't be offended. Thanks!

BAD THINGS TO DO
- Calling into *Headquarters Casting* fishing for work is not such a great idea.
- Do not automatically call the CD back on the number shown on your Caller ID – listen to any message and use the number he or she provides!
- DON'T ask needless questions about cast, wrap time, etc. Make it easy for Casting Directors to book you – they will tell you everything you need to know as soon as they know!

Headquarters Casting

BAD THINGS TO DO (cont'd)

- Failing to keep your children's work permits and Coogan Accounts current and/or being unable to provide copies of that paperwork.

DO YOU USE CALLING SERVICES OR ONLINE RESOURCES?

Carla tells **HOS**®: "Yes. I most often use *Cameo* and *Atmosphere* Calling Services, although I don't 'not use' anyone. Online, I post on **HOLLYWOOD OS**®."

INSIDE SCOOP

The best way to say "hi" and drop Carla a line is to send her a postcard which is very much appreciated. She "loves" to receive "updates, hellos and thanks yous." But please refrain from following up online submissions with a phone call. If she can use your type, you will be contacted.

Primary Contact Info

Main Line:
310-556-9006

Registration/Info Line:
310-556-2626

E-Mail:
hqctalent@gmail.com

act four

Innovative Casting Group

12400 Ventura Blvd., Suite 207
Studio City, CA 91604

Website:
www.innovativecasting.tv

Email:
innovativecastinggroup@yahoo.com

Casting Directors/Staff
Dan Shaffer

Main Line:
n/a

Registration Line:
818-843-0072

Info Line/Hotline:
818-843-0045

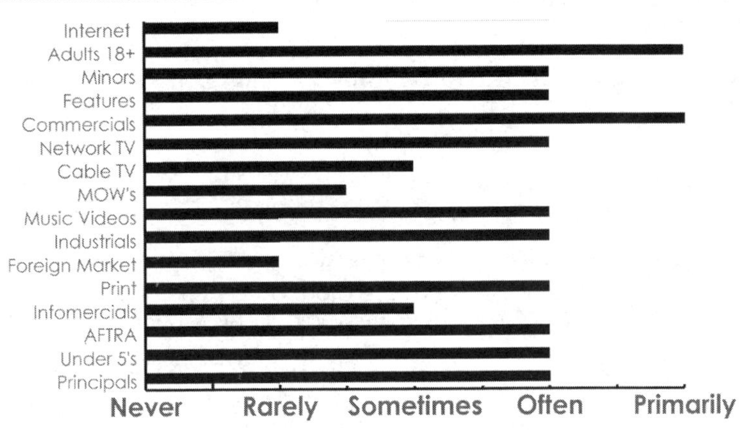

YEAR OPENED

2004

CREDITS INCLUDE

Finish Line (Industrial), *Tonight Show with Jay Leno, South of Pico* (Feature), commercials for a variety of companies including Circuit City, a music video for Carl Henry, as well as promos for ESPN, Jeep/Chrysler, Nissan, F/X, T-Mobile, Spike TV, The Science Channel, and Animal Planet among others.

TYPE OF AGENCY

An extras casting agency which handles adults for commercials, television, industrials, and features.

Company Fees	SAG Members	AFTRA & Non-Union Talent
Registration Fee:	$20	$20
Photo Fee:	$0	$0
Photo Update Fee:	$0	$0
TOTAL:	***$20***	***$20***

act four

Innovative Casting Group

REGISTRATION
They accept headshot submissions by mail and will give you a call if they're looking for your type. They also hold periodic open calls and registrations.

PROCEDURE TO FOLLOW ONCE REGISTERED
Dan will blast out an unexpected flurry of phone calls when he needs to fill specific roles.

INNOVATIVE CASTING GROUP CASTING APPRECIATES
Innovative tells HOS®: "Being on time and having a good attitude. If you're gonna be a pin, stay home, we'll replace you."

PET PEEVES
Not fond of: "Bad attitudes, being late, people who don't listen to direction."

ABOUT SAG VOUCHERS
Dan tells HOS®: "If a person proves to be a good worker, on time, and has a good attitude, we have no problem helping out any way we can."

DO YOU USE CALLING SERVICES OR ON-LINE RESOURCES?
When searching online, *Innovative Casting Group* hunts for talent using HOLLYWOOD OS®, *NowCasting.com* and *LACasting.com*.

ABOUT SPECING
Dan tells HOLLYWOOD OS® he has no problem with it as long as talent doesn't "circle the A.D. like a vulture." Just "let them know you're there, then give them space."

COMPANY PHILOSOPHY
Innovative says: "If you take care of us we'll take care of you (all you gotta do is be on time and in good spirits)."

INSIDE SCOOP!
Dan tells HOS®: "Look, we all know that background work can get to you, but you know what you're getting into before you get there, so show up with a great attitude please! If anything is wrong on set, feel free to call us and we will take care of it. Our goal is to have a small database, so everyone can work as often as possible."

Primary Contact Info

Registration Line:
818-843-0072

Email:
innovativecastinggroup@yahoo.com

Rich King Casting

Crossroads of the World
6671 Sunset Blvd., Suite 1597
Hollywood, CA 90028

Website:
n/a

Email:
n/a

Casting Directors/Staff
Rich King,
Kelly Hunt & Kean Cronin

Main Line:
n/a

Registration Line:
323-993-0186, ext. 301

Info Line/Hotline:
(Boys) 323-634-2556
(Girls) 323-634-2542

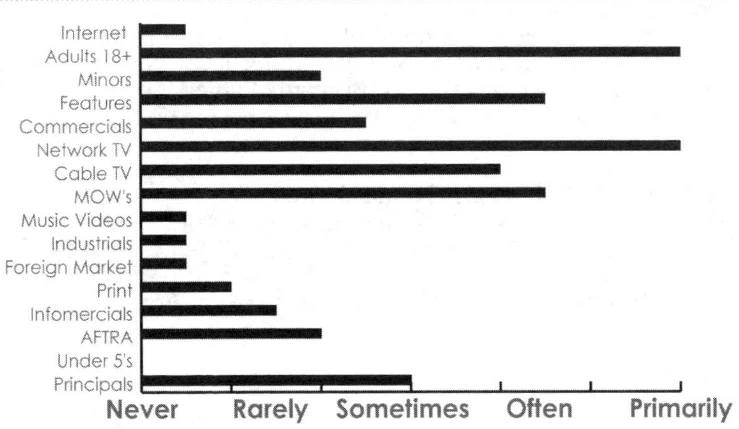

YEAR OPENED

1995

CREDITS INCLUDE

Big Momma's House 2, Lucky You, El Muerto, Black Dawn, Numb3rs, Ocean's 12, Elizabethtown, Herbie Fully Loaded, 2001 Maniacs, Eyes, Zoey 101, On Air Dare, Underclassmen, Shopgirl, Sleepover, Gigli, Kill Bill Volume 1 & 2, Solaris, Laurel Canyon, Duplex, The Shape Of Things, Traffic, Vanilla Sky, Family Man, Ocean's Eleven, Beautiful, The Next Best Thing, Erin Brockovich, Out of Sight, Next Friday, Nurse Betty, The Limey, The Wood, Boogie Nights, Almost Heroes, Volcano, Ghosts of Mississippi, Forrest Gump, Bound, True Lies, Another Day in Paradise, Best Laid Plans, Goodbye, Lover, Eye for an Eye, Reality Bites.

Company Fees	SAG Members	AFTRA & Non-Union Talent
Registration Fee:	$0	$0
Photo Fee:	$15	$15
Photo Update Fee:	$0	$0
TOTAL:	***$15***	***$15***

Rich King Casting

TYPE OF AGENCY
Adults, ages 18 and older for mostly big, big feature films. When casting minors, they primarily use *Studio Kids*.

REGISTRATION
Rich King Casting has registration for new folks every Tuesday 11AM-12:30PM. Be sure to bring all of your "General Information," as well as two photos (headshots and/or 3"x5"'s) and a Stand-In resumé if you have one. When submitting photos include the following information on the back of each photo: name, contact number(s), height, weight and Union affiliation(s). Please submit a MAXIMUM of 2 photos.

PROCEDURE TO FOLLOW ONCE REGISTERED
Call the appropriate hotline for casting needs and details. Rich and gang will often call out to you too, so don't worry – you will be contacted by one of the Casting Directors when there is work for your type. Additionally, feel free to stop by for a visit any 2nd Thursday of the month from 11AM-12PM.

PET PEEVES
Rich tells **HOS**®: "Visiting the office unannounced or outside of regular visitation. Also, calling the office directly fishing for work without first calling the hotline to see what I'm looking for!"

IF YOU HAVE A PROBLEM ON SET
Rich tells **HOS**®: "Call us first and then call SAG or the Labor Board. We look out for our talent and we want you to get your due. We like to know what is going on – sometimes we can help. Please know, it is sometimes embarrassing for us when someone files a claim and we have no idea there was a problem in the first place."

DO YOU USE CALLING SERVICES OR ON-LINE RESOURCES?
Rich uses and places his casting notices on the **HOLLYWOOD OS**® website.

Primary Contact Info

Registration Line:
323-993-0186, ext. 301

Guys' Hotline:
323-634-2556

Girls' Hotline:
323-634-2542

LA Casting Group

Los Angeles Center Studios
Los Angeles, CA 90017

Website:
www.lacgroup.com

Email:
info@lacgroup.com

Casting Directors/Staff
Michael Schiavone

Main Line:
213-534-3888

Registration Line:
n/a

Info Line/Hotline:
n/a

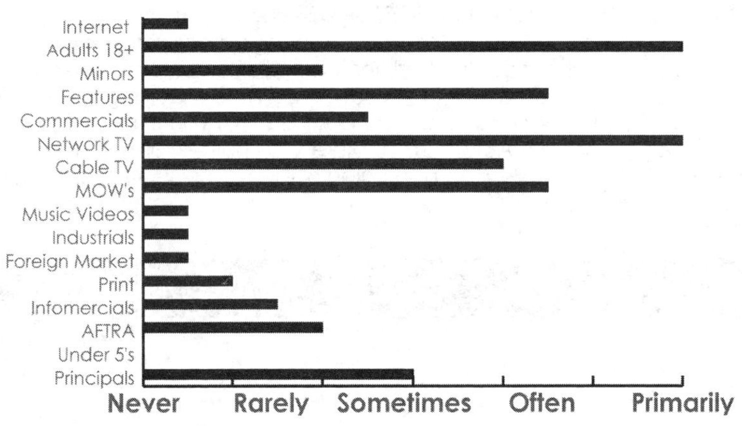

YEAR OPENED
2002

CREDITS INCLUDE
King of the Ants, A Lousy Ten Grand, Devils Knight, Vengeance, Grand Theft Parsons, Igby's Day Off, Paradise Hotel, The Surreal Life, Dog Eat Dog, The Steve Harvey Show and a variety of commercials.

TYPE OF AGENCY
LA Casting Group casts both principals and background talent.

Company Fees	SAG Members	AFTRA & Non-Union Talent
Registration Fee:	$0	$0
Photo Fee:	$0	$20
Website Listing:	$12*	$12*
Photo Update Fee:	$5	$5
TOTAL:	***$12****	***$32****

* According to the website, all talent has the option of having a web page on their website for the yearly fee of $12.00.

act four

LA Casting Group

REGISTRATION
LA Casting Group offers registration through their website. Apparently, an appointment can be made through their website to register in person as well. Quick registration note - security will NOT allow entrance without an appointment. Bummer.

PROCEDURE TO FOLLOW ONCE REGISTERED
According to their website: "Once you are registered with us, we recommend that you call our casting hotlines if you are non-union. These hotlines will have about 50 percent of the productions we are casting weekly. We will also call you directly if we have a booking that you fit into. If you're a member of the Screen Actors Guild, there is no hotline, all union bookings are done by direct calls. (The non-union hotline is for CA residents only)." Whoo-hoo, enough said!

Primary Contact Info

Main Line:
213-534-3888

Email:
info@lacgroup.com

act four

Landsman/Kaye Casting Partners

9002 Collett Avenue
North Hills, CA 91343

Website:
n/a

Email:
hk2sl1@msn.com

Casting Directors/Staff
Stan Landsman, Helene Kaye, Sarah DiGiacomo & Mishey Singer

Main Line:
818-895-7577

Registration Line:
n/a

Info Line/Hotline:
n/a

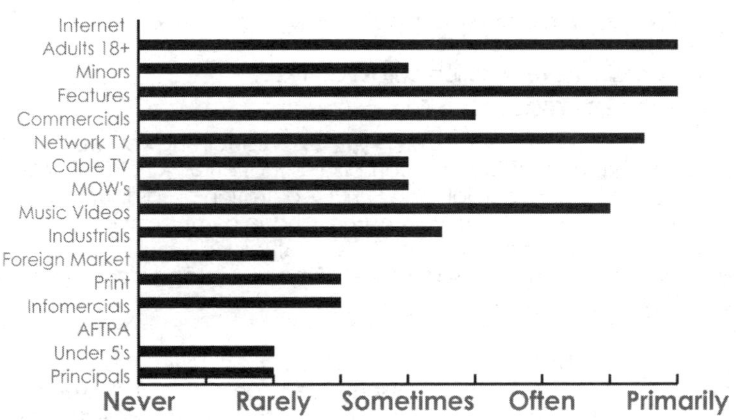

YEAR OPENED
2000

CREDITS INCLUDE
The Music Within, Long Dark Kiss, Lethal Eviction, Demon Hunter, Graveyard, Mortuary, Love Stories From Harvard, Untold Stories from the ER, The Battle of Shaker Heights, 23 Stories from the ER, Hollowmen, Emanuelle, Getting Played, Galaxy Hunter, Love Comes to the Executioner, The Deep End, Beholden, Dancing In The Dark, The Child, Force Of One, Would I Lie To You?, Lost In The U.S.A., The Medicine Show, The Perfect Tenant, High Stakes, Love Games, Ruse as well as music videos and commercials including Univision.

Company Fees	SAG Members	AFTRA & Non-Union Talent
Registration Fee:	$0	$0
Photo Fee:	$0	$0
Photo Update Fee:	$0	$0
TOTAL:	***$0***	***$0***

Landsman/Kaye Casting Partners

TYPE OF AGENCY
SAG and Non-Union background casting for music videos, television and film. They seek all types, ages and ethnicities.

REGISTRATION
The quickest way to register is to obtain and complete the official Registration cards and mail them along with your photos.

You may obtain the registration cards FOR FREE:

- Stop by the HOLLYWOOD OS® office -or-
- Send a 6"x9" or larger SASE to HOLLYWOOD OS® specifying you wish to register with the extras casting companies that offer FREE REGISTRATION. You will then be sent official (and FREE) registration cards for these companies. Please include your name, phone number, Union status and your gender (those named Chris, or others with multi-purpose nomenclatures can confuse matters). Be sure postage is attached to your SASE: six 39¢ stamps!

If you don't have the time to travel to the "hills," as in Beverly, to pick up their official registration card at HOLLYWOOD OS®, you can also mail off a color 3"x5" or headshot with all your General Information to Stan and Helene directly!

PROCEDURE TO FOLLOW ONCE REGISTERED
Once registered, sit tight, beloved background. Stan or Helene will contact you when there is work for you. You don't need to call them. And if you want to say "hello," please call for an appointment before stopping by *Landsman/Kaye Casting Partners*.

LANDSMAN/KAYE CASTING PARTNERS APPRECIATES
They tell HOS®: "A good attitude. We appreciate background actors who are reliable, on time and happy to be working."

PET PEEVES
Stan tells HOS®: "Not showing up on set on time. Not giving us enough time to replace you if a problem occurs. Poor wardrobe choices."

DO YOU USE CALLING SERVICES
The *Landsman/Kaye* casters use *Cameo, Extras Management,* and *Atmosphere* most often for Calling Services.

DO YOU USE ONLINE RESOURCES?
For internet resources Stan and Helene utilize HOLLYWOOD OS®.

Landsman/Kaye Casting Partners

ABOUT SPECING
They tell **HOLLYWOOD OS**®: "We welcome specs, sometimes they can save our [behind]."

WHAT DO YOU SEE FOR THE FUTURE OF BACKGROUND CASTING?
They also tell **HOS**®: "We believe that background casting brings to the project a positive force, a definite role in the success or failure of the film, show or commercial. So communication has got to be there. Connecting with talent has become quicker and more expedient because of cell phones, pagers and e-mail."

COMPANY PHILOSOPHY
Stan tells **HOS**®: "We care about our industry and the people we serve."

INSIDE SCOOP!
They're growing with more and more projects every day! Get registered already!

Primary Contact Info

Main Line:
818-895-7577

E-Mail:
hk2sl1@msn.com

act four

Magic Casting

1660 Cougar Ridge
Buellton, CA 93427

Website:
n/a

Email:
n/a

Casting Directors/Staff
Lee Sonja Kissik,
Stephanie Blake & Joell Kantor

Main Line:
805-688-3702

Registration Line:
n/a

Info Line/Hotline:
n/a

YEAR OPENED
1983

CREDITS INCLUDE
The Greener Mountain, *The Complete Guide To Guys*, music videos for Blink-182, Method of Mayhem, No Doubt and more. Mentos, Goodyear, McDonald's, Chesterfield, Mason's Apparel commercials for Europe, and lots of Korean principal casting for print and commercials.

TYPE OF AGENCY
Magic accepts submissions from both SAG and Non-Union talent for their digital casting files. They handle music videos, print jobs and commercials.

Company Fees	SAG Members	AFTRA & Non-Union Talent
Registration Fee:	$0	$45
Photo Fee:	$10	$0
Photo Update Fee:	$0	$0
TOTAL:	***$10***	***$45***

Magic Casting

REGISTRATION
Call the main line for the latest info or MAIL the following in LETTER FORM:

- How you heard about Magic Casting and the type of work you are interested in doing (EXTRA, PRINCIPAL, COMMERCIAL, PRINT, etc.).
- Your Union status and Union number(s) if applicable.
- Your Social Security number, address and at least two contact numbers (home, pager, service, etc.).
- Date of birth.
- Clothing sizes, measurements, special wardrobe, special abilities, type of auto (make, model, color) and any pet info.
- An 8"x10" and a resumé (if you have them).
- Recent photos (Polaroids, snapshots) with at least 2 different looks. These should be submitted whenever your look changes.
- Processing fees (REQUIRED – check or money order only – no cash).
- A photo of your car for the "Auto File."
- If you have an L.A.P.D. uniform, submit a photo of YOU IN IT for the "L.A.P.D. File."
- Please be sure to include the following on the back of all photos submitted: name, contact #'s and Union status.

ABOUT MINORS
Magic Casting does register minors. When appropriate talent can't be found in their files, they do utilize *Kids! Background*. *Magic* also finds minors through children's agencies via *Breakdown Services*.

PROCEDURE TO FOLLOW ONCE REGISTERED
After you mail your information, WAIT A COUPLE OF WEEKS and call Lee to make sure she has received your packet and information and then you can clarify any questions she may have. You will be contacted when there is work or an audition for you. Lee advises those already registered to "keep at it, be professional and if you live in L.A., get a Calling Service."

WHAT A BACKGROUND ACTOR MEANS TO MAGIC CASTING
"A very important part of the total picture. A film without props, set decorating, wardrobe and background would be a dull and incomplete film. But an extra overacting or improperly wardrobed can stand out and ruin the scene! When working properly, Background Actors enhance the scene but the background should NEVER steal the scene."

Magic Casting

ABOUT SAG VOUCHERS
SAG hopefuls may express their interest in obtaining vouchers "in writing and asking once is plenty." They also tell **HOS**®: "*Magic Casting* – casts! We cast the proper look and talent, SAG vouchers happen on set when an AD or Director deems it necessary."

COMPANY PHILOSOPHY
Magic tells **HOS**®: "Do a good job and the work keeps coming. Word of mouth is the best form of advertising. Be on time, be prepared, have whatever it takes to make you comfy on set and do not make a pest of yourself with the cast or the crew. Everybody has the random 'day or job from hell' but as I said in 1984, "I'll quit when it's not fun anymore" and that was a long time ago – and I'm still casting! You've got to have fun!"

MAGIC APPRECIATES
Magic tells **HOS**®: "A good attitude goes far. Flexibility, promptness, desire to learn. Taking a job for less pay after getting one that paid over scale [basic rate]."

DO YOU USE CALLING SERVICES OR ON-LINE RESOURCES?
They tell **HOS**®: "YES! Calling Services allow my job to become easier and swifter." *Magic* casters utilize *Cameo, Extras Management, Actors Access,* and *Booking Services.*

INSIDE SCOOP!
While *Magic Casting* is located in Santa Barbara County, they still cast lots of projects in Los Angeles. There is a lot of work going on Santa Barbara and Ventura County of late as well. *Magic* points out that background talent are generally treated exceptionally well, and tend to be treated with much more respect because of their distance from the L.A. movie-making machine. *Magic* encourages talent to "keep at it."

act four

Primary Contact Info

Main Line:
805-688-3702

Bill Marinella Casting

(no mailing address)

Website:
www.billmarinellacasting.tv

Email:
n/a

Casting Directors/Staff
Bill Marinella

Main Line:
n/a

Registration Line:
n/a

Info Line/Hotline:
n/a

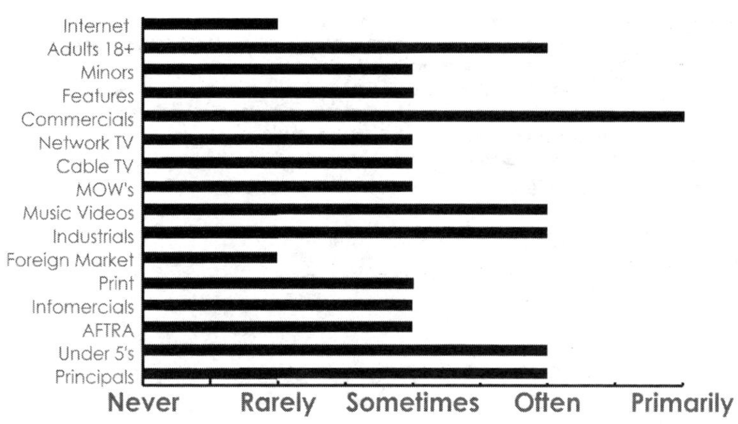

YEAR OPENED

2002

CREDITS INCLUDE

Seven Lives Exposed, Oblivious, Passion Cove, Sexy Urban Legends, The Rundown, Comic Book Villains, TLC's *Junkyard Wars,* Disney industrials, commercials for McDonald's, music videos for Creed, Blink-182, Eminem, etc.

TYPE OF AGENCY

Casts SAG and Non-Union principals and extras for a variety of projects.

INSIDE SCOOP!

Marinella worked as a CD at *Bill Dance Casting* for several years before going independent. He does not have a Registration process, but utilizes HOLLYWOOD OS® to find talent for his projects on a regular basis.

• No Primary Contact Info & No Fee Chart

• This Working Casting Director Does NOT Have Registration

act four

Millennium Casting

2763 West Avenue L, Suite 335
Lancaster, CA 93536

Website:
n/a

Email:
n/a

Casting Directors/Staff
Sherry Aude

Main Line:
n/a

Registration Line:
n/a

Info Line/Hotline:
(SAG) 310-225-5200
(NON-UNION) 310-255-5288

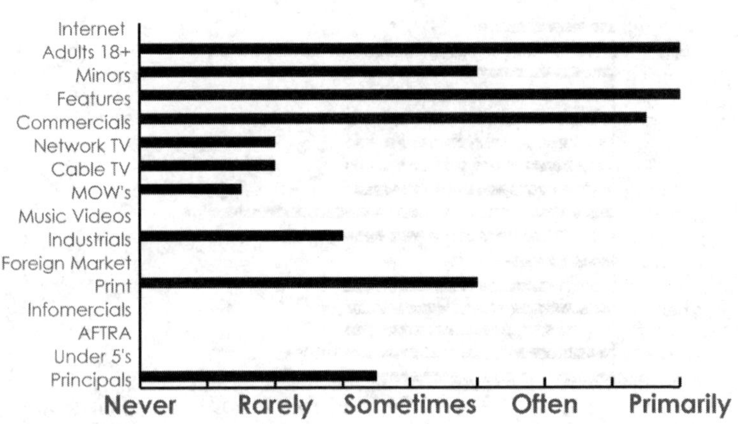

YEAR OPENED
1997

CREDITS INCLUDE
Head to Toe, Hearts Of Summer, and localized, high-desert extras casting for: *Planet Of The Apes, Best Laid Plans, Erin Brockovich* and commercials.

TYPE OF AGENCY
All ages may submit, but the majority of the work is for adults 18+. You should, however, be interested in working in Lancaster as a local hire. If you are not interested in working in Lancaster or the high-desert area, please do not submit unless there is a specific project she is currently casting closer to L.A.

Company Fees	SAG Members	AFTRA & Non-Union Talent
Registration Fee:	$0	$0
Photo Fee:	$0	$0
Photo Update Fee:	$0	$0
TOTAL:	***$0***	***$0***

Millennium Casting

REGISTRATION

Sherry has very specific requirements for those who wish to submit by mail. So please read her requirements carefully and be sure to follow them very, very closely. It is requested that all talent submit the following by mail, if and when she is accepting new talent :

- 4 - 6 Black & White 3"x5"'s **OR** 4 - 6 Color 3"x5"'s – These photos should be approximately waist-up, against a white background. They SHOULD NOT BE family portraits where your head is circled or the rest of the group is cropped out. No prom pictures, or vacation memories. Fun times, but not appropriate for extra work!
- All your GENERAL INFORMATION should be typed or written VERY CLEARLY on the back of EACH photo submitted. This information includes: NAME, PHONE NUMBER(S), UNION STATUS, MEASUREMENTS, etc.
- If you have one, a resumé is also a great idea – but this DOES NOT replace the requirement to have all your GENERAL INFORMATION on the back of each and every photo you submit to *Millennium Casting*.

PROCEDURE TO FOLLOW ONCE REGISTERED

Once registered, you will be contacted – if and when Sherry has anything exciting for you to do (often in the high-desert area)! When casting, Sherry also will post her casting notices on **HOLLYWOOD OS**®.

INSIDE SCOOP!

Sherry tells us that talent often submit any old photo they come across and that just ain't gonna cut it. Poorly scanned printouts from your ten year-old dot matrix printer may not get you booked for work. Be professional – have good photos! Uncle Ed's 35mm camera will work just fine as long as you're against a white wall and it's waist-up.

act four

Primary Contact Info

Info Line/Hotline:
(SAG) 310-225-5200
(NON-UNION) 310-225-5288

Mountain Ash Casting

(a.k.a. Pete Sutton)
P.O. Box 56687
Sherman Oaks, CA 91413

Website:
n/a

Email:
n/a

Casting Directors/Staff
Pete Sutton

Main Line:
818-759-1818

Registration Line:
818-759-1818

Info Line/Hotline:
n/a

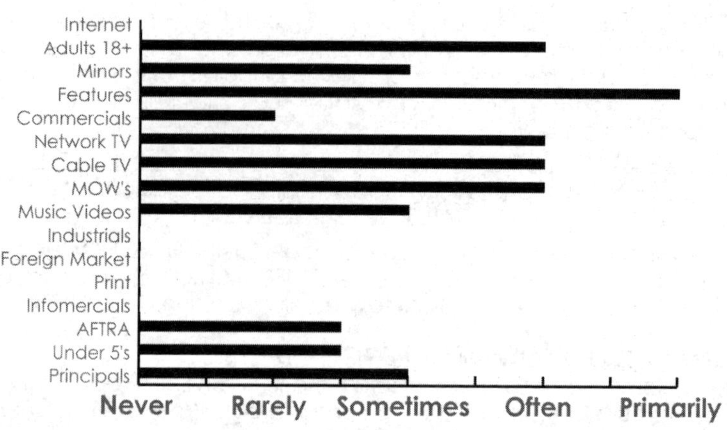

YEAR OPENED
1999

act four

CREDITS INCLUDE
Room 6, Dirty Love, Nip/Tuck, Point Pleasant (pilot), *Frankie and Johnny are Married, Sueño, The Breaks, Rancid, Doggie Fizzle Televizzle, Imaginary Heroes, Patient 14, Evolution, Made, An American Girl, Snoops, To Have and To Hold, The Trial of Old Drum, Durango Kids, Beyond Belief*, reshoots on *Fight Club* and *Detroit Rock City*, and commercials.

TYPE OF AGENCY
Pete accepts all types of talent and all ages – both SAG and Non-Union.

Company Fees	SAG Members	AFTRA & Non-Union Talent
Registration Fee:	$0	$0
Photo Fee:	$0	$0
Photo Update Fee:	$0	$0
TOTAL:	***$0***	***$0***

Mountain Ash Casting
(a.k.a. Pete Sutton)

REGISTRATION
The quickest way to register is to obtain and complete *The Mountain Ash* Official Registration Card .

You may obtain the registration cards FOR FREE:
- Stop by the HOLLYWOOD OS® office -or-
- Send a 6"x9" or larger SASE to HOLLYWOOD OS® specifying you wish to register with the extras casting companies that offer FREE REGISTRATION. You will then be sent official (and FREE) registration cards for different casting companies. Please include your name, phone number, Union status, and your gender (those named Chris, or Shawn, or others with multi-purpose nomenclatures can confuse matters). Be sure postage is attached to your SASE in the form of six 39¢ stamps or its equivalent.

If you don't have the time to travel to the "hills," as in Beverly, to go to HOLLYWOOD OS® (or you don't want/need cards for all the FREE places) you can also mail off a color 3"x5" or headshot with all your "General Information" to Pete himself. But no airbrushed versions please.

ABOUT PHOTOS
Pete tells HOLLYWOOD OS®: "Talent should send me a 3"x5" color photo of themselves, preferably stapled to the card supplied by HOLLYWOOD OS® and/or a resumé with a headshot that actually looks like you. No surprises, please. And just send that. Some of you are sending me dozens of pictures at a time or sending me pictures every other day. What this relays to me is that you like spending money on postage instead of on yourself, i.e., whatever money you have should go toward enhancing your wardrobe, enhancing your quality of life, etc. Don't send "Remember Me?" postcards. Take the money and remember yourself. You deserve it." Essentially, Pete is one of the few CDs who does not like postcard reminders - at least not excessively.

act four

PROCEDURE TO FOLLOW ONCE REGISTERED
Pete will call out to you when he has work for you. He also actively searches for talent on the HOLLYWOOD OS® website.

PETE APPRECIATES
"Good attitudes, good wardrobe and talent who follow directions!"

ABOUT SAG VOUCHERS
Pete shares his words of wisdom with HOS®: "Patience. When it happens, it happens. But only join SAG if you are serious about becoming an actor. There is an overabundance of SAG extras out there. If you do extra work as a way to learn about the business or if you are interested in doing crew work, stay Non-Union. You'll work more often, less money, but more often. The more often you work, the better your chances are of making connections."

Mountain Ash Casting
(a.k.a. Pete Sutton)

ABOUT RESUMÉS
What Pete had to tell HOS® on the subject of resumés: "I highly recommend that BG submit to me professional headshots and resumés ESPECIALLY with their agent's logo on it (with own home phone and pager on it also). Here's why: Oftentimes I am requested to submit photos of BG for featured parts and for interviews with the director. More often than not, they gravitate toward the BG with the most professional resumés (theatre references are a good thing), especially those with AGENCY REPRESENTATION because this telegraphs to the Director that he is dealing with a talented person who can follow directions.

Also, many Directors I have worked with have a soft spot and will oftentimes, especially on features, look for an excuse to throw this person a line. Also, I have seen Directors strike up conversations with these featured BG which is a great opportunity to schmooze and it sure beats waiting tables at *Louise's*. Get my drift? PLUS, you usually get more money doing these featured bits, and WE ALL LIKE MORE MONEY. Okay, now here's where I knock SAG... bring the silent bit back. I'm tired of negotiating on behalf of my background especially when just a few years ago these roles were AUTOMATICALLY ACCORDED a $150 base rate to begin with. End of tirade." Well, then, there you have it, people!

PETE'S PET PEEVES
- People who are late to set or fail to show up altogether.
- People who do not have pagers.
- Outdated phone numbers! Stay current, folks.
- "Remember Me?" postcards – Pete hates them! Don't call, don't mail. ("Spend your $$ on increasing your wardrobe.")
- People who whine about everything.
- People who ask, "When will I be wrapped?" when they just get to set.

Primary Contact Info

Main Line:
818-759-1818

Jeff Olan Casting

14044 Ventura Blvd., Suite 209
Sherman Oaks, CA 91423

Website:
www.jeffolancasting.com

Email:
jeffolancasting@yahoo.com

Casting Directors/Staff
Jeffrey G. Olan, Chef Gil, Whitney & Ryan

Main Line:
818-285-5462

Registration Line:
818-377-4475

Info Line/Hotline:
(SAG) 310-285-3375
(NON-UNION) 310-285-3376

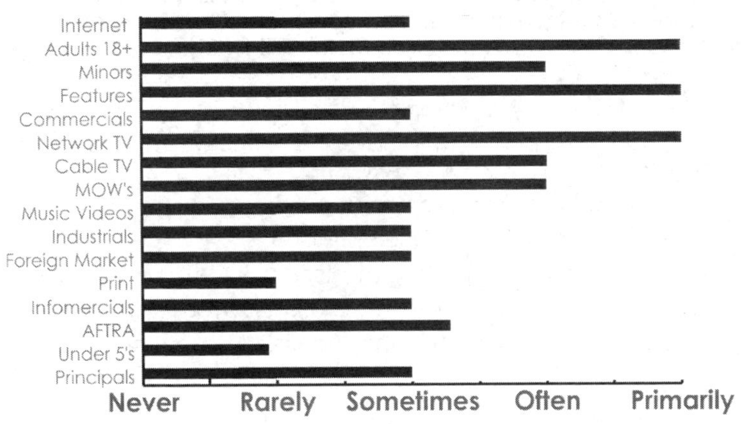

YEAR OPENED

1992 (as *Rainbow Casting*), 2002 (as *Jeff Olan Casting*)

CREDITS INCLUDE

Yours, Mine and Ours, Numbers, Grey's Anatomy, The L-Word, Sleeper Cell, Medium, The Law Firm, Taxi, Cheaper By The Dozen, Stuck On You, Just Married, Me, Myself, & Irene, The Good Girl, Come On Get Happy, Magnolia, My Best Friend's Wedding, Teaching Mrs. Tingle, Jello Shots, Jackie Brown, Chuck & Buck, The Net, Love Stinks, Say It Isn't So, Double Dragon, Springers, Holy Hollywood, Hurly Burly, The Joyriders, Gideon's Web, Basketball, Judas Kiss, Taxi, Rebound, Relative Strangers, Go, Criss Cross, High School High, A Streetcar Named Desire, From Dusk Till Dawn, My So Called Life, Martin, George Of The Jungle, Four Rooms, The Client, and Pulp Fiction.

Company Fees	SAG Members	AFTRA & Non-Union Talent
Registration Fee:	$0	$0
Photo Fee:	$25	$25
Photo Update Fee:	$5	$5
TOTAL:	***$25***	***$25***

act four

Jeff Olan Casting

TYPE OF AGENCY
The *Jeff Olan Casting* casters primarily cast adults, 18+ for big films, TV shows, commercials and all sorts of fun stuff like that.

REGISTRATION
Talent 18+ only, can register Monday-Friday 11AM-2PM. No earlier. If you don't make it by 2PM – please do not knock!! Simply slide any new photos under the door. When you're visiting for the first time and want to register be sure to bring:

- Two forms of ID – muy importanté!! Like a license, state ID, or passport.
- A recent 3"x5" color photo (if you have one – otherwise a Polaroid will be taken of you at NO EXTRA CHARGE).
- Union members bring your Union cards.
- KNOW ALL of your sizes and "General Info."
- A photo of your car (if it's not red, white or black – but you knew that!)
- If you have an L.A.P.D. uniform, a photo of snazzy you in your uniform.
- If you have a reel on VHS or DVD, they'll definitely take a look-see.

ABOUT PHOTOS
Jeff tells **HOLLYWOOD OS**®: "An upscale photo and a casual shot are just fine. Additional photos are good if you have specialty wardrobe (cop, nurse, homeless, rabbi, etc.) not just different color shirts. It helps determine where you can be placed." Be sure to list the following on the back of all photos submitted: full name, all contact #'s (except Calling Service), Union affiliation (including Union #'s) and all of your stats.

PROCEDURE TO FOLLOW ONCE REGISTERED
Call the hotline DAILY/HOURLY (every fourth minute of the day if you're so inclined) to hear invigorating casting notices and needs. Instructions will be given on the hotline for those FITTING the described needs. Do not call the office directly asking for work especially if you don't fit what they've asked for on the hotline – that will do you more harm, we promise! Send a postcard instead! Yeah, those are super-spiffy and cost-efficient to boot! Jeff also places many casting notices regularly on the **HOLLYWOOD OS**® website.

BEST WAYS TO GET WORK
- Call the appropriate hotline and keep your information CURRENT!
- Send postcards. Jeff recently told **HOS**®: "Marketing oneself with these is one of the easiest, quickest, greatest ways to reach one's goals."
- Be EASY to book by listening and following directions.
- Have a pen and paper ready to take down info – don't run to *Rite-Aid* to get these things while a CD is on hold!

Jeff Olan Casting

THE JEFF OLAN CASTING DON'T LIST

- Don't knock on the door when Registration and Visiting is not in progress – you will look silly!
- Don't call on the direct line asking for work.
- Don't CANCEL AT THE LAST MINUTE.
- Don't be late to the set or fail to show up altogether.
- Don't ask a zillion questions (cast, length of the day, etc.) when being booked – get the necessary facts and let the Casting Director continue booking the call.
- Don't be a pest and no begging for work!

AND SOME "REALLY BIG" DONT'S (with explanations even – rock on!)

- Don't call in for a job you do not fit!
  Jeff shares with **HOLLYWOOD OS**®: "What really annoys us is when talent calls in for the wrong thing... like a Caucasian person calling in for an ethnic spot or when a 45 year-old person will call in for something that is listed as 18-to-look-younger. Don't tell us that you can fit the bill and look younger. We do not arbitrarily make up what we need – that comes from the set and usually when they want a specific type... that is what they want. Do not question us on that."
- Don't call in for a job and fail to leave your info!
  Jeff elaborates (again) for **HOLLYWOOD OS**® (& you): "We get annoyed when someone will call in for a job letting us know that they are available and perfect for the job, but they will not leave a name or phone number or they simply leave a first name thinking we are going to know who they are. This is not very professional and you are losing work by not telling us who you are. If you only have one name like, 'Madonna' then that is a different story..."
- DON'T NOT pay attention to this list (Huh? C'mon, kids. Two negatives make a positive!) So, READ the list and FOLLOW the rules/requests!

THE JEFF OLAN CASTING DO LIST

- Do be on time to the SET (preferably 15 minutes early).
- Do be courteous, hassle-free, professional and darn reliable.
- Do be yourself.
- MOST DEFINITELY "folks who smile."
- Do visit, send flyers for plays and send postcards!
- Do have a pager.
- Do have a pen and paper ready when responding to a call!

Jeff Olan Casting

ABOUT GETTING BOOKED

Jeff shares with HOLLYWOOD OS®: "If you are taking extra work seriously, then you should invest in either a beeper or cell phone. We will leave a message for you at your house but we usually will not wait for an extended period of time for you to call us back. The people with cell phones or beepers who respond to our calls immediately will get the jobs first and usually get the better jobs. We enjoy booking talent and the best way to get booked through us is to be professional about it. Have a pen and paper ready when you call us. We do not have time to sit and wait for you to find a pen that writes."

THINGS THAT WILL NOT GET YOU BOOKED

Jeff also tells HOLLYWOOD OS®: "Sending 'zeds' of any sort does not mean that you are registered with us. You still need to register here in person so we can meet you. It is important for us to know those we cast. When you work for *Jeff Olan Casting*, you represent *Jeff Olan Casting* and we want to know the talent representing us." Can we (HOS®) get an "Amen?" Alrighty, we tried though, didn't we?

- Begging, pleading, throwing tantrums, or dispensing sob stories.
- Calling directly for work without checking those oh-so-snazzy *Moviefone*-esque hotlines.
- Arguing with them about any category or about fitting the bill.

ABOUT SAG VOUCHERS

Guess what? Jeff's gonna share with HOS® again: "If you are new talent and come into our office and tell us that you don't want to do Non-Union work, because you want to get your SAG vouchers – FORGET IT! – there are thousands of people who want to get into the Union and like everyone else, you need to pay your dues and put in your time. There are opportunities that come up for SAG vouchers, but you need to be professional about it to even be considered. The best way to get one is show up early on the set and let your set coordinator or AD know that you would appreciate them keeping an eye out for you. If there are any SAG vouchers to give, they will think of you as long as you are not pushy about it." Well said, Jeffrey. Kudos to you!

ABOUT SPECING

Jeff tells HOLLYWOOD OS®: "If you are not disrupting the set OR checking in as someone else – GO FOR IT! You must, however, understand if you can't be used and should leave with NO QUESTIONS ASKED! We don't take responsibility for anyone who is not booked."

ABOUT WORKING FOR JEFF OLAN CASTING

So much sharing. More words from Jeff for HOS® to pass on to you: "The absolute best way to establish a successful working relationship with us, or any agency for that matter, is basically MAKE OUR JOB EASY!"

Jeff Olan Casting

ABOUT WORKING FOR JEFF OLAN CASTING (cont'd)

We love booking people who have a great, positive attitude, who we can rely on, and who cause us as little work as possible! Most background actors don't understand how crazy it gets booking shows and all of the time-consuming tasks involved. You may say, "How difficult could it be?"

Well, just think of how difficult it can be to plan a simple lunch date with a few friends. Now multiply that by 10, 50 or 100 on a day-to-day basis! With that in mind, many background actors also don't know how even the smallest of unnecessary interruptions can turn into a big annoyance. Though the intention may be harmless, those calling to say "Hi" or "Keep me in mind" are keeping us away from casting. Imagine the hundreds of similar calls we receive throughout the course of a single day!

Imagine how a hundred calls to say "Hi" could become counter-productive and become an annoyance. While "Thank-You's" are nice, they, too, have the same unfortunate effect. If you really wish to thank us for a job you enjoyed, simply remain your reliable self. Be dependable, professional and MAKE OUR JOB EASY! This is the truest form of thanks. Keep your questions to a minimum and trust that you will receive your answers if you simply listen and follow instructions. Those who understand this are, by nature, the easiest to book."

DO YOU USE CALLING SERVICES OR ON-LINE RESOURCES?

The *JOC* casters DO NOT typically use Calling Services, but DO use **HOLLYWOOD OS**® as an online casting resource.

INSIDE SCOOP!

Jeff Olan Casting was formerly known as *Rainbow Casting* so don't be confused, fine friends. Jeff's the same cool caster; the company's name has simply changed a few years back.

act four

Primary Contact Info

Main Line:
818-285-5462

Work Line:
(SAG) 310-285-3375
(NON-UNION) 310-285-3376

Email:
jeffolancasting@yahoo.com

On Location Casting

1223 Wilshire Blvd., #409
Santa Monica, CA 90403

Website:
n/a

Email:
n/a

Casting Directors/Staff
Tina Kerr

Main Line:
310-772-8181

Registration Line:
310-229-5332

Info Line/Hotline:
310-284-3549

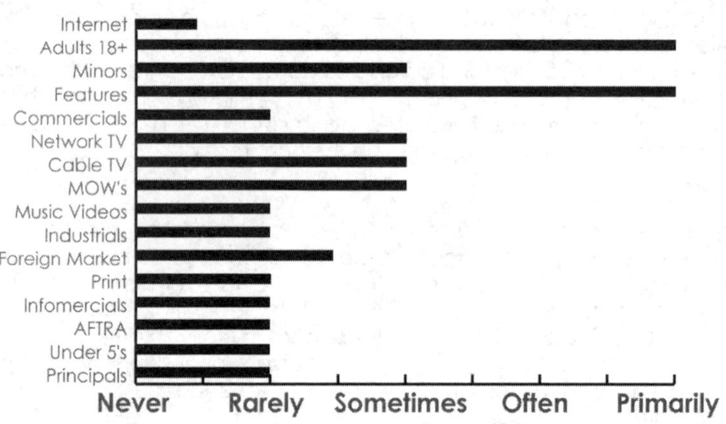

YEAR OPENED

1992

CREDITS INCLUDE

Edmond, Alpha Dog, The Tenants, A Lot Like Love, Coach Carter, Stephen King's Desperation (TV miniseries), *Little Black Book, Soul Plane, Hollywood Homicide, Terminator 3, Pearl Harbor, Bedazzled, Ready to Rumble, Any Given Sunday, Three Kings, Deep Blue Sea, Varsity Blues, Practical Magic, The Waterboy, Titanic, Celtic Pride, Assassins, Ace Ventura: When Nature Calls, Georgia, Disclosure, Free Willy II, Sleepless in Seattle, The Vanishing* and *Running Mates*, as well as principal casting on various UK commercials.

Company Fees	SAG Members	AFTRA & Non-Union Talent
Registration Fee:	$0	$0
Photo Fee:	$15	$15
Photo Update Fee:	$0	$0
TOTAL:	***$15*** (cash only)	***$15*** (cash only)

On Location Casting

TYPE OF AGENCY

They book all types, ethnicities and ages – including minors. Particuarly: upscale adults, 18TLY, beautiful women, African-Americans, and funky characters.

REGISTRATION

Tina tells **HOS**®: "The photo processing fee has changed to $15. This is a one-time only fee and all additional updates are free. The fee is for the digital database and commercial books only. We do still accept mail-in photos at no charge, but they are kept only in our paper files."

She and her staff hold random open calls and open registrations throughout the upcoming year to update the database. Once you are registered, be sure to call in when any important contact info changes – like phone numbers or union status. Call the Registration Line to learn about the next Registration: 310-229-5332.

COMMERCIAL BOOK

The $15 photo fee covers your inclusion in the *On Location* Commercial Book.

PROCEDURE TO FOLLOW ONCE REGISTERED

Tina tells talent through **HOLLYWOOD OS**®: "Background should send postcards concentrating on your best character-look and highlight that aspect. Also, if you are part of a working couple, be willing to work individually."

ABOUT SAG VOUCHERS

Tina tells **HOS**®: "If someone has a specific look/skill that can't be found in our SAG pool, we will gladly give an appropriate Non-Union person a voucher. Also, if a SAG person fails to report for work, we will upgrade a Non-Union person on set. I generally won't upgrade someone who 'demands' a voucher or complains that they deserve it. And don't beg for them!! Good things come to those who wait! Stay Non-Union as long as possible! Although the money/benefits are better as SAG, there is more Non-Union work available. If and when you do join, be sure to stay current on your dues so you will be in good standing."

PET PEEVES

- People who show up with the WRONG WARDROBE and then blame the person who gave them their information.
- Phones that don't accept blocked calls.
- People who play music on their voice mail/answering machine.
- People who cancel at the last minute or don't show up at all.
- People who don't return calls/pages promptly and then complain about a missed booking.

On Location Casting

THE ON LOCATION DO LIST

- Show up when you are booked and be on time!
- Respect others, have a good attitude and always be PROFESSIONAL!

DO YOU USE CALLING SERVICES OR ON-LINE RESOURCES?

When the *OLC* casters look outside of their files for background actors they use *Atmosphere, Networks* and *Cameo.*

COMPANY PHILOSOPHY

Tina tells **HOLLYWOOD OS**®: "Hands-on approach to casting by becoming familiar with each extra as an individual rather than part of the crowd. We get the best results by treating people with courtesy and respect. We go out of our way to make sure our background has a good time on our sets."

IF YOU COULD TELL BACKGROUND ACTORS ANYTHING...

Tina says: "Thanks so much for helping us get where we are today! We couldn't have done such high-profile shows without the support of the background community."

Primary Contact Info

Main Line:
310-772-8181

Registration Line:
310-229-5332

Info/Hotline:
310-284-3549

Ron Polk Casting

P.O. Box 2633
Hollywood, CA 90078

Website:
www.polkcasting.com

Email:
ronpolkcasting@sbcglobal.net

Casting Directors/Staff
Ron Polk

Main Line:
323-860-8766

Registration Line:
n/a

Info Line/Hotline:
n/a

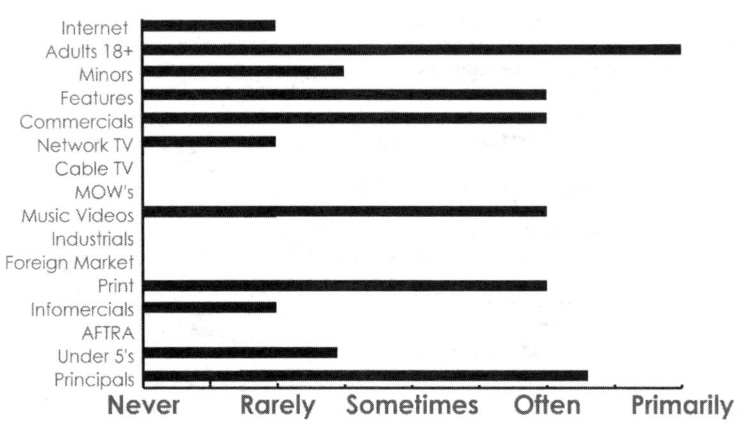

YEAR OPENED

1991

CREDITS INCLUDE

Music videos for Christina Aguilera, Celine Dion, Snoop Dog and Pharell, Arrested Development, and Nate James (U.K.), *Second Time Around* (UPN), commercials for Puma, MTV, Sony Playstation, Mountain Dew, Apple One, and Best Mexico Phone Cards.

TYPE OF AGENCY

An independent CD, Ron previously worked with *Anissa Williams Casting*. You may send hard copies of your photos with all your contact information to the above address. Be sure to write your name on the back of the picture. Check out his website for more details and be sure to check out the HOLLYWOOD OS® website for the cool project he occasionally posts.

- No Primary Contact Info & No Fee Chart

- This Working Casting Director Does NOT Have Registration

act four

Prime Casting

6430 Sunset Blvd., Suite 425
Hollywood, CA 90028

Website:
www.primecasting.com

Email:
primecasting@aol.com

Casting Directors/Staff
Peter, Andrew, Heather, Clare, Miyuki & Meg

Main Line:
323-962-0377

Registration Line:
n/a

Info Line/Hotline:
323-962-5846

YEAR OPENED
1991

act four

CREDITS INCLUDE
Pray For Morning, Akeelah and the Bee, Jane Doe, McBride, Crash Landing, Downtown, Seatfiller, Wild Things II, Salsa From Scratch, Gone But Not Forgotten, Hijacking, Adam & Eve, Imposter, Crossroads, Green Dragon, What Are Friends For?, Who's Your Daddy?, MTV's *Scratch & Burn, America's Dumbest Criminals,* commercials for Macy's, Lexus, L'Oreal, Oscar Meyer, Old Spice, and music videos for Madonna and Depeche Mode.

TYPE OF AGENCY
All ages are accepted – kids included – both SAG and Non-Union.

Company Fees	SAG Members	AFTRA & Non-Union Talent
Registration Fee:	$0	$10
Photo Fee:	$20	$20
Photo Update:	$0	$0
TOTAL:	***$20***	***$30***

Prime Casting

REGISTRATION
Monday - Friday, 11AM-4PM, and dress casually or upscale casual (unless coming in for an audition – this would be a specific look). Bring at least 5 - 10 3"x5" color photos and come knowing all of your "General Information." Registration is cash only. They tell **HOLLYWOOD OS®**: "Many of our projects are cast by picture submissions. Higher paying jobs usually ask for pictures." They suggest you call the hotline daily once registered, but also advise that you DO NOT CALL the office directly. Check out their website for more info.

DIGITAL UPDATES
Prime is digitally updating their files. If you've registered in the past but didn't stop by for the free digital update before January 1st, 2005, you'll have to re-register because your punk tush is no longer in their system.

PRIME CASTING APPRECIATES
Prime tells **HOS®**: "Politeness. Punctuality on set. Being prepared."

PET PEEVES
Prime tells **HOS®**: "Talent who repeatedly call our office line begging for vouchers or work." Heed their words, people, and leave them be!

ABOUT SAG VOUCHERS
Peter tells **HOS®**: "Only when SAG talent can't be found. It is possible." They advise that joining SAG is a good idea "if you plan to move on with your career."

DO YOU USE CALLING SERVICES OR ON-LINE RESOURCES?
When the casters look outside of their files for background actors they use the Calling Services *Networks, Cameo, Extras Management,* and also regularly post casting notices on the **HOLLYWOOD OS®** website. They recognize that "there is a move to utilizing the internet and we are slowly moving to accommodate that change."

act four

Primary Contact Info

Main Line:
323-962-0377

Info/Hotline:
323-962-5846

Payroll:
323-962-0573

E-Mail:
primecasting@aol.com

Tina Real Casting

3108 Fifth Avenue, Suite C
San Diego, CA 92103

Website:
n/a

Email:
n/a

Casting Directors/Staff
Tina Real,
Chris Real & J.K.

Main Line:
619-298-0544

Registration Line:
619-298-1766

Info Line/Hotline:
619-298-1766

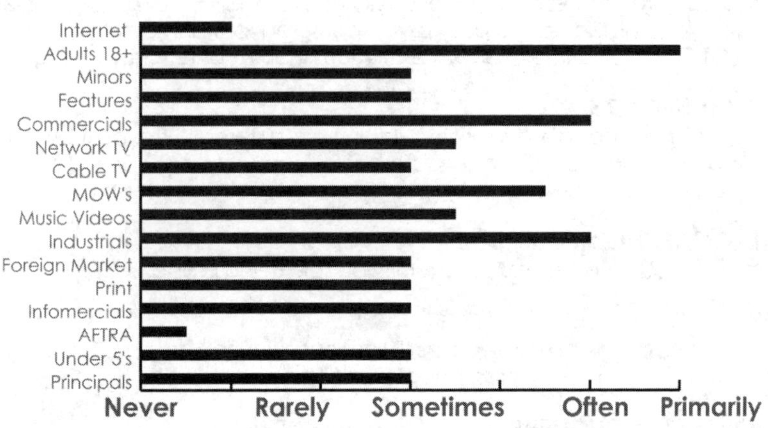

YEAR OPENED
1972

CREDITS INCLUDE
The Month of August, Santa Jr., JAG, The Antwone Fisher Story, Top Gun, Apollo 13, K-9, Mr. Wrong, Heartbreak Ridge, My Blue Heaven, In God We Trust, Raise The Titanic, The Devil & Max Devlin, Hardcore, Mr. Jones, Little Nikita. Some commercials including: Pechanga Casino & Resort, AT&T and Peter Piper Pizza.

TYPE OF AGENCY
These folks typically cast 18+, all shapes, sizes, looks and ethnicities.

Company Fees	SAG & AFTRA Members	Non-Union Talent
Registration Fee:	$0	$25
Photo Fee:	$0	$0
Photo Update:	$0	$0
TOTAL:	***$0***	***$25***

act four

Tina Real Casting

REGISTRATION

Call the Hotline for current Registration info. Always call first! Registration is usually held on Saturdays from 11AM-3PM. Be sure to bring two or three current 8"x10" headshots or composites AND current snapshots along with your resumé (if you have one). ALSO:

- Tina suggests you submit 10 -12 color snapshots with 5-6 different looks (if you have them) in order to be considered for extra work. "Just like you guys do at HOLLYWOOD OS® – they're perfect," (hey, her words, not ours)!
- A photo of your car if it is NOT red, white or black.
- Also bring photocopies of 2 forms of I.D. (such as your driver's license AND your Social Security card) and SAG members must bring their current paid-up SAG card.
- Be sure you have ALL of the information outlined in the "Checklist of General Information" with you when you register. Tina is not a seamstress or any such thing and doesn't wanna measure inseams no matter how cute you are – so know your sizes!

Tina wants photos of you looking natural and SMILING! Be sure to include the following on the back of all photos submitted: name, contact numbers, stats, credits and special abilities.

PROCEDURE TO FOLLOW ONCE REGISTERED

Check the hotline periodically to see if there are any current casting tidbits that apply to you. Additionally, Cool Chick Tina will call you when there is work for you. DO NOT CALL the office asking for work unless you have checked the hotline first! You can always check the HOLLYWOOD OS® website since Tina often places her casting notices there.

INSIDE SCOOP

Random tidbit, so it goes here... Tina Real is so cool that folks who are AFTRA members need not pay a Registration/Photo fee. She thinks a Union is a Union and you paid your dues just like SAG!

Primary Contact Info

Main Line:
619-298-0544

Registration Line:
619-298-1766

Info/Hotline:
619-298-1766

Deedee Ricketts Casting

8205 Santa Monica Blvd., #1-229
West Hollywood, CA 90046

Website:
www.ddcasting.com

Email:
n/a

Casting Directors/Staff
Deedee Ricketts & Stacy

Main Line:
n/a

Registration Line:
n/a

Info Line/Hotline:
n/a

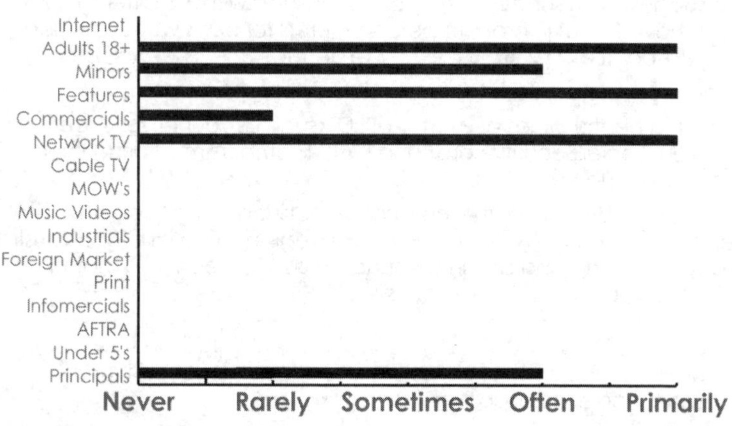

YEAR OPENED

1993

CREDITS INCLUDE

Fast and the Furious 3, Jake in Progress, Lady in the Water, Jarhead, Skeleton Key, Lords of Dogtown, The Village, Thirteen, The Big Bounce, Tears Of The Sun, 8 Mile, Training Day, Bedazzled, Ready To Rumble, Hard Ball, Three Kings, Varsity Blues, Waterboy, Titanic, Any Given Sunday, Without Limits, Northern Exposure, The Hand That Rocks The Cradle, and various print jobs.

Company Fees	SAG Members	AFTRA & Non-Union Talent
Registration Fee:	$0	$0
Photo Fee:	$0	$0
Photo Update Fee:	$0	$0
TOTAL:	***$0***	***$0***

Deedee Ricketts Casting

TYPE OF AGENCY

Deedee is an independent extras Casting Director who generally works out of the production office for the film she is currently casting. She typically casts 18+, all shapes, sizes, and ethnicities, but occasionally books minors and principals as well depending upon the production's needs.

REGISTRATION

Deedee tells **HOS**®: "There is no formal registration. I prefer a new photo for each show I do specific to the needs of that show. A snapshot outside in natural light – of a real person looks great." No airbrushing, people! It's okay to submit photos, but she generally holds an open call before each project and wants a look for *that* show. She advertises open calls and posts her casting notices on on-line services like **HOLLYWOOD OS**®. At one of these spiffy open calls or registrations, talent should bring a current, recent snapshot (remember, she loves natural light!), a resumé if you have one, contact info, sizes and measurements, your Driver's License, and Social Security card.

DEEDEE APPRECIATES

She tells **HOS**®: "Background who are on time, and who come prepared. I appreciate what energy they bring to the scene they work in."

DEEDEE'S PET PEEVES

Deedee tells **HOS**®: "When I see an extra somewhere he shouldn't be. Example: all background are on set and extra 'x' is at base camp. Also, an extra who separates himself from the crowd and manipulates his way in front of the camera."

WHAT DO YOU SEE FOR THE FUTURE OF BACKGROUND CASTING?

Deedee tells **HOS**®: "Having online access to services has opened up a tremendous resource – though I still like to cast location specific. In the future I think there will be complete access online in L.A. and more work on location for authentic 'flavors.' "

IF YOU COULD TELL BACKGROUND ACTORS ANYTHING...

Deedee tells **HOS**®: "I really want to focus my approach (to casting) into bringing the client (or producer) a 'real, natural, unique, off-the-street' look. If you are a strong 'type,' accentuate that and send it in. I want to show producers people they've never seen before. A big reason that big shows shoot out of town (aside from locations) is because of the non-Hollywood faces they get there. I know that they're in L.A. too and I want to see them! Figure out 'who' you are, find your own 'type' or character and go with it. Glossing up blends into a crowd. I hear too many Directors say they "hate L.A. extras... bland, boring-looking." Trust the Casting Director called you because they want you and your look – be yourself. Come to terms with why you are in this business..."

Deedee Ricketts Casting

INSIDE SCOOP:
Deedee gives HOS® some noteworthy random tips: "Put your phone numbers on your headshots or pictures. Give us a way to get in touch with you. Not just your agents."

"You don't have to be a supermodel, be you. All types are needed. Be your type. That's more interesting than pretending to be something or someone else."

"If people make it to an open call, they are my first calls. Always. I honor that. They came to see me, I'm going to give the director the people who want to be a part of [his or her] film." Okay, cool! Enough said!

Primary Contact Info

Website:
www.ddcasting.com

Scottie's Bodies

Casting Directors/Staff
Scottie Lazarus &
Greg Cotton

Website:
www.scottiesbodies.com

TYPE OF AGENCY
Scottie's Bodies was the premiere casting agency for Music Video principals and background for a hell of a long time!

Scottie Lazarus passed away in March of 2005, prematurely ending one of the rockingest careers in casting. We didn't have the heart to remove his page, and decided to leave it in as our own form of tribute.

Although the agency that bears his name has closed (Greg Cotton has gone on to open *Faceplant Casting*), his website remains up, filled with kind words from those who knew and worked with him.

You f@*#ing rocked, dude! No one could ever say that quite like you. Scottie, you will be missed.

Tina Seiler Casting

P.O. Box 2001
Toluca Lake, CA 91610

Website:
n/a

Email:
n/a

Casting Directors/Staff
Tina Seiler

Main Line:
818-628-1953

Registration Line:
n/a

Info Line/Hotline:
n/a

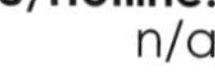

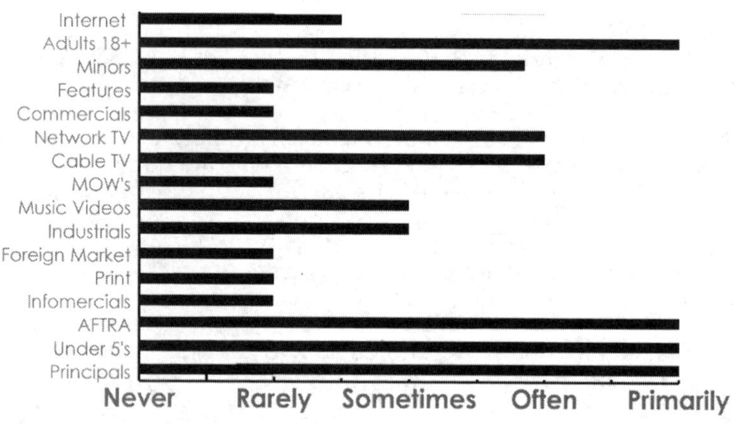

YEAR OPENED

1990

CREDITS INCLUDE

It's A Miracle, Trading Lives, Marriage Proposal, Husband Hunters, 5th Wheel, Anything But Love, The Snow Prince, makeover and Food Network shows such as *BBQ with Bobby Flay,* reenactments for Court TV and Discovery Channel shows such as *Strictly Sex with Dr. Drew.*

TYPE OF AGENCY

Tina is a Casting Director, who sometimes uses extras for the projects she is working on. Most often she does a ton of principal casting.

• No Primary Contact Info & No Fee Chart

• This Working Casting Director Does NOT Have Registration

Smith & Webster-Davis Casting

4924 Balboa Blvd., PMB 431
Encino, CA 91316

Website:
n/a

Email:
n/a

Casting Directors/Staff
Tammy Smith &
Dixie Webster-Davis

Main Line:
n/a

Registration Line:
310-364-3521

Info Line/Hotline:
310-364-3521

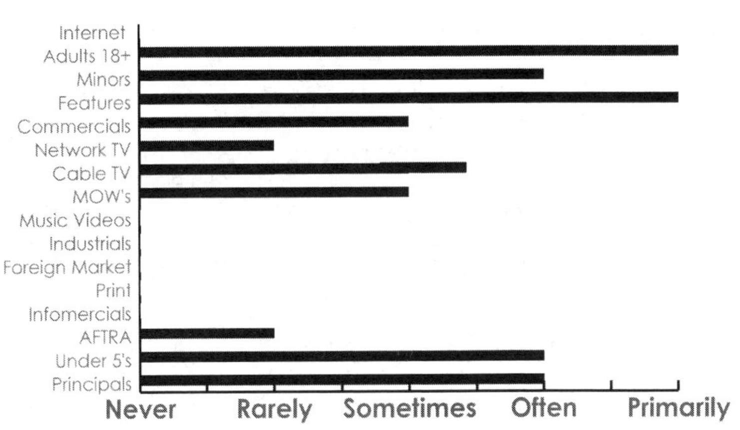

YEAR OPENED

Both Tammy and Dixie had worked as independent Casting Directors for many years prior to forming their partnership in 1999.

CREDITS INCLUDE

Dreamgirls, Jump Shot, Big Love, Thank You For Smoking, American Pie - Band Camp, Good Night and Good Luck, Art School Confidential, Fat Albert, Meet the Fockers, Fun with Dick and Jane, Flight Plan, Ray, Sideways, Christmas With The Kranks, Chumscrubber, Surviving Christmas, Be Cool, Mrs. Harris, The Mogul, Alex & Emma, Spartan, The Kid and I, The Dying Gaul, Kicking and Screaming, Bringing Down The House, Biker Boyz, Matchstick Men, Bruce Almighty, The Whole Ten Yards, Coyote Ugly, Thirteen Days, Men In Black, The Insider, Bulworth, Heat, Bugsy, Windtalkers, Dragonfly, Enough.

Company Fees	SAG Members	AFTRA & Non-Union Talent
Registration Fee:	$0	$0
Photo Fee:	$0	$0
Photo Update Fee:	$0	$0
TOTAL:	***$0***	***$0***

act four

Smith & Webster-Davis Casting

TYPE OF AGENCY
Tammy tells HOLLYWOOD OS®: "Dixie and I take pride in being a very hands-on, smaller casting company that provides a project with personalized, quality extras casting." They primarily cast adults ages 18+.

REGISTRATION
The quickest way to register is to obtain and complete their official Registration Card and mail it along with your photos.

You may obtain the registration cards FOR FREE:

- Stop by the HOLLYWOOD OS® office -or-
- Send a 6"x9" or larger SASE to HOLLYWOOD OS® stating that you wish to register with the extras casting companies that offer FREE REGISTRATION. We will then send you registration cards for those companies. Include your name, phone number, Union status and gender (those named Chris or Bryce, can confuse matters). Be sure postage is attached to your SASE (six 39¢ stamps).

Or you can just wait for one of their frequent open calls they hold when they are casting a new project. Dixie tells HOS®: "We would really like to keep our mail-in registration to only 3"x5" photos on our pink and blue cards available through HOLLYWOOD OS®. Headshots are NOT needed!"

PROCEDURE TO FOLLOW ONCE REGISTERED
If Tammy and Dixie have work for you, they will contact you directly or through your service. Send postcards and call the hotline! LOOK LIKE YOUR PHOTO and include all your "General Info" on the back of each photo submitted, and don't forget to include pet(s) and auto info!

If they give you a direct number to call during a project, it is for use on that project and ONLY that project. It is not for general publication or for calling to check in for work at a later time. Tammy tells HOS®: "It is not only detrimental to our day's work, but more importantly, it is just unnecessary. We don't have that kind of need considering we are only doing one or two specific projects at a time."

THE DON'T LIST

- Don't submit photos that look absolutely NOTHING like you.
- Don't show up on set unprepared or looking wrong!
- Don't say "Keep Me In Mind" when booked on one of their sets. If you are on their set, they obviously do . . . "Keep You In Mind!"
- Don't complain unnecessarily – save it for a legitimate situation.
- Don't bring the wrong or incomplete wardrobe – if you don't have the right stuff, say so!

Smith & Webster-Davis Casting

ABOUT SAG VOUCHERS
Tammy tells **HOS**®: "We do it when it is needed (i.e., the project calls for a type not commonly found in abundance in the SAG pool. We also love giving SAG vouchers to talent who are really pursuing acting and don't just want it so they can be a professional SAG extra."

DO YOU USE CALLING SERVICES OR ON-LINE RESOURCES?
Dixie tells **HOS**®: "Computers are, or should I say, have become such an essential part of casting for us now. We use the **HOLLYWOOD OS**® website which is so great – it is a staple in our everyday casting world. We also use *Cameo* and *Extras Management*'s files... what we see is immediate and that is so helpful. It's very cool."

COMPANY PHILOSOPHY
Their slogan is: "When the look counts." Tammy tells **HOS**®: "We take pride in our films and how we not only cast the right faces every time, but we treat people the way we want to be treated. The latter helps us ensure we get what we need."

IF YOU COULD TELL BACKGROUND ACTORS ANYTHING...
Dixie tells us: "The best thing you can do to perpetuate further work with us, is to have realistic pictures of yourself in our files, a normal attitude and be as low key as possible."

INSIDE SCOOP!
Tammy tell **HOS**®: "PLEASE DO NOT send candy in the mail! Although it is a very nice gesture. 1.) We don't need it. 2.) Sometimes a couple of weeks go by without us picking up the mail and it is stale and very sad candy."

Primary Contact Info

Info/Hotline:
310-364-3521

Starr Entertainment

554 S. San Vincente Blvd., Suite 200
Los Angeles, CA 90048

Website:
www.starrentertainment.net

Email:
hyoon@starrentertainment.net

Casting Directors/Staff
Heirim Yoon & Monisha Brewer

Main Line:
323-653-2900

Registration Line:
n/a

Info Line/Hotline:
n/a

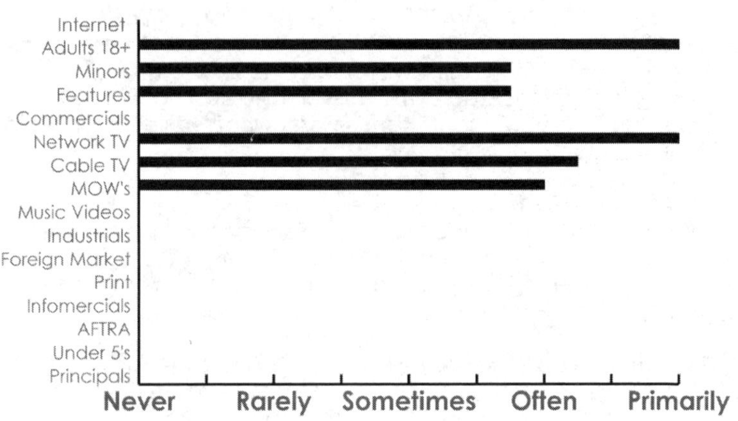

YEAR OPENED
1997

act four

CREDITS INCLUDE
Films including: *Sacred as the Flesh* and *Book of Love,* various print jobs, and music videos for folks like Frankie J, Seal, and Cypress Hill.

TYPE OF AGENCY
Primarily Adults 18+ for commercials, music videos, and print jobs.

SUBMISSION POLICY
They accept photos and resumés by mail. After that, it's just sit and wait - they'll call ya if they need ya. They post the types they are seeking on the HOLLYWOOD OS® website when they have projects.

• No Primary Contact Info & No Fee Chart

• This Working Casting Director Does NOT Have Registration

Stewart & Bernard Casting

(a.k.a. Casting By Teddy & Faye)
P.O. Box 341469
Arleta, CA 91334

Website:
n/a

Email:
n/a

Casting Directors/Staff
Teddy & Faye

Main Line:
323-860-6551

Registration Line:
n/a

Info Line/Hotline:
n/a

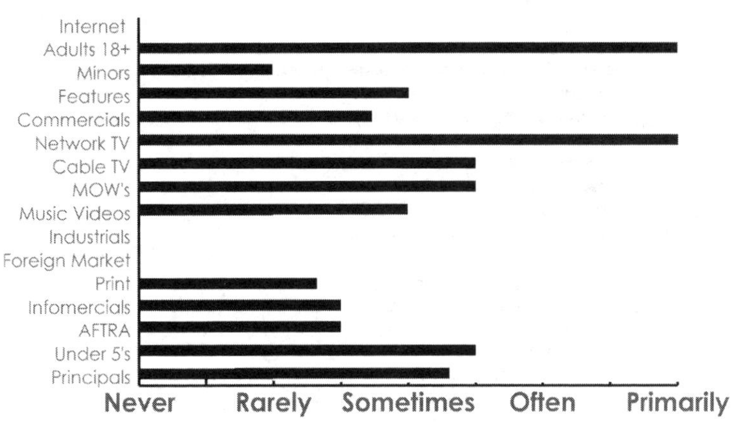

YEAR OPENED

2001 (*formerly Casting By Teddy & Faye*)

CREDITS INCLUDE

The Parkers

TYPE OF AGENCY

These independent, in-house casters generally work from the production office where they're filming at the time.

REGISTRATION

Feel free to submit photos and resumés. They will contact you if there is work you're appropriate for.

Company Fees	SAG Members	AFTRA & Non-Union Talent
Registration Fee:	$0	$0
Photo Fee:	$0	$0
Photo Update Fee:	$0	$0
TOTAL:	***$0***	***$0***

act four

In The Twink Of An Eye Casting
(no mailing address)

Website:
n/a

Email:
n/a

Casting Directors/Staff
Twinkie Byrd & Av Acton

Main Line:
n/a

Registration Line:
n/a

Info Line/Hotline:
n/a

YEAR OPENED
1990

CREDITS INCLUDE
King's Ransom, commercials for Pepsi, Dodge, Sylvania, etc. Music videos for The Game, Lil' Mo, Ying Yang Twins, Madonna, Black Eyed Peas, Notorious B.I.G., Ice Cube, Brandy, Blink-182, Lauryn Hill, Metallica, Christina Aguilera and more.

TYPE OF AGENCY
She's an independent who casts principals and extras of all ages.

SUBMISSION POLICY
No official registration. When Twinkie has work, she regularly places her casting notices on the HOLLYWOOD OS® website.

• No Primary Contact Info & No Fee Chart

• This Working Casting Director Does NOT Have Registration

act four

Blanca Valdez Casting

1001 N. Poinsettia Place
West Hollywood, CA 90046

Website:
www.blancavaldez.com

Email:
info@blancavaldez.com

Casting Directors/Staff
Blanca Valdez

Main Line:
323-876-5700

Registration Line:
n/a

Info Line/Hotline:
n/a

YEAR OPENED
2002

CREDITS INCLUDE
Spanish soap operas and television shows such as *Te Amare En Silencio*, commercials including Miller Beer, Verizon, Best Buy and random print jobs.

TYPE OF AGENCY
An independent CD who casts principals and extras of all ages. Primarily seeks Latino talent for her many projects – speaking español is a plus!

SUBMISSION POLICY
No official registration but you can send pictures with contact numbers and resumé to show your experience. When Blanca has work for background talent, she often places her casting notices on the HOLLYWOOD OS® website.

• No Primary Contact Info & No Fee Chart

• This Working Casting Director Does NOT Have Registration

Debe Waisman Casting

11684 Ventura Blvd., PMB 415
Studio City, CA 91604

Website:
n/a

Email:
debeatwork@earthlink.net *(no photos)*

Casting Directors/Staff
Debe Waisman

Main Line:
818-752-7052

Registration Line:
n/a

Info Line/Hotline:
310-535-1325

YEAR OPENED
1992

CREDITS INCLUDE
Commander in Chief, Single White Female 2, American Fusion, Dirty, Crazy, D-War, Phat Girlz, American Gun, Lucky 13, When Do We Eat?, U-Boat, Grind, Glory Days, L.A. Pool Party, Scorched, Donnie Darko, Teacher's Pet, Chicken Soup for the Soul, Gods and Monsters, Beethoven's III, Even Stevens, Broken Vows, What's Cooking?, Python, Jawbreaker, K-9 II, Michael Jordan: An American Hero, Shiloh, Shiloh II: A Dog's Tale, The Life of the Party, Deterrence, Epoch, Men in White, Richie Rich: A Christmas Wish, Addams Family Reunion, The Cowboy and the Movie Star, Just a Little Harmless Sex, music videos for Alterbridge to Bon Jovi to Insane Clown Posse.

Company Fees	SAG Members	AFTRA & Non-Union Talent
Registration Fee:	$0	$0
Photo Fee:	$0	$0
Photo Update Fee:	$0	$0
TOTAL:	***$0***	***$0***

Debe Waisman Casting

TYPE OF AGENCY

All ages may submit, but the majority of the work is for adults 18+. When Debe needs to book children that she can't find in her own files, she initially calls *Kids! Background*.

REGISTRATION

The quickest way to register is to obtain and complete Debe's official Registration Card and mail it along with your photos.

You may obtain the registration card FOR FREE:

- Stop by the **HOLLYWOOD OS**® office -or-
- Send a 6"x9" or larger SASE to **HOLLYWOOD OS**® specifying you wish to register with the extras casting companies that offer FREE REGISTRATION. You will then be sent official (and FREE) registration cards for the different casting companies. Please include your name, phone number, Union status, and your gender (those named Chris, or Shawn, or others with multi-purpose nomenclatures can confuse matters). Be sure postage is attached to your SASE (six 39¢ stamps). Way cool, right? Sí!

Debe no longer accepts mail or email submissions without her official registration card. Also, if you aren't in a mailing mood, feel free to leave your photos and completed registration card at **HOLLYWOOD OS**® as Debe often swings by to pick them up.

Include a photo of your car (NO red, white or black) – especially if it is unique or classic. If you have an LAPD uniform, submit a photo of you in your uniform for the "LAPD File." Debe recently completed a major overhaul of her files. If you registered before 2003, please stop by the **HOLLYWOOD OS**® office and re-register. Fun!

PROCEDURE TO FOLLOW ONCE REGISTERED

If Debe has work for your type, she will contact you. She regularly places casting notices on the **HOLLYWOOD OS**® website and lists what types she is looking for.

Please understand, when you do get booked, Debe will contact you with your details as soon as she has that information herself. She takes great efforts to make that clear when she is initially booking you. It is a very bad thing to accept another job once you have already been booked – you all should know that! Given Debe's nature, however, if you get some killer job offer, give her a jingle and explain the situation. She is a "human" Casting Director after all.

Debe Waisman Casting

ABOUT PHOTOS

Submitting a variety of pictures (looks) is a good thing. But, if you only have ONE LOOK/PHOTO, then send that one look. All photos submitted should be recent (please indicate the date taken on the back of each photo along with your name, union status and contact #'s). As Debe puts it, "Versatile looks are great! Production people surprisingly don't have much 'vision' and need to see background performers as they want them (i.e., in uniform)."

Debe DOES NOT require a certain format. She told us she did not want talent to be required to take a special photo just for her. It is STILL A GOOD IDEA to submit professional looking photos, considering production often looks through them. What Debe DOES REQUEST is that your photos are CURRENT and REALISTIC (not phony glamour shots!) She tells **HOLLYWOOD OS**®: "I have found that most commercials are very specific and usually producers/directors are NOT looking for the typical, attractive, normal person. I pull specific photos for each job."

ABOUT RESUMÉS

Debe does not require resumés but she does like to see them. "It certainly indicates professionalism but is not critical for easy background crosses! If I am casting Under 5's, I definitely look at resumés. Directors will always look at resumés when I show pictures, even if all they are looking for is a certain look. I think it is a good thing to have – it can't hurt, even for normal background work. It reflects experience."

ABOUT CALLING

Please know Debe REALLY IS QUITE BUSY and does not have extra time to sit around and chat. At the same time, however, she DOES NOT wish to alienate talent and make you feel she is not accessible. Debe tells **HOS**®: "Most people do not call me directly. I do look forward to listening to people's messages on the hotline since I do not have the time to chat during office hours, and I think most people realize this. Of course, feel free to call me directly if you must speak with me or my staff regarding a problem or emergency or cancellation or anything important, but if you are just calling to say "hi" and check for work, please don't. Thanks!" No visiting, but Debe WILL visit you on set – so BEWARE AND BEHAVE!!

DEBE'S DON'T LIST

- Don't call to simply ask:
  - "Did you get the pictures I mailed you?" No offense of course...
- Don't tell Debe you are SAG when in fact you are Non-Union – in hopes of getting a SAG voucher. Bad! Bad! Bad! You will be found out!
- Don't accept a job and then when called with information claim: "I made other plans because I did not hear from you."

Debe Waisman Casting

DEBE'S DON'T LIST (cont'd)

- Don't call begging for work:
  - "I only need one more job until I make my insurance,"
  - "My rent is due so I need to work."
  - "My sister's baby's father's brother needs groceries!"

  (You will be booked if you are right for the job – not because of your hardship or 'special' circumstance!)
- DON'T call Debe and complain that you haven't worked "in a long time" or any variation thereof. Debe tells **HOLLYWOOD OS**®: "I love all of my background actors – but sometimes the productions I'm working for do not call for their specific age, race or type – it's not my decision." She asks that you please remember that – even if you haven't worked in a while.
- When booked for the following day, don't call the office to see if there is info for the next day's shoot when you have already been told you will be contacted. They will call you as soon as they have the info. Be patient!
- Do not cancel at the last minute.

DEBE'S DO LIST

- ALWAYS include the date the photo was taken, your SS#, name, phone # and Union status on the back of each photo you submit.
- If you decide you no longer wish to work as a background performer and are registered – please let Debe know.
- A nice "Thank-You" card or a short note (a sincere one) after working a job you enjoyed goes over pretty well.
- Even if you have a Calling Service, be sure to "officially" register with her – it's FREE, after all!
- Always return phone calls ASAP!
- If you join SAG, let Debe know – she will gladly change your file!
- Make sure your answering machine/ voice mail has a short outgoing message and allows a person to leave a message for longer than 15 seconds!!

ABOUT SAG VOUCHERS

Debe tells **HOS**®: "Basically, please never request a SAG voucher. You may let me know you are interested in receiving SAG vouchers (do so via mail – i.e., postcard), but I would only consider it AFTER you have worked for me many times as Non-Union and you have been super professional. The only other circumstance would be if I can't find someone who is already SAG and right for the part and I know you (Non-Union) would be perfect. You have to be lucky and professional."

Debe Waisman Casting

WHAT A BACKGROUND ACTOR MEANS TO DEBE

Debe tells HOS®: "A very integral part of the creative process since he or she creates the general feel or atmosphere by means of particular wardrobe, specific look and actions." Whoa, spoken like a true Casting Director who does not just cast bodies, but people, real people.

BEST WAYS TO GET WORK FROM DEBE

- Have the look Debe is searching for at the moment.
- Always be on time, be responsible, dependable and bring the correct wardrobe – essentially – BE PROFESSIONAL!
- Debe places casting notices on the HOLLYWOOD OS® website - be sure to check them out!
- Debe tells HOS®: "Send a postcard with your latest look. They are much more convenient than receiving a "hello" call at an inopportune time."

DEBE'S THOUGHTS ON SPECS

"I always tell my coordinator or the AD never to take on a SAG spec. This protects the production company from a Station 12 situation where the supposed SAG extra might be behind on his/her dues. If the coordinator or AD calls me and I am able to 'clear' that person, only then can a SAG member get on my show by 'specing' – but this rarely happens. Usually, SAG players show up when they have been booked."

As far as Non-Union 'SPECING,' you MUST:

- Have all the CORRECT WARDROBE, have no time restraints, be AVAILABLE the next day if recalled, be honest (don't say you were booked, don't say you are replacing someone, don't claim to be a rush call.)

"Specs must understand that just because someone got there first, does NOT mean they are entitled to get on the show first! I might be seeking a very specific look, age, ethnicity, etc., and will need to replace the no-show with the same type. "Specing" is always a risk, but if you are willing to drive somewhere, have the right attitude, right wardrobe, and won't ask for a SAG voucher, then fine, go ahead. The Casting Director always wants to be sure that there are the requested number of extras on the set."

WHY DEBE OFFERS FREE REGISTRATION

Debe tells HOS®: "The desire to put people to work for the right reason – because he/she was right for the part and not because he/she paid me a certain chunk o' change. I do not wish to make money by taking money away from extras, but from the production company that pays me to cast their project."

Debe Waisman Casting

HOW DEBE GOT STARTED

Debe tells **HOS**®: "I have a degree in Theater from the University of Texas in Austin but I didn't want to pursue acting even though I love the art of acting. I loved being on the set of an *AT&T* commercial in Texas as the Casting Director's assistant, and moved to L.A. to pursue casting. I met different producers and directors and started casting AFI films. I fell into doing extras casting after working for a particular extras casting company that charged extras a lot of money to register. I left, knowing I enjoyed extras casting immensely and not wanting to take any money from extras! So I did what I wanted to do..."

COMPANY PHILOSOPHY

Debe tells **HOS**®: "Work hard, have fun, smile, be a pro and don't charge anyone!" Enough said...

Primary Contact Info

Main Line:
818-752-7052

Info/Hotline:
310-535-1325

E-Mail:
debeatwork@earthlink.net

act four

Renita Whited Casting

c/o Casting Studios
200 South La Brea Blvd., 2nd Floor
Los Angeles, CA 90036

Website:
www.renitawhitedcasting.com

Email:
renitaw@renitawhitedcasting.com

Casting Directors/Staff
Renita Whited

Main Line:
n/a

Registration Line:
n/a

Info Line/Hotline:
n/a

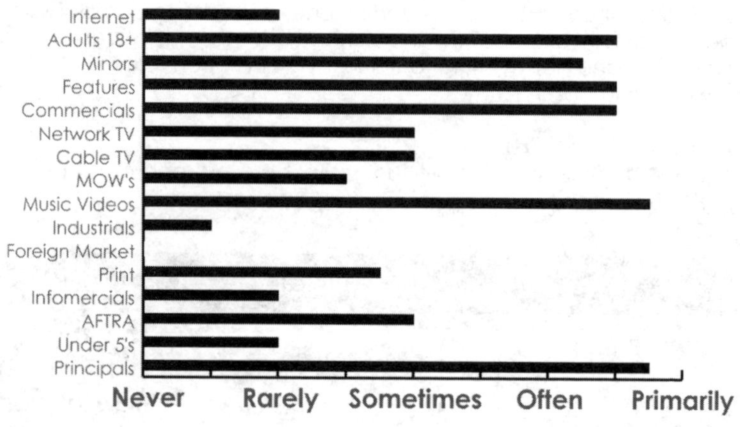

YEAR OPENED
1999

CREDITS INCLUDE
Music videos for Clay Aiken, Ruben Studdard, Madonna, Kid Rock, Stevie B, Hanson, Britney Spears, Def Leppard, Ol' Dirty Bastard, Moby and many more, as well as commercials for Pepsi, IKEA, Islands, Sears, Mattel, KFC, Jolly Rancher, Reebok, 1-800-Call-ATT, and many more. Feature films include *Spun, Sex and a Girl,* and *Roomies* along with various television, print and industrial credits to boot!

TYPE OF AGENCY
Renita is not an extras casting agency – she is a principal Casting Director who only casts background talent when it is called upon for a particular job. She looks for all ages, types and ethnicities depending upon the project.

• No Primary Contact Info & No Fee Chart

• This Working Casting Director Does NOT Have Registration

act four

Renita Whited Casting

SUBMISSION POLICY

No darn formal registration. Again, Renita is a PRINCIPAL Casting Director who only OCCASIONALLY casts extras. She places her casting notices on the HOLLYWOOD OS® website when seeking background talent. Sending postcards is a great way of reminding Renita that you are available for work.

DO NOT call her office and ask to register! You will be contacted IF and when there is work for you – there is NO NEED for you to call the office looking for work EVER! And sorry, folks... there's absolutely no visiting here!

PHOTO SUBMISSIONS

Renita accepts photo submissions BY MAIL from those interested in working on a project by project basis only. But, please remember she is not set up to keep photos at her office long-term. Be sure your photos look like you. "It does neither of us any good if you don't look like your photo!"

PET PEEVES

- Actors who book but then fail to show up – be it a job or an audition.
- Don't expect a job and start complaining after six hours that you want to go home!
- DO NOT call her office and ask to register!

WHAT RENITA APPRECIATES MOST

- A pleasant phone manner and quick responses to her calls.
- Actors who are willing to work for both the big bucks and the small bucks!
- Promptness.
- Actors with fax machines.

MARKETING TIPS

Renita tells HOS®: "I like receiving postcards as long as people understand that this DOES NOT register them with me. I don't register people, period. And they DO NOT follow up with a phone call."

INSIDE SCOOP

Renita tosses ya the following bon mot (thank you to our 7th grade French teacher) regarding principal casting: "We want you to book the job! So, PLEASE, KNOW that! Prepare the way you've been asked to prepare, walk in, do your very best, and know that I am there (either in the room with you or watching you on a TV monitor in my office) hoping, praying and wanting you to completely "ROCK IT!" You and I are always on the same team!"

Anissa Williams Casting

6605 Hollywood Blvd., #218
Hollywood, CA 90028

Website:
n/a

Email:
awilliamscasting@yahoo.com

Casting Directors/Staff
Anissa Williams, Yolanda Hunt, Marlon, Michelle & Venus

Main Line:
n/a

Registration Line:
n/a

Info Line/Hotline:
n/a

YEAR OPENED

1995

act four

CREDITS INCLUDE

Method and Red, Gang Tapes, The Breaks, music videos for Jennifer Lopez, No Doubt, Janet Jackson, Eminem, Dr. Dre, Missy Elliot, Shakira, Life House, Stacey Orrico and many more.

TYPE OF AGENCY

Anissa is not an extras casting agency – she is a full-service Casting Director who casts background talent when it is called upon for a particular job. She specializes in music videos and commercials. She looks for all ages, types and ethnicities depending upon the project she is currently casting.

• No Primary Contact Info & No Fee Chart

• This Working Casting Director Does NOT Have Registration

Anissa Williams Casting & Associates

SUBMISSION POLICY
There is no formal registration, however, Anissa accepts photo submissions from those interested in working on a project-by-project basis only. She is not set up to keep photos at her office long-term, so submit every few months. Be sure your photos look like you – the REAL you, not the airbrushed, "if I lost 35 lbs. pose" you might ideally want to look like!

Anissa and her staff no longer have a hotline, but they do use the **HOLLYWOOD OS**® website to post notices for specific types they are seeking!

MARKETING TIPS
Anissa tells **HOS**®: "I've always enjoyed postcards as a quick reminder about someone or something (a play, a showcase, etc.). A postcard is like a flash-card to jolt you, the actor, into the memory of each and every casting director."

INSIDE SCOOP!
Anissa tells **HOLLYWOOD OS**®: "We are a full-service casting company to help producers and directors find a wide variety of talent they need for their projects. We're always looking for cool, trendy, "real" people, hot models – male and female, skateboarders, and people with special talents, i.e., fire-eating, contortionists, etc."

act four

Xtraz Casting

P.O. Box 4145
Valley Village, CA 91617

Website:
n/a

Email:
n/a

Casting Directors/Staff
Tom Thacker

Main Line:
818-781-0066

Registration Line:
n/a

Info Line/Hotline:
n/a

YEAR OPENED

1993

CREDITS INCLUDE

Adventures of Johnny Tao, The Crush, Mostly True Stories, Pacific Blue, Children of The Corn 666, Innocent Victims, Day The World Ended, How To Make A Monster, War of The Colossal Beast, Teenage Caveman, The Spider, Tales From The Crypt: Demon Knight, and Japanese commercials.

act four

TYPE OF AGENCY

Primarily casts talent 18 and older for cable television shows, MOWs, and various foreign market projects, industrials and print jobs. Tom casts both principals and extras.

Company Fees	SAG Members	AFTRA & Non-Union Talent
Registration Fee:	$0	$0
Photo Fee:	$0	$0
Photo Update Fee:	$0	$0
TOTAL:	***$0***	***$0***

Xtraz Casting

REGISTRATION
The quickest way to register is to obtain and complete Tom's official Registration Card and mail it along with your photos.

You may obtain the registration cards FOR FREE:

- Stop by the **HOLLYWOOD OS**® office -or-
- Send a 6"x9" or larger SASE to **HOLLYWOOD OS**® specifying you wish to register with the extras casting companies that offer FREE REGISTRATION. You will then be sent official (and FREE) registration cards for these casting companies. Please include your name, phone number, Union status and your gender (those named Chris, or Shawn, or others with multi-purpose nomenclatures can confuse matters). Be sure postage is attached to your SASE (six 39¢ stamps). Way cool, right?

This doesn't work for ya? Okay. You can mail 3"x5"'s and/or 8"x10"'s (Tom LIKES 8"x10"'s) with your resumé and all your General Information. Include a bathing suit picture if you want to be considered for bathing suit work. Tom also accepts car photos for his auto file.

Once you have submitted by mail, consider yourself registered.

PROCEDURE TO FOLLOW ONCE REGISTERED
You may then check in with your availability every so often, but he has projects very sporadically. Check the **HOLLYWOOD OS**® website periodically for his most up-to-the-minute casting notices.

act four

Primary Contact Info
Main Line: *818-781-0066*

soap operas

Finding work on the world famous in-house shows...

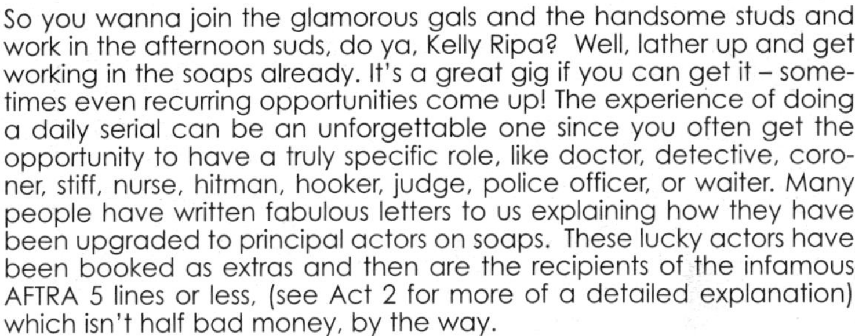

So you wanna join the glamorous gals and the handsome studs and work in the afternoon suds, do ya, Kelly Ripa? Well, lather up and get working in the soaps already. It's a great gig if you can get it – sometimes even recurring opportunities come up! The experience of doing a daily serial can be an unforgettable one since you often get the opportunity to have a truly specific role, like doctor, detective, coroner, stiff, nurse, hitman, hooker, judge, police officer, or waiter. Many people have written fabulous letters to us explaining how they have been upgraded to principal actors on soaps. These lucky actors have been booked as extras and then are the recipients of the infamous AFTRA 5 lines or less, (see Act 2 for more of a detailed explanation) which isn't half bad money, by the way.

In this section you will find listings and information for daytime soap operas (like *General Hospital* and *Days Of Our Lives*) that film in the Los Angeles area. We haven't included the sudsers that shoot in New York or elsewhere since we truly doubt NY-based CD's will pick an LA actor to partake in their shows (and poor *Port Charles* has been docked permanently).

Tips for Finding Work!

Remember daytime soap operas are AFTRA shows which means you gotta join AFTRA (again, see Act 2) OR agree to join AFTRA when working with the sexy soap stars or the Union will come find you and MAKE YOU JOIN! AND remember: you don't REGISTER with soaps, you simply SUBMIT photos to them... and wait. We know, it sucks! But here's some novel advice: be proactive about getting work on these shows. The worst thing that happens is they never use you, but you could also land some killer gig with John and Marlena and make some decent money!

- Remind the Casting Directors you are alive by sending some postcards of your sexy-self.
- Call their hotlines on a regular (but not an annoying/stalking) basis.

Remember, No Fees!!

Again, there are no fees when you submit to the soap operas or any other in-house casting office. For this obvious reason, there is no fee chart listed in this exciting section of the book. Hello... duh...

So read on, fine thespians, and see if working in the soaps is something you wanna sink your teeth into!

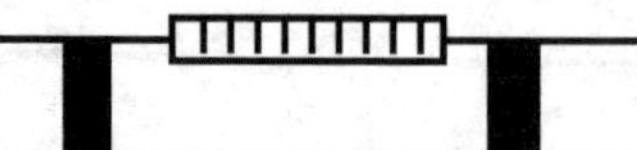

a soap story

Lathering your way into the soaps

by Laura Drake Mancini,
HOLLYWOOD OS®

FADE IN:

Chiseled STONE and gorgeous FAITH are tangled in a web of satin bed sheets.

STONE
I love you!

FAITH
What about my sister?

STONE
I love her too!

FAITH
But I'm pregnant with your father's child

STONE
My father's alive!?

DISSOLVE TO:

I know this may not be the most accurate dialogue (although it could be), but the parody is close enough that most would easily guess what type of television genre I'm referring to – Daytime Soap Operas!

Growing up, I learned very quickly that those who watched were immersed in *Another World*. Soaps were an integrated part of our society. I recall my grandmother watching her daily "stories." At school, I would hear friends *Passion(s)*ately discussing Luke & Laura, Bo & Hope, Jack & Jennifer, while casually discussing murder, sex, loving, deceit, birth... even demonic possession. I envied how they all seemed to know the intimate details of these people's lives.

After hearing about a serious fire one day, I unknowingly exclaimed "Oh my God... which *General Hospital*? Did anyone go to our school?" I felt as though someone had told a joke and I didn't get the punchline.

I began to grow curious about this soap world of *The Bold And The Beautiful* actors, not just *The Young And The Restless* teenagers that knew the stories as if they had lived them. I wondered, "Who were *All My Children*? Why didn't I know where *Port Charles* was? Why did it take so darn long for Susan Lucci to finally win a Daytime Emmy?"

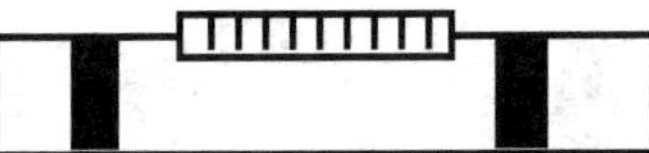

a soap story

Lathering your way into the soaps

I was certain that the viewing experience of a soap opera was very different from partaking in the taping. So, since we only have so many *Days Of Our Lives*, and I'm living in the right city to investigate, I prepared a mailing to every soap opera. Each envelope included a headshot, resumé and a short cover letter explaining my great desire to work as background on that particular show. There were also several availability lines to call after the mailing, but of course I procrastinated horribly. Fortunately, I was contacted by Linda Poindexter of *Days Of Our Lives*. Her call was short and sweet...

"Hi Laura, this is Linda over at *Days*. Are you available to work tomorrow morning at 7:30am. The pay is $105 and you would be a patron in an Italian restaurant." (The pay varies depending on the number of background artists booked on the call).

When I agreed she told me what type of wardrobe to supply and reminded me to come hair/make-up ready, and to bring a pen and paper, for notes. NOTES...What did she mean by notes? This was definitely going to be different from other background work.

To enter Sudsville I knew I was going to studios 2 and 4 at NBC. I pulled up to the guard shack, got a visitor's pass and was directed to park in the lot. I proceeded to lug my wardrobe across the street and through the gate. Finding the building was easy, after asking directions from every person who smiled back. I went in through what appeared to be a loading entrance. Nobody yelled at me so I figured it was okay.

After stating my name, I strolled past the guard and down the hallway into the studio. He told me to sign in on the clipboard hanging by the stage manager's desk, so I initialed by my name, wrote my arrival time and just stood there. That seemed easy enough, but where was the stage manager? Who officially "checks me in"? It turns out that I check me in.

A wardrobe woman read the confusion on my face and took me a few doors back up the hallway to have my wardrobe checked. I began holding up all fifty outfits...okay, so it wasn't fifty, but I probably could have opened a small boutique. "Oh you look fine in what you have on," she declared. I thought to myself, "I do? What do I have on? You mean you're not going to change me fifteen times? How about fitting me into two pieces of clothing that nobody in their right mind would ever consider an outfit"?

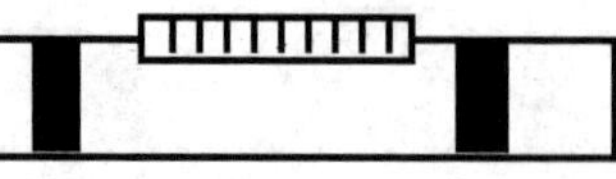

a soap story

Lathering your way into the soaps

Okay, I passed the soap preliminaries, now onto the finals. I walked all the way down the hall and discovered a lobby in which bagels, doughnuts, fruit and other yummies blanketed the tables. The local news was on one television hanging above my head and whatever was taping on the sound stages could be viewed on the other. I heard some of the other background talking about going upstairs, but I wasn't sure If I needed to do that. I had no idea there even was an upstairs. Well, yup, I did indeed need to do that. After following the others up a side staircase, I saw a clipboard with all our names on it. I signed my full name and followed the girls down to our holding area.

Right away I was realizing how imperative it was to keep my eyes and ears completely open. I was expected to be professional and to know what I was doing, even though I had no idea. This sense of independence was liberating...scary, but liberating. The holding was down a set of stairs near wardrobe. Several actors' dressing rooms, along with the female holding area, were on this ground floor. (Males and females had separate holdings). It was nice to see comfy couches, a mirror, clothes rack, a telephone and television. I sat for a while, with the others, when suddenly I heard, "Rehearsal for scene one, Italian restaurant, in five minutes." A few of the principal actors' names were then rattled off before mentioning, "and I need all background." The voice boomed through a loudspeaker and could be heard just about everywhere, including the bathrooms.

As we entered the soundstages, I felt an icicle form on my nose, but I warmed up once the lighting came on. Three video cameras, on wheels, rolled over to the stage as the actors walked onto set. It was so strange to see each stage already set with several lights and no need, or time, for stand-ins. We watched the quick rehearsal, but were told very little regarding our actions. The truth was, I had no clue.

They gave vague movement suggestions (this is where the "note taking" may come in handy) and during taping, motioned for us to cross back and forth as the scene progressed. You see, since all three cameras were working, taking turns taping and realigning themselves according to the scene's movement, the director didn't need to worry about continuity problems. They shot the scene until all aspects, including background, appeared the way they wanted. Then it's on to the next scene.

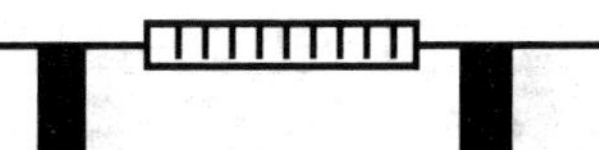

a soap story

Lathering your way into the soaps

As my visit to little Italy came to an end, I politely pretended to eat my gourmet, microwave dinner. We all then heard, "Thank you, background." As I followed everyone off the stage, I realized that after 3 hours, we were wrapped. The day was over. I went over to the same stage manager's clipboard that greeted me that morning and wrote my out time. My day here was done, and as I walked out through the loading dock, and past the front gate, I began anticipating my next visit to the soap opera world.

FADE TO:

A Full Day?

In my experience, a background actor's average day on a soap opera set is about 3-4 hours, but that is not assured. You are hired for the full 9 hour day. One Saturday, on *Days*, we worked 9 hours to catch up on the current shooting schedule. Several background had made beach plans and complained every 2 minutes. Believe me, this did NOT make the day go any faster.

When working on a soap, I was ecstatic to learn that if I work one day and we film 2 or 3 different scenes for different episodes, I would be paid double or triple my rate. Also, if a scene that I taped is aired again in a different episode, I receive an additional day's pay. YEAH!!!!

It can also be common for a background performer to receive an "Under Five." This is basically considered a role and consists of the performer doing something that progresses the plot. You could say, "Hi, you're sexy," or any number of lines under five. If you have an annoying voice, you can simply move a plate from one table to another, preferably not dropping it, and receive the same performer rate.

CUT TO:

SAG vs. AFTRA

Before working on a soap opera, I was only previously familiar with working on projects that were under SAG (Screen Actors Guild) contracts. Soaps, as they are taped, not filmed, fall under AFTRA (The American Federation of Television and Radio Artists). Most television, at one time, was considered AFTRA, but now a large portion records on film and is SAG.

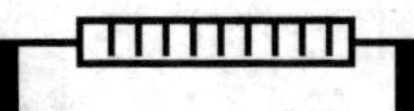

a soap story

Lathering your way into the soaps

AFTRA works much differently from the Screen Actors Guild. Any person can sign up with AFTRA if you have about $1,000 sitting in your sock drawer. Whereas in SAG, you need to have earned speaking lines or have received SAG vouchers doing background work. And if you are interested in working AFTRA projects, and are unable to pay the $1,000+ initiation fee, you can work it off.

Once you work one day on an AFTRA show, you have 30 days to work all the AFTRA shows you want. But after those days have passed, and you work AFTRA again, your paycheck will be taken to go towards your membership dues. You'll receive a comforting little statement showing how much money you'll owe now that your last check was deducted from your membership total. Isn't that sweet. So, after you sign in on set, many of you may find yourselves filling out a small paper allowing AFTRA to take the check. Paid-up members will simply sign in.

The odd part about working an AFTRA soap is that only the Gods know you worked that day. The performer doesn't acquire any proof. On a SAG set, when working as background, one usually takes home a carbon-copy of the voucher. This way, if payment isn't received, you had proof that you did indeed work. AFTRA doesn't have something of that nature, so it's important to try and keep your own accurate records.

CUT TO:

Working on a Soap

Overall, I learned:

- Pay full attention to the actors' blocking during rehearsal. You don't want to step on "Sammy" like I did.
- When taping, watch to see which camera has a red light on... if you are not in front of that camera, you are not on camera. I know it sounds silly, but it's always good to be watching. Soaps encourage you to take initiative and to fill in or move through any dead space.
    - If possible, inconspicuously watch the monitors, especially if you cannot see which camera is on. If you can see yourself on the screen, try to make sure you look alive.

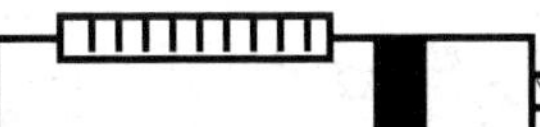

a soap story

Lathering your way into the soaps

- As you watch the monitors, don't forget that you are working. Even if you are not on camera for a moment, don't lose track and find yourself watching like you're at home on the sofa. Yes, I kinda caught myself just watching a couple times... whoops. This could be very bad!
- Please don't lip-synch the words on the actors' cue cards while the actors are saying them. No, I didn't try this, but please... just don't.
- Remember, soap operas usually air five, one-hour episodes a week. This means they need to tape, then move on quickly in order to be fully productive and keep their tight schedule.

It was a very positive experience to be a part of this different form of entertainment. As long as the background actor remembers to be responsible, respectful and attentive, then I believe anyone would have a good day lathering it up on "Days" or on any of the various soap operas. Why not submit and give it a try? After all, we only have *One Life To Live*!

FADE TO BLACK.

THE END

act five

The Bold & The Beautiful

CBS Television City
7800 Beverly Blvd., #3371
Los Angeles, CA 90036

Website:
www.theboldandthebeautiful.com

Lot Location:
CBS TV, City 31

Casting Directors/Staff
Shannon Bradley (Background & Under-5's)
Christy Dooley (Principals)

Main Line:
323-575-4138

Office Line:
323-575-4501

Info Line/Hotline:
n/a

YEAR OPENED

The Bold & The Beautiful premiered on March 23, 1987.

TYPE...

In-house casting for the CBS daytime serial. This is an AFTRA show that accepts submissions from anyone, but you must be willing to join AFTRA.

BASE RATE

$108 for an 8 1/2 hour work day for this 1/2 hour daytime soap opera, not including your meal break. If there are 20 or MORE extras booked on this call, your Base Rate is discounted 20% giving you $86.40 for an 8 1/2 hour workday.

SUBMISSION POLICY

For extra work, submit pictures and resumés to SHANNON BRADLEY at the above address. And PLEASE, folks, DO NOT call in. Shannon tells **HOLLYWOOD OS**®: "Just because you submit a picture doesn't mean you should call to check in, to see if we got it. We get so many submissions, we can't possibly check on every one. Please do not call." Talent who have never worked on an AFTRA program will be Taft-Hartleyed. If talent has already been Taft-Hartleyed and owes money to AFTRA, they will have their check forwarded to the AFTRA office.

HOW LONG ARE SUBMISSIONS KEPT ON FILE?

Shannon tells **HOS**®: "Usually about three or four months. We'll call you if we can use you." If you have worked on a daytime soap before, this is a good thing to list on your resumé. This lets Shannon know you are already familiar with the protocol involved in working on a daytime soap.

WHAT SHANNON APPRECIATES MOST

Talent who follow directions, are on time and bring plenty of wardrobe choices and are PROFESSIONAL at ALL TIMES. When on set: Don't be afraid to say "hi" when filling out your paperwork – just no lurking or special trips up to the Casting area. ALWAYS LISTEN to PAGES – in case she is looking for you. Be nice to fellow performers.

The Bold & The Beautiful

SHANNON'S PET PEEVES

- People who call asking for work after they have already been told they will be contacted when there is work for them.
- Talent who accept jobs and then fail to show up without calling or actors who cancel at the last minute.
- Photos that don't have info attached to them!
- People who call in looking for work. Don't do it!

INSIDE SCOOP!

Shannon tells HOLLYWOOD OS®: "Once I know someone is reliable I will use them because I know I can rely on them. [In seasons past] there have been a lot of the same scenes with the same talent. The look we need can vary but we're always looking for young, attractive people."

Shannon also wanted us to tell you not to get discouraged or mad if she can't use you. Casting for soaps is "very much about the look" and not everyone who submits is going to get to work. Fair enough.

Primary Contact Info

Main Line:
323-575-4138

Office Line:
323-575-4501

AFTRA Representative

Kathy Ewers:
323-634-8179

act five

Days Of Our Lives

Corday Productions
3400 W. Olive Blvd., #315
Burbank, CA 91505

Website:
www.daysofourlives.com

Lot Location:
NBC Studios, Stages 2 &4 in Burbank

Casting Directors/Staff
Linda Poindexter
(Background & Under-5's)

Main/Office Line:
818-295-2832

Availability Line:
818-295-2830

Info Line/Hotline:
n/a

YEAR OPENED

Days Of Our Lives premiered in November 1965.

TYPE...

In-house casting for the NBC daytime serial. This is an AFTRA show that accepts submissions from anyone, but you must be willing to join AFTRA.

BASE RATE

$140 for a 9 hour work day on a ONE HOUR DAYTIME SOAP OPERA not including your meal break. If there are 20 or MORE extras booked on this call, your Base Rate is discounted 20% giving you $112 for a 9-hour workday.

SUBMISSION POLICY

For extra work, submit pictures and resumés to Linda Poindexter at the above address. Once you've mailed in your photo, wait a week or so and then you are officially ALLOWED to call the Availability Line and leave your availability for the UPCOMING WEEK. You should only call to leave your availability once a week. Then wait PATIENTLY for them to call you – trust us, it will be well worth it once you get booked on this show! You must be an AFTRA member in good standing or be willing to join AFTRA in order to work on *Days*.

HOW LONG ARE SUBMISSIONS KEPT ON FILE?

Linda tells HOLLYWOOD OS®: "On average, we keep photos for a year or so." Be sure to include a resumé with any relevant soap opera experience as well as your contact info and measurements. Update your photo submissions whenever your look or contact info has changed.

WHAT LINDA APPRECIATES MOST

- PROFESSIONAL behavior and actors who take their job seriously.
- Talent who arrive on time, pay attention and follow directions.
- Talent with lots of excellent wardrobe choices.
- Talent who pay attention and take notes on blocking (and don't scam on the hot actors).

LINDA'S PET PEEVES

- Actors who try to schedule other work or auditions on the same day they are booked with her.
- Actors who try to replace themselves when they are unable to make a call – Linda ASKS that you call her to tell her!
- People who call to complain because they have not worked.
- Actors who refuse to sign the authorization form when they owe AFTRA money. It's the Union that's looking out for YOU!

LINDA'S ULTIMATE PET PEEVE

Talent who leave the set during lunch, or on a break, in an attempt to make an audition. If you accept the job, you're there for the day. Just because it may have been a short day the last time you worked the show, don't expect it to be that way every time!

INSIDE SCOOP!

Linda tells **HOS**®: "I am always looking for new faces, preferably 18-to-look-younger talent who are AFTRA and who are responsible!"

Primary Contact Info

Main Line:
818-295-2832

Availability Line:
818-295-2830

AFTRA Representative

Christina V. Hagstrom:
323-634-8182

act five

General Hospital

ABC Television Center
4151 Prospect Ave., Stage 54
Los Angeles, CA 90027

Website:
www.generalhospital.com

Lot Location:
ABC TV, Stage 54, City 31

Casting Directors/Staff
Gwen Hillier
(Background, Under-5's, Principals)
Mark Teschner (Principals)

Main Line:
n/a

Availability Line:
310-520-CAST (2278)

Info Line/Hotline:
n/a

YEAR OPENED

General Hospital premiered in April 1963.

TYPE...

In-house casting for the ABC daytime serial. This is an AFTRA show that accepts submissions from anyone, but you must be willing to join AFTRA.

BASE RATE

$140 for a 9 hour work day on a ONE HOUR DAYTIME SOAP OPERA not including your meal break. If there are 20 or MORE extras booked on this call, your Base Rate is discounted 20% to $112.

SUBMISSION POLICY

For extra work, submit pictures and resumés to Gwen Hillier at the above address. Once you HAVE BEEN CONTACTED, check in on the Availability Line ONCE a week to see what the heck is going on. Please DO NOT call UNLESS you have been contacted. You must be an AFTRA member in good standing or be willing to join AFTRA in order to work. Gwen tells **HOS**®: "I expect talent who work for me to be honorable and do the right thing by joining the union and not trying to step around it."

HOW LONG ARE SUBMISSIONS KEPT ON FILE?

Gwen tells **HOS**®: "Forever. Well, a long, long time. If your look or phone number changes, send a new pic too. Don't just send a letter with phone number changes. We'll have no idea who you are. Make it easy for me."

WHAT GWEN APPRECIATES MOST

- Talent who have a pager and return calls promptly.
- Actors who arrive on time, pay attention and are ready to work.
- DO be SURE you are listed on the sign-out sheet BEFORE you leave the building if you feel you were UPGRADED.

GWEN'S PET PEEVES

- DO NOT call UNLESS you have been contacted by them!
- Pictures and resumés that are not stapled together.
- Talent who call on lines OTHER THAN the Talent Availability Line.

General Hospital

ALWAYS REMEMBER...

Your photos should have contact info ATTACHED to them. She tells **HOS**®: "You would be surprised how many people submit pictures and resumés that aren't stapled together." Gwen looks for professional experience and training when casting background and Under-5's, so be sure to include any relevant experience on that rad resumé.

INSIDE SCOOP!

Do NOT call the Availability Line unless you have worked at least once. Gwen tells **HOS**®: "People will call and leave their names and phone numbers and availability, but I'll have no idea who they are. I don't know them. How can I book them without knowing what they look like? It's a waste of their time and mine to call that line unless I've booked them before and know them."

Primary Contact Info

Availability Line:
310-520-CAST (2278)

AFTRA Representative

Jennifer Holland:
323-634-8229

Passions

4024 Radford Avenue
Administration Bldg., #280
Studio City, CA 91604

Website:
www.nbc.com/passions

Lot Location:
NBC Stages, Burbank

Casting Directors/Staff
Jackie Briskey

Main Line:
n/a

Availability Line:
818-655-5299

Info Line/Hotline:
n/a

YEAR OPENED

Passions premiered July 5, 1999.

TYPE...

In-house casting for the NBC daytime serial. This is an AFTRA show that accepts submissions from anyone, but you must be willing to join AFTRA.

BASE RATE

$140 for a 9 hour work day on a ONE HOUR DAYTIME SOAP OPERA not including your meal break. If there are 20 or MORE extras booked on this call, your Base Rate is discounted 20%.

SUBMISSION POLICY

Jackie Briskey casts all background actors and Under-5's for *Passions*. On your resume, make sure to include height and your three-year age range as well as all contact numbers. He will call you if he can use you. You may also leave your availability on the Availability Line once every TWO WEEKS – after you have submitted! You must be willing to join AFTRA. *Passions* tells **HOS**®: "The Availability Line is cleared every day so don't panic if it's full." Just call back the next day, people.

Primary Contact Info

Availability Line:
818-655-5299

AFTRA Representative

Billie Murphy:
323-634-8178

The Young & The Restless

CBS Television City
7800 Beverly Blvd., #3305
Los Angeles, CA 90036

Website:
www.youngandtherestless.com

Lot Location:
CBS TV, City 43 & 44

Casting Directors/Staff
Marisa Rodriguez
(Background, Under-5's)
Marnie Saitta (Principals)

Main Line:
323-575-2532

Availability Line:
323-575-3319

Info Line/Hotline:
n/a

YEAR OPENED

The Young & The Restless premiered March 26, 1973.

TYPE...

In-house casting for the CBS daytime serial. This is an AFTRA show that accepts submissions from anyone, but you must be willing to join AFTRA.

BASE RATE

$140 for a 9 hour work day on a ONE HOUR DAYTIME SOAP OPERA not including your meal break. If there are 20 or MORE extras booked on the call, your Base Rate is discounted 20% which would give you $112 for a 9 hour workday.

SUBMISSION POLICY

For extra work, submit pictures and resumés to Marisa at the above address. She casts all background actors and Under-5's for *The Young & The Restless*. Be sure to include a resumé and make sure to include all contact numbers. She will CONTACT you if she can use you. Once you have WORKED, you can leave your availability on the Availability Line on MONDAYS, between 10AM–1PM. You must be an AFTRA member in good standing or be willing to join AFTRA in order to work.

HOW LONG ARE SUBMISSIONS KEPT ON FILE?

Marnie has always kept excellent records and files everyone who submits photos. We would imagine (and hope) that caster Marisa follows her lead. If you haven't heard from these ladies, it's probably because they have NOT NEEDED to use your type (sorry, do not take this personally). If a few months pass by and you still haven't heard anything, you may try resubmitting your picture and resumé to stay current.

WHAT MARISA APPRECIATES MOST

- Actors who return pages and phone calls quickly.
- Resumés that are ATTACHED to the headshot they accompany.

The Young & The Restless

MARISA'S PET PEEVES

- People who call in just to "see what's up."
- Calling at any time other than Mondays at the specified times and leaving long messages rather than your availability.

INSIDE SCOOP!

The *Y&R* folks NOW tell **HOS**®: "Please only call with your availability once we have already contacted you to work." They are so overwhelmed with phone calls.

Primary Contact Info

Main Line:
323-575-2532

Availability Line:
323-575-3319

AFTRA Representative

Kathy Ewers:
323-634-8179

commercials

The contract, the cash
and the casting companies...

The 2003-2006 SAG Commercials Contract

(in effect 10/30/03 through 10/30/06)

For those of you interested in commercial extra work – and that should be everybody since background work in commercials can be some of the most lucrative work out there for background talent – check the SAG website for the FULL and complete contract (*www.sag.org*).

A few of the basic points of which every extra should be aware before setting foot on set are:

Background Rate (Unlimited Use):	\$291.80
Stand-In Rate:	\$291.80 (yes, it's the same)
BG Rate for 13-week cycle:	\$169.40
Extension of 13-week cycle:	\$218.50 (additional)
Hand Model:	\$445.30
Wet, Snow, Smoke or Dust Adjustment:	\$40.00 (min)
Specified Wardrobe Bump:	\$16.90
Evening/Period Wardrobe Bump:	\$28.20
Number of SAG Extras Required:	40 SAGsters

If these numbers seem familiar, it's because they're the same as the AFTRA commercial figures listed in Act 2. SAG and AFTRA negotiate together. Which accounts for the suspiciously similar rates. Look at you, paying attention and stuff - you rock!

The LA-based extras casting companies that specialize in casting commercials are listed on the pages that follow. These outfits PRIMARILY book talent for commercials but may also occasionally cast TV, features, music videos, etc. Keep in mind that many other extras casting companies (like the ones listed in Act 4) also cast commercials – they just do not primarily cast them and are more likely to work in various areas like features and what not!

Atmosphere Casting

9903 Santa Monica Blvd., #412
Beverly Hills, CA 90212

Website:
n/a

Email:
n/a

Casting Directors/Staff
Robert Lewis, Greg Bull

Main Line:
n/a

Registration Line:
888-858-7090

Info Line/Hotline:
888-858-7090

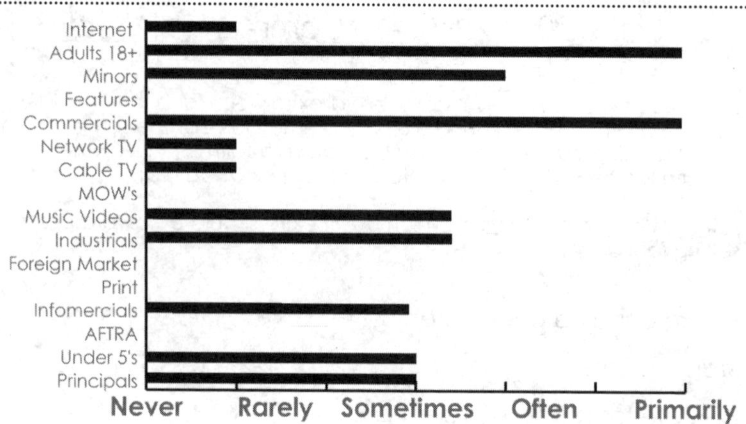

YEAR OPENED
2002

TYPE OF AGENCY
Robert primarily casts background for SAG and Non-Union commercials.

REGISTRATION
Mail a current headshot or snapshot with all your current contact information and he will contact you if he can use you. He frequently posts his jobs on the **HOLLYWOOD OS**® website.

Company Fees	SAG Members	AFTRA & Non-Union Talent
Registration Fee:	$0	$0
Photo Fee:	$40	$40
Commissions:	0%	0%
TOTAL:	***$40***	***$40***

ABOUT SPECING
Robert bluntly tells HOS®: "I don't like it."

ATMOSPHERE CASTING APPRECIATES
Robert tells HOS®: "[Have a] great attitude, be early, and bring an abundance of wardrobe."

ATMOSPHERE CASTING PET PEEVES
- People who sleep on the set.
- People who ask to leave set for callbacks or auditions.
- People who are moody.

DO YOU USE CALLING SERVICES OR ON-LINE RESOURCES?
Atmosphere Casting mainly uses *Extras Management, Big Daddy's Certified Extras*, and HOLLYWOOD OS® (when hunting for talent online).

IF YOU COULD TELL BACKGROUND ACTORS ANYTHING...
Robert tell HOS®: "Everybody gets one, and only one, screw-up. And if it's severe enough, you don't even get that one." Ouch!

Primary Contact Info

Registration/Info Line:
888-858-7090

Background Artists

12021 Wilshire Blvd., #632
Los Angeles, CA 90025

Website:
www.backgroundartists.tv

Email:
chad@backgroundartists.tv

Casting Directors/Staff
Chad Floyd & Tony Perkins

Main Line:
888-44ACTOR(442-2867)

Registration Line:
n/a

Info Line/Hotline:
n/a

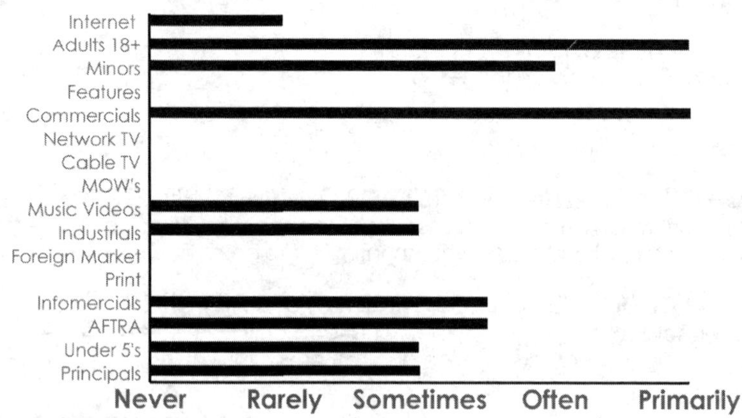

YEAR OPENED
1998

TYPE OF AGENCY
Chad and Tony cast both SAG and Non-Union background talent of all ages, ethnicities and types – primarily for commercials. They have begun to work on the web and will create a webpage for you should you decide to join. For more fun details, contact the casters yourself!

REGISTRATION
They are in the digital world now, so you gotta get a computer to get access! You can still mail photos to their address, but with so many people using the internet these days, it's anybody's guess if they'll get back to you.

Company Fees	SAG Members	AFTRA & Non-Union Talent
Registration Fee:	$0	$0
Photo Fee:	$50	$50
Commissions:	0%	0%
TOTAL:	***$50***	***$50***

REGISTRATION (cont'd)

Basically, *Background Artists* would prefer their background actors to register via their website: www.backgroundartists.tv (as opposed to the old-fashioned way of responding to your submission via snail mail). Once you are logged on to the site, click on JOIN, SELECT Los Angeles, SUBMIT the form, then call the hotline for digital photo session information.

The website will list all the particulars you'll need to get onboard with these folks, but rest assured, these include the usual: Driver's License, resumé, etc. So have that stuff ready.

Chad tells **HOLLYWOOD OS**®: "Talent who are already registered can update their information online or mail in any new photos."

BACKGROUND ARTISTS APPRECIATES

They tell **HOS**®: "Professionalism and a good attitude – knowing their job and representing the company well."

INSIDE SCOOP!

Chad tells **HOS**® that he thinks the future of casting is the internet (we suppose that's why he does his registration that way now). He hopes to see his company expand with the widespread use of the internet and he thinks *Background Artists* will be able to open satellite offices in New York, Miami, Dallas, Chicago and San Francisco.

Primary Contact Info

Main Line:
888-44ACTOR

E-Mail:
chad@backgroundartists.tv

DGS Extras

(a.k.a. ACT)
11054 Ventura Blvd., #475
Studio City, CA 91604

Website:
www.commercialextras.com

Email:
client@commercialextras.com

Casting Directors/Staff
Zach Schary & Laura Skill

Main Line:
n/a

Registration Line:
n/a

Info Line/Hotline:
323-645-2356

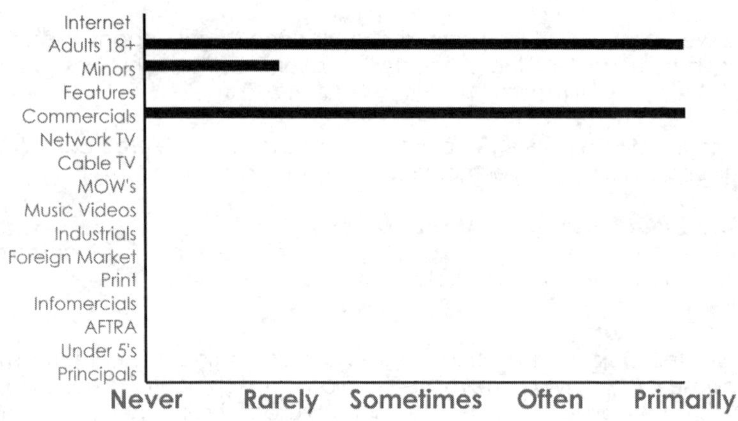

YEAR OPENED

November 2002

TYPE OF AGENCY

Commercial extras casting company. Zach formerly worked with *Producers Casting* as their photographer.

They tell **HOS**®: "*DGS Casting* only does commercials so there is no 'Checking In.' Please only call with changes of phone, address, personal appearance, etc. Also, there is no 'guarantee of work.' As with any casting, work is based on 'look,' wardrobe, on-the-set attitude, etc."

Company Fees	SAG Members	AFTRA & Non-Union Talent
Registration Fee:	$0	$0
Photo Fee:	$25	$25
Commissions:	0%	10%
TOTAL:	***$25***	***$25 + COMMISSIONS***

DGS Extras
(a.k.a. ACT)

REGISTRATION

Registration dates and times will be listed on the info line (323-645-2356). All new registrants must dress nice but don't wear white or a light color as your photo will be taken against a white background. Also, Union members should be sure to bring their SAG or AFTRA cards and everyone should bring their Driver's License.

Commercials are typically picture-picked jobs, so you will be contacted if your photo was chosen for a job. There is no need for you to contact the office with your availability. Once registered, your best bet is to have a good attitude and keep Zach and Laura up to date with postcards.

Primary Contact Info

Info Line:
323-645-2356

Email:
client@commercialextras.com

act six

Alice Ellis Casting

P.O. Box 1828
Venice, CA 90294

Website:
n/a

Email:
n/a

Casting Directors/Staff
Alice Ellis

Main Line:
n/a

Registration Line:
n/a

Availability Line/Hotline:
310-314-1488

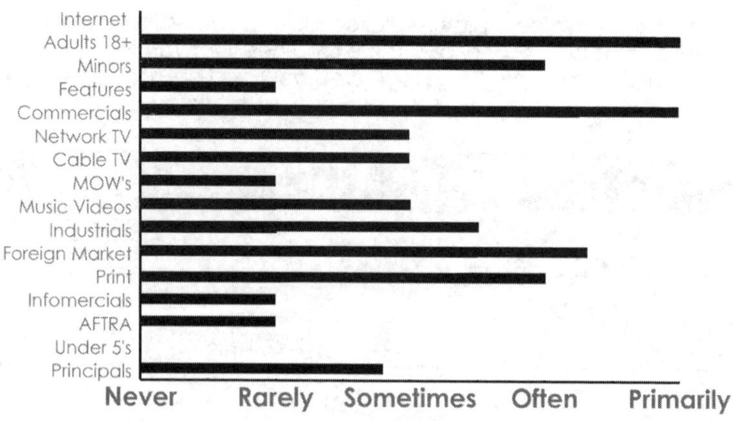

YEAR OPENED
1997

TYPE OF AGENCY
Primarily Alice casts SAG talent for commercials. She does not actively seek Non-Union talent as she doesn't cast many Non-Union folks.

REGISTRATION
In order to get OFFICIALLY REGISTERED with her, SAG applicants must be invited to register. Non-Union talent are not being formally registered at this time, but are still invited to send photos that she will keep on file.

Company Fees	SAG Members	AFTRA & Non-Union Talent
Registration Fee:	$0	n/a
Photo Fee:	$30	n/a
Commissions:	0%	n/a
TOTAL:	***$30***	***N/A***

Alice Ellis Casting

REGISTRATION (cont'd.)
Okay, SAG people, pay attention. Any Tom, Dick, Harry or Henrietta who mailed in a photo thought they were OFFICIALLY REGISTERED with Ms. Ellis – this is not so! SAGsters who submitted and who have been selected will be called when Alice is having an OFFICIAL REGISTRATION. She tells HOS® she generally has 4-6 of these a year. If you are SAG and Alice feels she can use you in her files, you will be invited to one of these formal registrations, whereupon you will pay your $30 smacks and be OFFICIALLY REGISTERED. A digital photo will be taken, so you should be wearing UPSCALE/BUSINESS attire if that is the type you play best.

THE PROCEDURE TO FOLLOW ONCE REGISTERED
You will be contacted if there is work for you. Additionally, for those formally registered, if you will NOT BE AVAILABLE for a LONG PERIOD of time, please call the Voice Mail after 8PM and leave a message letting her know, otherwise she will assume you are ready and willing to work.

BAD THINGS TO DO
- Don't be late – zero tolerance for tardiness!
- Don't call with your availability before 8PM. Some people have actually called earlier saying, "I know I am not supposed to call until after 8PM, but I'm going to see a movie and I won't be able to call later so I'm calling now." What?! Really think that will help you get work?!

GOOD THINGS TO DO
- Arrive to Set 15 minutes before your call time with a sunny attitude!
- Have a brief outgoing message on your Voice Mail – NOT a long soliloquy, or some song from your favorite film!

ALICE ELLIS ON "SPECING"
"On BIG shoots, we appreciate NON-UNION specs. We always need people because there are "no-shows." SAG talent should NEVER spec!"

INSIDE SCOOP!
Alice submits EVERYONE who is registered for each commercial. Generally, it is up to production as to who is actually chosen. Alice goes out of her way to promote all of the talent in her files. She will even go so far as to rearrange her casting books in an effort to highlight those chosen less often.

Primary Contact Info

Availability Line:
310-314-1488
(call after 8 PM only)

Extra Extra Casting

11693 San Vicente Bl., PMB 279
Los Angeles, CA 90049

Website:
www.extraextracastings.com

Email:
xtraxtracasting@aol.com

Casting Directors/Staff
Kristen Greenberg, Mariah Roncetti, Fiona Rouse & Alison Watters

Main Line:
310-552-1888

Registration Line:
n/a

Info Line/Hotline:
310-859-6951

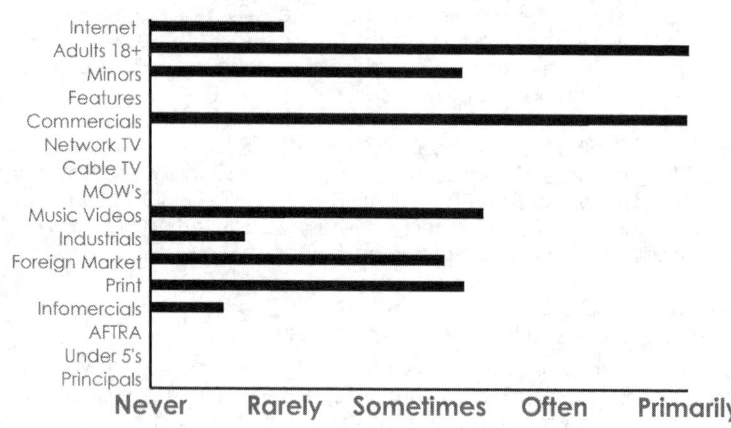

YEAR OPENED

1997

TYPE OF AGENCY

Primarily SAG and Non-Union commercial casting for talent ages 18 and older, but they sometimes cast music videos, industrials, infomercials, and print work. When minors are needed *Extra Extra* primarily uses *Kids! Background*.

REGISTRATION

Registration is only held two or three times a year and is always by "Invitation Only." What does this mean? Well, you should submit a picture and resumé. You will be contacted if Kris and the gang feel they can find you work.

Company Fees	SAG Members	AFTRA & Non-Union Talent
Registration Fee:	$0	$0
Photo Fee:	$30	$30
Commissions:	0%	10% (if talent makes more than $100)
TOTAL:	***$30***	***$30 + COMMISSIONS***

Extra Extra Casting

REGISTRATION (cont'd)

If your look or type is needed or wanted, an invitation to register will be made and you will have your photo taken for the *Extra Extra* Commercial books by a professional photographer.

PROCEDURE TO FOLLOW ONCE REGISTERED

If you are already OFFICIALLY REGISTERED, hang tight – there is NO NEED to call and ask endless questions. They do not list jobs on their hotline. You should only phone them if your availability has changed drastically. *Extra Extra* tells **HOLLYWOOD OS**®: "Registered talent should call in to 'BOOK OUT' only. Otherwise we assume they are available." Translation (that's our job)? This means, ONLY CALL if you are going to be leaving town for an extended amount of time. This DOES NOT mean to call the office every time you receive another job and are not available for a day or two.

EXTRA EXTRA APPRECIATES

- Talent who are early to set and bring great wardrobe!!!
- Talent who answer pages quickly!!

PET PEEVES

- Talent who call "just to chat" or constantly ask to be put on jobs.

ABOUT SPECING

Extra Extra welcomes Non-Union specing only on large calls. They have also posted jobs on the **HOLLYWOOD OS**® website.

COMPANY PHILOSOPHY

Extra Extra tells **HOS**®: "Be professional ALWAYS and know we are working hard for you."

INSIDE SCOOP!

Their website is up and running. It looks as though you can submit a photo online with your info to be considered for INVITATION to one of their OFFICIAL registrations. Check it out: www.extraextracastings.com. They tell us they're especially seeking great character types, the hip & cool crowd, and 18TLYs.

Primary Contact Info

SAG Info Line:
310-859-6951

Non-Union Info Line:
310-281-5553

E-Mail:
xtraxtracasting@aol.com

Idell James Casting

15332 Antioch Street, PMB 117
Pacific Palisades, CA 90272

Website:
n/a

Email:
n/a

Casting Directors/Staff
Idell,
Victoria & Tina

Main Line:
310-230-9344

Registration Line:
n/a

Info Line/Hotline:
310-230-9344

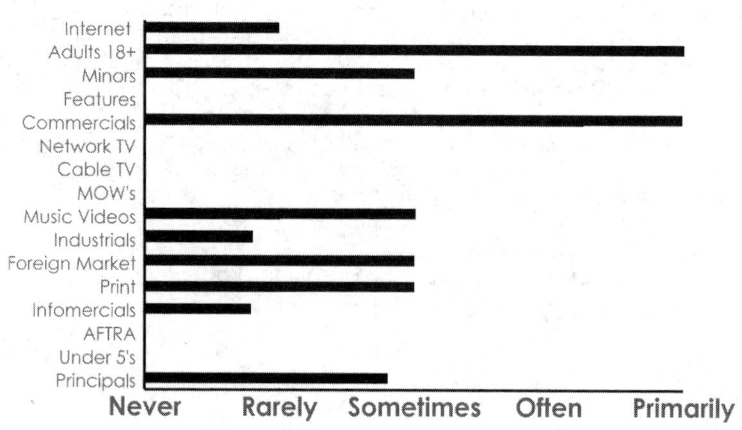

YEAR OPENED

1988

TYPE OF AGENCY

Primarily a SAG commercial extras casting agency that occasionally casts music videos and print jobs as well.

REGISTRATION

SAG members may submit a photo and resumé. If you fall into a category that Idell is currently seeking – you will be contacted for an interview. They also post jobs on the HOLLYWOOD OS® website.

Company Fees	SAG Members	AFTRA & Non-Union Talent
Registration Fee:	$0	$0
Photo Fee:	$25	$0
Commissions:	0%	15%
TOTAL:	***$25***	***COMMISSIONS ONLY***

Idell James Casting

REGISTRATION (cont'd)

It is recommended that you keep sending postcards after you have formally submitted a photo and resumé with current phone numbers, "General Information," etc. In the event they need your 'type,' they will call you and invite you to register. You will be contacted when there is work for you. Once registered, only call the office if you plan to go out of town for an extended period of time. This way, Idell does not submit you and production does not get all excited about using you, only to discover you are gallivanting around Guam or New Guinea or some such place.

FYI

If it's been three years or more since your last photo with the *Idell* casters, you must take another photo so they can have a current pic on file.

IDELL'S DON'T LIST

- Don't call in for work if you are behind on your SAG dues.
- Don't cancel at the last minute!
- Don't constantly ask why you are not booked more often.

IDELL'S DO LIST

- When booked, confirm bookings by 8PM the day before your booking (if the call is for Monday, confirm on Friday by 8PM).
- Arrive to set at least 15 minutes early.
- Be sure to bring and wear the correct wardrobe.
- Have a good attitude and be a hard worker!

INSIDE SCOOP!

Idell tells **HOLLYWOOD OS**®: "I have worked in this business for 35 years doing extra work, stunt work, principal work, etc. I am fully aware of all aspects from both sides (extras and producers). I loved being an extra throughout my life. I took it very seriously and I expect the people I hire to feel the same way. I have HIGH expectations."

Primary Contact Info

Talent Line:
310-230-9344

act six

Producers Casting

P.O. Box 1527
Pacific Palisades, CA 90272

Website:
n/a

Email:
n/a

Casting Directors/Staff
Virginia

Main Line:
n/a

Registration Line:
310-454-5233

Info Line/Hotline:
310-454-5233

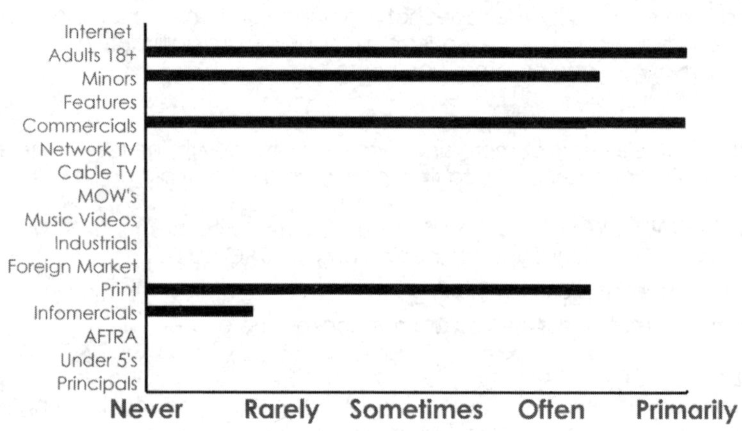

YEAR OPENED

1975

TYPE OF AGENCY

SAG-only commercial extras casting company. The Non-Unions division is *Sunset Casting.*

REGISTRATION

Producers Casting DOES NOT encourage AVERAGE people to register, as they are a "Specialized Boutique Commercial Company."

Company Fees	SAG Members	AFTRA & Non-Union Talent
Registration Fee:	$0	n/a
Photo Fee:	$30*	n/a
Commissions:	0%	n/a
TOTAL:	***$30***	***N/A***

* You may supply your own photos if they are taken precisely as they require – although they do not encourage nor particularly recommend this.

Producers Casting

act six

REGISTRATION (cont'd)

They have a ton of folks registered already and as they put it, "We do our best to get everyone seen, then it is all luck of the draw." If you are still determined to register, you can call and try to get an appointment to take your photo with a photographer who specializes in the format required for *Producers'* Commercial Books. If you can supply the appropriate 4"x6" color photos taken from the waist up against a WHITE background (you should wear upscale professional attire and be smiling!), you are welcome to submit them by mail, as opposed to going to the photographer. But you MUST SUBMIT photos in the aforementioned format ONLY and you will be contacted if they choose to accept you for their files. (Things at this company and *Sunset Casting* may soon change - just a brief FYI from Virginia herself.) For now...

Once registered, call in for work ONCE A MONTH: 310-454-5233, between 11am and 3pm. Don't call on weekends or holiday. It is also a good idea to send postcards because there is NO VISITING. Having a Calling Service will also help you land jobs through *Producers*. Above all, however, registered folks who check in (once a month) and have a GOOD ATTITUDE will have the best chances of landing a gig. Producers tells **HOLLYWOOD OS®**: "With the over-population of extras in ratio to the jobs that actually exist... it's not PERSONAL if you don't get picked – someone else did."

PET PEEVES

Virginia tells **HOS®**: "Tardiness, sloppiness and bad attitudes. Don't have the attitude that *Producers* works for YOU and don't carry on as if *Producers* owes you a job."

ABOUT SPECING

Virginia tells **HOS®**: "NEVER! Specing is highly unprofessional for commercials."

COMPANY PHILOSOPHY

Virginia tells **HOS®**: "We are a highly customized commercial shop. We do not seek out volume work. We emphasize QUALITY, PROFESSIONALISM and ABILITY. Our casting assignments are very specific."

Primary Contact Info

Registration Line:
310-454-5233

Availability Line:
310-454-5233

Sunset Casting

1680 Vine Street, #1110
Hollywood, CA 90028

Website:
n/a

Email:
n/a

Casting Directors/Staff
Colleen & Rich

Main Line:
n/a

Registration Line:
323-467-9326

Info Line/Hotline:
310-398-5904

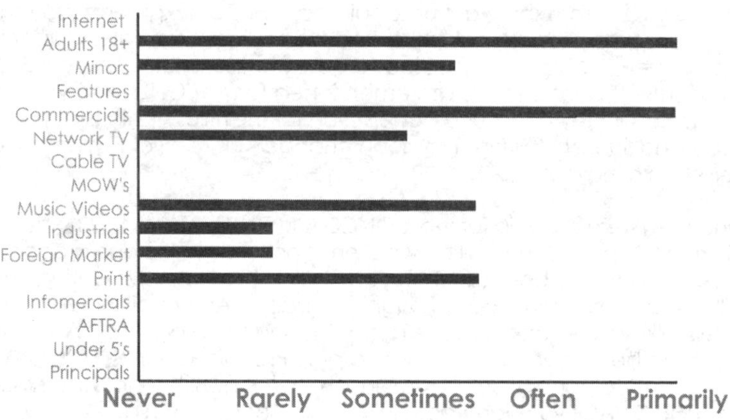

YEARS OPENED
1988

TYPE OF AGENCY
Non-Union extras casting primarily for commercials. The SAG division is *Producers Casting*.

REGISTRATION
Registration is usually held twice a month on various days (usually one weekday and one weekend day). You should call the Registration Line to learn when the next registration is and make an appointment to visit – registration takes place in Hollywood, on the corner of Hollywood Blvd. and Vine.

Company Fees	SAG Members	AFTRA & Non-Union Talent
Registration Fee:	n/a	$0
Photo Fee:	n/a	$30 (cash only)
Commissions:	n/a	15%
TOTAL:	***N/A***	***$30 + COMMISSIONS***

Sunset Casting

REGISTRATION (cont'd)

When you go to register be sure to dress in upscale clothes and don't wear white. Be prepared with all your "General Information" since you will fill out paperwork.

You need not bring pictures since photos will be taken of you on that day – so look your spiffiest and leave the headshots at home!

ONCE REGISTERED

- If you're booked, BE ON TIME – early is even better! If you are running late – CALL and let someone know, otherwise your voucher could be given to a spec.
- Have the proper wardrobe, be courteous and listen to directions.

ABOUT SPECS

"We welcome all specs – especially on LARGE CALLS. We do what we can to get specs on the call – if possible."

SUREFIRE WAYS NOT TO GET BOOKED BY SUNSET

Tardiness, no-shows and overall unprofessional behavior. Talent who, when booked, wander off (i.e., at the pay phone) and are not on set when needed will drastically reduce their chances of getting future jobs from *Sunset Casting*.

INSIDE SCOOP!

Sunset tells **HOLLYWOOD OS**®: "We try to work as many people as possible. Due to the fact that the ad agency usually picks the extras out of our books, we only have so much control as to who gets picked and who does not. We have much more control over larger calls as to who gets booked on a job." Also, things at this company and *Producers Casting* may soon change according to Virginia at *Producers Casting*. Just a random FYI.

Primary Contact Info

Registration Line:
323-467-9326

Availability Line:
310-398-5904

services

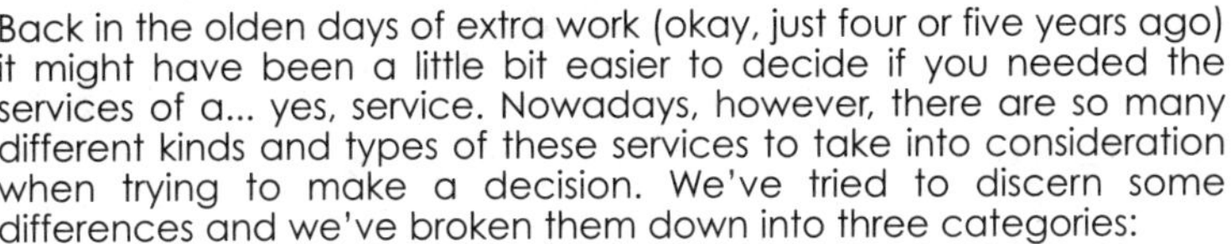

Back in the olden days of extra work (okay, just four or five years ago) it might have been a little bit easier to decide if you needed the services of a... yes, service. Nowadays, however, there are so many different kinds and types of these services to take into consideration when trying to make a decision. We've tried to discern some differences and we've broken them down into three categories:

1.) Traditional Calling Services

2.) Online/Internet Services

3.) Specialty Companies/Services (i.e., military, punk rockers, etc.)

Traditional Calling Services

Basically these services are companies to which you pay a monthly fee and they seek out work on your behalf. They are sort of like the agents or managers of the extra world, except their sole purpose by acting as your agent or manager is to seek out extra work on your behalf. The only difference is that they do not charge a commission. They instead charge a monthly fee ranging from $45 - $80, with first and last month's fees often due on sign-up. Some now also charge an upfront registration or photo fee as well.

Online Services

Oh, yes. With computers so prevalent in all our lives these days, this was inevitable. There are literally hundreds of sites on the World Wide Web that claim to have current casting notices and connections with CD's around the globe. Be careful. Yes, the internet is most definitely a huge asset to many Casting Directors nowadays, but be sure you know if Casting Directors are actually using such websites and how often. These types of companies' fees can range from $10 to $100 a month depending upon where you look. As always, just do your research.

Speciality Companies

These places generally charge no fees or very minimal fees and have a very select, core group of clients. These groups can vary in number depending upon their "speciality." One group might be for biker types, another for people with military or police experience. They take on new clients depending on the needs or amount of work each place might have. Car "casting" companies fall under this banner as well.

Acting Express Casting

P.O. Box 5761
Newport Beach, CA 92662

Website:
www.actingexpress.com

Email:
robertmconrad@hotmail.com

Staff
Bob Conrad

Main Line:
949-633-1580

Registration Line:
n/a

Info Line/Hotline:
n/a

act seven

YEAR OPENED
2003

CLIENT ROSTER
SAG and Non-Union talent of all ages are welcome.

TYPE OF COMPANY
This is tricky. This is a background casting company that also acts as a Calling Service of sorts for Orange County when the need arises. You pay $60 for six months of membership and there are no real guarantees of how much work you will get, but Bob tells HOS®: "People will definitely gets their money's worth in work." Hmmm, fairly vague, but okay...

REGISTRATION
Orange County talent interested in registering should call directly for a Registration date or appointment or log on to their website for all the latest info. Dress age-appropriate and bring all the regular stuff (Driver's License, applicable Union cards, etc.) and, of course, know all your sizes!

ACTING EXPRESS SPEAKS OUT
Bob tells HOS®: "I hope to give as many folks in OC and San Diego possible the ability to work with us and enjoy the filmmaking process."

INSIDE SCOOP!
Bob Conrad is a SAG and DGA member who has been a teacher in film and stage for over twenty years.

Company Fees	SAG Members	AFTRA & Non-Union Talent
Registration Fee:	$0	$0
Processing Fee:	$0	$0
Semi-Annual Fee:	$60	$60
Commissions:	0%	0%
TOTAL:	***$60/SIX MONTHS***	***$60/SIX MONTHS***

Actor's Reps

7060 Hollywood Blvd., Suite 504
Los Angeles, CA 90028

Website:
www.actorsreps.com

Email:
n/a

Staff
Richard Brannan
& Peter Tilleli

Main Line:
323-790-7992

Fax:
323-790-7995

Info Line/Hotline:
n/a

act seven

YEAR OPENED
1975 (in New York); 2003 in Los Angeles

CLIENT ROSTER
SAG and Non-Union talent of all ages are welcome.

TYPE OF COMPANY
A casting service and resource that places extras, principals and more.

REGISTRATION
You must CALL for an appointment: 323-790-7992. Talent can register Monday - Thursday from 11:30AM-1:30PM or 4PM-5:30PM. Bring your state-issued I.D., Union card(s) (if you're Union) and know your measurements.

PROCEDURE TO FOLLOW ONCE REGISTERED
Actor's Reps tells **HOS**®: "It's okay to call the office." So, if you want to work or want to see what's up, call in and let them know you are available.

ACTOR'S REPS APPRECIATES
They tell **HOS**®: "Good attitudes and professionals. Leave your egos at home. Never be late, always be early, and always be the first to volunteer for anything requested on set."

INSIDE SCOOP!
These folks are still fairly new to LA, but have worked in New York for almost 30 years – placing actors in *Sex And The City, SNL, All My Children* and more.

Company Fees	SAG Members	AFTRA & Non-Union Talent
Registration Fee:	$0	$0
Processing Fee:	$0	$0
Bi-Annual Fee:	$0	$0
Commissions:	10%	10%
TOTAL:	***DEPENDS ON COMMISSIONS***	***DEPENDS ON COMMISSIONS***

Alpha Company

P.O. Box 931042
Los Angeles, CA 90093-1042

Website:
www.alphacompany.com

Email:
info@alphacompany.com

Staff
Kristian Sorensen

Main Line:
n/a

Registration Line:
n/a

Info Line/Hotline:
n/a

YEAR OPENED
1999

TYPE OF COMPANY
Alpha Company helps cast extras when dealing specifically with military-type roles. Registered members of *Alpha Company* all have prior military or police service, or have had extensive training by an official military technical advisor. *Alpha Company* deals with both Union and Non-Union casting, men and women 18+ for all types of projects.

REGISTRATION
Send submissions to the address above. PLEASE INCLUDE:

- A current photograph (3"x5" preferably in uniform).
- Any professional headshots.
- A military resumé listing MOS qualifications and special skills.
- A theatrical resumé with phone numbers and mailing address.
- A list of any military or police uniforms you currently own.
- Your wardrobe sizes and any union affiliations.

You will indeed be contacted if you are accepted. Also, understand they do not guarantee work – it all depends upon what projects are shooting around town!

Company Fees	SAG Members	AFTRA & Non-Union Talent
Registration Fee:	$0	$0
Processing Fee:	$0	$0
Monthly Membership:	$0	$0
Commissions:	0%	0%
TOTAL:	***$0***	***$0***

Atmosphere Talent

6671 Sunset Blvd., #1525-1
Hollywood, CA 90028

Website:
www.atmospheretalent.com

Email:
atmospheretalent@aol.com

Staff
Dave Ott, Michel Verdi & Johnny

Main Line:
323-469-7700

Registration Line:
n/a

Info Line/Hotline:
323-634-4877

act seven

YEAR OPENED
2002

CLIENT ROSTER
SAG and Non-Union adults ages 18 +.

TYPE OF COMPANY
Atmosphere is a traditional Calling Service for background actors ages 18+.

AVERAGE BOOKINGS
Dave tells HOS® that if those who register don't get work or aren't satisfied they'll refund the month's dues "no questions asked." Gotta love that!

REGISTRATION
Atmosphere Talent accepts registrants 18+ of all types for their service. They are looking for new talent in all categories – especially Non-Union. So if you're in the market for a Calling Service, submit to these fine folks and see if they contact you for an interview or a date. Okay, just JOKING, simmer down - it's called quality control, people, just making sure you are reading carefully, duh!! Anyhoooo - submit a current photo of any type and you will be contacted if the nifty folks at *Atmosphere* feel they can keep you working. They'll call you for an interview/appointment and you'll hopefully be invited to register. When you go in, make sure you bring 4 different looks they can photograph you in.

Company Fees	SAG Members	AFTRA & Non-Union Talent
Registration Fee:	$50	$50
Processing Fee:	$0	$0
Monthly Membership:	$50	$50
Commissions:	0%	0%
TOTAL:	***$100***	***$100***

Atmosphere Talent

ATMOSPHERE TALENT APPRECIATES
To quote Dave: "Professionalism, reliability, and good communication skills!"

PET PEEVES
Quoting again: "No show, no call! And constantly asking for vouchers." Ouch. They're also not down with "constant, frivolous paging and lateness."

WHAT DO YOU SEE FOR THE FUTURE OF BG CASTING?
They tell **HOS**®: "We see more and more independent companies becoming successful. Background casting is finally starting to get the respect it deserves."

COMPANY PHILOSOPHY
Atmosphere Talent tells **HOS**®: "We love to help those who want to help themselves. We find no greater joy than helping people achieve their goals. It may sound corny, but we like to treat people like family."

IF YOU COULD TELL BACKGROUND ACTORS ANYTHING...
Atmosphere Talent tells **HOS**®: "Always be on time – never ever flake! Communicate, because communication is the key to success! Always let your service know any changes you may have, the minute you find out. Never pester CD's for vouchers – you can make your point by requesting one time! CD's and Services have memories like elephants – we never forget! 'Thank you' is a great phrase to use!"

INSIDE SCOOP!
Don't confuse these folks with the peeps at *Atmosphere Casting*. They are two entirely different companies. *Atmosphere Talent* is a Calling Service not the commercial extras casting company! They're always on the lookout for new talent and they guarantee work, so inquire within already!

Background Talent Services

4804 Laurel Canyon Blvd., Suite 414
North Hollywood, CA 91607

Website:
n/a

Email:
n/a

Staff
Debbie

Main Line:
818-760-7090

Registration Line:
818-771-5727

Info Line/Hotline:
818-771-5727

act seven

YEAR OPENED
1997

CLIENT ROSTER
Non-Union adults ages 18+.

TYPE OF COMPANY
BTS is a Calling Service for Non-Union background actors 18+ that specializes in TV commercials and music videos.

AVERAGE BOOKINGS
BTS guarantees to offer you work each month or you do not have to pay the monthly fee.

REGISTRATION
Submit a current photo with your name, "true age" (not Hollywood age), phone number, height and weight and you will be contacted if the nifty folks at *BTS* feel they can keep you busy with work. If you are contacted to register, be sure to bring the following: driver's license and Social Security card along with your "General Info." Be sure to look super spiffy at registration because they will take photos of you for their Commercial Books.

PROCEDURE TO FOLLOW ONCE REGISTERED
You will be contacted if and when there is a project for you, so you need not call the office looking for work or to just "check in."

Company Fees	SAG Members	AFTRA & Non-Union Talent
Registration Fee:	n/a	$35
Processing Fee:	n/a	$0
Monthly Membership:	n/a	$25
Commissions:	n/a	0%*
TOTAL:	***N/A***	***$60***

* While *Background Talent Services* does not take a commission for themselves, the casting company (i.e., *Idell James Casting*) may take a commission.

Bat Pack

2123 South Bronson Avenue
Los Angeles, CA 90018

Website:
www.batpack.net

Email:
casting@batpack.net

Staff
Randy & Amy

Main Line:
323-737-5991

Registration Line:
n/a

Info Line/Hotline:
n/a

YEAR OPENED

1996

TYPE OF COMPANY

Specializes in alternative types ONLY. Think goth/industrial, punk, ravers, club kids, 70's, 80's rockers, tattoos, multiple piercings, etc. They accept both SAG and Non-Union background talent (primarily 18-30) for TV, film, commercials and music videos. "We specialize in extreme looks. If you are not covered in metal, ink or dye, or have some other extreme attribute (i.e., bald), please don't waste our time or yours." Well, there you go!

REGISTRATION

You can sign up via their snazzy online registration form at www.batpack.net. But call first and let them know that you're interested in registering. You can then check their online message board once you're registered. Also feel free to drop them a postcard and call to say "howdy" from time to time.

Company Fees	SAG Members	AFTRA & Non-Union Talent
Registration Fee:	$50*	$50*
Processing Fee:	$0	$0
Monthly Membership:	$25	$25
Commissions:	0%	0%
TOTAL START-UP:	***$50***	***$50***

* Registration fee is first and last month's monthly fee.

Booking Services

1112 Montana Ave., #431
Santa Monica, CA 90403

Website:
www.bookingservices.com

Email:
ebookingservices@yahoo.com

Staff
Craig, Angela, & Lindsey

Main Line:
323-882-6400

Registration Line:
n/a

Info Line/Hotline:
n/a

act seven

YEAR OPENED

1987

CLIENT ROSTER

Accepts both SAG and Non-Union talent.

TYPE OF COMPANY

A commission-based Calling Service for SAG and Non-Union talent ages 18+.

AVERAGE BOOKINGS

Angela tells **HOLLYWOOD OS**®: "I feel confident to say three days a week for Non-Union." Craig explains they are very selective with SAG talent and the amount of work can vary. Good answer. Commission-based could be fairly interesting. It seems like they would have to work damn hard for you.

REGISTRATION

By appointment only, kiddies. No walk-ins. Call to set up a time. They'll talk to you for a little bit and see if there's a match. To register with these folks you MUST be registered with *Central Casting*. People say the darnedest things...

POLICY ON GIVING OUT SAG VOUCHERS

Booking Services tells **HOLLYWOOD OS**®: "We don't want any psychos who are going to bug the casting people for SAG vouchers. We want solid people only. If you're a beginner, that's okay, but we want solid people with transportation and a great wardrobe. Then, eventually the vouchers may come."

Company Fees	SAG Members	AFTRA & Non-Union Talent
Registration Fee:	$25	$49
Processing Fee:	$0	$25
Monthly Membership:	$0	$0
Commissions:	10%	0%
TOTAL:	**$25 + COMMISSIONS**	**$74**

Cameo Casting Services

6115 Selma Ave., Suite 203
Hollywood, CA 90028

Website:
www.cameocasting.com

Email:
russ@yocameo.com

Staff
Russ Reynolds &
Christine Reynolds

Main Line:
310-535-5781

Registration Line:
323-460-4475

Info Line/Hotline:
310-535-5781

act seven

YEAR OPENED

1995 (Non-Union), 1998 (SAG), 2004 Under New Ownership.

CLIENT ROSTER

Adults ages 18+, SAG and Non-Union. *Cameo*'s Primary SAG Roster is strictly limited to 75 men and 75 women. Fabulous people for whom there is currently no space available are invited to join the Reserve Roster to wait for space to open up.

TYPE OF COMPANY

Cameo is a Calling Service for Background Actors. They are no longer affiliated with any company marketing principal acting submissions, and they no longer take a cut if they refer you for a principal gig. Whew!

SAG RESERVE ROSTER

Because of *Cameo*'s strict SAG limits, they offer the Reserve Roster as a waiting list with fringe benefits. Reserve clients are submitted for work when all Primary clients who fit the job are booked or unavailable. These folks are kept on a "check first" basis and control their own schedules. The best news is... if you don't get at least one day of work in any quarter, you don't pay until *Cameo* books you again. Way rad!

RESERVE ROSTER FEES

$99 for 3 months plus a $29 registration fee.

PRIMARY ROSTER FEES

See neat chart below!

Company Fees	SAG Members	AFTRA & Non-Union Talent
Registration Fee:	$29	$29
First Month:	$75	$75
Last Month:	$75	$65
Commissions:	$0	$0
TOTAL:	***$179***	***$169***

Cameo Casting Services

AVERAGE BOOKINGS

The *Cameo* casters tell **HOLLYWOOD OS**®: "Our goal is twice a week for SAG, though the majority of our members do much better than that. Non-Union can generally work as many days as they like."

REGISTRATION - By Appointment Only

SAG peeps (short for people, but almost as long...) should mail a headshot and resume. *Cameo* will call if they have space for you. Most SAG spaces are filled by Non-Union clients who go SAG and outstanding Reserve Roster clients who are invited to go Primary. Like most things Hollywood, if you're a 23-year-old hottie, your chances are better.

Lucky Non-Union hipsters/folks can phone the registration line directly for an appointment to interview. Before your meeting, print an application from CameoCasting.com and fill it out. Bring it with you, as well as a pen (this is a test!), and plenty of change for parking meters, as *Cameo*'s Hollywood office is diligently patrolled by the most rabid, ravenous meter maids in LA. Plan to spend at least an hour, come camera-ready in the look you are booked in most often, and do not wear white. If you are invited to join, your photo will be taken that day.

COLOR PHOTO UPDATES

Cameo offers its clients FREE quarterly photo updates at the Hollywood office, and requires members to update their photo at least once a year. "It's vital to casting directors that we have a current, undoctored photo of every client, and it is our commitment to them that each and every client REALLY looks like their photo." Clients are encouraged to upload their headshots, costume shots, car and pet photos to their page on the *Cameo* website so that these can also be made available to casting when needed.

COMPANY PHILOSOPHY

Cameo is a Cooperative Network of Actors; a stress-free alternative designed to accommodate an exclusive group of the sharpest, most reliable SAG and Non-Union background talent. "We are a boutique calling service for actors who do background work. We take pride in the fact that many of our members are working actors. As a *Cameo* member you are an individual, and you are important!"

PET PEEVES

If you're looking for a job that allows you to sleep on set and fill your duffle bag with craft service after you've emptied it of the wadded-up wardrobe that smells like parmesan, *Cameo* is not for you. Cancelling without an amazing excuse is a big no-no (so do be creative). Replacing yourself and double bookings, however, are the biggest no-no's of all, and either of these fine stunts result in instant walking papers.

Cameo Casting Services

IF YOU COULD TELL BACKGROUND ACTORS ANYTHING

Remember all those little things you learned in kindergarten. Be kind to others, clean up after yourself, don't lie, cheat or steal. Always come to work well groomed with great wardrobe and a great attitude. Expect to work, not sleep, when you're on the clock (unlike kindergarten). Know that the future opportunities of each and every *Cameo* member are directly linked to your performance on set and your reputation with Casting Directors, so never take that responsibility lightly. Enough said!

"Cars"

Make your Car a Star!
(addresses listed below)

Website:
(addresses listed below)

Email:
n/a

Staff
n/a

Main Line:
(numbers listed below)

Registration Line:
n/a

Info Line/Hotline:
n/a

act seven

Car "Representation"

Yes, you are reading correctly. These way-cool places "represent" your cars! Say, wha-huh? Basically, you can go in, take some pictures, fill out some paperwork and get YOUR CAR on file with these places. Most accept registration of any and ALL vehicles from just about anywhere!

Cars need not always be antique or in mint condition – but those are often preferred. There is usually no fee at all (or just a modest, one-time fee of $5 - $10). Call and check for yourself. We've listed those which are most "friendly" to BG actors who want to make their rides famous.

- **Hollywood Picture Cars**
  1028 North La Brea Avenue
  West Hollywood, CA 90038-2324
  Website: www.hollywoodpicturecars.com
  Main Line: 323-466-2277 (CARS)

- **Show Mobiles**
  5542 Cahuenga Blvd.
  North Hollywood, CA 91601
  Website: www.showmobilesinc.com
  Main Line: 818-762-0700

- **Picture Vehicles Unlimited**
  10615 Chandler Blvd.
  North Hollywood, CA 91601
  Website: www.extremeperformances.com/pvu/
  Main Line: 818-766-2200

- **Nationwide Picture Cars**
  8491 Sunset Boulevard #269
  Hollywood, California 90069
  Website: www.nationwidepicturecars.com
  Main Line: 310-659-1711

Casting Networks

Crossroads of the World
6671 Sunset Blvd., Suite 1517
Hollywood, CA 90028

Website:
www.lacasting.com

Email:
talentsupport@castingnetworks.com

Staff
Beau Bonneau

Main Line:
323-462-8200

Registration Line:
n/a

Info Line/Hotline:
n/a

act seven

YEAR OPENED

2005

CLIENT ROSTER

All ages and types, both SAG and Non-Union.

TYPE OF COMPANY

Casting Networks, the company behind online principal casting service *LACasting.com*, has created a division for background work called *Extras Connection*. It is an online database where your profile can be viewed by casting directors. You can also submit yourself to notices placed on the site.

REGISTRATION

Registration for *Extras Connection* is free until April 1st 2006 only. For Non-Represented Members there is no charge as it is included in your *Casting Networks* monthly or prepaid membership (which ranges from between $8 and $10 per month depending on the length of your contact).

Represented and *Extras Connection* only Members pay $5 per month or $50 pre-paid per year. This includes 2 digital photos and $5 per every photo thereafter.

Note: *Extras Connection* only members are not able to submit their profile for principal Direct Cast projects and are not searchable by principal casting directors.

Company Fees	SAG Members	AFTRA & Non-Union Talent
Registration Fee:	$0*	$0*
Yearly Fee:	$0*	$0*
Per Submission:	$0*	$0*
Commissions:	$0*	$0*
TOTAL:	***$0****	***$0****

* After April 1st 2006, the montly fee for *Extras Connection* goes to $5/month as discussed above.

Combat Casting

P.O. Box 46159
Los Angeles, CA 90046

Website:
www.combatcasting.com

Email:
combatcasting@yahoo.com

Staff
Jody Heart &
Deryl Michael

Main Line:
310-686-2718

Registration Line:
n/a

Info Line/Hotline:
n/a

act seven

YEAR OPENED

2002

CLIENT ROSTER

Accepts both SAG and Non-Union talent.

TYPE OF COMPANY

Combat Casting provides Actors, Background Actors, and Technical Advisors with real Military, SWAT, and other law enforcement experience for anything and everything from features to television to music videos.

REGISTRATION

Download the Information Sheet from their website and mail it in along with: a DD214 or other proof of military or police service, headshots, an acting resumé, a military/police resumé, and an acting reel if available. The more they know about your skills, the better.

PROCEDURE TO FOLLOW ONCE REGISTERED

Once registered, you will be placed in their database, casting book, and on their website. *Combat Casting* is not a casting agency and does not guarantee work. Check in occasionally, preferrably by email, and let them know ASAP about any changes in your contact information or Union status.

They also schedule periodic get-togethers for their members: everything from BBQ's to paintball games to training sessions. Showing up definitely helps them know you and your skills.

Company Fees	SAG Members	AFTRA & Non-Union Talent
Registration Fee:	$0	$0
Processing Fee:	$0	$0
Monthly Membership:	$0	$0
Commissions:	10% on Principal Roles	10% on Principal Roles
TOTAL:	**COMMISSION**	**COMMISSION**

Combat Casting

act seven

COMBAT CASTING APPRECIATES:
"Loyalty, honor, dedication, punctuality, good attitudes, working hard. Knowing your job and your Chain of Command while on set."

COMBAT CASTING PET PEEVES:
Combat Casting tells us: "Not showing up for work on time and ready to go. EVERYONE in the film business should show up at least 30 minutes before their call time. We have a Chain of Command to make it easier for the Technical Advisors and ADs to do their jobs. If you are stepping over their heads and telling the Director your ideas and advice, you will not work for us again."

COMBAT CASTING'S POLICY ON SAG VOUCHERS
They tell **HOLLYWOOD OS**®: "We can and have helped our members get their SAG vouchers. Work hard for us and we will work hard for you."

POLICY ON SPECING
Combat Casting tells us: "Never, please."

IF YOU ARE RUNNING LATE TO SET...
Always let them know about it. They'll help out any way they can. Just make sure it doesn't happen more than once or twice.

COMPANY PHILOSOPHY
Jody tells **HOLLYWOOD OS**®: "*Combat Casting*'s motto is: Adding realism to your production. We tell all members this: First, represent yourself to *Combat Casting* at 100%. Second, represent *Combat Casting* at 110%. Third, represent the Military/Police at 120%. If you do that, then *Combat Casting* will be hired again and so will you."

Direct Line

23945 Calabasas Road, Suite 113A
Calabasas, CA 91302

Website:
www.directlinecasting.com

Email:
n/a

Staff
Jean & Charlie

Main Line:
818-223-3590

Registration Line:
n/a

Info Line/Hotline:
n/a

act seven

YEAR OPENED
1993

CLIENT ROSTER
They accept both SAG and Non-Union talent 18+, all types and ethnicities.

TYPE OF COMPANY
Direct Line is a traditional Calling Service for all background actors 18+.

REGISTRATION
Monday, Tuesday, Thursday and Friday (NO Wednesdays) 11AM - 1PM and 3PM - 5PM. But you should always call first. When you register – dress UP-SCALE. A 35mm photo will be taken of you – which will be reproduced for the *Direct Line* Casting Books (included in the registration fee). Per website, "cash is required at registration." Italians rule!

COMPANY PHILOSOPHY
"We don't control or intimidate. Our door is always open and our phone is always answered. We are available for casting 24/7."

INSIDE SCOOP!
Charlie and Jean tell **HOLLYWOOD OS®**: "We feel that our contacts will enable us to provide our clients quality jobs – commercials, Stand-In jobs – in addition to regular background work." They asked that we remind backgrounders to always answer your phone when possible or return calls and pages immediately so they can confirm with casting – or else you could lose the job!

Company Fees	SAG Members	AFTRA & Non-Union Talent
Registration Fee:	$30	$30
Processing Fee:	$0	$0
Monthly Membership:	$60	$60
Commissions:	0%	0%
TOTAL:	***$90***	***$90***

Extras Access

2140 Cotner Ave.
Los Angeles, CA 90025

Website:
www.extrasaccess.com

Email:
info@extrasaccess.com

Staff
Gary Marsh

Main Line:
310-276-9166

Registration Line:
n/a

Info Line/Hotline:
n/a

act seven

YEAR OPENED

New in 2005.

CLIENT ROSTER

SAG and Non-Union talent of all ages.

TYPE OF COMPANY

Extras Access is a spin-off of the online principal casting service *Actors Access* (run by *Breakdown Services*). Background talent can scan casting notices and submit themselves to gigs that fit their profile or catch their interest or (ideally) both.

REGISTRATION

Registration can be done online at www.extrasaccess.com. With the Free Membership you can upload 2 photos and pay $2.00 per submission. If you wish to upload additional pictures, the cost is $10.00 for each additional photo. The Los Angeles Regular Membership is $50.00 per year and includes 4 free photos and submissions. Additional pictures may also be uploaded for $10.00 per photo. If *Extras Access* staff is required to scan and manually upload pictures, members will be charged $10.00 for each picture. Also, membership to *Extras Access* does not include membership to *Actors Access*, which is a separate membership with different pricing rates.

Company Fees	SAG Members	AFTRA & Non-Union Talent
Registration Fee:	$0	$0
Yearly Fee:	$50*	$50*
Per Submission:	$2**	$2**
Commissions:	0%	0%
TOTAL:	***$50* OR $2*****	***$50* OR $2*****

*For Regular Los Angeles Membership.
**For Free Membership, the charge is $2.00 per submission.

Extras! Management

207 S. Flower Street, 2nd Floor
Burbank, CA 91502

Website:
www.extrasmanagement.com

Email:
n/a

Staff
Cynthia, Sandra, Chris, Brett, Eden, Elaine, Brittney, David, Jeanette & Richard

Main Line:
818-972-9474

Registration Line:
818-771-8466

Info Line/Hotline:
n/a

YEAR OPENED
2000

CLIENT ROSTER
Both SAG and Non-Union talent ages 18 and older.

TYPE OF COMPANY
Extras! Management is a Calling Service for all background actors 18+.

REGISTRATION
SAG members can submit their photos to the above MAILING address and see if they call to INVITE you to register. Non-Union folk may register 10AM OR 12PM, Monday through Friday. Of course you can, fun times over at *EM*.

AVERAGE BOOKINGS
"Based upon work available."

INSIDE SCOOP!
This company is the result of many a merger between *Extra Effort*, *Extra Phone* and *American Casting*... gobbling up the town bit by bit by bit!

Company Fees	SAG Members	AFTRA & Non-Union Talent
Registration Fee:	$10	$10
Processing Fee:	$0	$0
Monthly Membership:	$70**	$70**
Commissions:	0%	0%
TOTAL:	**$150***	**$80**

* Your registration fee plus first and last month's monthly fee must be paid at sign up.
** If you are 55+, the monthly fee is reduced to $55. Bargain. Cool!

Gunmetal Group

11271 Ventura Blvd., #369
Studio City, CA 91604

Website:
www.gunmetalgroup.com

Email:
jonathanbarton@gunmetalgroup.com

Staff
Matt Sigloch, Jon Barton, Sam, Erik, & Sean

Main Line:
310-709-0751

Casting Line:
323-839-7233

Info Line/Hotline:
n/a

act seven

YEAR OPENED
2004

CLIENT ROSTER
Accepts both SAG and Non-Union talent.

TYPE OF COMPANY
Gunmetal handles MIlitary Special Ability Casting (principal, background, stunt performers, and technical advisors) for film and television projects. Credits include: *JAG, NCIS, Threshold, Invasion, Over There, 24, E-Ring, American Dreams*, and *The Unit*. They are currently on a recon mission for "good-looking military professionals."

REGISTRATION
Registration is typically held once a month. Time, place, and procedure to follow will be announced on their website (www.gunmetalgroup.com). You must be able to present military documentation upon request (DD214).

PROCEDURE TO FOLLOW ONCE REGISTERED
Once registered, talent will be contacted as work arises. You can also check in at: admin@gunmetalgroup.com. They request talent keep them advised of both schedule conflicts and new gigs they've booked.

Gunmetal Group schedules monthly meetings for its members (details are announced on the website).

Company Fees	SAG Members	AFTRA & Non-Union Talent
Registration Fee:	$0	$0
Processing Fee:	$0	$0
Monthly Membership:	$0	$0
Commissions:	10% on tech. advisors	10% on tech. advisors
TOTAL:	**COMMISSION**	**COMMISSION**

Gunmetal Group

GUNMETAL GROUP APPRECIATES:
"We charge [production] between $150 and $250 per 8 hours on voucher for our talent, so we expect the best, because we give the best. Our Military Special Ability performers are the best in the business."

GUNMETAL GROUP PET PEEVES:
Gunmetal Group tells us: "Lack of physical fitness. Never bring a chair to set. Never fall asleep. No books. We demand 100%."

GUNMETAL GROUP'S POLICY ON SAG VOUCHERS
They tell **HOLLYWOOD OS**®: "We fill the needs dictated by the production. We are really good about taking care of military men and women. Non-Union performers become SAG eligible through us very fast."

POLICY ON SPECING
Gunmetal Group tells us: "We don't tolerate specing. If we invite you to our set, please come out and meet us. If not, just stay at home and wait for a call."

IF YOU ARE RUNNING LATE TO SET...
You must call the lead technical advisor for the show and let him or her know.

COMPANY PHILOSOPHY
Jon tells **HOLLYWOOD OS**®: "We strive for and demand perfection in all military areas on our shows. *Gunmetal* is more than a company name, it's an idea and a way of doing things."

IF YOU COULD TELL BACKGROUND ACTORS ANYTHING...
"Being in the military, we have a unique perspective on the film industry. Most of us are combat veterans that started working on *JAG* for Matt Sigloch years ago, so we are not new to film and TV. It's a foreign concept to us to complain about working for 12 hours without a place to sit, or not having food prepared for you on time. The film industry doesn't owe anyone anything. Have pride in yourself and what you are doing, and always strive to achieve the next promotion. If you are playing an extra today, you might be a principal tomorrow. Don't let your attitude ruin your future work, and never be afraid of hard work... work as if the camera is always on you!"

Hollywood OS®

400 S. Beverly Drive, Suite 307
Beverly Hills, CA 90212

Website:
www.hollywoodos.com

Email:
info@hollywoodos.com

Staff
Stuart, Jared, Angela, Nicolas, Alexis & TJ

Office Line:
310-289-9400

Subscription Line:
310-277-1007

Info Line/Hotline:
n/a

YEAR OPENED

1997

CLIENT ROSTER

Anyone - SAG, AFTRA, Non-Union talent, all ages, can subscribe/register with *Hollywood OS®* (*Hollywood Operating System®*) in addition to inclusion in the free Talent Search Engine™! Our goal is to help get you cast and provide you with the necessary tools! We appreciate reliable and professional talent. Whether you are a character actor, a model or a background actor, Casting Directors using the *Hollywood Operating System®* are searching for your type on a daily basis. Actors, Background Actors, Kids, Voice-Over Talent, Pets and Cars are all listed with us.

REGISTRATION

FREE! Yup, it's free, baby! 100%. Promise. For those of you new to background work, tight on cash, or just not sure that you're ready to subscribe to *Hollywood OS®*, we offer a free, one week trial, complete with all online options! Get your booty down to our office any weekday between 1pm and 4pm (yes, you have to come in person so we know that you're really you). We'll snap a photo, create your Account Profile and get your mug out there for the casting directors who use *Hollywood OS®*. They'll see you, and you'll be able to submit to any and all casting notices that you fit for a full week!

Give us a test drive, baby! Here's the best part – if you don't use it, decide you don't even like background work or you don't land any gigs (although we would hope that you would be proactive about using your free week and submit for projects daily) – guess what – you haven't spent a darn dime! If you like it, great, if you don't, no big deal!

How's that for believing in our system and the Casting Directors who utilize *Hollywood OS®*. We are so confident that you will get called for work and land a gig, we are willing to let you try us out for a full week, experiencing ALL online options. This not only benefits you and your pocketbook (our hope is that you can make some moolah) but will also benefit the Casting Directors using our website. Everyday these CD's need new faces for their projects. If you are a person who needs to create a free account, you are automatically a new searchable face to those CD's. It's a win-win for everyone, and you still haven't spent a penny! (How cool are we?!)

REGISTRATION (cont'd)

Once your free week of complete access is up, even if you choose not to officially subscribe, your photo and profile will remain in the *Hollywood OS®* Talent Search Engine™. Forever. Or until your phone number goes bad. Or you call/email us and ask to be removed. While you'll no longer be able to submit yourself without being a current subscriber, your Account Profile will remain fully searchable to Casting Directors hunting for your type. So keep your stats current.

FREE BENEFITS

- Your online profile will be searchable by CDs seeking your type
- One free photo taken
- Receive casting alerts via email & text message for roles that fit your profile
- View, manage and update your online profile
- Schedule your availability daily for work
- Review casting information, production information and industry events

To ensure that everyone from all walks of life is given the opportunity to be seen and cast, the *Hollywood OS®* Talent Search Engine™ has always been, and will continue to remain, free of charge to anyone who wishes to be available to Casting Directors. Actors of all ages, shapes and sizes are welcome to come into the office, complete the paperwork, take a free digital photo and fill out their online Account Profile – all of it for FREE! No registration fee, no commission, no strings attached.

SUBSCRIPTION

Hollywood Operating System® is a casting and information resource. A subscription to *Hollywood OS®* gives you exclusive complete access to all content in print and online. The subscription includes advance casting notices and information that appears online before the print magazine edition. Subscription also enables you to create your own free online account profile for the Talent Search Engine™.

TO SUBSCRIBE

Initially this may be done in the office or online. It is highly suggested that you go into the office so they can take your photo(s) for your account. Why not, it's free!

You can visit anytime during office hours and (depending on your subscription choice) get up to 10 photo updates so CD's can view your different looks. They can also scan in your professional photos (please, no headshots - shots of just your head) and add them as well, no charge. When you go in for photos, do NOT wear white since your photo will be taken in natural light against a white background – bright colors or dark colors are best! Dress according to your type. If you look like a mad scientist, dress like one!

TO SUBSCRIBE (cont'd)

Be sure to know your accurate sizes and bring the following information:

- Current photo ID and original (non-laminated) Social Security card OR a receipt from the Social Security office OR
- Current photo ID and birth certificate OR current U.S. passport OR current green card
- Current SAG card and /or your AFTRA Card (or a receipt from SAG or AFTRA) if you are union.

FOR MINORS

Bring what you have of the above AND you MUST bring in PHOTOCOPIES of the following:

- Current entertainment work permit
- Proof of your child's Coogan Account

SUBSCRIPTION OPTIONS:

Day Pass: $9.99
Unlimited Submissions
2 Free Photos
Hollywood OS® - Casting Magazine
No Commitment

1 Week Pass: $14.99
Unlimited Submissions
2 Free Photos
Hollywood OS® - Casting Magazine
No Commitment

1 Month: $39.99
Unlimited Submissions
4 Free Photos
"EXTRA" WORK for Brain Surgeons®
Hollywood OS® - Casting Magazine
No Commitment

3 Months: $89.99
(averages out to $29.99/a month)
Unlimited Submissions
10 Free Photos
"EXTRA" WORK for Brain Surgeons®
Hollywood OS® - Casting Magazine
No Commitment

6 Months: $149.99
(averages out to $24.99/a month)
Unlimited Submissions
10 Free Photos
"EXTRA" WORK for Brain Surgeons®
Hollywood OS® - Casting Magazine
No Commitment

1 Year: $199.99
(averages out to $16.66/a month)
Unlimited Submissions
10 Free Photos
"EXTRA" WORK for Brain Surgeons®
Hollywood OS® - Casting Magazine
No Commitment

MONTHLY SUBSCRIPTIONS:

6 Months: $29.99/a month
($29.99 on 6 month commitment with a credit or debit card)
Unlimited Submissions
10 Free Photos
"EXTRA" WORK for Brain Surgeons®
Hollywood OS® - Casting Magazine

12 Months: $19.99/a month
($19.99 on 12 month commitment with a credit or debit card)
Unlimited Submissions
10 Free Photos
"EXTRA" WORK for Brain Surgeons®
Hollywood OS® - Casting Magazine

PROCEDURE TO FOLLOW

Check the website often, that way you can see what CD's are booking and what types are needed. CD's also call us daily and ask for booking assistance. Talent should make sure their account profile is current. We try to call out to talent and help them get work, however, just remember we are NOT a calling service and cannot vouch for your availability. You can vouch for your own availability by submitting directly to the online casting notices.

New projects are posted 24/7: Commercials, Print, Film, Music Videos, Infomercials, Industrials, Interstitials, Television, SAG Jobs, AFTRA Jobs, Non-Union Jobs, Photo Double Work, Stand-In Work, Principal Work, Extra Work and Voice-Over. As a current subscriber, there is no charge per submission.

APPRECIATES

"Common sense and people genuinely interested in working in this business. We love the professional folks and sincerely appreciate polite, friendly, honest people. Our business is to provide you with the information and if you have questions, be sure to ask – it never hurts!"

PET PEEVES

"Non-professional, rude, mean, arrogant, all-knowing people with bad attitudes, this goes for CD's as well. Being rude is not necessary. It doesn't take any more effort to be nice to people and treat others as you would like to be treated. We reserve the right to refuse service. No one wants to book talent with poor attitudes and work ethic. Also, no boozing on set, people, it's not a party. I know... you think I'm kidding, I'm so NOT kidding...

Also, please DO NOT submit to *Casting Notices* if you do NOT fit what the CD states they are seeking. Many CD's have been miffed when looking in their submission box to find people who look nothing like the TYPE they specifically stated they were looking for. It wastes their time and ultimately hurts your chances of getting booked when you do actually fit the criteria. They're like "Dude, why'd that dude submit?!"

SORT OF PET PEEVES

"People who insist upon using their 1978 disco picture because they believe it still looks like them. It's hard to give someone bad news about their photos. This is why it's standard policy to have your photos taken with us (it's free) and to only accept 3/4 headshots and color zed cards for scanning purposes. Extras Casting Directors sincerely love the standard 3"x5" color photos, waist-up against a white wall. It is what you really look like. Ultimately, you will get more work from that type of photo in the extras business. I know, people hate to hear that... "

"DEEP THOUGHTS"

"They say what doesn't kill you makes you stronger. This is a tough competitive business infested with people who go for the jugular. Believe in yourself, and your talent. Never lose sight of your goals and keep the faith."

"Houses"

Make your House a Star!
(information listed below)

Website:
www.eidc.com

Email:
n/a

Casting Directors/Staff
n/a

Main Line:
n/a

Registration Line:
n/a

Info Line/Hotline:
n/a

act seven

House "Representation"

Yes, this may seem sort of random to mention in a city where thirteen new-to-town thespians usually share one cramped and crowded studio apartment at the foot of the Hollywood Hills, but for those of you who may have homes or houses that are a bit bigger – this info is for you! Production scouts are constantly scouring within the city limits and beyond to locate that perfect home for location filming.

QUESTION: *How do you go about this, you ask?*

Well, rather than wait for said him or her scout to show up at your doorstep taking photos of your perfect shutters and frame, you can go to the Entertainment Industry Development Corporation website:

ANSWER: *www.eidc.com*

Once there, click on "Public Information." From the cool drop-down menu. Now click on "Make Your Property A Star." Now you're well on your way. Be sure to read EVERYTHING. There's a booklet of sorts you can print out that will detail all the things you should know about "making your property a star."

If you still feel like your abode is just the type for stardom, you have great relationships with your neighbors (productions tend to cause chaos and curious crowds of onlookers), and you're ready to make some money for your property, now's the time to contact a location manager. Yes, that's right – your house gets a manager for its career! Only in Hollywood, people!

Depending upon who you contact, this manager will ask you various questions regarding your property before he or she will make a determination to "represent" your home. You can forgo the manager altogether if you feel like luck and the good graces of the gods are on your side.

You can also find a listing of location services and scouts (and managers for that matter) in *LA 411*. They all get a cut of your profit, of course, but your house still gets all the screen time!

Hey, you never know, right? Make your home work for you!

Joey's List

13619 Moorpark St., Suite G
Sherman Oaks, CA 91423

Website:
www.joeyslist.com

Email:
info@joeyslist.com

Staff
Joey Stafura

Main Line:
818-286-3078

Registration Line:
n/a

Info Line/Hotline:
n/a

act seven

YEAR OPENED
2005

CLIENT ROSTER
Accepts both SAG and Non-Union talent.

TYPE OF COMPANY
A calling service for Adults 18+ with a small and selective roster.

REGISTRATION
Joey is currently accepting Non-Union talent. Submit your photo and info to: Info@joeyslist.com. His Union roster is currently full (except by referral), but feel free to email him your photo/info. He'll put you on the waiting list and you'll be contacted when there's an open spot. Joey also wants all of his talent to be registered with *Central Casting*.

PROCEDURE TO FOLLOW ONCE REGISTERED
Joey's List is an "available service." He likes all of his clients to call in every day that they are available to work. He accepts calls the day before, but does not accept availability for the week or month. His office hours are 10am to 7pm. Joey says he likes to hear from his people daily as it helps him build relationships with each of his clients.

JOEY'S LIST APPRECIATES
To quote Joey: "Not cancelling and showing up on time."

Company Fees	SAG Members	AFTRA & Non-Union Talent
Registration Fee:	$0	$0
Processing Fee:	$0	$0
Monthly Membership:	$50	$50
Commissions:	$0	$0
TOTAL:	***$50***	***$50***

Joey's List

PET PEEVES
Joey says: people who ask "am I booked yet for tomorrow?"

COMPANY PHILOSOPHY
Joey's List goes by the motto: "It is, what it is?" Very zen.

IF YOU COULD TELL BACKGROUND ACTORS ANYTHING...
Joey tells **HOS**®: "If you just show up on time, bring additional wardrobe, and never cancel, you can create a good name for yourself as well as increase your bookings."

INSIDE SCOOP!
Joey Stafura was formerly a CD over at mega-casters *Central Casting*. In January of 2005, he set out to create his own calling service, with a limited roster of "high quality, groomed people." He hand-picks members of his roster, and seeks to develop a rapport with each of them. He also rocks the bass guitar in his very own alternative band, *High School Logic*. Yeah, that last part doesn't really have anything to do with background casting, but we thought it was cool, so we threw it in anyway. Rock on!

Kalifornia Kasting

30 North Raymond Avenue, Suite 408
Old Town Pasadena, CA 91103

Website:
www.kaliforniakasting.com

Email:
info@kaliforniakasting.com

Staff
Jennifer, Jeanie, Jerry & Ted

Main Line:
n/a

Registration Line:
n/a

Info Line/Hotline:
888-282-2623

act seven

YEAR OPENED

1994

CLIENT ROSTER

A limited client roster of "quality" talent. Represents adults ("18 to a million"), all ethnicities, mostly Non-Union. About 200 folks.

25% (SAG) **75% (Non-Union)**

TYPE OF COMPANY

Kalifornia is a traditional Calling Service for background actors ages 18+.

AVERAGE BOOKINGS

Jennifer tells **HOLLYWOOD OS**®: "Non-Union clients work a minimum of three days a week – usually five. We keep our SAG clients limited and they tend to work a couple of times each month." Remember CD's make the final choice, so Jen and gang CAN'T guarantee work.

REGISTRATION

Registration is by appointment only! Call their spiffy new toll-free # and leave your name, Union status, phone number and the best time to reach you. Referrals preferred. If you are referred by someone, please tell Jen the name of the individual who referred you to her. SAG applicants should understand they have a very limited number of spots available, if at all, and that's because they want their clients working and they don't want to take your money if they can't get you work (SAG members generally work 3 - 5 days a month).

Company Fees	SAG Members	AFTRA & Non-Union Talent
Registration Fee:	$40	$40
Processing Fee:	$0	$0
Monthly Membership:	$55 or $65*	$55 or $65*
Commissions:	0%	0%
TOTAL:	***$95 or $105***	***$95 or $105***

* Ok. If you set up an automatic pay-plan which is deducted from your credit card or checking account each month, the monthly fee is $55. Otherwise the monthly fee is $65.

Kalifornia Kasting

POLICY ON GIVING OUT SAG VOUCHERS

Jennifer tells **HOLLYWOOD OS**®: "A SAG voucher is up to you – how you handle yourself on the set, following directions, being a professional... if you've proven yourself, and I know of an opportunity, it can happen."

WHAT JENNIFER APPRECIATES MOST

act seven

Jennifer tells **HOLLYWOOD OS**®: "Honesty, professionalism, common courtesy, keeping me updated on your schedule. I also love when CD's rave about my clients – positive feedback is great!" Yeah it is! She also believes communication is key and wants to remind talent to use common sense. Enough said.

"DEEP THOUGHTS"

Jen shares some more good stuff with **HOLLYWOOD OS**®: "Our company is kind of like a mom and pop store – a family. We've been around long enough to establish ourselves in the casting community and to earn a (well-deserved) reputation with casting agencies and our clients alike. While there are many "choices" at our feet, we always suggest looking into a service before jumping into a service. We are limited on the amount of clients that we will accept. We have always been a firm believer in bigger doesn't necessarily mean better. We pride ourselves on knowing the face with the name and voice. Once you pass our top-secret investigating, we will set up an appointment with you, but not everyone gets to this point.

We represent you and you represent *Kalifornia Kasting*, Inc. Having a "me" mentality is not what *Kalifornia Kasting* is looking for in a client. Clients must realize that what they do, will and does effect their fellow members as well as *Kalifornia Kasting* as a whole. So please know that no person or persons will remain with this company or be allowed to put in jeopardy the name that *Kalifornia Kasting* has built and earned in this casting community." Well said, Jen. Team work, everyone working together, working as one. Sweet!

Knota Ko Casting

4845 N. Maywood Avenue
Los Angeles, CA 90041

Website:
www.punkrawkstunts.com

Email:
n/a

Staff
Eaglebear, Mike & Paul

Main Line:
323-255-1001

Registration Line:
n/a

Info Line/Hotline:
n/a

YEAR OPENED
2001

TYPE OF COMPANY
SAG and Non-Union adults ages 18+ who are unique character types and/or Native American.

REGISTRATION
By mail only. Submit a headshot and resumé and/or General Info. Be sure to include your contact numbers and they will get in touch with you if they can use you. Once they contact you, you may need to supply them with 20 - 30 headshots or 5"x7" prints.

Eaglebear tells **HOLLYWOOD OS**®: "We will contact you as needed, so please don't get mad if you don't hear from us. Please be on time when booked. Be ready to go and ready to work. Don't hide on set and have a lot of fun!"

INSIDE SCOOP!
Eaglebear would like to make it clear that he did at one time own *Casting To The Four Winds,* but sold the company and is no longer affiliated with them in any way. Okay. Enough said.

Eaglebear, however, is now partnered with a place called *Punk Rawk Stunts,* which handles stunt performers and extreme "unique looks" casting - think "goth and whips and chains." To quote their website: "Scary People, Professional Performers, Reasonable Rates." Whoa!

Company Fees	SAG Members	AFTRA & Non-Union Talent
Registration Fee:	$0	$0
Processing Fee:	$0	$0
Monthly Membership:	$0	$0
Commissions:	0%	0%
TOTAL:	***$0***	***$0***

Latin Connection Management

1426 North Avenue 55
Los Angeles, CA 90042

Staff
Betty

Main Line:
323-257-9748

Website:
n/a

Registration Line:
n/a

Email:
n/a

Info Line/Hotline:
n/a

YEAR OPENED
1990

TYPE OF COMPANY
The Latin Connection is a management company that specializes in Latin and Hispanic talent but they accept all types (Caucasian, Asian and African-American) as long as you are "serious, respectful and reliable."

REGISTRATION
Call Tuesday - Friday AFTER 7:30PM for specifics. Referrals and recommendations are especially welcome. Betty tells **HOLLYWOOD OS®**: "Remember, quality not quantity is what we are about. Follow instructions, and please DO NOT call in for work – we will call you."

INSIDE SCOOP!
Betty also tells **HOLLYWOOD OS®**: "We provide Union and Non-Union principals and extras for features, TV shows, commercials, videos, industrials, print, dubbing and we're VERY STRONG in voice-overs."

She does not like talent who spec her sets and she does not guarantee work! She says: "The only guarantees in life are death and taxes." Okay then...

Company Fees	SAG Members	AFTRA & Non-Union Talent
Registration Fee:	$0	$0
Processing Fee:	$0	$0
Monthly Membership:	$0	$0
Commissions:	10%* to 15%**	10%* to 15%**
TOTAL:	**DEPENDS ON COMMISSIONS**	**DEPENDS ON COMMISSIONS**

*10% if you make less than $100.
**15% if you make over $100.

Margarita's Casting

1128 S. Marietta Street
Los Angeles, CA 90023

Website:
n/a

Email:
n/a

Staff
Margarita & Maria

Main Line:
323-268-1584

Registration Line:
n/a

Info Line/Hotline:
n/a

act seven

YEAR OPENED

1990

TYPE OF COMPANY

This company specializes in ethnic talent of all ages, especially Hispanic talent. Although all ethnicities are welcome to submit, Margarita explained to us that most productions seek her services when they are looking for Hispanic talent. This company usually provides talent for commercials, print, features, music videos and some television.

REGISTRATION

You may call to register Monday through Friday, 11AM-2PM ,to see if you are what they are currently looking for. If so, you will then mail photos. It is suggested that you submit six headshots and resumés for consideration. Please be sure to have a current resumé along with your "General Information" and contact numbers.

Margarita tells **HOLLYWOOD OS**®: "I will contact you when I have work for you – please do not call in looking for work." She is very busy, boys and girls, so behave – Margarita will do her best to get you working if she's got something to cast!

Company Fees	SAG Members	AFTRA & Non-Union Talent
Registration Fee:	$0	$0
Processing Fee:	$0	$0
Monthly Membership:	$0	$0
Commissions:	10% of Base Rate only	10% of Base Rate only
TOTAL:	**DEPENDS ON COMMISSIONS**	**DEPENDS ON COMMISSIONS**

Media Access

1255 S. Central Ave.
Glendale, CA 91204

Staff
Gloria Castaneda
(Casting Liaison/Program Coord.)
Gail Williamson
(Talent Dev./Industry Relations)

Website:
www.disabilityemployment.org/med_acc.htm

Main Line:
818-409-0448

Email:
n/a

Info Line/Hotline:
n/a

YEAR OPENED

1980

TYPE OF COMPANY

An advocacy group and casting liaison for performers with disabilities. Read all about *Media Access* at their website.

REGISTRATION

If you have a disability, you should call and request a new client packet. You then make an appointment to return the paperwork and submit photos. You should submit a headshot and a photo that shows your disability (if it can be visible in your photo). Check them out on the web!

ABOUT THE CASTING DIVISION

"Talent files include actors with seen and unseen disabilities, Non-Union and Union performers with and without agent representation. The office submits headshots and resumés to Casting Directors, and can provide information on accessibility and special services."

MEDIA ACCESS TALENT DEVELOPMENT

Services include: individual career development, reviewing and setting career goals, industry referrals, acting workshops, business of the business classes, low-cost headshot clinics, and young performer and parent seminars.

Company Fees	SAG Members	AFTRA & Non-Union Talent
Registration Fee:	$0	$0
Processing Fee:	$0	$0
Monthly Membership:	$0	$0
Commissions:	0%	0%
TOTAL:	***$0 - STATE-FUNDED***	***$0 - STATE-FUNDED***

Nandinee Productions

3736 Watseka Avenue, #9
Los Angeles, CA 90034

Website:
www.nandineeproductions.com

Email:
nandineeprods@yahoo.com

Staff
Toufiq Tulsiram &
Nandinee Tulsiram

Main Line:
310-876-0404

Registration Line:
n/a

Info Line/Hotline:
n/a

act seven

YEAR OPENED

2000

TYPE OF COMPANY

This company primarily focuses on SAG and Non-Union East Indians, Native Americans, Middle Easterners, Asians and African-Americans of all ages. However, they encourage all ethnicities to submit a photo as you never know.

REGISTRATION

They accept both SAG and Non-Union talent. You should submit a photo (headshot or 3"x5" with all your "GENERAL INFORMATION"), a resumé if you have one, a copy of your Social Security card and all of your current contact numbers. If they like your look, they will call you.

COMPANY PHILOSOPHY

They tell **HOS**®: "Be happy. Don't worry. Follow your heart." Sounds like a tune right out of the 70's.

INSIDE SCOOP!

Check out their website: *www.nandineeproductions.com* and see for yourself what kind of talent they generally take on.

Company Fees	SAG Members	AFTRA & Non-Union Talent
Registration Fee:	$0	$0
Processing Fee:	$0	$0
Monthly Membership:	$0	$0
Commissions:	10%	10%
TOTAL:	***DEPENDS ON COMMISSIONS***	***DEPENDS ON COMMISSIONS***

Networks Casting

224 E. Olive Avenue, Suite 204
Burbank, CA 91502

Website:
www.networkscasting.com

Email:
tyler@networkscasting.com

Staff
Tyler, Jacqlyn, Nader, Ronnie, Kim & Sherry

Main Line:
818-260-8989

Registration Line:
818-260-0992

Info Line/Hotline:
n/a

YEAR OPENED

1997

CLIENT ROSTER

Adults ages 18+, but specializing in talent ages 18-35. Traditionally, their roster has broken down as follows:

60%	**18-25 Year Olds**	**350 (SAG)**
25%	**25-35 Year Olds**	**100 (Non-Union)**
15%	**35-50 Year Olds**	

TYPE OF COMPANY

Networks is a Calling Service for background actors ages 18+. Tyler, formerly of *Central Casting* fame, recently purchased *Networks Casting*, but tells us he will be preserving the majority of the policies and philosophies that have made *Networks Casting* a success. With his 8 years of centralized casting experience, (come on - it was funny, we couldn't resist!) Tyler prides himself on knowing "what a Casting Director wants to see in a calling service."

AVERAGE BOOKINGS

This varies depending on your age and the projects. The former Union policy was if they couldn't get you a minimum of two days of regular background work OR one commercial that month, then you didn't pay for that month. However, the new ownership has discontinued this policy citing too much "abuse" of the privilege.

Company Fees	SAG Members	AFTRA & Non-Union Talent
Registration Fee:	$20	$20
Processing Fee:	$0	$0
Monthly Membership:	$80	$60
Commissions:	0%	0%
TOTAL:	***$100***	***$80***

Networks Casting

act seven

REGISTRATION
Both SAG and Non-Union must call for an appointment. Registration hours are Monday through Friday, 9:30AM to noon. Once registered, photos and resumés can be updated at any time on their website. You can call in for work twice a week. Otherwise you will be contacted with work information. If you are not booked on a particular day (Non-Union only) you may call in between 8AM-9AM to check for "rush call" work which happens frequently.

POLICY ON GIVING OUT SAG VOUCHERS
They don't give them out, so don't even bother asking. Instead, they put people in the position where they can receive them.

WHAT NETWORKS EXPECTS FROM THEIR CLIENTS
Networks tells **HOLLYWOOD OS**®: "Professionalism and honesty. Everyone's schedule varies from time to time. We understand that. We simply want the common courtesy of you letting us know if and when your availability changes. This will only help us be of better service to our clients. We want to avoid double-bookings and schedule conflicts. The flaw with calling services is when the "service" books an extra with a Casting Director for the next day only to find out that the client cannot do the job for whatever reason. Then the Casting Director gets mad for wasting their time replacing them. We then look bad and everyone loses. That's why communication is vital for a service to perform at its best."

KIDS CASTING
New for this year, *Networks* has started a children's division entitled, fittingly, *Kids Casting Network*. Check them out at *www.kidscastingnetwork.com*.

ABOUT PROFESSIONALISM
Networks tells **HOLLYWOOD OS**®: "We do expect the utmost professionalism. We love self-motivated people. Please arrive 15 minutes early to set and please bring the appropriate wardrobe. Always follow the A.D.'s instructions."

COMPANY PHILOSOPHY
And lastly, but not leastly (??? – so not a word, but we like it), *Networks* tells **HOLLYWOOD OS**®: "Our policy is straight-forward. Of course we will get our clients jobs. Unlike other services who take your money, promise you the world, then fall short – we are not like that. We do not guarantee work. However, if you do not work during that month and you were available, we will credit your payment for that month to the following month. We will also consult with you on what we can do to try and get more bookings. Possibly new pictures or going into visit a casting agency or possibly moving on."

Performing Arts Studio West

P.O. Box 1441
Inglewood, CA 90308

Website:
www.pastudiowest.com

Email:
pastudiowest@earthlink.net

Staff
John, Randy, Zander, Teresa, Carmel, Ayana, Diana, Maia

Main Line:
310-674-1346

Registration Line:
818-260-0992

Info Line/Hotline:
n/a

act seven

YEAR OPENED

1998

TYPE OF COMPANY

Performing Arts Studio West is not a calling or casting service, but they're so cool we had to find room for them somewhere, and they do provide an incredibly way cool, valuable service, helping adults with disabilites excel in the performing arts. Let's let them tell you about it in their own words.

From their rad website:

"Performing Arts Studio West began as a concept by studio director and owner John Paizis, in October of 1997. Since the studio opened its doors with five performers in June of 1998, Los Angeles area adults with disabilities have been provided the opportunity to find new avenues to healthy lifestyles, personal success, creative learning, vocational skills and self-expression through our innovative acting, music and dance programs, technical training and live performances. The studio currently serves forty-seven combined full and part-time clients. *PASW* is a working acting studio and production facility that is funded in part by the State of California Department of Developmental Services through Westside Regional Center in Culver City, California."

INSIDE SCOOP!

Whether you're a CD in need of talent or a disabled individual looking for the resources to pursue acting, singing, or dancing, try giving John and the gang a call. They might just be the folks you're looking for. Jeez, that sounded like an ad. But it's not, they're really cool. Call them already, people!

TCA

(a.k.a. Talent Calling Associates)
6116 Fulton Avenue, Space A
Van Nuys, CA 91401

Website:
www.tcaextrascasting.com

Email:
tcatcatca@aol.com

Staff
Teri & Paul

Main Line:
818-997-7867

Registration Line:
n/a

Info Line/Hotline:
n/a

act seven

YEAR OPENED
1994 (Teri took over in 1994, but *TCA* has been around since 1990)

CLIENT ROSTER
SAG and Non-Union, ages 18-80. Approximately 50 SAG members and 50-75 Non-Union members.

TYPE OF COMPANY
TCA is a traditional Calling Service for SAG and Non-Union background talent 18+.

AVERAGE BOOKINGS
"If you are good, reliable and dependable you will work a lot. But it all depends on how busy the casting season is."

REGISTRATION
Call their main line for an appointment. Registration is typically held Monday-Friday from 11AM-5PM and again, by appointment only. Be sure to come knowing your "General Information" and bring a headshot and resumé (if you have one). Please note, fine people, the above listed address is for mailing purposes only – don't just show up unannounced! Not a super "Brain Surgeon" idea.

Company Fees	SAG Members	AFTRA & Non-Union Talent
Registration Fee:	$0	$0
Processing Fee:	$0	$0
Monthly Membership:	$50	$50
Commissions:	0%	0%
TOTAL:	***$100****	***$100****

* Your first and last month's monthly fee must be paid at sign up.

TCA
(a.k.a. Talent Calling Associates)

RESERVE ROSTER
TCA also has a FREE Reserve Roster, but because EWFBS® publicized this last year, Teri told us she was overwhelmed with thousands of requests! So, please understand that work from the Reserve Roster is very, very rare. If you still want to be included, submit a current photo along with your "General Information" and contact numbers. If *TCA* can hook you up with work, they will give you a call. This is a free service and no commissions will be taken. Cool!

TCA PROFESSIONALISM DEFINED
- If you call and get the voicemail, please do not call back until some one answers. Understand that the CASTING LINES are the top priority and the folks at *TCA* will not hang up on a Casting Director in order to answer the phone. Sorry!
- Please call at DECENT HOURS! The *TCA* office is a HOME OFFICE!
- Have the correct wardrobe.
- Do NOT cause problems on the set.
- Let *TCA* know if you are not available – immediately!!!

When Casting requests you and *TCA* books you and it turns out you are not available – that is a bad thing! It frustrates the Casting Director, it annoys *TCA* and it jeopardizes the likelihood that the Casting Director will use *TCA* again. *TCA* will not let one person ruin it for everyone!

TCA PET PEEVES
Teri tells **HOS**®: "Background should not leave the set and plan to come back when they are checking people out or hassle AD's for SAG vouchers." She also wants to remind her talent not to harass the stars or cancel or replace themselves because they booked themselves on a better job. And never, never lie and say "*TCA* never told me . . ."

GOOD THINGS TO DO...
Follow the AD's instructions, act professionally, be on time, have a positive attitude, the correct wardrobe and remember that every day is a new day and while one job may be downright lame the next job may be absolutely amazing!

INSIDE SCOOP!
Teri tells **HOS**®: "Anybody can be a star. Extra work is a stepping stone to other things! The people who are booking extras today might be booking principals tomorrow (including me) – don't burn any bridges!"

Uncut Casting Services

11925 Wilshire Blvd., Suite 313
Los Angeles, CA 90025

Website:
www.uncutcasting.com

Email:
help@launcut.com

Staff
Scott, Jacques, Matt & Beatriz

Main Line:
310-444-2929

Registration Line:
n/a

Info Line/Hotline:
n/a

act seven

YEAR OPENED

2003

TYPE OF COMPANY

Uncut is an online Calling Service for SAG and Non-Union background talent ages 18+.

REGISTRATION

Call their office line (818-990-9009) to set up an appointment to head down to their office and register. Bring your IDs and Union Cards. Photos are not required as they take photos in-office at no additional charge.

POLICY ON SAG VOUCHERS

Uncut tells us: "Should casting allow us to submit non-union talent for a SAG spot, we always consider our most professional people first. But really your best bet is working as non-union on SAG productions as much as possible and being on your best behavior. Most of our people seem to get their vouchers by getting upgraded on set or being requested back by the casting director or production."

UNCUT APPRECIATES

They tell **HOS**®: "If you follow instructions carefully, are always on time, and you are generally enthusiastic about working on set - you are gold in our eyes. A positive attitude can really motivate us to go the extra mile for you."

Company Fees	SAG Members	AFTRA & Non-Union Talent
Registration Fee:	$50	$25
Processing Fee:	$0	$0
Monthly Membership:	$35	$35
Commissions:	0%	0%
TOTAL:	***$85***	***$60***

Uncut Casting Services

UNCUT PET PEEVES

Uncut tells **HOS**®: "Even though we like *50 Cent*, it doesn't mean we want to listen to the first 2 minutes of *In Da Club* every time we get your voice mail." Save the music for the club.

IF YOU COULD TELL BACKGROUND ACTORS ANYTHING...

"Never forget that a bad day working on set is usually better than a good day working in an office."

INSIDE SCOOP!

Uncut is always in search of character types and especially 18TLYs. "If you are as cute as a button and you still look like you are in high school, expect to work a lot with us."

If you are accepted into their monthly service, they "guarantee multiple bookings every month." If you are available to work and they can't book you during the month, they will "refund your money - no questions asked." Well, that's hella cool!

Vision Casting

3629 Cahuenga Blvd. West
Los Angeles, CA 90068

Website:
www.visioncasting.biz

Email:
visioncasting@sbcglobal.com

Staff
Elise & Stef

Main Line:
323-874-2681

Registration Line:
n/a

Info Line/Hotline:
n/a

act seven

YEAR OPENED

2005

TYPE OF COMPANY

This calling service is, as you've likely surmised from our spiffy YEAR OPENED section, a recent addition to the Los Angeles background world. Registered talent are featured in their online database.

REGISTRATION

Registration is Tuesday through Friday at 12 noon. Call first to schedule an appointment (323) 874-2681.

INSIDE SCOOP!

These guys are always looking for enthusiastic talent. Particularly Asian men and women, women of any ethnicity between 30 and 50, and folks of all type over the age of 65. Apparently maybe some sort of spinoff or other division of *Print Models Network*, (see Fabulous Other section) at least that's what the Caller I.D. states. We hear that *Vision* is working hard to get their clients killer gigs. Cool!

Elise tells **HOS**®: "Enjoy being a background artist. If you have a good attitude, as with any job, it will be noticed and rewarded." Awesome!

Company Fees	SAG Members	AFTRA & Non-Union Talent
Registration Fee:	$25	$50
Photo Fee:	$0	$25
Monthly Fee:	$25*	$50
Commissions:	0%	0%
TOTAL:	***$50***	***$75****

*Bumps up to $50/month after you book 3 days of work.
**Fee can be paid after you get work. Cool!

The Wild Bunch of Hollywood

5854 Jamieson Avenue
Encino, CA 91316

Website:
www.thewildbunchofhollywood.com

Email:
management@thewildbunchofhollywood.com

Staff
Ron, Rico, Jacque & Antonio

Main Line:
818-342-8282

Registration Line:
n/a

Info Line/Hotline:
n/a

act seven

YEAR OPENED
1995

TYPE OF COMPANY
A self-supporting Actors' Group, neato! This is a highly specific group of performers who fall into a unique category. They are extreme character types ranging from experienced stunt people, homeless, hippies, hookers, gang bangers, druggies, prisoners, pimps, scary tattooed bikers, strippers, pro wrestlers, thugs, bikers with Harley's, gothic, punk, etc.

REGISTRATION
The Wild Bunch accepts both SAG and Non-Union talent who have alternative looks. If you have a funky look – submit a photo (3"x5", 4"x6", headshot – they're not too picky, as long as it's a character look). If your photo intrigues them, they'll give you a call to talk about getting registered.

INSIDE SCOOP!
This super-specific group often negotiates for a higher base for its members. Gotta love that! But no guarantees, folks. They will give out hotline numbers to those who are registered with them officially and they suggest you check the lines daily so you don't miss out on work!

Company Fees	SAG Members	AFTRA & Non-Union Talent
Membership Fee:	$40	$40
Processing Fee:	$0	$0
Quarterly Fee:	$20	$20
Commissions:	0%	0%
TOTAL:	***$40****	***$40****

* The $40 Registration Fee covers an initial Processing Fee plus your first four months.

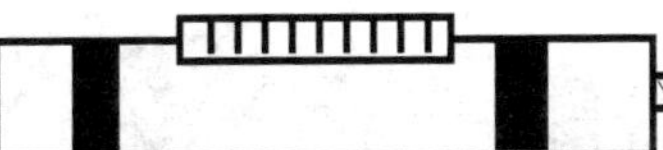

finding an agent

A report straight from the frontline

by Laura Drake Mancini,
HOLLYWOOD OS®

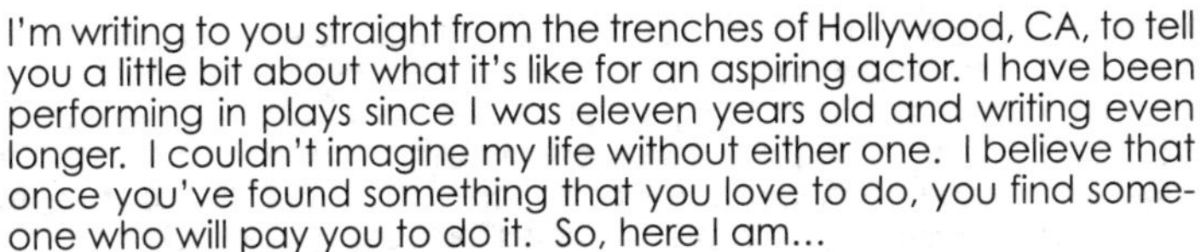

I'm writing to you straight from the trenches of Hollywood, CA, to tell you a little bit about what it's like for an aspiring actor. I have been performing in plays since I was eleven years old and writing even longer. I couldn't imagine my life without either one. I believe that once you've found something that you love to do, you find someone who will pay you to do it. So, here I am...

Each and every day a Jimmy from Wisconsin or a Cindy from Texas arrives to join the forces. They, like thousands of others, will struggle to attain a successful career in the entertainment field. While they're here, far from home, they'll experience just about every emotion known to man.

Living out here, I have learned that film and television are very different from theatre, and that physical appearance plays a much greater role in determining whether or not you're RIGHT for a particular part. I am 5'7", have short dark brown hair and dark brown eyes. I weigh about 125 pounds (I know, girls should never tell their weight, but this is for a good cause). I wish I was in better shape, but I'm working on that (no, I haven't joined a gym yet). You see, I'm not very unique... MANY people may look like me! And MANY people will be considered for the same roles.

Nonetheless, I took my first steps towards finding MY place in this industry and I want to share my experiences with you. Although they're not incredibly exciting, I hope you can chuckle with me (or at me) and perhaps relate to my adventures! Here goes...

They Like Me…
They Really... Like Me?!

My left arm ached as I stood in line at the Hollywood Station Post Office for twenty-five minutes, holding a *Big K-Mart* bag containing one hundred and nine 9"x12" envelopes. Each envelope snugly held my headshot and resumé and for the low cost of only $59.95 (55¢ a piece, at the time) I could mail ALL of them to those eagerly awaiting agents.
Well, at least I could hope that they were eager, right?!

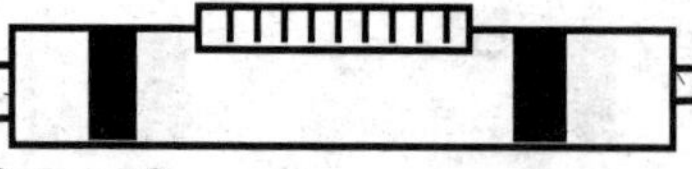

finding an agent

A report straight from the frontline

The day after I mailed my submissions I received two pages and an answering machine message. A total of three agents contacted me! I was overjoyed!!! "YEAH! They like me, they really like me!" – for about a week! That first week I received a total of six responses. In the weeks to follow I would receive one more call making the total seven agencies. About five of those agencies represented only commercial talent and I wondered if that had anything to do with my submissions arriving during pilot season.

Anyway, I quickly made appointments with each agency and dreamt of the meeting where they would announce, "There she is, finally. You are exactly what we've been looking for." This didn't happen, but I must admit that I met a great deal of wonderful, down-to-earth agents.

• Interview I

The first agency I met with, we'll call them "Sexy People Inc.," told me that they wanted to represent me immediately. The agent explained that I would be their only female client with short hair. Yes, they were very small, but that doesn't mean they're not a good agency. However, I did find it strange that they didn't have me read or audition in any way AND the agent was also an actor himself, which I thought could be a conflict of interest.

• Interview II

The next interview was the worst. . . BECAUSE I NEVER GOT THERE! Stupid me got completely lost and I found myself calling both the agency we'll call "Tip-Top Folks," and my friends. "Where in God's name am I!? I think I'm at the L.A. Zoo," I yelled over my cell phone. Yes, folks, I was completely lost! To make a long story even longer, the folks at "Tip" told me I could reschedule my appointment, but I was never able to reach them to do that. They were a full-service agency and I wonder what would have happened had I actually met with them. Who knows? I hold the belief that everything happens for a reason - I just have absolutely NO IDEA what this reason could be!

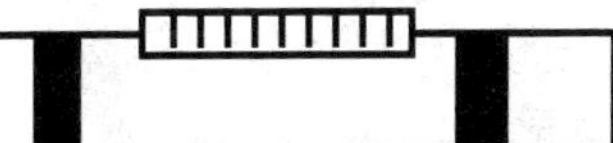

finding an agent

A report straight from the frontline

• Interview III

The next agency really excited me. Let's call them "Exciting Agency Inc.," (I know, I'm really inventive with names). I met with the agent and he called me back the next week to do a scene. I couldn't find just the right piece, so I wrote a monologue of my own and performed it the following Friday afternoon. They seemed to love it! I felt that it was the best agency audition I'd ever given. Technically, so far, it was the ONLY agency audition I'd ever given. Well, they called the following Monday, like they promised, and said, "You're a great actress and we really enjoyed your piece, BUT (here it comes) we are unable to take you on as a client at this time." Yes, my heart sank, but look how far I got. Plus, I really felt like I gave a solid, true performance. I think that's the most important part.

• Interviews IV & V

The two agency visits to follow were brief and uneventful (no, I didn't get lost again)! The first I'll call "Che Che," and they didn't ask me to audition. Rather, they gave me the name and number of a commercial teacher that I might wish to look into, so I could create a commercial reel for myself. They were very nice and told me to come back when I HAD a commercial reel because, "How do you know you like doing commercials if you've never done one?" Those were her words.

I did audition at the next agency, which was quite a drive; we'll call them "Faraway Folks." I had never done a commercial audition and I actually got to say, "When I have a headache, I use *Excedrin*." I wasn't videotaped, and I was told to direct my speech to the corner of a hanging picture. It felt pretty weird. I was nervous, at first, but then I remembered how my sister and I used to make up our own little commercials in front of the bathroom mirror as kids: "Look how my teeth shimmer and my hands are so soft because of this dishwashing liquid." We were pretty strange children, true, but these memories helped to ease the building tension. Not much happened with these agencies...

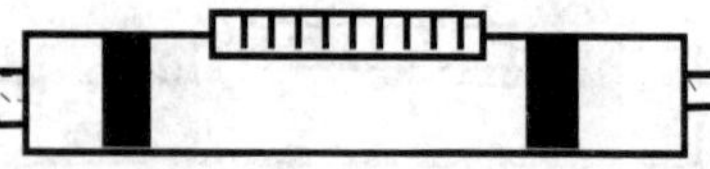

finding an agent

A report straight from the frontline

• Interview VI

The next audition was my first in front of a camera. I had to say my name, turn left, turn right and begin reading a candy commercial. I then had to do the same commercial in a fit of hysterical laughter. It was really fun! I was told that if they liked me I would be called back. Yes, a week later I WAS called back. I really liked everyone at this commercial agency and I wanted to sign with them, but I still had one more audition. So, I told "Candy People Inc.," (yes, another unique, fabricated name) that I would probably be back.

act eight

• Interview VII

Well, I went on my last agency audition a week later and announced, "When I went for my physical, I asked my doctor what to take for my headaches. He told me that two *Advil* work better then two *Extra Strength Tylenol Gelcaps*. For my tough headaches *Advil* just works better." (I think I have a thing for headache commercials!) I auditioned in a long empty room with two young women peering back at me. Before I auditioned, they asked whether I had ever been in a commercial or had taken commercial classes. Since I hadn't, they gave me the name of a teacher that they recommend (déja vu from interview II, eh?) It went pretty well, but I never heard from them after that day.

Whew!

I can't tell you how much I learned! It was all quite an adventure! I am now with the commercial agency, "Candy People Inc." and they are really sweet...no pun intended. I do plan to do this all again soon, however, in hopes of finding television and theatrical representation. It should be quite an adventure!

Good luck and happy trails to you all!

principally speaking

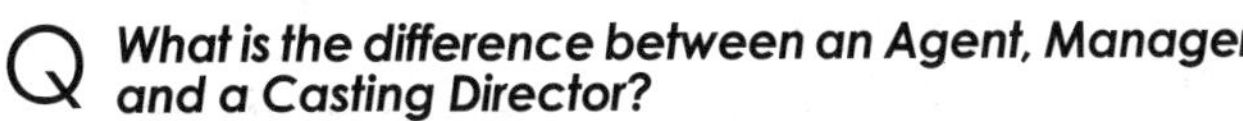

Principal actors' most commonly asked questions..................................

Q ***What is the difference between an Agent, Manager and a Casting Director?***

A

- ***AGENTS*** are franchised by one or more performers' unions (SAG, AFTRA, ACTRA, AGVA, AGMA, & AEA...), but it isn't as important as it once was. They have a fixed commission and get the dough after you get paid for an acting job . You can find a comprehensive list of SAG franchised talent agencies in this Act.
- ***PERSONAL MANAGERS*** are not franchised by the union and can collect more commission from you than an agent, but only AFTER you work! They're more like legal advisors or financial/business managers, and cannot secure work for you. They will, however, put a heck of a lot of time and money into your career, so that's good.
- ***CASTING DIRECTORS*** are casting consultants! They are hired by studios, networks, producers and advertising agencies. They make their bread and butter from these places, NOT from the sexy actors they hire!

Q ***What is the difference between a legitimate talent agency and one that wants money?***

A A legitimate talent agency doesn't charge a lame upfront, advance fee for registration, resumés, photos, screen tests, acting lessons, public relations services, or other "expensive" stuff. If they love you and sign you, nothing leaves your wallet until you work as a performer – that's the rule! Once your booty finally lands that infamous gig, then you pay 10% of your earnings after, never before, the job. F.Y.I.: Legitimate agencies don't typically advertise in newspapers, classifieds, or through the mail!

Q ***Does the state of California license talent agencies and if so, how can I obtain that information?***

A Yes! The state licenses legitimate agencies as "talent agents." Most established agencies in movies and television are franchised by SAG or AFTRA. Watch out for any talent agency not licensed by this good ol' state of CA! Call 415-703-4846 for more info or check their website: www.dir.ca.gov/databases/dlselr/Talag.html

principally speaking

Principal actors' most commonly asked questions

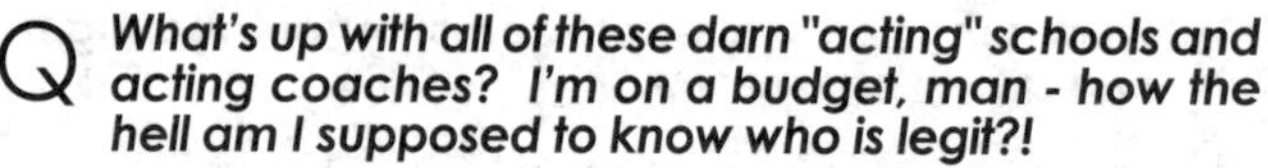

Q ***What's up with all of these darn "acting" schools and acting coaches? I'm on a budget, man - how the hell am I supposed to know who is legit?!***

A This is Hollywood for cryin' out loud – the entertainment capital of the world! Of course there are several fine acting schools, as well as the money-hungry purse-snatching lemons. A couple of tips, my innocent young tulips: When looking for a school or teacher watch for the same signs as choosing a talent agent or photographer. A lame school or teacher may request outrageous fees or demand pictures be taken by their photographer. Not good. Watch out for suspicious teachers who "claim" to have produced incredible TV shows, theatrical productions and movies. The unions do not recommend a school. You may think of contacting a local Community College for theatre, radio and television classes too. This, too, is a good way to test the waters.

Q ***How in the heck do I find a good, honest and reputable photographer!?***

A There are many photographers that you should consider in your quest for a truly special headshot. We suggest that you pick your favorite 3 - 5 and meet with each of them in person and check out their portfolio! You will get a much better headshot from a photographer that you really "CLICK" with (pun entirely intended)! If you think about it, a headshot is your billboard for the industry. It is often your first and last impression! Many talented actors are often over looked because of poor headshots. This market is simply too competitive to sabotage yourself with an unflattering representation.

Q ***What do I do if a talent agent is insistent on sending me to a certain photographer for pictures?***

A Run for the exit clutching your money! He or she may be a scam who sneaks down into the basement and then splits the photographer's fee. Recommendations are fine, requirements are not so fine. Choose your own photographer if you need pictures. You might want to try a different agent if this were to happen.

principally speaking

Principal Actors' most commonly asked questions

Q ***When I do meet with a potential photographer, what questions should I ask them?!***

A ***Ask about their EXPERIENCE . . .***

- How long have you been specializing in Headshot Photography?
- Are you a professional or just a struggling actor with a stupid camera?

Ask about LOCATIONS AND LIGHTING . . .

- Do you have a professional studio, do you shoot on location, or both?
- Can you shoot natural, studio and hot lights and what would you recommend for my skin tone?

Ask about your MARKETABLE APPEARANCE . . .

- Approximately how many different looks can I expect?
- What about Hair and Makeup – is that included in the cost?
- Should I come "Camera Ready" or will I be able to get ready at the studio (if there is one)?

Ask about THE SHOOT . . .

- How many appointments are scheduled in a day?
- How long is a usual session?
- What if something comes up & I have to reschedule?
- Can you shoot a Polaroid so I can see "the shot" before we shoot?
- Can you shoot medium format for higher quality?

Ask about THE NEXT STEP. . .

- How soon after the shoot can I see the proof sheets?
- Will you go over the proof sheets with me and make suggestions?
- What photo lab should I use?

Ask about ADDITIONAL (i.e., HIDDEN) COSTS . . .

- Do you offer inexpensive proof prints to help me find "the shot"?
- How much should an 8"x10" print cost?
- Which is better for multiple reproductions – photograph reproductions or lithos?
- Is there an outrageous fee to own my negatives after the shoot? Ouch!

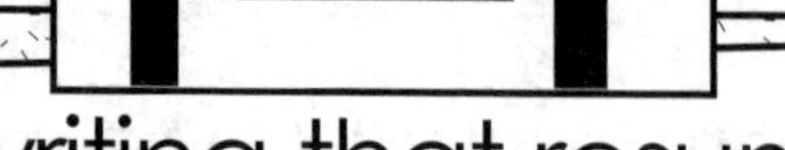

writing that resumé

Hot Brain Surgeon tips for the professional actor

by Mike Wood,
HOLLYWOOD OS®

So you wanna be a star? Okay, let's not even go there. But how about a working actor? Sounds great, right? Ready to sign on the dotted line, aren't ya? Well, there's lots you gotta do first. And we at **HOLLYWOOD OS®** want to help.

So, first things first – you gotta get your so-sexy-self out there! And how do you that, you ask? Impress the heck out of them, with a kick-ass, killer RESUMÉ.

Many of you have asked how to write a REAL resumé – one that looks professional, gets you noticed, and most importantly, gets you the darn job! You want to make sure you include all the right elements (and leave out those little tid-bits no one really cares about except your mother or your really bored friends... i.e., your favorite color, the last time you got a truly bad haircut, etc.).

There is no standard format or font for a resumé (centered, right-justified, etc.), but there are a few key things no resumé should be without. And that's what we'll be talking about here. First, the resumé should always look PROFESSIONAL. If you wanna be funky, wait for the audition! Don't put it on the paper. Chances are, the person reading your resumé doesn't know you from Shirley, and he or she might not realize what a funky, fun person you are – you might just look like a flake or a freak or worse! Your resumé is your ticket in – it's a key element of your first impression – and professionalism will win every time.

Your resumé should present you, the REAL YOU (no lying, folks – it doesn't benefit anybody – and worse yet, you could get caught...): "You can juggle seven flaming samurai swords while standing on your pinky finger? Cool. Demonstration, please." You need to present yourself as YOU, not some fictionalized, idealized version of you. Be proud of what you have done and who you are. Everyone has to start somewhere. Remember that. The trick is to present yourself in the most favorable light that will reflect the talents and traits you do, in fact, have. After all, it's just a piece of paper – but you gotta make this baby fly! You wanna wow them with a doozy of a resumé. And here's how...

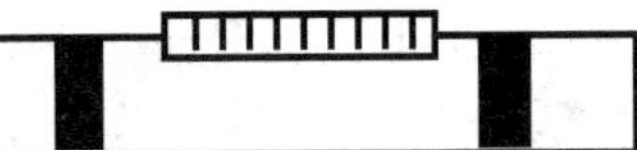

writing that resumé

Hot Brain Surgeon tips for the professional actor

• THE NITTY GRITTY •

YOUR NAME

Big, bold and SPELLED CORRECTLY. This may seem silly to mention, but you don't even know how many times we've seen names on resumés that don't match the spelling of the name on the headshot it's attached too! And you know what that big blunder spells? UNPROFESSIONAL and UNFOCUSED among other things (um, dumbass?). And the Agent or Casting Director is back in the pile searching for someone else who learned how to spell their name in second grade. Your name should be spelled EXACTLY as it appears elsewhere (headshot, attachments, letters, etc.). Also, if your name is Pete – keep it Pete. Don't choose that you want to sound more formal on your resumé and call yourself Peter... it's confusing and inconsistent. Pick Pete or Peter or Guenivere for that matter, but use ONLY ONE NAME and spell it correctly, for the love of Pete (ouch, bad joke... okay, moving on...)

CONTACT INFORMATION

Use your discretion here. Some people choose to list their address as well as their phone number(s). Just remember that this resumé might be circling town (which would be a good thing), but some weirdo who thinks you're a cutie might decide to stalk you (this would be the bad thing), and if your address is on it, you may as well just invite the freak in for dinner. PMB's (private mailboxes) are good for actors and are relatively cheap, too! You may not want to offer your home phone number either (now, don't start getting paranoid – it's just a precaution), but be sure you have a pager number or cell phone or answering service so the LEGITIMATE people can get in touch with you! And if you have an agent or manager, by all means, have that here too (first, in fact). F.Y.I.: E-mail addresses are showing up with the contact info these days too.

UNION AFFILIATION

Only if applicable, of course. SAG? Be proud of it, gosh darn it. AFTRA, AEA... people will wanna know and you should want to tell them.

act eight

writing that resumé

Hot Brain Surgeon tips for the professional actor

STATISTICS
"Just the stats, ma'am, and only the stats." Remember, that means no fibbing. None. Do people do it? Sure. An inch or two here, ten pounds less there... but be careful. If you insist on presenting yourself differently than you actually appear, you may be setting yourself up for failure. Giving yourself an extra inch or two or three on the resumé really serves nobody. When you show up with lifts inserted in eight inch stilettos, they're gonna know something is up – besides your height. You're 5'4", then you're 5'4". Period. You wanna be 130 lbs instead of 140 lbs? Then, put the dang brownie down and get on the Lifecycle! Don't try to trick anyone in your resumé. And don't forget to tell them about your gorgeous hair and eyes. Date of birth? Optional. Age range works just as well.

OBJECTIVE
Okay, we're back to judgment calls – like with the contact information. The fact that you're sending out a headshot and resumé is in itself pretty self-evident of what your objective is... although some people want to assure the whole world that they are indeed an actor/writer/singer/songwriter/dancer/model. It's your call.

EXPERIENCE
That means film, television, commercials and theatre. Generally in that order. Most resumés list this experience in reverse chronological order (most recent first). Do student films count? Sure. How about the home video your cousin Ed catches you in every Christmas? Probably not. And while the footage from drunken Spring Break shenanigans might make for good laughs, it doesn't make for good credits and it isn't worth listing either. Nice try, though. You get the drift? Same goes for TV. If you have none, don't feel the need to make them up. Again, if you tell them you played patty-cake with Chandler Bing, they may call you on it and ask to see that tape of you in your featured role on *Friends*. With commercials, even if you have none at all, it might be a good idea to write: List Available Upon Request - or - Conflicts Available Upon Request. The latter simply ensures that if they're considering you for a *Duracell* battery commercial, you didn't already shoot one with that cute little pink bunny. They won't want you hawking the same product for different companies at the same time – I mean where's your loyalty for heaven's sake!?

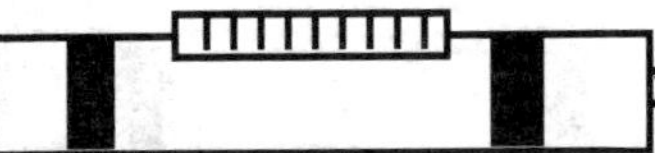

writing that resumé

Hot Brain Surgeon tips for the professional actor

RELATED EXPERIENCE
Some people include this in their resumés and others don't. If you think it's important to let people know you were a PA on a popular sitcom, tell them. Stage manager for a local theatre group? Looks good too and lets them know you're dedicated to the arts. You go with your supersonic-self!

EDUCATION
Heck, let the world know how smaht you are (smaht = smart, for all you non-Bostonians)! If you graduated with a Bachelor's or a Master's from an artsy-fartsy film school or acting academy, let them know. Heck, impress them! Maybe they're an alumni too – you never know what hook will reel in that shark... I mean agent (or manager or CD). The bigger the worm, the better the bite. Did I just write that? Wow. Moving on...

TRAINING
Here's where you get to impress them even more. Let them know that you're still involved, still learning. Tell them about the acting class/teacher you go to religiously every Wednesday instead of watching lame-o sitcoms. Name-drop. Go for it! Singing? Tenor? Baritone? Maybe the person knows your teacher. Dancing? Tell them who taught you to tango. They might be looking for a versatile performer who can do a little ditty. List voice training, stage combat, etc. You get it, right? Cool.

SPECIAL SKILLS
Remember the story about sword juggling? Don't lie! List only those things you can do at least FAIRLY well. It would sure be embarrassing to show up on the set of a football-themed film claiming to be your high school's star quarterback, yet when the director yells, "Action," you throw like your Great Aunt Bertha or the biggest super-wuss of all time! Ouch. Bye-bye, ego.

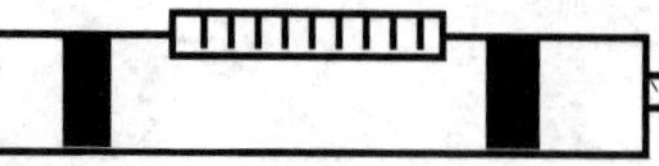

writing that resumé

Hot Brain Surgeon tips for the professional actor

AWARDS & HONORS
Some people skip this, but if you place first, second or third in a well-known or reputable screen or stage contest, why not include it? Heck, scream it from the rooftops (and write it in the resumé). This includes the smallest to the biggest... won an Oscar? Put that baby in there! But, you probably wouldn't need to be sending out resumés then, would you, wise guy?

SPELL CHECK
Double check ALL your spelling, folks. We can't spell to save our lives either, but Spell Check is always at the ready to save the day. One big tip: when noting a Principal role on your resumé, the correct spelling in this case is "Principal" NOT "Principle." This is a very common mistake and detracts from the overall impression of professionalism.

I AIN'T NOTHING BUT EIGHT LI'L LETTERS (Mike Wood)
These are tips, folks, not the final word. That's my own disclaimer just in case you don't get the grooviest of jobs, the perfect part, that magnificent manager, or the best-looking date for Friday night...

But seriously, why am I saying this, my dearest Brain Surgeons? Because these are the basic elements to writing a clear, concise, professional resumé. Use these tips as a GUIDE and mold YOUR resumé to suit YOUR needs. As I've mentioned, some elements are optional and the standard look for a resumé can vary depending upon your intention. Look at the examples that follow, sit down at the dang computer, write that resumé, and rock this town with your bad self!

Good luck, Brain Surgeons!

Ernie Capellini
SAG/AFTRA

HAIR: Black	**Big Fat Representatives**
EYES: Brown	**223 Avenue of the Stars**
HEIGHT: 5'10"	**Suite 3105**
WEIGHT: 175	**Los Angeles, CA 90037**
	(310) 555-1212

FILM

MR. & MRS. SMITH	Co-star	Touchstone
HOW TO MARRY RICH	Principal	Paramount
HALLOWEEN 16	Justin Diaz	Warner Bros.

TELEVISION

24	Guest Star	Ho-Hum Productions
YOUNG & THE RESTLESS	Recurring	CBS Productions
SHE WANTS A DIVORCE	Co-star	CBS Productions
THE PRACTICE	Guest Star	David E. Kelley Prods.

THEATRE

A FEW GOOD MEN	Lt. Kaffe	My Waterfall Theatre
PRE-NUP BLUES	K-Fed	New Bedford Playhouse
ROMEO AND JULIET	Mercutio	Shakespeare Park
BOY DID I SCORE	Matt Stoner	Fools Playhouse
WEST SIDE STORY	Tony	Dartmouth Theatre

TRAINING

IMPROV	Kevin Federspenderliner Institute, CA
COLD READING	Shar Anderson Institute, NY
VOICE/MUSIC	Brittany Life Workshop, LA

SKILLS & INTERESTS

Fluent in Spanish & French. Dialects: English, Cockney, French, Italian, German, Russian, New York. Baseball, Basketball, Football, Watching Television for Long Periods of Time, Soccer, Skateboarding, Tennis, Track & Field, Eating, Snowboarding, Golf, Spending Other People's Money.

Shirley Smith
SAG

HAIR: Blonde
EYES: Blue
HEIGHT: 5'9"
WEIGHT: 110

1240 Wing Nut Road, Apt. 2
Sherman Hills, CA 90034
(818) 555-1212

FILM

RETURN OF THE ANT	Lead	"B " Movie Ent. Group
THE INCREDIBLE SHRINKING POTATO	Spud	Image Entertainment
I SMELL CHEESE	Reporter	Dairy Product Pictures

INDUSTRIAL FILM

PARKING SAFETY	Details Inc.
LABORATORY PROCEDURES	Chemical Pro

TELEVISION

BOSTON LEGAL	Recurring	David E. Kelley Prod.
GENERAL HOSPITAL	Day Player	ABC Productions
GREY'S ANATOMY	Guest Star	NBC Studios

COMMERCIALS
Conflicts Available Upon Request

STAGE

77th STREET	Sarah	Hamilton Playhouse
DOHICKEY'S ROOM	Lee	Dudley Theatre
AN AWFUL APPLE OR TWO	Grace	Carrington Players

RELATED EXPERIENCE

IMPROV IMAGES	Performer/ Teacher	(Improv Troupe– Touring)
COMEDY CART	Performer	(Comedy Troupe– clubs, school events)

TRAINING

ACTING	George James, NY
ACTOR'S STUDIO	Elizabeth Jones (Stanislavski Method)
SINGING / SPEECH AND DICTION	Robert Smith

SKILLS
Stand-up comedy, Improv, Stage Combat, Stage Tech, Softball, Volleyball, Tennis, Mountain Climbing, Surfing, great with animals

act eight

Patty Purple
SAG

915 Meatball Lane
Beverly Hills, CA 90212
310-555-1212
September 21, 2006

To Whom It May Concern:

I am submitting the enclosed resumé for your consideration. As visible in my resumé, I'm a versatile and energetic performer with extensive experience in film, television, theatre, and commercials. I am eager to expand my career and would appreciate any opportunities.

Thank you for your time and consideration. I look forward to meeting with you.

Sincerely,

Patty Purple

Olivia Mustard
Actress

29971 Dip Drive
Studio City, CA 91506
(310) 555-1212
November 27, 2006

A. B. Seedy Casting
P.O. Box 5489
Hollywood, CA 90028

Dear A.B. Seedy Casting:

Please review my enclosed picture and resumé. I have successfully obtained roles on several feature films and anticipate an opportunity to work with you on your upcoming productions. I would be grateful for the chance to meet with you and possibly audition.

Thank you for your time and consideration. I eagerly await your response.

Regards,

Olivia Mustard
Enclosures: resumé/photo

sag-franchised agencies

Important Note...

For those aspiring background actors who desire to become speaking actors, we've included a listing of the SAG-franchised talent agencies in Southern California. The following is as fully updated as possible (as we go to press) and includes agencies that represent adults and those that represent children (these are indicated with an asterisk). Also, please keep in mind that many companies often move and change their numbers at the drop of a hat – just thought we'd throw that in as a mini-disclaimer!

It's also important to note that many reputable agencies that were once SAG-franchised no longer retain this status because SAG recently rejected a renewal of the tentative agency agreement with the Association of Talent Agents (ATA)/National Association of Talent Representatives (NATR). The result of that rejection is that members/agencies represented by the ATA/NATR are no longer SAG-franchised. This includes well-respected agencies like *CAA*, *William Morris*, *Endeavor*, and *Innovative*. So what does this mean for you? Frankly, just more confusion.

While SAG literature (and its website) insists that SAG members' agents MUST be SAG-franchised, several phone calls to SAG's office revealed that SAG RECOMMENDS you not sign with these agencies unless and until you have SAG read over the contract (which we're told is most often very, very similar anyway), but they do not truly forbid you from doing so.

Call SAG's Agency Department: 323-549-6729.

As far as we know, there are no penalties for signing with a non-franchised agency. The problem is there are many, many very SKETCHY so-called "agencies" that are not SAG-franchised and these DO pose a danger to prospective clients because of their unscrupulous ways.

The talent agencies listed here ONLY represent those agencies still SAG-franchised as of this printing. Check the SAG website for more info on non-franchised agents and to better understand how these recent changes affect your relationship with a current or potential ATA/NATR agent (like *CAA* or *WMA*). SAG, of course, recommends: "If you're looking for representation, start your search with [our] list of SAG-franchised agents."

sag franchised agencies

Updated List for **2006**

In past editions of **"EXTRA" WORK for Brain Surgeons®** we included specific types the agencies may have been seeking at that time. Since this is now an annual publication, however, and the needs of each agency change so frequently, we have decided to include their phone numbers and let you call to see if they are accepting new talent and what types they may be looking for. These agencies represent creative professionals in all different categories and this may also fluctuate depending upon their day-to-day needs.

We hope our information is useful to you in your search for an agent or representation for your children. Please remember to verify addresses and try to get a contact name at the particular agency before randomly submitting photos and resumés since things can change very quickly in this crazy town!

ASA
4430 Fountain Ave., Suite #A
Los Angeles, CA 90029
(323)662-9787

ACTORS LA/LA GROUP
12435 Oxnard Street
North Hollywood, CA 91606
(818) 755-0026

AIMÉE ENTERTAINMENT
15840 Ventura Blvd., Suite 215
Sherman Oaks, CA 91403
(818) 783-9115

ALLEN TALENT AGENCY
3832 Wilshire Blvd., 2nd Floor
Los Angeles, CA 90010
(213) 605-1110

AMATRUDA BENSON & ASSOCIATES*
9107 Wilshire Blvd., Suite 500
Beverly Hills, CA 90210
(310) 276-1851

ARTIST MANAGEMENT AGENCY
1800 East Garry Street, Suite 101
Santa Ana, CA 92705
(714) 972-0311

THE ARTISTS GROUP, LTD.
10100 Santa Monica Bl., Ste. 2490
Los Angeles, CA 90067
(310) 552-1100

THE AUSTIN AGENCY
6715 Hollywood Blvd., Suite 204
Hollywood, CA 90028
(323) 957-4444

BADGLEY CONNOR AGENCY
1680 Vine Street, Suite 1016
Los Angeles, CA 90028
(323) 463-8355

BAIER/KLEINMAN INTERNATIONAL
3575 Cahuenga Bl. West, Ste. 500
Los Angeles, CA 90068
(323) 874-9800

*** Indicates agencies that work with children.**

sag-franchised agencies

Updated List for **2006**

BALDWIN TALENT, INC.
8055 W. Manchester Ave., Ste. 550
Playa Del Rey, CA 90293
(310) 827-2422

BARON ENTERTAINMENT, INC*
5757 Wilshire Blvd., Suite 659
Los Angeles, CA 90036
(323) 936-7600

MARC BASS AGENCY, INC
415 N. Crescent Dr., Ste. 320
Beverly Hills, CA 90210
(310) 278-1900

MARIAN BERZON AGENCY*
336 East 17th Street
Costa Mesa, CA 92627
(949) 631-5936

BICOASTAL TALENT AGENCY*
3489 Cahuenga Blvd. West, Ste. A
Los Angeles, CA 90068
(818) 845-0150

BONNIE BLACK TALENT AGENCY*
12034 Riverside Dr., Suite 103
Valley Village, CA 91607
(818) 753-5424

THE BLAKE AGENCY*
1327 Ocean Avenue, Suite J
Santa Monica, CA 90401
(310) 899-9898

BLOC TALENT AGENCY, INC.*
5651 Wilshire Blvd., Suite C
Los Angeles, CA 90036
(323) 954-7730

BOUTIQUE
10 Universal City Plaza, Suite 2000
Universal City, CA 91608
(818) 753-2385

BRAND MODEL & TALENT*
1520 Brookhollow Drive, Suite 39
Santa Ana, CA 92705
(714) 850-1158

CAREER ARTISTS INTERNATIONAL*
11030 Ventura Blvd., Suite 3
Studio City, CA 91604
(818) 980-1315

CARRY COMPANY TALENT AGENCY
3875 Wilshire Blvd., Suite 402
Los Angeles, CA 90010
(213) 388-0770

CASTLE-HILL TALENT AGENCY
1101 South Orlando Avenue
Los Angeles, CA 90035
(323) 653-3535

CAVALERI & ASSOCIATES*
178 South Victory Blvd., Suite 205
Burbank, CA 91502
(818) 955-9300

CERISE TALENT AGENCY
13412 Moorpark St., Suite C
Sherman Oaks, CA 91423
(818) 995-1775

NANCY CHAIDEZ & ASSOC.*
1555 N. Vine St., Suite 223
Los Angeles, CA 90028
(323) 467-8954

THE CHARLES AGENCY
11950 Ventura Blvd., Suite 3
Studio City, CA 91604
(818) 761-2224

THE CHASIN AGENCY
8899 Beverly Blvd., Suite 716
Los Angeles, CA 90048
(310) 278-7505

*** Indicates agencies that work with children.**

sag-franchised agencies

Updated List for **2006**

CHATEAU-BILLINGS TALENT*
8489 W. 3rd St., Suite 1032
Los Angeles, CA 90048
(323) 965-5432

CHIC MODELS & TALENY AGENCY
5353 Paoli Way
Long Beach, CA 90803
(562) 433-8097

W. RANDOLPH CLARK AGENCY*
13415 Ventura Blvd., Suite 3
Sherman Oaks, CA 91423
(818) 385-0583

COLLEEN CLER TALENT AGENCY*
178 South Victory, Suite 108
Burbank, CA 91502
(818) 841-7943

CONTEMPORARY ARTISTS, LTD
610 Santa Monica Blvd., #202
Santa Monica, CA 90401
(310) 395-1800

CORALIE JR. THEATRICAL AGENCY
4789 Vineland Ave., Ste. 100
North Hollywood, CA 91602
(818) 766-9501

DDO ARTISTS AGENCY
8322 Beverly Blvd., Suite 301
Los Angeles, CA 90048
(323) 782-0070

THE DANGERFIELD AGENCY
4063 Radford Avenue, Ste. 201-C
Studio City, CA 91604
(818) 766-7717

DRAGON TALENT, INC.*
8444 Wilshire Bl., Penthouse
Beverly Hills, CA 90211
(323) 653-0366

ELITE OF LOS ANGELES TALENT
345 N. Maple Dr., Ste. 397
Beverly Hills, CA 90210
(310) 274-9395

ELLIS TALENT GROUP
4705 Laurel Canyon Bl., Ste. 300
Valley Village, CA 91607
(818) 980-8072

EQUINOX MODELS & TALENT*
8455 Beverly Blvd., Ste. 304
Los Angeles, CA 90048
(323) 951-7100

FERRAR-MEDIA ASSOCIATES
8430 Santa Monica Bl., Ste. 220
West Hollywood, CA 90069
(323) 654-2601

FILM ARTISTS ASSOCIATES
4717 Van Nuys Blvd., #215
Sherman Oaks, CA 91403
(818) 386-9669

FLICK EAST-WEST TALENTS, INC.
9057 Nemo Street, Suite A
West Hollywood, CA 90069
(310) 271-9111

FONTAINE TALENT*
205 S. Beverly Drive, Suite 212
Beverly Hills, CA 90212
(310) 471-8631

ALICE FRIES AGENCY
1927 Vista Del Mar Avenue
Hollywood, CA 90068
(323) 464-1404

DALE GARRICK INTERNATIONAL*
1017 N. La Cienega Blvd., Ste. 109
West Hollywood, CA 90069
(310) 657-2661

*** Indicates agencies that work with children.**

sag-franchised agencies

Updated List for **2006**

THE GEDDES AGENCY
8430 Santa Monica Bl., Ste. 200
West Hollywood, CA 90069
(323) 848-2700

THE LAYA GELFF AGENCY
16133 Ventura Blvd., Suite 700
Encino, CA 91436
(818) 996-3100

PAUL GERARD TALENT AGENCY
11712 Moorpark Street, Ste. 112
Studio City, CA 91604
(818) 769-7015

THE DON GERLER AGENCY
3349 Cahuenga Blvd. West, #1
Los Angeles, CA 90068
(323) 850-7386

MICHELLE GORDON & ASSOC.
260 S. Beverly Drive, Suite 308
Beverly Hills, CA 90212
(310) 246-9930

GRANT, SAVIC, KOPALOFF & ASSOCIATES
6399 Wilshire Blvd., Suite 414
Los Angeles, CA 90048
(323) 782-1854

GREENE & ASSOCIATES
7080 Hollywood Bl., Suite 1017
Hollywood, CA 90028
(323) 960-1333

MITCHELL J. HAMILBURG AGENCY
149 S. Barrington Ave., Ste. 732
Los Angeles, CA 90049
(310) 471-4024

HENDERSON/HOGAN/MCCABE
247 S. Beverly Drive
Beverly Hills, CA 90212
(323) 650-3738

HERVEY-GRIMES TALENT AGENCY*
10561 Missouri Avenue, #2
Los Angeles, CA 90025
(310) 475-2010

HILLTOP TALENT AGENCY*
2550 Imperial Hwy, Suite 200
El Segundo, CA 90245
(310) 727-2642

THE DANIEL HOFF AGENCY*
1800 N. Highland Ave., Ste. 300
Los Angeles, CA 90028
(323) 962-6643

HOLLANDER TALENT GROUP*
14011 Ventura Blvd., Suite 202
Sherman Oaks, CA 91423
(818) 382-9800

IFA TALENT AGENCY
8730 Sunset Blvd., #490
West Hollywood, CA 90069
(310) 659-5522

JB TALENT AGENCY
9150 Wilshire Blvd., Suite 270
Beverly Hills, CA 90212
(310) 344-2881

JLA (JACK LIPMAN AGENCY)*
9151 Sunset Blvd.
West Hollywood, CA 90069
(310) 276-5677

JFA (JAMIE FERRAR AGENCY)
4741 Laurel Canyon Blvd., Ste. 110
Valley Village, CA 91607
(818) 506-8311

JS REPRESENTS
6815 Willoughby Avenue, Ste. 102
Los Angeles, CA 90038
(323) 462-3246

*** Indicates agencies that work with children.**

sag-franchised agencies

Updated List for **2006**

KAPLAN-STAHLER-GUMER AGENCY
8383 Wilshire Blvd., #923
Beverly Hills, CA 90211
(323) 653-4483

SHARON KEMP TALENT AGENCY
447 S. Robertson Blvd., Ste. 204
Beverly Hills, CA 90211
(310) 858-7200

WILLIAM KERWIN AGENCY
1605 N. Cahuenga Blvd., Ste. 202
Hollywood, CA 90028
(323) 469-5155

ERIC KLASS AGENCY
139 S. Beverly Drive, Suite 331
Beverly Hills, CA 90212
(310) 274-9169

LJ AND ASSOCIATES
5903 Noble Ave.
Van Nuys, CA 91411
(818) 345-9274

L.W. 1, INC.
7257 Beverly Blvd., Suite 200
Los Angeles, CA 90036
(323) 653-5700

LEAVITT TALENT GROUP
6300 Wilshire Blvd., Ste. 1470
Los Angeles, CA 90048
(323) 658-8118

THE LEVIN AGENCY*
8484 Wilshire Blvd., Suite 750
Beverly Hills, CA 90211
(323) 653-7073

KEN LINDNER & ASSOCIATES
2049 Century Pk. East, Ste. 3050
Los Angeles, CA 90067
(310) 277-9223

JANA LUKER TALENT AGENCY*
1923 ½ Westwood Blvd., Suite 3
Los Angeles, CA 90025
(310) 441-2822

LYNNE & REILLY AGENCY
Toluca Plaza Building
10725 Vanowen St., Ste. 113
N. Hollywood, CA 91605
(323) 850-1984

MGA/MARY GRADY AGENCY*
4400 Coldwater Canyon Ave., # 315
Studio City, CA 91604
(818) 763-8400

MADEMOISELLE TALENT AGENCY*
10835 Santa Monica Bl. Ste. 204A
Westwood, CA 90025
(310) 441-9994

MALAKY INTERNATIONAL*
10642 Santa Monica Blvd., Ste 103
Los Angeles, CA 90025
(310) 234-9114

MAXINE'S TALENT AGENCY
4830 Encino Avenue
Encino, CA 91316
(818) 986-2946

MEDIA ARTISTS GROUP*
6300 Wilshire Blvd., Suite 1470
Los Angeles, CA 90048
(323) 658-5050

MIRAMAR TALENT AGENCY*
7400 Beverly Blvd., Suite 220
Los Angeles, CA 90036
(323) 934-0700

MODELINQUE TALENT AGENCY
9595 Wilshire Blvd., Suite 900
Beverly Hills, CA 90212
(310) 300-4047

*** Indicates agencies that work with children.**

sag-franchised agencies

Updated List for **2006**

H. DAVID MOSS & ASSOCIATES*
733 N. Seward St., Penthouse
Los Angeles, CA 90038
(323) 465-1234

NTA TALENT AGENCY*
8899 Beverly Blvd., Suite 612
Los Angeles, CA 90048
(310) 274-6297

NU TALENT AGENCY
117 N. Robertson Blvd.
Los Angeles, CA 90048
(310) 385-6907

OH MY NAPPY TALENT AGENCY
805 S. La Brea Ave.
Los Angeles, CA 90036
(323) 939-3435

OMNIPOP, INC.
10700 Ventura Blvd., Suite 2C
Studio City, CA 91604
(818) 980-9267

ORIGIN TALENT
4705 Laurel Canyon Blvd., #306
Valley Village, CA 91607
(818) 487-1800

PTI TALENT AGENCY*
9000 Sunset Blvd., Suite 506
West Hollywood, CA 90069
(818) 386-1310

PACIFIC WEST ARTISTS
12500 Riverside Drive, Suite 202
Valley Village, CA 91607
(818) 755-8544

PAKULA/KING & ASSOCIATES
9229 Sunset Blvd., Suite 315
West Hollywood, CA 90069
(310) 281-4868

THE PARTOS COMPANY
227 Broadway, Suite 204
Santa Monica, CA 90401
(310) 458-7800

PEAK MODELS & TALENT
28065 Avenue Stanford
Valencia, CA 91355
(661) 288-1555

THE JOHN PIERCE AGENCY
8127 Melrose Ave., Suite 3
West Hollywood CA 90046
(323) 653-3976

PLAYERS TALENT AGENCY*
7700 Sunset Blvd.
Los Angeles, CA 90046
(323) 851-6111

PRIVILEGE TALENT AGENCY*
14542 Ventura Blvd., Suite 209
Sherman Oaks, CA 91403
(818) 386-2377

PROGRESSIVE ARTISTS AGENCY
400 S. Beverly Drive, Suite 216
Beverly Hills, CA 90212
(310) 553-8561

Q MODEL MANAGEMENT
8618 W. 3rd Street
Los Angeles CA 90048
(310) 205-2888

QUALITA DELL' ARTE
5353 Topanga Canyon Rd., Ste. 220
Woodland Hills, CA 91364
(818) 598-8073

CINDY ROMANO MODELING & TALENT AGENCY*
414 Village Square West
Palm Springs, CA 92262
(760) 323-3333

*** Indicates agencies that work with children.**

sag-franchised agencies

Updated List for **2006**

SDB PARTNERS, INC.
1801 Ave. of the Stars, Ste. 902
Los Angeles, CA 90067
(310) 785-0060

THE SAMANTHA GROUP
300 S. Raymond Ave., Suite 11
Pasadena, CA 91105
(626) 683-2444

THE SARNOFF COMPANY, INC.
10 Universal City Plaza, 20th Fl.
Universal City, CA 91608
(818) 753-2377

JACK SCAGNETTI AGENCY*
5118 Vineland Ave., Suite 102
North Hollywood, CA 91601
(818) 762-3871

IRV SCHECHTER COMPANY
9460 Wilshire Blvd., Suite 300
Beverly Hills, CA 90212
(310) 278-8070

SANDIE SCHNARR TALENT
8500 Melrose Avenue, Suite 212
West Hollywood, CA 90069
(310) 360-7680

KATHLEEN SCHULTZ & ASSOC.
6442 Coldwater Cnyn., Ste. 206
North Hollywood, CA 91606
(818) 760-3100

DON SCHWARTZ ASSOCIATES
1604 N. Cahuenga Blvd., Ste. 101
Los Angeles CA 90028
(310) 860-4718

SCREEN ARTISTS AGENCY, LLC*
4526 Sherman Oaks Avenue
Sherman Oaks, CA 91403
(818) 789-4896.

DAVID SHAPIRA & ASSOCIATES
15821 Ventura Blvd., Suite 235
Encino, CA 91436
(310) 967-0480

SHAPIRO-LICHTMAN, INC.
8827 Beverly Boulevard
Los Angeles, CA 90048
(310) 859-8877

JEROME SIEGEL ASSOCIATES
1680 N. Vine Street, Suite 613
Los Angeles, CA 90028
(323) 466-0185

SIGNATURE ARTISTS AGENCY
6700 W. 5th Street
Los Angeles CA 90048
(323) 651-0600

SKY TALENT AGENCY
8228 W. Sunset Blvd., Suite 206
Los Angeles, CA 90046
(323) 656-0962

MICHAEL SLESSINGER ASSOC.
8730 Sunset Blvd., Suite 270
West Hollywood, CA 90069
(310) 657-7113

THE SOHL AGENCY
669 Berendo Street
Los Angeles CA 90004
(323) 644-0500

SOLID TALENT, INC.
6860 Lexington Ave.
Hollywood, CA 90038
(323) 978-0808

SCOTT STANDER & ASSOCIATES*
13701 Riverside Drive, Suite 201
Sherman Oaks, CA 91423
(818) 905-7000

*** Indicates agencies that work with children.**

sag-franchised agencies

Updated List for **2006**

STARCRAFT TALENT AGENCY
1516 N. Formosa Avenue
West Hollywood, CA 90046
(323) 845-4784

STARWILL TALENT AGENCY*
433 N. Camden Drive, 4th Floor
Beverly Hills, CA 90210
(323) 874-1239

STEINBERG'S AGENCY
6399 Wilshire Blvd., Ste. 220
Los Angeles, CA 90048
(323) 653-3146

THE STEVENS GROUP*
14011 Ventura Blvd., Suite 201
Sherman Oaks, CA 91423
(818) 528-3674

SUPERIOR TALENT AGENCY*
11712 Moorpark Street, Suite 209
Studio City, CA 91604
(818) 508-5627

THE THOMAS TALENT AGENCY
6709 La Tijera Blvd., Suite 915
Los Angeles, CA 90045
(310) 665-0000

ARLENE THORNTON & ASSOC.
12711 Ventura Blvd., Suite 490
Studio City, CA 91604
(818) 760-6688

TILMAR TALENT AGENCY
4929 Wilshire Blvd., Suite 830
Los Angeles, CA 90010
(323) 938-9815

TISHERMAN AGENCY, INC.
6767 Forest Lawn Dr., Suite 101
Los Angeles, CA 90068
(323) 850-6767

US TALENT AGENCY
485 S. Robertson Blvd., Suite 7
Beverly Hills, CA 90211
(310) 858-1533

UNIVERSAL ARTISTS GROUP
4444 W. Riverside Dr., Ste. 308
Burbank, CA 91505
(818) 848-8183

VISION ART MANAGEMENT
9200 Sunset Blvd., Penthouse 1
Los Angeles, CA 90069
(310) 888-3288

THE WALLIS AGENCY*
4444 Riverside Dr., Suite 105
Burbank, CA 91505
(818) 953-4848

WARNING TALENT, INC.
9440 Santa Monica Blvd., Ste. 400
Beverly Hills, CA 90210
(310) 860-9944

BOB WATERS AGENCY, INC.
4311 Wilshire Blvd., Suite 622
Los Angeles, CA 90010
(323) 965-5555

ANN WAUGH TALENT AGENCY*
4741 Laurel Canyon Bl., Ste. 200
Valley Village, CA 91607
(818) 980-0141

SHIRLEY WILSON & ASSOCIATES*
5410 Wilshire Blvd., Suite 510
Los Angeles, CA 90036
(323) 857-6977

ZANUCK, PASSON & PACE, INC.*
4717 Van Nuys Blvd., Suite 102
Sherman Oaks, CA 91403
(818) 783-4890

*** Indicates agencies that work with children.**

Entertainment Industry

California Child Labor Laws

The following is an overview/summary regarding main points which concern children employed in film, TV, commercials, etc. See the complete version of the Entertainment Industry California Labor Laws for full and complete explanations and interpretations of these laws.

Child Labor Laws Summary

• Minors

MINORS may work between 5AM to 10PM on nights preceding the school days, or 5AM to12:30AM on nights preceding non-school days. There must be a 12 hour turnaround. If 12 hours have not elapsed between the minor's dismissal and the next day's school start time, the minor MUST be schooled by the employer. With permission from the school's authority, minors between the ages of 14 through 18 may work up to 8 hours a day for a maximum of two consecutive days. Written requests must be submitted to the California Division of Labor Standards Enforcement 48 hours in advance for an employer to receive an extension, a PARENT and/or GUARDIAN must be within eyesight of ALL MINORS UNDER the age of 16.

• Studio Teachers

The TEACHER must be CERTIFIED by the DLSE. These teachers must be provided for the education of ALL MINORS up to 18 years of age. Furthermore, these teachers must also care for and attend to the health, safety, and morals of ALL minors under the age of 16. Additionally, there must be ONE STUDIO TEACHER for every TEN CHILDREN on school days and ONE STUDIO TEACHER for every TWENTY CHILDREN on non-school days. Minors MUST carry a VALID WORK PERMIT with them at all times. Employers MUST have a permit to EMPLOY minors. ALL CHILDREN are required to bring school supplies and the employers are required to provide "adequate" school facilities.

• Working on Location

If a minor has to go to a location, the TRAVEL TIME from the studio to the location counts as part of the minor's work day. When on a distant location with an overnight stay, a grace period of 45 minutes each way from "HOTEL" to the shoot location is NOT COUNTED toward work time. ALL REGULATIONS are fully applicable to EMANCIPATED minors age 15 and under. OUTSIDE CALIFORNIA, ALL LAWS are FULLY APPLICABLE including the use of a California Certified Studio Teacher when hiring a California State Resident minor. Minors from OUT OF STATE working in California MUST ALSO adhere to the California State Laws.

kid requirements

So, your kid wants to be a (rock) star, huh?..

"Your kid should be in pictures!"

Did some sleazy man solicit you at the bus stop or outside the market, telling you to get that cute kid of yours in the movies? Well, before you jump the gun and sign on with some less-than-established outfit – KNOW THE FACTS!

We've broken down some of the basics for you, so you can understand what it takes to get your kid in pictures and to keep 'em working.

If you want the end-all in books about kids in the industry, pick up our directory **KIDS' ACTING for Brain Surgeons**™. This newly revised publication is busting at the seams with ALL the information you and your child will ever need!

For now, you can use the fabulous tips in the beginning of this chapter to set your child up with a cool resumé and maybe find him or her representation. The agencies that specialize in children or work specifically with kids are listed in the SAG-franchised agency list earlier in this chapter and indicated with an asterisk (*). But, first things first:

• Registering •

BEFORE you register your kid for work, your child MUST have:

- A current Entertainment Work Permit
- A Social Security Card
- A Birth Certificate
- The Last Report Card received – with no lower than a "C" in EACH subject!

• Work Permit •

For a Work Permit application, call or write to:

State Labor Commission
6150 Van Nuys Blvd., Room 206
Van Nuys, CA 91401
(818) 901-5315 or (818) 908-4556

act eight

kid requirements

So, your kid wants to be a (rock) star, huh?

• What's a Work Permit •

A work permit will allow your child to work in the state in which you reside. It is your duty as a responsible adult to obtain one for your child or children. The regulations which govern these groovy work permits may vary from state to state and even from city to city within the same state (just to confuse us all a little bit more). So where do you get one of these nifty numbers known as a work permit? Refer to the previous page and continue to read further.

• Where to Get a Work Permit •

Go down to the Labor Commission or write to the address on the previous page for an application. Although, some Los Angeles schools may have entertainment work permit applications on-site since filming in the area is so prevalent. In fact, most public high schools can provide work permits for students sixteen and over, through their guidance counselor. But, if your li'l star is still in school, the school principal will probably have to sign off on the application, stating his or her "okay" that the little (or big) tyke is gonna be taking time off from school to work on set.

- You may also contact any LOCAL chapter.
- Applications can also be downloaded at: www.dir.ca.gov/dlse/DLSE-Forms-CL.htm
- Include a SASE with your application. It usually takes about 3 days to process (not including the unpredictable time spent in the mail). But it can take longer, so apply ASAP once you know junior needs one. AND KEEP THEM UP-TO-DATE. Expired permits are useless permits!

• Social Security Card •

There's this little ole' law that was passed way back in 1987 that requires everyone five years old or older to obtain a Social Security number (Uncle Sammy wants his share of wages). To be in check with The Tax Reform Act, get down to your local Social Security office and apply for one for your child. Processing could take several weeks, so get it done – your child will not be paid without one. You may call (800) 772-1213 to locate the nearest social security office.

kid requirements

So, your kid wants to be a (rock) star, huh?

• Birth Certificate •

You have got to have proof the kid exists. If you have lost or tossed your child's birth certificate AND your child was born in the state of California, you may call (916) 445-2684 or check out the website www.vitalchek.com.

• Report Cards •

Okay, first off, your child's got to make the grade! He or she will not be allowed to work unless he or she has a "C" or better in EVERY subject – that DOES NOT mean a "C" average overall. Once your children get to set (with the principal's blessing – remember, he or she will most likely have to sign off on your kid's work permit) your kids will get to learn while they work. When it's required under the contract, schooling will be provided by the Producer(s) of the movie or TV show your offspring are working on. But, you – the ever-diligent parent/ guardian – are responsible for bringing your child's books, notebooks, assignments, homework, favorite pen, etc. to set. Since your child's regular classroom structure is going to be interrupted by working on set, you should make arrangements with your child's teachers and principal to make sure it's as smooth a transition as possible for the young people. Although, the school's principal is often required to sign off on your child's work permit application (as we've already mentioned... ahem!), you should be sure of what's in store for your out-of-school, on-the-set kid.

• School Attendance •

"What is the school's policy on attendance? And will this absence be classified as an excused absence?" Good question, people! We know it's been a while since you sat in the classroom, parents, but that makes a difference! You might want to ask who the primary contact will be at the school – a teacher, guidance counselor, the principal? You'll want to discuss with ALL your child's teachers how you'll obtain and exchange daily assignments. And, a biggie – who will be responsible for grading daily assignments, tests, & quizzes, and who will determine grades if the child's not in the classroom for the teacher to assess?

kid requirements

So, your kid wants to be a (rock) star, huh?

• School Hours •

Minors must be taught an average of three hours a day with no period of time less than 20 minutes acceptable as actual school time. And all teaching and learning has to be completed in a place which allows uninterrupted instruction (no quickie quizzes en route to set in the Range Rover – that doesn't constitute classroom learning time!) For a more detailed explanation and a breakdown of schooling requirements based on your child's age, check the nifty chart below.

•School Chart

Act, Work & Play

• AGES •	• TIME ON SET	• TIME AT WORK	• SCHOOL	• R&R	• TOTAL TIME+ MEAL
• 15 Days to 6 Mo.	2 Hours	20 Minutes	•	1 Hour & 40 Min.	2 1/2 Hours
• 6 Mo. to 2 Years	4 Hours	2 Hours	•	2 Hours	4 1/2 Hours
• 3 to 5 Years Old	6 Hours	3 Hours	•	3 Hours	6 1/2 Hours
• 6 to 8 Years Old	6 Hours	4 Hours 6 Hours	3 Hours Vacation	1 Hour 2 Hours	8 1/2 Hours
• 9 to 15 Years Old	6 Hours	5 Hours 7 Hours	3 Hours Vacation	1 Hour 2 Hours	9 1/2 Hours
• 16 & 17 Years Old	6 Hours	6 Hours 8 Hours	3 Hours Vacation/ Graduation	1 Hour 2 Hours	10 1/2 Hours

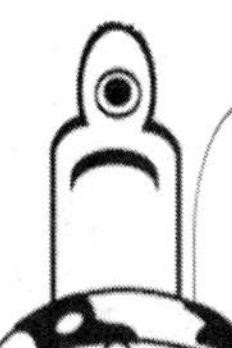

kid requirements

So, your kid wants to be a (rock) star, huh?

• Playing an Active Role •

Yikes! You've got a lot of things to consider and that's not even all the things you need to think about BEFORE getting your children in the movies. As parents, you should, of course, take an active role to ensure that the highest academic standards are maintained on the set your children are working on. You want them edu-ma-cated(??), don't you? As a responsible adult/guardian the responsibility for your child ultimately rests with YOU (and your child).

• KIDS' ACTING for Brain Surgeons™ •

Remember, if you need additional information or more specifics about your kids working in the entertainment industry, **HOLLYWOOD OS**® writes and publishes **KIDS' ACTING for Brain Surgeons**™.

This directory is the definitive source for parents and kids who want to learn the ins and out of the tricky entertainment industry.

To order go to www.HollywoodOS.com or call the office direct at (310) 289-9400.

act eight

tips for kids & parents!

ACT 1:
"DO'S" WHILE AT THE AUDITION, please . . .

- DO have those darn resumés/pictures with you at all times – even have a few extras in the trunk of your car, for crying out loud!
- DO know what your child is wearing and what clothing is appropriate.
- DO be on time, if not ahead of schedule – you are an adult, make this happen!
- DO sign in and out with a pen only. Crayons, markers or pencils are not acceptable (and no eating the paste, parents)!!
- DO let your cute kid relax & concentrate on the darn script or copy and try not to irritate your children!
- DO be supportive and teach your child to cope with disappointment and rejection.

ACT 2:
"DON'TS" WHILE AT THE AUDITION, please . . .

- DON'T wait until the last minute to get details (i.e. addresses and directions). Come on, parents, grow up, get the info you need already!
- DON'T change your child's clothes or appearance for the callback. Make sure your little cutie wears the same thing.
- DON'T bring other children, cousin Patrick, friends or Fido – the 5 lb. poodle (this could be distracting... cute, but distracting).
- DON'T let anyone else sign in or sign out for you or your cute kid.
- DON'T pressure your child – they have their own problems to worry about (i.e., tying shoelaces, driving your car on the weekends, etc.).
- DON'T let your child waste time playing. Work with them instead – review the script or copy with 'em, for cryin' out loud, but...
- DON'T interpret the copy/script or coach your child on line reading. Let them do it – it'll come naturally.

ACT 3:
"DO'S" WHEN WORKING ON SET, please . . .

- DO know the rules and regulations for child employment .
- DO know your responsibilities. At least one of you needs to be responsible, and the kid's gotta act!
- DO have social security number, work permit and I-9 identification .

tips for kids & parents!

- DO be responsible for your child's safety and welfare (be within sight and sound of your child while on set), then chauffeur them home in your super-cool minivan.
- DO arrive on set 15-30 minutes early (yes, that's EARLY, not late).
- DO check in with the designated person on set, usually an A.D. or Stage Manager.
- DO check in with the teacher. Do not avoid the teacher, parents!
- DO have at least 3 hours of schoolwork if your child has a tutor. . . fun!
- DO supervise your child during set time, breaks, meals and non-school times (and don't encourage food fights either)!
- DO sign a completed copy of the contract before your child begins work (all blanks should be filled in). Be sure to call his/her/your agent should you have any problems, questions or concerns.
- DO speak up if you feel your child is working too long without a break or being asked to do something you feel he/she should not be doing... it's okay, you won't get in trouble for asking.
- DO be sure to tell your agent ahead of time if: your child has special food, medication and or unusual educational requirements.
- DO sign out at the end of the work day.

<u>*ACT 4:*</u>
"DON'TS" WHEN WORKING ON SET, please . . .

- DON'T assume anything – always call the stinkin' union if you've got a concern! (You know what they say about people who assume. . .)
- DON'T allow your child to work if you have not received a contract – this could spell trouble!
- DON'T sign the contract if it's different from your understanding of the employment terms (never, never, ever sign anything you are unsure of)!
- DON'T bother other actors, the director or crew members (and no flirting, come on, parents!).
- DON'T get in the way while watching your child on the set! (Give 'em a break & cut the apron strings – they're working, for Godsakes!)
- DON'T interrupt the classroom during school time (you already went to school, right? Do you really miss it *that* much?).
- DON'T allow unreasonable requests or make exceptions to provisions in the contract, it could end up causing confusion in the end.
- DON'T let anyone else sign out for your children, they're your kids – sign them out already!

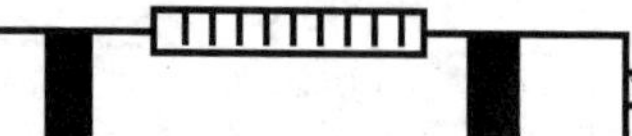

the "coogan law"

Bank accounts, percentages, and trust funds: understanding your your kids' cash..

Anyone remember poor li'l Jackie Coogan? Go way back into those dusty memory banks... or just hit a local video store that offers more than New Releases. Jackie Coogan was a child actor of silent films. He was that cute kid with the big brown eyes and the Dutch boy haircut that starred in lots of funny-man Charlie Chaplin's films. Well, anyway... the little tyke got ripped off! He made mega-mega amounts of money as a child star, but discovered upon reaching adulthood, that his cold, hard cash had not been conserved. Holy crap! Ouch.

Thus, the creation of the COOGAN LAW. Some states have adopted similar legislation (under different names) which allows a judge to specify a certain amount or percentage of a minor's earnings to be set aside in a blocked trust for the minor's future (adulthood) under certain circumstances. I bet Jackie wishes this were the case in his day! Well, today in California, 100% of all minors' contracts are protected by the Coogan Law – and the minimum amount set aside for any minor's contract signed on or after January 1, 2000, is 15% of gross earnings.

The most well-known of any such laws is this one we refer to in our grand old state of California as the "Coogan Law" – named after (guess whom?) Jackie Coogan. Each state which has a "Coogan Law" in effect sets the particular rules by which a judge makes a decision in regards to amounts or percentages saved for the child actor's future. The judge in each case has sole discretion, and there are usually no predetermined amounts described in other state laws that suggest how much should be reserved for the trust. The judge in those states bases his or her decisions upon the individual case and the circumstances surrounding the child actor and his or her living situation.

In California, however, any child who works under contract on or after January 1, 2000, is protected under the revised Coogan Law. It is now in effect 100% of the time (even for extra work). Parents must set aside at least 15% of the minor's gross earnings in a trust (or some other such account) that the child has sole right to – but cannot withdraw from until his or her 18th birthday.

Well, poor Jackie may have been broke as an adult, but at least Jackie Coogan got a real, full-fledged LAW named after him! How many of us can say that? He's a bazillionaire in our book!

CR Kids Talent Management

6433 Topanga Canyon Blvd., #400
Canoga Park, CA 91303

Website:
n/a

Email:
CRKidsMgmt@aol.com

Casting Directors/Staff
Cyndee Romley

Main Line:
818-206-3490

Registration Line:
n/a

Info Line/Hotline:
n/a

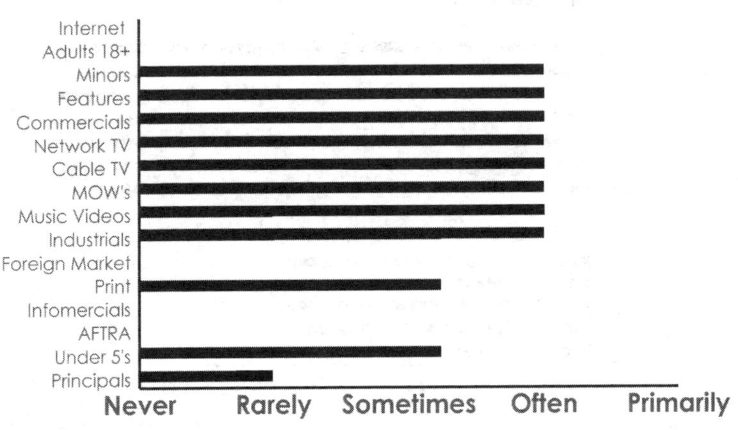

YEAR OPENED
1995

TYPE OF COMPANY
Cyndee looks for kids of all shapes, sizes and ethnicities. She primarily concentrates on extra work for television and film, but also works in commercial and print.

REGISTRATION
You can register by mail or call 818-206-3490 for an appointment. You will then be advised as to how to go about getting your kids started with *CR Kids*.

Company Fees	SAG Members	AFTRA & Non-Union Talent
Registration Fee:	$25	$25
Photo Fee:	$0	$0
Commissions:	15%	15%
TOTAL:	***$25 + COMMISSIONS***	***$25 + COMMISSIONS***

act eight

Jet Set Kids

P.O. Box 2302
La Jolla, CA 92038

Website:
www.jetsetmodels.com

Email:
lindsay@jetsetmodels.com

Casting Directors/Staff
Lindsay Stewart

Main Line:
858-551-9393 ext. 103

Registration Line:
n/a

Info Line/Hotline:
n/a

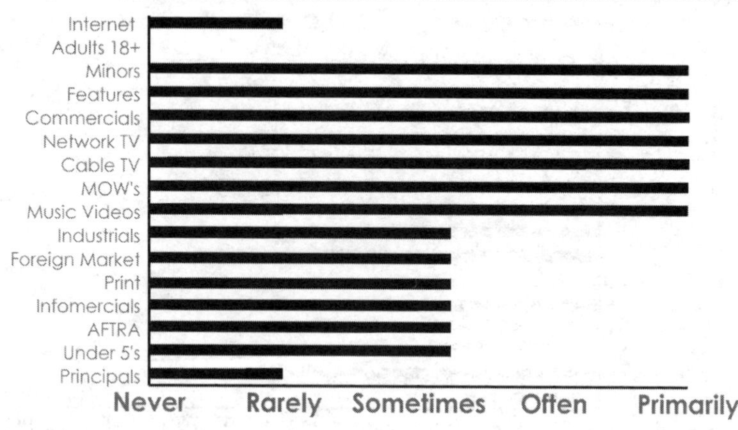

act eight

YEAR OPENED

1995

TYPE OF COMPANY

Jet Set Management Group, Inc. (of which *Jet Set Kids* is a division) is a SAG franchised agency based in the San Diego area, though most of the work they book is in Los Angeles.

REGISTRATION

Mail ONLY! Send 4 to 5 "natural home snapshots" of your child along with his/her info. If *Jet Set* is interested, they will contact you within 2 weeks.

Company Fees	SAG Members	AFTRA & Non-Union Talent
Registration Fee:	$0	$0
Photo Fee:	$0	$0
Commissions:	10%	20%
TOTAL:	***COMMISSION***	***COMMISION***

Kids! Background Talent

207 S. Flower Steet, Second Floor
Burbank, CA 91502

Website:
www.kidsmanagement.com

Email:
n/a

Casting Directors/Staff
Eric, Laura, Amber, Kim, & Jackie

Main Line:
661-964-0131

Registration Line:
n/a

Info Line/Hotline:
n/a

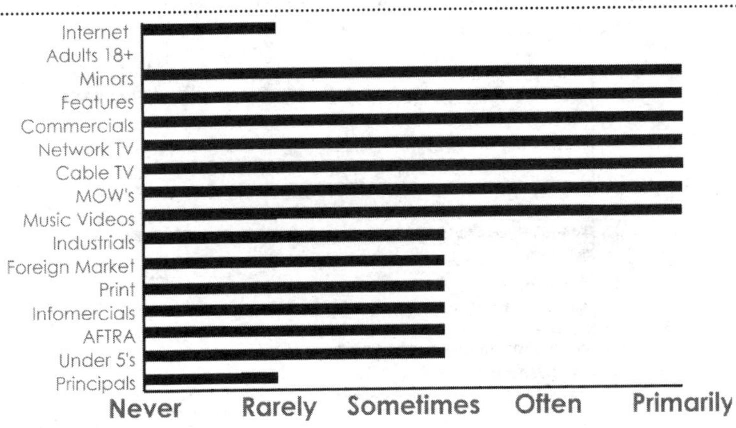

YEAR OPENED

2000 (Previously known as *Academy Kids* and *March Hare*)

TYPE OF AGENCY

They look for kids of all sizes and ethnicities. They concentrate on extra work for television and film, as well as some print work. *Kids! Background Talent* is a division of the calling service *Extras! Management* with a shared staff.

REGISTRATION

Call 661-964-0131 for an appointment or to request the paperwork for your child. You will need the COMPLETED paperwork at the time you come in.

Company Fees	SAG Members	AFTRA & Non-Union Talent
Registration Fee:	$0	$0
Photo Fee:	$30	$30
Semi-Annual Dues:	$18* or $27**	$18* or $27**
Commissions:	20%	20%
TOTAL:	***$30 + 18* or 27** + COMMISSIONS***	***$30 + 18* or 27** + COMMISSIONS***

*Children under 5 years old pay $18 every June & December ($36 a year).

**Children over 5 years old pay $27 every June & December ($54 a year).

Lang Talent Group

21601 Vanowen Steet, Suite 202
Canoga Park, CA 91303

Website:
www.langtalent.com

Email:
info@langtalent.com

Casting Directors/Staff
De Lang, Linda & Rhonda

Main Line:
818-592-6990

Registration Line:
n/a

Info Line/Hotline:
n/a

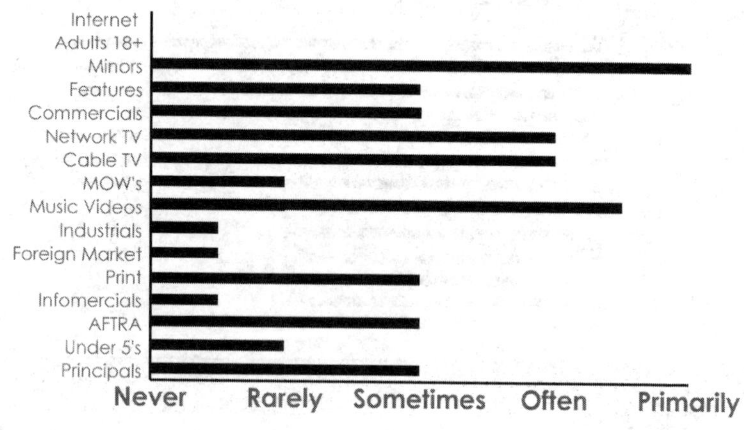

act eight

YEAR OPENED

1985

TYPE OF COMPANY

This is a management company of sorts for children 15 days old to 18 years old. They also offer acting classes for children, but be sure you're not paying a boatload of money for your kids to take these as a prerequisite to taking your cute one on as a client. Rock on!

Company Fees	SAG Members	AFTRA & Non-Union Talent
Registration Fee:	$50* (kids under 3, kids 4 & up FREE)	$50* (kids under 3, kids 4 & up FREE)
Extra/Print Commissions:	20%	20%
Principal Commissions:	15%	20%
TOTAL:	***$50* + COMMISSIONS***	***$50* + COMMISSIONS***

*Children UNDER 3 years old are charged $50. Children OVER 4 years old are FREE!!

Lang Talent Group

REGISTRATION

They know how many Moms and Dads across the country think their kids are cute enough to be in the movies, so they want to make it clear that you MUST live in or around Los Angeles in order for them to consider your children.

You can apply by mail if you send a PICTURE or VIDEO of your child with all his or her pertinent info attached to the submission. Be sure to enclose a SASE if you choose this method to apply. You can also submit via the internet (sign of the times, parents!). Call the main line and ask for registration information or check 'em out on the net: www.langtalent.com

INSIDE SCOOP!

It's our understanding that these folks are now some type of a personal management outfit. They don't strictly cast background talent, and supposedly have other interests in your child's career. Remember, you should pay nothing up front for a manager. Managers don't get paid until your child gets his bucks!

Primary Contact Info

Main Line:
818-592-6990

E-Mail:
info@langtalent.com

Screen Children's Casting

4000 Riverside Drive, Suite A
Burbank, CA 91505

Website:
n/a

Email:
n/a

Casting Directors/Staff
Jill, Ron, Erin, Amber & Ashley

Main Line:
818-846-4300

Registration Line:
n/a

Info Line/Hotline:
n/a

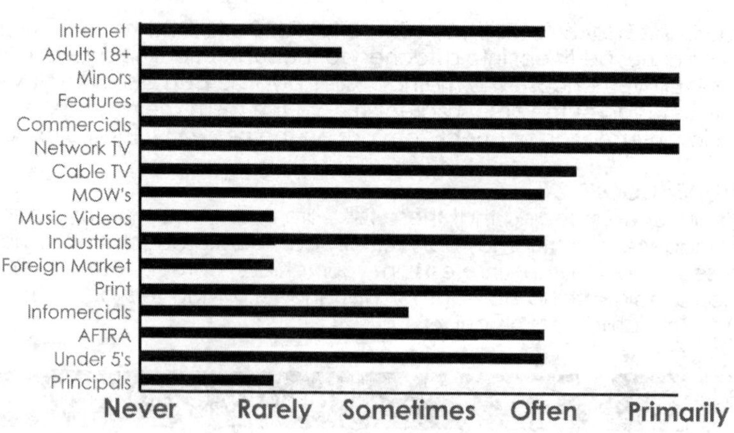

act eight

YEAR OPENED

1936 – yes indeed, 1936. NOT a typo, people.

TYPE OF COMPANY

A children's casting agency (imagine that, with a name like *Screen Children's* even!) that primarily seeks newborns (15 days +) to young adults through their swell Young Adult Department for 18-23 year olds. They tell **HOLLYWOOD OS**®: "Keep in mind that while parents are sometimes booked to work with their children, parents are ALWAYS REQUIRED TO REMAIN ON THE SET with their child or children regardless."

Company Fees	SAG Members	AFTRA & Non-Union Talent
Registration Fee:	$0	$0
Photo Fee:	$40	$40
Commissions:	15%	15%
TOTAL:	***$40 + COMMISSIONS***	***$40 + COMMISSIONS***

Screen Children's Casting

REGISTRATION

You can call the Main Line and ask for Registration information or stop by during their scheduled visiting times: Tuesdays from 11AM - 12PM. But be sure to CALL first because *Screen Children's* does not take walk-ins for Registration.

THE PROCEDURE TO FOLLOW ONCE REGISTERED

You will be contacted when there is work for your child. You SHOULD NOT call the office more than once a month to check in – unless you are returning a call or page. If you haven't heard from *Screen Children's* in a while and your child is registered, instead of calling, try dropping A CURRENT SNAPSHOT IN THE MAIL with new sizes (heck, kids change/grow daily!!).

THE ALL-TIME NO-NO'S

Don't accept a job and then later cancel claiming your child has finals, play-offs, a recital or anything else planned that you should have been aware of at the time your child was initially booked.

act eight

GOOD THINGS TO DO

- Have a pager, arrive early to set, and listen to instructions about wardrobe, and be sure to bring selections.
- Never bring extra people along – there is to be ONE adult accompanying the child booked at all times.
- Children should be on set with a backpack filled with between 3 and 5 hours of school work (yikes – lotsa fun, huh??!).

INSIDE SCOOP!

Screen Children's Casting tells **HOLLYWOOD OS**®: "We have been providing children for the Entertainment Industry since 1936. Children attend school on the set with a certified, credentialed studio teacher. There MUST be a Studio Teacher on all jobs that last over one hour. We encourage the children registered with us to get EXCELLENT GRADES at their home schools. Children learn good work habits at an early age."

Primary Contact Info

Main Line:
818-846-4300

Fax:
818-846-3745

Studio Kids Management

15068 Rosecrans Avenue, #198
La Mirada, CA 90638

Website:
n/a

Email:
studiokids@comcast.net

Casting Directors/Staff
Lisa Marie

Main Line:
562-902-9838

Registration Line:
562-902-9838 ext. 2

Info Line/Hotline:
562-259-1824

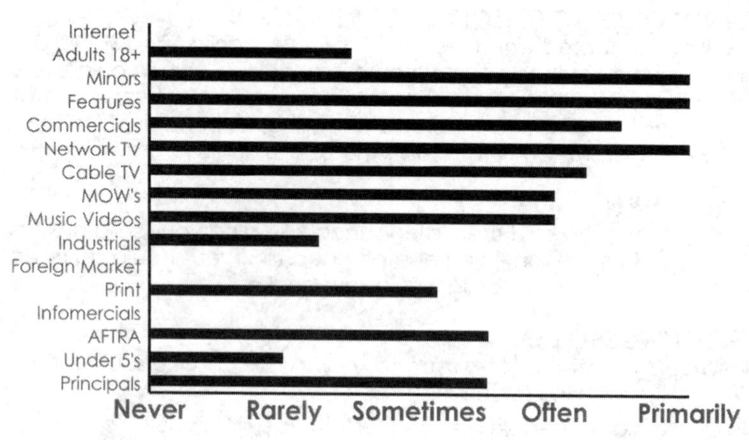

YEAR OPENED

1998

TYPE OF COMPANY

To quote Lisa Marie: "We are a unique management company for children." She and her fine staff look for children ages 15 days to 18 years and work hard to put their clients to work in all types of projects. Lisa Marie also tells **HOLLYWOOD OS**®: "We are always accepting twins, triplets, quads too!"

Company Fees	SAG Members	AFTRA & Non-Union Talent
Registration Fee:	$50*	$50*
Photo Fee:	$50**	$50**
Commissions:	15%	15%
TOTAL:	***$100*** *(+COMMISSIONS)*	***$100*** *(+COMMISSIONS)*

* Twins, triplets & quadruplets are FREE!

***SKM uses KelliMac Photography* ONLY... yet Lisa says you are welcome to bring your own pictures.

Studio Kids Management

REGISTRATION

Call the hotline for registration information and the next registration dates. They are usually held every six to eight weeks. You can send them a picture of your child or children with a SASE (business size) and they will send you a *Studio Kids* information packet with all the important info you'll need to get started.

PROCEDURE TO FOLLOW ONCE REGISTERED

You will be contacted when there is a project for you or your child.

WHAT SKM APPRECIATES

Lisa Marie tells **HOS**®: "When our parents' "yes's" mean YES and their "no's" mean NO. If they want the project – do it! If for some reason, you cannot take a job – say no! We do understand!" They also love when parents keep on top of their kids' Coogan accounts and make sure their work permits stay current. And their pictures.

SKM PET PEEVES

Lisa Marie tells **HOS**®: "Parents who don't follow through. If parents express that they want their child in the business – but fail to send current photos or don't get their paperwork in current working order. We do not tolerate lateness, cancelling jobs, expired work permits and old photos."

TYPES OF CHILDREN SKM IS ALWAYS LOOKING FOR

Lisa Marie tells **HOS**®: "All sorts of delicious types of children. Every day always accepting new types, sizes, color, ages, etc. The studios are always looking for twins, triplets and quadruplets. And all SAG kids are welcome."

ABOUT SAG VOUCHERS

Lisa Marie tells **HOS**®: "If the child is seeking SAG – we will help the families get them. However, we do help the 18+ kids in that area too! Most kids are Non-Union to start and we help guide their way to becoming SAG."

WHAT DO YOU SEE FOR THE FUTURE OF BACKGROUND CASTING?

SKM tell **HOS**®: "We would love to see the recognition of children's extras management companies on the big screen!"

COMPANY PHILOSOPHY

Lisa Marie tells **HOS**®: "*Studio Kids* specifically allows the parent to choose what is best for their child. We work very hard to allow parents to pick what projects best benefit the child and their families and their own family issues."

Studio Kids Management

SIDE NOTE
SKM encourages our families not to spend very much money. We all know it is not necessary! We honestly approach the parents as if this was a 'sport' for the child. Today they want to be an actor, next month, next year, they want to play baseball. This is why we encourage parents NOT to spend their hard-earned money on something their child may not be too interested in later. We do, however, have children in our files that are obviously destined to act."

INSIDE SCOOP!
These ladies have a policy of not turning anyone down as long as the child wants to do this. They also have a fair rotation policy where those who haven't worked lately will get the first calls to work when there is a project (unless the production is looking for a specific type, of course!).

Primary Contact Info

Main Line:
562-902-9838

Email:
studiokids@comcast.net

fabulous other

"Frankly, my dear(s), we DO give a damn!"

This chapter is for YOU, the background actor, and it is mainly filled with companies we are confused about for any number of reasons:

- HUGE Fees
- Too Many "Promises"
- Advertiser-Driven
- "Unique" Sales Pitches
- Unexplained Or Unnecessary Name Changes
- Supposed "State-of-the-Art" Technology

So you just got off the bus (plane, train or automobile – we're gonna borrow from the fun film) from Wichita, Harlem, Harrisburg, San Antonio or some such place in between... now what? Maybe you've been here in Hollywood for years, but have only just realized your dream to be in the movies. Whatever the case, you've got those stars in your eyes and a few pennies in your pockets, and you wanna break into the business known as show business! What do you do? Well, you put on the brakes, sit down somewhere real comfy-like and read the pages that follow – before someone tries to shake you down for all your hard-earned dough!

Your uncle's boss's baby brother's poker partner says you got the look (eyes, ears, nose, figure, face – whatever!) to make it as a successful model or actor and you jump at the words and decide a career in Tinseltown is just what you're after. Well, what you need to take with a grain of salt (besides the poker partner's words) is the "promises" that certain individuals or companies may throw at ya claiming they can get you work in this tricky industry. There are lots of sketchy and unscrupulous so-called talent or modeling agencies in this town that will lead you to believe they can make you a "star." Unfortunately, consumers are all-too-often victimized by such fraudulent agencies promising mucho money and that much sought-after stardom.

When you walk into a place and they ask you to pay BIG up-front fees for pictures, screen tests, photography, consultation, classes or other things of that nature – beware! You'll want to do some investigating before signing your life (or your small fortune) away.

fabulous other

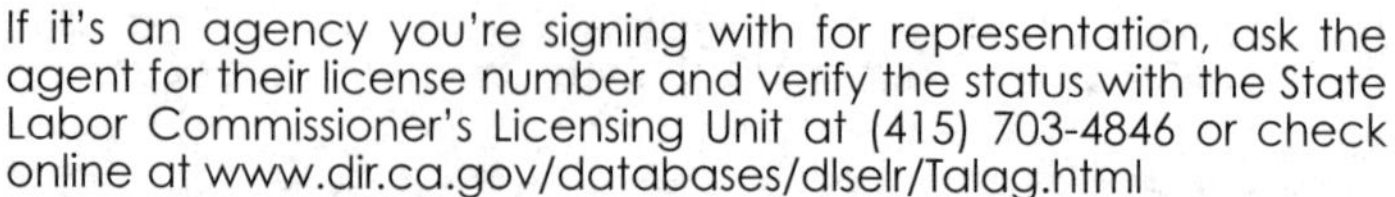

If it's an agency you're signing with for representation, ask the agent for their license number and verify the status with the State Labor Commissioner's Licensing Unit at (415) 703-4846 or check online at www.dir.ca.gov/databases/dlselr/Talag.html

If the company is offering classes and charging tuition, contact the Council of Private, Post Secondary Vocational Education at (916) 445-3428 to determine their licensing status. And while photography is a tool of the trade and you may be required to provide your own photos, you should not be required to use a photographer that the agent recommends.

In this section of **"EXTRA" WORK for Brain Surgeons**®, we've done a lot of that investigating for you, but ultimately it's your decision to find the place or places that are right for you. There are many different types of businesses operating in this industry: extras casting agencies, acting schools, talent agencies, modeling schools, photography studios, management companies, and most recently the huge glut of on-line casting resources that promise the world, but often deliver significantly less.

As we do with every new edition, we have conducted some significant trimming and reassessing of those companies listed here. Simple reason being: THERE ARE JUST TOO MANY! AND they DO NOT deserve recognition AT ALL. With this said (or written), please understand, we have tried to include ONLY those that predominately target newcomers and most appropriately "extras" – did you forget the title of the book already, people?

Your duty is to know what you want going into a situation AND finding out what the company does before signing or paying anything. Those too-good-to-be-true verbal promises they made? Chances are, they're words spoken to get you to pick up the pen and sign on that dotted line. Make sure they put all their "promises" in writing so that if and when you do sign an agreement, you know EXACTLY what you're getting.

Reputations are built and earned. Good or bad. Don't fall prey to promises. Look at their productivity. Do they have a track record? And if they're "new," who are the players involved? Are they just has-beens and rejects from five other unsuccessful, scammy companies under a brand-new banner or are they trusted, legitimate professionals?

fabulous other

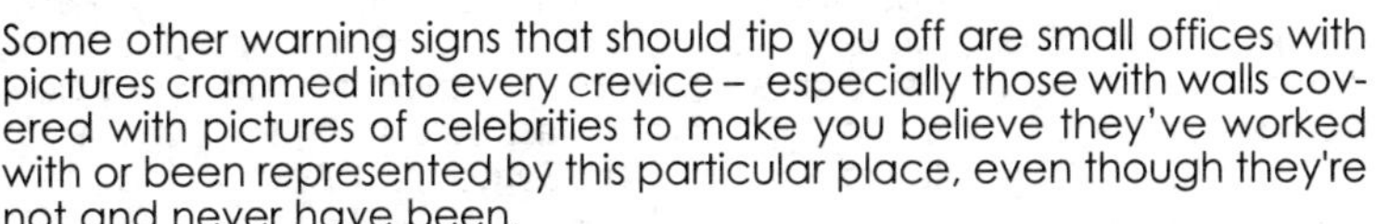

Some other warning signs that should tip you off are small offices with pictures crammed into every crevice – especially those with walls covered with pictures of celebrities to make you believe they've worked with or been represented by this particular place, even though they're not and never have been.

Some companies will also use names which sound so similar to well-known agencies that you can become confused. Don't fall for it. Fraudulent companies are trying to confuse you and give an impression of legitimacy that they are by no means entitled to. And the biggest, flashing-red warning sign of all? Phony ads placed in the help wanted section of newspapers like *L.A. Weekly* that read: "New Faces Wanted," "No Experience Necessary," or the most obvious "Be A Star!" Yuck, come on, people!

While not ALL of the companies listed in Fabulous Other are unscrupulous, sketchy or otherwise scary, they're listed here to make you aware of their existence. So just heed our words as "a heads-up" of sorts – so you know what you're getting yourself into. Decide for yourself which company or companies you want to contact! Good luck! (P.S. Where applicable, we've provided the Better Business Bureau's (BBB's) two cents also!)

• *Disclaimer (read me)!* •

Legitimate questions, concerns or complaints about a casting company, modeling school, casting website, agent or agency may be referred to the following places:

- *Better Business Bureau*
- *Department of Licensing and Regulation*
- *Consumer Protection Agency*
  (in the city or town where the company is located)

If at anytime, however, you come across any new and/or interesting companies not listed in this directory, feel free to let us at **HOLLYWOOD OS®** *know. We'll do our part to try to help you in finding out more information. Our email address is info@hollywoodos.com.*

Also, if you have had any quality experiences with companies included in Fabulous Other, let us know that too. It's important to share information with others. . . heck, isn't that what **"EXTRA" WORK for Brain Surgeons®** *is all about anyway?! Thanks for reading! Enjoy!*

act nine

2000 CASTING
3115 Sunset Blvd.
Los Angeles CA 90028
CONTACT: Morena Moncada

Who knows, we are just covering our bases in case they decide to change their names to *2006, 2007, 2008 Casting* (see *CNTV* and *Hollywood Casting*). Kidding, people.

It amazes us how often some of these clever folks open up shop under one name and then a year or so later, change names and change locations. Such, it seems, is the story with *2000 Casting*, formerly *Hollywood Casting* and now *CNTV Casting*. Same game, different name. They charged a yearly fee of $45 and advertised all over the darn place. Unfortunately for talent, they have in the past advertised for shows they were not actually casting and worse yet – for shows that we couldn't find listed as being in production! Ouch. Now, listen up, Brain Surgeons, because the following is a true story:

One poor guy came into our office and proceeded to tell us that he was to be booked on *Pearl Harbor* for an entire week and he rushed to our office because he was told he would be booked by... *2000 Casting*. Huh?! Needless to say, we were flustered because this guy was adamant and he was not leaving without a call time! We got the lowdown and then called *On Location Casting* and spoke with Tina Kerr who didn't even know who *2000 Casting* was. Further, she confirmed that the casting for *Pearl Harbor* would not begin for weeks. We then put the *2000 Casting* "victim" on the phone with Tina – the actual, real and true Casting Director for *Pearl Harbor*. After a few minutes, they resolved to call *2000 Casting* together to get to the bottom of things. Luckily for you, our beloved readers, it was a speaker-phone conversation, so we can tell you all the juicy lowdown of what happened next.

Tina, who had just wrapped *Bedazzled*, was cleaning out her office there and was quickly put on the line with the owner of *2000 Casting*. The owner, Morena, proceeded to question Tina as to who she was and from what company she was calling. Tina patiently explained. Tina also pointed out that she was the Casting Director for *Pearl Harbor* and she did not understand why this gentleman, one whom she had never before laid eyes on, was told to rush down to be booked for a week on a movie she was casting.

Morena feigned exasperation and said that he must have misunderstood – *2000 Casting* was not booking *Pearl Harbor* now, they were presently booking *Bedazzled*. WHAT?? Morena was now taking credit for *On Location*'s other gig! Not only had Morena tried to take credit for casting *On Location*'s films, but when challenged about the validity of her claims, Morena pronounced herself to be the Casting Director on films that the *real* Casting Director had just wrapped! To make matters worse, Morena didn't even know who Tina Kerr was. How many marbles can these people be missing?!

A & A, LLC
ACTOR AND ACTRESS
16161 Ventura Blvd., Suite 341
Encino, CA 91436
PHONE: 818-481-3998
EMAIL: incredibletalent2010@yahoo.com
CONTACT: Ian Mickelson II

A CD-ROM "talent search magazine" which supposedly goes out to all sorts of casting agencies and production companies (at least the ones supposedly willing to pay the $10/month subscription fee). Actors and actresses looking to get their mugs in Actor and Actress are also expected to pony up 10 George Washington's a month. In our experience, casting services of any kind that try and charge both ends of the biz are usually destined to crash and burn. Maybe this one will survive, who knows?

The "magazine" itself is just a loose collection of files and folders loaded onto a CD-ROM which then taped inside a "cover" that looks like it came off a home printer.

Despite all the facts, if this idea somehow sounds so good to you that you want to jump onboard in a big way, Ian's apparently offering 50% ownership in A&A to the first lucky investor with an extra $120,000. Side note, the buy-in price was set to balloon to $347,000 after July of 2005. Um...ok then.

A & B CASTING
3575 Cahuenga Blvd. West
Suite 125-9
Universal City, CA 90068
PHONE: 323-850-0024
EMAIL: abcasting@sbcglobal.net
WEBSITE: www.abcasting.net

What to say about these folks? Hmmm, well they never return our phone calls, for one. They're new (which doesn't necessarily mean bad, just new). They advertise themselves (online and in the *LA Weekly*) as a casting service covering the spectrum from commercials to feature films. Registration is free, but they'll charge you a one-time $20 photo imaging fee to take your picture. Recent credits include "Love Story In Harvard" (though Landsman/Kaye reportedly booked the bulk of the 600 extras needed) and a couple Union and Non-Union commercials. If anyone out there knows of more credits, feel free to drop us a line - we'd love to know what they are.

ACTINGZONE.COM
WEBSITE: www.actingzone.com

A basic membership is free, but an upgraded membership to view all their casting notices will cost you 6 bucks a month. Not a bad deal at about 20¢ a day *if* you had any inkling if these notices are accurate, if they're coming from the source itself or some third-party wannabe.

We welcome input from our readers regarding any gigs they've booked via ActingZone.com. Or any heads-up as to exactly where their casting notices might be originating.

ACTOUT.COM

WEBSITE: www.actout.com

Gone. They were an on-line database for "casting professionals," but their site has been under construction for almost two years now. How much did it/does it cost? Who used/uses it? When or will the website be back up? Big fat questions abound. Help us out here, folks!?!

ACTORS PROMOTIONAL SERVICES
APS PRODUCTIONS
HOLLYWOODSUCCESS.COM

6464 Sunset Blvd., #750 or 5564 Sunset Blvd.
Hollywood, CA 90028
PHONE: 323-462-2777 or 323-980-3375
WEBSITE: www.hollywoodsuccess.com

People! Please, people! Help us help you! How does this place do it? Genius, we tell you. We get many phone calls, letters and emails about *APS*. Help inform your fellow extras/actors, will ya?!

Let's momentarily forgive them the fact that there are supposedly two addresses and supposedly two different names for the supposedly same outfit. Let's also forget that their so-called "services" can apparently cost $1000's (that's thousands, not hundreds) of dollars. Likewise, we won't chastise them for the numerous typos/misspellings/omissions (and they're going to do your resumés? Ouch) in their "professional" (low-resolution, ink-jet printed) mailings. We too have typos, expertly crafted and strategically placed, but typos nonetheless (they send us their cool mailings).

Let's also set aside the fact that we've never heard (maybe we're brain dead) of any of their "internationally-known" writers, producers or directors that supposedly attend their "Industry Insider" seminars that take place at posh (read: trying to impress the heck outta ya) "private estates" where the prizes they give out are "gift certificates" to their OWN events – so you can help potentially hook your friends! Genius! Let's even forget for just a moment that the man who runs this whole operation has a name that sounds more like that of a used car salesman or late-night Infomercial host... hey, it is so damn catchy, maybe it's real! They do, after all, want to help you... right? You have been paying attention, haven't you?

Rock Riddle is the cool man (hiding?) behind this "accelerated success" program on "the business of acting," and it seems to be quite a fabulous racket indeed. They claim to have been around since 1976 in some incarnation or another (*APS Productions, Associated Producers Services, Actors Promotional Services*... you get the idea). They also claim to have helped "many" actors get gigs. Who? Um... yes, exactly. We can't even bring ourselves to share all they claim to offer. It might be a waste of ink. In fact, we just anonymously got an email about how we can help Mr. Riddle raise money so that he can buy his own personal jet. No, we are not kidding...

"It's show business - not show art." That's their *Kraft®* macaroni line, not ours, but apparently it's worked since people have been buying into it for some twenty-seven years. Last year, they were developing a very special "on-line magazine" for members only! Apparently it no longer exists! But, heck, at least they got all your personal/pertinent info – like names, phone numbers and email addresses so they can contact you endlessly in case they want to pitch their products and hand off your info to Lord knows who.

You could be chosen to join their limited numbers of "professional actors & actresses." We're still waiting to meet the poor person who had hundreds of $$ in hand and actually got turned away by the Riddler. And one last benefit/service/selling point of *APS*? And we quote: "An Investigative Service for *APS* members (the truth – who's legitimate, professional, and ethical in the industry and who isn't!)." Enough said. We can't take any-more.

ACTOR'S RESOURCE
38 Rockview
Irvine, CA 92612
CONTACT: Randall Stewart
PHONE: DISCONNECTED
WEBSITE: www.actors-resource.com

This Calling Service opened in 2003 and closed by the same year's end. They had a good rep with most of their roster, but found it too difficult to compete in an already-crowded field and told us they couldn't break through *Central*'s impenetrable connection with *Extras Management*. What, and that was some big news flash?!

ACTORSNOW.COM
WEBSITE: www.actorsnow.com

All the exciting info we wanted to share with you guys is now mysteriously missing from their website. In December 2002 the website was shut down and undergoing construction. In August 2003, it read "COMING SOON!" In October, November... the same. You get the idea. Could that mean they just disappeared after making enough bucks on those who did sign up for so-called services? We do not know. But it's been TWO YEARS, people! Perhaps they are addressing issues of actors' concerns or perhaps they're sunning themselves in Barbados with the cash some poor talent paid for what seems to be a now-nonexistent-nothing. Let us know.

AFFINITY MODEL & TALENT
AFFINITY TALENT AGENCY
8721 Santa Monica Blvd., Suite 27
West Hollywood, CA 90069
PHONE: 323-525-0577
WEBSITE: www.affinitytalent.com

The name doesn't say "extras" or "background" anywhere, and their fancy-looking website totes pretty-looking people. At one point they supposedly claimed to help find featured "extras" for films. Two women who contacted us thought they just wanted their money – with no return on their investment, who knows? Keep us posted; we are interested in your personal experiences with these folks.

ALLIANCE DEVELOPMENT CENTER

6430 Sunset Blvd., Suite 1000
Hollywood, CA 90028
PHONE: 323-301-4263
EMAIL: alliancedevelopment@yahoo.com

New to town? Need an agent? Need headshots? Need advice on breaking into the industry? Well, you've come to the right place, sweetheart, ADC is a management company/acting school/headshot studio here to help you make...oh, wait, you do have the purported $500 sign-up fee and supposed $200 per month membership fee, don'tcha?

This engine of entertainment education fired to life around October of '04, promising to guide the young and confused along the winding paths to Hollywood superstardom. They apparently have an acting coach, a go-to headshot guy, a buddy-buddy relationship with a production company called *Shusett Productions* (headed by Ronald Shusett - a writer/producer with some actually legit credits), and, we love this one, their very own ADC Discount Card - good for discounts at local restaurants (*Red Lobster*, here we come!) Their self-proclaimed "main goal" is to place talent in ADC/Shusett-produced projects. Hmm, so, essentially, unless we've read the facts wrong, you have to pay them for the chance to be cast in their films. Sounds fair. That's the way the film biz works, right? These folks have posted on Craig's List and a few other hotbeds of online chicanery.

ARTIST ENTERTAINMENT GROUP

12346 Santa Monica Blvd.
Santa Monica, CA 90404

The young woman who called our office was so upset with these folks – she almost took a job with them! Yikes. She responded to an ad in her school newspaper that stated they were looking for telemarketers. Okay, fine... she thought. She went on a series of interviews and began to learn what it was this place was actually selling. Her job was to go to her college or other local colleges and try to recruit students or as she said, supposedly "scam them out of lots of money." How? With photo packages and acting classes taught by "nobodies," she said. They even asked her if she could teach a class on acting – the young lady was a Nursing major who had never even taken an acting class herself or even once expressed an interest in acting! She ran. Then called us and wanted us to warn all you – because, although she didn't take the job, she's sure someone with less of a conscience did. If you have any cool feedback on this company, let us know.

ARTISTWEBSITE.COM

P.O. Box 1168
Studio City CA 91604
PHONE: 310-328-5405
WEBSITE: www.artistwebsite.com

What is this - a website where you can order Van Gogh knock-offs and finger paints?! No. For now, this company has a website that supposedly lets Casting Directors see YOU! They have pics of people young and old and from as far away as the Dakotas. Do CD's use this site to cast? We can't say. Is it likely? Who knows, but stranger things have happened.

A Casting Director in LA is likely not going to fly in your cute six-year-old from Tampa to audition when there's plenty of talent in the area. *Artistwebsite.com* will build a web page for you or your child with head-shots and photos and stuff – but be careful! Anyone can look at it on the web! Do you really want any possible creep in the world to get a look at your kid via the internet? They supposedly e-mail casting notices to you every week too... and they'll forward requests from casting agents that want to meet you from your page. There's a yearly $25 fee that doesn't seem so bad. If you've had experiences with these guys, fill us in.

BACK TO ONE CASTING

P.O. Box 753
Hollywood, CA 90078
FAX: 818-255-3699
CONTACT: Cullen Chambers
WEBSITE: www.backtoone.net

Chambers publishes a book, comprised mostly of photos, that pretends to be a directory it clearly isn't. Ours. Why do we say this? The moron does this under our legal trademark as well, *"EXTRA" Work for Rocket Scientists®* – yes, owned by us, **HOLLYWOOD OS®**. He also tried to emulate our quarterly casting magazine by using our tagline "Extra, Extra, Read All About Ya!" They say imitation is the sincerest form of flattery. Confused customers have been misled by uninformed sales help who confuse his "book" with our "directory." Yuck! We are sorry. We know you work hard for your money and want the best. Can you say bait and switch, people? We can't imagine intentionally misleading the consumer with deceptive name confusion is complementary to one's character.

Our publication "EXTRA" WORK for Brain Surgeons® has no substitute, and you know that – that's why you're reading us (woo-hoo!). The man behind this madness has in the past dubbed himself a Casting Director for commercials. What commercials, you may ask? We don't know, so if you know, let us know, 'cause we'd love to know. Know what we mean? He's previously held a "Commercial Extras Casting Registration & FREE Career Expo." What's free? The parking. And some seminars with "industry pros" (who exactly, we don't know) – or a lot of vendors that seem to have had things to sell to the unassuming and unsuspecting background actors. Apparently, he is putting a spin on what he used to do years ago when he would advertise seminars, sell talent tickets and then reportedly cancel with no refunds (back in the 90's according to some old timers in the biz).

A while back, three background actors who attended a "Commercial Extras Casting Registration & FREE Career Expo" in April of 2002, contacted us to tell us they've never booked a gig or even been called since their wondrous registration day. Hhhm? In fact, we have yet to hear of a single person who has even landed a commercial through this company. But we bet that if jobs were landed, he'd throw himself on the call and book himself out from *Extras Management*, his Calling Service. Who knows? If this is not the case, we apologize in advance...but really, don't use our registered trademark to sign folks up.

Apparently there is a one-time $25 Photo Imaging Fee for the Registration, cool! However, the Registration Line (aka cell phone) seems to have been disconnected. Best we could do was a fax number. We just wonder what was done with all of those photo-imaging fees. We assume one could assume whatever the hell they want.

BAM
BOOKING ACTORS & MODELS
BLAKE ARI MODELS
STUDIO CITY MODELS & TALENT

7083 Hollywood Blvd., Suite 304
Hollywood, CA 90028
(also located in Studio City, Santa Monica & Beverly Hills)
PHONE: 323-468-9188
WEBSITE: www.bammodels.com

"Wham! Bam! Thank you, Ma'am!" Sorry, we couldn't resist. *Booking Acting & Models* agency (just one of the five names). Boy, does that sound impressive. What's our take on it? There was once a $200 set-up fee that was divided into three monthly payments, and then some other lovely fees that brought the INITIAL grand total to an apparent $349 smacks just to get started. Well, now the set-up fee "varies" depending on what you want to do with them. Hhhm? There is also either a $20 or $40 monthly website fee depending upon which service you choose. In the summer of 2002, there was a scandal of sorts where some background actors were getting cold calls from *BAM*. The Bammers (funny, huh) told the talent that they had been referred to them by a current satisfied client. Who referred them? *BAM* apparently wouldn't say.

A few of the extras who contacted us thought an extras casting company was selling their names and contact info... hhhm. It seems someone at a really big casting company sold them names, numbers, and socials of registered talent for $2 bucks a head. How do we know this? Because some slimy guy from *BAM* wanted to buy our clientele list as well. Did they not know who we were and think that we would not report this back to you?! Stupid people amaze us. Sketchy indeed. We told the actors to contact the Better Business Bureau, and boy did they get an earful. Read the end of this ditty for that fantastic info!

So, anyway, the Bamsters market their models online and supposedly claim that "[BAMmodels.com] is the only service of its kind in the world." Are they joking? Who uses them? We don't know. Will you get booked, or just whammed, bammed and thank you ma'am-ed? We'd like to know. We could render a guess. Check out their website if you wish and test the tepid waters for yourself. And, as always, keep us posted on your adventures.

act nine

BARBIZON SCHOOL OF MODELING

All over the country
PHONE: 562-799-2985
WEBSITE: www.barbizonmodeling.com

Oh, dear. We wish, we wish, we only wish... we were joking. But, alas, fine people, we are not. In late July 2003, we were contacted by a regional office asking to take part in a mutual referral program – with *Barbizon* – yeah, whatever! Most of their franchises have a satisfactory record with the BBB, but to solicit us for customer leads? We're not sure if they've purchased our fine directory. Oh well, you win some and you lose some.

Since this company's scope is nationwide, refer to the specific franchise in your area when looking for info at www.bbb.org.

BEVERLY HILLS STUDIOS, INC.

CONTACT: Kevin James O'Brien

This place filed for bankruptcy a couple of years ago. Gosh, we're shocked. We thought it would still be pretty educational to explain how this place really "functioned," so you can stay on the lookout for similar scam tactics! They used to rent out hotel space and hold cheesy inspiring seminars, which were announced on the radio. Nice. They enticed you into spending several thousand dollars (negotiable, of course) on photos, classes, etc. and the opportunity to supposedly meet big-time agents and big-time *California Dream* stars (or at least that's who we believe we saw, we may be wrong. It could've been some *Saved by the Bell* folks). Cool. Screech rules!

Anyway, they informed everyone that this was the place to be discovered! Sure. *Beverly Hills Studios* was not even in Beverly Hills, darn it – try Santa Monica by the Santa Monica Airport. . . but it sounded good, didn't it?! They then called you approximately 2 weeks later to inform you that you had been selected to attend a different event or that you should come in for a consultation. That's when Angie (author of this fabuloso directory) found out that she was not the only "selected one." How depressing for her. All the other THOUSANDS of people were SELECTED ONES as well. After all – she did fill out their questionnaire with all of her pertinent information. Of course they're going to call. When she went in, she told them she was broke and suddenly the $2,500 headshot/acting class negotiable quote was lowered to $2,100. She made a joke that she'd have to sell her car for that. . . she was then told that was a good idea and in the end, she'd be making a wise investment. Huh? Needless to say, she didn't do it.

B.J.'S CASTING SERVICE
WIZARD'S TOUCH MANAGEMENT
BRESLER CASTING & ASSOCIATES
BRESLER & ASSOCIATES CASTING

3760 Cahuenga Blvd., West, Suite #104
Universal City, CA 91604
PHONES: 818-786-1212 (office), 818-773-7867 (work line)

Okay, we got a new phone number. But it just rings and rings, and... yeah, rings. Wow, lots of names already! This company touts itself as "The Star Makers of Today. " Cool! They charge a "Filing Fee" (wow, that's a good one – but still not better than the ultra-original "Safety & Security Course Fee" Wizard used at *Casting 2000*). The so-called "Filing Fee" is supposedly $25 per year for SAG and AFTRA talent. For the poor Non-Union folks, there is a purported $50 yearly "Filing Fee." There is a 20% commission on all principal work through *Wizard's Touch Management*, otherwise *B.J's* supposedly doesn't take a commission and they accept talent from age one and up.

You can call 818-773-7867 to schedule a registration appointment, Monday-Friday, 11AM - 4PM. When you arrive, make sure you have your: union cards, social security card, driver's license (photocopies of all), stats and all your pertinent info. Once registered, call the same number once a week for work and leave availability. Make sure you leave your name, number, ethnicity, age range and union status... if it doesn't ring and ring and ring! Keep us posted. Feedback is awsome!

BRAVO CASTING
BRAVO ENTERTAINMENT GROUP

6052 Beeman Avenue
North Hollywood, CA 91606

Owners Mike Arutinyan and Albert Bravo opened shop in early 2003 and took $40 bucks from lots of folks who expected work – only to, as was previously reported to us, apparently get none! Claimed to be casting *Background Players* shows and also Monica Cooper's projects. Apparenty they convinced a few people that they needed to register with them in order to be considered for work on those shows. So wrong. Let us know what you hear or what happens.

BRENTWOOD CASTING

9663 Santa Monica Blvd., Suite 261
Beverly Hills, CA 90210
PHONE: 310-837-3009
CONTACT: Eli Mathieu
EMAIL: brentwoodcasting@yahoo.com
WEBSITE: www.brentwoodcasting.com

A casting agency/management company/online actor database which fired to life in 2005. As we go to press, registering with them is currently free (though there's an optional $25 photo fee and it's $15 to be included in their commercial book). They also offer, sigh, management packages (Silver, Gold, or Platinum - you're choice) which include headshots and breakdowns and such. They run from several hundred dollars to a thousand dollars plus. As a general rule, we advise folks out there to be a bit cautious of "management" companies that require upfront fees or insist that you use their photographers. Managers, like agents, should make their money as a percentage of the jobs they help you book. Use your best judgement.

act nine

C2 ENTERTAINMENT

These folks have been impossible to locate this year and may well have gone under. However, if you should stumble across them, here's what we know:

Hispanic or Latino talent need only apply. Apparently they want you to call for an appointment to register, but good luck getting a return phone call after leaving several messages on a voice mail that seems nothing like a casting line. They charge no registration fees of any kind (that we know of). Cool. Apparently, they seek Non-Union talent 18+ of all ethnicities, but you MUST speak fluent Spanish and be able to improv in the language if necessary. We guess. Oh, boy... we mean "Oh, niño!" Be sure to keep us posted. We'd love feedback.

Make sure you don't confuse this C2 Entertainment with the identically monikered C2 Entertainment at www.C2tv.net. These guys (so they say) are completely unrelated producers of (coincidence time?) Hispanic programming.

CARBON COPIES MANAGEMENT

P. O. Box 1158
Lakeside, CA 92040
PHONE: 619-749-0002
CONTACT: Tracy Gruhot
WEBSITE: www.carboncopies.tv

This company exclusively manages twins under 18. Fun. We wish we could give you more exciting information, but alas that's all we've been able to get. Check out their website and give 'em a call – maybe they will be more thorough with you... like how kids can get management representation and how much money one supposedly has to pay and what, if any, commission is taken. We always seem to get an answering machine and zero return faxes. Let us know! Thanks!

CARMA CASTING

5770 Melrose Avenue, 3rd Floor
Los Angeles, CA 90038
PHONE: DISCONNECTED
HOTLINE: DISCONNECTED

Really, sometimes the name just says it all. A very pleasant woman named Victoria didn't return our fax in 2003, but she seemed lovely enough in our two brief conversations. Then she vanished! She used to hold a Registration of sorts once a week, but the day varied each week, so you'd have to call her Hotline to find out which day it is in a particular week – but guess what? The Hotline isn't working. This was also the day to stop in and say, "hi." If you want to register by mail, it used to cost ya $15 smacks – but we'd guess the address is also no good now since the phones are dead. She may be there, she may not. Good luck. And keep us posted.

CARROT FILMS

PHONE: 323-468-3990
FAX: 323-468-3989

In-House casting for music videos, films and commercials. Kimberly Ogeltree (sorry, if we butchered the spelling) is a producer and Tanya is casting (she used to run *Creative Image* on Wilshire (??) that closed down a few years back). There was a $20 registration fee, (last time we heard from them), and that's about all we can tell ya. Call 'em up for more info if you're interested in seeing what *Carrot*'s all about, but the number just seems to be a random voicemail box these days. We left a message in November '04, but never heard back from them – if the number is even still for them! Let us know.

TOLLEY CASPARIS

A rad independent Casting Director with way cool high-profile projects. In 2003, Tolley asked to have her fabulously larger and more detailed listing removed from future editions of EWFBS®. Why, you may ask? Too many people called and harassed her at home at odd hours of the day and night, even though the book said not to. People! Read!

CAST OF THOUSANDS

We've got nothing exciting to report about this place. We just wanted to let you know that these lovely ladies have packed up shop and moved north – to San Francisco as of December 2003. They asked that we pass along their "thanks" to all background who have worked with them through the years. They also wanted us to let you know they have destroyed/shredded all Los Angeles files – so you can rest assured that your SS# isn't floating around somewhere for the unscrupulous to find! Still miss ya, Lisa & Joni!

CASTAWAY STUDIOS

8899 Beverly Blvd.
Los Angeles, CA 90048
PHONE: 310-248-5296
WEBSITE: www.castawaystudios.com

Now this place may seem familiar to some. In fact, maybe you auditioned in their studios or attended an open call at their facilities. Could be. Supposedly, a couple years ago, the *Castaway* crew (or at least some associated with it) decided to become Casting Directors of sorts themselves and started charging crazy fees to unsuspecting talent. Apparently for $99 smacks a year they would "store" (yes, "store" is the word they used) your photos and info/pictures/demo reel/videotapes at their facilities (Actor's Digital Library as they call it) for "potential" use by "artists, producers and directors that may make use of the the Studio premises." POTENTIAL use? MAY make use of? What? Confused? So are we.

For $99 a year, we'd hope someone would have been reading and reviewing your "stored" stuff daily. Not a single soul came through our doors in the last 2+ years to tell us they got any work. Maybe one of you folks had a different experience you'd like to tell us about? Mercifully, they tell us the Actor's Digital Library has been discontinued and *Castaway* has returned to what they do best, renting out studio space. Ok, that's cool.

act nine

CASTING 2000

CONTACT: Wizard aka Wizzard (that's two zz's)

This was supposed to be different than *2000 Casting*, but, well... you can do the math and see what's what. The guy who seemed to run the show, Wizard, faxed us with a statement that *Casting 2000* exists no longer, but he is still interested in managing talent and coordinating on set... in fact, last we heard the dude works at *B.J.'s Casting*. Interesting. We do feel sorry for all of the people who originally paid to join *Casting 2000* way back when and are now left hung out to dry. In its time of glory, *Casting 2000* was the home of the original catch phrase "Safety and Security Course fee" that no longer exists. Bummer, they'd win the best "original fee" award in our book if they were still around!

CASTING DAILY.COM
CASTING NET.COM
333 Washington Blvd., # 507
Marina Del Rey CA, 90292
WEBSITE: www.castingnet.com

Just as the first part of the dot.com address suggests, these folks apparently claim to post new casting notices daily – for SAG and Non-Union roles, principal and background on both coasts. And that's fantastic. It costs $19.95 a month to view the casting notices and surf through some of their other features. Ok, cool. We are still waiting for word if casting directrors really use it or if talent are actually booking jobs through this site. If you know anything, please let us know. Swell. Thanks!

CASTING ENTERTAINMENT
500 Esplanade Dr., Suite #333
Oxnard, CA 93030
PHONE: DISCONNECTED

In their advertising, they claimed to be casting shows which were not theirs (how original) and for $65 smacks a year, that's quite a bold maneuver! Apparently they've since closed their doors. They ran an ad in a Ventura Paper for *Scorpion King* a few years ago and we all know that film was cast by *Background Players*, not this outfit called *Casting Entertainment*. One of our readers specifically asked *Casting Entertainment* why they were advertising for this show and they claimed they were supposed to cast it but the contract fell through. Hmm? Oh well.

A couple of years ago, they told us that they were a "Marketing Referral Service." It would have been nice if they put such information in their ads rather than the names of movies that were not theirs to cast. This company should not be confused with the now-defunct *Entertainment Casting* also in Oxnard. Oh yeah, they also had (and may still have) an office in Las Vegas... for what? We don't know – maybe showgirls, maybe porn (just kidding), who knows?!

CASTING HEADQUARTERS
CONTACTS: Michael and Sebastian
WEBSITE: www.castingheadquarters.com
EMAIL: info@castingheadquarters.com

Despite their suspiciously similar name, these folks are in no way affiliated with *Headquarters Casting*. *Casting Headquarters* is, we guess, an online database where, so it seems, for $8/month or $60/year, actors can have their photos and profiles posted online for theoretical review by Casting Directors and Agents and such.

The membership also includes access to the CHQ Casting Notices, which are apparently whipping in at the blistering rate of...uh...possibly one or two a month (subject to change of course). Though they've only been online for a few months, they claim to already have 1100 subscribers to their website. How, we have no idea. But who knows, keep us posted. The reason they state on their website for not having a phone is that a "receptionist can be costly."

So, in a nutshell, you pay $8 a month for the privileges of having your photos seen by...well...um...whoever... and getting to never talk to a human being if you have a problem. And if you want to go see them in person, well, they don't list an address and the one their website is registered under doesn't even exist. Hello, weird! You can sign up with the mysterious Michael and Sebastian for free. They offer a gratis basic membership (with one photo posted) which might be a darn good way to go until they figure out their business communication.

CASTING TO THE FOUR WINDS
PHONE: 213-204-6107

They specialized in Ethnic and Native American talent. The former owner, Eaglebear, sold this place, but he has re-emerged as *Knota Ko Casting* – same phone number, different address and some new people.

CHRISTAL BLUE CASTING
C.B.C.
5723 Melrose Ave.
Los Angeles, CA 90038
PHONE: 323-960-5057
WEBSITE: www.christalblue.com

Different registration fees going on here. Ok, let's see if we can map this one out for ya. Last we heard, there is a $100 lifetime membership fee or something and they apparently take a whopping 10% commission on Non-Union jobs. Yikes, not cool! We got *Central Casting* busted for doing this since it drives actors' wages below minimum wage. And that, it seems, is just for the BASIC membership. Or supposedly you can opt for a $2,000 package of classes etc., etc., ad nauseam. Non-Union talent need to bring in/send in $20 and then the remaining $80 is either taken out of their checks until paid off or you can just pay in full (we think you can still do this). Give *C.B.C.* a call. They used to advertise in *BackStage West®* about selling SAG vouchers or something to that effect and they now apparently say (through their website) that talent need not live in CA to register.

In the Arizona Film Commission Book, they also claim to have cast *Men in Black* (can you say Casting Director Tammy Smith?) and *Dante's Peak* (can you say Tammy Smith – AGAIN?). If you find out anything new about this puzzling situation, drop us a line.

If the casting thing doesn't work out, Christal apparently also offers addiction counseling services through her website. Anything and everything from alcohol to porn to clutter - if you're addicted, Christal Blue says she can help. That's cool. We like people who care.

CKM CASTING
10907 Magnolia Blvd., Suite 419
North Hollywood, CA 90027

These fellas of the *CKM* popped up in *LA Weekly* like so many of those other lovely outfits who love to advertise there for the newbies. They wanted you to send 'em $10 bucks with your headshot and resumé.

They apparently accepted only checks and money orders, but didn't tell ya if or when they'd contact you. Usually when people are soliciting you for money, it's nice if they at least tell you what you're paying for, right?! We're hoping you are all a lot smarter than to send money to a random address without having any idea of how to contact them or know whom you're dealing with! No names, no phone numbers, just the claim of supposedly casting three nameless features. Come on, do we look like we just fell off the *U.S.S. Dumbass*?! Keep us posted.

CMT
COLOURS TALENT & MODELS
COLOURS MANAGEMENT
8344 1/2 West 3rd Street
Los Angeles, CA 90048
PHONE: 323-658-7072

They were a SAG-franchised talent agency in early 2003, but willingly surrendered their license when accusations of charging talent surfaced. Yuck. We've been told SAG members aren't allowed to have anything to do with them anymore per their SAG contract, but Non-Union folks should be alert to their supposed ways as well. We had conversations with two "agents" at *CMT* in the summer of 2003 and they both insisted that talent paid nothing – only the standard 10% was taken after talent worked and were paid – but SAG and some of its actors definitely disagreed. Do your own research and let us know if you turn up something different.

CNTV TALENT AGENCY
CNTV CASTING
PG CASTING
PRODUCERS UNION CASTING
5455 Wilshire Blvd., 3rd Floor
Los Angeles, CA 90036
PHONE: 323-850-3803
HOTLINE: 323-433-4880
CONTACT: Morena Moncada

Oh man...so many names, so many addresses, so many numbers, so little time. Their 2004 address, miraculously, seems to still be good. (A certified A+ for unique names, by the way. I mean, really, on a scale of 1 to 10, these guys get an eleventeen on the names.) Morena's many companies have had more changes in the last two years than we've had bathroom breaks. Sorry we went there. And here's yet another incarnation. Well, two to be precise (as afar as we know). *PG* and *CNTV*. Ho-hum. See *2000 Casting* and *Hollywood Casting*. Or would that be four names for the same people? (Side note...not that you asked...) We can't help but wonder why they need so many random names? It's prolific. Anyone want to make a bet as to how long they go until they add a new name and another office address and start all over yet again? (We can only imagine the moving costs...)

Apparently, books audience work like *Change of Heart, Talk Or Walk, Judge Judy* (rocks!) and *Joe Brown*. Which is fine. In 2003, a young woman in their office claimed they were booking *Moesha* – but when we told the girl that the show was cancelled the year before, she said, "I'm tired and it's on my list." Whatever, good answer.

She then tried to say she never said that, but we digress... Last time they responded to us, they apparently charged: $29 a year for students and $39 year for all "regular" folk. They seem to work like an overflow company or calling service of sorts, we guess. That's what they seem like, anyway. When we spoke to the fabulous owner, she claimed to be everything (short of the President of the USA) – a production company with three films in development (with apparently top secret titles), a personal manager, a casting company, a modeling outfit (*CNTV Models*) – you name it.

It seems at one point their ads (complete with plenty of typos and misplaced apostrophes) used big movies (*Matrix II* & *Men in Black II*) and fancy words like "exclusive" and "professional" to lure in new talent. One time we spoke with them they were casting *Austin Powers 3* among other *Casting Couch* projects. Hmmm. Who knows? Morenna used lots of "sweetie" and "honey" talk and gave us some other numbers to call: 323-850-3898 and 310-936-4722. Circles and rings? Give a call, and find out for yourself if you're game.

COAST TO COAST CASTING

17200 Newhope St. #40C
Fountain Valley, CA 92708
PHONE: 714-444-1555
CONTACT: Mark Munro

Mark advertises his services in free OC newspapers supposedly promising he can get your child in the movies. But what exactly does he do? The apparent 5 year (yes, 5 year, with options for an additional 4 years!) contract he gives prospective clients states that he is not an employment agency, a theatrical talent agency, a booking agency, or an advance fee talent service. He is, instead, a "casting representative." What in the hell does that mean? What does he do to earn the $40 upfront fee and 20% commission? If he ever returned our phone calls maybe we could tell you. We know he supposedly told at least one mother that he handled extras casting for, among other big films, *Bad Santa*, which is totally untrue. One thing's for sure, given the length of the contract you're expected to sign, little Billy's gonna be shaving before that sucker's expired.

CREATIVE ENTERTAINMENT GROUP CEG

8057 Beverly Blvd., 2nd Floor
Los Angeles, CA 90048

This company allegedly uses Non-Union talent only for various infomercials, print work and foreign market projects. As far as we know, there are no fees or commissions. So, that's good. Submit two photos (matte finish) and your "General Info" by mail only. One photo should be commercial, the other a natural or glamour shot. Include your name, contact #'s, sizes and special skills on the back of each photo. You will be contacted if there is a job for you. Unfortunately, we have received complaints about checks that were late from those who have worked projects through this place. So, be forewarned that it may take a while to get paid. Just let us know how it goes.

JANET CUNNINGHAM CASTING

Janet is an independent Casting Director who has been casting on and off since 1981 and there are no fees or commissions that we know of. Super swell. She uses all types and ethnicities for various films, MOW's, television and cable. Not to discourage you or anything, but... she relies pretty heavily on calling services and generally uses the same core group of extras (sorry, folks). Further, she does not like to receive photo submissions or phone calls – hence no address and no number listed. Again, sorry, folks. Well, at least you know this happy camper's name!

PATRICK CUNNINGHAM & AKUA CAMPANELLA CUNNINGHAM AND CAMPANELLA CASTING

2630 Lacey Street
Los Angeles, CA 90031
PHONE: 949-609-1600; 310-858-3300; 323-222-1656

In late August 2002, we were sitting down to write parts of our new kids' book and we hear one of those commercials on the radio we like to warn you about. It goes something like this: "A leading Casting Director is currently looking for new faces. If you or your child are between the ages of 6 and 25, Patrick Cunningham wants to meet you. If you've ever wanted to be in the movies or be a star – this is your chance!"

Stop! Holy bat crap! Put on the brakes! Typically, legitimate talent agencies DON'T solicit via radio ads. Generally, big outfits like *JRP* pay gobs of moolah to the CD to attend or promote these "talent scout" events. We hope this isn't the case here. What's doubly disconcerting about this is:

1.) Patrick Cunningham is a member of *CSA* (*Casting Society of America*) and you would think his name would not be associated with such things (though weirder stuff has happened).

2.) The number we were ultimately given to call was actually a phone number for *JOHN ROBERT POWERS*! You can read all about these lovely people later in this very Act, including Angie's (your friendly author's) own personal story. So what's the dealio?

We're not sure how Cunningham's name got connected with this outfit or if he even knows about the *JRP* track record. If he has no idea, we apologize in advance, because this connection is el bizzaro. The woman we spoke to first answered the phone as *BET Entertainment* (*Black Entertainment Television*) we believe, but she was quick to give us another phone number for the LA area. God, we are confused. This man then gave us YET ANOTHER number – to Mr. Cunningham? No. His staff? No. The third number was to *John Robert Powers*. Fun.

We called the third number and explained that we had heard the ad on a popular radio station and were interested in "becoming stars" (who isn't?). She was very enthusiastic and commented on what a lovely speaking voice [we] had. Boy, the bull@#$% already begins. "When could we meet Mr. Cunningham?" Well, we would need an appointment. Okay. "When is he available?" He wasn't. Not until after we met with the grand folks at *JRP* to see if we were the "right material" (possibly code for: did we have enough money to spend?), then we MIGHT be invited to a seminar where Cunningham would speak. How wonderful. Gag us with a rubber spoon, people.

We thanked her for her time (it was Friday night after 9PM by the way), but she didn't want us to hang up. We should come in. She was sure Mr. Cunningham would meet with us because [we] SOUNDED like exactly what he needed. Sounded like? And we're talking about our VOICE here, people – because we never told her WHAT [WE] LOOKED LIKE. The sound of my voice was going to get me cast? So now he does voiceovers, huh?! Good sales tactic! We're sold; we've always wanted to do voiceover work. (How desperate are they?) Hopefully, you get the point here.

Apparently, as of late, Patrick has partnered up with Akua Campanella, granddaughter of baseball great Roy Campanella, and they've done several smaller budget features. Has he changed his business affiliations? We hope so, but who knows?

D'S CASTING
740 N. Kings Road, #112
Hollywood, CA 90069

We couldn't get in touch with *Devan of D's Casting* last year, and now this year he's still missing. The latest address we have for him is above, but it's three years old. Any and all phone numbers we had got us nowhere. He opened this company under this name some time in late 2001, after a stint at *Film Casting*. It was free to submit to *D's*, so if you feel so inclined, drop him a pic or two and let him know you're available. But we don't know if he's still around or still casting. If you hear anything, let us know! Last we heard, talent had payment problems.

D.B.D. ENTERTAINMENT
4804 Laurel Canyon Blvd., #113
Studio City, CA 91607
PHONE: 323-850-4417, 714-648-2258, 323-960-1652
CONTACT: Ellen Lauren

Apparently, they advertise "NO CRAZY FEES" (no, we did not make that up) and supposedly claim to be the best way in town to get extra work. We scream, "pu-leeezzze!" There's some sort of $48 Registration Fee they want you to send to them with your paperwork – and they may never even call you, but sure, send 'em a check! We're not kidding, people. Pay attention already!

So they tout their revolutionary "Medical Directory." Gee, we wonder if the big advice these people give you is to join SAG and make enough money to qualify for that new, even more expensive, more-impossible-to-meet-the-minimums health plan... ya think?! Or better yet, could it be a whole booklet of FREE MEDICAL CLINICS in the Los Angeles area (which have been closing their doors on what seems like a daily basis now)? Could that be the revolutionary new program? FREE Medical Clinics throughout the Los Angeles area?! Fine, but probably not eactly the extras info you wanted. Oh well.

In any event, they send you some 5-page pamphlet that lists Calling Services in big, bold type, real Casting Directors' projects to maybe imply they may be the ones doing the casting and those, yup, FREE medical clinics. How random is that?! Again, did we mention that you can get all of this advice in a bulk-rate pamphlet for $48 bucks?!

Oh, and the best new addition to this listing? These folks say that you don't need a car to do extra work – the buses will get you to any set you have to find! If the bus lines you need run THAT early in the morning and THAT late at night, maybe. But, agreed, it's a good way to save on gas money.

THEDAILYCALL.COM
FIFTH MEDIA INC.
9663 Santa Monica Blvd., #274
Beverly Hills, CA 90210
PHONE: 818-878-9079
WEBSITE: www.thedailycall.com

Another online casting resource. For $9.99 a month you get casting notices sent to your "wireless mobile device." They contacted us in September '03 after a "casting contact" informed them they were listed in FAB OTHER in our 2003 directory. We actually wrote nothing disparaging about them and only asked readers to keep us posted. No one has actually reported anything to us, period. We asked for their fax number and mailing address so we could send them an info form. We wanted them to provide us with their company/service information in their own words. We sent over our excitingly extensive 12-page questionnaire, but oddly enough, never got a response. In fact, we never heard from them again, period. Weird. Again, if your experiences are postive, let us know. We like to find good companies.

GARY DAVIES

Gary is a cool CD known to work at *Bill Dance Casting*. Occasionally he will jet-set off on his own to cast a project or two. He usually posts his jobs on the **HOLLYWOOD OS**® website or advertises so talent can submit for the jobs he may be casting. He has no permanent files of his own at this time and works with talent on a project by project basis. Cool!

DELUXE MODELS

"A $450 rip-off!" shouted one happy parent in our lobby (August '03) to another Mom who asked about this place that seems to have disappeared as quickly as it emerged. Yikes, she sounded angry! This outraged Mom claimed they "preyed on kids and their dreams" and had her shell out megabucks for nothing... "nothing except long lines and promises they never kept," she said. Ouch. Remember the name... or better yet – don't! If you hear anything, keep us posted.

DIGITAL EXPOSURE, INC.
EXTRASONCALL.COM
FRONTIER PUBLISHING
AMERICAN DATA CORP
AMERICAN DATA GROUP
817 Garden St., Suite 100
Santa Barbara, CA 93101
- or -
5276 Hollister Avenu,e #158
Santa Barbara, CA 93111
PHONE: 800-260-3949, 805-683-5636, 805-683-3811 or maybe 805-899-3245
CONTACT: William Clayton, Jerry Brasa

Digital Exposure had a website: www.pickme.tv that let you get your sexy mug on the web. Cheese. But it's so closed. Their newest creation is www.extrasoncall.com.

Let's re-tell a tale from 2002 and let you be the judge. Undercover, **HOS**® calls and some guy named Guy (yes, we're serious) says he is in the Sales Department (that should tip you off right there, people) for online Casting for Extras. Ouch! He claimed he worked directly with CD's (in sales? Hhmm?) but the only two he could name were *J.P. Talent* and *CMP Models* – who we're pretty darn sure have never been hired by productions to cast background talent (but let us know if you've heard differently).

Okay, moving on...apparently they used to charge $59 for 12 months, but now it's $59 for just the first month and $9.95 for each subsequent month you stick around (unless you SOMEHOW happen to live in CA, then it's reportedly $63.57/first month and $10.72/month thereafter). He goes on to tell us that you have 60 days to get your $$ back and 12 months if you never get a job (by then they're probably hoping you have forgotten about it/them). Guy then told us to call Customer Service (the second phone number listed above) if we had other specific questions because he is "just trying to make a living (in sales) and has to support his kids." When we told him he might be making a living taking advantage of talent he supposedly said "thank you" and hung up.

This was actually our second phone call – the first was disconnected (??) when we told him we wanted to know which CD's in Southern California use his website to cast talent. He put us on hold to get a few names and we were mysteriously disconnected. Before things became elevated, he told us that every conversation was recorded for their protection and ours – he told us this well into the conversation (umm..can you say "inappropriate?"). We told him he was an advance-fee talent service and that they had to be bonded – he had had enough apparently, because it was at this point he gave us the *Frontier Publishing* name and told us they ran the show and they were located in Santa Barbara, CA.

Well, that show is now www.extrasoncall.com, (not to be confused with www.extrasonbootycall.com - ha, we made that up!) so be sure to do your research. In late 2003, a young woman called us and wanted us to "warn" our readers about the name change to www.extrasoncall.com because she had dealt with them earlier as *Digital Exposure*. Sounds like she might have a case of bad luck.

DIRECTCAST
DIRECTCAST.COM
KEITH WOLFE CASTING
WOLFE PRODUCTIONS
Sunset Gower Studios
1438 N. Gower St. #39
Hollywood CA 90028
PHONE: 323-469-5595
-or-
11271 Ventura Blvd., #238
Studio City, CA 91604
WEBSITE: www.keithwolfe.com

Okay, we believe there may be two mailing addresses here and we're not sure if they are the same outfit. If not, sorry in advance. You see, both share the name *DirectCast*, but one is affiliated with *Keith Wolfe Casting* and the other may or may not be (we can't be sure). We saw an ad for the second address in *Back Stage West®* a while back. As for the first mailing address: for $49 smacks, your photo was apparently listed on the website for a year! As we go to press, it no longer seems to work and we are not sure what CDs may have used it. Sorry.

The second address seems to be Wolfe's "Silver Screen" program. For $10 smacks a month you can get access to all sorts of industry information that you may or may not be able to research on your own. Current information is cool. According to www.IMDB.com, "entertainment professional" Keith Wolfe's listed credits as a Casting Director are for *Shadow Warriors* (1996) and *Dead Girls Don't Tango*. As for Keith himself, he's the guy sporting a darn sexy Tom Selleck moustache in his online photo. Hello, hot!

DIVERSE CASTING
303 S. Crescent Heights Blvd.
Los Angeles, CA 90048
PHONE: 323-634-2151 (info)/ 323-951-9936 (office)
EMAIL: diversecasting@yahoo.com

Matthew Gray, brother of Christopher Gray, has hung out his own shingle, *Diverse Casting*. There's a $25 annual registration fee. We've tried to get more 411 on *Diverse*, but they're pretty tight-lipped about the particulars. As we go to press, they may have a few feature films in the pipeline.

DREAM CASTING
415 S. Topanga Canyon Blvd., #192
Topanga, CA 90290

These folks seem to come and go with the Santa Ana winds. They had a random Industrial in April 2003, but never reemerged. They have never returned email requests for updated information. Going once, going twice...

DREAMCAST
P.O. Box 2706
Culver City, CA 90231-2706
-or-
2118 Wilshire Blvd. #582
Santa Monica, CA 90403
PHONE: DISCONNECTED

There were no fees associated with this place, but we have the hardest time keeping up with these peeps. They pop up every six months or so with a random commercial, then disappear again. Major bummer because they are nice folks! You used to be able to send current 3"x5"'s with a resumé to be considered for work, but we're not sure if the above P.O. Box is still active or what. We've also tried to send emails, but to no avail. And the Wilshire spot? Well, we're not even sure they're the same casters! Sorry, no phone numbers. If you hear any news on these folks, let us know, we'd love to hear from them.

ECAST².COM
269 S. Beverly Drive, Suite 411
Beverly Hills, CA 90212
WEBSITE: www.ecast2.com

Our neighbors on Beverly Drive like to advertise in *Back Stage West®* looking for everyone and your mother (yes, your mother!) – actors, athletes, bands, cheerleaders, comedians, dancers, DJ's, extras (ah, there you are), newscasters, talk show hosts... and the list went on and on.

We're not kidding. That's their ad – not our take on it! They want you to send your pictures and resumé along with your reels, but when you email or call for info they want you to come by for a "consultation." Consultation (for what - your senior thesis on photosynthesis?) possibly sounds a lot like – "give us your dime if we're gonna give you our time." As for the definition of *ecast²* (or the strange math reference) they're a not-yet-fully-functioning website. It seems like they've been "not-yet-fully-functioning" for a few years. Keep us posted.

EXPLORETALENT.COM
7060 Hollywood Blvd., #802
Los Angeles, CA 90028
PHONE: 323-790-2244
CONTACT: Robert Berg
WEBSITE: www.exploretalent.com

Explore Talent? Try explore getting boned out of an apparent $1500 or explore getting possibly scammed by BAM all over again. Remember BAM from a few pages back? Although www.Exploretalent.com claims to be an independent company, guess whose name comes up in the Caller ID when they call you? Oh no. You got it, the Baminators. Sigh. Don't these guys ever give up? And couldn't they have at least shelled out for a new phone line? Who knows? Inquire within and keep posted. We'd love to hear from ya.

EXTRAS & MODELS
EXTRASANDMODELS.COM
EXTRACAST
EXTRACASTING.COM
15720 Ventura Bl. #608
Encino, CA 91436
PHONE: 310-659-9555 or 818-995-3342
STAFF: Gigi Cossar
WEBSITE: www.extrasandmodels.com

The location is the same as last year, but apparently not the year prior. You used to pony up $65 a year for a listing on their website – now it's an apparent $950 (!!!) membership fee and a reported $150 (???) upload fee. Sounds like what's getting "uploaded" is your cash into their bank account. Gigi was formerly involved with *Glamour Models* (see listing this section) and says that the shenanigans that took place with *Glamour* are not taking place at *Extracast*, um, now *Extras & Models/ ExtrasandModels.com*. It seems the suite-sharing Modeling Co. that had its home in her offices has joined with her... and, thus, increased fees.

In July of 2003 a young couple emailed us to say that they had seen a market research ad on *Craigslist.com* and responded. They were invited for an interview for the market research, but upon arrival, they were told that all the spots were filled up for the study. The "market researchers" then tried to pitch this cute young couple the model/actor/extra package. They were not the only ones in the lobby who were refused a place on the market research panel either... others in the lobby smelled the same possible rat. Furious, they all left together without paying a dime. But some unfortunate *Craigslist* surfer may not be so lucky! Its other namesake, *ExtraCast*, has an interesting past of questionable goings-on. But, maybe they've changed things. Keep us informed.

EXTRAS NETWORK CASTING
P.O. Box 95349
Hollywood, CA 90093
STAFF: Barbara Klein & John Laccetti
WEBSITE: www.extrasnetwork.com

Major fabulous *Extras Network Casting* is a long-time background agency which has cast extras for some really fun projects such as *Late Friday*, *What Planet Are You From?*, and *Dropping Out*. They tend to get cool, random projects every now and again, and are major rock stars. Registration is via mail, using a form which can be downloaded from their website. So register - it's free, what the hell. Free places are rad!

FAIR BUSINESS ASSOCIATION OF AMERICA
FBAA
11138 W. Arizona Avenue #6
Youngtown, AZ 85363
WEBSITE: www.fbaa.us

Ok, ok, these guys have nothing to do with casting or the entertainment industry. But you really need to know about them anyway, ok... promise. The FBAA is apparently a knock-off version of the Better Business Bureau.

Cool. This is the place where businesses with bad, or darn bad, or just good ol' downright stinkin' bad BBB ratings (or so it seems) can go and buy themselves a "satisfactory" rating (and some online advertising) from an offical-sounding organization. Brilliant.

We're not saying that all the varied companies listed on their website are in the slightest bit questionable, but when you see that FBAA Seal of Approval, definitely take a closer look at the company you're about to get involved with. You guys like doing your research, right? Hell, you're reading this book.

FAME CASTING GROUP
FAME ENTERTAINMENT
369 S. Doheny Drive, Suite 1205
Beverly Hills, CA 90211

"Fame – I'm gonna live forrr-evver..." Or not. Okay, we'll stop singing; we like to sing. Not sure if these people THOUGHT their *Fame Entertainment* was gonna live forever and all, but here's what we know so far – they're NOT alive at all! All phones were disconnected and mail was returned to sender in March 2003. We told you about these folks in our Fall/Winter 2002 magazine supplement. *Fame* was on SAG's list of extras agencies as late as August '03.

FILM CASTING
FACES INTERNATIONAL
9255 Sunset Blvd.
Hollywood CA 90069
PHONES: DISCONNECTED

In the summer of 2003, two young ladies wandered into our office with lots of queries about this place. We didn't know, but we promised to look into it. Well, come time for investigation, they had apparently closed up shop and shut off the phones (or at the very least – moved yet again!). Oy vey.

FILM CASTING ASSOCIATES
SCREEN ARTISTS AGENCY
STUDIO CASTING
7060 Hollywood Blvd., #320
Hollywood, CA 90028
PHONE: DISCONNECTED

This company charged talent an advance fee but never registered with the State of California as an Advance-Fee Talent Service. They have been open for 14 years, but now their phone is disconnected, so we don't know if they're still operating. They used to advertise heavily on phone poles and in newspapers. Go figure. The most common complaint we heard regarding *Film Casting* was that talent had a difficult time getting paid for jobs *Film Casting* had gotten for them.

Devan Gaudry ventured off on his own (see *D's Casting* earlier in this Act). It's like another bad future installment of the next *Austin Powers 4: International Casting Men of Mystery*.

FLASHCAST, INC.
FLASHCAST KIDS
FLASHCAST COMPANIES
3575 Cahuenga Blvd., Suite 120
North Hollywood, CA 91604
PHONE: 323-969-9006
WEBSITE: www.fbaa.us/companies/flashcast.htm

They supposedly cast commercials and specialize in print work and magazine covers for your cute children. They've got a fancy-schmancy website they've apparently called "the first and only casting website in the nation" and are widely misguided in their claims, but their more pressing troubles include the CA courts.

Deputy city attorney Mark Lambert filed charges in 2002 alleging that *Flashcast* was an unlawful job-listing service and engaged in false advertising. There were 26 counts against the company and as many as eight alleged victims testified. Although the court's decision fined them several thousand dollars, the *Flashcast* folks avoided jail time. Bummer.

Long ago, in a Hollywood-infested galaxy far, far away from the way things are today... we remember a pompous owner who bombarded us with threatening phone calls and letters from attorneys. For what reason, we are not sure. It seems that their own previous business practices got themselves busted, but we digress. Interesting how things evolve. Maybe things have changed, so totally inquire within and keep us posted.

Remember, just for the record, your children do not uber-need zed cards, acting classes and expensive headshots – wait for a reputable agent's advice for when these are necessary if ever at all. A child's look changes every single month, and with that said, geez, you'd need to get your child's headshot re-taken every single month. Gosh, that could be expensive. Apparently this place also specializes in animals, too. At least that's what it said on their letterhead, but we don't really have any enthralling information on that either...

MEGAN FOLEY CASTING

In 2003, Megan asked to be removed from future editions of EWFBS® because background were not heeding our disclaimers about not contacting her, via phone, at all hours of the day and night. That totally sucks! She currently casts principals and gets really cool gigs. She formerly owned part of the now-defunct Calling Service *Extra En Masse*.

FOUR SISTERS CASTING
CONTACT: Tom Daniels

No comment.

FUTURE CASTING 2000

Edwards & Hill Communications, LLC
P.O. Box 1490
Washington Grove, MD 20880-1490
WEBSITE: www.futurecasting2000.com

"Become a member at the low monthly rate of just $14.95 and get access to the most sought after casting/crew job notices online." Okay, but, um... should someone tell these folks that they're in MARYLAND?! This is generally far, far, far from the hustle and bustle of Hollywood film shoots, but let's dig in here a little further, shall we? Your headshot and resumé are supposedly listed in a talent and crew database for FREE, but we're not sure what that gets you if you're nowhere near the location of a working film set – let's just say it: it's very unlikely that a CD or production is going to cast you from an obscure website based out of MARYLAND.

The *Future Casting 2000* peeps also say you can upload your own headshots and resumé and such and mess with 'em whenever your look or credits change. Swell. If you're not savvy enough, they'll help you with the process on-line, but, regardless... who is looking at you here? Get specific names, people. If you are paying for something, get the facts and find out what Casting Directors may be utilizing the website.

They also produce a newsletter to "help" those who want to break into the industry. There are FREE features on the website that you may want to check out. Keep us posted. We want you working!

The BBB reported last year and still reports in December 2004: "We are currently attempting to develop information on this company. Our file does not contain enough information to enable us to issue a report at this time."

PAM GILLES CASTING

11425 Moorpark St.
Studio City, CA 91602
PHONE: 818-508-1020
WEBSITE: www.pamgillescasting.com

She's an acting teacher. Cool. She's a Casting Director. Way cool! She maybe charging "non-represented talent" $50 a year to remain in a file she will use from time to time should the need arise. Huh? Apparently you can send her your photos and resumés with a check for $50 smacks, or you can call for an appointment so she can meet you personally to see if you're a match. Huh? We are confused as well. Um... we think she'll find lots of matches for $50 a head per year. Who knows. Let us know if you land a gig.

GLAMOUR MODELS
FACTORY CASTING
MODELS FOR FILM & TV

CONTACT: Gigi Cossar

Models for Film and Television... the place formerly known as *Glamour Models*, formerly sharing an office with *Factory Casting*. How would you like to be part of a company known as *Factory Casting*? Yikes, makes you feel like another pretty-face-number or a slab of beef.

At least three different possible name changes in a short span of time? Gosh, we'd love to find someone who has had a great experience with the aforementioned outfits.

We had in our possession at one time, a business card with an estimate for $769. Yes, you read that correctly. Apparently this $769 covered a photo shoot, some reproductions, $19 tax and the negatives or something. Another time, a couple with a child accidentally stumbled into our office wanting to know if they should go back to this place and fork out this type of money to get their child into the business. Did we mention they were visiting and didn't even live in Los Angeles?

Yet another time, an older woman, maybe in her 60's, came into our office and proceeded to explain how they were going to guide her career in commercials and print work. Well, after she spent $850+ on zed cards (remember, these aren't needed for extra work) they pretty much forgot about her and hadn't talked to her since. They instead gave her a photocopied article from *Back Stage West®* and told her to find some extra work. (This is not why she spent almost $1,000, by the way). She was told she could do print work and they'd help. Did we mention, in our opinion, that the quality of those zed cards was less than stellar for the moolah?? This story gave us heartburn. We needed *Rolaids*. A whole pack. Cherry flavor. They're the best.

GLOBAL ENTERTAINMENT STUDIOS
GLOBAL STUDIOS
ACTORS UNLIMITED
ENTERTAINMENT STUDIOS
ENTERTAINMENT UNLIMITED

It appears to possibly be one large up-front fee – perhaps 1,000's of dollars. Apparently, they may do it all – who knows? They may even want you to spend money on cooking classes, but we can't tell ya 'cuz our inquiries go unanswered. You do not need acting classes, zed cards or super-duper expensive headshots for extra work. Haven't we already said this? The last time we ever spoke to them, they thought WE had them confused with some porno place. We were not confused.

Since this story was first published *Global Entertainment Studios* has supposedly been shut down, but for some reason, we have heard reports that they are back in business supposedly advertising here and there. We'll see... sometimes places pop back up in the oddest of locations with such unique, worldly and renowned names.

VICKI GOGGIN CASTING
1723 Nichols Canyon Road
Hollywood, CA 90046
PHONE: 323-851-8871

We came across Vicki right as we were going to press with the last edition. We spoke with her for the 2004 edition, but she asked not be included in Act 4 (extras casting) because she very rarely needs extras. She's an independent CD who casts principals for random cool projects, but feel free to drop her a snapshot if you're so inclined and see what happens. She seemed very nice. And we like nice people.

HALO ENTERTAINMENT GROUP
HALO TALENT

PHONE: 800-764-4266
WEBSITE: www.halotalent.com -or- www.hegcorp.us
EMAIL: info@hegcorp.us

Halo Entertainment Group started popping up this year on *Craigslist* boards throughout the country, implying that they're casting such films as *Pirates of the Caribbean 2, The Dukes of Hazzard,* and *Superman*. Two small snags - they're not casting these projects and they're not actually even a casting agency.

What they are, in fact, is a standard-issue online database (charging from $10 to $35.95 per month) where actors and models can post their portfolios. With so many of these friggin' sites it's hard to say if this one is worth it. Let's look at the facts as observed on their website: they have no contact information outside of an 800 number (for Cancellations only) and an email address, they use misleading ads to get folks to sign up, and their website is apparently registered to some fella named Valdron Hirmisavo with an address in the Ukraine of all places. Interesting.

HIGH DESERT TALENT AGENCY

139 Balsam Street
Ridgecrest, CA 93555
PHONE: 800-517-3272
WEBSITE: www.highdeserttalent.com

Elena Vitale heads this talent agency that's about a three-hour drive from L.A., through the Antelope Valley, up the CA 14 freeway. Quite a trip. She tells us she has more than 20 years experience in theatre and casting, but after our initial conversation, she never returned our fun fax for all the fun facts! She is a Calling Service of sorts too for those casting companies with productions seeking talent in the high desert area – from extras to principals, to production personel. There is a $25 yearly fee for SAG and Non-Union talent and commissions may be taken depending upon the situation.

According to her website, she also provides acting and directing lessons, as well as a modeling course in association with another place in the same area. Yes, you read correctly – DIRECTING LESSONS – a new option that will no doubt start a trend for folks in this Act. It's uncertain what fees apply to these courses, or if part or all are included. You can check out her website and see for yourself what the deal is. But, pack some snacks if you venture out to visit – it's a hike and a half! Keep us posted. We want the dirt! (Get it, High Desert, dirt...oh, never mind!)

HOLLYWOOD ACTORS CENTER FOR ASIAN TALENT

6401 Riverton Avenue, #206
North Hollywood, CA 91606
CONTACT: Lily Zhou

Specifically for Asian talent back in 2002. They said they were charging a $10 photo fee to be included in their casting files for 'upcoming Chinese features.' They also took a 10% commission on higher base jobs as well. The number we had was disconnected and the address was temporary.

In early 2003, Lily cast a Non-Union TV show, but we haven't heard from her since. Bummer, she was nice, and she did have some cool projects. So keep us posted and we will do the same. We are always up for real companies who have legitimate opportunities to offer talent.

HOLLYWOOD CASTING
6253 Hollywood Blvd., Suite 917
Hollywood CA 90028
PHONE: 310-497-6337
CONTACT: Morenna Moncada (one "n," two "n's," ten "n's" – we don't know)

Gee, what to say, what to say..? Morenna is an extremely busy woman. After reading about *2000 Casting* and *CNTV* we are sure you will be shocked to hear this company has previously claimed to cast other people's projects. Apparently they call you every now and then and tell you where you can "spec" a job. This place apparently charges $75 bucks or so. It is our understanding that low paying audience jobs can be found through this company.

We have heard sob stories of talent waiting months for their checks. We have published complaint letters from our readers about this darn place. *Hollywood Casting* had apparently spawned a lovechild/brainchild offshoot called *2000 Casting* (not to be confused with *Casting 2000*) and the latest is simply called *CNTV*. Both of them can be found in this section as well. Yawn.

HOLLYWOOD GROUP
HOLLYWOOD HANDBOOK
SCOUT SERVE
2050 South Bundy Drive, Suite #202
Los Angeles, CA 90025
PHONE: 310-882-7602
EMAIL: info@hollywoodgroup.com
WEBSITE: www.hollywoodgroup.com or www.hollywoodhandbook.com

Hollywood Group/Handbook offers a "comprehensive" and "quality-assured" program supposedly designed to prepare your child for a successful career in show biz. This map to superstardom consists of "information, referrals, discounts, and ongoing support" for you and your kid. All of it culminating in a...drumroll please...kick-butt, awesomely-cool-beans SHOWCASE with sister company *Scout Serve*. Sweet! Hey, wait a sec, what exactly does all that mean? Who exactly is at these $25 per kid showcases? And what does the rest of it cost? Hello?

Vague promises about vague services and an unwillingness to discuss costs upfront. An address nearly identical to the name-changing, and missing-in-action, *Kids and Teens Casting*. You guys do the math on this one.

HOLLYWOOD MODELS
PRO ARTISTS GROUP
SHOW CASTING
CASTING EXPRESS
HOLLYWOOD MODELS AND TALENT
SMASH CASTING
HOLLYWOOD EXTRAS GUILD
LA EXTRAS
7080 Hollywood Blvd., Suite 306
Hollywood, CA 90028
PHONE: 323-465-8500
WEBSITE: www.hollywood-models.com or www.la-extras.com

Fab Other favorite *Pro Artists Group* has adopted a new address, name(s) and phone number for the new year. Just thought we'd keep you posted. Advertises: "Actors Needed, 5 lines or less (or more?) and supporting roles." Or perhaps you've seen their popular "Movie Extras - Real People" flyers taped to telephone poles throughout Los Angeles.

If you call, they won't give you any information regarding their fees, which sucks. Instead, they will encourage you to set up an "audition." If you show promise during your 2 minute commercial monologue (apparently necessary to see if you're suitable for the "non-speaking" extra parts they advertise), maybe they'll consider taking you on. Sure. Somehow we bet if you've got the cash, you're gonna make the cut. Unless you suck...just kidding.

We did get through to Don, the ever-so-mafia threatening owner, and this is the lowdown as we understand it. (For kicks and giggles, check out the trouble this kid has gotten himself into under *Malibu Talent*.) Okay, you get a yearly website listing, that's $99. The yearly website listing, one roll of headshots and four weeks of free acting classes, $199 (how is that FREE?). Maybe it's a good deal, who knows?

All members are allowed to attend free showcases which are held about once a month. Cool. Who knows, maybe valuable info is provided. We hope so. They also manage talent and submit those clients as well. They supposedly have so-called "Talent Scouts" showing up on sets to solicit Background actors! They even apparently posted for a "talent scout" job on *Craigslist* saying that applicants should be "persuasive" so they could invite "selected talent and families" in to meet them. Nice. We asked you, our dear readers, to keep us posted with any experiences – and boy, did you ever!

The craziest letter we got was from a woman in September 2003 who responded to an *LA Weekly* ad for models and actors. When she arrived to her appointment, she was reportedly asked if she was there to be a "female escort" for celebrities at special events. We're not kidding, kids, this is what she reported to us. Interesting/weird that the BBB acknowledges the "escort" employment issue as well. *Pro Artists Group*, of course, claimed it was good clean fun, but apparently when pushed, mafia-Don asked if this woman would actually refuse "if a handsome actor laid down $5,000 to have sex with him." We'll just assume that he was kidding and that the aforementioned question was only a sarcastic hypothetical. We're not sure what any of this has to do with casting, so we apologize to all parties in advance. Keep us posted; we'd love to hear if someone works and what they were working on.

HOLLYWOOD TALENT ASSOC., LLC

7825 Fay Avenue, # 200
La Jolla, CA 92037
PHONE: 858-456-5770
CONTACT: Camie Carpenter

A management company of sorts that wanted to sell us the world over the phone and was very persuasive when trying to get our undercover spy's other phone numbers and address (for further solicitation, one could surmise). Okay, here's the scoop: supposedly for $500 smacks she'll give you the **HOLLYWOOD OS**® address so you can sign up for the companies with FREE registration and she will also discuss SAG vouchers with you. At least that's the info nice Camie provided Angela over the phone before Camie accidentally hung up on her.

Apparently she wasn't too fond of Angela pressing her to explain exactly what she meant by "voucher information." Go figure! Their bond was cancelled with the state of California as an Advance-Fee Talent Service. Not sure if this is a good thing. Ms. Carpenter is the former partner of *Starz* and *Hollywood Talent Management*. You should check out those companies' histories with the BBB as well.

HOLLYWOODAUDITIONS.COM
HITECH NETWORKS

5025 Ludgate Drive
Agoura Hills, CA 91301
PHONE: 800-827-2830
WEBSITE: www.hollywoodauditions.com
CONTACT: Maksim Muzichenko

In addition to working as "talent managers," this place charges up to $459 for a three year membership to their "Talent CD-ROM," which is supposedly mailed out to 5000 different casting directors, and production companies, and you get an online portfolio. Holy smokes! Which CD's and production companies get the CD-ROM? Is anyone in the business checking out their website? Good questions. Let us know if you manage to find out.

HUMBLE CASTING

3350 Wilshire Blvd., Suite 975
Los Angeles, CA 90010
PHONE: 213-417-8801

Nobody ever answers the phone, although office hours are supposedly 10AM-7PM, Monday-Friday. There is also no answering machine or voicemail, so it just rings and rings and rings. The one time we did get through, the man who answered the phone sounded as if he had just woken up, "Hello?" "Hi, is this *Humble Casting*?" "Um, no. Not right now. She's not here." And then he hung up. Hung up. Huh? I hate it when we get confused. $20 Registration Fee. The mysterious "she" *Humble* has apparently had one movie in the last year or so that we are aware of, a SAG Experimental that was surprise-surprise *Untitled*. Drop us an email if you hear of them casting anything new. We really do love to find good, new, busy companies.

IMT
IMAGE MODEL TALENT
Sunset Gower Studios
1438 N. Gower St. #22
Hollywood, CA 90028
PHONE: 323-468-7900

Sounds prestigious. Names are important, so we're off to a good start. They've been known to advertise in *Back Stage West*®, they charge fees that range from $200 - $450 depending on how hard they may have to work to sell you...or how much cash you've got on hand.

How do we know? Because of the countless emails and letters from people who came in contact with them and their, um, questionable practices. Their ad in *Back Stage West*® stated that if you have any questions to call them. We did. They got very irritated very quickly. Not as irritated as the family of four who drove down to the **HOLLYWOOD OS**® office from Temecula for an "audition" appointment with a password *IMT* supplied them with. There were no AUDITIONS at **HOLLYWOOD OS**®, just an open casting call for *Monica Cooper Casting*'s *Sucker-Free City* that was posted in *Back Stage West*®. And a password? Um, yeah, there were no passwords. Apparently it was totally fabricated to make their "appointment" or "audition" seem more legit. We provided the family with information we'd gathered from other parents who came in with their "contracts." Thankfully the family hadn't paid or signed anything.

IN THE PICTURE KIDS
PHONE: Disconnected

This outfit dropped off the radar in 2003 as quickly as they came. This, as you will see, may be a good thing – unless you paid them the hundreds of dollars it most likely would have cost to get your child started. See, the young man we spoke to on the phone didn't seem to know how much things cost and what exactly he did, or what the company did.

Was it $20? More, he thought. $50? "More like $150," he offered. "For what?" we inquired. He eventually fessed to: "I just answer the phone." Oh, dear. Well, phone-boy didn't answer it a week later when we called back for more info – the number had been disconnected with no further information available. Oh well. We want to let you know of this place just in case you come across an old ad or an upcoming announcement for them sometime in the future.

INDIVIDUAL CASTING
7336 Santa Monica Blvd., #795
West Hollywood, CA 90048
CONTACT: Jeff Meyer
PHONE: 323-851-6133

An ultra-specific casting place, meaning they only have ultra-specific types (tattooed, piercings, gothic, punk, etc.) on file. Cool. We've heard that there is a $30 fee and a purported 10% commission on anything you work on. *Individual* mostly works on music videos. You will need to supply approximately 10 headshots and resumés. We're not proof-positive, but we believe this address may be an apartment. If this is the case, our advice is to call first before just happening by. Let us know.

INSTANT CAST

WEBSITE: www.instantcast.com

These folks appear to be a sorta spin-off of a New York text message direct-marketing outfit called *Kikucall* (who look to be the owners of the *Instant Cast* website). While *Kikucall* specializes in texting likely-unwanted ads for perfume and vodka and satellite TV straight to your cell phone (no, people, we are not making this up), the *Instant Cast* arm of the biz sends you casting notices for the fee of $3.99/week. Their ads and emails imply that they are somehow affiliated with the Casting Directors whose notices they are texting over. We don't believe this to be the case. Let us know if you hear something to the contrary.

INTERNATIONAL CREATIVE ARTISTS

Jamboree Promenade
2646 Dupont Drive, Suite C270
Irvine, CA 92612
PHONE: 949-250-9888
WEBSITE: www.internationalcreativeartists.com

From the outset, if you're driving by, the fact that the place looks like a restaurant should make you do a double take. Seriously, you'd think it was an *Applebee's*...we're not joking.

"Fed up with being ripped off with other "so-called" modeling schools? At International Creative (sic) Aritsits..." Their website schpeel began with a very noticeable typo in their opening/introductory paragraph (the second sentence!) Seems they couldn't even spell their own name (it does happen though). They fixed it by November 2003. Well, nonetheless, they claim to work with top agents in New York, LA, Milan... boy, they're everywhere – yup, even in Irvine, CA – at the mall, soliciting shoppers for supermodel-dom. Oh, boy! Milan and... Irvine? Yeah.

Contacted by several distressed/perplexed consumers, one version of the reported $6000 pitch goes like this: a young mother was approached at the mall by a "talent scout" with the duplicitous namesake that tries to sound too much like, not one, but two SAG-franchised talent agencies *International Creative Management* and *Creative Artists Agency* (CAA) – but has no relation or affiliation with either of the much-respected outfits. But that's probably the trick. Okay, now back to the pitch... the woman took the business card and agreed to an appointment for her daughter. Thank goodness, this is where we come in. A friend of hers refers the poor woman to us and informs us of the six thousand smacks – luckily she hadn't paid yet! She said she would call to cancel, but we offered to cancel for her. Hee-hee!

We contacted *ICA*, but they would not cancel or confirm if there was an appointment for a third party – but they would be willing to set an appointment up for us! What? We're trying to cancel, lady! Aren't you paying attention? We asked the woman on the phone at *ICA* if they often solicited clients at the mall. The woman we spoke to offered: "the mall, the market, post office, wherever there are people." Wherever there are people? Ok, we guess people with talent do live in other cities. Oh, boy – forget Milan – watch out, Boise, Idaho – here come "top model scouts" from Irvine, CA, looking for you at the local *EZ Lube* or *Kentucky Fried Chicken*! Keep us posted, though. We are interested in your experiences, both good and bad.

INTERNATIONAL TALENT GROUP
ITG
15720 Ventura Blvd.
Encino, CA 91436
PHONE: DISCONNECTED

Bling, bling. Another great name, actually. This nifty place in the Valley would probably love it if you went for their supposed expensive management resumé/headshot bonanza. Lots of people did, since numerous complaints have come into us from those who went to this place and realized they only got talked into buying stuff. Do keep us posted.

KTR CASTING, INC.
KIMBERLY RODGERS CASTING
12427 Riverside Drive
Valley Village, CA 91607

Kimberly is a fabulous chick who left *Christopher Gray Casting* a hell of a long time ago to cast on her own. We've tried to coax more info out of her, but with only limited success (she's a nice busy lady), so we don't really have enough intel to give her a big, shiny entry in Act 4. She has had the random project and occasionally assists with audience participation projects. Way cool!

KIDS & TEENS CASTING
KIDS AND TEENS, INC.
LOS ANGELES KIDS & TEENS CASTING
TALENT CASTING NETWORK
KIDS CASTING
10 CASTING
MARCH HARE MANAGEMENT
ERIK DESANDO CASTING
2050 South Bundy Drive, Suite 200
Los Angeles CA 90025
PHONE: 310-571-1516 (rings and rings and rings...)

Wow – so many names, so little space, time or trees to talk about 'em all. As such, we think the BBB should give you the breakdown. They tell it all...

Kids & Teens is defined by the Better Business Bureau as: "This company's business is an entertainment company which sells a product that shows how children can begin in the entertainment industry. The company sells the package at a seminar. This company is not a talent agency." Further, the BBB reports the following about *Kids & Teens*: "We rate this company as having an unsatisfactory business performance record.

"The company has a pattern of complaints alleging misrepresentation of the company's services, deceptive sales practices, and disputes regarding the company's non-cancelable agreement and non-refundable prepayments. Specifically, complainants state that they are contacted and told that the company wants to use their children as extras for television shows and other entertainment work. After making significant payments to the company, complainant's children do not receive any work."

"The company responded by offering explanations of their policies and disputing the complainants allegations. In some cases partial refunds were offered. Some complaints were closed as disputed, meaning the customer was not satisfied with the company's response. Other complaint responses did not address the complaint allegations and were referred back to the company for re-consideration. This company is not licensed by the Labor Commissioner as a talent agency. Accordingly, it is unlawful for the company to promise or offer to procure employment in the entertainment industry to anyone. It is also unlawful to collect any money in advance of actually providing the promised services."

In one of its other incarnations, *March Hare Management* is defined by the BBB as: "This company's business is a talent management company that advises and counsels actors. The company works with talent agents, casting directors and employment agencies."

Further, the BBB reports the following about *March Hare Management*: "We rate this company as having an unsatisfactory business performance record. The company has a pattern of complaints alleging misrepresentation of the company's services, deceptive sales practices, and disputes regarding the company's non-cancelable agreement and non-refundable pre-payments. Specifically, complainants state that they are contacted and told that the company wants to use their children as extras for television shows and other entertainment work."

"After making significant payments to the company, complainant's children do not receive any work. The company responded by offering explanations of their policies and disputing the complainants' allegations. In some cases partial refunds were offered. Some complaints were closed as disputed, meaning the customer was not satisfied with the company's response. Other complaint responses did not address the complaint allegations and were referred back to the company for re-consideration."

It is believed that *Kids & Teens* and *March Hare Management* may also have offices in Brisbane and Hermosa Beach, California... see *Young Entertainment Artists* near the end of this Act for the ditty on the Hermosa locale. What we do know is that years ago *March Hare,* the kids division, was eaten up by *Kids! Background Talent* owned by *Extras Management*. Interesting course.

act nine

KIDS HOLLYWOOD CONNECTION
1151 Dove Street, Suite 225
Newport Beach, California 92660
PHONE: 949-851-0920

What is this, a dating service for Tinseltown's kids?! Way joking. This company isn't even located in Hollywood, for cryin' out loud! Whatever! Okay, they say right up front that they are an Advance-Fee Talent Service bonded by the state of California. Which is cool. Honesty is the best policy. The fact that they don't shy away from this is good news. The bad news is we have no idea how much this place will cost you! If they decide to take your child on as a client they claim they will help you find an agent. The phone-friendly person we spoke to seemed very sales savvy but didn't want to tell us much about actual prices until we set up an appointment to come in. Hmm? They probably believe that once they have you in the office, the sale will be easier 'cuz they can gush about your gorgeous li'l kid – and you'll sign the big, fat check then and there.

If you do call, have your wits about you. Ask questions, people, and find out specifically what you may or may not be getting. And let us know if you find out anything interesting. Maybe they rock! Maybe it's a bargain.

KINGSTON CORP.
9663 Santa Monica Blvd., Suite 3000
Beverly Hills CA 90210
PHONE: 888-440-9888, 323-960-3069, 800-750-3069,
708-450-8282, 323-960-5577
CONTACT: Rita Summers

Whoa, lots of phone numbers. This cool place advertised in non-industry publications and basically promised you commercials if you mailed them a check for $495!!! Yes, you read us correctly – four hundred and ninety-five dollars! They didn't ask for a resumé, they didn't ask for a headshot, they just asked for your well-earned megabucks! We just wonder how many people fell prey to this not-so-ingenious schpeel.

If you've got a few minutes to kill, just start dialing numbers from the Kingston Company's own personal phonebook listed above and see if you can actually reach a human being to talk to. Some are disconnected, some are unidentified voicemails, some are fax numbers...sometimes, some are just "temporarily" disconnected.

The BBB reports in October 2003: "Our files show disconnected phone numbers, returned mail or both. The company appears to be out of business. The Bureau cannot trace addresses of companies or principals. General information is available upon request which may assist you. We rate this company as having an unsatisfactory business performance record. This company has a pattern of complaints alleging misrepresentation of services offered. Complainants reported after paying the company the requested fees, commercials never materialized and return calls were never made. To date, all complaints remain unanswered."

KUKER CASTING
256 S. Robertson Blvd., Suite 150
Beverly Hills, CA 90211
PHONE: 310-659-8859

Founded in 2001 by Sandra Kuker, *Kuker Casting* did a few killer projects such as *Punch Drunk Love* and *Spun*. They seem to be more or less in hibernation at present; they haven't had a new project in many, many moons. *Kuker Casting* accepts photos by mail, but don't have a real registration per se (though they do have a reported $20 Non-Union Registration Fee). If you hear of Sandra exploding back into action again, drop us a line and let us know. Apparently, she's been pretty involved in the theatre scene here in Los Angeles which is pretty cool!

LAEXTRAS.COM

10790 Ocean Drive
Culver City, CA 90230
WEBSITE: www.laextras.com

At one time, this place apparently had 100's of people coming in on a daily basis, yet could not name a single Extras Casting Director in town or a single project. This place will threaten to file harassment charges against you if you call and ask too many questions, yet the supposed owner, Daniel or something, claims everyone in town "knows him." Hmm?!? They know him so well that this man-about-town couldn't name a single extras casting company when pressed. Odd, isn't it? But, it's a non-issue – they're apparently gone-zo! If you hear of them popping back up, drop us a line.

Recently *Pro Artists Group* aka *Hollywood Models* have started going under the name *LA-Extras.com*. They don't seem connected to the old, unhyphenated LAExtras.com, but they've got a very special story all their own. Check 'em out under the *Hollywood Models* listing.

LADYBUG MANAGEMENT

PHONE: 323-801-2222

Okay, "The Tale Of Two" goes like this: We (our unnamed, anonymous **HOS**® spy) walk into a teeny-tiny windowless room posing as an office. Zed cards plaster the walls surrounding Dionne. She sets out to give me (okay, first person narration now) a registration form – but she is out of them so instead she begins to explain things to me. They are, it seems, a Management Company – they supposedly use the Breakdowns (that are faxed to them from *Models Guild*) to submit talent for jobs. The photos are the "all-important" factor, she tells me. To have them done through *Ladybug* it's $175 (this includes a free make-up artist, three changes and film – you develop on your own). Ok, good deal indeed. Then, from these "all-important" pics, the single-sided zed cards can be made at a cost of $200 to $500!

If you can't afford the zed cards (this might be the pricey part), you can take your negatives across the street to some photo lab and get laser prints made and they will "stamp" their logo on the back. Oh, boy! When I asked about the *Models Guild* name at the top of a fax – I was told that *Models Guild* was the Union division of their company – *Ladybug* is Non-Union only. I asked where they were and she said, "Somewhere in the building." I then asked, "How do you not know where they are if you are part of the same company?" Which is a reasonable question, or so I thought. She then said she felt very uncomfortable – like I was interrogating her. Ooops.

I told her I was SAG and was simply interested in Union work. She then made it pretty clear that she wanted me to leave. So I did. As it turns out – *Ladybug Management* is supposedly not the Non-Union division of *Models Guild*. Speaking with Gary Marsh, the owner of *Breakdown Services*, I was informed that *Models Guild* could lose their SAG-franchised status if they had such a relationship with *Ladybug*. Turns out SAG pulled their license in June 2003. Oh, by the way, those "all-important photos", they're apparently taken in a garage across the street from the building – one subscriber said there was a long line of folks getting their pictures taken on the day she was there.

This subscriber, however, was actually sent to an audition by *Ladybug* and did land the job. Cool. But (PART 2)... she never got paid and we found this out just days after having visited *Ladybug* ourselves. She was told by *Ladybug* that her pay rate was $100. About four weeks after the shoot she called the music video production company to inquire about payment. They told her they sent the check to *Ladybug* weeks ago.

After she made several calls to *Ladybug*, leaving messages to request her check, and being totally ignored – she got in her car and drove down to their office to find... they were no longer there! What?! She had heard of their so-called affiliation with *Models Guild Talent* at the same address, so she went to their office to see if she could rectify the situation. After all, it had been over a month since she did the job and she hadn't been paid yet! And the office had suddenly gone missing!

The president of *Models Guild Talent* supposedly told her that someone by the name of Dionne Corona of *Ladybug* "had gone on to bigger and better things and had a part in a film." What? The *MGT* Prez offered no apologies for not answering or returning any of her phone calls, or about never paying her – she just said they were "so busy." The Prez eventually wrote the woman a check, but the scenario should not ever have gone to such extremes. If you've got any additional info, give us the heads-up.

LEGENDARYTALENT.COM

321 Anacepa St.
Santa Barbara, CA 93101
PHONE: DISCONNECTED
WEBSITE: OFFLINE

Another one bites the digital dust. Based on BBB files, the company is "no longer in business." This was apparently a website for talent to have their pics on. It was supposedly only $40 bucks per pic, and you could sign up in person or online. If you hear of them popping up again, do let us know.

act nine

LEGENDS 2000

This company made a go at it again in 2003 – trying to pick up where *Entertainment Casting* left off. *Entertainment Casting* went under, taking all of their clients who spent money with them. Our paperwork was enthusiastically filled out and promptly sent back though. "I'm going to welcome the clients, all the clients, that were from *Entertainment Casting*. I will waive the registration fee at this time. I want to do the right thing. What happened in the past stays there. I will say this, what goes around comes around."

Our sentiments exactly. These folks were, it appears, also likely known as: *Universal Casting, Universal of Oxnard, Universal Entertainment, Entertainment Casting*, some sort of record company, and even apparently *John Robert Powers* in Oxnard. WOW – so prolific!!

In our humble opinion, if this new organization wanted to do the right thing, they would have refunded everyone who never worked, (with checks that don't bounce, mind you) instead of saying it's free for everyone (who already paid) to register. In any event this company is gone. We wonder what happened to all of those new folks who registered.

Like clockwork, we were contacted by yet another friend of the original founder Robert Lewis (not to be confused with the *Atmosphere Casting* CD of the same name) – who started yet another new company in Oxnard called *Prime Time Casting*. Oy vey. See the listing in this Act.

MAC MODELS INTERNATIONAL, INC.

9454 Wilshire Blvd., Suite M1
Beverly Hills, CA 90210
PHONE: 310-273-2566

These peeps purportedly advertise in obscure publications and those free newspapers we've warned you about with ads like "Are You A Model?". The first gentleman who called us back in April of 2003 said he saw their ad in *Easy Reader* near his home in Redondo Beach. He called the number in the ad and set up a meeting since the ad said they were "looking for people – all types for modeling and print jobs."

He called us back two weeks later to tell us that he was asked nothing about his modeling experience or aspirations, just about his personal/professional life – fishing for details on his finances, no doubt. No doubt that helps them figure out how much you might be able to spend. We received subsequent calls from others who were skeptical about the opportunity at *Mac Models*. It is not clear what it may or may not cost. If you have any great experiences with this company, let us know.

MAGIC EYE CASTING

PHONE: DISCONNECTED

We don't want to give any place free advertising if they're just out to get your money, but we were never actually able to talk to a live person when we'd call their now-disconnected number – so we don't know their true dealio. We always got the same friendly answering machine asking for our name and number; it was always there when we needed it. But, no more! Where have you gone, *Magic Eye Casting* Answering Machine? We miss you! Was it something we said? Can't we work it out?

MALIBU TALENT
HAVEN INDUSTRIES
MALIBU CASTING

2001 West Magnolia Avenue, Suite F
Burbank, CA 91506
PHONE: 818-972-2900

Malibu...in Burbank. Huh? They advertise in non-industry publications, and remote towns such as Lancaster and Bakersfield, likely in hopes of appealing to the wide-eyed newcomer who is eager to sign some ridiculous contract and get overpriced headshots. And, again, it's in Burbank, people – not ultra-posh Malibu! This establishment may charge hundreds and claimed in previous ads to cast just about every darn commercial and TV show known to mankind. How can this be possible?! We have yet to find anything solid that they are supposed to be casting, but we've been known to be off our darn rockers!

One of the ever-so-polite owners, Don, has called us on several occasions (we think he likes us) to invite us down (at least we think that's what he was saying... we were "accidentally" disconnected a few times – actually, we think we were hung up on, but we digress). Extras have called to complain too, and one poor **HOS**er claimed to have paid $256 bucks for one year's non-service. He's apparently part of the contingent looking for a refund through the courts.

ANNA MILLER-SHARMA CASTING

5400 McConnell Avenue
Los Angeles, CA 90066

Anna had been doing principal casting and extras casting on several "sensual erotica" films for *Playboy*, but she disappeared for a little while. In late 2005, she was busy casting a TV show for *HBO* and a neat feature film. Cool.

MINDTRIPP.COM

WEBSITE: www.mindtripp.com
E-MAIL: support@mindtripp.com

We don't even like to give certain places exposure (even if it is in *Fab Other*) because it makes people notice them. We've taken out many of the web-based extras casting places because there are just so many of them, but we figured they're off in cyberspace somewhere and most only make their money from unsuspecting surfers who happen upon them by accident. Apparently this is not one of those places.

They supposedly sought out clients at shopping malls and cineplexes in LA and one poor girl paid $100+ to get casting notices that this place appeared to have simply regurgitated from *Back Stage West*® and other legitimate places. The website claims to only charge $45/year, however, our source supposedly paid the $100+ rate as well. Inquire within. *Mindtripp* also lets anyone view your information and they apparently "sell" other things too, web design, discount airline tickets. As of November 2004, the "actors database" section seemed to consist of around 14 headshots and the "casting notices" were limited to two MTV open calls.

MODELS-ACTORS.COM

PHONE: 212-228-6400
WEBSITE: www.models-actors.com

Original. Are we tired of having to tell you fine folks all about these dot coms that pop up all over the internet? Well, sort of. But we want you informed. A call into our office prompted us to check out these dudes. The woman we spoke to was worried she'd be spending too much money for a website listing for her little girl. Her daughter was just turning two. Our answer would have to be, "Heck yeah!" We first called this place on a Friday afternoon in mid-August 2002. The man who answered the phone simply said: "Hello?" as if he was answering his home phone. We asked about the website and he promptly asked how we got this number... um, two ads in *LA Weekly* – one in the classifieds and one in red type on the inside of the back cover!

He wasn't too happy with having to answer our tough question. What was this "tough" question? "How much does it cost?" His reply: "You'll have to call back on Monday." And then he hung up. Click. Very professional. Maybe he should have read his own ad in *LA Weekly*, which apparently stated that it was $195 for the year. The site features adults as well as children. The "headquarters" for this place moved in 2004. No longer situated in the clueless dude's apartment, *Models-Actors* has found its new homebase in NYC. If it is indeed the same place, the fee has bumped up another Ben Franklin – yeah, that's a $100 more smacks. Keep us posted with your experiences.

MODELS GUILD INTERNATIONAL
VANTÉ MODELS
VANTE MORNING SUN MODELING AGENCY
1382 North Main Street, Suite 8
Walnut Creek, CA 94596
PHONE: 925-947-0789
WEBSITE: www.modelsguild.com

We didn't know that the *Little House* peeps had a modeling guild on their *Prairie*! Okay, okay. So that was Walnut Grove and this is Walnut Creek, but still... come on, people! Yes, they're far, far away from LA – closer to San Francisco, but they supposedly still have an LA presence on community corkboards and telephone poles. So, we wanted to give you a heads-up. We left messages to ask about fees associated with membership, or how to qualify, but we never heard back. Even the BBB doesn't know too much about these guys.

MODELS GUILD OF CALIFORNIA TALENT AGENCY
8489 W. 3rd St., #1107
Los Angeles, CA 90048
PHONE: 323-782-0393 or 323-801-2132
CONTACT: Pamela Roberts
WEBSITE: www.modelsguildtalent.com

We are sure you're surprised that the website no longer works and it redirects you to some random search engine. And also that their phones just ring and ring (at least when we call). You will always need better photos and preferably by someone recommended by them. How do we know this? Our very own Brain Surgeon Angela spent a ton of dough at this place for the stuffola they were selling. She never heard from them again (which sucks by the way).

They will also want you to get your darn zed card through their acquaintances (of course). They have also advertised in legit newspapers like *LA Times* – that's scary! Aside from that, we're not sure what the heck they do! Once you get the stuff (from them), that seems to be it, they are done with you... at least that was also another former staffer's personal experience with this place! "Thanks for getting your photos done through us, unfortunately there is nothing more we can do for you at this time..." Not nice.

MYSTIC ART CASTING

1918 West Magnolia Blvd., Suite 206
Burbank, CA 91506
PHONE: 818-563-4121
CONTACT: Katy Wallin
WEBSITE: www.katywallin.com

Credits include: *Where the Red Fern Grows, The Trouble With Frank*, and "Ozzfest 2004." Seems to concentrate heavily on reality TV projects with some feature and commercial work. It's free to register, just send a headshot or a 3x5 photo of your sassy self to the above address. Drop us a line if you hear about any other projects or book work through them.

NE'VON STUDIO PRODUCTIONS

600 Wilshire Blvd., Suite 1200
Los Angeles, CA 90017

Apparently advertised in *Back Stage West®* and on *CraigsList.com* in the summer of 2003. They were charging a $25 photo fee, for supposed "upcoming projects." What these projects were or if they still have (or ever had) work is anybody's guess. We haven't seen or heard from them.

NEW ENTERTAINMENT INDUSTRIES

Okay, *New Entertainment Industries* apparently popped up in *Back Stage West®* in March 2003, but it's really not even a singular industry, let alone a pluralized one. It... HE, rather, is just one dude named Dan. And get this: on a now-defunct webpage, Dan supposedly stated that he was an out-of-work actor who needed money (nice research, *Back Stage West®*). Can you believe that? Yup, so try and get it from other unsuspecting, out-of-work actors! He was apparently charging $25 for a digital photo fee. We're just hoping he didn't even make $25 smacks off his wet noodle of an idea.

We emailed Dan on four different occasions and he responded to only the first one saying he had lots of projects. No names or dates, of course. The number was a cell phone for the out-of-work actor – who lives in Palmdale! Oh, and you're waiting for the clincher, right? On his *AOL* profile under Hobbies and Interests...? We quote: "acting in movies and buying cars walking on the beach having sex with nice women." Please, people...come on!

NEWFACESLA.COM

8112 W. 3rd Street
West Hollywood, CA 90048
PHONE: 323-651-3601
WEBSITE: www.newfacesla.com

Boldly going where no other casting dot com has gone before. Just kidding. These folks dropped their business cards in our office and ran. We can't say we're all too pleased that they use our catchphrase of "get connected." Nor can we say we love the idea that they ran out the door without so much as a "hello" or "sayonara."

Their website has some pretty people posing on it, but try finding a price for any of their "services" and you're out of luck. The man we spoke to seemed to be a little bit confused with what he or they actually did. Apparently, they're a management company of sorts, but they won't take on all clients that come through their doors! Of course not! Where have we heard that before? You can call for an appointment and meet with their photographer (who may even be the same man we spoke to). He seemed nice enough, but with lots of "ums" and "ahs" and uncertainties peppering his responses. Commissions? Not sure. Pricing? We don't know. Do us a favor and let us know if you hear of anything.

NIMBUS PRODUCTIONS
NIMBUS ENTERTAINMENT
1626 North Wilcox Avenue, Suite 728
Hollywood, CA 90028
PHONE: 213-989-0540
WEBSITE: www.nimbusentertainment.com

They've been a *New Times* mainstay. When we called in 2002, we learned that some guy named Tony supposedly runs the place – except there is no "place," no office. Calls this year for this edition were always met with the same recorded message telling us to leave our name or check out their website. Beep. Then it hangs up. Lovely. *Nimbus* is/was a Calling Service of sorts that primarily books audience work. Cool.

They charge a $35 registration fee per year (1/2 off the second year). The only casting companies that the young lady on the phone could name who use their service were *Sunset* and *Central*. Oh, and the reason there's no "place/office?" She had lots of creative explanations, " It had to close down – it was a circus – looking for larger space," etc... So, if you still want to get registered, it looks like you either pay over the phone, by mail, or via their website. They will then put you in their online database and grant you access to their online "casting board." This Tony fella is supposedly calling us back. We're not holding our breath. It's been three years... and counting.

act nine

NOWCASTING.ORG
PHONE: DISCONNECTED
WEBSITE: DISCONNECTED

Not to be confused with *NowCasting.com* (to whom the www.nowcasting.org address now links) which is an online service for principal actors. This dot org version emerged in the summer of 2003, and was an apparent copycat version of the real *NowCasting.com* and posted notices in many random internet forums. They supposedly tried to solicit membership by intentionally misleading readers and web surfers (by simply re-posting notices from legitimate sites or providing info about projects they were in no way casting).

The company (term used loosely) used several aliases to lure in actors – usually from free email accounts with the word CASTING somehow incorporated into their email address – and has disappeared from the World Wide Web (for the time being anyway!).

ON CALL TALENT

3111 S. Valley View Blvd, B-203
Las Vegas, NV 89102
PHONE: 877-662-2558 or 702-227-4544
EMAIL: info@oncalltalent.com
WEBSITE: www.oncalltalent.com

Based in Las Vegas, this is an on-line database for Models, Singers, and Non-Union Actors. *On Call Talent* offers the standard online photo/resumé package for $195 per year. You can also add video and audio clips for an extra Benjamin (we coulda just said $100, but we're way hip).

They provide casting notices to subscribers, but most of the work being booked off the site seems to be stuff like infomercials, or tradeshow modeling in other states, or wedding singer gigs. I guess if you're a wedding singer looking for a juicy role on a tradeshow infomercial shooting in Maryland, this is the place for you. If you're looking for extra work in Los Angeles, maybe not so much the place to drop two or three hundred smackers. Who knows? Keep us posted.

ONE SOURCE TALENT

6120 Paseo Del Norte, Suite G2
Carlsbad, CA 92009
(many other locations)
CONTACTS: Anthony Toma and Mike Fomkin
PHONE: 760-268-1123
WEBSITE: www.onesourcetalent.com

This is yet another online acting/modeling/model-marketing/model-placement/model...whatever website. Toma and Fomkin, the two guys who run the place, have a long history in the online modeling industry. Unfortunately, that history happens to be as big cheeses in the ultra spectacular, highly combustible *Transcontinental Talent/Wilhelmina Scouting Network* (check out that fat entry for more info).

They claim (as does pretty much everyone associated with the *TCT* debacle) that they weren't the ones in the company responsible for cheating the starry-eyed masses out of millions of dollars. Well, that's good. All is fair in love and war. *TCT/Wilhelmina* is such a mess of finger-pointing and lawsuits that it's honestly hard to tell. But *One Source Talent* seems to be running on pretty much the same model as *TCT*. So be on high alert if they start telling you that your photos aren't up to snuff and that, for the supposed "bargain price" of $995, they can fix you up with a brand spanking new *One Source* approved set of shots.

OPTIONS MODELS
EMODEL MANAGEMENT

PHONE: DISCONNECTED

Even though these tykes are part of *TCT* (listed later in this Act), we're keeping them here under *Options* too, so people will recognize the name in case a particular franchise hasn't adopted the *Transcontinental* logo, etc. An investigative news team in Atlanta did an exposé on these fabulous folks early in 2003 and uncovered the less-than-kosher tactics that they were trying with all the fine residents of Georgia.

But since there are franchises throughout the country, we thought we should inform you about the *Option Models* experience in LA. These pilgrims basically took our friend's money, as he tells it, and left him nothing but a few photos to show for it. They told him he was "hot," "perfect," "model material," blah, blah, blah. $600 smack-a-roos and three weeks later with just a few pics in his pocket, he called them to ask what was up. They acted as if they didn't even know who he was.

Then he explained his situation, and the woman on the phone told him that he should "take a couple of modeling classes." And wouldn't you know? They offered them, for a "modest" fee of course, supposedly $300-$400 for a class. Where are *Options Models* now? Well, it seems they've merged with or were bought out by *Transcontinental*. To read more about them, go to the "T's" in – where else? *Fabulous Other*! Our friend? He sucked it up and went on to bigger and better things.

RAQUEL OSBORNE

Raquel is a fantastic CD and has cast some killer projects including *24* (season 1), *American Beauty, Town And Country, Mermaids, Malice*, and *The Good Son*. At present, she's on permanent vacation. Good for her!

PARENT GUIDE
SLATE ENTERTAINMENT

12211 Washington Blvd, #100
Los Angeles, CA 90066
CONTACT: Michelle Zahn
PHONE: 310-397-3277, ext. 101
WEBSITE: www.parentguide.biz

If you ever see a parent on set with their child actor, clutching a red book and allowing no one else to take a gander at its contents, they probably just came from *Parent Guide* (or they're completely paranoid and crazy - back away slowly, avoid eye contact - kidding, of course!). You'd be overprotective of your 'top secret' book too if you apparently just dropped eight hundred bucks on it.

Parent Guide representatives scout kids at malls, implying that they can get them work, inviting them over for screen tests and advice (and maybe cookies), and then drop the bomb that their counseling and super-duper wonder book costs around $800. But maybe you've found it to be worthwhile. Keep us posted. Under the *Slate Entertainment* banner, Michelle and company just rent out audition space in their building. Good work, people! Excellent way to make some extra cash!

MARSHALL PECK

This Independent CD works with talent on a project by project basis – usually from the film's production office. His casting credits include: *Holes, Sweet November, My Dog Skip,* and *Ladder 49*. He has no fees, and will find folks when he has work (though it is pretty sporadic and random) by holding random open calls when needed.

PHANTOMCASTING.COM
1255 S. La Cienega Blvd.
Los Angeles, CA 90035
CONTACT: Kenny Johnson
PHONE: 323-839-5881
WEBSITE: www.phantomcasting.com

Online casting for films, TV, commercials, etc. Advertised in *Back Stage West*® in late 2003 suggesting that "actors get noticed." How? Producers can find talent for projects. Are these *phantom* "producers" using it? Excuse the lame pun. The problem is, we don't know who uses it. We do know it costs $79.95 a year to maintain a webpage with the standard resumé, headshots, etc. + $50 to renew each year thereafter. Other than that, we're in the dark, *Phantomcasting.com* indeed, funny.

PLANETEXTRAS.COM
15720 Ventura Blvd., Suite 601
Encino CA 91436
PHONE: 818-990-9009
WEBSITE: www.planetextras.com

First this place was *ExtraCast*. Then it morphed into *PlanetExtras*. Which then evolved into the calling service *Uncut Casting* (see Act 7), which seems to be on the right path. So there you have it. Brief synopsis indeed! Unusual for us, we know...

POSH ENTERTAINMENT
POSH ENTERTAINMENT GROUP
POSH AND GO MODELS
GO MODELS & TALENT
9454 Wilshire Blvd., Suite 204
Beverly Hills, CA 90212
PHONE: 310-385-5869
WEBSITE: www.poshentertainmentgroup.com

It's as if a Spice Girl owns this joint! And what's with this "Go Models"?! "Go" where? Home? Back to bed? Under a rock? "Go" away? What are we "Go" (ing) for here, people? Well, this prompted enough speculation, we had to "Go" and investigate – the shooting star imagery in their ad sold us! Plus, the open call they were advertising was in just a few days.

What were they looking for? Kids five and up, as well as juniors and adults. Hhmm? "What kind of talent are you looking for?" we asked the woman on the phone. She responded (rather rudely), "Didn't you see the ad? Anyone. Anyone can come in. Two to seventy-five. You fit that?"

Seems someone didn't have their morning coffee, but that's ok, we understand. She said they accept SAG and Non-Union and there were no fees. No fees? "For the open call," she corrected. "What does it cost after that?" Long pause. "IF..." (it was a BIG, emphasized 'if')... "IF we accept you, it all depends." On what? " We'll see you at the open call." And click. She hung up. Simmer down, people. Don't be so disgruntled. If you don't like your job, quit!

We got a similar story in late 2004 when we tried to get answers for this new edition, although the woman who answered the phone was much, much happier. Pricing, however, could only be discussed once we scheduled an appointment.

JOHN ROBERT POWERS
Anytown, USA

You fine folks should know ALL about this place by now, they spend a hell of a lot on advertisting! This place has franchises across the state. These franchises are owned by various people, but it's our understanding that this place could charge anyone from a couple hundred dollars to thousands and thousands of dollars for headshots, acting classes, etc. – but you get the idea – super-expensive stuff (some of the franchises are registered in the state of California as Advance-Fee Talent Services).

The fact of the matter is that this stuff is not necessary for extra work (we love to repeat ourselves). Anyway, a man who claimed to be John Robert Powers (who incidentally died in 1977) called to complain about what we had written. When we told him about the personal experience one of us has had with his organization, he became exceedingly enraged and began threatening us. He informed us that we were "sick" and he hung up! We love maturity.

The following is a true story of Angela's personal experience with the *John Robert Powers* franchise in Sacramento, California, many years ago. "When I was 14 or so, an older gentleman who worked for *JRP* called me every single night (as I was doing my algebra homework) and tried to persuade me to convince my parents to spend upwards of two thousand dollars on the various services they provided. This harassment went on for months – even when I said I was not interested. I still don't know how they go my contact info. Weird. Can you believe that – calling and asking for me, the 14-year-old, to tell me I should convince my parents that I wanted to take the classes and that I needed photos?!

When I told him he should speak to my parents and I proceeded to hand the phone over to them, he always SUDDENLY had to go. And I was called the sick one?? Whatever. I'm sure everyone has a different experience with different franchises, some good, some not so good. This company has franchises all over the darn place and each one may operate a little differently.

Quite frankly, I would much rather hear a positive story than a negative story. The negative gets rather old, to be honest with you. If you've had a positive experience with them or any of the companies mentioned, we'd love to hear them. Write to me. Send your less-than-positive experiences as well. Why not? It's a free country."

If you need more info, check with the Better Business Bureau (www.bbb.org) for information regarding a particular franchise of *John Robert Powers*.

PREMIERE CASTING
7985 Santa Monica Blvd., PMB 292
West Hollywood, CA 90046

Fees? Who knows. Projects? Oy vey! Couldn't tell ya. We don't even know if they are still around since we have no phone number and they're operating from a P.O. Box in West Hollywood. They advertised a few projects mid-2003 in *Back Stage West®*, and spies submitted pictures, but no one ever heard from them. Hhhm?

PREMIUM-ACCESS.COM
WEBSITE: OFF-LINE

This website address wants you to sign-up for reality TV casting notices. But what you may not know is that it's just one small piece of a much larger entity called *Colonize* that: "... is a leading direct marketing firm that specializes in acquiring large numbers of customers for businesses." Yeah, we're serious. You enter your email address and they'll apparently share it with the world. They supposedly tell you that in the fine print, but many of the lazier peeps won't read the small print, so we'll inform you that if you give 'em your email address you MAY get notices about reality TV casting projects, but ALSO much, much more of STUFF you may not want!

PRIME STAR ENTERTAINMENT AND CASTING
500 Esplanade Drive, Suite 1444
Oxnard, CA 93030
PHONE: DISCONNECTED

What is this? A *USDA* prime cut slab of beef, *Prime Star*, huh?! Kidding... do not confuse this with the very reputable *Prime Casting*. This is a company that popped up in Oxnard in 2002 – although *Prime Star* sounds more like a beer and ribs joint to us. Anyway, it's run by a Mr. Vincent McCowan who wasn't so sure if he's partners with Robert Lewis (who owned the now-defunct *Entertainment Casting* – also in Oxnard – and shouldn't be confused with Robert Lewis of *Atmosphere Casting*).

In the very same conversation McCowan stated that Mr. Lewis was his partner, but when we mentioned our concerns about Mr. Lewis's business history, Mr. McCowan changed his mind and decided that Lewis was merely a "consultant." Fine, we'll play the game. *Prime Star* (not a steak house) still supposedly charges a $60 annual fee for Non-Union talent (that's once a year, folks) to be registered with this company in bustling Oxnard. Okay.

They also sell a "Headshot Package" for $275 and an "Actors Package" for $375. Hmm? When asked about standard 3"x5" photos for extra work, he suggested that background talent only needed headshots (HIS headshots presumably). Okay. Who knows? Maybe he's got good stuff to offer. One thing's for sure, as of December 2004 he no longer had a working phone line. So, if you want to reach the elusive Mr. McCowan, guess it has be by mail or road trip (gas is expensive though, these days...).

PRIME TIME ENTERTAINMENT
SHOWTIME CASTING
SHOWTIME ENTERTAINMENT
STAR SEARCH CASTING
HOSPITALITY TRAINERS
215 1/2 N. Coast Hwy
Oceanside, CA 92054
-or-
P.O. Box 1100
Oceanside, CA 92054
PHONE: 800-863-0238
EMAIL: support@primetimecasting.com
WEBSITE: www.primetimecasting.com

Oy vey! Do not confuse this with the very reputable *Prime Casting* (whoa...deja vu). In addition to apparently offering (sigh) bartending classes, *Prime Time Entertainment* is also a sorta-kinda-unlicensed talent/casting agency. They apparently offer online posting of actors' photos for $99.95/year. They place ads for their services in a variety of non-industry publications throughout the U.S. Supposedly they have offered cash to angry ex-clients who file negative reports with the Better Business Bureau for them to withdraw their complaints against *Prime Time*.

PRINT MODELS NETWORK
PMN
MODELS NETWORK
LASER LENZ
3629 Cahuenga Blvd., West
Universal City, CA 90068
-or-
(Three other locations that appear to be affiliated)
PHONE: 323-882-6495
STAFF: Stefan Valero
WEBSITE: www.printmodelsnetwork.com

Huh?! Have office furniture, movie posters, will travel. Where *Booking Services* Calling Service resided, *Print Models* was not far behind. What's the connection? Keep reading, you'll understand the possible dealio. Apparently, they are still advertising in *LA Weekly,* appealing to the newbies fresh off the bus. Their advertisements shout, "BREAK INTO SHOWBIZ, no advance fee!" Uh...huh.

Stefan claims they don't cast for extra work (even though it says so in their ads - fine) or charge their clients fees, but may gladly show you some "state of the art" computer database. Cool. They may also encourage you to take some classes and hook you up with some zed cards and/or headshots (of course, by their recommended photographer) but who knows, maybe it's a good deal, inquire within. They might then hook you up with one of their Calling Service buddies for a free month using that service – Hhhmm?? – could that possibly be *Booking Services* or not? You see, in the past, these two have been located at the same address! Clever.

Several years back, we received a phone call from this Stefan fellow in regards to the complaint letter that we published. He personally invited Angela to come down to his office to see his "database of talent" and review the way he operates, which was nice of him.`

He claimed that he does not provide headshots or acting classes and that talent makes their money back in 6 weeks. Cool. That is if they land an audition he supposedly sends them on – by the way, what are the odds of nailing your first audition? Stranger things have happened, who knows?

In any event, we were then informed that we should really be "commending him on the services [he] provides talent." Wait a minute, we're confused. We thought he didn't offer any services? Furthermore, (here's what's frustrating) we have been writing this book for 9 years. We have previously been in his establishment and heard the whole pitch personally – not to mention random newcomers come over to our office complaining and rat out all of the sales tactics. Whatever! A while back, during a 3-day period, we had five girls come into our office who informed us that they all paid a lump sum of $445 bucks. Yikes! They said that was the only package-type offer available, completely contradictory to what Stefan says. Oh well. Maybe we're all confused.

Before brain surgery, one of our staff was looking for a job through his college (UCLA) job board. He came across *Print Models Network* (*PMN*) listed as a "submission service for actors, models and extras." He got some work alright, but paid big-time for what little he was offered. The start-up cost was $300 – but our trooper only had half. He was then threatened with legal action if he failed to pay them the rest – and this was apparently before he even handed over half the dough or signed a thing. He was later sent several letters regarding his "delinquent account" because he had failed to send his payment vouchers from set directly to *PMN* offices. They wanted him to sign his checks over to them in exchange for their "services" and they would then "cut him a check" for his share. Ouch, a cut indeed. Let us know if you've had similar experiences or maybe landed a killer gig directly from *PMN* which would rock! They now may have a calling service offshoot call *Vision Casting*. Neat!

PRO CASTING
c/o Madilyn Clark Studios
10852 Burbank Blvd.
North Hollywood, CA 91601
PHONE: DISCONNECTED

act nine

Advertised in *Back Stage West®* in early 2003 charging talent $20 cash to register. Their credits? Um, none...that we know of, but let us know. Their whereabouts now? Unknown. All phone numbers disconnected. Emails never responded to. Staff at *Pro Casting* told us they only rented space... yeah, that sucks!

PRODUCERS GENIUS CASTING
PRODUCERS GENIUS CAST
P.G. CASTING
5254 Melrose Avenue
Hollywood, CA 90026
PHONE: 323-960-3469

Question... did some drunk person lose a bet in a bar and get stuck naming their next business the aforementioned name? Come on, people, is production really gonna call *Producers Genius Casting* – we mean, what if they do and *Producers Genius* screws up? Then who is the dumbass?

Just a joke, people. Food for thought though, okay... moving on... last we knew, you could register with them by calling the number above and setting up an appointment, M-F, 10AM-5PM. But when we tried four or five times in late 2002, it just rang and rang and rang. Guess what? The same uneventful outcome occurred everytime since!

They previously had an address on Van Ness, but we think the Melrose address is more current. There *was* apparently a $29 registration fee for the year, but now we hear that it costs $39 for six months. Supposedly you can get extra work, or audience work through them that pays $7-$9 an hour – CASH! Which is cool. We'd love more insight from anyone who's signed up with them to gauge whether or not it's worth the dough! From what we have heard in the office, this company is most likely another spin-off from Morenna/*Hollywood Casting*/*CNTV*'s brain cells. (*Brain Surgeon* humor, get it?!)

RAZOR CASTING

1831 Colorado Ave., Suite 800
Santa Monica, CA 90404
PHONE: 310-909-8572
WEBSITE: www.razorcasting.com

An established Voice-Over casting company, Razor is transitioning into On-Camera work. Which is cool. Apparently they're diving into principal commercial and feature film roles and may possibly plan to start casting background. There are no fees at present, which is great. Inquire within.

REASURE CASTING

PHONE: 818-386-9723 or 323-687-9723
EMAIL: reasurecasting@aol.com

Run by mystery man Reasure Jacobs (formerly of *Fabulous Other* all-star *CNTV*?), this place/dude seems to advertise almost exculsively on *CraigsList.com*, mostly for low-paying modeling gigs and audience work. We've been unable to locate an address for Reasure. Which isn't really a surprise, since we've had a report that he apparently casts via cell phone out of an internet cafe somewhere just off of Hollywood Boulevard. A mixed bag of complaints have trickled into our offices about this fellow, everything from sending folks to the wrong address for commercial work to bumming lunch from his models at a photo shoot. We'd ask him to tell us his side of the story, but messages left on his phone and email go unreturned. Guess we'll have to find reassurance elsewhere. C'mon, that one was funny!

SANTA CLARITA CASTING PRODUCTION

In the *Valley Recycler* they advertise that they need extras. Do they need or want recycled extras? Kidding. Get it? That was funny! Maybe not. Anyway, they also advertise in other publications in the ever-so-remote Valencia area. They may charge talent $75 to get registered. But who knows? These people hung up on us. Maybe it was an accident. Now, the phone number no longer works. Are they still around? We don't know. But take this little ditty as a heads-up in case you come across their name in the future.

SCOUTING ENTERTAINMENT GROUP
SEG

1680 North Vine Street, Suite 600
Hollywood, CA 90028
PHONE: 323-790-2900
WEBSITE: www.segstudios.com

No! Say it isn't so. In April 2003 FOX News did an exposé on these dudes, yet people apparently keep falling prey. One woman who emailed us in May 2003 told us how *SEG* had called her and persuaded her to come in for an interview. The woman brought her friend with her (also an actress). They were then told that *SEG* didn't usually work with talent who had not been in LA for at least two years, but they would schedule a "screen test" for them because some French dude named Francois "liked" them. Ugh.

Well, they scheduled screen tests on SEPARATE days, of course (divide and conquer, after all). One woman was turned down, believe it or not, and one was accepted based on her supposed "screen test." But this tactic only serves to add legitimacy to the one woman who WAS chosen – "Well they did PICK me... they don't pick everyone." They'd rather make their money from one person who believes than TWO skeptics.

The catch, of course, was that the "chosen woman" would need to pay $900 for a photo package. This was never mentioned until she was ready to sign on the dotted line. Thankfully, she had contacted us ahead of time and DIDN'T sign the contract! Let us know your stories.

SHOWBIZKID.COM

Newport Beach Office
2715 West Coast Hwy., Suite A
Newport Beach, CA 92663
PHONE: DISCONNECTED
WEBSITE: OFF-LINE

act nine

With their old phone number now a private residence and their website seemingly down for the count, these folks seem to have gone extinct sometime in the last year. But, for your personal edification, get a load of these little ditties. They said as their introduction: "You've never seen anything like *ShowBizKid.com*." Um, actually we have. All over the place, in fact. When you're paying upwards of $175 bucks for the year, you want to make sure the website is being utilized by real industry pros with legitimate work to offer.

They claimed to help you "connect" your children with producers, directors, casting directors and the like on a daily basis. But where are the specific names? They offered the standard online resumé, photo thingy and they kept your children's info confidential (which is very important). They also claimed to have a daily bulletin board listing broken down by region and location so little Larry and Luanne could break a leg at the local level.

If you know anything we may have missed or if you've had a great experience, let us know.

SOUNDSTAGE STUDIOS, INC.
SOUNDSTAGE OF BEVERLY HILLS
BEVERLY HILLS SOUND STAGE STUDIOS
SOUND STAGE MODEL AND TALENT MANAGEMENT
SOUND STAGE ENTERTAINMENT
OC IMAGE AND TALENT
2901 W. MacArthur Blvd, #104
Costa Mesa, CA 92701
PHONE: 714-979-8450

Yowzer! First off, did you get through the long run-on of multiple company names? This place supposedly charged wide-eyed talent $450 for overpriced something-or-others. They had several "top secret" divisions but they were simply not tellin'. We went up the street to visit their exciting Beverly Hills office in 2002, but sadly enough there was a note on the door saying that they were out of town at some modeling event or something! Guess they never made it back home. But, who knows, due to (what seems to be) expansion, maybe they needed bigger office space.

Their latest incarnation seems to be *OC Image and Talent*, based down in (appropriately enough) the OC.

STAR CASTING
24307 Magic Mountain Parkway, PMB 46
Valencia, CA 91354
PHONE: 310-289-2278
CONTACT: Cheryl Faye

These fine folks have cast random commercials in the past but formal registration is rarely if ever held (it's been years actually). Last word was you can mail a headshot or some pictures and a resumé along with a SASE and they would notify you if and when they had work. Cool!

STAR SEARCH CASTING
4360 E. Main St., #306
Valencia, CA 93003
PHONE: 206-984-4408
EMAIL: info@starsearchcasting.com
WEBSITE: www.starsearchcasting.com

Some of you eagle-eyed readers out there might have noticed that *Star Search Casting* was also listed as one of the many aliases of *Prime Time Entertainment*. Well, fine, you're right. Happy? The reason we're also listing them separately is because *Star Search* has supposedly, SUPPOSEDLY, split off from *Prime Time* to become its own separate, independent company. Well, that's fantastic! Double the Registration opportunity! They offer the same type of online performer portfolio and the start-up fee appears to be exactly the same ($99.95/year). We'll just have to wait and see if this place is what it claims to be, and if casting directors are really using it (which would be cool). One less-than-promising omen: their phone number is just a recorded line telling you to email them. Customer service rocks! Keep us posted.

STARMAKER MODELS
STARMAKER MODELS, CASTING & TALENT
4223 N. Scottsdale Road
Scottsdale, AZ 85251
PHONE: 480-949-0180
WEBSITE: www.starsusa.com

For your convenience, this star-making casting office is located in Arizona. Yes, we are aware that Arizona is several hours away, but a call into our office from a confused California mommy made us do a little investigating and landed *Starmaker* in *Fabulous Other*. Seems someone told them about *Starmaker* and she sent 'em some money she wished she hadn't. It's $175 smacks for a year of "exposure" for your child on their website. Seemingly the same stuff as many other companies – standard webpage deal, etc..., but all contact from any potential casting directors who happen to be looking for the stars of tomorrow on the AZ-based website apparently MUST go through them. Anyhow, you can send them photos which they will scan and put on a webpage. Do keep us abreast and drop us a line if you hear anything.

PAUL STEWART CASTING
1236 1/2 Cloverdale Ave.
Los Angeles, CA 90019
PHONE: 323-933-2005
WEBSITE: www.next-thing.com

Sexy Paul is an independent CD who casts talent for music videos, commercials, industrials, and print work. He has cast videos for the likes of Busta Rhymes and MC Breed among others. Duh, how cool is that?! Paul typically casts a couple shoots a month, and finds his talent using online services such as *LA Casting* and the **HOS**® website.

act nine

STUDIO KIDZ
STAR KIDZ
PACIFIC SCOUTING
1828 Pandora Ave., Suite 2
Los Angeles, CA 90025
-or-
8670 Wilshire Blvd., Suite 112
Los Angeles, CA 90025
CONTACT: Alisa Poplofsky
PHONE: 310-487-3477 or 310-864-2273

Oh fun times! Another company supposedly specializing in scouting kids out of shopping centers and getting them to come down to showcase/audition/screen tests which apparently turn into sales pitches for their paid services. Not sure about the costs, so let us know if you get a firm price.

Although we haven't been able to confirm that *Studio Kidz* is affiliated with fellow kiddie-scouters *Hollywood Handbook*, one of *Studio Kidz*'s old addresses is the same as *Hollywood Handbook*'s current 2050 South Bundy location (interesting detective work, huh?). And they seem to work off a very similar (if not identical) business model.

Studio Kidz pseudonym "*Pacific Scouting*" is also one of the old monikers of *Fab Other* all-stars *Kids and Teens Casting*, who also work from that pesky 2050 South Bundy address. One thing is for sure, *Studio Kidz* are IN NO WAY affliated with the similarly named kids agency *Studio Kids Management*.

STUDIO PHONE

P.O. Box 34481
Los Angeles, CA 90034
PHONE: 310-202-9872

A place that, by their own definition, can be translated into "selling SAG vouchers." This service is supposed to be an all-SAG calling service, but many a Casting Director has expressed a bit of shock when *Studio Phone* has either offered up a Non-Union person or they, *Studio Phone*, had the audacity to replace SAG members (who apparently didn't know they'd been booked) with voucher-needing, Non-Union folks. Our latest phone calls have been encouraging, because they, it seems, politely refused submissions from various Non-Union talent... cleaning up their act? They told us they charge $55 per month, with first and last month's membership fees due at sign up. You are only charged if you get work. So that's cool. Let us know about your experiences.

TALENT ENTERTAINMENT NETWORK, INC.
T.E.N.

6399 Wilshire Blvd, #700
Los Angeles, CA 90048
PHONE: 323-655-2233
WEBSITE: www.in2talent.com

These guys were formerly a "consulting service" for actors and models. Now *T.E.N.* has metamorphosed into a fully licensed talent agency. Here's the tale: When a woman came into our office with an $800-plus contract for a headshot/zed card deal, we almost flipped out! That's a lot of dough for anything these days! Of course we immediately called the young chap, Louis Molinsky, whose name was listed on the business card of this place. We explained who we were and what we did. He was so excited that we called (we are pretty nice) and he couldn't wait to tell us about, what we percieve to be, his painfully overpriced services. Maybe he thought we wanted the photos or something, but the guy just didn't get it. He was praising us left and right! In fact, he said our book sounded like such a great idea, he couldn't wait to rush out and buy a copy so he could use it as a reference on the industry. HUH?! (He's right, though, we are cool!)

Smart Louis also went on to explain that his prices are really nominal, etc. Little did he know that if he buys an issue for his "research," he'd be a topic of discussion in it! The latest update to this sad story is that another young woman spent a wad of cash-olla – this time for pictures and classes and a grand total of $1,035. He apparently "guaranteed" that he could place her in commercials within a few weeks. Well, a few weeks became a few months. You get the idea. Supposedly, if she signed up for another acting class through him, he could again guarantee her placement in commercials. Apparently he did not realize he had already made that guarantee. Well, this fella had the same sort of stories as our first example.

TALENTMATCH.COM
WEBSITE: www.talentmatch.com

Sounds like an actors' dating site, but we digress. This website is just one arm within a sisterhood of websites of sorts whose focus is apparently something involving "developing world communities." TalentMatch.com, DataDate.com, and M.com which was top-secret in August 2003, but seems to have emerged as an all-inclusive talent community for on-the-rise peeps of all varieties – extras, singers, dancers, writers, actors, etc. Basic sign-up is free. Which is cool. There is, however, a 'Pro-Level' membership that costs $99.99 a year. Exactly who is looking up your profile, photos and resumés is up for debate. Keep us posted regarding your experiences.

TALENTPAGES.COM
7095 Hollywood Blvd., Suite 874
Hollywood, CA, 90028
PHONE: 323-851-1900
WEBSITE: www.talentpages.com

Another *LA Weekly* mainstay. Claims to be the "real deal" and even advertises no "BS." Dude, what does that stand for?! Does that mean what we think it means, or is that just their way of saying NO BACKGROUND SERVICES? Or that they're another dating service? Just kidding.

Claim to have cast for *Coors*, and Saggy (which we assume is Shaggy the singer) but we don't really know (oddly enough, it's their typo, not ours). So, are they casting directors or an online resource? It appears to be the latter. SAG members can join for FREE and there's a $10 charge for a premium listing if you're Non-Union. If you can figure out how to sign up at all, that is.

There are two separate web pages you may find yourself tumbling through. The "old" page (on which talent are supposedly listed) was barely functional when we checked it out. The "new" page, as they call it, appears to be little more than a defunct forum with a broken sign-up system. Maybe they're working on it. If casters go to talentpages.com to read up on you, we don't know. Please keep us posted and we will do the same.

TALENTEDFACES.COM
P.O. Box 702224
Dallas, TX 75370
WEBSITE: www.talentedfaces.com

What, does my face look talented to you?! Just kidding. This is an online talent showcase for models, actors and children (both amateur and pro). And the good news here, people, for those interested in soft-core... is that *TalentFaces.com* is an authorized *Playboy* store affiliate. And they accept children? Huh, ok, confused? They charge a one-time, $20 set-up fee payable to some place called *The Beber Group* in Dallas, Texas. If you need to know more, visit the site and send 'em an e-mail. Holy smokes, let us know...

TALENTEDKIDS.COM
P.O. Box 54963
Irvine, CA 92619
WEBSITE: www.talentedkids.com

Yes, another dot com. They'll send you a FREE membership kit for your cute kids and they claim to keep all the info strictly private. They help advise against scams (just like us – yay!) and they suggest contacting the Better Business Bureau to report the bad guys. At least they're putting that info out there which is more than we can say for most other internet-based "casting" resources. There is another level of membership that looks as though it has a fee of $19.95 (that'll keep you linked in for three months). This seems to include more features than the basic membership kit – like audition links, casting agent lists, etc. Is it worth it? Choose wisely, parents. We do want you to spend money on things that do work. Check out the website and see for yourself. Keep us posted, people.

TBS CASTING
8831 Sunset Blvd., Suite 310
West Hollywood, CA 90069
PHONE: 310-854-1954
HOTLINE: 310-854-1955

They've mostly booked 18+ talent, Non-Union and SAG (mostly through Calling Services). They claim to have Registration/Visitation on Tuesdays from 12PM-3PM, but be sure to call first, since sometimes they supposedly DON'T SHOW UP – whoops! There's a one-time $20 Processing Fee for Non-Union talent and a $5 Photo Fee (for all) unless you provide your own recently taken Polaroid snapshot. Cash only. Of course, that's the biz. They advise updating once a year if it's been at least that long since you've worked for them. They apparently haven't had a project in what seems like years.

act nine

TORCH ENTERTAINMENT GROUP
1620 26th Street, 3rd Floor
Santa Monica, CA 90404
PHONE: 310-255-8647

Torch this, baby! Sorry, we don't get it either. Another lovely place that offers up info about **HOLLYWOOD OS**® so people can find the FREE Registration places. Apparently, they do this, of course, only after those not in the know may have already spent big bucks. *Torch* promises no up-front fees. Umm, that's totally cool, um, except that new talent may, of course, want to purchase a $750 photo package. Apparently if you resist long enough, they may agree to "sponsor" $200 of that fee, so you'll only owe $550. What a bargain. Seriously people, if you have any fantastic experiences, let us know.

TOTALLY XTRAS CASTING
6399 Wilshire Blvd.
Beverly Hills, CA 90211
PHONE: DISCONNECTED

Totally disconnected! Supposedly a $20 fee to register for SAG and Non-Union talent. Not sure if this was a website, a Calling Service, a hot dog stand that sold extras... but seemingly not a bona fide casting company.

TRANS CONTINENTAL TALENT
TCT
EDGE TALENT
EMODEL
ENTERTAINMENT GROUP
OPTIONS TALENT
OPTIONS TALENT GROUP
T C TALENT
T C TALENT AGENCY
TRANS CONTINENTAL CLASSICS, INC.
TRANSCONTINENTAL TALENT
WILHELMINA SCOUTING NETWORK
STUDIO 58
WHY MODEL/WHY TALENT
WEB STYLE NETWORK
FASHION ROCK LLC
FASHION ROCK NOW
TALENT ROCK
1701 Park Center Dr., Suite 220
Orlando, FL 32835
-or-
127 W. Church Street, Suite 300
Orlando, FL 32801
PHONE: 866-582-4201
WEBSITE: www.webstylenetwork.com and www.talentrock.com

Holy Mac & Cheese. Another year gone by and even more names added to this ever-evolving, world renowned, mother of all mothers. This place re-invents itself more than Madonna. Cool! They apparently employ(ed?) an army of so-called "talent scouts" to recruit folks with that *American Idol* mindset, folks with big dreams who are just waiting for someone to recognize their talent. Anyone with the cash to pony up can get their very own weblisting and the CHANCE to supposedly be seen by industry pros. Not sure who these industry pros were or are, so let us know if you talk to one. Now they apparently also host talent events/competitions where singers, dancers, models, actors, and comics can all compete for FABULOUS PRIZES! Oh, goodie, we'd love a trip for two.

Here's a little history on the place: it started out (we think - it's such a bizzare mess, even they're probably not sure anymore how it all began) as possibly rockin' *Emodel, Inc* and morphed into even more ingenious *Options Talent* a few years later. Lou Pearlman, the way-hip Florida tycoon/teenage-talent monger who discovered *N'SYNC* and the *Backstreet Boys*, took a liking to the place, hopped onboard as chairman, and changed the name to *Trans Continental Talent* (not to be confused with an airline company).

Every Tom, Dick, and Britney now thought they had a direct line to the top. Plunk down your apparent $595 sign up fee and $19.95 a month and you could be off to *TRL* with Justin Timberlake (that's an MTV show for you folks over 25 who might not know). Pearlman got a license to use the "Wilhelmina" name from the respected folks at the *Wilhelmina Model Agency* and (trumpets sounding) the *Wilhelmina Scouting Network* was born. With a respectable-sounding moniker and a successful boy band mogul at the helm, the dinero really started to flow in, it seems. Still with us? Good, 'cause here's where stuff gets juicy - put the kids to bed and call in Judge Judy, it's lawsuit time!

Realizing the possibly uncool business practices of their new buds, *Wilhelmina* sued Pearlman for fraud and it was "Bye Bye Bye" to the *Wilhelmina Scouting Network* name - hello *Web Style Network* and *Fashion Rock LLC* (which recently evolved into, dum dum dum, *Talent Rock*).

In September of 2003, the New York State Consumer Protection Board apparently decided that the company was officially full of crappola, and demanded that they leave the state (random). Let's mention that again because it's so bizzare, they got kicked out of a whole state (which probably doesn't happen too often)! After Pearlman and company were shown the exit door to NY, Lou decided it was time to abdicate his chairman's throne to the company formerly know as the *Wilhelmina Scouting Network*.

Pearlman admitted that deceptive practices were used to rook people out of their cash, but said that he wasn't personally responsible, it was others in his company that tricked folks. It all collapsed in one big mess, but, somehow, through the haze of lawsuits and bankruptcies and corporate restructurings, Lou Pearlman's *Talent Rock* aka *Fashion Rock* aka *Web Style Network* aka *Trans Continental Talent* has managed to emerge intact, with Pearlman still very much at the helm and their very own talent search TV show on the *Fuse Network*. So they're more like *American Idol* than ever...except on *American Idol*, the contestants don't have to pay an entry fee for the chance to compete. Ugh! With fraud estimated at over 100 million bucks, court battles and investigations are sure to continue in this case for a while to come.

Contact the BBB of Central Florida for any questions or to file a complaint. The Bureau's address to write to is 151 Wymore Road, Suite 100, Altamonte Springs, FL 32714 or call (407) 621-3300. The website address is www.orlando.bbb.org."

VIP CASTING
TAKE ACTION CASTING
JD CASTING

3575 Cahuenga Blvd. West, Suite 125-9
Los Angeles, CA 90068
PHONE: 818-339-5061
WEBSITE: www.takeactioncasting.com
EMAIL: takeactioncasting@sbcglobal.net and vipcasting@sbcglobal.net

This place is a spicy goulash of intriguing fees and credits. Whenever they change names, talent is apparently asked to re-register, and get the chance to pay their registration fee all over again.

We've heard that they spin some sort of malarky involving multiple CD's working from the same office, and each CD is rumored to require his or her own registration fee. Their credits are mostly low budget indie fair and commercial work. Although, when last we talked to them, they claimed to be casting background for the NBC show *Las Vegas*. Guess they forgot to let *Central Casting* and the production staff at *Las Vegas* in on that little secret, because nobody we talked to at either of those companies seemed to know anything about *Take Action* or *VIP* or *JD*. And yes, as always, we love to hear from ya if you have anything spicy to say.

VISIONAIRE
BAMBINI LA
BAMBINI KIDS
SPECTRUM MANAGEMENT
1010 S. Robertson Blvd., #2
Los Angeles, CA 90035
PHONE: 310-652-7368
CONTACT: Theingi Cossar (as listed with BBB)
WEBSITE: www.spectrumtalent.com

Not again, people. Are Gigi and Theingi and Morenna the same person?! Who shot J.R.? When is the next leap year? Is Eminem really a genius? These are all questions we want the answers to. Moving on... Although Theingi (Gigi, see *ExtraCast* and *Glamour Models*) claims to not be affiliated with this company or its new name (*Spectrum*), it is interesting that the Better Business Bureau reports otherwise, but, who knows. Now we may have people changing their personal names as well as their company names (soap opera indeed).

Currently, *Visionaire* is apparently all about selling pricey headshots and Zed cards. A "development company" as Gigi would put it. Possible business tip: Gigi and Morenna should just get together with all of their many companies and form one big conglomerate (maybe that wouldn't be as interesting, huh)? *Bambini LA/Bambini Kids*, by the way, is their kids' division – which we'd bet may be run like their adult division.

WEST COAST CASTING
7200 Franklin Ave., #308
Hollywood, CA 90046
PHONE: 517-410-1236
CONTACT: Brian Lindensmith
EMAIL: casting@digiclipproductions.com
WEBSITE: www.westcoastcasting.com (site down)

This is supposedly a casting agency which also does everything from website design to demo reel editing. However, in terms of casting, as we go to press, our research hasn't yet turned up one single project credited to these guys. The casting side is free to actors who wish to register. Which is fantasic, woo-hoo! Registration is done primarily via email, so feel free to send over your photos and resume - they say they accept about 75% of those who apply to the database. There are fees for all the other services, including a $75/year fee for a "featured section" on the website. Swell. Keep us posted about your experiences.

SAMUEL WARREN & ASSOCIATES

2244 Fourth Avenue, Suite D
San Diego, CA 92101
PHONE: 619-264-4135
WEBSITE: www.samuelwarrenandassociatescasting.com

Whew! Have fun typing that ultra-long web address into your computer. Sam teaches acting classes and casts principal and background talent for projects such as commercials and industrials. He's been around town for a pretty long time, booking neat, random killer, high paying gigs.

JENNIFER WELLINGS

16581 Greenview Lane
Huntington Beach, CA 92649

This swell young lass used to specialize in club, edgy, goth, tattooed, glam raver types ONLY – ages 18-to-look-younger to about 50 years old. Problem is, we couldn't get any updated info for this updated edition of our directory. The address may work, but the phone numbers were all disconnected. Which sucks. If you feel lucky, mail off some pics, but you MUST have an alternative look. Cool! Let us know how you fare.

WINNING IMAGE

4444 Riverside Drive, Suite 105
Burbank, CA 91505
PHONE: DISCONNECTED

Oh, Lord. Where do we start? *Winning Image*... sounds like a bad before-and-after etiquette/beauty program your mom and dad would've sent you to had you insisted on living your life as an Osbourne in the 90's.

We've been contacted by quite a few people who've been much more than simply displeased with the tactics of this outfit. There is apparently a $300 start-up fee, a photographer whose photos "sucked" (we're quoting here), more money ($50) to develop photos from the proof sheet, and an apparent additional $50 fee to take some "half-baked " (we're quoting again here) cold-reading class from a teacher who was (it is rumored) also the Receptionist/Director/Manager and couldn't "act her way out of a wet paper bag," and more unoriginal shenanigans. The class was to prepare students for an audition in the film *Ali*. Cool, except the audition was merely for extra work – no lines to be given out whatsoever! But folks were out $50 smacks nonetheless and embarrassed when they showed up on set to "audition."

A seemingly rotating staff informed the folks who contacted us that of the "hundreds" that come to them only a "select few, maybe fifteen" were accepted. Lucky them. Well, wouldn't you know – these two gentlemen who contacted **HOS**® were among the lucky fifteen to be invited back from the hundreds to pay $300 bucks to get the ball rolling?! In later meetings, these two guys were told they were the "pick of the litter" and they were going to get a "special offer." How special? $2,000 smackeroos special. For this price they would be "invited" to participate in a special modeling-type seminar in North Carolina (of course, the two grand did not include airfare, supposedly mandatory "modeling" photos, food, accommodations, etc.).

The short version of a very long story ends with the fact that neither of the men we refer to in this piece were ever offered paying work through *Winning Image*. *Winning Image* does, however, continue to call them and offer them additional "special seminars" at the average price of just $125! That's nice. Much better deal! Keep us posted.

WIZZARD'S ENTERTAINMENT
PHONE: 818-754-4385

By now, you are hundreds of pages into this book, so we really don't need to place a lot of worthless text here. If you have been paying any attention to us at all, you've seen this character's name a half-dozen times or more. Wizzard? (Kind of like Morenna and Gigi, very popular people back here in *Fab Other*!) Ring a bell? Go back to the *2000 Casting, Hollywood Casting,* or the *CNTV Fabulous Other* entries if you really need to be refreshed. Inquire within and keep us posted.

TIFFANY WOODS CASTING
11260 Overland Drive, #19G
Culver City, CA 90230
WEBSITE: OFF-LINE

Sometimes randomly works in LA but is based in Northern California. She casts mostly low-budget features here and there and works with both SAG and Non-Union talent. There appear to be no fees when working for her, and that's a good thing! You can submit "8x10"'s or "3x5"'s to the above address with all your contact info (or a resumé). You used to be able to email photos and resumés to her online, but with her website MIA in 2004, that no longer appears to be an option. Feel free to enlighten us if you come across new info.

WORLDWIDE CASTING
ENTERTAINMENT CASTING
6430 Variel Avenue, #102
Woodland Hills, CA 91367
PHONE: 818-598-8889 or 818-598-8723

We can't even believe some poor tree had to die so we could inform you about what's going on here (partially because we're not clear). Lets just start by telling you that they copy entire pages from OUR book and hand them out to their potential customers as their own. Huh? Can you say copyright infringement?! They appear to promise talent auditions, SAG vouchers, and lots of work for $60, but we are still confused as to what's going on. For an additional $75, the supposed CD will find you more work and the manager/dude will "fix up" your resumé. Nice. According to the recorded message on their phone lines, all casting reps are currently (and perpetually) too busy to pick up. We'd love to know what they're casting, so keep us posted.

XTRAS ONLINE

5694 Mission Center Road, #259
San Diego, CA 92108
WEBSITE: www.xtrasonline.com

At one point there was a company with the same name that dealt with porn – the "X" stood for, well, you are smart and now casting-educated. But you need not fret, neither company seems to be in business at present.

YOUNG ENTERTAINMENT ARTISTS
MARCH HARE MANAGEMENT

230 Manhattan Avenue
Hermosa Beach, CA 90254

March Hare has re-emerged...yet again...sort of...apparently (you already read about 'em in "K" for *Kids & Teen*-something-or-other agency in this very *Fab Other* section!). The supposedly defunct kids casting place is, it would seem, back with the next new name (look what the BBB said... go back to *Kids & Teens Casting*). They are bonded as an Advance-Fee Talent Service with the state of California which means they are at least following the law of the land (that's cool). But under other names, they also quickly broke several laws as well. It is NOT necessary to pay huge upfront fees or rely on empty promises that are not written down on paper! Those seldom amount to much. But you know this already, right, people? C'mon, it's the last listing in this section... you gotta know what's up in this town by now!?! Enough said. Keep us posted.

scammed submission form

SCAMMED!!?

. . .tell us about it!

As you probably know by now, one of the crucial reasons we write this directory is to protect talent from corrupt organizations that charge exorbitant fees and empty promises. After spending their hard-earned money, many actors find themselves without any means to acquire work because these companies they have visited are nothing but a big, fat joke.

We want you to help us so that we can help you prevail against these "scammers." If this has ever happened to you, please cut out this questionnaire, answer the following questions, mail it into us and let HOLLYWOOD OS® work for you!

If you do not want to mutilate your personal edition of EWFBS®, copy the pages that follow and mail those answers to us. You may also email us with your complaint, or log onto www.HollywoodOS.com, click on "Report a Scam," and follow the instructions listed on screen. Our goal is to help you in any way we can.

Please Fill Out the Enclosed Form and Return it ANY of the Following Ways

- ADDRESS: HOLLYWOOD OS®
  ATTN: SCAMMED!
  400 S. Beverly Drive, Suite 307
  Beverly Hills, CA 90212
- EMAIL: info@HollywoodOS.com
- FAX: 310-277-3088

scammed submission form

- What was the name of the company/organization?

- Where were they located? Address & phone number?

- Where did you hear about them (*Back Stage West*®, *LA Weekly*, telephone pole, internet, on a set, at mall, a friend, etc.)? And when did you sign up with them?

- What was their initial fee?

- How much was your total payment?

- What were you promised/guaranteed? (i.e., photos, phone numbers, stardom, etc.)

- What did you actually receive for your money?

scammed submission form

• Did they ever find you work?

• Did you ever ask for a refund? If so, what was their response?

• Do you know of anyone else who had the same experience, or a similar one, with this company? Can we contact them?

• Please comment on how this experience made you feel. This can be anonymous! Be as candid as you like and attach additional paper if you need to.

act nine

scammed submission form

• Please comment *(cont'd.)*

• Please provide us with your name, address and phone number so we may contact you with any further questions if you feel comfortable. We will not share this information with anyone else. Again, you may remain anonymous if you'd like... although, in order to help ya out, it would be better if we did have your name!

• NAME ____________________

• ADDRESS ____________________

• PHONE NUMBER(S) ____________________

• E-MAIL ____________________

• OTHER ____________________

• Thanks for helping others NOT get scammed! •

act nine

T H E   L A W   O F F I C E S   O F

SACINO, BERTOLINO & HALLISSY

A Professional Corporation

Richard P. Bertolino

Attorney at Law

916.649.2214
fax 916.649.9241

IN LOS ANGELES
818.506.7445

740 UNIVERSITY AVENUE, SUITE 100 • SACRAMENTO • CA 95825

hollywood os® paychart

HOURS	$54/8	$122/8	$137/8	HOURS	$54/8	$122/8	$137/8
0-8	54.00	122.00	137.00	**12:48**	112.05	237.90	267.15
8:06	55.01	124.30	139.57	**12:54**	113.40	240.95	270.58
8:12	56.03	126.58	142.14	**13:00**	114.75	244.00	274.00
8:18	57.04	128.86	144.71	**13:06**	116.10	247.05	277.43
8:24	58.05	131.15	147.28	**13:12**	117.45	250.10	280.85
8:30	59.06	133.44	149.84	**13:18**	118.80	253.15	284.28
8:36	60.08	135.73	152.41	**13:24**	120.15	256.20	287.70
8:42	61.09	138.01	154.98	**13:30**	121.50	259.25	291.13
8:48	62.10	140.30	157.55	**13:36**	122.85	262.30	294.55
8:54	63.11	142.59	160.12	**13:42**	124.20	265.35	297.98
9:00	64.13	144.88	162.69	**13:48**	125.55	268.40	301.40
9:06	65.14	147.16	165.26	**13:54**	126.90	271.45	304.83
9:12	66.15	149.45	167.83	**14:00**	128.25	274.50	308.25
9:18	67.16	151.74	170.39	**14:06**	129.60	277.55	311.68
9:24	68.18	154.03	172.96	**14:12**	130.95	280.60	315.10
9:30	69.19	156.31	175.53	**14:18**	132.30	283.65	318.53
9:36	70.20	158.60	178.10	**14:24**	133.65	286.70	321.95
9:42	71.21	160.89	180.67	**14:30**	135.00	289.75	325.38
9:48	72.23	163.18	183.24	**14:36**	136.35	292.80	328.80
9:54	73.24	165.46	185.81	**14:42**	137.70	295.85	332.23
10:00	74.25	167.75	188.38	**14:48**	139.05	298.90	335.65
10:06	75.60	170.04	190.94	**14:54**	140.40	301.95	339.08
10:12	76.95	172.33	193.51	**15:00**	141.75	305.00	342.50
10:18	78.30	174.61	196.08	**15:06**	143.10	308.05	345.93
10:24	79.65	176.90	198.65	**15:12**	144.45	311.10	349.35
10:30	81.00	179.19	201.22	**15:18**	145.80	314.15	352.78
10:36	82.35	181.48	203.79	**15:24**	147.15	317.20	356.20
10:42	83.70	183.76	206.36	**15:30**	148.50	320.25	359.63
10:48	85.05	186.05	208.93	**15:36**	149.85	323.30	363.05
10:54	86.40	188.34	211.49	**15:42**	151.20	326.35	366.48
11:00	87.75	190.63	214.06	**15:48**	152.55	329.40	369.90
11:06	89.10	192.91	216.63	**15:54**	153.90	332.45	373.33
11:12	90.45	195.20	219.20	**16:00**	155.25	335.50	376.75
11:18	91.80	197.49	221.77	**16:06**	209.25*	457.50	513.75
11:24	93.15	199.78	224.34	**18:06**	317.25*	701.50	787.75
11:30	94.50	202.06	226.91	**20:06**	425.25*	945.50	1061.75
11:36	95.85	204.35	229.48				
11:42	97.20	206.64	232.04				
11:48	98.55	208.93	234.61				
11:54	99.90	211.21	237.18				
12:00	101.25	213.50	239.75				
12:06	102.60	216.55	243.18				
12:12	103.95	219.60	246.60				
12:18	105.30	222.65	250.03				
12:24	106.65	225.70	253.45				
12:30	108.00	228.75	256.88				
12:36	109.35	231.80	260.30				
12:42	110.70	234.85	263.73				

* It is a VIOLATION of California State Labor Law for Non-Union extra performers to work in excess of 16 hours. This 16 hours INCLUDES meal breaks and is exactly 16 hours from your call time. If a production chooses to break the law by insisting you work beyond 16 hours, you may want to bring this to the Labor Commissioner's attention.

Call 213-620-6330 for information on filing a claim. The asterisk(*) reflects rates that were *once* the INDUSTRY STANDARD "Golden Time" provision for Non-Union performers. This INDUSTRY STANDARD was an unwritten understanding that Non-Union performers who work beyond the 16th hour should be compensated as their SAG counterparts would be compensated. BUT as the law reads it is still ILLEGAL for Non-Union actors to work more than 16 hours.

commercial paychart

• UNLIMITED USE •

HOURS	Weekday: $291.80/8	Weekend/Holiday: $583.60/8
0-8	291.80	583.60
8:06	346.51	638.31
9:06	401.23	693.03
10:06	474.18	765.98
11:06	547.13	838.93
12:06	620.08	911.88
13:06	693.03	984.83
14:06	765.98	1057.78
15:06	838.93	1130.73
16:06	1130.73	1422.53
17:06	1422.53	1714.33
18:06	1714.33	2006.13

• 13-WEEK USE •

HOURS	Weekday: $169.40/8	Weekend/Holiday: $338.80/8
0-8	169.40	338.80
8:06	201.16	370.56
9:06	232.93	402.33
10:06	275.28	444.68
11:06	317.63	487.03
12:06	359.98	529.38
13:06	402.33	571.73
14:06	444.68	614.08
15:06	487.03	656.43
16:06	618.57	778.20
17:06	778.20	937.83
18:06	937.83	1097.46

• OVERVIEW OF THE COMMERCIAL CONTRACT •

The first 40 background performers hired on commercials must be hired under the SAG contract. See Act 6 for more info on the commercial contract! ,

• Adjustments (These $$ amounts go on your BASE RATE):

Wet, Snow, Smoke & Dust =	$40
Body Make-up/Oil, Skull Cap =	$31.40

• Bumps (Additional pay, not on BASE RATE):

Auto, Trailer, Motorcycle =	$36.05
Mileage =	$0.315/mile
Skates, Skateboard =	$9.05
Bicycle =	$12.05
Moped =	$18.05
Regular Wardrobe =	$17.20
Evening, Pre-1950's, Uniform =	$28.65

important numbers

Academy of Motion Picture Arts & Sciences	310-247-3000
Academy of Television Arts & Sciences	818-754-2800
Academy Players Directory	310-247-3058
Actors Equity Association	323-634-1750
Actors Equity Association Hotline	323-634-1776
Actors Fund of America	323-933-9244
The Actors Work Program	323-939-1801
AFI (American Film Institute)	323-856-7600
AFTRA Casting Line Los Angeles	323-634-8263
AFTRA Health & Retirement Fund	323-937-3631
AFTRA Office Los Angeles	323-634-8100
AFTRA Sexual Harassment Hotline	323-634-8132
AFTRA Showcase Hotline L.A.	323-634-8262
Alliance of Motion Picture & Television Producers	818-995-3600
American Assoc. of Composers, Authors & Publishers	323-883-1000
American Federation of Musicians	213-251-4510
American Guild of Variety Artists (AGVA)	818-508-9984
American Humane Association	818-501-0123
American Screenwriting Association	866-265-9091
Association of Talent Agents	310-274-0628
Back Stage West (Editorial)	323-525-2356
Better Business Bureau	909-825-7280
Breakdown Services	310-276-9166
CFI Film Preservation	818-260-3841
California Film Commission	323-860-2960
Career Transition for Dancers	323-549-6660
Casting Society of America (CSA)	323-463-1925
Commercial Casting Director Association	818-782-9900
Department of Consumer Affairs	800-952-5210
Department of Industrial Relations	415-703-5070
Directors Guild of America (DGA)	310-289-2000
Division of Labor Standards Enforcement	213-620-6330
Entertainment Industry Foundation	818-760-7722
Filmmakers Alliance	213-228-1152
HOLLYWOOD OS®	310-289-9400
Hollywood Reporter	323-525-2000

important numbers

IATSE (West Coast Office)	818-980-3499
International Stunt Association	323-874-3174
L.A. City Attorney's Office Consumer Prot.	213-974-1452
L.A. County Dept. Consumer Affairs	213-974-1452
Las Vegas Motion Picture Hotline	702-486-2727
Los Angeles Public Library	213-228-7000
Motion Picture Association of America	818-995-6600
Motion Picture and TV Fund	800-876-8320
Multicultural Motion Picture Association	310-358-8300
Museum of Television and Radio	310-786-1000
Performers Guild Alliance of MP & TV Producers	818-995-3600
Producers Guild of America (PGA)	310-358-9020
Publicists Guild	323-876-0160
Recording Musicians Association	323-462-4762
SAG/AFTRA Hotline San Francisco	415-433-6266
SAG/AFTRA Credit Union – Studio City	818-509-3690
SAG/AFTRA Credit Union – Hollywood	323-461-3041
SAG Agent Seminars: Information Line	323-549-6745
SAG Conservatory	323-856-7736
SAG Ethnic Performers Directory	323-549-6644
SAG Film Society	323-549-6657
SAG Foundation	323-549-6708
SAG Global Rule One Hotline	323-549-6650
SAG Info Cast Hotline L.A.	323-937-3441
SAG Office Los Angeles	323-954-1600
SAG Residuals Office	800-205-7716
San Francisco Film Commission	415-554-4004
Scriptwriters Network	323-848-9477
Society of Composers & Lyricists	310-281-2812
Stuntman's Association	818-766-4334
Talent Managers Association	310-205-8495
Theatre Authority West	323-462-5761
Variety	323-857-6600
Women In Film	310-657-5144
Writers Guild of America West (WGA)	323-951-4000

joblines & hotlines

ABC-7 TV	818-863-7562
Capitol Records Job Posting Hotline	323-871-5763
Disney Studios Jobs line	818-558-2222
Disneyland Resort Jobline	714-781-1600
Dreamworks Job Hotline	818-695-5000
Dreamworks Animation Job Hotline	818-695-7252
E! Entertainment TV Internship Hotline	323-954-2710
E! Entertainment TV Jobline	323-954-2666
E! Style Network	323-954-2666
FOX 11 KTTV	310-584-2280
ICM Job Hotline	310-550-4000 ext. 3131
KCET (PBS)	323-953-5236
KFMB (CBS) San Diego	858-495-8640
KGTV's Jobline in San Diego	858-237-6250
KNBC (NBC) Los Angeles	818-840-4397
Knotts Berry Farm	714-995-6688
KTLA Job Line	323-460-5500
KMEX-TV	310-348-3590
Legoland Job Hotline	760-918-5454
MTV Job Line	310-752-8008
NBC Job Hotline	818-840-4397
New Line Cinema Job Hotline	310-967-6553
Nickelodeon Job Line	310-752-8008
Paramount Studios Jobline	323-956-5216
San Diego Wild Animal Park	760-738-5006
Sony/Columbia/Tristar Job Hotline	310-244-4436
Spelling Entertainment Job Hotline	323-634-3700
Time Warner Communications/Cablevision	818-998-2238
Turner Broadcasting Job Line	310-788-4255
Universal Studios Job Line	818-777-5627
UPN Job Line	310-584-2280
VH-1 Job Line	310-752-8008
Warner Bros. Job Hotline	818-954-5400

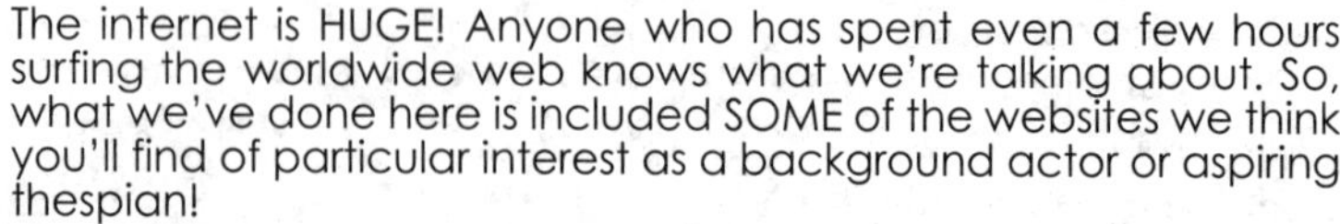

rad internet links

The internet is HUGE! Anyone who has spent even a few hours surfing the worldwide web knows what we're talking about. So, what we've done here is included SOME of the websites we think you'll find of particular interest as a background actor or aspiring thespian!

PLEASE NOTE: the official website addresses for those extras casting agencies or services which maintain websites are included in their listings in the appropriate chapter. Happy surfing!

www.HollywoodOS.com
This, of course, is our rad website!

www.sag.org
Um... the SAG home page.

www.aftra.org
AFTRA's home page. Follow links to the local chapter of your choice.

www.imdb.com
The ultimate resource for movie info on just about anyone in the biz, as well as cool trivia, etc.

www.eidc.com
AKA Entertainment Industry Development Corporation. Different links on this site can sometimes tell you what is shooting in and around L.A. and where.

www.ftc.gov
Got Scammed? Yeah, this is the Federal Trade Commission, a devoted consumer advocate!

www.bbb.org
File a complaint online with the Better Business Bureau.

www.dir.ca.gov/t8/11120.html
The Industrial Welfare Commission/Industry and Occupation Orders for the Motion Picture Industry.

www.dir.ca.gov/databases/dlselr/Talag.html
The Division of Labor Standards Enforcement talent agency license database. Check them out and make sure they're legit!

rad internet links

www.actorsfund.org
This site is for anyone in entertainment – in front of the camera or behind the scenes – coast to coast!

www.unclaimedcoogan.org
Administered by the fine folks at The Actor's Fund, this site lists the unclaimed wages of child performers.

www.producersguild.org
You guessed it, you clever Brain Surgeon, you! It's the Producers Guild's website filled with fun facts!

www.castingsociety.com
The *Casting Society of America* website is full of info about the casting industry and how it works!

www.wif.org
The "Women In Film" website promotes, nurtures, and mentors women in the industry through valuable industry contacts.

www.hollywoodu.com
Short for Hollywood University, it's really the website for the Hollywood Film Institute, not a university, but it's pretty cool, nonetheless!

www.hollywoodreporter.com
Latest breaking Hollywood news from a leading industry resource!

www.backstage.com
The online version of the popular weekly newspaper.

www.variety.com
Looking for more of the lowdown in movieland? Check out *Daily Variety* online!

www.playersdirectory.com
Check out parts of the *Academy Players Directory* right online.

www.hcdonline.com
These folks at the *Hollywood Creative Directory* have lots of great, useful info. But the books can cost a bundle. Look online and see what info you can gather for FREE!

rad internet links

www.minorcon.org
This children's advocacy group founded by a former child actor looks after the rights of kids working in the entertainment industry. Parents with kids interested in the biz should definitely check this out!

www.mpaa.org
This is the homepage for the *Motion Picture Association of America.*

www.emmys.tv
Want to learn all about the awards show circuit? This is for you!

www.moviefone.com
Get showtimes, and tickets right on the web!

www.hollywood.com
Check out movie times and download movie trailers and other cool stuff!

www.hsx.com
The *Hollywood Stock Exchange* lets you have some fun with the stars by trading and selling celebrities like they're stock!

www.boxofficeguru.com
Just for fun. Lists film grosses, opening weekend stats and more!

www.cinematter.com
Read movie reviews that you and your peers write and not those stuck-up film snob critics!

www.thefutoncritic.com
They style themselves as "the web's best television resource." And with the vast amount of up-to-the-minute info they post, they just might be right!

www.umds.us
Cool discounts for Union members on all sorts of different stuff. Google-search "union discounts" for even more sites.

http://cityguide.aol.com/losangeles/hollywood
Where and when do all your most favorite TV shows tape? Believe it or not, America Online knows! Just click on the link for TV Tapings. It's a doozy to type in, but the information is pretty good - especially if you have relatives from out of town coming in and they want to see some live tapings!

payroll companies

AXIUM PAYROLL
5800 Wilshire Blvd.
Los Angeles, CA 90036
PHONE: (866) 295-3954
WEB: www.axium.com

BTL PAYROLL
100 E. Tujunga Ave., 2nd Floor
Burbank, CA 91502
PHONE: (818) 848-1562
FAX: (818) 848-9484

CAPS/UPS
666 Dundee Road, Suite 1502
Northbrook, IL 60062
PHONE: (847) 480-7366

CAST & CREW ENT. SERVICES
100 E. Tujunga Ave., 2nd Floor
Burbank, CA 91502
PHONE: (818) 848-6022
FAX: (818) 848-9556
WEB: www.castandcrew.com

ENTERTAINMENT PARTNERS
2835 N. Naomi St.
Burbank, CA 91504
PHONE: (818) 955-6000
FAX: (818) 845-6507
WEB: www.entertainmentpartners.com

FILM AUDITORS
849 N. Occidental Blvd.
Los Angeles, CA 90026
PHONE: (213) 413-0033
FAX: (213) 413-0088
WEB: www.filmauditors.com

FILM PAYMENT SERVICES/ MEDIA SERVICES
500 S. Sepulveda Blvd., Fourth Fl.
Los Angeles, CA 90049
PHONE: (310) 440-9600
FAX: (310) 472-9979
WEB: www.media-services.com

MACC PAYROLL
P.O. Box 1979
Burbank, CA 91507
PHONE: (866) 840-5497

NETPAY, INC.
12881 Knott St., Suite 206
Garden Grove, CA 92841
PHONE: (714) 379-6891
FAX: (714) 379-6890
WEB: www.netpayinc.com

THE PAYROLL FACTORY, INC.
1426 Aviation Blvd., Suite 103
Redondo Beach, CA 90278
PHONE: (310) 376-5577
FAX: (310) 379-8539

PES PAYROLL
4000 W. Burbank Blvd.
Burbank, CA 91505
PHONE: (818) 729-0080
FAX: (818) 295-3886
WEB: www.pespayroll.com

PRIME CASTING & PAYROLL
6430 Sunset Blvd., Suite 425
Hollywood, CA 90028
PHONE: (323) 962-0573
WEB: www.primecasting.com

SESSIONS PAYROLL MANAGEMENT, INC.
303 N. Glenoaks Blvd., Suite 810
Burbank, CA 91502
PHONE: (818) 841-5202
FAX: (818) 841-9112
WEB: www.sessionspayroll.com

TALENT PARTNERS
101 S. First St., Suite 302
Burbank, CA 91502
PHONE: 818-556-4700
WEB: www.talpar.com

studio addresses

ABC TV NETWORK
4151 Prospect Ave.
Hollywood, CA 90027
PHONE: 818-460-7477
WEB: www.abc.com

ACME STAGE
7404 Fulton Ave., #3
North Hollywood, CA 91605
PHONE: 818-765-2484

ATWATER VILLAGE STUDIOS
3018 Carmel St.
Atwater Village, CA 90065
PHONE: 818-546-2289

AVALON
6918 Tujunga Avenue
North Hollywood, CA 91605
PHONE: 818-508-5050

AXEL STAGES
3050 Lima St.
Burbank, CA 91504
PHONE: 818-556-6182

BARKER HANGAR
3021 Airport Avenue
Santa Monica, CA 90405
PHONE: 310-390-9071
WEB: www.barkerhangar.com

BARWICK INDEPENDENT STUDIO
4585 Electronics Place
Los Angeles, CA 90039
PHONE: 818-543-1828
WEB: www.barwickstudios.com

BEATRICE STUDIOS
12636 Beatrice Street
Los Angeles, CA 90066

BEN KITAY STUDIO
1015 N. Cahuenga Blvd.
Hollywood, CA 90038
PHONE: 323-466-9015
WEB: www.benkitay.com

BOYINGTON FILM PRODS.
5907 W. Pico Blvd.
Los Angeles, CA 90035
PHONE: 323-933-7500

BRUCE AUSTIN STAGE
727 N. Victory Blvd.
Burbank, CA 91502
PHONE: 818-842-0820
WEB: www.bapi.com

CBS STUDIO CENTER
4024 Radford Avenue
Studio City, CA 91604
PARKING TIP: Enter on Colfax, Gate C north of Ventura Blvd.

CBS TELEVISION CITY
7800 Beverly Blvd.
Los Angeles, CA 90036
PHONE: 323-575-2345

CENTINELA STUDIOS
321 Hampton Dr.
Venice, CA 90291
PHONE: 310-396-3688

CENTURY STUDIO CORP.
8660 Hayden Place, Suite 100
Culver City, CA 90232
PHONE: 310-287-3600
or 310-287-3601
FAX: 310-287-3608
WEB: www.centurystudio.com

CHANDLER TOLUCA LAKE STUDIOS
11405 Chandler Blvd.
North Hollywood, CA 91601-2617
PHONE: 818-763-3650

CHANDLER VALLEY CENTER STUDIOS
13927 Saticoy St.
Van Nuys, CA 91402
PHONE: 818-763-3650
WEB: www.valleystudios.com

studio addresses

CHAPLIN STAGES
1416 N. La Brea Ave.
Los Angeles, CA 90028
PHONE: 323-856-2682

CHELSEA STUDIOS, INC.
451 N. La Cienega Blvd.
Los Angeles, CA 90048
PHONE: 310-492-6500
FAX: 310-492-6499
WEB: www.chelseastudios.com

THE COMPLEX
2323 Corinth Ave.
West Los Angeles, CA 90064
PHONE: 310-477-1938

CULVER STUDIOS
9336 W. Washington Blvd.
Culver City, CA 90232
PHONE: 310-202-1234
WEB: www.theculverstudios.com

DELFINO STAGES
12501 Gladstone Ave.
Sylmar, CA 91342
PHONE: 818-361-2421
WEB: www.delfinostudios.com

DISNEY'S GOLDEN OAK RANCH
19802 Placerita Canyon Rd.
Newhall, CA 91321
PHONE: 661-259-8717
or 818-560-5298
WEB: www.goldenoakranch.com

DOS CARLOS (DC) STAGES
1360 E. Sixth St.
Los Angeles, CA 90021
PHONE: 213-627-7635

EDGEWOOD STAGES
1150 S. La Brea Avenue
Los Angeles, CA 90019
PHONE: 323-938-4762

EMPIRE STUDIOS
1845 Empire Ave.
Burbank, CA 91504
PHONE: 818-840-1400

eOFFICESUITES, INC.
13101 Washington Blvd., Suite 100
Los Angeles, CA 90066
PHONE: 310-566-7000
FAX: 310-566-7400
WEB: www.eofficesuites.com

FOX CABLE SPORTS WEST
10000 Santa Monica Blvd.
Los Angeles, CA 90067
PHONE: 310-286-3800
WEB: www.fxnetworks.com

FOX TELEVISION CENTER
5746 W. Sunset Blvd.
Hollywood, CA 90028
PHONE: 310-856-1000
PARKING TIP: Limited street parking - if approved by security, lot parking enter on Wilton Pl.

GLAXA STUDIO I
246 S. Spring St.
Los Angeles, CA 90013
PHONE: 323-663-5295

GLAXA STUDIO II
3707 Sunset Blvd.
Los Angeles, CA 90026
PHONE: 323-663-5295

GLENDALE STUDIOS
1239 S. Glendale Ave.
Glendale, CA 91205
PHONE: 818-550-6000
WEB: www.glendalestudios.com
PARKING TIP: Limited parking behind the studio or street parking.

studio addresses

GMT STUDIOS
5751 Buckingham Parkway
Culver City, CA 90230
PHONE: 310-649-3733
WEB: www.gmtstudios.com

GOSCH PRODUCTIONS
2227 W. Olive Avenue
Burbank, CA 91506
PHONE: 818-729-0000
WEB: www.goschproductions.com

HOLLYWOOD CENTER STUDIOS
1040 N. Las Palmas Ave.
Hollywood, CA 90038
PHONE: 323-860-0000
FAX: 323-860-8105
WEB: www.hollywoodcenter.com
PARKING TIP: Lots A and B at Santa Monica/ Seward or street parking

HOLLYWOOD PROD. CENTER
1149 N. Gower St.
Los Angeles, CA 90038
PHONE: 323-785-2100
WEB: www.hollywoodpc.com

HOLLYWOOD STAGE
6650 Santa Monica Blvd.
Hollywood, CA 90038
PHONE: 323-466-4393

HYPERION STAGE
2012 Hyperion Ave.
Los Angeles, CA 90027
PHONE: 323-665-9983

HANGAR 9 STUDIOS
2828 Donald Douglas Loop North
Santa Monica, CA 90405
PHONE: 310-392-5084

HAVENHURST STUDIOS
7021 Havenhurst Ave.
Van Nuys, CA 91406
PHONE: 818-909-6999

ICN PRODUCTIONS
12401 W. Olympic Blvd.
West Los Angeles, CA 90064
PHONE: 310-442-2371

INTERVIDEO
1500 W. Burbank Blvd.
Burbank, CA 91506
PHONE: 800-843-3626

KCAL TV
6121 Sunset Blvd.
Los Angeles, CA 90028
PHONE: 323-467-9999
WEB: www.kcal.com

KCBS
(Local CBS, Channel 2)
6121 Sunset Blvd.
Hollywood, CA 90028
PHONE: 323-460 3000
WEB: www.cbs2.com

KCET
4401 Sunset Blvd.
Los Angeles, CA 90027
PHONE: 323-666-6500

KCOP
(Local Channel 13)
1999 S. Bundy Drive
Los Angeles, CA 90025
PHONE: 310-584-2000
WEB: www.upn13.com

KTLA
5800 Sunset Blvd.
Hollywood, CA 90028
PHONE: 323-460-5500
WEB: www.ktla.trb.com

KTTV
(Local Channel 11)
1999 S. Bundy Drive
Los Angeles, CA 90025
PHONE: 310-584-2000
WEB: www.fox11la.com

studio addresses

LOS ANGELES CENTER STUDIOS
1201 W. 5th Street
Los Angeles, CA 90017
PHONE: 213-534-3000
WEB: www.lacenterstudios.com

LACY STREET PROD. CENTER
2630 Lacy St.
Los Angeles, CA 90031
PHONE: 323-222-8872
WEB: www.lacystreet.com

LINDSEY STUDIOS
25241 Avenue Stanford
Valencia, CA 91355
PHONE: 661-257-9292
PARKING TIP: Street parking only. There are posted limitations.

LINE 204 STUDIOS
1034 N. Seward St.
Hollywood, CA 90038
PHONE: 323-960-0113
WEB: www.line204.com

THE LOT
1041 N. Formosa Ave.
West Hollywood, CA 90046
PHONE: 323-850-3180
WEB: www.skyepartners.com

MACK SENNETT STAGE
1215 Bates Ave.
Los Angeles, CA 90029
PHONE: 323-660-8466

MGM
2500 Broadway Street
Santa Monica, CA 90404
PHONE: 310-449-3000
WEB: www.mgm.com

MEDIA CITY PROD. CENTER
2525 N. Naomi St.
Burbank, CA 91506
PHONE: 818-848-5800
WEB: www.mediacitystudios.com

NBC BURBANK
(KNBC Burbank Studios Channel 4)
3000 W. Alameda Ave.
Burbank, CA 91523
PHONE: 818-840-4444
WEB: www.nbc4.tv
PARKING TIP: Limited lot parking off Bob Hope Drive or street parking

NEW DEAL STUDIOS
4105 Redwood Ave.
Los Angeles, CA 90066
PHONE: 310-578-9929

NORWOOD STAGE
9023 Washington Blvd.
Culver City, CA 90232
PHONE: 310-204-3323

OCCIDENTAL STUDIOS
201 N. Occidental Blvd.
Hollywood, CA 90026
PHONE: 213-384-3331

OCEANSIDE STUDIOS
3350 Ocean Park Blvd., #100
Santa Monica, CA 90405
PHONE: 310-399-7704

PALADIN STAGE
1001 N. Poinsettia Pl.
Los Angeles, CA 90046
PHONE: 323-851-8222

PANAVISION STAGES
6219 DeSoto Ave.
Woodland Hills, CA 91367
PHONE: 818-316-1000
WEB: www.panavision.com

PARAMOUNT PICTURES
5555 Melrose Ave.
Los Angeles, CA 90038
PHONE: 323-956-5000
WEB: www.paramountpictures.com
PARKING TIP: Street parking or pay to park structures on Melrose or lot on Van Ness.

studio addresses

PARAMOUNT RANCH LOCATIONS
8800 Grimes Canyon Rd.
Moorpark, CA 93021
PHONE: 805-530-1967
FAX: 805-531-0436
WEB: www.movielocations.com

PASADENA PROD. STUDIOS
39 E. Walnut Street
Pasadena, CA 91103
PHONE: 626-584-4090
FAX: 626-584-4099

PKE STUDIO
8621 Hayden Place
Culver City, CA 90232
PHONE: 310-838-7000

POST GROUP
6335 Homewood Ave.
Hollywood, CA 90028
PHONE: 323-462-2300
WEB: www.postgroup.com

PRO CAM
140 East Tujunga Blvd.
Burbank, CA 91502
PHONE: 818-954-9300

PRODUCTION GROUP
1330 N. Vine St.
Hollywood, CA 90028
PHONE: 323-469-8111
WEB: www.production-group.com

PRODUCTION SPACE
6427 Sunset Blvd.
Hollywood, CA 90028
PHONE: 323-469-2195
FAX: 323-962-8028
WEB: www.productionspace.net

QUIXOTE STUDIO
1011 N. Fuller Ave.
West Hollywood, CA 90046
PHONE: 323-851-5030
WEB: www.quixotestudios.com

RALEIGH STUDIOS
5300 Melrose Ave.
Hollywood, CA 90038
PHONE: 323-466-3111
WEB: www.raleighstudios.com
PARKING TIP: Street parking or park in the structures on Van Ness and Melrose

RALEIGH STUDIOS MANHATTAN BEACH
1600 Rosecrans Ave.
Manhattan Beach, CA 90266
WEB: www.raleighstudios.com

RAY-ART STUDIOS
6625 Variel Ave.
Canoga Park, CA 91303
PHONE: 818-887-2400
WEB: www.rayartstudios.com

REN-MAR STUDIOS
846 N. Cahuenga Blvd.
Hollywood, CA 90038
PHONE: 323-463-0808
WEB: www.renmarstudios.com

SAN MAR STUDIOS
861 Seward Street
Hollywood, CA 90038
PHONE: 323-465-8110

SANTA CLARITA STUDIOS
25135 Anza Drive
Valencia, CA 91355
PHONE: 661-294-2000
WEB: www.sc-studios.com
PARKING TIP: Street parking unless permitted to park on top of hill.

SANTA MONICA PROD. SUITES
1513 Sixth Street, Suite 104A
Santa Monica, CA 90401
PHONE: 310-395-4620

SANTA VENTURA STUDIOS
5301 N. Ventura Avenue
Ventura, CA 93001

studio addresses

SHADES OF LIGHT STUDIOS
2980 Ontario Street
Burbank, CA 91504
PHONE: 818-556-6182

SHRINE AUDITORIUM
649 W. Jefferson Blvd.
Los Angeles, CA 90007

SHUTTER STUDIO
1107 N. El Centro Ave.
Hollywood, CA 90038
PHONE: 323-957-1672
WEB: www.bassodesign.com

SMASH BOX STUDIOS
8549 Higuera St.
Culver City, CA 90232
PHONE: 310-558-7660
WEB: www.smashboxstudio.com

SOLAR STUDIOS
1601 S. Central Ave.
Glendale, CA 91204
PHONE: 818-240-1893
WEB. www.solarstudios.com

SONY PICTURE STUDIOS
10202 W. Washington Blvd.
Culver City, CA 90232
PHONE: 310-244-4000
WEB: www.sonypictures.com
PARKING TIP: Parking structure is on Overland & Washington.

SOUTH BAY STUDIOS
20434 S. Sante Fe Ave.
Long Beach, CA 90810
PHONE: 310-762-1360

SOUTH LAKE STAGE
293 S. Lake Street
Burbank, CA 91502
PHONE: 818-953-8400

STUDIO 57
5760 Tujunga Ave.
North Hollywood, CA 91601
PHONE: 818-985-1908

STUDIO WEST
2220 Colorado Ave.
Santa Monica, CA 90404
PHONE: 310-315-4350

SUNSET STAGE
6063 Sunset Blvd.
Hollywood, CA 90028
PHONE: 323-461-6308
WEB: www.sunsetstage.com

SUNSET-GOWER STUDIOS
(NBC-Hollywood)
1438 N. Gower St.
Hollywood, CA 90028
PHONE: 323-467-1001
PARKING TIP: Street parking if pre-approved structure B or lot parking (both located on Gower street)

TEN9FIFTY
10950 Washington Blvd.
Culver City, CA 90232
PHONE: 310-202-2330
WEB: www.skyepartners.com

TWENTIETH CENTURY FOX
10200 Pico Blvd.
Culver City, CA 90067
PHONE: 310-369-1000
WEB: www.fox.com

UNIVERSAL / MCA
100 Universal City Plaza
Universal City, CA 91608
PHONE: 818-777-3000
WEB: www.universalstudios.com
PARKING TIP: Enter from Lakeside Plaza and park in River Road lot or if told, structure 488 enter from Lankershim

VALENCIA STUDIOS
26030 Avenue Hall, Suite 5
Valencia, CA 91355
PHONE: 661-257-8000

studio addresses

VISUALINER STUDIOS
3629 Holdrege Avenue
Los Angeles, CA 90016
PHONE: 310-558-8393
WEB: www.visualinerstudios.com

VPS STUDIOS
800 N. Seward St.
Hollywood, CA 90038
PHONE: 323-469-7244
WEB: www.vpsstudios.com

WALT DISNEY STUDIOS
500 S. Buena Vista St.
Burbank, CA 91505
PHONE: 818-560-1000
WEB: studioservices.go.com
PARKING TIP: Zorro parking structure is off of Riverside Drive

WARNER BROS. BURBANK
4000 Warner Blvd.
Burbank, CA 91522
PHONE: 818-954-2577
WEB: www.wbsf.com
PARKING TIP: Gate 8 on Forest Lawn Drive

WARNER HOLLYWOOD STUDIOS
1041 N. Formosa Ave.
Hollywood, CA 90046
PHONE: 323- 850 2500
WEB: www.wbsf.com
PARKING TIP: Street parking corner of Santa Monica/Formosa

WARNER BROS. RANCH
411 N. Hollywood Way
Burbank, CA 91505
PHONE: 818-954-2577
WEB: www.wbsf.com

WARNER DRIVE WAREHOUSE
8461 Warner Dr.
Culver City, CA 90232
PHONE: 310-841-6572

WEST VALLEY STUDIOS
9260 Topanga Canyon Blvd.
Chatsworth, CA 91311
PHONE: 818-998-2222

WORLD TV PRODUCTIONS
6611 Santa Monica Blvd.
Hollywood, CA 90038
PHONE: 323-469-5638

STUDIO INFORMATION DISCLAIMER:
We have provided studio address and contact information as accurately as possible at press time. Please verify any and all information before trekking across town to get there... people move.

Mapping it out!

On the pages that follow, we have included a few super-exciting studio maps of some of the bigger or better-known studios in and around L.A. just in case you find yourself wandering around one of these suckas when you're working as an extra and you're lost! Plus, you wanna be able to find the commissary, don't ya..?

Maps Included:

- Culver Studios
- Fox Studios
- Paramount
- Raleigh Studios
- Ren-Mar
- Sony Studios
- Sunset-Gower
- Warner Brothers

Some of the information included within the maps on the pages that follow has been derived from one or more of these three sources:

The American Film Industry: A Historical Dictionary, by Anthony Slide. Greenwood Press ©1986

The New Historical Dictionary of The American Film Industry, by Anthony Slide. The Scarecrow Press, Inc. ©1998

International Motion Picture Almanac, Editorial Director Tracey Stevens. Quigley Publishing Company, Inc. ©1999

Dumb Disclaimer (revisited):

We have provided studio addresses and contact information as accurately as possible at press time. Again, please verify any and all information before trekking across town to get there!

. . . culver studios

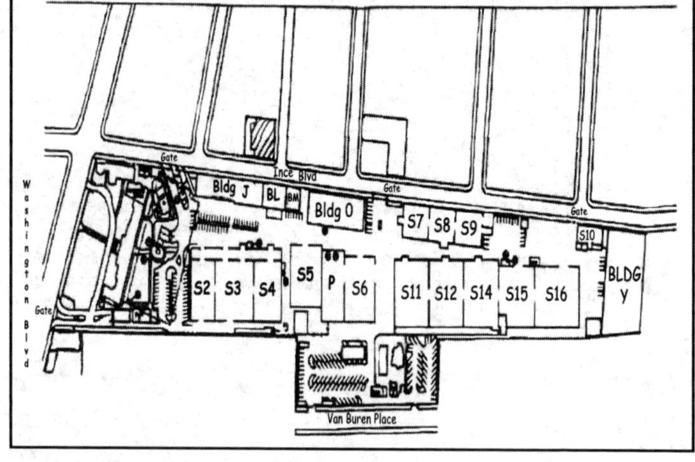

FAMOUS QUOTE: Culver City is known to be "a sleepy little town with a big Hollywood history."

ORIGINAL OWNER: Producer Thomas H. Ince

ORIGINAL NAME: The Laird International Studios

INCORPORATED: 1919

OTHER OWNERS/NAME CHANGES:
(1925) Cecil DeMille took over studios upon Ince's death.
(1928) DeMille tired of the studios and they became Pathe Studios.
(1930) A merger took place & RKO-Pathe Studios was born.
(1935) David O. Selznick leased the studios which became Selznick International Studios. Desilu Productions took over the studios with RKO's demise
(1968) Perfect Film and Chemical bought the studios.
(1969) OSF Industries, Ltd acquired the studios.
(1970) The studios were renamed to Culver City Studios.
(1977) Laird International Studios bought the lot and returned it to its original name.

MORE TIDBITS:
- The colonial style building at the front of the studio was built by Ince and was used as the trademark for Selznick International Pictures.

SIZE & SPACE:
The Culver Studios have 14 stages and 154,638 square feet.

ADDRESS:
9336 W. Washington Blvd.
Culver City, CA 90232-2600

to

...fox studios

point 

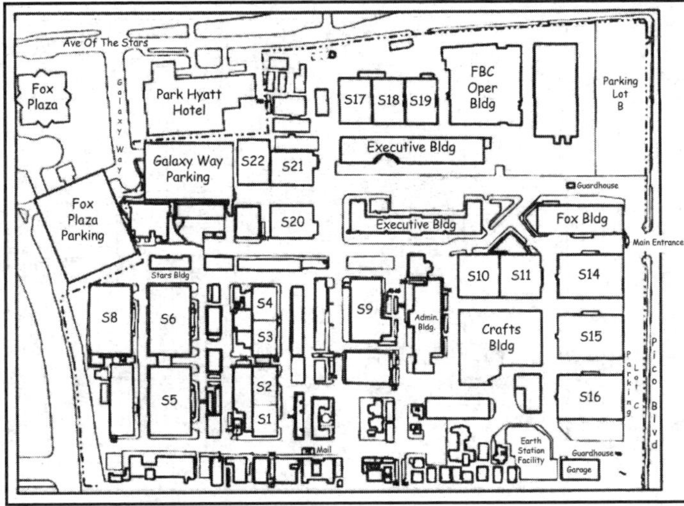

ORIGINAL OWNER: William Fox

ORIGINAL NAME: Fox Film Corporation

INCORPORATED: February 1, 1915

OTHER OWNERS/NAME CHANGES:
(1903) Fox buys his first theatre.
(1904) Begins Greater New York Film Rental Co. to distribute films.
(1913) Fox changes name to Box Office Attractions Film Rental Co.
(1914) First feature is released, "Life's Shop Window."
(1915) Fox Film Corp. founded. Fox leases Selig studio in Edendale.
(1916) Fox gets his own studio at Sunset Blvd. and Western.
(1919) Fox opens offices in Paris, Rome, Berlin, London & Dublin. Fox News is established.
(1925) West Coast Theatres are purchased and the Fox Theatre Corp. begins in November.
(1926) Movietone (a sound-on-film process) is introduced.
(1930) Fox is forced out of the company.
(1935) Fox Film Corporation & Twentieth Century Pictures merge. Twentieth Century-Fox Film Corp. becomes the official name.
(1981) A company owned by Marvin Davis merges with Fox.
(1985) Davis sells the company to Rupert Murdoch's News Corp. Fox, Inc. is formed and now operates Twentieth Century Fox Film Corp., Fox TV Stations, Inc. & Fox Broadcasting Co.
(1989) Fox's filmmaking unit is renamed Fox Film Corporation.

SIZE & SPACE:
Fox has 18 stages and 323,161 square feet.

ADDRESS:
10200 Pico Blvd.
Culver City, CA 90067

...location, location, location...

point 

act ten

to ...paramount ...point b

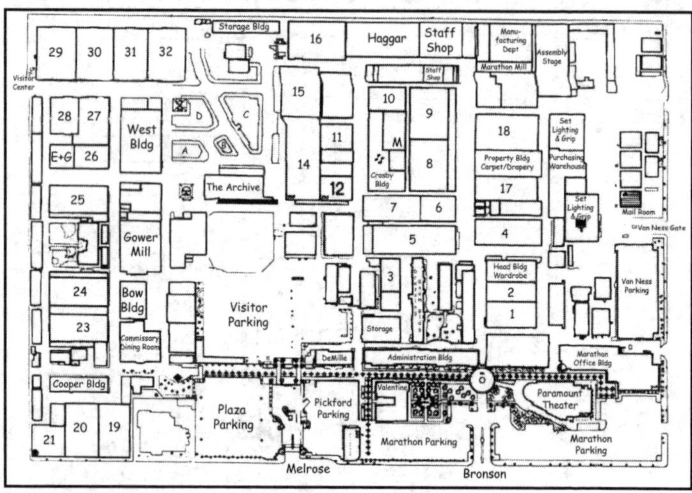

ORIGINAL OWNER: W. W. Hodkinson

ORIGINAL NAME: Paramount Pictures Corporation

INCORPORATED: May 8th, 1914

OTHER OWNERS/NAME CHANGES:

(1912) Paramount's prod. origins begin with Famous Players Film Co.
(1913) In Nov. the Jesse L. Lasky Feature Play Co. is incorporated.
(1914) Paramount is founded as a distribution organization.
(1916) Zukor & Lasky acquire 50% of Paramount's stock. Famous Players-Lasky Corp. is incorporated, but maintains the name Paramount.
(1917) A merger with twelve companies, Artcraft and Paramount integrates production and distribution.
(1919) The lesser Paramount productions are handled by Realart Pictures Corporation.
(1926) Paramount moves from Sunset Blvd. and Vine Street studios to its current location.
(1927) The name is changed to Paramount Famous Lasky Corp.
(1930) Name changed to Paramount Publix Corporation which declared bankruptcy in 1933.
(1935) Company arises from financial setback as Paramount Pics., Inc.
(1949) Paramount splits: Paramount Pictures Corp. handles prod. and dist. while United Paramount Theatres handles theatre operation.
(1958) All rights to Paramount's features from 1929-1949 are sold to MCA.
(1966) Paramount becomes a subsidiary of the Charles Bludhorn conglomerate when acquired by Gulf & Western.
(1989) Another name change to Paramount Communications, Inc. was formed when Gulf & Western decided to focus on publishing and entertainment.
(1997) Company taken over by Viacom, Inc.

SIZE & SPACE:
Paramount has 29 stages and 352,391 square feet.

ADDRESS:
5555 Melrose Avenue
Hollywood, CA 90038

...raleigh studios

to ...point b

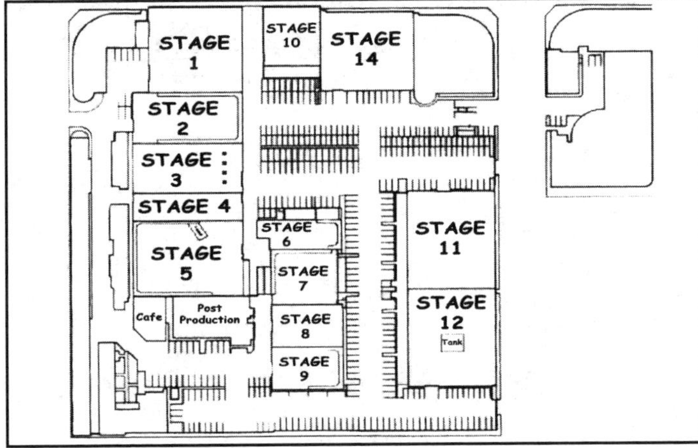

ORIGINAL OWNER: Clune Family

ORIGINAL NAME: Clune Studios

INCORPORATED: 1920's

OTHER OWNERS/NAMES:
(1933-1936) Prudential Studios.
(1934) Harry Sherman leased the studios from the Clune Family and they became known as the California Studios.
(1944) Howard Hughes formed California Pictures Corp. on the lot.
(1946-1948) The studio was renamed to Enterprise Studio when Sherman leased the studios to Enterprise Productions, Inc.
(1961) Producers Studios Incorporated acquired the studio and it was renamed to Producers Studios.
(1980- CURRENT) The studio was purchased by Raleigh Enterprises, Inc., and renamed Raleigh Studios.

MORE TIDBITS:
- Dating back to 1915, Raleigh Studios is one of the oldest Hollywood studios.
- California Studios became the home of many productions in the fifties, namely those of Albert Zugsmith (from 1952), Horizon Productions (1952), Stanley Kramer (from 1955), and the television series "Superman."
- Jack Lemmon, Richard Quine, and American International Pictures all used the studios as a rental lot. Today, Raleigh Studios rent lots to other studios.
- It now manages the Manhattan Beach Studios and is "the area's largest independent studio group in terms of stages."

SIZE & SPACE:
Raleigh Studios has 14 stages and 123,509 square feet.

ADDRESS:
5300 Melrose Ave.
Hollywood, CA 90038

...ren-mar studios

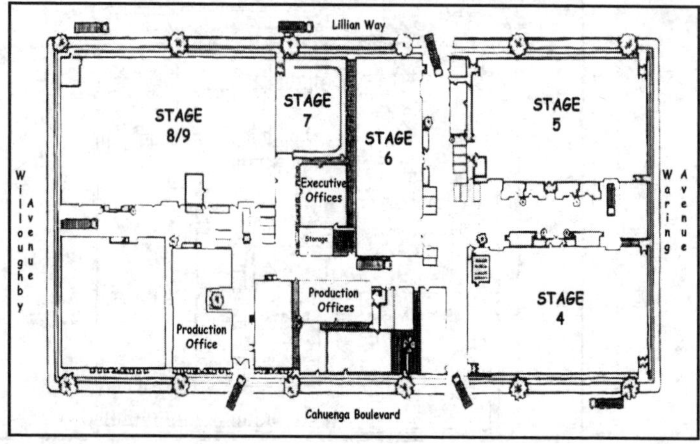

ORIGINAL OWNER: Metro Studios

OTHER OWNERS/NAMES:
Metro merged and became Metro-Goldwyn-Mayer (MGM). 1940's- Known as Motion Pictures.

PRODUCTIONS:
"Seinfeld," "Make Room for Daddy," "Empty Nest," scenes from "Who Shot Roger Rabbit," "Mother," "The Birdcage" and "The Relic."

MORE TIDBITS:
- Ren-Mar served as the headquarters for David E. Kelley Productions until June 1998 when he moved to the Manhattan Beach Studios.
- In present day, Ren-Mar functions as a rental studio. The lots and soundstages are leased to independent filmmakers and other studios for television, commercials and video games.

SIZE & SPACE:
Ren-Mar Studios has 6 stages and 76,298 square feet.

ADDRESS:
846 N. Cahuenga Blvd.
Hollywood, CA 90038

to ...sony studios ...point b

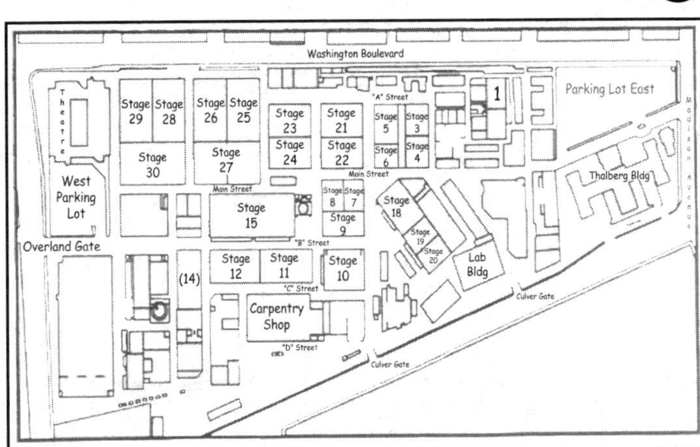

ORIGINAL OWNERS: Harry Cohn, Jack Cohn, & Joe Brandt

ORIGINAL NAME: C.B.C. Film Sales Co.

INCORPORATED: January 10th, 1924

OTHER OWNERS/NAME CHANGES:

(1920) Screen Snapshot (off-screen activities of movie stars) are created.
(1924) C.B.C. becomes Columbia Pictures.
(1926) Columbia now has a studio containing an office building and two stages.
(1929) "The Donovan Affair," their first all-talking feature is released.
(1935) A 40 acre ranch located in Burbank is purchased by Columbia.
(1946) Incorporated as Tokyo Telecommunications Engineering Corporation (TTEC).
(1951) Screen Gems is created for producing television programs.
(1958) TTEC adopts the name Sony.
(1972) Columbia shares the Burbank Studios with Warner Bros.
(1980) Columbia moves to the old MGM lot in Culver City.
(1982) Columbia is purchased by Coca-Cola Co.
(1987) Columbia Pictures Entertainment is formed to reorganize Coca-Cola's entertainment business.
(1989) Sony takes over Columbia.
(1991) Renamed to Sony Pictures Entertainment.

MORE TIDBITS:

- Considered to be a "poverty row" studio, it transformed its image to become a major corporation.
- Columbia's best known director: Frank Capra (1897-1991).
- Major Stars: Grace Moore, Rita Hayworth, Kim Novak, William Holden, Glenn Ford and Judy Holliday.
- Columbia was the first to release a group of youth-oriented features.
- Columbia was the first of any major studio to actively be involved in TV.

SIZE & SPACE:
Sony has 24 stages and 407,074 square feet.

ADDRESS:
10202 W. Washtington Blvd.
Culver City, CA 90232

point a

to ...sunset gower

point 

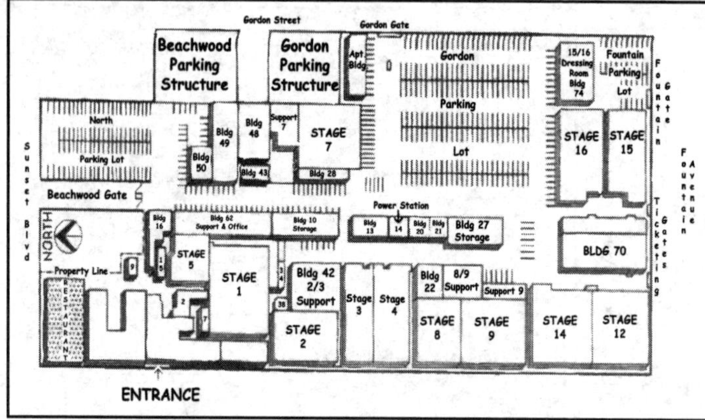

ORIGINAL OWNER: Columbia Pictures Studios

BUILT IN: 1921

OTHER OWNERS/NAME CHANGES:
It wasn't until Columbia was bought by Sony and moved to Culver City that it was renamed Sunset-Gower.

PRODUCTIONS:
"Married with Children," "Fresh Prince of Bel-Air," "Six Feet Under," "Moesha," "The John Larroquette Show" and "City Guys."

MORE TIDBITS:
- Sunset-Gower rents its soundstages for various television and independent film productions.

SIZE & SPACE:
Sunset-Gower has 12 stages and 156,646 square feet.

ADDRESS:
1438 N. Gower St.
Hollywood, CA 90028

a point

to

...warner bros.

point 

...location, location, location...

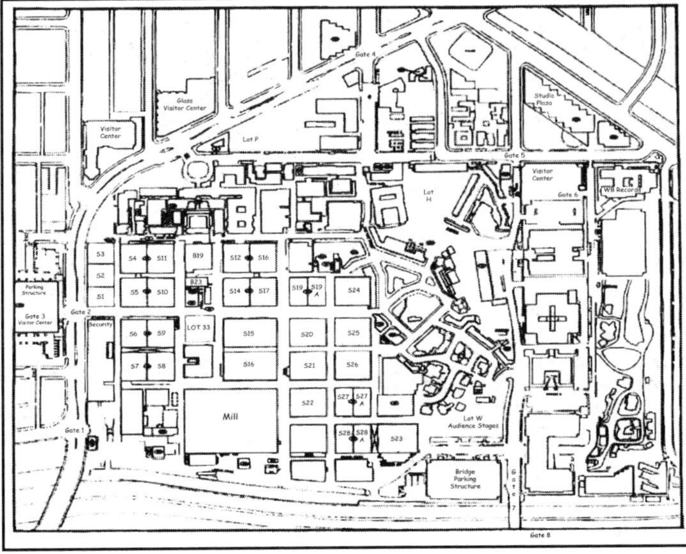

ORIGINAL OWNERS: Harry, Sam, Albert & Jack Warner

ORIGINAL NAME: Warner Bros.

INCORPORATED: 1923

(1905) Warners set up the 90-seat Cascade Theatre in New Castle, PA.
(1907) They branch into distribution and open the Duquesne Amusement Supply Company.
(1909) The company folds.
(1913) The brothers move into film production with Warner Features.
(1925) Warner acquires the Vitagraph, Inc. and experiments with sound.
(1926) First Vitaphone (sound-on-disc process) premieres with synchronized film sound.
(1927) "The Jazz Singer" is released with dialogue and some musical numbers in sound.
(1928) The first 100% all-talking picture, "Lights of New York," is released with box office records. Warner Bros. purchases the First National Pictures and Fox West Coast Theatres and moves to First National Pictures' Burbank studios and back lot containing 135 acres.
(1953) Warner Bros. separates. The theatres are sold to Fabian Enterprises, Inc. which is renamed Stanley Warner Corp. Warner Bros. Pictures remains the production & distribution company.
(1956) Pre-1948 film library sold to United Artists: 850 features, 1,000 shorts.
(1967) All the business and assets of WB Pictures, Inc. is acquired and renamed Warner Bros. - Seven Arts Limited.
(1969) Purchased by Kinney National Service, Inc.
(1971) Company is renamed Warner Communications, Inc. while the studio uses the original name of Warner Bros.
(1989) In a merger, Time, Inc., purchases Warner Communications. Time-Warner now includes Time Publishing, Home Box Office, Cinemax, HBO Video and American Television & Communications Corp.
(1993) Warner Bros. Family Ent. is created for the children's market.

SIZE & SPACE:
Warner Bros. Studios has 24 stages and 369,578 square feet.

ADDRESS:
4000 Burbank Blvd.
Burbank, CA 91522

a point

act ten

Hundreds of years ago. . .

. . . someone may have stood tall as a guard in an ancient Greek Tragedy, or another may have slithered across stage as a begging peasant in a Shakespearan performance. Although these individuals didn't have lines, they played a crucial part in creating the production's believable atmosphere. Then they were called "supernumeraries." Now, on the silver screen, they are referred to as "background artists" or "extras." (21)

With the popularity of silent moving pictures came the need for a few people to stand around and make a room look full or a street look busy. Extras belonged to studio stock companies and were often interchangeable with bit players. In 1918, after WWI, the extra ranks began to grow and grow with war veterans, past stage players and vaudeville performers. They crowded Hollywood with their dreams of movie stardom! (21)

Many people went to agencies and stood at the doors of Casting Directors in hopes of a big break. The CD's eyes would float over the crowd as if he were searching for someone who wasn't there. All he saw were pieces of "human furniture" as he pulled out five or six types who were most likely to fit the background call. Those lucky few automatically relinquished a percentage of that day's pay to the agency. (5 & 24)

Like the many scammers of today, greedy people were everywhere, waiting to empty wallets and create false hopes. Among them were employment agencies, service bureaus and even make-up studios. After they took the money, they would send those aspiring actors to the major studios' open lots, (21) also known as the "bullpens." (4) Many waited for hours hoping for a day of work. Others would head over to another studio, then another. . . all in a 20 mile radius of each other. (25) By noon the bullpens were empty. The day's extras were already selected and would receive cash payment at the end of the day. (4) The others went home, until tomorrow.

A Li'l History Lesson

In the early 1900's, a young John Henaberry stood in the bullpens in the late afternoon and became an extra who was able to work up to bit parts. He recognized that, as an extra, he was "a piece of scenery." As a rule, when he worked as background, he felt that "when anyone's talking, pay them a little attention. Follow the conversation around." Henaberry later became Assistant Director to D.W. Griffith of Griffith Studios and he grew into a top Director. (4)

Although Casting Directors often became familiar with certain people and would call them for work directly, it was much more difficult to find the required number of extras for mob scenes. John Henaberry recounts going down to "skid row," a Los Angeles slum, and picking up drunkards, homeless

people, prostitutes, or those poor people who were just unlucky. The crew would also gather up what they called "IWW's," Industrial Workers of the World. They nicknamed them "I won't works" and "wobblies." Many of these "booze hounds" and "Down-and-outers" just couldn't hold a job or they had physical ailments that made it impossible to work. They'd toss them in wardrobe and then onto the set in a massive crowd. (4)

In the 1916 film *Intolerance*, there were as many as 2,000 extras needed for one day. Henaberry set up costume booths and about 150 people reported to each booth. This was their method of getting everybody ready to film by 8 am. *Intolerance* was also quite a dangerous set where extras were given little or no regard. In one day, as many as 67 people suffered minor injuries when background was dressed as a Persian army, placed on the "walls of Babylon" and armed with real spears and arrows to throw at one another. Well, they did all receive carfare, a 35¢ brown-bagged lunch (which was considered very good) and $1.25 per day. Henaberry also recalled a heartbreaking image of an elderly man passing half his lunch under the studio fence to his starving wife. This was the life of an extra! (4)

Studios saw the corrupt nature of how things were working. They saw the many criminals and hustlers who were among the extra ranks. Some type of structure was needed, so on December 4, 1925, they decided upon one focused background organization to simplify background casting for studios and players. The Association of Motion Picture and Television Producers (AMPTP) contacted the Russell Sage Foundation (a New York research organization).

On January 25, 1926, Mr. Will H. Hays established the Central Casting Corporation and was believed to have cleaned things up. (21) But when bribery and favoritism began showing up, Howard Philbrick was employed to take over. He had been an FBI agent and Head of Californias Motor Vehicle Department and was hired to instill good morals and employ honest, trustworthy Casting Directors. (21)

Central Casting Corporation Takes Flight

First of all, the extra paid no fee. Central's expenses were paid by the studios that utilized it: "Colombia, Samuel Goldwyn, MGM, Paramount, RKO, Pathe, Republic, Hal Roach, Fox, Universal and Warners." (10) Yes, a few of those names are foreign to us today!

So, like the workings of a clock, Central Casting functioned in the following manner: Production assistants notified the casting dept. in terms of what would be needed for background the next day. Studio Casting Directors sent their requirements through "Teletype" to Central. A bell and light went off as the information (including date, time, production, director, clothing/make-up requirement, etc.), was all obtained. Assistant casting directors received the orders, and sat before "call boards" which specified thousands of background not working that day. Each extra had colored dots beside their name to indicate wardrobe. Geez, hard on the eyes if you ask me.

Anyway, if you were unable to work for two or more weeks, you were required to let them know that you are "withdrawing from the labor market." (10) There were four people sitting at switchboards who received as many as 4,000 calls an hour between 4-7 pm. Although these were their busiest times, they were open from 6 am until whenever the day ended.

By early 1940's they were receiving only about 750 calls an hour between 5:30 and 7:30 pm. Central was filling about 250,000 jobs a year. (6) The calls were then transmitted over a loudspeaker. If an assistant CD heard the name of an extra who would be suitable for a job that day, he had no more than 20 seconds to press a button that transferred the call directly to his line. He then relayed the work information to the extra extremely quickly. No time to chat!

Assistant Casting Directors remembered players through photographs, from the required interviews every six months or from checking them in at the studio. They also had a machine called a "Hollerith" (12) which was a type of "mechanical casting director." (5) It sorted through files and selected certain players according to the numbers labeled on their cards. Although this was utilized, CD's relied greatly on their memory and extraordinary ability to immediately associate the name of an extra with the face, wardrobe, attributes, etc.

How The Heck Did They Cast?

All background was separated into four categories; "Atmosphere, Character, Specialized and Dress." Each category had its own phone number and different day's wages. (22) In the late 1940's the phone lines were split between males and females. The files contained everything including physical attributes and abnormalities. They also have alphabetized subcategorizes of talent including "Girls – Sweet Looking," "Strong Men," "Short Men," and "Cigarette and Hat-Check Girls" (25) They were forced to look outside of their office files for specialty calls. When looking for American Indians, Casting Director "Many Treaties" would contact reservations. "Bessie Loo" was called upon for Chinese extras. (25)

When their character "call" board was in operation, and there was no need for extras on a particular day, the phones were answered "NO WORK." Players were encouraged to continue calling in case the phrase changes to "TRY LATER." (25) After all of the extras needed were booked for the following day, the vouchers and call sheets are prepared and messengered over to the studio.

Who Was Working?

Central Casting was bursting with more extras than there were jobs. In an *LA Times* article by Harrison Carroll, dated July 18, 1931, it was discovered that with each application, registrants were given a document to read that explained the "hopeless odds against success." As many as 17,541 men, women and children were registered as extras at Central Casting in 1929. (In 1951, however, when Philbrick died and Art Bronson took over, the great numbers of registered extras decreased to 6,000.) (21) Meanwhile, others longed to join, but there was only an average of 840 extra jobs daily. Many of those jobs were going to non-registered members working in huge mob scenes. Other jobs were going to those with special talents for dancing, singing, etc. The remaining background were those extra veterans requested by studio CD's. Carroll explained that 65 men, out of 6095, worked approximately 3 or more days of work per week. Only 21, out of 10,000 women, averaged the same. He encouraged extras to "back off." But, you see, "the extra is a peculiar hypnotic case. He reads the damning facts and reaches for a pen to sign the application." (23)

What Kind Of Moolah Were They Makin'?

I was lucky enough to discover an N.R.A Motion Picture Code Provisions pamphlet, of Supplemental Rules and Regulations, issued by Central as of November 22, 1934. The pamphlet clearly outlines the four classes of extras and what they would earn. Wardrobe was the key! "You take care of your clothes the way a plumber does his wrenches." (3)

The following is "the Price-Caste System:" (17)

Atmosphere: $5.00 Extras, simply stated created atmosphere. They were mobs, crowds..."Miscellaneous people." They would arrive and be filmed in basic street attire.

Character: $7.50 Extras were better dressed. Besides an ordinary wardrobe, they were expected to own clothing to play a period piece, soldier, sailor, peasant, maid, nurse, etc.

Specialized: $10.00 Extras had to have a good wardrobe. Their clothes were to be "suitable for motion picture purposes." They were required to keep an upscale wardrobe. Suits, coats, "Palm Beach suits," sport clothes...all in light and dark colors. Also, it was noted, that "for this type of work, clothes must be strictly up to date."

Dress: $15.00 Extras had the best wardrobes of all! Full formal dress of a tuxedo, gloves, silk hat and cane, "boulevard complete, riding habit complete" or, for women, gowns (evening differed from dinner) furs, exquisite wraps, etc. were all required. The note in this category was that "this type of work wardrobe must be an 'acceptable modern' wardrobe."

Payment for all extras was cash at, the day's end, or a negotiable check. If overtime was not paid by the day's end, it must be mailed to the extra within 24 hours. Overtime for those working on a weekly basis received payment with their weekly check.

By 1940, mob extras received 50¢ more. Also going up, $7.50 and $15.00 extras each received a dollar more per day.

During these days, stories circulated about how different classes of extras looked upon one another. The "Vine Street Story," which circulated in the early 1940's, told of the shadow of a $5.50 extra passing across the body of a $16.00 extra. The higher paid extra commented to friends that he felt "unclean" for a month. (17)

Yet, in contradiction, when Frank Capra needed 3,000 mob extras for a production, $16.00 extras took the $5.50 work so that Capra would not have to get a waiver and go outside of SAG and Central for extras. He did end up using a waiver, partly because many $8.50 extras felt that they earned their status and were not going to take less, although many were actually starving. They considered it the principle. (17)

Speaking extras were a bit different. Those extras who spoke "Atmospheric words," otherwise known as "omnies" got paid upward of $25 a day. Unfortunately by 1947 it was reduced to $14. (10) That's Hollywood!

Central Changes

In 1961, Central became the employer of the extras, not employees of the studios hiring them. (1) Then in 1976, Central passed into private ownership and was taken over by Production Payment Inc. (PPI) and Paul Roth who was President of Talent and Residuals Inc. (Central Casting is now a private business firm.) By 1977 Central's registration process would begin by going through hundreds of composites, resumés and applications once a week and deciding who they could use. Acceptance or rejection letters were then issued.

Other casting companies began to creep into existence. Well, although Central was still the main company for casting extras, a 1959 article in the *Saturday Evening Post* pointed out that "Three smaller casting agencies [had] sprung up to feed the Television and independent movie producers." (21) I believe this was a small beginning in the expansion of extra casting.

One Day In The Life...Sound Familiar?

"Now, folks, you are in a swell European nightclub. You're having a gay time. See? How's to looking like you're enjoying yourselves?" (16) These were the words bellowed by a 1944 Assistant Director, also referred to as the "Sheepherder." (21) Pete Martin, Reporter for the Saturday Evening Post, went undercover in February, 1944, to show the general public what it's like. In his article titled, "Letter from Hollywood: A Day as a Dress Extra," he made mention of extras requesting whether they'd be needed for the next day. If not, they'd run to the phone and try to book the next day's job through Central. Also, after eight hours, extras were automatically paid overtime for two hours, even if they only worked two minutes more. So Martin noticed the "coughing and shuffling of feet" shortly before the eight hours were up...and silence thereafter. (16)

Screen Actors Guild

Before the Screen Extras Guild, most extras joined SAG as Class B members. They were not considered actors and were not given the same voting right as Class A members. There was much controversy as extras felt this was unfair.

SAG, in connection with Central, placed restrictions on how often a person could call in. Extras were calling so frequently that lines were tied up. SAG implemented Guild charges against anyone who called more than once every 15 minutes. (13)

Joining the guild was quite different from today. If you were able to secure a letter from a studio executive that explained that you had a part in a film, you paid a $100 fee and you were in. The fee was $50 in New York. For extra work, you would be asked to appear before a board. They would examine you and decide whether or not they thought you were "employable." (12) If you passed, you paid and that was that.

SAG jurisdiction extended 300 miles from either Hollywood or New York. Past those limits productions could, and often did, hire non-guild members... especially for crowd scenes. They'd run ads stating, "Like to see Yourself in the Movies?" (12)

Screen Extras Guild

SEG was formed in 1945 as a SAG breakaway for extras. It dealt with producers when negotiating background wages and was successful in achieving higher wages. In 1949, a new contract with producers emphasized that only SEG members could be hired unless what was needed for background players wasn't in the guild's lists. Then they were allowed to reach outside the guild. (24) Also, Central felt that all of its registrants should be SEG. Within 30 days of working as a Non-Union extra, you must join SEG.

Merger Time

SEG and SAG talked and talked and attempted a merger in 1982 and again in 1984. After all, New York extras fell under SAG contracts, why couldn't Hollywood work the same? Although SEG members were in favor of the alliance, SAG members were not! In a 1982 article published in the *LA Herald Examiner*, then-SAG-President Ed Asner was pushing for the merger. "It would upgrade the extra to the Actor's Status," he argued. Strong opposition came from Charleton Heston. He feared that the union would bring higher costs and force producers to go outside of the guild's jurisdiction, thereby hiring non-union talent. Well, although the "merger" never happened, SEG was going broke and SAG was considering absorbing the union. By 1988, SEG membership had fallen from 6900 to 3800 in only two years. (20) SEG President Peter Eastman was thrilled at the idea of a take-over. (9) The only thing needed was approval from the Associated Actors and Artists of America. Heston threatened that many actors would leave SAG and "opt for financial core status" which would allow them to cross a SAG picket line. (9) However the take-over went through.

Were Extras/Stand-Ins Appreciated?

Believe it or not, there were awards. In the early 1940's, the Associated Stand-Ins of Hollywood voted for the best stand-in performance of that year and were awarded "Elmer Awards." These were stand-in equivalents to Academy Awards and were awarded the week after Academy Awards were presented. (11) Although extras didn't have this type of award presentation, in September of 1963, Barbara Stanwyck presented "SEG Gold Life Membership cards to veteran extras." (8)

A Future For Extra Performers

Background work has dramatically changed with the times. In 1939, Central's general manager, Campbell MacCulloch, stated that "extra work has no future." He didn't see it as a beginning, but rather a place where former stars were "finishing their careers." (6)

Now we view "extra work" as a wonderful means of learning about productions. We see the inner-workings of television sitcoms, soap operas, feature films and commercials close-up. Working as an extra not only allows us to watch how each scene comes together... we create the atmosphere and play an important part of the "big picture" (no pun intended).

And Mr. MacCulloch might rethink his words if he knew that stars like Clint Eastwood, Brad Pitt, Burt Reynolds, Bruce Willis, Mary Tyler Moore, Robert Duvall, Sly Stallone, Bill Cosby, Robert Redford, Tom Selleck, Jack Nicholson and Laurence Fishburne (among others) are all rumored to have begun their careers as background actors... but who knows?

1. Association of Motion Picture and Television Producers Release. December 4, 1975
2. "Actors, Extras Protest Proposed Merger of Their Unions" LA Herald Examiner, by Nicole Szulc. 1982
3. "Blah is the Word! It describes a film Extra's Personality" Citizen News, by Virginia McPherson. January 1,1948.
4. Brownlow, Kevin. The Parade's Gone By. New York, Alfred A. Knopf, 1968.
5. Carmody, John M. Los Angeles-A Guide to the City and Its Environs. Hasting House Publishers, 1941.
6. "Central Casting, an Interview with Mr. Campbell MacCulloch, General Manager of Central Casting Corporation" It's Happening in Hollywood, Weekly News of Pictures in Production, March 27,1939
7. "Central Casting Now is Private Business Firm" Variety, June 30,1976
8. "Extras Air Pact Demands at Meet of over 5 Hours" Variety, Sept. 9,1963
9. "Foes Denounce SEG Takeover" by David Robb, Variety, December 11,1989
10. "Hollywood Extras" Look, Feb. 18,1947
11. "Hollywood's Stand-Ins Make Elmer Awards" LA Times, March 11,1944
12. "How to Get Rich in Films" Sunday Evening Post, June 1,1947
13. "Hundreds of Extras Face Guild Charges" Variety, May 18,1944
14. "I am an Extra" LA Times Sunday Magazine by Helen Tensing May 23,1937
15. "Industry Notes - The Break a Leg Business, An Interview with Central Casting" T.G.I.F. Casting News, May 5, 1977
16. "Letter from Hollywood: A Day as a Dress Extra" Saturday Evening Post by Pete Martin Feb. 19,1944
17. "NNW" Citizen News by Morton Thompson Sept. 9, 1940
18. N.R.A. Motion Picture Code Provisions, Issued by Central Casting Corporation, Nov. 22, 1934
19. "Roaming Around" with Austin Conover, Citizen News, July 1,1946
20. "SAG Considers Takeover of SEG" Variety by David Robb, August 30, 1988
21. "So you Want to be a Hollywood Extra" Saturday Evening Post, Jan. 24,1959
22. "System for Film Extras Simplified" Citizen News, May 11, 1944
23. "The World holds no Greater Optimist than the Hollywood Extra" LA Times by Harrison Carroll, July18, 1931
24. "Want to Break in as an Extra? You can if you have 3 Heads" Examiner, Feb. 1,1949
25. "What's Happening in Hollywood" Weekly News of Current Pictures, Trends and Production, Vol. 4, No. 13, Nov. 30, 1946

Works Cited Page!

by Laura Mancini

HOLLYWOOD OS®

how to claim unemployment

What's A Struggling Actor To Do (And Not Do) When Waiting For The Dough To Roll In?

Who can apply for UI (Unemployment Insurance) benefits?
To be entitled to benefits you must be:

- Out of work due to no fault of your own
- Physically able to work
- Actively seeking work
- Ready to accept work

Anyone who meets the above requirements and is unemployed or working part-time can apply for UI benefits by contacting the Employment Development Department (EDD): 1-800-300-5616.

Where do Unemployment (UI) benefits come from?
UI benefits are financed solely from taxes paid by your employers. In reference to actors (principal & background, Union & Non-Union), the unemployment benefits that you may be eligible for have already been funded by your previous employers (those are the exciting payroll companies whose names you find on your vouchers).

How can I qualify for UI benefits?
Most work performed in California or in other states qualifies you for UI benefits. Self-employment does not usually qualify for UI benefits coverage.

How do I file a claim?
Contact EDD 1-800-300-5616 to file a claim.

Be prepared to provide the following:

- Name and social security number
- Address and telephone number
- Date of birth and gender
- Name, address (including ZIP code), telephone number (including area code) of your last employer (this will be the PAYROLL COMPANY that issued your last check – NOT the organization that booked you) regardless of the length of time you worked for the employer.
- Last date worked and the reason you are no longer working (i.e., When it comes to principal or background jobs, the "Job" ended.
- Citizenship status (which may include your alien registration number)

how to claim unemployment

How are UI benefits calculated?
Benefits are calculated using an individual's earnings during a specific twelve month period (this is called a base period). The base period begins approximately 15-17 months prior to the date the claim is filed. The amount paid each week is calculated based on the calendar quarter with the highest earnings during the base period.

Essentially, if you decide to file for Unemployment on Jan 1, 2006, the amount of money you will be eligible for will depend on how much you made between July 1, 2004-June 30, 2005. That will be your qualifying year. The actual dollar amount will then be based on your highest quarter of that year – July-Sept., Oct.-Dec., Jan.-March, April -June. The higher your income during any one period, the higher your benefits will be up to a maximum. Since your base period is determined by the date you file your claim, you should choose the quarter in which you know you were paid the most, then ensure that this quarter will be included in the base period for your filing date. Whoa – you get all that? You may want to read that sucka again.

How much can I receive in benefits after filing a claim?
Weekly benefit amounts range from $40 (minimum) to $450 (maximum) depending on your quarterly earnings. To qualify for the maximum amount each week you must earn at least $11,674.01 in a calendar quarter during the base period (your earnings during a specific twelve-month period).

How long do my UI benefits last?
When you file a claim, it's effective for one year. So you can receive anywhere from 12 to 26 weeks of full benefits. The number of weeks varies based on your total earnings during the base period. Additional benefits may be granted by Congress, or the State Legislature should a period of high unemployment exist. Let's hope it doesn't come to that.

When should I apply for UI benefits?
You should apply for benefits as soon as you are not gainfully employed, or working less than full-time. And as struggling actors/artists/singers/dancers, aren't we all?

When do UI benefits start?
They start with the effective date of the claim, which is the Sunday prior to your filing. There's a one-week, non-paid waiting period. Confusing? Yeah, we know. Sorry.

Am I required to pay taxes on UI benefits?
You bet. You may voluntarily request that EDD withhold 15% of weekly benefits for federal taxation of UI benefits. You must request that taxes be taken out each week or some weeks Uncle Sam won't take out his share, and you'll owe come tax time!

how to claim unemployment

Next item of business. . .
After you've filed your claim you will either be accepted or your claim will be questioned (ouch!) and an "Eligibility Rights Interview" will be scheduled. What's an ELIGIBILITY RIGHTS INTERVIEW, you ask? And what do you need to KNOW/DO/SAY?

The Employment Development Department may attempt to establish that you can and should work in areas other than acting (say it ain't so!). See, they may think you're trying to take an easy out so you can kick back on the couch and watch the soaps or re-runs of *What's Happening!!* rather than functioning as a responsible citizen. Let them know you really ARE an actor, put don't pull a De Niro-esque *Taxi Driver* moment on them. Stay calm and pleasant, and make your case. Unfortunately, just working a day or two every so often isn't going to cut it to convince the skeptics at EDD. So be prepared.

Things to bring that may help your cause:

- Recent paycheck stubs (from acting gigs, folks – not *Carl's Jr.*)
- Receipts from SAG or AFTRA dues and current membership cards
- A detailed record of all auditions you've gone on, etc. (date worked, film or commercial title, Director, Casting Director – any tidbit that shows how truly dedicated you are to your craft).
- Additionally, bring your acting resumé and a headshot along, including training and schooling that shows your commitment to the trade. You might also have your agent or manager write a letter explaining that you are a star on the cusp of greatness (or at least that you've been going on a lot of auditions). You've got to make your case, and such tangible proof as this might very well make the difference of convincing that hard-nosed EDD representative.

For more information. . .
For more specific questions about the intricacies of filing and what your benefits may or may not include or be limited to (gosh, now we sound as confusing as them – yikes!) contact the Employment Development Department directly: 1-800-300-5616.

WEBSITE TIP: You can also gain lots of insight from www.edd.ca.gov

This concludes our super exciting summary of main points. They are simply meant as an overview to be useful to background actors who want to obtain unemployment benefits entitled to them under the laws of our great land! Woo-hoo!

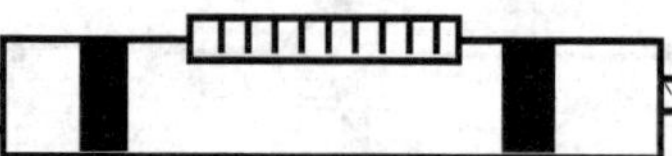

stock free advice

Damn fine advice from a stockbroker guy out of Chicago

by Pete Sutton, Mountain Ash Casting

Uneventful Intro. . .
Now for all my background artist friends who are poor as church mice, who don't have two nickels to rub together, who involuntarily took a vow of poverty. . . my advice to you is, first and foremost, when you get that paycheck, no matter how measly it is, whether you are union or non, 18-to-look-younger, fifty-four, forty or fight. . . the first thing you need to do is:

Pay Yourself!
Okay, this is what I mean. . . take ten percent of that check, that's right, move that decimal point over one place to the left. . . see that amount? That's your fee to yourself that is going to go to your future. Store it in a savings account, then move it over to a money market or a three-month CD, then put it into a Mutual Fund or a DRIP (I'll explain all that later). And the ninety percent that's left over you're going to live on. Why? Because to be honest with you, the chances of you becoming the next 20 million per picture star is a million to one against you, but the chance of you reaching the age of retirement at 65 is a million to one in your favor. And the sooner you start saving and investing the better off you'll be. Want me to prove it? Get out your calculators and I'll show you the Eighth Wonder of the World! For the past 60 years, the S&P 500 has gone up an average of 11% per year, so that means if you went out and bought a no-load mutual fund like Vanguard 500 stock index:

- AT AGE 25, if you invest $117 per month ($3.90 per day) or
- AT AGE 40, if you invest $547 per month ($18.23 per day) or
- AT AGE 50 if you invest $1,650 per month ($55 per day)

You will have a million bucks by the time you reach your 65th birthday. Not bad, eh? Just leave that money alone and look what happens. Now if you can afford to double the amounts you pay yourself each month that's even better. Why? Because if you are twenty-five years old and put away $234 each month into a stock fund, you'll have one million bucks by the time you reach age 48.

Now for a Reality Break. . .
Although the stock market environment can be tricky, there are some opportunities in individual stocks that one can invest in quite cheaply. Most of these, however, are on the web, so you would need to have access to a computer to use them.

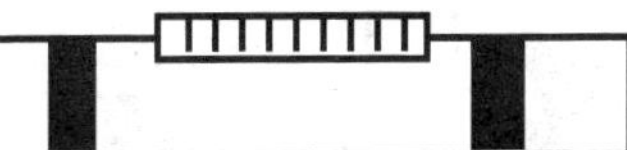

stock free advice

Damn fine advice from a stockbroker guy out of Chicago

Credit Cards & Debt Check...
I would say that before anyone invests in stocks, check out your debt first. I mean, get rid of that credit card debt, car loans and student loans. I mentioned that the stock market goes up an average of 11% per year, but if you are paying off your credit cards and they are charging you 18, 19, 20%, then do the math...pay them off first! That way you are guaranteeing yourself a return of 18, 19, 20%. You need to become rich first; the credit card companies are already rich. With all due respect, there aren't that many millionaires who got that way doing background work. If your income is less than your outgo, we all know the outcome, right? So if you are living off the Credit Cards, then something is wrong. It means that:

1) You need to cut back on expenses. Even a bargain is not a bargain if you cannot afford it.

2) Find additional income elsewhere. Granted, I know how erratic background work can be, but even working one weekend day in an unrelated field can at least help with the gas money.

3) Be honest with yourself. If acting is your passion but the pesos aren't flying in, take a few months away from this dream you have to instead work a steady 9 to 5, 40 hour a week job. It may be mundane, but then you're building up a financial cushion, paying off that credit card and car payment debt methodically so that you don't have to worry as much. Trust me, I know all this from all the phone calls the payroll company gets from people needing their checks the day after they worked on a movie or commercial.

In a perfect world, you will have no debt, have saved up 6 months worth of income to cover expenses, and then slowly, methodically start saving money in an IRA. I'm sure a lot of you right now are saying, "Yeah, right," but let's face it, we live in a fickle business. There is always summer hiatus, always Christmas hiatus. When times are good, don't go and spend the money all at once. Save some for that hiatus, take a second job, do a market research survey, be an election judge, etc.

Whatever you do, keep that income flowing. It's a shame, but I have had a few SAG people turn down one day's work because they figure they will receive more from their unemployment benefits. If only they could try and save money from the busy times to cover the leaner periods, that way they would take the one day of SAG work (which, by the way often turns into a two day call or a three day call, trust me on this), and the unemployment benefits will still be there when they really need it.

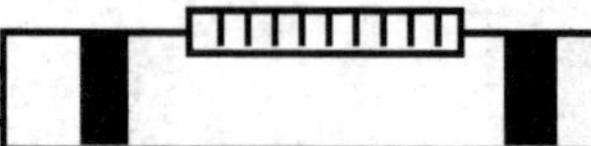

stock free advice

Damn fine advice from a stockbroker guy out of Chicago

Websites to Check Out!

Sharebuilder.com: To open an account, the first year is free, then about 12 bucks per year after that to maintain. If you have, let's say, $25 bucks to invest in GE, then they will buy $25 worth of GE stock for you, minus the $2 fee. That is much better than a broker because a broker will charge you much more, plus, a broker will never let you buy fractional shares.

BuyandHold.com: Similar to Sharebuilder.com, but there is no fee after the first year. However, the transaction fee is $2.99 per trade, so that's the trade off.

DripInvestor.com & NetStockDirect.com: Gives you information on about 1600 stocks in which one can invest in individual stocks directly from the company. However, some of the individual companies have pretty high initial investment requirements (like as much as $1,000, most require an initial investment of $250). In this type of investing you talk with the company's transfer agent (a toll free number) and they send you out a packet of information which you fill out and return with a check. Almost every large company in the universe offers direct investing.

Mutual Funds: My advice is to only invest in no-load mutual funds with low expense ratios. Why? Because with load funds you are basically helping the investment manager make payments on his Porsche. Do some research on these (like go to the library and ask for Morningstar). Off the top of my head, the best no-load mutual funds I can think of are Vanguard, Janus and TIAACREF. Most of these funds require $1000 minimum for IRA's so beware.

Speaking of IRA's...

First try to put investment money into an IRA. Why? Because no matter what your income is (assuming it's below $110,500 per year), the first $2000 you invest is, of course, tax deductible. This means you can't touch it until you reach age 59 1/2. Uncle Sam will not tax you on withdrawals until you reach retirement age, so you save tons of money in income taxes. Roth IRA's work in a different fashion. You put in $2000 per year (or as much as you can afford), you don't take the yearly deduction, and LO & BEHOLD, when you retire, you don't pay any income taxes on it at all!

PETE'S DISCLAIMER:
Use this advice as a guide, since nothing is etched in stone when it comes to stocks. But remember to put yourself first. Put a little money aside. Be resourceful and be patient.

...charting your work

track

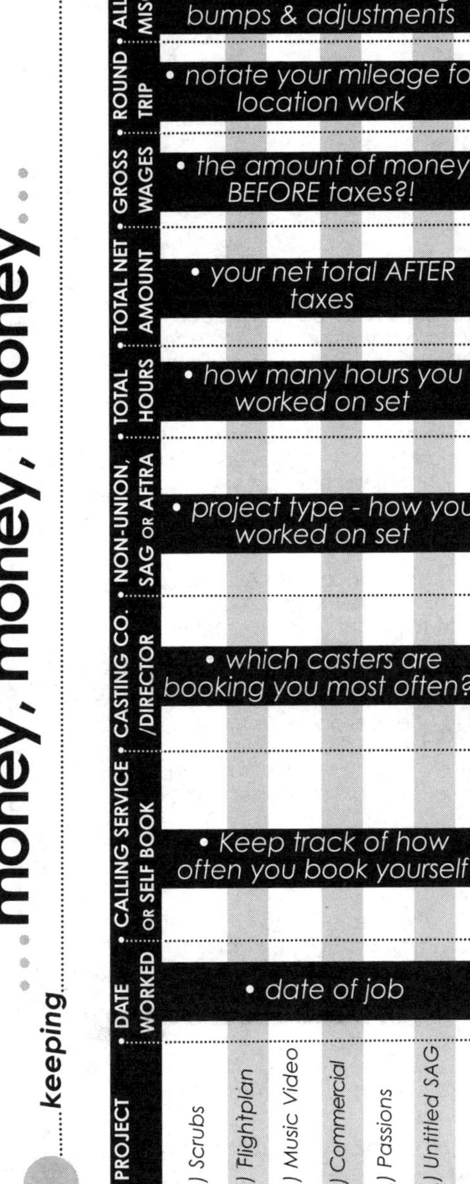

Organize Your Career...

Yep, we know, charts can be a pain in the big toe, but this non-intimidating chart is intended to make your life simple.

This is about money, people, and keeping track of your moolah is important! Get organized! Even if you don't have a sophisticated money tracking program for your computer, or an accounting background, you can re-create a simple chart like this one in minutes. Or buy one from a company such as Holdon Log (www.holdonlog.com).

Extra Benefits...

You can add on other elements like meal penalties or bumps for smoke/wet or take out those options which you don't feel are necessary. However, be sure to keep track of the project, the date worked, and the casting company or CD who cast you in case you are entitled to late payments.

Financial Benefits...

The reward is in your wallet! Accurately recording when and what you work on will keep you aware of your income for budget, as well as those darn taxes for tax season. Cool!

Heath Benefits...

For SAG & AFTRA members, keeping detailed records will also assist in calculating whether or not you will be eligible for the union's health insurance.

taxes suck!

Two words for you, organization and itemization, folks

Brain Surgeon(-ified) Notes

Behold, our compiled non-exciting list of things you should be itemizing and keeping track of.

Remember that taxes are mandatory – you cannot hide from them forever!! The following expenses have been placed in a category so that you may carefully review each section. Hopefully this rough guideline will help you determine whether or not certain deductions apply to you.

Please remember that the government likes to play tricks with us. Because of their sarcasm, just know that the Federal and State tax laws are continually changing, making it virtually impossible to list every darn item that could be considered a deduction in the acting profession.

As a general policy, it is a wise decision to save ALL receipts, with specific, detailed information as to the nature of the expense. If you are claiming entertainment dining expenses, be sure to conduct business during the meal and keep a record of who was there, what was discussed, when the meal took place, etc. Your checkbook and daily planner will come in handy to trace your expenses / deductions. A majority of the deductions listed have been allowed in the past, however, this list is intended as a GENERAL GUIDELINE ONLY. Again, please consult your tax accountant or business manager with your super-specific questions.

AGENCY-RELATED

- Calling Service Fees/Registration Fees/Photo/Computer Imaging Fees/Agency Commissions/Agent, Publicist and Manager Fees/Union or Guild Dues/Fees/Casting Website Fees

PROMOTIONS

- Headshots, photos, postcards, photo reproduction – almost anything publicity-related.
- Resumé design, resumé reproduction, Academy Players Directory – if you are listed.

taxes suck!

Two words for you, organization and itemization, folks...

MONTHLY BILLS

- Telephone, voice mail, pager, cell phone, answering service, internet provider – all of which are partially business-related.

RESEARCH

- Trade papers, subscriptions (**HOLLYWOOD OS**®), plays, books, journals and various other materials – **"EXTRA" WORK for Brain Surgeons**®
- Movies, movie rentals, plays, showcases, comedy clubs.

EXPENSES

- Postage, faxing, photocopying, office supplies and expenses.
- Tapes (video & audio), sheet music, compact discs, laser discs, records, dvds, etc.
- Acting lessons, dramatic coaching, comedy showcases/training, and music training.

PERSONAL BUSINESS ENHANCEMENT

- Make-up, styling/grooming (must be for business only)
- Special clothing purchased for specific roles/parts
- Costumes purchased, alterations, dry cleaning, laundry.

BUSINESS-RELATED

- Auto mileage (gas) to casting offices, meetings, agents, studios, and work.
- Location and tour expenses.
- Airfare and travel.
- Business gifts ($25 limit for each gift and promotion).
- Hotels, lodging, and meals.
- Depreciation of items purchased (computer, answering machine, televisions, VCRs, stereos)

TAX BRACKET TIP

- Do not forget to check and see if you fall into the ***"Qualified Performing Artist"*** Category!

audience participation

Applause! The Audience Company: *310-450-2074*
1818 Ocean Park Blvd., Suite A
Santa Monica, CA 90405
Procedure:
We're told there is no need to call. Just send a headshot and resumé or a pic with all your pertinent info so they can call you when there is work. They do random sitcoms and awards shows.

Atwork Audiences: *323-472-6719*
8229 Santa Monica Blvd., #201
West Hollywood, CA 90046
Procedure:
Call in and get recorded info on how to be a member of the audience on numerous shows and get paid $6.75/hr. No fee.

Audiences Unlimited: *818-753-3470*
100 Universal City Plaza, Bldg. 3153
Universal City, CA 91608
www.tvtickets.com OR www.audiencesunlimited.com
Procedure:
Call the phone number above for show info or you can check them out on the web at: www.tvtickets.com. You usually can get tickets for any of the new shows and sometimes the more popular sitcoms that are taped all around LA like Emmy winners *Will & Grace*, etc.

First Call: *818-242-9988*
1111 N. Brand Blvd., Suite J
Glendale, CA 91202
Procedure:
This company does not strictly fill seats in audiences. They are a temp agency of sorts that provides all kinds of temporary employees for clerical positions and office staff, etc. In order to be considered for audience work (it pays from $7.75 to $8.50 an hour), you MUST attend an orientation (usually held every other week on Wed. or Thurs. at 3PM). Arrive early (as they only accept the first 25 people in line) and have two government-issued ID's with you (i.e., Driver's License and Social Security card). Once you've completed an orientation, you can call in to see what shows they have each day or week.

On-Camera Audiences: *818-295-2700*
www.ocatv.com
Procedure:
Call the phone number above for show info or you can check them out on the web at www.ocatv.com. *OCA* has audience tickets for *American Idol, MAD TV, The Late Late Show* and lots of talk and reality shows that can come and go quickly.

audience participation

Seatfiller: *818-407-7434*
P.O. Box 2830
Victorville, CA 92393
www.seatfiller.com
Procedure:
In the past, talent was told to send their pictures and resumés to be kept on file. Now it seems they've enabled sign-up through their website. You can look through their shows and leave your contact info if you're interested. They do MTV concert films, award shows and things like that!

Standing Room Only: *818-762-9936*
20929 Ventura Blvd., Suite 47-533
Woodland Hills, CA 91364
www.standingroomonly.tv
Procedure:
Info on what TV shows you can get free tix for are recorded on their hotline and also listed on their website. Apparently you can also register with the casting arm of this company. Any fees associated with this are not known.

Studio Audiences: *818-753-3470*
www.studioaudiences.com
Procedure:
Get tix for game shows taped in LA – most tape at Sony Studios in Culver City or at Paramount. This is an offshoot of Audiences Unlimited, and you are often redirected to their website for ticket availability.

TV Tickets AKA Audience Associates: *323-653-4105*
7471 Melrose Avenue, Suite 10
West Hollywood, CA 90046
www.beinamovie.com
Procedure:
Call the phone number above for the TV shows they are currently booking or visit them at www.beinamovie.com to see what film they can get you in (usually a freebie with no pay, i.e., think big calls for stadium filling scenes in *Seabiscuit*).

TV Tix: *323-653-4105*
www.tvtix.com
Procedure:
Just like Studio Audiences, you can get audience tickets for game shows and sometimes "special events" or tapings.

• F.Y.I. #1:
Some of the companies we have listed in the past are gone. These "companies" often last as long as the particular show they're booking.

quick bucks for actors

Making "Extra" Money. . .

Sometimes, when you're dedicated to acting full time but aren't booking as many jobs as you need to pay the bills, it comes time to get a real job. Relax, this is NOT that time. One of the most valuable attributes any background actor can have is a flexible schedule. If you're available when the Casting Directors call with a Rush booking, they're going to keep on calling you. A 9 to 5 day job can really throw a wrench into your availability. So, if the landlord's pounding on your door looking for the rent check and you're living off the free samples at Ralph's, there are alternative ways to make cash, from the mundane to the adventurous (c'mon now – not THAT adventurous!)...but all short-term, flexible, and (let's be honest) disposable at a moment's notice when the next acting job jumps into your lap.

Art Class Modeling:

Myth #1: You have to be naked. Nope, not always, you usually get paid more to be naked, but figure drawing classes also usefully clothed models. Myth #2: You have to be in great shape. Nope, skinny or fat, short or tall - anything goes. Just like being an Extra. Teachers like different looks. If you can hold a pose and you've got the confidence to stand in front of a group, then give art class modeling a shot. Design schools, art colleges, community drawing classes, private artists: they all need models. Gigs can pay anywhere from $10 to $50 or more an hour.

Banquet/Party Staff:

Are you a waiter with no restaurant? A bartender with no bar? A doorman with no club to keep goofy folks like us out of? A valet with no expensive cars to ding up? If so, party and banquet staffing might be just the thing for you. Get in with a few different companies and work events as they come up. And keep an eye out for random gigs being staffed by the people throwing the party. Weekends, holidays, evenings – there's always a party going on somewhere in this town. Get paid to be there.

Canvassing/Paid Activism/Petitions:

You really have to be a people person for this job. And like the outdoors. Ever have someone come up to you and ask you to sign a petition for something. Annoying, right! Well, you can be that person! Companies, politicians, environmental groups – these folks all need people out there spreading the word, gathering donations and signatures. Many places pay a flat hourly wage with bonuses for the number of people you sign up. So...there it is. Do it for a day and quit. Or maybe you can find some cause that you actually care about. Then you'd feel good on top of getting the paycheck.

quick bucks for actors

Child's Party Performer:

Clowns, magicians, suited characters of all shape, size and species: make kids laugh for money. It's not glamorous, it can be pretty trying at times, but it's not a set schedule and you might just have some fun from time to time.

Concert/Venue Staff:

Ushers, parking attendants, concession, clean-up, etc. Big venues bring on people to work concerts and sporting events. You work when the show or team is in town, and are off when the venue is dark. It's intermittent work, and you'll get to see a lot of games and concerts for free (in between whipping bags of peanuts up into the cheap seats).

Election Judge:

Get involved in the voting process and get paid for it. Election Judges (a.k.a. Election Officials or Poll Workers) supervise the voting process on election day. They check in voters, make sure no chads are left hanging, and generally ensure that there's no funny business going on at the poll. Aspiring Election Judges just have to be eligible voters who aren't running for office and who are willing to take an orientation class. Stipends and specifics vary from county to county. For more info contact your local county elections official; the list of contact numbers is available at: www.ss.ca.gov/elections/elections_d.htm

Flyer Distribution:

Easy but boring work. Stand around and hand out little pieces of paper to passers by, or stick them to telephone poles, or slap them on cars in a parking lot. Many flyer places only pay you a percentage of the money they make from people who got your flyer and actually spent cash on whatever service it offers. Avoid these and stick to the jobs that pay an hourly wage. It likely isn't going to be much, but it's some fast extra moolah.

Game Shows:

Pick your fave and sign up to Come On Down! Some shows just pull contestants out of the audience (ala *The Price is Right* – line up outside CBS at dawn and hope for the best), but most accept applications and audition their contestants. Yep...another audition. But, heck, it never hurts to try, and if you make it on you might win a stinky wad of TV cash, or at least a bling-blingin' new toaster oven.

quick bucks for actors

General Temp Work:

If you have office skills, temp work is not a bad way to pay the bills. It's flexible, short-term assignments can be found, and many gigs can pay somewhere between $10 and $15 an hour, especially if you are a speedy typist, know a scooch (FYI - a "scooch" is a bit more than a "little bit", but less than "a lot") about business software (like MS Office and QuickBooks) and don't mind dressing the part. There are a number of general temp agencies, and even a few which specialize in temp gigs in the entertainment industry. If you gotta work for The Man for a while, it might as well be in an environment where you can make contacts which may further your real goal of being a working actor.

Market Research Surveys:

Do you buy stuff? And do stuff? With things and...stuff? Then marketing companies want to know your opinion about that stuff! There are PAID surveys and focus groups out there on everything from cell phones to spray cheese to anxiety attacks (will we ever finish this book in time! Breathe, breathe...phew!). Craigslist.com is a great place to find Market Research studies looking for all sorts of folks, many of them paying a quick $50 or more for a couple hours "work." To start out, try registering for free at Adept Consumer Testing (www.adeptconsumer.com).

Medical/Drug Studies:

We are NOT recommending this one. Just letting you know it's out there. Drug companies and universities pay to have human guinea pigs test out their new drugs, talk about their problems, or just undergo a physical. Some studies pay several thousand bucks to their victims...uh, test subjects. If you're feeling lucky and don't mind needles, you can turn your insomnia, psoriasis, or rotten childhood memories into cold, hard cash.

Movie Screening Recruiter:

Every big film (and lots of little ones too) has test screenings of the semi-completed flick to determine what audiences like and dislike about it. Ending too sad? Acting too cheesy? The producers want to know. Places like Nielsen and The Screening Exchange hire folks (and especially outgoing actory types) to recruit John and Jane Q. Public into seeing these free test screenings. Basically you drive to a mall and hand out flyers for the film. Much like other flyer-related jobs, some pay a base hourly wage, some only pay based on the number of audience members who show up with your flyer.

quick bucks for actors

Mystery Shopping:

You are paid to shop! (Come on ladies and metro-sexual men - it's like our dream job!!) Yes, paid to shop! And write up reports telling how your steak at Norm's was the bomb, or how that clerk at The Gap is a snooty little so-and-so. Drive around town and be a secret agent of commerce. It's easy, flexible, and a lot of times you get to keep the stuff you bought (or ate – it's hard to return a used turkey burger). Visits might only pay $10 or $15 bucks a pop, but you can conceivably schedule a few in any given day.

SAT Tutoring:

This one's for all you smarty-pants out there. If you've got a college degree, know that Calculus isn't some sort of horrible skin condition, and is more gooder at English than we is, SAT tutoring might be right up your alley. Travel around to students' homes or meet them at the tutoring center. You only work a few hours a day and the wage can be anywhere from $15 to $40 an hour depending on experience. This job requires a bit more commitment than the others (since you can't really quit and leave a kid hanging halfway through the lesson plan), but the limited hours/days make it worth a look if you're qualified.

Seasonal/Holiday Positions:

I think we all realize that Hollywood pretty much grinds to a halt at the holidays. With a bazillion places hiring seasonal workers to cover the Xmas shopping rush, this hiatus is a great time to find a short-term gig and clock a lot of paid hours fast. Retail stores, shipping companies, warehouses, the U.S. Post Office: you name it, they're hiring. And if you're fat, jolly, have a long white beard, and like sitting in a throne in the middle of the mall...well, your ship has just come in, pal!

Telemarketing:

We apologize for including this one. And if you call us to sell something we apologize for hanging up on ya. If you've got a thick skin and don't mind sittin' on your tush for a few hours, these gigs are still plentiful and fairly easy to come by. It's an "ugh!" kind of job for many folks, but calling centers offer uber-flexible work schedules and bonuses for selling the most time-shares or...umm...whatever.

...key terms! on set & off

ABBY SINGER: The second to last shot of the day named in honor of former first A.D. Abby Singer, who perpetually called the last shot of the day one shot too early.

ABOVE THE LINE: This refers to the peeps whose credits used to appear before the title of the film in the good ol' days. Now it still refers to these people (the stars, the director, the producer, the screenwriter) even if their names do not appear above the line/title; this term is generally used in reference to the money budgeted for them.

ACADEMY STANDARDS: These are technical requirements set by the Academy of Motion Picture Arts and Sciences that enforce standard practices throughout the industry. They are a bit outdated in the day and age of CGI and all, but minimum standards of any kind are a cool idea.

ACTION: When the Director yells, "Action," this will begin the scene. This is the actors' cue to start their action or dialogue. Background actors begin their movement on "background action" (see definition on the next page).

ACTION STILL: This is a photo that is blown up directly from the negative of a film – not like a traditional "still" that is taken during production by a separate photographer and his or her still camera.

AD LIB: Means there is no prepared script or lines – make it up as you go along!

ADAPTATION: This usually means making a film or TV show based upon some other form or forms of art. Think of a movie based on a book.

ADJUSTMENT: Added pay to your base rate (i.e., Smoke Work, Wet Work). This is better than a BUMP because it increases your overtime earnings.

AEA: Actors Equity Association; often called "Equity." This is SAG's sister union which represents stage actors.

AFI: The American Film Institute. AFI films are typically non-paying jobs taken for experience and networking.

AGENT: You need a definition here? Okay, a person authorized to negotiate for and act on behalf of talent.

ANAMORPHIC LENS: This lens will squish and squeeze a large image until it fits snugly in a standard frame.

APERTURE: Fancy-schmancy camera talk going on here, but the simplest explanation is that it's the opening in a lens that is adjusted by the iris of the camera. Yeah, we know, now you gotta skip ahead to "iris."

APPLE BOX: You're always bound to hear this one on sets (especially if the Stand-In for Shaq is only 5'4"). These are boxes of different sizes used to elevate actors or objects – so called because apple boxes were originally used.

ART DIRECTOR: This person is in charge of the set's overall look in terms of construction and decor.

ARTIFICIAL LIGHT: We're gonna go out on a limb here and say you can probably guess this one, but for the dimmer bulbs out there (pun entirely intended)... a source of light other than natural daylight or moonlight, etc.

ASPECT RATIO: The width to height ratio of a film frame.

ASSISTANT DIRECTOR (A.D.): This is the production's Assistant Director who makes sure the Big Cheese's (Director's) directions are followed!

AUDITION: Your shot at stardom! A "tryout" of sorts for a role in a movie, play or TV show. Usually auditions involve reading from the script, but they can also require improvisation.

AVAIL: A courtesy situation extended by a performer or agent to a producer indicating the performer's availability to work a certain job. Avails have no legal or contractual status.

BACKGROUND ACTION: This is the Background Artists' cue to start their action. Don't wait for "action," always go on "background action" unless the A.D. has specifically told you otherwise.

BACKGROUND CROSS: A cross behind the actors in relation to the camera.

BACK LIGHTING: Lighting the scene in a film from behind the actors and towards the camera.

BACK TO ONE (FROM THE TOP/RESET): The whole darn shot will be done again from the beginning. This means you return to your starting position and do the same action you did before – kinda like reading the same crappy book OVER and OVER... and over... and... well, you get the point!

BANANA: A diagonal cross but with a curve so it's shaped like a banana (this does not mean you take the curve around craft service and get a Banana!).

BARN DOORS: These are the folding metal flaps around a light source that control its stream and spread.

BEST BOY: The Key Grip's right hand guy (or girl) in charge of ordering and maintaining equipment and manpower. Technically this is a grip department title but lately you see a lot of lighting crews using the term Best Boy electric instead of Assistant Chief Lighting technician. It's usually the second in command...they order the gear, do all the paperwork, hire the crew and crew day players. There are actually two separate best boy positions - the best boy/electric and the best boy/grip - who are second in command to the gaffer and to the key grip. The best boy/grip is in charge of the rest of the grips and grip equipment. The best boy/electric is in charge of the rest of the electricians and the electrical equipment.

BIT: This is a small speaking part in a film or TV show. And yes, it's dated, but you'll still hear it used on sets today.

BLOCKING: The planned-out movement that an actor is to do in a scene. Very important for Stand-Ins to watch when working on set.

BLUE SCREEN: Fun times for the actors – they gotta pretend something is there that truly isn't. The crew shoots against a large blue or green backdrop-type-thingy, which allows a background or object (spaceship, dinosaur) to be superimposed later in the final image.

BODY DOUBLE: For some shots, a Director may consider that a particular actor's body may not be suitable for the impression desired. In these situations, the actor is "doubled" (replaced) by a person whose body is more suitable. Typically, body doubles are used for shots requiring nudity or depictions of physical fitness (like when Sam Rosen doubles for Brad Pitt or Governor Arnold Schwarzenegger... okay, maybe not).

BOOKING: A solid confirmation and/or commitment to work a job. This means you were contacted by an agency or casting director and they asked you if you were available to work on a set. If the answer is "yes" you were available to work, the casting director will then "book" you on the call which means you will be asked to confirm, show up, and act responsibly while working on set.

BOOM: A microphone that is usually on an extended pole and held above or below the actors to record their lines.

BOOM OPERATOR: The member of the sound department responsible for holding the boom pole (see above, kids), with a microphone attached.

BOX OFFICE: We've all heard this term before, but we thought it would be way-fun to tell you how it originated. It used to be a booth in a movie theatre where the tickets were sold that was little more than a BOX of an OFFICE – now it means the monetary potential of a film or the amount a film makes.

BREAKAWAY: Props that appear to be solid and perfectly intact, but will shatter or "break" on purpose.

BREAKDOWN: An extremely detailed list of roles/characters available to actors in various productions.

BRIDGE MUSIC: This music is used to enforce the images on the screen during scene transitions. It sets the mood for the cuts in a picture from one place to another. It is not music you hear while sitting on or driving over a bridge.

BUMP: Something everyone wants! A Bump is added money written onto your voucher (example: Car Bump). Note: It is not an adjusted Pay Rate (see Adjustment). This is very good – everyone seems to like more money.

BURY: To hide or conceal someone or something out of sight in a scene. You will often find seasoned Background Actors burying themselves so they are not "established" on camera.

BUZZ TRACK: Non-distinct background noise or "room tone" as it is often known, so the editor can fill in the gaps between dialogue with a natural sound of nothingness. Hhhmm.

C-STAND: A type of light stand with fixed legs that swing out or together when not in use. Equipped with an arm and typically used to hold a flag.

CALLBACK: A follow-up interview or audition. When you are called back or booked to work an additional day of extra work, SAG members must be notified by 5PM. If SAG members have already been given a callback, they may not be canceled after 4:30PM without a day's pay. There are a few extreme exceptions to this rule – which include floods and other "Acts of God." In these cases, callback talent must be canceled by 6PM.

CALLING SERVICE: A third party organization where you pay a monthly fee to obtain work. They receive bookings from the agencies actually hired by production. 1.) A company that is paid a monthly fee to manage your schedule, to keep your availability and picture accessible to casting on a daily basis and is authorized to accept work on your behalf. 2.) A liaison between Casting Directors and extras. (They are NOT Casting Directors and should NEVER guarantee jobs to extras.) See Act 7 for more.

CALL SHEET: A printed schedule of the day's work that is to be filmed, the cast and crew needed, the props and filming location, and times. This sheet contains just about everything there is to know about the filming events that will occur that day.

CALL TIME: The actual time you are to report to work ready to begin working for the day. . . although, as we know, it is always a good idea to be 15 to 30 minutes earlier than your call time.

CAMERA LEFT & CAMERA RIGHT: When facing the camera head on, Camera left is actually to your right. We know it sounds nuts, just read the aforementioned sentence over and over again and then you might just get it!

CAMERA READY: When you arrive to the set completely dressed with your hair and make-up done, ready to work at a moment's notice.

CANDLEPOWER: The power of a light source was originally measured by candle units, so the phrase has stuck. When you hear them shout: "How much candlepower we got there, Hal?" you'll know what the heck they're talking about.

CAR CALL: When you are booked with your car. Think about all of the freeway or parking lot scenes in movies and in television. These automobiles usually belong to the background actors, and they are given additional money to supply their own cars. Generally red, white and black cars do not work in the background that often... sorry.

CASTING DIRECTOR (C.D.): You better know who this hot potato is if you wanna get booked on a job! He or she is hired by a production to find the actors or background actors to work the shoot.

CATERER/ROACH COACH: Are you kidding?! This is the Mac Daddy catering truck that will hopefully provide you with an excellent, well-balanced, nutritional dessert, breakfast, lunch and dinner – yum.

CATTLE CALL: A casting call where a large group of people are expected to attend. So called because of, well, its cattle-like qualities... Moo!

CATWALK: Suspended high above the often-crowded studio stage, this platform allows crew members to access lights and such, way, way up there.

CGI: Computer Generated Images. A sign of the times, people. Fill a stadium with 500 background actors or CGI them in there?

CHANGES: This applies to the amount of clothing or costume changes you have endured throughout the course of the day. You always want to keep track of the changes because if the wardrobe department liked your clothing and picked out several items to wear and if you were asked to change into your own supplied outfits, you will be paid additional money.

CHEAT: When the actor has to adjust (cheat) his or her position or eye-line to accommodate the placement of the camera. Even though Ashley Judd looks as if she's staring right at Tom Cruise... she may really be looking to the right or left of him (at the yummy craft service table)!

CHECKING IN: Find an A.D. (Assistant Director) and check in when you arrive to set. If you haven't been given a voucher, chances are the Assistant Director doesn't know that you are there on the set ready to work.

CHECKING THE GATE: Usually means they have the shot they want – they simply have to make sure the lens on the camera does not have dust on it.

CHOKER: Actually just a slang term for a close-up of the actor's face.

CINEMATOGRAPHER: Otherwise known as the Director of Photography. In charge of setting up the shots, selecting the frame and lighting the shots.

CLOSE-UP (C.U.): A very tight shot of an actor's face... sometimes including their shoulders too – but close!

COLD READING: This usually takes place at an audition where you will perform something you have not previously seen or read. Sort of like flying blind – the ultimate improvisational test. Fun times!

COLOR COVER: When you work as a Stand-In you are asked to wear the same color clothes as the actor you are Standing In for.

COMMISSARY: This is where you chow down when you're working on a studio lot. It's their restaurant or cafeteria.

COMMISSION: You handing over your hard-earned cash! It's the percentage the performer pays to agents or managers for their services.

COMPOSITE: Photos of an actor's different "looks" all on one sheet.

CONFLICT: Used when referring to commercial principal work. If you are booked to hawk, say... *Bud Light*, you are contractually prevented from then publicly endorsing *Miller Lite*!

CONTINUITY: Anyone who has ever worked on set knows that most films are shot entirely out of sequence, so filmmakers must be careful to make sure all the elements remain continuous – that is making sure everything matches scene to scene. For an example of bad continuity, check out how Dorothy's pigtails are three or four different lengths throughout *The Wizard of Oz*, or how Sean Connery's shirt is buttoned all the way up, then not, then buttoned again all in one continous scene of *The Untouchables* obviously spliced together from different takes for the film's final cut.

COPY: What the "script" for a Voice-Over advertisement or commercial is commonly referred to as.

COUNTER: In this cross you will "counter" an actor or another Background Actor or a moving camera. This means you will be crossing on or near the same path the actor (or camera) is taking, but in the opposite direction.

COVERAGE: Coverage of a particular scene might include two-shots and close-ups or various angles on actors that cannot be captured from the Master Shot.

CRAFT SERVICES or CRAFTY: If you're an extra and you don't know what this is, your home planet cannot be Earth. It's the snack table with cookies, and chips, and dips and sodas and stuff!

CRANE SHOT: Let's see if you can follow this one. A camera raised on a crane above the set or the action to film it from above or afar. Think of a car chase scene.

CROSS: The ever-so-exciting action an extra makes when the scene is being filmed. If you have crossed (walked) from the living room to the kitchen in a scene, you have made a cross. See, extra work is exciting, people!

CUE: A signal of some sort (can be a hand sign, an off-set light, an action within a scene) to indicate an actor's entrance or action.

CUT!: A verbal cue for the action in a scene to cease. Don't try it on set, kids – for Directors to yell only!

CUTAWAY: A shot of something usually but not always directly related to the scene. If for instance we're watching that mega hunk Matthew McConaughey and Reese Witherspoon make-out, then we "cutaway" to a hatchet laying under the bed – yikes – and back to the bed – that's a cutaway!

DAILIES: The rough footage shot on a particular day before it is edited for print and inclusion in the final film or TV show.

DAY PLAYER (DAY PERFORMER): You get to "play" (act) for one day and one day only (or at least just a day at at time). A principal actor hired on day by day, rather than on a long-term contract.

DEMO TAPE: An audio or video tape that agents use for audition purposes.

DEUCE: We're including this one because we always hear this one on set and most people have no idea what's happening. A deuce is just a slang term for a 2,000 watt lamp used on set for lighting: "Hey, Stevie, snag me a deuce!"

D.G.A.: Abbreviation for Directors Guild of America.

D.G.A. TRAINEE: Someone who is in official training with the Directors Guild of America to soon become an Assistant Director. By the way, just to throw this random tidbit out there... this fabulous book, **"EXTRA" WORK for Brain Surgeons®** is the official textbook for the Directors Guild Training Program. Neato, huh?! How cool are we?!

DIAGONAL/OBLIQUE CROSS: A cross with a diagonal pattern in relation to the camera instead of a flat or straight across cross. It keeps you in the frame longer – hey, even better!

DIALECT: A very distinct speech pattern categorized by the region from which it comes (think Ben & Matt's Beantown tongue in *Good Will Hunting*) or the funny way New Yawkers talk! Just kidding – "We LOVE New York!"

DIALOGUE: The ever-so-important words that the magician known as a screenwriter has written for the actors to speak and/or exchange.

DIFFERENTIAL FOCUSING: As a backgrounder, you probably don't need to know this one, but a Stand-In might hear it while the Second Team is setting up a shot. It means: the actors are in sharp, sharp focus and the background is blurred.

DIRECTOR: This is the big cheese that is basically in charge of every creative aspect of the movie once filming begins.

DIRECTOR OF PHOTOGRAPHY (D.P.): The D.P. is otherwise known as the Cinematographer – the big cheese that sets up the shots.

DOLLY: The camera sits on this mobile device so as to have ease of movement. That sucka (read: camera) is heavy!

DOUBLE: A performer in some capacity (stunt double, body double, stuffed animal) who appears in place of another performer – usually the lead actors – who don't generally wish to jump from three-story buildings, be set on fire, reveal their breastises, or expose their pasty buttocks!

DOWNSCALE: The opposite of Upscale. Okay, this refers to the type or style of clothes you would or should wear as an extra who is requested to dress "downscale": usually T-shirts, jeans, very casual.

DRESS THE SET: After a set is built, the Set Dressers come in to make a living room look like a living room or a bedroom look like a bedroom by adding the appropriate features, like furniture, remote controls, dirty laundry, etc.

DRIVE-ON PASS: A pass to drive onto and park in a studio lot.

DRY RUN: A full-on rehearsal where the actors speak their lines and move as they'll move while the cameras are on so the lighting dudes can get a glimpse and the Director can see what works and what doesn't and adjust things accordingly.

8x10: Um, a headshot. A commonly used slang referring to the size of an actor's industry-standard, black & white photos (not necessarily the size of his or her ego). Color 8x10's are quickly becoming the industry standard.

18-TO-PLAY-YOUNGER: A performer who is legally 18 years old or older, but could pass for a minor. Used for high school scenes, etc.

EMPLOYER OF RECORD (E.O.R.): The company named on your voucher responsible for taxes, deductions, benefits and workers' comp and more. Nine times out of ten, this is usually the payroll company.

EQUITY: Refers to the Actors Equity Association (AEA) – the union representing stage actors.

EQUITY WAIVER: Now formally known as "Showcase Code," it's when Equity waives contract provisions for 99-seat (or less) theatres in L.A. under certain circumstances.

EXECUTIVE PRODUCER: This person's got the bucks! She or he is responsible for funding or finding funding for that mega-budget feature!

EXT. (EXTERIOR): Do you really need a definition for this one? Okay, fine. A scene that is to be shot outside (in the exterior).

EXTRA: You're joking, right? You've got this HOT directory in your hands, don't ya? It's a background actor who is used only in non-principal roles to add atmosphere to a scene.

FAVORING: When the camera "favors" an actor over another actor or an object, but both and/or all are included in the shot.

FICA: Fun stuff like taxes. Stands for: Federal Insurance Corporation of America; a.k.a. Social Security.

FINE CUT: An almost final version of the film that the editor prepares and approximates the length and continuity of the picture. Far beyond the "rough cut," though not quite as clean as the "final cut."

FIRST ASSISTANT DIRECTOR (FIRST A.D.): The First Assistant Director has the minor responsibility of running the set (that was a joke). This person is responsible for making the director's requests become a reality.

FIRST TEAM: The principal actors in a film or TV show.

4-A's: Associated Actors and Artists of America (get it, four "A"s?); An "overseer" organization if you will (please do) for SAG, AFTRA, Equity and other performers' Unions.

FLAG: Those black, flag-shaped things you see mounted around lights to deflect the glare and such.

FLAT RATE: A base rate often used for extras who work on music videos. A flat rate is generally paid for the entire day's work (i.e., flat rate = $150 for the day). As long as the flat rate does not break down to performers getting paid below the state-mandated hourly minimum wage, it is okay!

FORCED CALL: Yuck! Forced Calls are miserable! It's a call to work less than 12 hours after you were released the day before. For example, if your out time was 10PM Tuesday night and your call time is 8AM Wednesday morning – see, NOT fun!

FOREGROUND: This, my friends, is the area in front of the camera lens, solely between an object or the principal actors.

FOREGROUND CROSS: A cross in front of the actors in relation to the camera. Yes, really, in between the camera and the cast – we did not just make that up. This is the exciting cross. When you are making a foreground cross you should move more slowly than usual, as the closer you are to camera the faster you appear to move.

FOREGROUND WIPE: A foreground cross very close to camera so that your body or whatever you are carrying completely blocks the frame briefly. This gives the editors a place to cut.

FRAMES PER SECOND (F.P.S.): Those in the know will talk in the "FPS" mode, rather than spell it all out.

FRENCH HOURS: When you hear this on set it means there are no official meal breaks. Instead food is available all the time and you may eat when you're hungry.

GAFFER: A member of the crew who is involved in setting the lighting.

GATE: If you paid attention to the C's, we told you about "checking the gate." The gate is just that part of the camera where the film is momentarily held while a frame is being exposed (and it looks just like a li'l gate – on hinges and everything!).

GLIOMA: A tumor of the brain/spinal cord... Ooops! Wrong book.

GOLDEN TIME: The magical hour of pay – the 16th hour. Say, for example, your call time is 7: 00AM – count 16 hours later (including your exciting food breaks) and the minute after that 16th hour, which would be 11: 01PM, you receive Golden Time. Golden Time is your base rate. If you are SAG, your base rate is $118/8 (negotiable July 2005), so every hour from the 16th hour on, you are paid your base rate of $115 an hour until you are wrapped/released from work for the day.

GRACE: It refers to the twelve-minute period allowed by unions to delay meal period violations. If the director and crew are in the middle of a shot when you get to the sixth hour from your last meal, the Director may call "grace." This means the Director has twelve minutes to finish the shot before MPVs (meal penalty violations) begin. They may not move onto another shot, and this only applies to Union talent and crew.

GRIP: Someone in charge of arranging or rearranging the lighting equipment and/or various camera equipment.

HAND MODEL: Have you got hands to make the *Palmolive* lady proud? A person whose hands are used to double for another's.

HIATUS: Summer vacation for television shows/production. Usually begins in April or May until about August. Essentially, hiatus is when television production is down and we all must endure hellish re-runs of *According To Jim*.

act ten

HOLDING: Where you should be when you are not working on the set. Typically, Holding consists of a room full of people playing cards, reading **"EXTRA" WORK for Brain Surgeons**® and talking about who is casting what.

HONEYWAGON: This is a big, huge truck where you will find a clean bathroom and changing rooms.

HOT SET: A set that is currently being used for filming/taping. Basically, do not touch anything on a hot set. This way nothing will be changed or disturbed and continuity will be maintained. (No eating the damn yummy food props, by the way – this we have seen people do... and get fired!)

HOT SPOT: No, not the hippest club in all of Hollyweird, but an area in a particular scene that is purposely overlit.

HYPHENATES: The oh-so-important peeps who get two or more names, like Sam Rosen Writer-Director (see the nifty hyphen!).

IATSE: International Alliance of Theatrical Stage Employees represents most of a production's off-camera crew members.

IMPROV (IMPROVISATION): More than just a comedy club, this term describes a performer's ability to make up their own dialogue (humorous or serious) on set.

INDUSTRIAL: A non-broadcast film or video, typically of an educational nature (your foray into soft-core sex educational videos for high school seniors doesn't count).

INSERTS: Shots, usually close-ups, of hands or close business, inserted into previously shot footage.

INT. (INTERIOR): A scene shot indoors – or in the I-N-T-E-R-I-O-R... INT., get it?

"IN" TIME: The actual call time or start time. It's also, the return time from a break or meal.

IRIS: A circular opening in a camera that is adjustable allowing varying amounts of light to hit the film, or tape, or Hi Def imaging chips.

JUMP CUT: A very abrupt cut that is exceedingly popular at the moment thanks to *MTV* and the short-attention span of today's movie-going audience – jumping from one object or actor to another and sometimes back!

KICKER: A source of light that makes the actor's teeth and eyes appear whiter and brighter without basking his or her whole face in light. *Crest Whitestrips* are out – bring in the kicker!

LEFT TO RIGHT: Directions are always given from the camera's point of view. So this is camera left to camera right.

LIBRARY SHOT: More commonly known as "stock footage" – not a shot of an actual library.

LIVE SOUND: Dialogue or actual sounds that are recorded while the film is rolling rather than added or dubbed in later.

LOCATION: Where you are working.

LONG SHOT (L.S.): This camera shot captures the performer's full body – usually from a distance (a "long" ways away)!

LOOPING: A technique used to add, fix, or change dialogue already performed during principal photography. Dialogue is adjusted in the studio to match voices to the movements and images on the screen.

MAJOR ROLE PERFORMER: An actor (usually pertaining to Heather Locklear) who works on a specific project and gets special billing like "Special Guest Star," or "Special Appearance By" and is paid at least twice the established dayplayer rate.

MARK/MARKER: The camera assistant calls this out just before clapping the slate. It is the position you were placed at or in by the Assistant Director (on your mark!).

MARTINI: When you hear "Martini," know you will be going home soon because the "Martini" is the last shot of the day! (By the way, if you were looking for an alcoholic adult beverage suggestion, let us recommend the ultimate chick drink – a Chocolate Martini – it is a fabulous dessert!)

MASTER: This is the first shot made of a scene. Usually it is a wide shot and the camera sees all of the actors in the scene.

MATCHING: When filming the same scene over and over, you will need to match your action every time they shoot an area of the room. Again, this is still the same scene as they shot in the master, only the camera angle has changed, so you should continue to match your action. If your part of the room is off camera, the Assistant Director will let you know.

MATTE SHOT: Hardly ever used today thanks to Special Effects and CGI, but a popular method of combining a photographed background with live-action actors.

MEAL PENALTY: Per state law and SAG/AFTRA rules, production is to officially break you for a meal every six hours. If production does not break you, production must pay you a "meal penalty." The Non-Union penalty is an additional hour of your regular wage. The SAG & AFTRA penalties depend on the type of production (film, TV, commercial, etc.) you are working.

MEAT AXE: Not as scary as it sounds. It's just the slang term you may hear some gaffers use when they're looking for a pole to hold a flag or scrim.

MILLING: Basically means hanging around and making yourself look busy during a scene. Milling about – just keeping yourself busy while in the background during the scene whether it's engaging in mimed conversation with people, or walking over to pretend to file some papers in an office. Create your own busy action in a scene.

MINGLING/THE PARTY SCENE: The room needs to stay full without any empty spaces anywhere in the room. But they need to see movement and mingling. The best way to create movement without leaving any empty spaces is to form party groups of three or more, then you can leave your group to join another group. When a new member of the group arrives, an old member of the group should leave. Never leave one person alone. If you were at a party, would YOU want to be left alone?!

MISE EN SCENE: Okay, we know we're not a film school, but it's a French term that some fancy Directors may use. It simply and literally means: the placing of a scene.

MIXER: The big cheese of the Sound Crew who is responsible for recording quality sound on a shoot.

M.O.S.: A shot or scene without sound. (Random Trivia: apparently this originated from Director Erich Von Stroheim, who couldn't pronounce "without sound" correctly due to his accent and it came out "mit out sound.")

M.O.W.: Movie of the Week. (Ya know those Danielle Steele-Melissa-Gilbert-or-Bruce-Boxleitner-starring-three-hankie-enthralling-weepies? Yeah, them.)

MULTIPLE PICTURE: An actor is hired to work on two or more projects within the same time frame. Think Kelly Ripa. That sister is everywhere all at once!

NIGHT PREMIUM: Usually applies to commercial work where a surcharge is added for work performed after 8PM.

NON-DEDUCTIBLE MEAL (N.D.B.): A meal break that does not take you off the time clock and brings your meal time up to the crew call time. The purpose here is to avoid meal penalties. Example: N.D.B = Non-Deductible breakfast.

NON-DESCRIPT (N.D.): Definition pretty much tells itself, but for those who need more it means to wear clothes that will make you blend in and not stand out so much in the background. Everyday clothes.

OFF-CAMERA (O.C./O.S./OFF SCREEN): Dialogue or Voice-Over that is delivered without seeing the actor on the screen (the O.S. simply stands for, yep, "Off Screen").

OMNIES: Words background actors speak as part of a group that are common and not distinct. See "wild track/walla-walla" if you need more!

ON A BELL: This simply means that when you are working on a soundstage, they will alert the crew when the bell sounds off – everyone should stop working as the Director and actors are now ready to film the scene. If you are outside of the soundstage gossiping, flirting, smoking or trying to use your cell phone – always make sure the red light is NOT on before entering.

OPEN CALL/CATTLE CALL: A general audition for roles where many people turn out looking for the part. A mob scene! You may have caught this definition at CATTLE CALL, under the "C's."

OUT OF FRAME: An actor who is not in the camera's frame – too far to the left or right – so as to be at least partially cut out of the camera's frame and, thus, the scene.

OUT-TAKES: The best parts of the film or TV show that we don't get to see! Okay, so that's when we know them as bloopers, but out-takes were originally just the rejected scenes that didn't make the final cut of the film.

"OUT" TIME: The actual time one has been released from set. Your "out time" will also be written on your voucher.

OVER-THE-SHOULDER: A camera shot over the shoulder of one actor, focusing entirely on the face or upper body of another actor in a scene.

OVERTIME: This is when we start really making the big bucks, kids! Overtime typically begins after 8 hours of work for both Union and Non-Union talent (on some AFTRA programs, overtime doesn't begin until after the 9th hour).

PAN/TILT: The action of rotating a camera about its vertical axis.

PANTOMIME: The key term all professional background actors must know. Pantomime means just that. You pretend to talk and mouth the words as if you are having a real conversation. Get it, mime – miming?!

PAYMASTER: An independent talent payment service used in place of, or acting as, the employer of record.

PER DIEM: Fee paid by producer on location shoots to compensate performers for expenditures for meals that are not provided by the producer.

PHOTO DOUBLE: When talent is hired to take the place of the Principal actor. For example, let's take the television program *Law & Order*. Yeah, it's been on forever, but it's still a Nielsen ratings champ. So say sexy Dennis Farina goes psycho and decides to rob a bank. (It could happen, right – the show has been on forever, someone's got to snap sooner or later!) Let's then say ole' Denny pulls this heist off and there is a scene where we see the cops (his buddies) chasing the Den-ster down rambling hills. The shot is a long shot, showing only the back of Mr. Farina. What if, in real life, almost-geriatric Dennis can't run in those tight trousers or risk ruining his fine hair from a crisp breeze? Well, that's when production hires a Photo Double. They may hire a double or a stunt double for this, all depending on how dangerous the scene really is. The double hired should look somewhat like Dennis, with the exact measurements and sizes so the audience is not aware that the man sprinting expertly in that shot is not the real Dennis Farina but just someone who looks like the strapping Mr. Farina. Get it?! Cool.

PICKING UP (RESHOOTS/PICKUPS): This means that the Director is happy with the first part of the scene but wants to redo a later part of the scene. The A.D. will either tell you, "Picking up about 15 seconds into the scene," which means that you should return to your starting position and then go 15 seconds into your action to find your new start. Or the A.D. will say "Picking up from Joe kisses Sally," or Joe's line, "Well, I guess it's final, then." This means you will have to start from wherever you were at that moment in the scene. This is when paying attention pays off, Brain Surgeons!

PICTURE CAR: A vehicle shown in a movie. Hey, if you can't get the gig, maybe your car can!

PICTURE'S UP!: Or "too late to run to the bathroom!" It's a warning of sorts that the shooting of a prepped scene is about to begin.

PILOT: First show of a new TV series introducing characters and a storyline.

PITCH: The story idea a screenwriter tries to sell to a Director, studio head or production company so they'll hire him or her to write the script!

POINT OF VIEW (P.O.V.) SHOT: A camera angle from the perspective or Point-Of-View of an actor to make us believe that what is on the screen is what our actor is actually looking at.

POSITIVE: A print made from a... negative. Cool.

POST-PRODUCTION: After the film has been shot and wrapped, this stage begins where editing, scoring, dubbing, and such comes into play.

PRE-PRODUCTION (PREP): The phase before shooting begins on a project. It includes writing (very, very important... ahem!), budgeting, location scouting, casting, hiring crews, ordering equipment, etc.

PRINCIPAL: A performer who typically has lines of dialogue in a production. It can refer to those actors with one or two lines, but most typically it refers to the Julias and Toms of the world.

PRINCIPAL PHOTOGRAPHY/PRINCIPAL FILMING: The filming of a movie which involves the lead actors.

PRINT: When the take is developed or printed, it will then be looked at or considered to be in the film or TV show by the powers-that-be.

PRODUCTION ASSISTANT (P.A.): A person responsible for various odd jobs, such as stopping traffic, acting as a courier, fetching items from craft service, etc. Basically, this person is like a gofer.

PRODUCTION COMPANY: The organization that is behind the actual making of the movie or television show.

PROP: An object on the set used by an actor (i.e., briefcase, phone, gun). Not an extra.

PSA: Public Service Announcement. Think *Smokey The Bear*.

PUBLICITY STILL: A picture taken before, during or after the filming to be used for publicity purposes.

RAIN OR SHINE: You will work, regardless of whether it is raining or shining.

RAW STOCK: You'll often hear the camera-folk asking for some. It's simply unused film that has not been exposed.

READER: Yes, one who reads. So, yes, maybe even you. But when talking in industry circles, it means a person at a literary agency or studio who reads screenplay submissions before they are passed on to the higher-ups.

RECALL: When background actors get asked back for an additional day's work. See "callback."

RESIDUALS: When commercials, films or TV programs are rebroadcast, the principal performers are paid additional compensation. Gotta love that!

RESUMÉ: A list of a performer's credits, contact information, etc., that is usually attached to his or her fabulous headshot.

REVAMPING: This can apply to many different things on a film set, most typically, however, it refers to altering a set – whether for the same movie or to suit another production.

REWRITES: Changes, additions or deletions in the script that are often re-distributed to the cast on color-coded pages to indicate the most current version (usually a writer's nightmare).

RIGHT TO LEFT: Directions are always given from the camera's point of view. So this is camera right to camera left.

RIGHT-TO-WORK STATES: The states the USA, which do not honor certain provisions of established Unions (SAG, etc.).

ROLLING: This means the scene is about to begin shooting. Essentially, the film is rolling in the camera's coils and the camera is ready to shoot a scene.

ROLLING TITLE: Not the title of the film, but its credits. So called because they are "titles" that roll up from the bottom of the screen and magically disappear at the top.

ROOM TONE: A sound recording (sometimes made upon completion of a scene) to record existing noise at the location. The things you hear in a silent room. Very Zen.

RUSH CALL: When a Casting Director calls you last minute to book you because (generally) someone needed to be replaced and you will be replacing that person. Always be sure to get the name of the person you are replacing, that way when you get on set, there will not be any confusion.

RUN-THROUGH: In theatre the players have dress rehearsals, in movies they have "run-throughs" where they run through the dialogue and actions of the script.

SCALE: Minimum payment for services under union contracts.

SCENE: A continuous block of storytelling either set in a single location or following a particular character. The end of a scene is usually followed by a change in location, style, or time.

SCREENPLAY or SCRIPT: It's the written words on the page that tell the film's story through action and dialogue.

SCRIM: They hang from meat axes, remember? Were you paying attention back in the M's? It's a translucent (nice word) screen used in front of a studio light to filter, soften or diffuse the light's projection on an actor or object.

SCRIPT SUPERVISOR: Ensures continuity by recording any and all changes or significant actions in the script – page by page, throughout the entire production.

SDI: State Disability Insurance.

SECOND ASSISTANT DIRECTOR: An assistant to the Assistant Director. This person hustles and bustles. Duties include overseeing the movements of the cast and preparing call sheets.

2ND-2ND ASSISTANT DIRECTOR/3RD ASSISTANT DIRECTOR: An over-exhausted assistant to the Second Assistant Director mainly responsible for directing the background talent. 2nd-2nd's are kind of like the Background Actors' boss. Canadians generally use the "3rd Assistant Director" term.

SECOND TEAM: Or "get the Stand-Ins away from craft service and put them to work!" The cue to inform Stand-Ins they are being called to set to begin their "lighting mode" functions.

SECOND UNIT/2ND UNIT: A smaller crew typically responsible for filming uneventful shots of less importance, such as inserts, crowds, scenery, etc.

SECOND UNIT DIRECTOR/2ND UNIT DIRECTOR: The Director of the second unit. He or she may direct scenes where no principals or speaking actors are involved.

SEGUE: A clean transition from one shot to another in a film or TV show which should not distract or disorient viewers.

SELECTIONS: Different "selections" of wardrobe. This means that you bring several options of the same type of wardrobe. Example – three completely different color business suits equal three selections.

SET: The location where a scene is being filmed.

SET-UP: Each time the camera changes position.

SEVENTH ART: This is the art of Motion Pictures. Way back in 1916 an Italian poet and film theorist coined the phrase explaining that film deserved recognition as art. What are the first six? Good question, people. That's your homework – find out the first six. Have your people contact our people.

SFX: Sound effects. Just like it sounds!

SHOT: A continuous block of unedited footage from a single point of view.

SKINS: A list of who is booked on the call. Remember the roll call in school? It's kinda like the roll call list except it's for extra work.

SIDES: Mini photocopied pages of the script or scene. When auditioning for a principal role, an actor will typically use sides to read and rehearse from. If you are a Stand-In always ask the 2nd A.D. or P.A. for sides so you will know what the heck is going on.

SIGNATORY: An employer who has agreed to produce a project under the terms of a union contract.

SILENT BIT: An actor has a specific action in a scene. And no, to answer your next question, this does not automatically mean you will get a bump or a SAG Voucher! Another example is when an A.D. instructs you to have a specific main action – not just walking in the background making crosses.

SLATE (CLAPPER): 1.) The slate refers to an actor identifying him or herself at an audition. The actor would state his or her first name and last name, then turn to the right, then to the left, showing his or her side profile to the camera/Director. 2.) The clapper or chalkboard used to identify the shots being filmed.

SNOOT: A cone-shaped instrument attached to a lamp to send light in a certain direction.

SOUND SPEED: The rate at which film passes through the camera when it is accompanied by a sound.

SOUP: Not the caterer's surprise stew, but slang for the solution used in developing and processing film.

SPEC: A background actor who shows up to a set who is not OFFICIALLY booked. They show up in hopes of being added to the call.

SPEED: Usually heard right after rolling. When the sound mixer yells "speed," they are letting the camera people know that the tape is up to the proper speed for recording dialogue.

SPIDER: It can be a creepy-crawly arachnid or a three-legged (or armed) metal device used to support a camera on unsteady surfaces.

SPIDER BOX: A multi-outleted "box" that the studio electricians can plug all sorts of lights into. No, people, not a place to keep spiders of any variety.

SPIKING THE LENS: Looking directly into the lens during a scene, since it destroys the illusion of realism, you should never spike the lens unless specifically directed to do so for specific effect.

SQUIB: No guns involved, but it sure looks like it. A device that explodes, implodes or otherwise shatters to look as if hit by a bullet.

STAGE MANAGER: An Assistant Director on a TV show is generally called a stage manager.

STAGE RIGHT (CAMERA LEFT): To the performer's right side, to the audience's (camera's) left side. Likewise, STAGE LEFT (CAMERA RIGHT) is to the performer's left, the audience's (camera's) right.

STANDARDS & PRACTICES: The departments where people in tight-fitting suits work to cut out all the "good" stuff from network TV shows! They're the censors – less violence, less sex... etc.

STAND-INS: Also known as part of the "Second Team," these background actors are used as substitutes for featured players or lead actors, so the D.P. (Director of Photography) can set lights and rehearse camera moves.

STICKS: Catchy slang for the slate or clapboard used to mark scenes for the camera during shooting.

STOPPING DOWN: It means to reduce the aperture (which we covered earlier, people!) of a camera lens to change the way a scene will appear on film.

STORYBOARD: Drawings that act as a layout for the entire film, scene for scenes that are prepared before filming begins so the Director can "see" exactly how the film will look.

STRIKE: To destroy or dismantle a set after the film is wrapped!

STUDIO: That big soundstage/lot/studio where a film or TV production gets filmed (usually on a soundstage).

STUNT COORDINATOR: This person gets to WATCH them jump through fire and fun stuff like that. He or she is in charge of supervising those spectacular stunts and other hazardous activities.

STUNT DOUBLE/STUNTPERSON: A stuntperson who performs stunts for a principal. When George Clooney or Catherine Zeta-Jones would rather not jump from a speeding train to a wild bronco.

SUBMISSION (ONLINE SUBMISSION): 1.) For principal work, this is usually a headshot & resumé submitted by an agent or an actor to a casting director for consideration for a role. 2.) For extra work, this is usually a 3" X 5" color photo, waist up, against a white background. 3.) For "online submissions" this is generally a website-based program where casting directors can do a search to find actors, place casting notices and view responses. Also can be known as "Electronic Submissions."

SUN GUN: Sounds more fun than it really is. It's just a hand held, battery-powered light that crew members can use on the go when outlets aren't readily available or accessible. Think *Blair Witch* or other docu-style films.

S.W.: An abbreviated notation on a call sheet that an actor is starting ("S") on this day and working ("W") on this day.

S.W.F.: Another abbreviated notation on a call sheet that an actor is... c'mon, let's sound it out together: starting ("S"), working ("W"), and... finished ("F") all in the same day. Can you say, "Day Player"?

SWEETENING: The ever-so-exciting process of adding additional voices or sounds to previously recorded work – usually music.

SYNDICATION: When a TV show is sold to local affiliates, rather than the BIG (now) FOUR networks (CBS, NBC, ABC, FOX). It can be a mega-success like *Friends* or a syndie only like *Babylon 5*.

TAFT-HARTLEY: A federal statute which gives a performer thirty (30) days after first being employed under a Union contract before being required to join a Union (SAG).

TAKE: The clapboard indication that a shot has been "taken" or printed. There are usually lots of "takes" for any given scene until the Director gets exactly what he or she wants from the actors.

TAKE 5: This is what is yelled when you get to take a five-minute break.

TELEPROMPTER: Ready? It's TelePrompTer (Big "T," big "P," and big "T" again). That's cuz it's a fancy-schmancy brand-name of the device which enables a performer, President or some fabulous other actor to read a line-by-line script while looking into the camera lens.

TERM PERFORMER: Not really used today, but back in the day, stars were committed to a studio without necessarily knowing the project he or she would work on. Thus, he or she agreed to work under the terms of the studio, not the project.

THEATRICAL: In the industry, this refers to TV shows or feature film work, as opposed to commercials.

THREE BELLS: A warning bell sounds off three times. It means to shut your trap and stop making any noise. Simply be QUIET because a scene is about to be filmed.

THROW: The distance between the projector the film is running through and the screen it is displayed on.

TIGHT SHOT (GO IN TIGHT): When the camera frames a shot very closely, with little or no space around the central focus – be it an actor's mug, nose, leg, pinky finger or a prop; ya know, like a close-up.

TILT: When the camera "tilts." The up and down movement of the camera.

TIME-AND-A-HALF: This deals with overtime. It's the overtime rate of pay that is 1 and 1/2 times the standard hourly rate.

TRACKING SHOT: It's that shot that keeps on going in one continuous flow while the camera is moving, either on a dolly, a track, or mounted on a moving vehicle.

TRADES: Slang or shortened version of "trade papers." These are newspapers like *The Hollywood Reporter* and *Variety* that concentrate specifically on the workings of the entertainment industry.

TRAILER: 1.) These "coming attractions" (movie previews) used to come after the feature film years ago, thus the trailer nomenclature. 2.) It can also be that place on a set where the ultra-cool-big-time movie stars get to chill out on a comfy couch all their own... "trailer."

TURNAROUND: We got us a word here that has three very distinct definitions in the entertainment circuit: 1.) The number of hours between dismissal one day and your call time the next day. 2.) To shoot the same scene from the reverse direction. 3.) A project that was stalled in development hell and miraculously goes back into production full steam ahead.

TWO-SHOT: A shot of two people – usually very close and tight. Thus, a "two-shot." Easy. You like that?

UNDER 5 (U-5): This applies to the Union AFTRA. An Under 5 is a contract under AFTRA which means you have FIVE speaking lines or less.

UNDERSTUDY: Hey, we're a multi-purpose, multi-faceted type of outfit, so we'll throw this theatre reference out at ya just to make sure you're paying attention. This poor performer only gets to hit the stage if the featured performer is unable to make the play.

UPGRADE: Exactly what it sounds like! An actor is upgraded from an Extra to a Stand-in, Photo Double, or Principal Player (also equals more money!).

UNIT PRODUCTION MANAGER (U.P.M.): This is usually the penny-pinching tightwad in charge of the budget and financial matters concerning the film. When the crew is about to go into overtime, needless to say, this is the last kid you'd want to be sitting next to. Usually in a bad mood – but you'd be in a bad mood too if you had studios yelling at you all the time to keep your budget in check!

UPSCALE: Expensive-looking clothing, manicured bodies and all-around fancy-looking, Gucci/Armani wearing people. The opposite of Downscale.

UP STAGE: We got us a noun AND a verb. How riveting is that all in one word? 1.) Noun = in theatre, it's at the back of the stage (down stage is the area in front of the performer). 2.) Verb = to draw attention to yourself, usually at the expense of a fellow performer. An English lesson within a definition – how excited are you right now?

VAULT: It's a temperature and humidity-controlled storage space for films used to ensure they are safe from outside elements that might otherwise cause deterioration of the print. Also, *Def Leppard*'s greatest hits album. Highly recommeded (with an adult cocktail) for those in their late 20's to mid-30's. Pour some sugar on me, baby...

VOICE-OVER (V.O.): It's an off-camera voice from an actor not in the frame of the camera, or the voice over an intercom or answering machine or some other inanimate object.

VOUCHER: A time card/time slip with all the pertinent info needed for getting paid properly. You will be given this upon "checking in."

W: A notation on the call sheet indicating that an actor is working that day.

WAIVERS: When SAG or another Union allows a production to deviate from the standard practices of their contract, they grant "waivers."

WALKAWAY: This means you gotta feed your own mouth. It's a meal break (usually on TV shows filmed at a lot) where the cast and crew are up to their own devices to get lunch, generally at the commissary.

WARDROBE ALLOWANCE: This means wardrobe has chosen you to wear one of your outfits in a particular scene and they will pay you to wear your snappy clothing. Wardrobe allowances are great and can add up! Remember, the first wardrobe is a freebie – except with AFTRA or on SAG commercials. Wardrobe allowances typically begin when you change into your SECOND On-Camera getup. 2nd Outfit = 1st Wardrobe Allowance. 3rd On-Camera Outfit = 2nd Wardrobe Allowance.

WARDROBE FITTING: The amount of moo-lah an actor is paid for the time they spent going on a wardrobe fitting. Essentially, you are paid 1/4th of a regular day's check. It is STATE LAW that all extra performers who are sent on a Wardrobe Fitting are GUARANTEED ONE DAY of paid work on that production. Cool!

WEATHER PERMITTING: This means that because weather is a factor, the call could be canceled for the day – in which case, you will not be paid unless you are held on set for more than 4 hours.

WIGWAG: The "wigwag" is that flashing red light outside of the set doors that warns you that filming is in progress and if you like your job (and your life) you better not enter or exit until the red warning wigwag stops flashing.

WILD TRACK/WALLA-WALLA: Large group of Background conversation such as "crowd unrest" or "murmuring" (i.e., like during a big party scene). You will not be given onscreen credit or a bump. Walla-Walla does not count as a speaking role – sorry. SAG defines a "Crowd" to be five or more performers in a scene.

W/N: Stands for "will notify." Yet another exciting notation on a call sheet that tells the actor that he or she will probably work that day but the specific time has not yet been decided by the powers-that-be.

WRAP: To finish shooting, either for the day or the entire production. When you are "wrapped," you are released from working to go home.

ZOOM: Without moving the camera the lens adjusts the depth of the shot. It zooms!

OUR PERSONAL, CHEESY DISCLAIMER: *WE ARE NOT PERFECT (believe it, or not)! We realize there will, no DOUBT, be nuances to the above definitions that are not wholly correct. Sorry! This list is designed to give the newcomer an overview of commonly used terms. Essentially, please refer to the SAG Supplement and the California Labor Law Supplement for the end-all in definitions. We don't work for Webster's, thus, we are not up for debates on semantics (how's that for a $100 dollar word?)!*

index................

act ten

act ten

act ten

act ten

act ten

page
531

page
532

page
533

advertiser index

act ten

act ten

act ten

Where to purchase our products

- "EXTRA" WORK for Brain Surgeons®
- HOLLYWOOD OS® - The Casting Magazine
- KIDS' ACTING for Brain Surgeons™

HOLLYWOOD • newsstands & book stores

- **Larry Edmunds**
  6644 Hollywood Blvd.
  Hollywood, CA 90028
  PHONE: 323-463-3273
  WHERE: Hollywood & Cherokee, 3 Blocks East of Highland

- **World Book & News**
  1652 Cahuenga Bl.
  Hollywood, CA 90028
  PHONE: 323-465-4352
  WHERE: Cahuenga & Hollywood, just below Hollywood Blvd.

- **Hollywood Sunset**
  7225 Sunset Blvd.
  Hollywood, CA 90046
  PHONE: 323-969-9310
  WHERE: Sunset & Pointsettia, next to *Ralph's*

- **Woodey/La Brea News**
  1110 N. La Brea Avenue
  W. Hollywood, CA 90038
  PHONE: 323-465-1153
  WHERE: La Brea & Santa Monica, in front of *Rite Aid* & *RadioShack*

- **The Daily Planet**
  5931 1/2 Franklin Ave,
  Hollywood, CA 90028
  PHONE: 323-957-0061
  WHERE: Tamarind & Franklin between Bronson & Beachwood

- **La Cienega News**
  745 N. La Cienega Blvd.
  Los Angeles, CA 90046
  PHONE: 310-652-6851
  WHERE: South of Santa Monica Blvd., near *Mark's* restaurant

- **Book Soup**
  8818 Sunset Blvd.
  W. Hollywood, CA 90069
  PHONE: 310-659-3110
  WHERE: Across from *Tower Records,* between Holloway & Larrabee

- **Centerfold News**
  716 N. Fairfax Ave.
  Los Angeles, CA 90046
  PHONE: 323-651-4822
  WHERE: On the corner of Fairfax, just above Melrose

- **Swing Brothers News**
  8224 Sunset Blvd.
  W. Hollywood, CA 90069
  PHONE: 323-848-9070
  WHERE: Sunset & Crescent Heights

- **Sheltham's News**
  633 West 3rd Street
  Los Angeles, CA 90036
  PHONE: 323-924-0318
  WHERE: Two locations in the Farmer's Market!

BEVERLY HILLS • order direct

Order through HOLLYWOOD OS® & receive the magazine for FREE! Call 310-289-9400 or find a location near you. All credit cards accepted.

HOLLYWOOD OS®

• Where to purchase our products

- "EXTRA" WORK for Brain Surgeons®
- HOLLYWOOD OS® - The Casting Magazine
- KIDS' ACTING for Brain Surgeons™

THE WESTSIDE • newsstands & book stores

- **Midnight Special**
  1450 2nd Street
  Santa Monica, CA 90401
  PHONE: 310-393-2923
  WHERE: One block from the old store!

- **Lido Village Books**
  3424 Via Oporto
  Newport Beach, CA 93663
  PHONE: 949-673-2549
  WHERE: Off Via Lido, turn right onto Via Oporto

- **Brentwood News**
  11737 San Vicente Blvd.
  Brentwood, CA 90049
  PHONE: 310-447-2080
  WHERE: Right next to *Whole Foods.*

- **Hollywood OS®**
  400 S. Beverly Drive, Ste. 307
  Beverly Hills, CA 90212
  PHONE: 310-289-9400
  WHERE: At the corner of Olympic Bl. & Beverly Drive

THE VALLEY • newsstands & book stores

- **Sherman Oaks News**
  14500 Ventura Blvd.
  Sherman Oaks, CA 91403
  PHONE: 818-995-0632
  WHERE: Ventura & Van Nuys Blvd.

- **Para's News**
  3911 30th Street
  San Diego, CA 92104
  PHONE: 619-296-2859
  WHERE: 30th & University

- **Studio City Newsstand**
  12605 Ventura Blvd.
  Studio City, CA 91604
  PHONE: 818-761-0632
  WHERE: Next to *Jerry's Deli*!

- **Laurel Canyon News**
  1210 Ventura Blvd.
  Studio City, CA 91604
  PHONE: 818-769-3327
  WHERE: Ventura & Laurel Canyon

OTHER SOURCES • online retailers

- **Amazon**
  www.Amazon.com

- **Hollywood OS**
  www.HollywoodOS.com

Too many other RAD locations to mention! Thanks for carrying the little suckers!

HOLLYWOOD OS®

• Order Form

CONTACT • information

Name:____________________

Address:____________________

City:____________________ State:________

Zip: __________ Phone(s):______________

Email: ____________________

PRODUCTS

	•price	•copies
•"EXTRA" WORK for Brain Surgeons® ($33.72 total includes tax & s/h)	$27.50	#_____
• HOLLYWOOD OS® - Quarterly Magazine ($6.13 total includes tax & s/h)	$4.95	#_____
•KIDS' ACTING for Brain Surgeons™ ($33.72 total includes tax & s/h)	$27.50	#_____

• be sure to include the price with tax, shipping & handling •*TOTAL$*_______

PAYMENT • credit card info

☐ **Visa #:**____________________ ***EXPIRES:***______

☐ **MC #:**____________________ ***EXPIRES:***______

☐ **Amex #:**____________________ ***EXPIRES:***______

☐ **Disc. #:**____________________ ***EXPIRES:***______

☐ **Check*** Driver's Lic.# ____________________
* When paying by check, you MUST include your Driver's License Number and the state it is issued from.

☐ **Cash**

☐ **Money Order**

...order today...

RETURN ORDER FORM TO: **HOLLYWOOD OS®**
400 S. Beverly Dr., Ste. 307 • Beverly Hills, CA 90212
Office: 310-289-9400 • Fax: 310-277-3088